GENERAL MOTORS NOVA/CHEVY II
1962-79 REPAIR MANUAL

CHILTON'S

Covers all U.S. and Canadian models of
Chevrolet Chevy II, Concours, Nova, Nova Custom,
Nova Hatchback and Nova LN

by **Christine L. Nuckowski**, S.A.E.

CHILTON *Automotive Books*

PUBLISHED BY **HAYNES NORTH AMERICA. Inc.**

Manufactured in USA
© 1997 Haynes North America, Inc.
ISBN 0-8019-9067-X
Library of Congress Catalog Card No. 97-65896
6789012345 9876543210

Haynes Publishing Group
Sparkford Nr Yeovil
Somerset BA22 7JJ England

Haynes North America, Inc
861 Lawrence Drive
Newbury Park
California 91320 USA

ABCDE
FGHIJ
KLMNO
PQR

Contents

1 GENERAL INFORMATION AND MAINTENANCE

1-2 HOW TO USE THIS BOOK
1-3 TOOLS AND EQUIPMENT
1-7 SERVICING YOUR VEHICLE SAFELY
1-8 FASTENERS, MEASUREMENTS AND CONVERSIONS
1-14 SERIAL NUMBER IDENTIFICATION
1-16 ROUTINE MAINTENANCE
1-41 FLUIDS AND LUBRICANTS
1-55 TRAILER TOWING
1-56 TOWING THE VEHICLE
1-56 JUMP STARTING A DEAD BATTERY
1-57 JACKING
1-60 HOW TO BUY A USED VEHICLE

2 TUNE-UP

2-2 SPARK PLUGS AND WIRING
2-8 FIRING ORDERS
2-9 BREAKER POINT IGNITION SYSTEM
2-13 HIGH ENERGY IGNITION
2-13 IGNITION TIMING
2-13 VALVE LASH
2-15 IDLE SPEED AND MIXTURE ADJUSTMENTS

3 ENGINE AND ENGINE REBUILDING

3-2 ENGINE ELECTRICAL
3-18 ENGINE MECHANICAL
3-50 EXHAUST SYSTEM
3-52 ENGINE REBUILDING

4 EMISSION CONTROLS

4-2 AIR POLLUTION
4-3 AUTOMOTIVE EMISSIONS
4-6 EMISSION CONTROLS
4-16 VACUUM DIAGRAMS

5 FUEL SYSTEM

5-2 FUEL SYSTEM

6 CHASSIS ELECTRICAL

6-2 UNDERSTANDING AND TROUBLESHOOTING ELECTRICAL SYSTEMS
6-12 HEATER
6-13 RADIO
6-15 WINDSHIELD WIPERS
6-17 INSTRUMENT PANEL
6-17 SEATBELT SYSTEM
6-19 LIGHTING
6-24 TRAILER WIRING
6-25 CIRCUIT PROTECTION
6-30 WIRING DIAGRAMS

Contents

7-2 MANUAL TRANSMISSION   **7-21** DRIVELINE
7-5 CLUTCH   **7-25** REAR AXLE
7-12 AUTOMATIC TRANSMISSION

DRIVE TRAIN   7

8-2 WHEELS   **8-14** REAR SUSPENSION
8-4 FRONT SUSPENSION   **8-18** STEERING

SUSPENSION AND STEERING   8

9-2 BRAKE SYSTEM   **9-15** DRUM BRAKES
9-9 FRONT DISC BRAKES   **9-21** PARKING BRAKE

BRAKES   9

10-2 EXTERIOR   **10-9** INTERIOR

BODY   10

10-21 GLOSSARY

GLOSSARY

10-25 MASTER INDEX

MASTER INDEX

SAFETY NOTICE

Proper service and repair procedures are vital to the safe, reliable operation of all motor vehicles, as well as the personal safety of those performing repairs. This manual outlines procedures for servicing and repairing vehicles using safe, effective methods. The procedures contain many NOTES, CAUTIONS and WARNINGS which should be followed, along with standard procedures to eliminate the possibility of personal injury or improper service which could damage the vehicle or compromise its safety.

It is important to note that repair procedures and techniques, tools and parts for servicing motor vehicles, as well as the skill and experience of the individual performing the work vary widely. It is not possible to anticipate all of the conceivable ways or conditions under which vehicles may be serviced, or to provide cautions as to all possible hazards that may result. Standard and accepted safety precautions and equipment should be used when handling toxic or flammable fluids, and safety goggles or other protection should be used during cutting, grinding, chiseling, prying, or any other process that can cause material removal or projectiles.

Some procedures require the use of tools specially designed for a specific purpose. Before substituting another tool or procedure, you must be completely satisfied that neither your personal safety, nor the performance of the vehicle will be endangered.

Although information in this manual is based on industry sources and is complete as possible at the time of publication, the possibility exists that some car manufacturers made later changes which could not be included here. While striving for total accuracy, the authors or publishers cannot assume responsibility for any errors, changes or omissions that may occur in the compilation of this data.

PART NUMBERS

Part numbers listed in this reference are not recommendations by Haynes North America, Inc. for any product brand name. They are references that can be used with interchange manuals and aftermarket supplier catalogs to locate each brand supplier's discrete part number.

SPECIAL TOOLS

Special tools are recommended by the vehicle manufacturer to perform their specific job. Use has been kept to a minimum, but where absolutely necessary, they are referred to in the text by the part number of the tool manufacturer. These tools can be purchased, under the appropriate part number, from your local dealer or regional distributor, or an equivalent tool can be purchased locally from a tool supplier or parts outlet. Before substituting any tool for the one recommended, read the SAFETY NOTICE at the top of this page.

ACKNOWLEDGMENTS

Portions of materials contained herein have been reprinted with the permission of General Motors Corporation, Service Technology Group.

HOW TO USE THIS BOOK 1-2
WHERE TO BEGIN 1-2
AVOIDING TROUBLE 1-2
MAINTENANCE OR REPAIR? 1-2
AVOIDING THE MOST COMMON MISTAKES 1-2
TOOLS AND EQUIPMENT 1-3
SPECIAL TOOLS 1-6
SERVICING YOUR VEHICLE SAFELY 1-7
DO'S 1-7
DON'TS 1-8
**FASTENERS, MEASUREMENTS AND
 CONVERSIONS 1-8**
BOLTS, NUTS AND OTHER THREADED
 RETAINERS 1-8
TORQUE 1-9
 TORQUE WRENCHES 1-11
 TORQUE ANGLE METERS 1-12
STANDARD AND METRIC MEASUREMENTS 1-12
SERIAL NUMBER IDENTIFICATION 1-14
VEHICLE 1-14
ENGINE 1-14
TRANSMISSION 1-15
ROUTINE MAINTENANCE 1-16
AIR CLEANER 1-18
 REMOVAL & INSTALLATION 1-18
FUEL FILTER 1-19
 REMOVAL & INSTALLATION 1-19
PCV VALVE 1-20
 REMOVAL & INSTALLATION 1-20
CRANKCASE VENTILATION FILTER 1-22
 REMOVAL & INSTALLATION 1-22
FLAME ARRESTER 1-22
EVAPORATIVE CANISTER 1-22
 SERVICING 1-22
BATTERY 1-23
 GENERAL MAINTENANCE 1-23
 BATTERY FLUID 1-23
 CABLES 1-25
 CHARGING 1-26
 REPLACEMENT 1-26
BELTS 1-26
 INSPECTION 1-26
 TENSION CHECKING & ADJUSTING 1-27
HOSES 1-29
 INSPECTION 1-29
 REMOVAL & INSTALLATION 1-29
AIR CONDITIONING 1-30
 SAFETY PRECAUTIONS 1-30
 GENERAL SERVICING PROCEDURES 1-31
 SYSTEM INSPECTION 1-32
 DISCHARGING, EVACUATING &
  CHARGING 1-32
WINDSHIELD WIPERS 1-32
 ELEMENT (REFILL) CARE &
  REPLACEMENT 1-32
TIRES AND WHEELS 1-37
 TIRE ROTATION 1-37
 TIRE DESIGN 1-38
 TIRE STORAGE 1-38
 INFLATION & INSPECTION 1-38
 CARE OF SPECIAL WHEELS 1-40
FLUIDS AND LUBRICANTS 1-41
FLUID DISPOSAL 1-41
FUEL AND ENGINE OIL
 RECOMMENDATIONS 1-41
 FUEL 1-41
 ENGINE OIL 1-41
ENGINE 1-42
 OIL LEVEL CHECK 1-42
 OIL CHANGE 1-43
 OIL FILTER CHANGES 1-44
MANUAL TRANSMISSION 1-45
 FLUID RECOMMENDATIONS 1-45
 LEVEL CHECK 1-45

DRAIN & REFILL 1-45
AUTOMATIC TRANSMISSION 1-45
 FLUID RECOMMENDATIONS 1-45
 LEVEL CHECK 1-45
 DRAIN & REFILL 1-46
REAR AXLE 1-47
 FLUID RECOMMENDATIONS 1-47
 LEVEL CHECK 1-47
 DRAIN & REFILL 1-47
COOLING SYSTEM 1-48
 FLUID RECOMMENDATIONS 1-49
 LEVEL CHECK 1-50
 COOLING SYSTEM INSPECTION 1-50
 DRAIN & REFILL 1-51
 FLUSHING & CLEANING THE SYSTEM 1-52
MASTER CYLINDER 1-52
 FLUID RECOMMENDATONS 1-52
 LEVEL CHECK 1-52
MANUAL STEERING GEAR 1-53
 FLUID RECOMMENDATION 1-53
POWER STEERING PUMP 1-53
 FLUID RECOMMENDATION & LEVEL
  CHECK 1-53
CHASSIS GREASING 1-54
BODY LUBRICATION 1-54
 HOOD LATCH 1-54
WHEEL BEARINGS 1-54
TRAILER TOWING 1-55
GENERAL RECOMMENDATIONS 1-55
TRAILER WEIGHT 1-55
HITCH (TONGUE) WEIGHT 1-55
COOLING 1-55
 ENGINE 1-55
 TRANSMISSION 1-55
HANDLING A TRAILER 1-56
TOWING THE VEHICLE 1-56
JUMP STARTING A DEAD BATTERY 1-56
JUMP STARTING PRECAUTIONS 1-56
JUMP STARTING PROCEDURE 1-57
JACKING 1-57
JACKING PRECAUTIONS 1-59
HOW TO BUY A USED VEHICLE 1-60
TIPS 1-60
 USED VEHICLE CHECKLIST 1-61
 ROAD TEST CHECKLIST 1-62
COMPONENT LOCATIONS
 MAINTENANCE COMPONENT LOCATIONS—
  EARLY MODEL V8 ENGINE 1-16
 MAINTENANCE COMPONENT LOCATIONS—
  LATE MODEL NOVA INLINE ENGINE 1-17
SPECIFICATION CHARTS
 STANDARD TORQUE SPECIFICATIONS AND
  FASTENER MARKINGS 1-10
 STANDARD AND METRIC CONVERSION
  FACTORS 1-13
 1962–68 ENGINE OIL VISCOSITY
  RECOMMENDATIONS 1-42
 1969–71 RECOMMENDED SAE VISCOSITY
  NUMBER 1-42
 1972–77 RECOMMENDED SAE VISCOSITY
  NUMBER 1-42
 1978–79 RECOMMENDED SAE VISCOSITY
  NUMBER 1-42
 LUBRICATION AND MAINTENANCE
  SCHEDULE 1-63
 CAPACITIES 1-65
 ENGLISH TO METRIC CONVERSION
  CHARTS 1-68

1

GENERAL INFORMATION AND MAINTENANCE

HOW TO USE THIS BOOK 1-2
TOOLS AND EQUIPMENT 1-3
SERVICING YOUR VEHICLE SAFELY 1-7
FASTENERS, MEASUREMENTS
 AND CONVERSIONS 1-8
SERIAL NUMBER IDENTIFICATION 1-14
ROUTINE MAINTENANCE 1-16
FLUIDS AND LUBRICANTS 1-41
TRAILER TOWING 1-55
TOWING THE VEHICLE 1-56
JUMP STARTING A DEAD BATTERY 1-56
JACKING 1-57
HOW TO BUY A USED VEHICLE 1-60

HOW TO USE THIS BOOK

Chilton's Total Car Care manual is intended to help you learn more about the inner workings of your vehicle while saving you money on its upkeep and operation.

The beginning of the book will likely be referred to the most, since that is where you will find information for maintenance and tune-up. The other sections deal with the more complex systems of your vehicle. Operating systems from engine through brakes are covered to the extent that the average do-it-yourselfer becomes mechanically involved. This book will not explain such things as rebuilding a differential for the simple reason that the expertise required and the investment in special tools make this task uneconomical. It will, however, give you detailed instructions to help you change your own brake pads and shoes, replace spark plugs, and perform many more jobs that can save you money, give you personal satisfaction and help you avoid expensive problems.

A secondary purpose of this book is a reference for owners who want to understand their vehicle and/or their mechanics better. In this case, no tools at all are required.

Where to Begin

Before removing any bolts, read through the entire procedure. This will give you the overall view of what tools and supplies will be required. There is nothing more frustrating than having to walk to the bus stop on Monday morning because you were short one bolt on Sunday afternoon. So read ahead and plan ahead. Each operation should be approached logically and all procedures thoroughly understood before attempting any work.

All sections contain adjustments, maintenance, removal and installation procedures, and in some cases, repair or overhaul procedures. When repair is not considered practical, we tell you how to remove the part and then how to install the new or rebuilt replacement. In this way, you at least save the labor costs. Backyard repair of some components is just not practical.

Avoiding Trouble

Many procedures in this book require you to "label and disconnect . . ." a group of lines, hoses or wires. Don't be lulled into thinking you can remember where everything goes—you won't. If you hook up vacuum or fuel lines incorrectly, the vehicle will run poorly, if at all. If you hook up electrical wiring incorrectly, you may instantly learn a very expensive lesson.

You don't need to know the official or engineering name for each hose or line. A piece of masking tape on the hose and a piece on its fitting will allow you to assign your own label such as the letter A or a short name. As long as you remember your own code, the lines can be reconnected by matching similar letters or names. Do remember that tape will dissolve in gasoline or other fluids; if a component is to be washed or cleaned, use another method of identification. A permanent felt-tipped marker can be very handy for marking metal parts. Remove any tape or paper labels after assembly.

Maintenance or Repair?

It's necessary to mention the difference between maintenance and repair. Maintenance includes routine inspections, adjustments, and replacement of parts which show signs of normal wear. Maintenance compensates for wear or deterioration. Repair implies that something has broken or is not working. A need for repair is often caused by lack of maintenance. Example: draining and refilling the automatic transmission fluid is maintenance recommended by the manufacturer at specific mileage intervals. Failure to do this can ruin the transmission/transaxle, requiring very expensive repairs. While no maintenance program can prevent items from breaking or wearing out, a general rule can be stated: MAINTENANCE IS CHEAPER THAN REPAIR.

Two basic mechanic's rules should be mentioned here. First, whenever the left side of the vehicle or engine is referred to, it is meant to specify the driver's side. Conversely, the right side of the vehicle means the passenger's side. Second, most screws and bolts are removed by turning counterclockwise, and tightened by turning clockwise.

Safety is always the most important rule. Constantly be aware of the dangers involved in working on an automobile and take the proper precautions. See the information in this section regarding SERVICING YOUR VEHICLE SAFELY and the SAFETY NOTICE on the acknowledgment page.

Avoiding the Most Common Mistakes

Pay attention to the instructions provided. There are 3 common mistakes in mechanical work:

1. **Incorrect order of assembly, disassembly or adjustment.** When taking something apart or putting it together, performing steps in the wrong order usually just costs you extra time; however, it CAN break something. Read the entire procedure before beginning disassembly. Perform everything in the order in which the instructions say you should, even if you can't immediately see a reason for it. When you're taking apart something that is very intricate, you might want to draw a picture of how it looks when assembled at one point in order to make sure you get everything back in its proper position. We will supply exploded views whenever possible. When making adjustments, perform them in the proper order; often, one adjustment affects another, and you cannot expect even satisfactory results unless each adjustment is made only when it cannot be changed by any other.

2. **Overtorquing (or undertorquing).** While it is more common for overtorquing to cause damage, undertorquing may allow a fastener to vibrate loose causing serious damage. Especially when dealing with aluminum parts, pay attention to torque specifications and utilize a torque wrench in assembly. If a torque figure is not available, remember that if you are using the right tool to perform the job, you will probably not have to strain yourself to get a fastener tight enough. The pitch of most threads is so slight that the tension you put on the wrench will be multiplied many times in actual force on what you are tightening. A good example of how critical torque is can be seen in the case of spark plug in-

stallation, especially where you are putting the plug into an aluminum cylinder head. Too little torque can fail to crush the gasket, causing leakage of combustion gases and consequent overheating of the plug and engine parts. Too much torque can damage the threads or distort the plug, changing the spark gap.

There are many commercial products available for ensuring that fasteners won't come loose, even if they are not torqued just right (a very common brand is Loctite®). If you're worried about getting something together tight enough to hold, but loose enough to avoid mechanical damage during assembly, one of these products might offer substantial insurance. Before choosing a threadlocking compound, read the label on the package and make sure the product is compatible with the materials, fluids, etc. involved.

3. **Crossthreading.** This occurs when a part such as a bolt is screwed into a nut or casting at the wrong angle and forced. Crossthreading is more likely to occur if access is difficult. It

helps to clean and lubricate fasteners, then to start threading with the part to be installed positioned straight in. Then, start the bolt, spark plug, etc. with your fingers. If you encounter resistance, unscrew the part and start over again at a different angle until it can be inserted and turned several times without much effort. Keep in mind that many parts, especially spark plugs, have tapered threads, so that gentle turning will automatically bring the part you're threading to the proper angle, but only if you don't force it or resist a change in angle. Don't put a wrench on the part until it's been tightened a couple of turns by hand. If you suddenly encounter resistance, and the part has not seated fully, don't force it. Pull it back out to make sure it's clean and threading properly.

Always take your time and be patient; once you have some experience, working on your vehicle may well become an enjoyable hobby.

TOOLS AND EQUIPMENT

Naturally, without the proper tools and equipment it is impossible to properly service your vehicle. It would also be virtually impossible to catalog every tool that you would need to perform all of the operations in this book. Of course, It would be unwise for the amateur to rush out and buy an expensive set of tools on the theory that he/she may need one or more of them at some time.

The best approach is to proceed slowly, gathering a good quality set of those tools that are used most frequently. Don't be misled by the low cost of bargain tools. It is far better to spend a little more for better quality. Forged wrenches, 6 or 12-point sockets and fine tooth ratchets are by far preferable to their less expensive counterparts. As any good mechanic can tell you, there are few worse experiences than trying to work on a vehicle with bad tools. Your monetary savings will be far outweighed by frustration and mangled knuckles.

Begin accumulating those tools that are used most frequently: those associated with routine maintenance and tune-up. In addition to the normal assortment of screwdrivers and pliers, you should have the following tools:

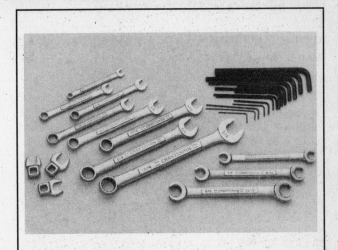

In addition to ratchets, a good set of wrenches and hex keys will be necessary

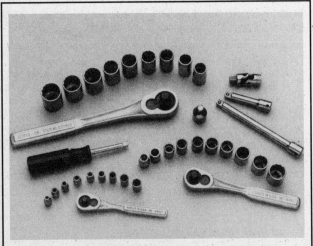

All but the most basic procedures will require an assortment of ratchets and sockets

A hydraulic floor jack and a set of jackstands are essential for lifting and supporting the vehicle

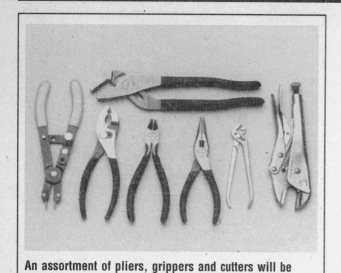

An assortment of pliers, grippers and cutters will be handy for old rusted parts and stripped bolt heads

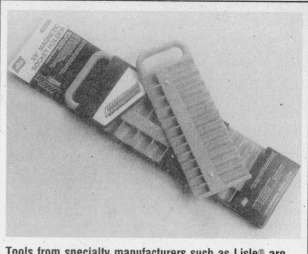

Tools from specialty manufacturers such as Lisle® are designed to make your job easier . . .

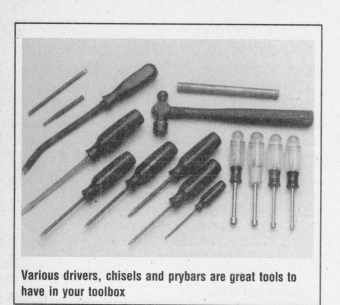

Various drivers, chisels and prybars are great tools to have in your toolbox

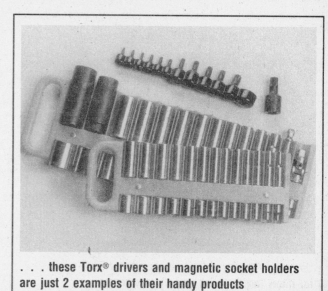

. . . these Torx® drivers and magnetic socket holders are just 2 examples of their handy products

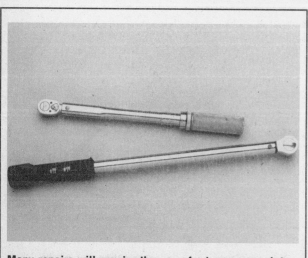

Many repairs will require the use of a torque wrench to assure the components are properly fastened

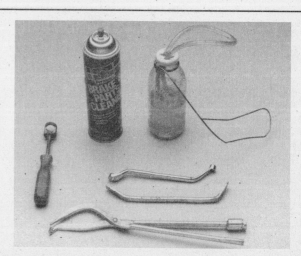

Although not always necessary, using specialized brake tools will save time

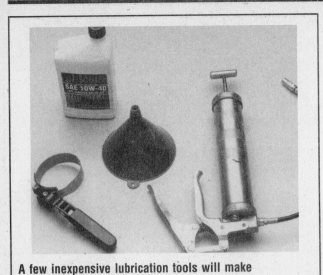

A few inexpensive lubrication tools will make maintenance easier

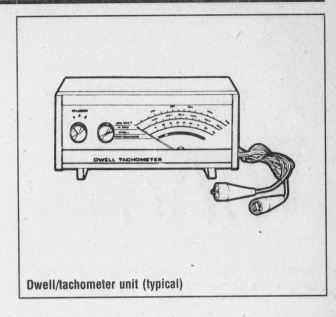

Dwell/tachometer unit (typical)

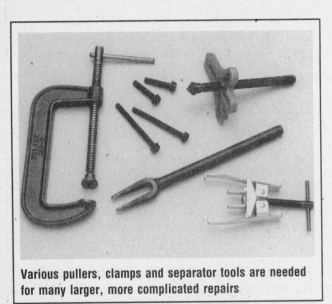

Various pullers, clamps and separator tools are needed for many larger, more complicated repairs

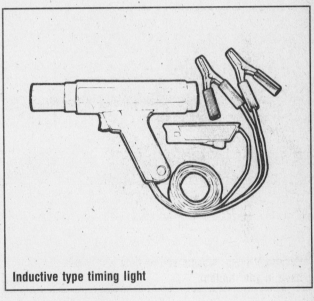

Inductive type timing light

A variety of tools and gauges should be used for spark plug gapping and installation

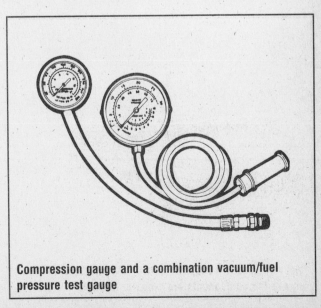

Compression gauge and a combination vacuum/fuel pressure test gauge

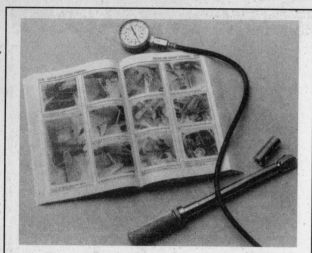

Proper information is vital, so always have a Chilton Total Car Care manual handy

• Wrenches/sockets and combination open end/box end wrenches in sizes from 1/8–3/4 in. or 3mm–19mm (depending on whether your vehicle uses standard or metric fasteners) and a 13/16 in. or 5/8 in. spark plug socket (depending on plug type).

➡ **If possible, buy various length socket drive extensions. Universal-joint and wobble extensions can be extremely useful, but be careful when using them, as they can change the amount of torque applied to the socket.**

• Jackstands for support.
• Oil filter wrench.
• Spout or funnel for pouring fluids.
• Grease gun for chassis lubrication (unless your vehicle is not equipped with any grease fittings—for details, please refer to information on Fluids and Lubricants found later in this section).
• Hydrometer for checking the battery (unless equipped with a sealed, maintenance-free battery).
• A container for draining oil and other fluids.
• Rags for wiping up the inevitable mess.

In addition to the above items there are several others that are not absolutely necessary, but handy to have around. These include Oil Dry® (or an equivalent oil absorbent gravel—such as cat litter) and the usual supply of lubricants, antifreeze and fluids, although these can be purchased as needed. This is a basic list for routine maintenance, but only your personal needs and desire can accurately determine your list of tools.

After performing a few projects on the vehicle, you'll be amazed at the other tools and non-tools on your workbench. Some useful household items are: a large turkey baster or siphon, empty coffee cans and ice trays (to store parts), ball of twine, electrical tape for wiring, small rolls of colored tape for tagging lines or hoses, markers and pens, a note pad, golf tees (for plugging vacuum lines), metal coat hangers or a roll of mechanics's wire (to hold things out of the way), dental pick or similar long, pointed probe, a strong magnet, and a small mirror (to see into recesses and under manifolds).

A more advanced set of tools, suitable for tune-up work, can be drawn up easily. While the tools are slightly more sophisticated, they need not be outrageously expensive. There are several inexpensive tach/dwell meters on the market that are every bit as good for the average mechanic as a professional model. Just be sure that it goes to a least 1200–1500 rpm on the tach scale and that it works on 4, 6 and 8-cylinder engines. (If you own one or more vehicles with a diesel engine, a special tachometer is required since diesels don't use spark plug ignition systems). The key to these purchases is to make them with an eye towards adaptability and wide range. A basic list of tune-up tools could include:

• Tach/dwell meter.
• Spark plug wrench and gapping tool.
• Feeler gauges for valve or point adjustment. (Even if your vehicle does not use points or require valve adjustments, a feeler gauge is helpful for many repair/overhaul procedures).

A tachometer/dwell meter will ensure accurate tune-up work on vehicles without electronic ignition. The choice of a timing light should be made carefully. A light which works on the DC current supplied by the vehicle's battery is the best choice; it should have a xenon tube for brightness. On any vehicle with an electronic ignition system, a timing light with an inductive pickup that clamps around the No. 1 spark plug cable is preferred.

In addition to these basic tools, there are several other tools and gauges you may find useful. These include:

• Compression gauge. The screw-in type is slower to use, but eliminates the possibility of a faulty reading due to escaping pressure.
• Manifold vacuum gauge.
• 12V test light.
• A combination volt/ohmmeter
• Induction Ammeter. This is used for determining whether or not there is current in a wire. These are handy for use if a wire is broken somewhere in a wiring harness.

As a final note, you will probably find a torque wrench necessary for all but the most basic work. The beam type models are perfectly adequate, although the newer click types (breakaway) are easier to use. The click type torque wrenches tend to be more expensive. Also keep in mind that all types of torque wrenches should be periodically checked and/or recalibrated. You will have to decide for yourself which better fits your purpose.

Special Tools

Normally, the use of special factory tools is avoided for repair procedures, since these are not readily available for the do-it-yourself mechanic. When it is possible to perform the job with more commonly available tools, it will be pointed out, but occasionally, a special tool was designed to perform a specific function and should be used. Before substituting another tool, you should be convinced that neither your safety nor the performance of the vehicle will be compromised.

Special tools can usually be purchased from an automotive parts store or from your dealer. In some cases special tools may be available directly from the tool manufacturer.

SERVICING YOUR VEHICLE SAFELY

It is virtually impossible to anticipate all of the hazards involved with automotive maintenance and service, but care and common sense will prevent most accidents.

The rules of safety for mechanics range from "don't smoke around gasoline," to "use the proper tool(s) for the job." The trick to avoiding injuries is to develop safe work habits and to take every possible precaution.

Do's

• Do keep a fire extinguisher and first aid kit handy.

• Do wear safety glasses or goggles when cutting, drilling, grinding or prying, even if you have 20–20 vision. If you wear glasses for the sake of vision, wear safety goggles over your regular glasses.

• Do shield your eyes whenever you work around the battery. Batteries contain sulfuric acid. In case of contact with the eyes or

Using the correct size wrench will help prevent the possibility of rounding off a nut

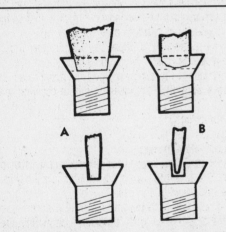

Screwdrivers should be kept in good condition to prevent injury or damage which could result if the blade slips from the screw

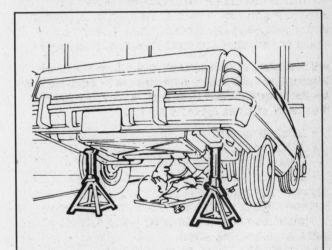

NEVER work under a vehicle unless it is supported using safety stands (jackstands)

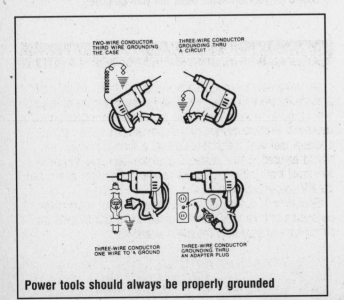

Power tools should always be properly grounded

skin, flush the area with water or a mixture of water and baking soda, then seek immediate medical attention.

• Do use safety stands (jackstands) for any undervehicle service. Jacks are for raising vehicles; jackstands are for making sure the vehicle stays raised until you want it to come down. Whenever the vehicle is raised, block the wheels remaining on the ground and set the parking brake.

• Do use adequate ventilation when working with any chemicals or hazardous materials. Like carbon monoxide, the asbestos dust resulting from some brake lining wear can be hazardous in sufficient quantities.

• Do disconnect the negative battery cable when working on the electrical system. The secondary ignition system contains EXTREMELY HIGH VOLTAGE. In some cases it can even exceed 50,000 volts.

• Do follow manufacturer's directions whenever working with potentially hazardous materials. Most chemicals and fluids are poisonous if taken internally.

• Do properly maintain your tools. Loose hammerheads, mushroomed punches and chisels, frayed or poorly grounded electrical cords, excessively worn screwdrivers, spread wrenches (open end), cracked sockets, slipping ratchets, or faulty droplight sockets can cause accidents.

• Likewise, keep your tools clean; a greasy wrench can slip off a bolt head, ruining the bolt and often harming your knuckles in the process.

• Do use the proper size and type of tool for the job at hand. Do select a wrench or socket that fits the nut or bolt. The wrench or socket should sit straight, not cocked.

• Do, when possible, pull on a wrench handle rather than push on it, and adjust your stance to prevent a fall.

• Do be sure that adjustable wrenches are tightly closed on the nut or bolt and pulled so that the force is on the side of the fixed jaw.

• Do strike squarely with a hammer; avoid glancing blows.

• Do set the parking brake and block the drive wheels if the work requires a running engine.

Don'ts

• Don't run the engine in a garage or anywhere else without proper ventilation—EVER! Carbon monoxide is poisonous; it takes a long time to leave the human body and you can build up a deadly supply of it in your system by simply breathing in a little every day. You may not realize you are slowly poisoning yourself. Always use power vents, windows, fans and/or open the garage door.

• Don't work around moving parts while wearing loose clothing. Short sleeves are much safer than long, loose sleeves. Hard-toed shoes with neoprene soles protect your toes and give a better grip on slippery surfaces. Jewelry such as watches, fancy belt buckles, beads or body adornment of any kind is not safe working around a vehicle. Long hair should be tied back under a hat or cap.

• Don't use pockets for toolboxes. A fall or bump can drive a screwdriver deep into your body. Even a rag hanging from your back pocket can wrap around a spinning shaft or fan.

• Don't smoke when working around gasoline, cleaning solvent or other flammable material.

• Don't smoke when working around the battery. When the battery is being charged, it gives off explosive hydrogen gas.

• Don't use gasoline to wash your hands; there are excellent soaps available. Gasoline contains dangerous additives which can enter the body through a cut or through your pores. Gasoline also removes all the natural oils from the skin so that bone dry hands will suck up oil and grease.

• Don't service the air conditioning system unless you are equipped with the necessary tools and training. When liquid or compressed gas refrigerant is released to atmospheric pressure it will absorb heat from whatever it contacts. This will chill or freeze anything it touches. Although refrigerant is normally non-toxic, R-12 becomes a deadly poisonous gas in the presence of an open flame. One good whiff of the vapors from burning refrigerant can be fatal.

• Don't use screwdrivers for anything other than driving screws! A screwdriver used as an prying tool can snap when you least expect it, causing injuries. At the very least, you'll ruin a good screwdriver.

• Don't use a bumper or emergency jack (that little ratchet, scissors, or pantograph jack supplied with the vehicle) for anything other than changing a flat! These jacks are only intended for emergency use out on the road; they are NOT designed as a maintenance tool. If you are serious about maintaining your vehicle yourself, invest in a hydraulic floor jack of at least a 1½ ton capacity, and at least two sturdy jackstands.

FASTENERS, MEASUREMENTS AND CONVERSIONS

Bolts, Nuts and Other Threaded Retainers

Although there are a great variety of fasteners found in the modern car or truck, the most commonly used retainer is the threaded fastener (nuts, bolts, screws, studs, etc). Most threaded retainers may be reused, provided that they are not damaged in use or during the repair. Some retainers (such as stretch bolts or torque prevailing nuts) are designed to deform when tightened or in use and should not be reinstalled.

Whenever possible, we will note any special retainers which should be replaced during a procedure. But you should always inspect the condition of a retainer when it is removed and replace any that show signs of damage. Check all threads for rust or corrosion which can increase the torque necessary to achieve the desired clamp load for which that fastener was originally selected. Additionally, be sure that the driver surface of the fastener has not been compromised by rounding or other damage. In some cases a driver surface may become only partially rounded, allowing the driver to catch in only one direction. In many of these occurrences, a fastener may be installed and tightened, but the driver would not be able to grip and loosen the fastener again. (This could lead to frustration down the line should that component ever need to be disassembled again).

If you must replace a fastener, whether due to design or damage, you must ALWAYS be sure to use the proper replacement. In all cases, a retainer of the same design, material and strength should be used. Markings on the heads of most bolts will help determine the proper strength of the fastener. The same material, thread and pitch must be selected to assure proper installation and safe operation of the vehicle afterwards.

Thread gauges are available to help measure a bolt or stud's thread. Most automotive and hardware stores keep gauges available to help you select the proper size. In a pinch, you can use another nut or bolt for a thread gauge. If the bolt you are replacing is not too badly damaged, you can select a match by finding another bolt which will thread in its place. If you find a nut which threads properly onto the damaged bolt, then use that nut to help select the replacement bolt. If however, the bolt you are replacing is so badly damaged (broken or drilled out) that its threads cannot be used as a gauge, you might start by looking for another bolt (from the same assembly or a similar location on your vehicle) which will thread into the damaged bolt's mounting. If so, the other bolt can be used to select a nut; the nut can then be used to select the replacement bolt.

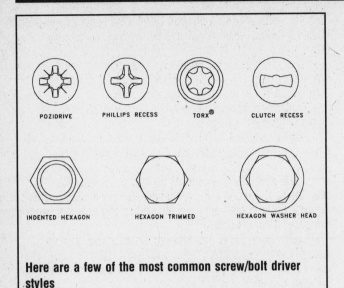

Here are a few of the most common screw/bolt driver styles

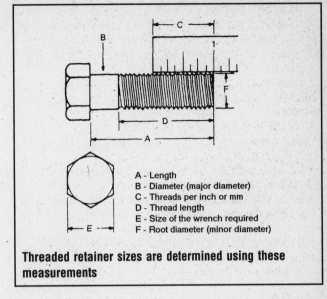

A - Length
B - Diameter (major diameter)
C - Threads per inch or mm
D - Thread length
E - Size of the wrench required
F - Root diameter (minor diameter)

Threaded retainer sizes are determined using these measurements

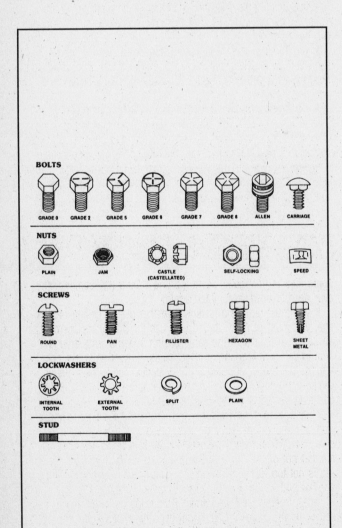

There are many different types of threaded retainers found on vehicles

Special fasteners such as these Torx® head bolts are used by manufacturers to discourage people from working on vehicles without the proper tools

In all cases, be absolutely sure you have selected the proper replacement. Don't be shy, you can always ask the store clerk for help.

✳✳ WARNING

Be aware that when you find a bolt with damaged threads, you may also find the nut or drilled hole it was threaded into has also been damaged. If this is the case, you may have to drill and tap the hole, replace the nut or otherwise repair the threads. NEVER try to force a replacement bolt to fit into the damaged threads.

Torque

Torque is defined as the measurement of resistance to turning or rotating. It tends to twist a body about an axis of rotation. A common example of this would be tightening a threaded retainer such as a nut, bolt or screw. Measuring torque is one of the most

Standard Torque Specifications and Fastener Markings

In the absence of specific torques, the following chart can be used as a guide to the maximum safe torque of a particular size/grade of fastener.
- There is no torque difference for fine or coarse threads.
- Torque values are based on clean, dry threads. Reduce the value by 10% if threads are oiled prior to assembly.
- The torque required for aluminum components or fasteners is considerably less.

U.S. Bolts

SAE Grade Number	1 or 2			5			6 or 7		
Number of lines always 2 less than the grade number.									
Bolt Size (Inches)—(Thread)	**Maximum Torque**			**Maximum Torque**			**Maximum Torque**		
	Ft./Lbs.	Kgm	Nm	Ft./Lbs.	Kgm	Nm	Ft./Lbs.	Kgm	Nm
¼ — 20	5	0.7	6.8	8	1.1	10.8	10	1.4	13.5
— 28	6	0.8	8.1	10	1.4	13.6			
5/16 — 18	11	1.5	14.9	17	2.3	23.0	19	2.6	25.8
— 24	13	1.8	17.6	19	2.6	25.7			
⅜ — 16	18	2.5	24.4	31	4.3	42.0	34	4.7	46.0
— 24	20	2.75	27.1	35	4.8	47.5			
7/16 — 14	28	3.8	37.0	49	6.8	66.4	55	7.6	74.5
— 20	30	4.2	40.7	55	7.6	74.5			
½ — 13	39	5.4	52.8	75	10.4	101.7	85	11.75	115.2
— 20	41	5.7	55.6	85	11.7	115.2			
9/16 — 12	51	7.0	69.2	110	15.2	149.1	120	16.6	162.7
— 18	55	7.6	74.5	120	16.6	162.7			
⅝ — 11	83	11.5	112.5	150	20.7	203.3	167	23.0	226.5
— 18	95	13.1	128.8	170	23.5	230.5			
¾ — 10	105	14.5	142.3	270	37.3	366.0	280	38.7	379.6
— 16	115	15.9	155.9	295	40.8	400.0			
⅞ — 9	160	22.1	216.9	395	54.6	535.5	440	60.9	596.5
— 14	175	24.2	237.2	435	60.1	589.7			
1 — 8	236	32.5	318.6	590	81.6	799.9	660	91.3	894.8
— 14	250	34.6	338.9	660	91.3	849.8			

Metric Bolts

Relative Strength Marking	4.6, 4.8			8.8		
Bolt Markings						
Bolt Size Thread Size x Pitch (mm)	**Maximum Torque**			**Maximum Torque**		
	Ft./Lbs.	Kgm	Nm	Ft./Lbs.	Kgm	Nm
6 x 1.0	2–3	.2–.4	3–4	3–6	.4–.8	5–8
8 x 1.25	6–8	.8–1	8–12	9–14	1.2–1.9	13–19
10 x 1.25	12–17	1.5–2.3	16–23	20–29	2.7–4.0	27–39
12 x 1.25	21–32	2.9–4.4	29–43	35–53	4.8–7.3	47–72
14 x 1.5	35–52	4.8–7.1	48–70	57–85	7.8–11.7	77–110
16 x 1.5	51–77	7.0–10.6	67–100	90–120	12.4–16.5	130–160
18 x 1.5	74–110	10.2–15.1	100–150	130–170	17.9–23.4	180–230
20 x 1.5	110–140	15.1–19.3	150–190	190–240	26.2–46.9	160–320
22 x 1.5	150–190	22.0–26.2	200–260	250–320	34.5–44.1	340–430
24 x 1.5	190–240	26.2–46.9	260–320	310–410	42.7–56.5	420–550

Standard and metric bolt torque specifications based on bolt strengths—WARNING: use only as a guide common ways to help assure that a threaded retainer has been properly fastened.

When tightening a threaded fastener, torque is applied in three distinct areas, the head, the bearing surface and the clamp load. About 50 percent of the measured torque is used in overcoming bearing friction. This is the friction between the bearing surface of the bolt head, screw head or nut face and the base material or washer (the surface on which the fastener is rotating). Approximately 40 percent of the applied torque is used in overcoming thread friction. This leaves only about 10 percent of the applied torque to develop a useful clamp load (the force which holds a joint together). This means that friction can account for as much as 90 percent of the applied torque on a fastener.

TORQUE WRENCHES

In most applications, a torque wrench can be used to assure proper installation of a fastener. Torque wrenches come in various designs and most automotive supply stores will carry a variety to suit your needs. A torque wrench should be used any time we supply a specific torque value for a fastener. A torque wrench can also be used if you are following the general guidelines in the accompanying charts. Keep in mind that because there is no world-wide standardization of fasteners, the charts are a general guide-line and should be used with caution. Again, the general rule of "if you are using the right tool for the job, you should not have to strain to tighten a fastener" applies here.

Beam Type

The beam type torque wrench is one of the most popular types. It consists of a pointer attached to the head that runs the length of the flexible beam (shaft) to a scale located near the handle. As the wrench is pulled, the beam bends and the pointer indicates the torque using the scale.

Click (Breakaway) Type

Another popular design of torque wrench is the click type. To use the click type wrench you pre-adjust it to a torque setting. Once the torque is reached, the wrench has a reflex signalling fea-

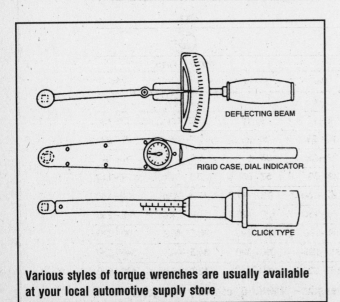

Various styles of torque wrenches are usually available at your local automotive supply store

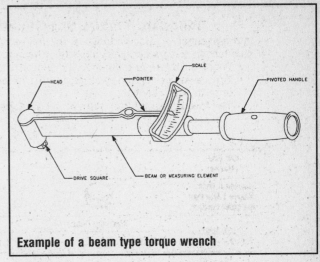

Example of a beam type torque wrench

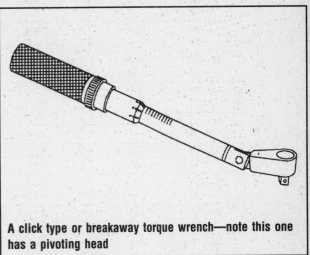

A click type or breakaway torque wrench—note this one has a pivoting head

ture that causes a momentary breakaway of the torque wrench body, sending an impulse to the operator's hand.

Pivot Head Type

Some torque wrenches (usually of the click type) may be equipped with a pivot head which can allow it to be used in areas of limited access. BUT, it must be used properly. To hold a pivot head wrench, grasp the handle lightly, and as you pull on the handle, it should be floated on the pivot point. If the handle comes in contact with the yoke extension during the process of pulling, there is a very good chance the torque readings will be inaccurate because this could alter the wrench loading point. The design of the handle is usually such as to make it inconvenient to deliberately misuse the wrench.

➡**It should be mentioned that the use of any U-joint, wobble or extension will have an effect on the torque readings, no matter what type of wrench you are using. For the most accurate readings, install the socket directly on the wrench driver. If necessary, straight extensions (which hold a socket directly under the wrench driver) will have the least effect on the torque reading. Avoid any extension that alters the length of the wrench from the handle to the head/driving point (such as a crow's foot). U-joint or Wobble extensions can greatly affect the readings; avoid their use at all times.**

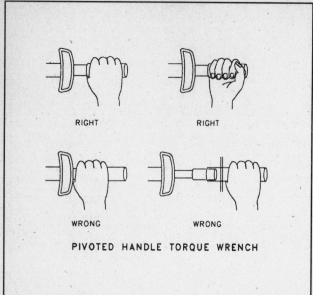

Torque wrenches with pivoting heads must be grasped and used properly to prevent an incorrect reading

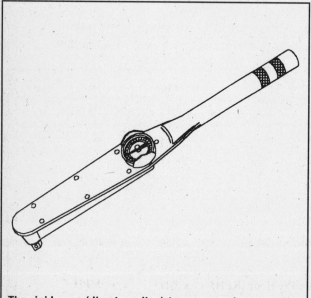

The rigid case (direct reading) torque wrench uses a dial indicator to show torque

Rigid Case (Direct Reading)

A rigid case or direct reading torque wrench is equipped with a dial indicator to show torque values. One advantage of these wrenches is that they can be held at any position on the wrench without affecting accuracy. These wrenches are often preferred because they tend to be compact, easy to read and have a great degree of accuracy.

TORQUE ANGLE METERS

Because the frictional characteristics of each fastener or threaded hole will vary, clamp loads which are based strictly on

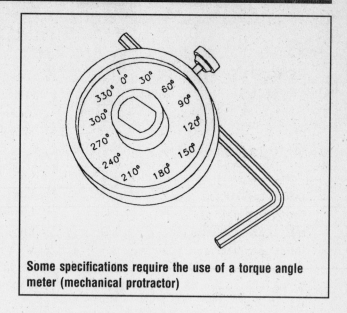

Some specifications require the use of a torque angle meter (mechanical protractor)

torque will vary as well. In most applications, this variance is not significant enough to cause worry. But, in certain applications, a manufacturer's engineers may determine that more precise clamp loads are necessary (such is the case with many aluminum cylinder heads). In these cases, a torque angle method of installation would be specified. When installing fasteners which are torque angle tightened, a predetermined seating torque and standard torque wrench are usually used first to remove any compliance from the joint. The fastener is then tightened the specified additional portion of a turn measured in degrees. A torque angle gauge (mechanical protractor) is used for these applications.

Standard and Metric Measurements

Throughout this manual, specifications are given to help you determine the condition of various components on your vehicle, or to assist you in their installation. Some of the most common measurements include length (in. or cm/mm), torque (ft. lbs., inch lbs. or Nm) and pressure (psi, in. Hg, kPa or mm Hg). In most cases, we strive to provide the proper measurement as determined by the manufacturer's engineers.

Though, in some cases, that value may not be conveniently measured with what is available in your toolbox. Luckily, many of the measuring devices which are available today will have two scales so the Standard or Metric measurements may easily be taken. If any of the various measuring tools which are available to you do not contain the same scale as listed in the specifications, use the accompanying conversion factors to determine the proper value.

The conversion factor chart is used by taking the given specification and multiplying it by the necessary conversion factor. For instance, looking at the first line, if you have a measurement in inches such as "free-play should be 2 in." but your ruler reads only in millimeters, multiply 2 in. by the conversion factor of 25.4 to get the metric equivalent of 50.8mm. Likewise, if the specification was given only in a Metric measurement, for example in Newton Meters (Nm), then look at the center column first. If the measurement is 100 Nm, multiply it by the conversion factor of 0.738 to get 73.8 ft. lbs.

CONVERSION FACTORS

LENGTH–DISTANCE

Inches (in.)	x 25.4	= Millimeters (mm)	x .0394	= Inches
Feet (ft.)	x .305	= Meters (m)	x 3.281	= Feet
Miles	x 1.609	= Kilometers (km)	x .0621	= Miles

VOLUME

Cubic Inches (in3)	x 16.387	= Cubic Centimeters	x .061	= in3
IMP Pints (IMP pt.)	x .568	= Liters (L)	x 1.76	= IMP pt.
IMP Quarts (IMP qt.)	x 1.137	= Liters (L)	x .88	= IMP qt.
IMP Gallons (IMP gal.)	x 4.546	= Liters (L)	x .22	= IMP gal.
IMP Quarts (IMP qt.)	x 1.201	= US Quarts (US qt.)	x .833	= IMP qt.
IMP Gallons (IMP gal.)	x 1.201	= US Gallons (US gal.)	x .833	= IMP gal.
Fl. Ounces	x 29.573	= Milliliters	x .034	= Ounces
US Pints (US pt.)	x .473	= Liters (L)	x 2.113	= Pints
US Quarts (US qt.)	x .946	= Liters (L)	x 1.057	= Quarts
US Gallons (US gal.)	x 3.785	= Liters (L)	x .264	= Gallons

MASS–WEIGHT

Ounces (oz.)	x 28.35	= Grams (g)	x .035	= Ounces
Pounds (lb.)	x .454	= Kilograms (kg)	x 2.205	= Pounds

PRESSURE

Pounds Per Sq. In. (psi)	x 6.895	= Kilopascals (kPa)	x .145	= psi
Inches of Mercury (Hg)	x .4912	= psi	x 2.036	= Hg
Inches of Mercury (Hg)	x 3.377	= Kilopascals (kPa)	x .2961	= Hg
Inches of Water (H$_2$O)	x .07355	= Inches of Mercury	x 13.783	= H$_2$O
Inches of Water (H$_2$O)	x .03613	= psi	x 27.684	= H$_2$O
Inches of Water (H$_2$O)	x .248	= Kilopascals (kPa)	x 4.026	= H$_2$O

TORQUE

Pounds–Force Inches (in–lb)	x .113	= Newton Meters (N·m)	x 8.85	= in–lb
Pounds–Force Feet (ft–lb)	x 1.356	= Newton Meters (N·m)	x .738	= ft–lb

VELOCITY

Miles Per Hour (MPH)	x 1.609	= Kilometers Per Hour (KPH)	x .621	= MPH

POWER

Horsepower (Hp)	x .745	= Kilowatts	x 1.34	= Horsepower

FUEL CONSUMPTION*

Miles Per Gallon IMP (MPG)	x .354	= Kilometers Per Liter (Km/L)
Kilometers Per Liter (Km/L)	x 2.352	= IMP MPG
Miles Per Gallon US (MPG)	x .425	= Kilometers Per Liter (Km/L)
Kilometers Per Liter (Km/L)	x 2.352	= US MPG

*It is common to covert from miles per gallon (mpg) to liters/100 kilometers (1/100 km), where mpg (IMP) x 1/100 km = 282 and mpg (US) x 1/100 km = 235.

TEMPERATURE

Degree Fahrenheit (°F)	= (°C x 1.8) + 32
Degree Celsius (°C)	= (°F – 32) x .56

Standard and metric conversion factors chart

SERIAL NUMBER IDENTIFICATION

Vehicle

♦ **See Figure 1**

On 1962–67 models, the vehicle serial number is on a plate attached to the left front door hinge pillar. The vehicle serial number plate for 1968 and later models is mounted on the top left-hand side of the instrument panel, visible through the windshield.

A typical vehicle serial number tag yields manufacturer's identity, vehicle type, model year, assembly plant, and production unit number as shown in the charts.

Engine

♦ **See Figures 2 and 3**

The engine identification numbers for four- and six-cylinder engines are found on a pad at the front right side of the engine block, just to the rear of the distributor. On eight-cylinder engines, the engine identification number pad is located at the front right-hand side of the engine block.

Fig. 1 Vehicle Identification Number (VIN) plate location—1962–67 Chevy II shown

On late-models, the Vehicle Identification Number (VIN) plate is visible through the windshield

Fig. 2 On 4 and 6-cylinder engines, then engine identification number is located on a pad at the front right side of the engine block

Fig. 3 Engine serial number location—8-cylinder engines

Transmission

▶ See Figure 4

The transmission identification number can be found at the location described below:

Muncie 3 speed: On the boss above the filler plug.

Muncie 4 speed: On the right side of the transmission case at the right side of the lower rear of the cover flange.

Saginaw 3 and 4 speed (83 mm): On the lower right side of the case adjacent to the rear cover.

76 mm 3 and 4 speed: On the right side below the side cover.

Powerglide, Torque Drive, Turbo Hydra-Matic 350 to 1972 and Turbo Hydra-Matic 400: On the left upper flange of the transmission housing converter opening.

Turbo Hydra-Matic 200: Tag on right side of the transmission extension.

Turbo Hydra-Matic 250, 350 (1973 and later): On the right vertical surface of the oil pan.

Fig. 4 On the Turbo Hydra-Matic, the identification number is located either on the left upper flange of the transmission housing converter opening or on the right side of the extension

ROUTINE MAINTENANCE

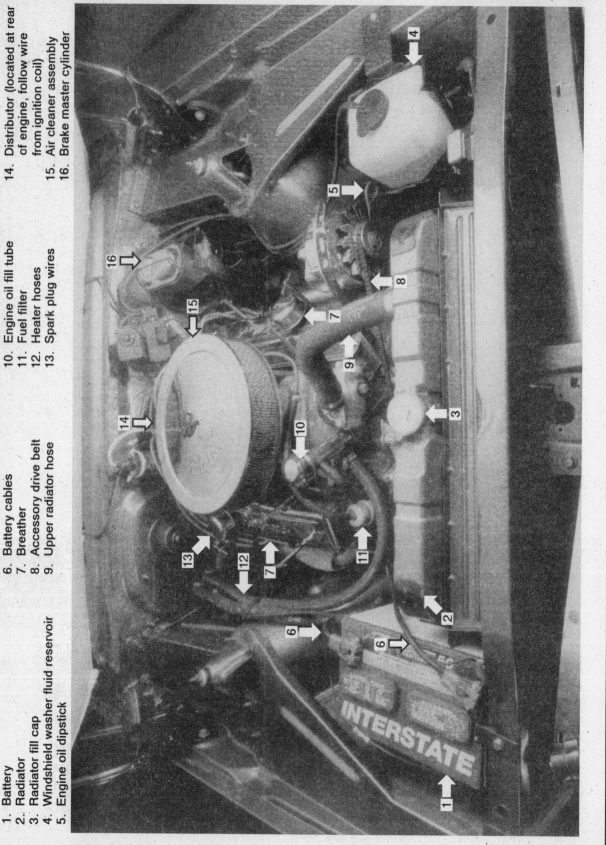

MAINTENANCE COMPONENTS LOCATIONS - EARLY MODEL V8 ENGINE

1. Battery
2. Radiator
3. Radiator fill cap
4. Windshield washer fluid reservoir
5. Engine oil dipstick

6. Battery cables
7. Breather
8. Accessory drive belt
9. Upper radiator hose

10. Engine oil fill tube
11. Fuel filter
12. Heater hoses
13. Spark plug wires

14. Distributor (located at rear of engine, follow wire from ignition coil)
15. Air cleaner assembly
16. Brake master cylinder

MAINTENANCE COMPONENT LOCATIONS – LATE MODEL NOVA INLINE ENGINE

1. Coolant recovery reservoir
2. Battery
3. Radiator cap
4. Lower radiator hose
5. Upper radiator hose
6. Evaporative canister
7. Windshield washer fluid reservoir
8. Power steering pump
9. Engine oil fill cap
10. Distributor
11. Heater hoses
12. Oil level dipstick
13. Spark plug wire
14. PCV valve
15. Automatic transmission fluid dipstick
16. Brake master cylinder
17. Air cleaner assembly

Air Cleaner

The air cleaner element should be inspected at 12,000 mile intervals and replaced, if necessary. Otherwise, the element should be replaced at every 24,000 miles on cars built up to 1974, and 30,000 miles on 1975–79 cars.

REMOVAL & INSTALLATION

▶ **See Figure 4a**

1. Disconnect the negative battery cable.
2. Unfasten the air cleaner lid retaining wingnut, then remove the lid.
3. Remove the air cleaner element by lifting it from the housing.

To install:

4. Place a new element in the air cleaner housing.
5. Install the air cleaner assembly lid and secure with the wingnut.
6. Connect the negative battery cable.

Unscrew the air cleaner wing nut

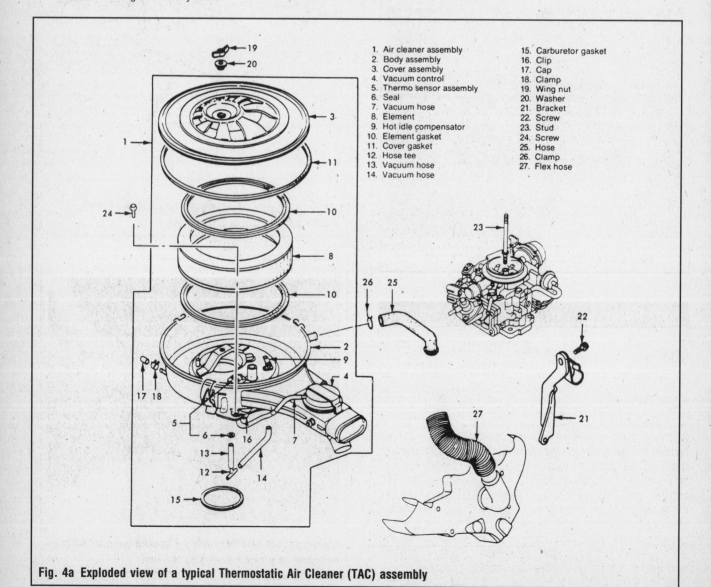

1. Air cleaner assembly	15. Carburetor gasket
2. Body assembly	16. Clip
3. Cover assembly	17. Cap
4. Vacuum control	18. Clamp
5. Thermo sensor assembly	19. Wing nut
6. Seal	20. Washer
7. Vacuum hose	21. Bracket
8. Element	22. Screw
9. Hot idle compensator	23. Stud
10. Element gasket	24. Screw
11. Cover gasket	25. Hose
12. Hose tee	26. Clamp
13. Vacuum hose	27. Flex hose
14. Vacuum hose	

Fig. 4a Exploded view of a typical Thermostatic Air Cleaner (TAC) assembly

Remove the air cleaner assembly lid . . .

. . . then remove the air cleaner element

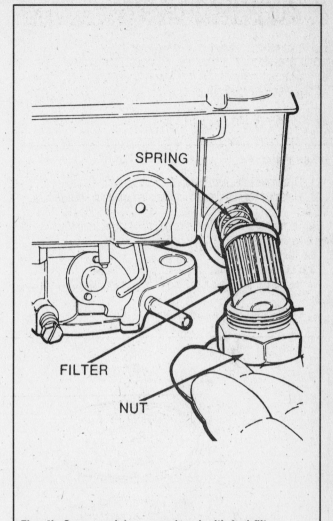

Fig. 4b Some models are equipped with fuel filters mounted in the carburetor fuel inlet

Fuel Filter

REMOVAL & INSTALLATION

◆ **See Figure 4b**

All models are equipped with a fuel filter located in the carburetor fuel inlet and/or an inline fuel filter positioned in the fuel line between the fuel pump and the carburetor. Either type of filter should be changed at 12 month or 12,000 mile intervals on cars built until 1974, and 12 month or 15,000 miles intervals on 1975 and later cars. To service the inlet type filter, disconnect the fuel line at the carburetor, unscrew the filter retainer, and withdraw the filter element from the carburetor. Install a new filter and refit the retainer and fuel line to the carburetor. For the inline type fuel filter, follow the instructions which are included with the replacement filter to remove the old filter and install the new unit.

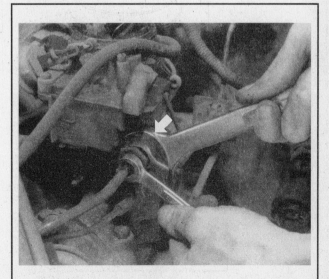

Disconnect the fuel line, using a backup wrench (noted by arrow) to prevent damaging the line

Loosen the fuel filter retaining nut . . .

. . . then remove the nut, washer and fuel filter from the carburetor

PCV Valve

REMOVAL & INSTALLATION

▶ **See Figures 5, 6 and 7**

The Positive Crankcase Ventilation (PCV) valve should be replaced every 24 months or 24,000 miles on cars built up to 1974, every 30,000 miles on 1975–77 cars, or every 15,000 miles or 12 months on 1978–79 cars. Symptoms of a defective PCV valve are: rough idle, oil in air cleaner, oil leaks, or excessive oil sludging or dilution.

Inspect the valve at every oil change by pulling the valve from the rubber grommet in the valve cover. Shake the valve, if a rattling sound is heard, the valve is in good condition.

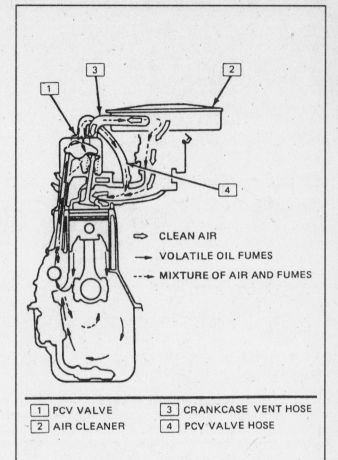

⇨ CLEAN AIR
→ VOLATILE OIL FUMES
--► MIXTURE OF AIR AND FUMES

| 1 | PCV VALVE | 3 | CRANKCASE VENT HOSE |
| 2 | AIR CLEANER | 4 | PCV VALVE HOSE |

Fig. 5 Typical Positive Crankcase Ventilation (PCV) system air flow schematic

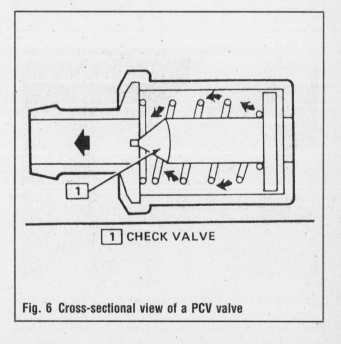

1 CHECK VALVE

Fig. 6 Cross-sectional view of a PCV valve

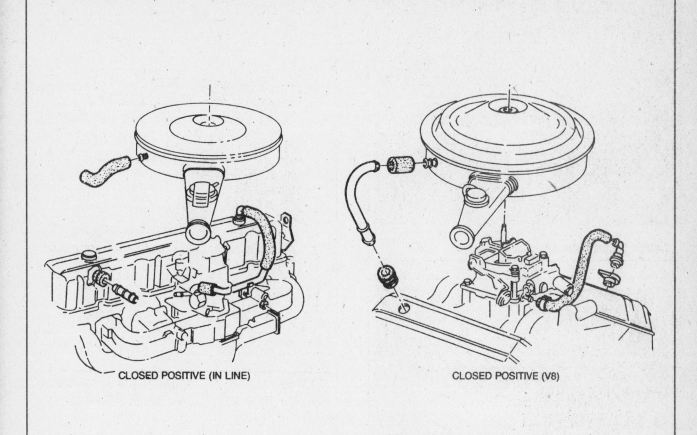

CLOSED POSITIVE (IN LINE)   CLOSED POSITIVE (V8)

Fig. 7 Positive Crankcase Ventilation (PCV) system component locations—6-cylinder engine on the left, 8-cylinder engine on the right

Remove the PCV valve from the grommet in the valve cover

If replacement is necessary, disconnect the PCV valve from the hose

Crankcase Ventilation Filter

REMOVAL & INSTALLATION

This filter, located within the air cleaner housing, should be replaced at least every 24,000 miles or 24 months on cars built up to 1974, every 30,000 miles or 24 months for 1975–77 cars, or every 12 months or 15,000 miles on 1978 and later cars. If the vehicle is driven under dusty conditions, replace the crankcase ventilation filter more often. Simply pry the old filter from its housing and install a new filter.

The crankcase ventilation filter is located inside the air cleaner housing

Flame Arrester

▶ See Figure 8

Clean the flame arrester, on 1962–77 cars so equipped, located in the base of the air cleaner, at 12,000 mile intervals with a safe solvent. Dry with compressed air.

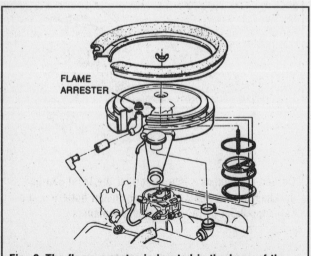

Fig. 8 The flame arrester is located in the base of the air cleaner

Evaporative Canister

SERVICING

▶ See Figures 9 and 10

The filter in the bottom of the evaporative canister must be changed every 24 months or 24,000 miles on cars built up to 1974, and every 24 months or 30,000 miles on later models (more often under dusty conditions). The canister is mounted on the left-side of the engine compartment.

To change the filter, proceed as follows:
1. Raise and securely support the front of the car.
2. Note the installed position of the hoses on the canister.
3. Disconnect the hoses from the top of the canister.
4. Loosen the clamps and remove the canister.
5. Remove the bottom of the canister from the canister body.
6. Remove and discard the old filter.

To install:
7. Install a new filter.
8. Reassemble the bottom to the canister body.
9. Install the canister in the mounting clamps. Tighten the clamp bolts.
10. Reconnect the hoses to the top of the canister in their proper positions.
11. Lower the car.

➡ **When replacing canister hoses, use only fuel-resistant replacement hose marked "EVAP."**

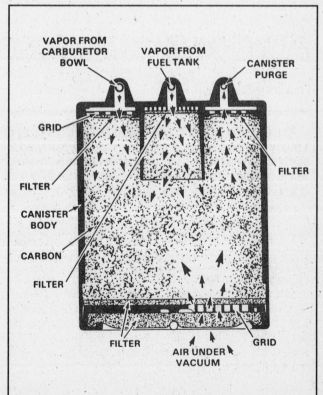

Fig. 9 Cross-sectional view of a typical evaporative canister

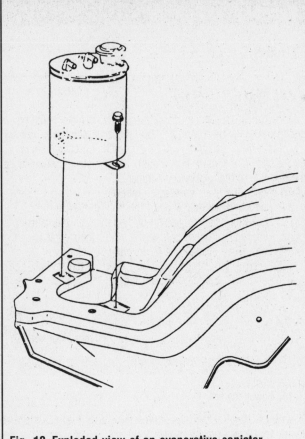

Fig. 10 Exploded view of an evaporative canister mounting

Battery

GENERAL MAINTENANCE

All batteries, regardless of type, should be carefully secured by a battery hold-down device. If this is not done, the battery terminals or casing may crack from stress applied to the battery during vehicle operation. A battery which is not secured may allow acid to leak out, making it discharge faster; such leaking corrosive acid can also eat away components under the hood. A battery that is not sealed must be checked periodically for electrolyte level. You cannot add water to a sealed maintenance-free battery (though not all maintenance-free batteries are sealed), but a sealed battery must also be checked for proper electrolyte level as indicated by the color of the built-in hydrometer "eye."

Keep the top of the battery clean, as a film of dirt can help completely discharge a battery that is not used for long periods. A solution of baking soda and water may be used for cleaning, but be careful to flush this off with clear water. DO NOT let any of the solution into the filler holes. Baking soda neutralizes battery acid and will de-activate a battery cell.

✳✳ CAUTION

Always use caution when working on or near the battery. Never allow a tool to bridge the gap between the negative and positive battery terminals. Also, be careful not to allow a tool to provide a ground between the positive cable/terminal and any metal component on the vehicle. Either of these conditions will cause a short circuit leading to sparks and possible personal injury.

Batteries in vehicles which are not operated on a regular basis can fall victim to parasitic loads (small current drains which are constantly drawing current from the battery). Normal parasitic loads may drain a battery on a vehicle that is in storage and not used for 6–8 weeks. Vehicles that have additional accessories such as a cellular phone, an alarm system or other devices that increase parasitic load may discharge a battery sooner. If the vehicle is to be stored for 6–8 weeks in a secure area and the alarm system, if present, is not necessary, the negative battery cable should be disconnected at the onset of storage to protect the battery charge.

Remember that constantly discharging and recharging will shorten battery life. Take care not to allow a battery to be needlessly discharged.

BATTERY FLUID

✳✳ CAUTION

Battery electrolyte contains sulfuric acid. If you should splash any on your skin or in your eyes, flush the affected area with plenty of clear water. If it lands in your eyes, get medical help immediately.

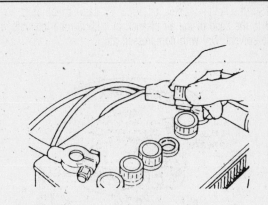

On non-maintenance free batteries, the level can be checked through the case on translucent batteries; the cell caps must be removed on other models

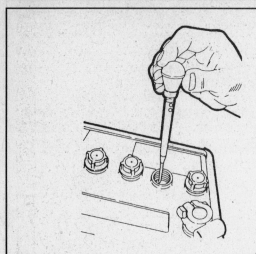

Check the specific gravity of the battery's electrolyte with a hydrometer

The fluid (sulfuric acid solution) contained in the battery cells will tell you many things about the condition of the battery. Because the cell plates must be kept submerged below the fluid level in order to operate, maintaining the fluid level is extremely important. And, because the specific gravity of the acid is an indication of electrical charge, testing the fluid can be an aid in determining if the battery must be replaced. A battery in a vehicle with a properly operating charging system should require little maintenance, but careful, periodic inspection should reveal problems before they leave you stranded.

Fluid Level

Check the battery electrolyte level at least once a month, or more often in hot weather or during periods of extended vehicle operation. On non-sealed batteries, the level can be checked either through the case on translucent batteries or by removing the cell caps on opaque-cased types. The electrolyte level in each cell should be kept filled to the split ring inside each cell, or the line marked on the outside of the case.

If the level is low, add only distilled water through the opening until the level is correct. Each cell is separate from the others, so each must be checked and filled individually. Distilled water should be used, because the chemicals and minerals found in most drinking water are harmful to the battery and could significantly shorten its life.

If water is added in freezing weather, the vehicle should be driven several miles to allow the water to mix with the electrolyte. Otherwise, the battery could freeze.

Although some maintenance-free batteries have removable cell caps for access to the electrolyte, the electrolyte condition and level on all sealed maintenance-free batteries must be checked using the built-in hydrometer "eye." The exact type of eye varies between battery manufacturers, but most apply a sticker to the battery itself explaining the possible readings. When in doubt, refer to the battery manufacturer's instructions to interpret battery condition using the built-in hydrometer.

➡**Although the readings from built-in hydrometers found in sealed batteries may vary, a green eye usually indicates a properly charged battery with sufficient fluid level. A dark eye is normally an indicator of a battery with sufficient fluid, but one which may be low in charge. And a light or yellow eye is usually an indication that electrolyte supply has dropped below the necessary level for battery (and hydrometer) operation. In this last case, sealed batteries with an insufficient electrolyte level must usually be discarded.**

Specific Gravity

As stated earlier, the specific gravity of a battery's electrolyte level can be used as an indication of battery charge. At least once a year, check the specific gravity of the battery. It should be between 1.20 and 1.26 on the gravity scale. Most auto supply stores carry a variety of inexpensive battery testing hydrometers. These can be used on any non-sealed battery to test the specific gravity in each cell.

The battery testing hydrometer has a squeeze bulb at one end and a nozzle at the other. Battery electrolyte is sucked into the hydrometer until the float is lifted from its seat. The specific gravity is then read by noting the position of the float. If gravity is low in one or more cells, the battery should be slowly charged and checked again to see if the gravity has come up. Generally, if after

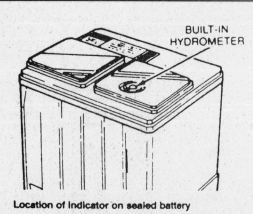

Location of indicator on sealed battery

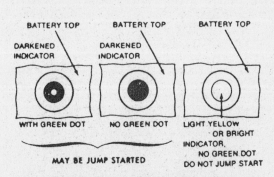

Check the appearance of the charge indicator on top of the battery before attempting a jump start; if it's not green or dark, do not jump start the car

A typical sealed (maintenance-free) battery with a built-in hydrometer—NOTE that the hydrometer eye may vary between battery manufacturers; always refer to the battery's label

charging, the specific gravity between any two cells varies more than 50 points (0.50), the battery should be replaced as it can no longer produce sufficient voltage to guarantee proper operation.

On sealed batteries, the built-in hydrometer is the only way of checking specific gravity. Again, check with your battery's manufacturer for proper interpretation of its built-in hydrometer readings.

CABLES

Once a year (or as necessary), the battery terminals and the cable clamps should be cleaned. Loosen the clamps and remove the cables, negative cable first. On batteries with posts on top, the use of a puller specially made for this purpose is recommended. These are inexpensive and available in most auto parts stores. Side terminal battery cables are secured with a small bolt.

Clean the cable clamps and the battery terminal with a wire brush, until all corrosion, grease, etc., is removed and the metal is shiny. It is especially important to clean the inside of the clamp

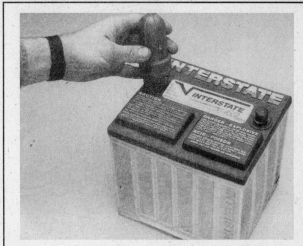

Place the tool over the terminals and twist to clean the post

Maintenance is performed with household items and with special tools like this post cleaner

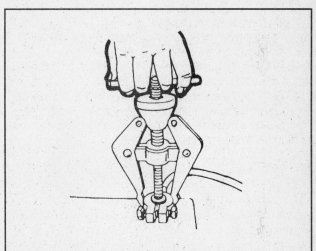

A special tool is available to pull the clamp from the post

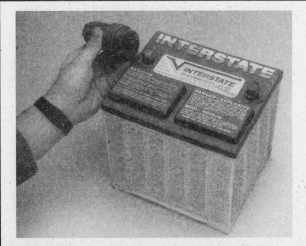

The underside of this special battery tool has a wire brush to clean post terminals

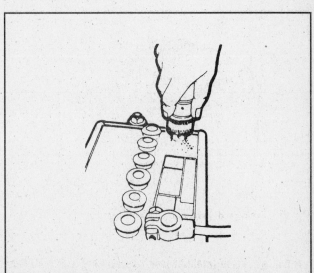

Clean the battery terminals until the metal is shiny

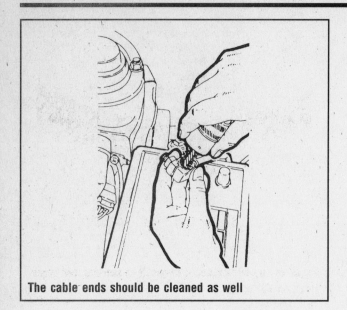
The cable ends should be cleaned as well

A battery should be charged at a slow rate to keep the plates inside from getting too hot. However, if some maintenance-free batteries are allowed to discharge until they are almost "dead," they may have to be charged at a high rate to bring them back to "life." Always follow the charger manufacturer's instructions on charging the battery.

REPLACEMENT

When it becomes necessary to replace the battery, select one with a rating equal to or greater than the battery originally installed. Deterioration and just plain aging of the battery cables, starter motor, and associated wires makes the battery's job harder in successive years. The slow increase in electrical resistance over time makes it prudent to install a new battery with a greater capacity than the old.

Belts

INSPECTION

Inspect the belts for signs of glazing or cracking. A glazed belt will be perfectly smooth from slippage, while a good belt will have a slight texture of fabric visible. Cracks will usually start at the inner edge of the belt and run outward. All worn or damaged drive belts should be replaced immediately. It is best to replace all drive belts at one time, as a preventive maintenance measure, during this service operation.

Every 4 months or 6,000 miles inspect the alternator and air conditioning drive belts for wear, fraying, cracking, and tension. Replace any defective belts immediately. Adjust loose belts to the proper deflection. Replace the drive belts every 24 months or 24,000 miles.

(an old knife is useful here) thoroughly, since a small deposit of foreign material or oxidation there will prevent a sound electrical connection and inhibit either starting or charging. Special tools are available for cleaning these parts, one type for conventional top post batteries and another type for side terminal batteries.

Before installing the cables, loosen the battery hold-down clamp or strap, remove the battery and check the battery tray. Clear it of any debris, and check it for soundness (the battery tray can be cleaned with a baking soda and water solution). Rust should be wire brushed away, and the metal given a couple coats of anti-rust paint. Install the battery and tighten the hold-down clamp or strap securely. Do not overtighten, as this can crack the battery case.

After the clamps and terminals are clean, reinstall the cables, negative cable last; DO NOT hammer the clamps onto post batteries. Tighten the clamps securely, but do not distort them. Give the clamps and terminals a thin external coating of grease after installation, to retard corrosion.

Check the cables at the same time that the terminals are cleaned. If the cable insulation is cracked or broken, or if the ends are frayed, the cable should be replaced with a new cable of the same length and gauge.

CHARGING

✳✳ CAUTION

The chemical reaction which takes place in all batteries generates explosive hydrogen gas. A spark can cause the battery to explode and splash acid. To avoid serious personal injury, be sure there is proper ventilation and take appropriate fire safety precautions when connecting, disconnecting, or charging a battery and when using jumper cables.

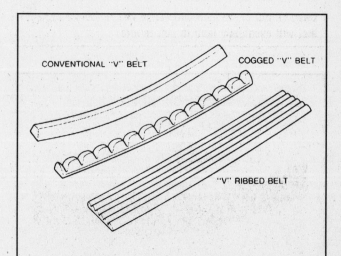

CONVENTIONAL "V" BELT   COGGED "V" BELT

"V" RIBBED BELT

There are typically 3 types of accessory drive belts found on vehicles today

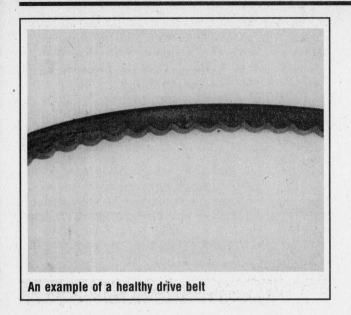

An example of a healthy drive belt

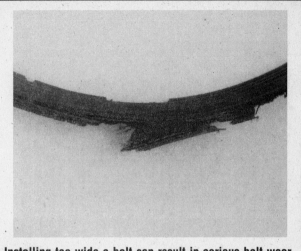

Installing too wide a belt can result in serious belt wear and/or breakage

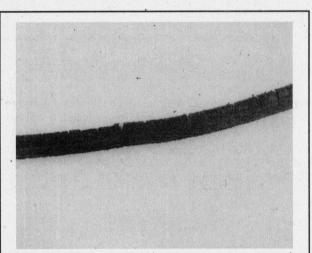

Deep cracks in this belt will cause flex, building up heat that will eventually lead to belt failure

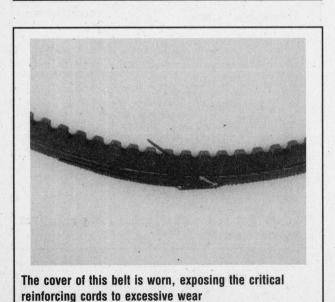

The cover of this belt is worn, exposing the critical reinforcing cords to excessive wear

TENSION CHECKING & ADJUSTING

▶ **See Figures 10a, 10b, 10c, 10d and 10e**

Check belt tension by applying moderate thumb pressure to the belt at a point midway between the pulleys. If the center-to-center distance between the pulleys is 13–16 inches, belt deflection should be ½ in.

Loosen the component's adjusting bolt and move the component until proper belt tension is achieved. Tighten the adjusting bolt.

7" TO 10"
1/4" DEFLECTION

13" TO 16"
1/2" DEFLECTION

Fig. 10a You can check belt tension with thumb pressure

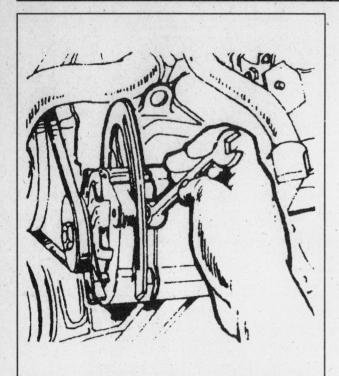

Fig. 10b To adjust belt tension or to replace belts, first loosen the component's mounting and adjusting bolts slightly

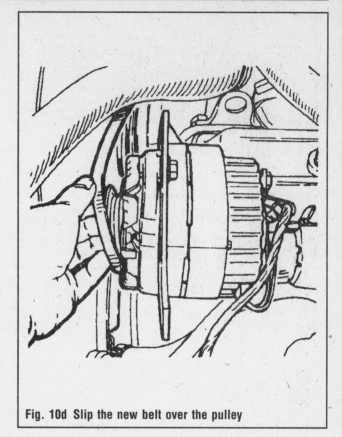

Fig. 10d Slip the new belt over the pulley

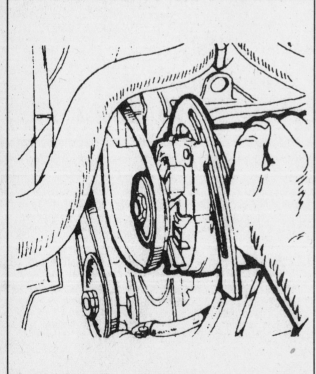

Fig. 10c Push the component toward the engine and slip the belt off

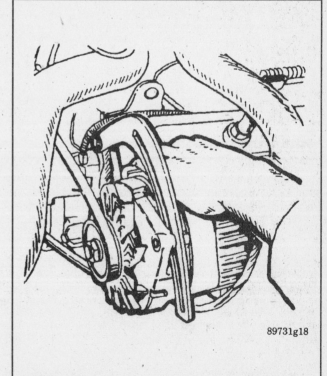

89731g18

Fig. 10e Pull outward on the components and tighten the mounting bolts

Hoses

INSPECTION

Upper and lower radiator hoses along with the heater hoses should be checked for deterioration, leaks and loose hose clamps at least every 15,000 miles (24,000 km). It is also wise to check the hoses periodically in early spring and at the beginning of the fall or winter when you are performing other maintenance. A quick visual inspection could discover a weakened hose which might have left you stranded if it had remained unrepaired.

Whenever you are checking the hoses, make sure the engine and cooling system are cold. Visually inspect for cracking, rotting or collapsed hoses, and replace as necessary. Run your hand along the length of the hose. If a weak or swollen spot is noted when squeezing the hose wall, the hose should be replaced.

REMOVAL & INSTALLATION

1. Remove the radiator pressure cap.

2. Position a clean container under the radiator and/or engine draincock or plug, then open the drain and allow the cooling system to drain to an appropriate level. For some upper hoses, only a little coolant must be drained. To remove hoses positioned lower on the engine, such as a lower radiator hose, the entire cooling system must be emptied.

3. Loosen the hose clamps at each end of the hose requiring replacement. Clamps are usually either of the spring tension type (which require pliers to squeeze the tabs and loosen) or of the

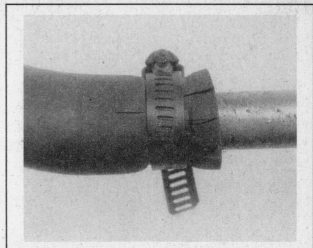

The cracks developing along this hose are a result of age-related hardening

A hose clamp that is too tight can cause older hoses to separate and tear on either side of the clamp

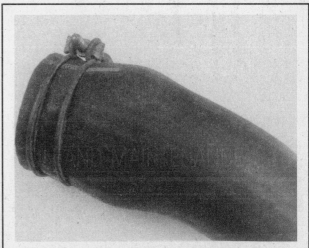

A soft spongy hose (identifiable by the swollen section) will eventually burst and should be replaced

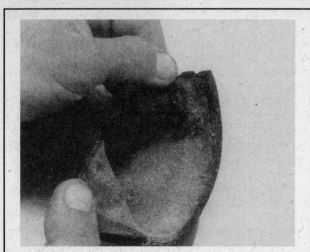

Hoses are likely to deteriorate from the inside if the cooling system is not periodically flushed

screw tension type (which require screw or hex drivers to loosen). Pull the clamps back on the hose away from the connection.

4. Twist, pull and slide the hose off the fitting, taking care not to damage the neck of the component from which the hose is being removed.

➡If the hose is stuck at the connection, do not try to insert a screwdriver or other sharp tool under the hose end in an effort to free it, as the connection and/or hose may become damaged. Heater connections especially may be easily damaged by such a procedure. If the hose is to be replaced, use a single-edged razor blade to make a slice along the portion of the hose which is stuck on the connection, perpendicular to the end of the hose. Do not cut deep so as to prevent damaging the connection. The hose can then be peeled from the connection and discarded.

5. Clean both hose mounting connections. Inspect the condition of the hose clamps and replace them, if necessary.
   To install:
6. Dip the ends of the new hose into clean engine coolant to ease installation.
7. Slide the clamps over the replacement hose, then slide the hose ends over the connections into position.
8. Position and secure the clamps at least ¼ in. (6.35mm) from the ends of the hose. Make sure they are located beyond the raised bead of the connector.
9. Close the radiator or engine drains and properly refill the cooling system with the clean drained engine coolant or a suitable mixture of ethylene glycol coolant and water.
10. If available, install a pressure tester and check for leaks. If a pressure tester is not available, run the engine until normal operating temperature is reached (allowing the system to naturally pressurize), then check for leaks.

✳✳ CAUTION

If you are checking for leaks with the system at normal operating temperature, BE EXTREMELY CAREFUL not to touch any moving or hot engine parts. Once temperature has been reached, shut the engine OFF, and check for leaks around

the hose fittings and connections which were removed earlier.

Air Conditioning

➡Be sure to consult the laws in your area before servicing the air conditioning system. In most areas, it is illegal to perform repairs involving refrigerant unless the work is done by a certified technician. Also, it is quite likely that you will not be able to purchase refrigerant without proof of certification.

SAFETY PRECAUTIONS

There are two major hazards associated with air conditioning systems and they both relate to the refrigerant gas. First, the refrigerant gas (R-12) is an extremely cold substance. When exposed to air, it will instantly freeze any surface it comes in contact with, including your eyes. The other hazard relates to fire. Although normally non-toxic, the R-12 gas becomes highly poisonous in the presence of an open flame. One good whiff of the vapor formed by burning R-12 can be fatal. Keep all forms of fire (including cigarettes) well clear of the air conditioning system.

Because of the inherent dangers involved with working on air conditioning systems and R-12 refrigerant, these safety precautions must be strictly followed.

• Avoid contact with a charged refrigeration system, even when working on another part of the air conditioning system or vehicle. If a heavy tool comes into contact with a section of tubing or a heat exchanger, it can easily cause the relatively soft material to rupture.

• When it is necessary to apply force to a fitting which contains refrigerant, as when checking that all system couplings are securely tightened, use a wrench on both parts of the fitting involved, if possible. This will avoid putting torque on refrigerant tubing. (It is also advisable to use tube or line wrenches when tightening these flare nut fittings.)

➡R-12 refrigerant is a chlorofluorocarbon which, when released into the atmosphere, can contribute to the depletion of the ozone layer in the upper atmosphere. Ozone filters out harmful radiation from the sun.

• Do not attempt to discharge the system without the proper tools. Precise control is possible only when using the service gauges and a proper A/C refrigerant recovery station. Wear protective gloves when connecting or disconnecting service gauge hoses.

• Discharge the system only in a well ventilated area, as high concentrations of the gas which might accidentally escape can exclude oxygen and act as an anesthetic. When leak testing or soldering, this is particularly important, as toxic gas is formed when R-12 contacts any flame.

• Never start a system without first verifying that both service valves are properly installed, and that all fittings throughout the system are snugly connected.

• Avoid applying heat to any refrigerant line or storage vessel. Charging may be aided by using water heated to less than 125°F (50°C) to warm the refrigerant container. Never allow a refrigerant storage container to sit out in the sun, or near any other source of heat, such as a radiator or heater.

• Always wear goggles to protect your eyes when working on a system. If refrigerant contacts the eyes, it is advisable in all cases to consult a physician immediately.

• Frostbite from liquid refrigerant should be treated by first gradually warming the area with cool water, and then gently applying petroleum jelly. A physician should be consulted.

• Always keep refrigerant drum fittings capped when not in use. If the container is equipped with a safety cap to protect the valve, make sure the cap is in place when the can is not being used. Avoid sudden shock to the drum, which might occur from dropping it, or from banging a heavy tool against it. Never carry a drum in the passenger compartment of a vehicle.

• Always completely discharge the system into a suitable recovery unit before painting the vehicle (if the paint is to be baked on), or before welding anywhere near refrigerant lines.

• When servicing the system, minimize the time that any refrigerant line or fitting is open to the air in order to prevent moisture or dirt from entering the system. Contaminants such as moisture or dirt can damage internal system components. Always replace O-rings on lines or fittings which are disconnected. Prior to installation coat, but do not soak, replacement O-rings with suitable compressor oil.

GENERAL SERVICING PROCEDURES

➡**It is recommended, and possibly required by law, that a qualified technician perform the following services.**

The most important aspect of air conditioning service is the maintenance of a pure and adequate charge of refrigerant in the system. A refrigeration system cannot function properly if a significant percentage of the charge is lost. Leaks are common because the severe vibration encountered underhood in an automobile can easily cause a sufficient cracking or loosening of the air conditioning fittings; allowing, the extreme operating pressures of the system to force refrigerant out.

The problem can be understood by considering what happens to the system as it is operated with a continuous leak. Because the expansion valve regulates the flow of refrigerant to the evaporator, the level of refrigerant there is fairly constant. The receiver/drier stores any excess refrigerant, and so a loss will first appear there as a reduction in the level of liquid. As this level nears the bottom of the vessel, some refrigerant vapor bubbles will begin to appear in the stream of liquid supplied to the expansion valve. This vapor decreases the capacity of the expansion valve very little as the valve opens to compensate for its presence. As the quantity of liquid in the condenser decreases, the operating pressure will drop there and throughout the high side of the system. As the R-12 continues to be expelled, the pressure available to force the liquid through the expansion valve will continue to decrease, and, eventually, the valve's orifice will prove to be too much of a restriction for adequate flow even with the needle fully withdrawn.

At this point, low side pressure will start to drop, and a severe reduction in cooling capacity, marked by freeze-up of the evaporator coil, will result. Eventually, the operating pressure of the evaporator will be lower than the pressure of the atmosphere surrounding it, and air will be drawn into the system wherever there are leaks in the low side.

Because all atmospheric air contains at least some moisture, water will enter the system and mix with the R-12 and the oil.

Trace amounts of moisture will cause sludging of the oil, and corrosion of the system. Saturation and clogging of the filter/drier, and freezing of the expansion valve orifice will eventually result. As air fills the system to a greater and greater extent, it will interfere more and more with the normal flows of refrigerant and heat.

From this description, it should be obvious that much of the repairman's focus in on detecting leaks, repairing them, and then restoring the purity and quantity of the refrigerant charge. A list of general rules should be followed in addition to all safety precautions:

• Keep all tools as clean and dry as possible.

• Thoroughly purge the service gauges/hoses of air and moisture before connecting them to the system. Keep them capped when not in use.

• Thoroughly clean any refrigerant fitting before disconnecting it, in order to minimize the entrance of dirt into the system.

• Plan any operation that requires opening the system beforehand, in order to minimize the length of time it will be exposed to open air. Cap or seal the open ends to minimize the entrance of foreign material.

• When adding oil, pour it through an extremely clean and dry tube or funnel. Keep the oil capped whenever possible. Do not use oil that has not been kept tightly sealed.

• Use only R-12 refrigerant. Purchase refrigerant intended for use only in automatic air conditioning systems.

• Completely evacuate any system that has been opened for service, or that has leaked sufficiently to draw in moisture and air. This requires evacuating air and moisture with a good vacuum pump for at least one hour. If a system has been open for a considerable length of time it may be advisable to evacuate the system for up to 12 hours (overnight).

• Use a wrench on both halves of a fitting that is to be disconnected, so as to avoid placing torque on any of the refrigerant lines.

• When overhauling a compressor, pour some of the oil into a clean glass and inspect it. If there is evidence of dirt, metal particles, or both, flush all refrigerant components with clean refrigerant before evacuating and recharging the system. In addition, if metal particles are present, the compressor should be replaced.

• Schrader valves may leak only when under full operating pressure. Therefore, if leakage is suspected but cannot be located, operate the system with a full charge of refrigerant and look for leaks from all Schrader valves. Replace any faulty valves.

Additional Preventive Maintenance

USING THE SYSTEM

The easiest and most important preventive maintenance for your A/C system is to be sure that it is used on a regular basis. Running the system for five minutes each month (no matter what the season) will help assure that the seals and all internal components remain lubricated.

ANTIFREEZE

In order to prevent heater core freeze-up during A/C operation, it is necessary to maintain a proper antifreeze protection. Use a hand-held antifreeze tester (hydrometer) to periodically check the condition of the antifreeze in your engine's cooling system.

➡**Antifreeze should not be used longer than the manufacturer specifies.**

RADIATOR CAP

For efficient operation of an air conditioned vehicle's cooling system, the radiator cap should have a holding pressure which meets manufacturer's specifications. A cap which fails to hold these pressures should be replaced.

CONDENSER

Any obstruction of or damage to the condenser configuration will restrict the air flow which is essential to its efficient operation. It is therefore a good rule to keep this unit clean and in proper physical shape.

➡**Bug screens which are mounted in front of the condenser, (unless they are original equipment), are regarded as obstructions.**

CONDENSATION DRAIN TUBE

This single molded drain tube expels the condensation, which accumulates on the bottom of the evaporator housing, into the engine compartment. If this tube is obstructed, the air conditioning performance can be restricted and condensation buildup can spill over onto the vehicle's floor.

SYSTEM INSPECTION

➡**R-12 refrigerant is a chlorofluorocarbon which, when released into the atmosphere, can contribute to the depletion of the ozone layer in the upper atmosphere. Ozone filters out harmful radiation from the sun.**

The easiest and often most important check for the air conditioning system consists of a visual inspection of the system components. Visually inspect the air conditioning system for refrigerant leaks, damaged compressor clutch, compressor drive belt tension and condition, plugged evaporator drain tube, blocked condenser fins, disconnected or broken wires, blown fuses, corroded connections and poor insulation.

A refrigerant leak will usually appear as an oily residue at the leakage point in the system. The oily residue soon picks up dust or dirt particles from the surrounding air and appears greasy. Through time, this will build up and appear to be a heavy dirt im-

An antifreeze tester can be used to determine the freezing and boiling levels of the coolant

pregnated grease. Most leaks are caused by damaged or missing O-ring seals at the component connections, damaged charging valve cores or missing service gauge port caps.

For a thorough visual and operational inspection, check the following:

1. Check the surface of the radiator and condenser for dirt, leaves or other material which might block air flow.
2. Check for kinks in hoses and lines. Check the system for leaks.
3. Make sure the drive belt is under the proper tension. When the air conditioning is operating, make sure the drive belt is free of noise or slippage.
4. Make sure the blower motor operates at all appropriate positions, then check for distribution of the air from all outlets with the blower on **HIGH**.

➡**Keep in mind that under conditions of high humidity, air discharged from the A/C vents may not feel as cold as expected, even if the system is working properly. This is because the vaporized moisture in humid air retains heat more effectively than does dry air, making the humid air more difficult to cool.**

Make sure the air passage selection lever is operating correctly. Start the engine and warm it to normal operating temperature, then make sure the hot/cold selection lever is operating correctly.

DISCHARGING, EVACUATING & CHARGING

Discharging, evacuating and charging the air conditioning system must be performed by a properly trained and certified mechanic in a facility equipped with refrigerant recovery/recycling equipment that meets SAE standards for the type of system to be serviced.

If you don't have access to the necessary equipment, we recommend that you take your vehicle to a reputable service station to have the work done. If you still wish to perform repairs on the vehicle, have them discharge the system, then take your vehicle home and perform the necessary work. When you are finished, return the vehicle to the station for evacuation and charging. Just be sure to cap ALL A/C system fittings immediately after opening them and keep them protected until the system is recharged.

Windshield Wipers

ELEMENT (REFILL) CARE & REPLACEMENT

For maximum effectiveness and longest element life, the windshield and wiper blades should be kept clean. Dirt, tree sap, road tar and so on will cause streaking, smearing and blade deterioration if left on the glass. It is advisable to wash the windshield carefully with a commercial glass cleaner at least once a month. Wipe off the rubber blades with the wet rag afterwards. Do not attempt to move wipers across the windshield by hand; damage to the motor and drive mechanism will result.

To inspect and/or replace the wiper blade elements, place the wiper switch in the **LOW** speed position and the ignition switch in the **ACC** position. When the wiper blades are approximately vertical on the windshield, turn the ignition switch to **OFF**.

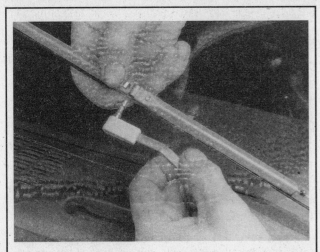

Press on the retaining clip, then remove the wiper blade from the arm

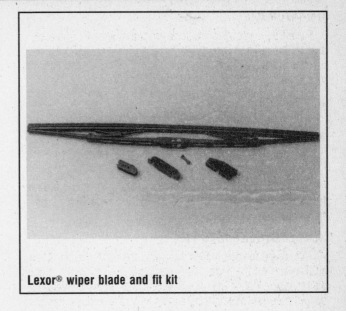

Lexor® wiper blade and fit kit

Pylon® wiper blade and adaptor

Examine the wiper blade elements. If they are found to be cracked, broken or torn, they should be replaced immediately. Replacement intervals will vary with usage, although ozone deterioration usually limits element life to about one year. If the wiper pattern is smeared or streaked, or if the blade chatters across the glass, the elements should be replaced. It is easiest and most sensible to replace the elements in pairs.

If your vehicle is equipped with aftermarket blades, there are several different types of refills and your vehicle might have any kind. Aftermarket blades and arms rarely use the exact same type blade or refill as the original equipment. Here are some typical aftermarket blades; not all may be available for your vehicle:

The Anco® type uses a release button that is pushed down to allow the refill to slide out of the yoke jaws. The new refill slides back into the frame and locks in place.

Some Trico® refills are removed by locating where the metal backing strip or the refill is wider. Insert a small screwdriver blade between the frame and metal backing strip. Press down to release the refill from the retaining tab.

Other types of Trico® refills have two metal tabs which are un-

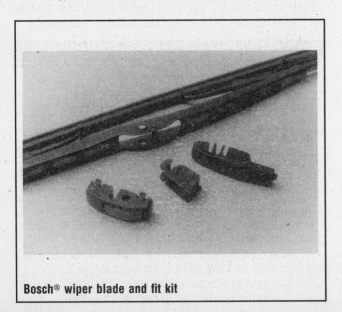

Bosch® wiper blade and fit kit

Trico® wiper blade and fit kit

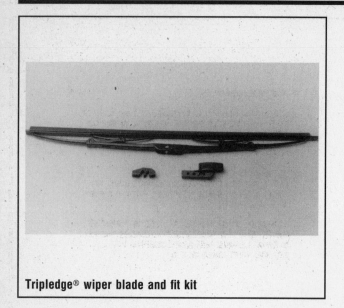

Tripledge® wiper blade and fit kit

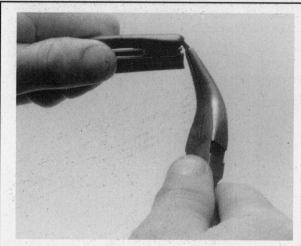

On Trico® wiper blades, the tab at the end of the blade must be turned up . . .

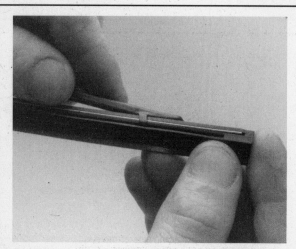

To remove and install a Lexor® wiper blade refill, slip out the old insert and slide in a new one

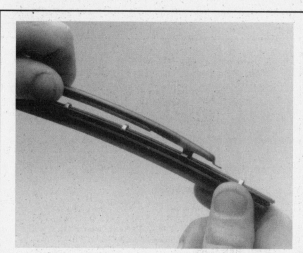

. . . then the insert can be removed. After installing the replacement insert, bend the tab back

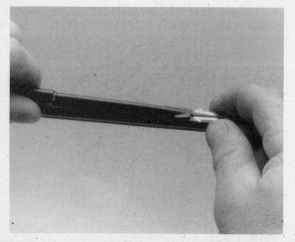

On Pylon® inserts, the clip at the end has to be removed prior to sliding the insert off

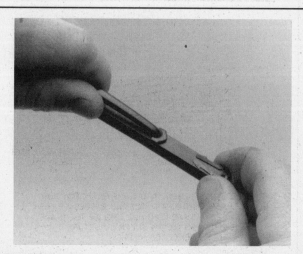

The Tripledge® wiper blade insert is removed and installed using a securing clip

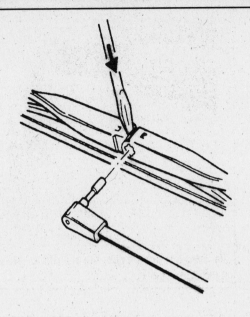

BLADE REPLACEMENT

1. CYCLE ARM AND BLADE ASSEMBLY TO UP POSITION—ON THE WINDSHIELD WHERE REMOVAL OF BLADE ASSEMBLY CAN BE PERFORMED WITHOUT DIFFICULTY. TURN IGNITION KEY OFF AT DESIRED POSITION.

2. TO REMOVE BLADE ASSEMBLY, INSERT SCREWDRIVER IN SLOT, PUSH DOWN ON SPRING LOCK AND PULL BLADE ASSEMBLY FROM PIN (VIEW A)

3. TO INSTALL, PUSH THE BLADE ASSEMBLY ON THE PIN SO THAT THE SPRING LOCK ENGAGES THE PIN (VIEW A). BE SURE THE BLADE ASSEMBLY IS SECURELY ATTACHED TO PIN

VIEW A

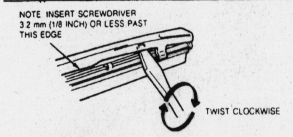

NOTE INSERT SCREWDRIVER 3 2 mm (1/8 INCH) OR LESS PAST THIS EDGE

TWIST CLOCKWISE

ELEMENT REPLACEMENT

1 INSERT SCREWDRIVER BETWEEN THE EDGE OF THE SUPER STRUCTURE AND THE BLADE BACKING DRIP (VIEW B) TWIST SCREWDRIVER SLOWLY UNTIL ELEMENT CLEARS ONE SIDE OF THE SUPER STRUCTURE CLAW

2 SLIDE THE ELEMENT INTO THE SUPER STRUCTURE CLAWS

VIEW B

4 INSERT ELEMENT INTO ONE SIDE OF THE END CLAWS (VIEW D) AND WITH A ROCKING MOTION PUSH ELEMENT UPWARD UNTIL IT SNAPS IN (VIEW E)

VIEW D

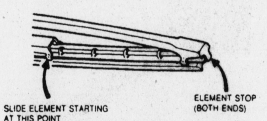

SLIDE ELEMENT STARTING AT THIS POINT

ELEMENT STOP (BOTH ENDS)

3. SLIDE THE ELEMENT INTO THE SUPER STRUCTURE CLAWS, STARTING WITH SECOND SET FROM EITHER END (VIEW C) AND CONTINUE TO SLIDE THE BLADE ELEMENT INTO ALL THE SUPER STRUCTURE CLAWS TO THE ELEMENT STOP (VIEW C)

VIEW C

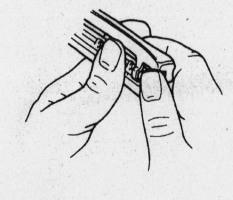

VIEW E

Trico® wiper blade insert (element) replacement

BLADE REPLACEMENT

1. Cycle arm and blade assembly to a position on the windshield where removal of blade assembly can be performed without difficulty. Turn ignition key off at desired position.
2. To remove blade assembly from wiper arm, pull up on spring lock and pull blade assembly from pin (View A). Be sure spring lock is not pulled excessively or it will become distorted.
3. To install, push the blade assembly onto the pin so that the spring lock engages the pin (View A). Be sure the blade assembly is securely attached to pin.

ELEMENT REPLACEMENT

1. In the plastic backing strip which is part of the rubber blade assembly, there is an 11.11mm (7/16 inch) long notch located approximately one inch from either end. Locate either notch.
2. Place the frame of the wiper blade assembly on a firm surface with either notched end of the backing strip visible.
3. Grasp the frame portion of the wiper blade assembly and push down until the blade assembly is tightly bowed.
4. With the blade assembly in the bowed position, grasp the tip of the backing strip firmly, pulling up and twisting C.C.W. at the same time. The backing strip will then snap out of the retaining tab on the end of the frame.
5. Lift the wiper blade assembly from the surface and slide the backing strip down the frame until the notch lines up with the next retaining tab, twist slightly, and the backing strip will snap out. Continue this operation with the remaining tabs until the blade element is completely detached from the frame.
6. To install blade element, reverse the above procedure, making sure all six (6) tabs are locked to the backing strip before installing blade to wiper arm.

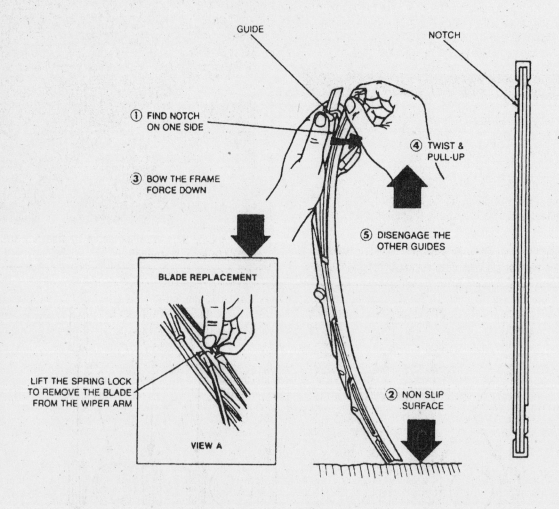

Tridon® wiper blade insert (element) replacement

locked by squeezing them together. The rubber filler can then be withdrawn from the frame jaws. A new refill is installed by inserting the refill into the front frame jaws and sliding it rearward to engage the remaining frame jaws. There are usually four jaws; be certain when installing that the refill is engaged in all of them. At the end of its travel, the tabs will lock into place on the front jaws of the wiper blade frame.

Another type of refill is made from polycarbonate. The refill has a simple locking device at one end which flexes downward out of the groove into which the jaws of the holder fit, allowing easy release. By sliding the new refill through all the jaws and pushing through the slight resistance when it reaches the end of its travel, the refill will lock into position.

To replace the Tridon® refill, it is necessary to remove the wiper blade. This refill has a plastic backing strip with a notch about 1 in. (25mm) from the end. Hold the blade (frame) on a hard surface so that the frame is tightly bowed. Grip the tip of the backing strip and pull up while twisting counterclockwise. The backing strip will snap out of the retaining tab. Do this for the remaining tabs until the refill is free of the blade. The length of these refills is molded into the end and they should be replaced with identical types.

Regardless of the type of refill used, be sure to follow the part manufacturer's instructions closely. Make sure that all of the frame jaws are engaged as the refill is pushed into place and locked. If the metal blade holder and frame are allowed to touch the glass during wiper operation, the glass will be scratched.

Tires and Wheels

Common sense and good driving habits will afford maximum tire life. Fast starts, sudden stops and hard cornering are hard on tires and will shorten their useful life span. Make sure that you don't overload the vehicle or run with incorrect pressure in the tires. Both of these practices will increase tread wear.

➡**For optimum tire life, keep the tires properly inflated, rotate them often and have the wheel alignment checked periodically.**

Inspect your tires frequently. Be especially careful to watch for bubbles in the tread or sidewall, deep cuts or underinflation. Replace any tires with bubbles in the sidewall. If cuts are so deep that they penetrate to the cords, discard the tire. Any cut in the sidewall of a radial tire renders it unsafe. Also look for uneven tread wear patterns that may indicate the front end is out of alignment or that the tires are out of balance.

TIRE ROTATION

Tires must be rotated periodically to equalize wear patterns that vary with a tire's position on the vehicle. Tires will also wear in an uneven way as the front steering/suspension system wears to the point where the alignment should be reset.

Rotating the tires will ensure maximum life for the tires as a set, so you will not have to discard a tire early due to wear on only part of the tread. Regular rotation is required to equalize wear.

When rotating "unidirectional tires," make sure that they always roll in the same direction. This means that a tire used on the left side of the vehicle must not be switched to the right side and vice-versa. Such tires should only be rotated front-to-rear or rear-

Unidirectional tires are identifiable by sidewall arrows and/or the word "rotation"

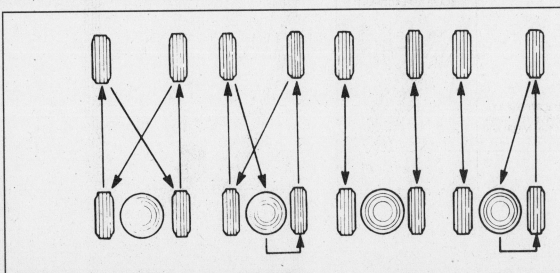

Common tire rotation patterns for 4 and 5-wheel rotations

to-front, while always remaining on the same side of the vehicle. These tires are marked on the sidewall as to the direction of rotation; observe the marks when reinstalling the tire(s).

Some styled or "mag" wheels may have different offsets front to rear. In these cases, the rear wheels must not be used up front and vice-versa. Furthermore, if these wheels are equipped with unidirectional tires, they cannot be rotated unless the tire is remounted for the proper direction of rotation.

➡The compact or space-saver spare is strictly for emergency use. It must never be included in the tire rotation or placed on the vehicle for everyday use.

TIRE DESIGN

For maximum satisfaction, tires should be used in sets of four. Mixing of different types (radial, bias-belted, fiberglass belted) must be avoided. In most cases, the vehicle manufacturer has designated a type of tire on which the vehicle will perform best. Your first choice when replacing tires should be to use the same type of tire that the manufacturer recommends.

When radial tires are used, tire sizes and wheel diameters should be selected to maintain ground clearance and tire load capacity equivalent to the original specified tire. Radial tires should always be used in sets of four.

✳✳ CAUTION

Radial tires should never be used on only the front axle.

When selecting tires, pay attention to the original size as marked on the tire. Most tires are described using an industry size code sometimes referred to as P-Metric. This allows the exact identification of the tire specifications, regardless of the manufacturer. If selecting a different tire size or brand, remember to check the installed tire for any sign of interference with the body or suspension while the vehicle is stopping, turning sharply or heavily loaded.

Snow Tires

Good radial tires can produce a big advantage in slippery weather, but in snow, a street radial tire does not have sufficient tread to provide traction and control. The small grooves of a street tire quickly pack with snow and the tire behaves like a billiard ball on a marble floor. The more open, chunky tread of a snow tire will self-clean as the tire turns, providing much better grip on snowy surfaces.

To satisfy municipalities requiring snow tires during weather emergencies, most snow tires carry either an M + S designation after the tire size stamped on the sidewall, or the designation "all-season." In general, no change in tire size is necessary when buying snow tires.

Most manufacturers strongly recommend the use of 4 snow tires on their vehicles for reasons of stability. If snow tires are fitted only to the drive wheels, the opposite end of the vehicle may become very unstable when braking or turning on slippery surfaces. This instability can lead to unpleasant endings if the driver can't counteract the slide in time.

Note that snow tires, whether 2 or 4, will affect vehicle handling in all non-snow situations. The stiffer, heavier snow tires will noticeably change the turning and braking characteristics of

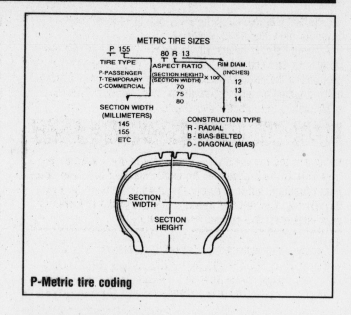

P-Metric tire coding

the vehicle. Once the snow tires are installed, you must re-learn the behavior of the vehicle and drive accordingly.

➡Consider buying extra wheels on which to mount the snow tires. Once done, the "snow wheels" can be installed and removed as needed. This eliminates the potential damage to tires or wheels from seasonal removal and installation. Even if your vehicle has styled wheels, see if inexpensive steel wheels are available. Although the look of the vehicle will change, the expensive wheels will be protected from salt, curb hits and pothole damage.

TIRE STORAGE

If they are mounted on wheels, store the tires at proper inflation pressure. All tires should be kept in a cool, dry place. If they are stored in the garage or basement, do not let them stand on a concrete floor; set them on strips of wood, a mat or a large stack of newspaper. Keeping them away from direct moisture is of paramount importance. Tires should not be stored upright, but in a flat position.

INFLATION & INSPECTION

The importance of proper tire inflation cannot be overemphasized. A tire employs air as part of its structure. It is designed around the supporting strength of the air at a specified pressure. For this reason, improper inflation drastically reduces the tires's ability to perform as intended. A tire will lose some air in day-to-day use; having to add a few pounds of air periodically is not necessarily a sign of a leaking tire.

Two items should be a permanent fixture in every glove compartment: an accurate tire pressure gauge and a tread depth gauge. Check the tire pressure (including the spare) regularly with a pocket type gauge. Too often, the gauge on the end of the air hose at your corner garage is not accurate because it suffers too much abuse. Always check tire pressure when the tires are cold, as pressure increases with temperature. If you must move the vehicle to check the tire inflation, do not drive more than a mile before checking. A cold tire is generally one that has not been driven for more than three hours.

A plate or sticker is normally provided somewhere in the vehicle (door post, hood, tailgate or trunk lid) which shows the proper pressure for the tires. Never counteract excessive pressure build-up by bleeding off air pressure (letting some air out). This will cause the tire to run hotter and wear quicker.

✳✳ CAUTION

Never exceed the maximum tire pressure embossed on the tire! This is the pressure to be used when the tire is at maximum loading, but it is rarely the correct pressure for everyday driving. Consult the owner's manual or the tire pressure sticker for the correct tire pressure.

Once you've maintained the correct tire pressures for several weeks, you'll be familiar with the vehicle's braking and handling personality. Slight adjustments in tire pressures can fine-tune these characteristics, but never change the cold pressure specifica-

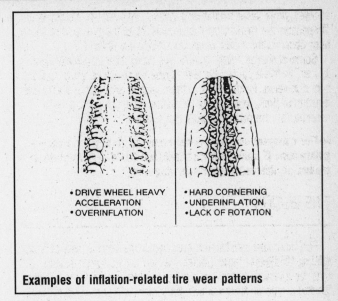

- DRIVE WHEEL HEAVY ACCELERATION
- OVERINFLATION
- HARD CORNERING
- UNDERINFLATION
- LACK OF ROTATION

Examples of inflation-related tire wear patterns

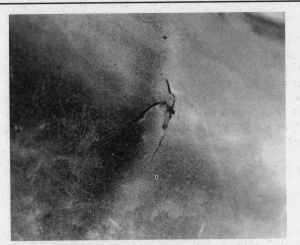

Tires should be checked frequently for any sign of puncture or damage

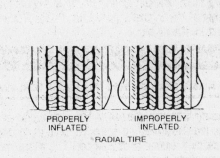

PROPERLY INFLATED IMPROPERLY INFLATED

RADIAL TIRE

Radial tires have a characteristic sidewall bulge; don't try to measure pressure by looking at the tire. Use a quality air pressure gauge

Tires with deep cuts, or cuts which show bulging should be replaced immediately

tion by more than 2 psi. A slightly softer tire pressure will give a softer ride but also yield lower fuel mileage. A slightly harder tire will give crisper dry road handling but can cause skidding on wet surfaces. Unless you're fully attuned to the vehicle, stick to the recommended inflation pressures.

All tires made since 1968 have built-in tread wear indicator bars that show up as ½ in. (13mm) wide smooth bands across the tire when 1/16 in. (1.5mm) of tread remains. The appearance of tread wear indicators means that the tires should be replaced. In fact, many states have laws prohibiting the use of tires with less than this amount of tread.

You can check your own tread depth with an inexpensive gauge or by using a Lincoln head penny. Slip the Lincoln penny (with Lincoln's head upside-down) into several tread grooves. If you can see the top of Lincoln's head in 2 adjacent grooves, the tire has less than 1/16 in. (1.5mm) tread left and should be replaced. You can measure snow tires in the same manner by using the "tails" side of the Lincoln penny. If you can see the top of the Lincoln memorial, it's time to replace the snow tire(s).

CARE OF SPECIAL WHEELS

If you have invested money in magnesium, aluminum alloy or sport wheels, special precautions should be taken to make sure your investment is not wasted and that your special wheels look good for the life of the vehicle.

Special wheels are easily damaged and/or scratched. Occasionally check the rims for cracking, impact damage or air leaks. If any of these are found, replace the wheel. But in order to prevent this type of damage and the costly replacement of a special wheel, observe the following precautions:

• Use extra care not to damage the wheels during removal, installation, balancing, etc. After removal of the wheels from the vehicle, place them on a mat or other protective surface. If they are to be stored for any length of time, support them on strips of wood. Never store tires and wheels upright; the tread may develop flat spots.

• When driving, watch for hazards; it doesn't take much to crack a wheel.

• When washing, use a mild soap or non-abrasive dish detergent (keeping in mind that detergent tends to remove wax). Avoid cleansers with abrasives or the use of hard brushes. There are many cleaners and polishes for special wheels.

• If possible, remove the wheels during the winter. Salt and sand used for snow removal can severely damage the finish of a wheel.

• Make certain the recommended lug nut torque is never exceeded or the wheel may crack. Never use snow chains on special wheels; severe scratching will occur.

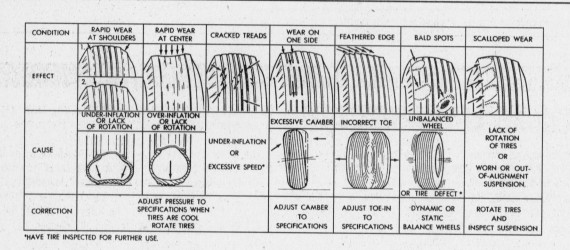

Common tire wear patterns and causes

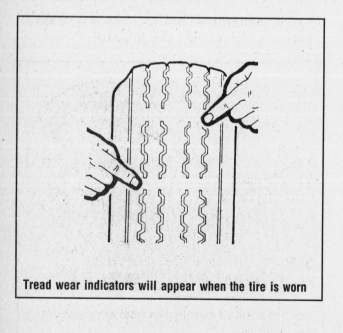

Tread wear indicators will appear when the tire is worn

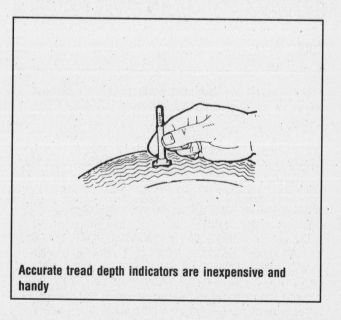

Accurate tread depth indicators are inexpensive and handy

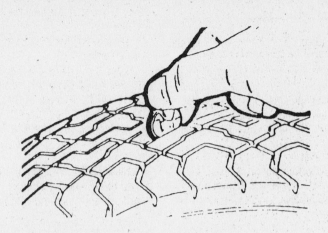

A penny works well for a quick check of tread depth

FLUIDS AND LUBRICANTS

Fluid Disposal

Used fluids such as engine oil, transmission fluid, antifreeze and brake fluid are hazardous wastes and must be disposed of properly. Before draining any fluids, consult with the local authorities; in many areas, waste oils, etc. is being accepted as a part of recycling programs. A number of service stations and auto parts stores are also accepting waste fluids for recycling.

Be sure of the recycling center's policies before draining any fluids, as many will not accept different fluids that have been mixed together, such as oil and antifreeze.

Fuel and Engine Oil Recommendations

FUEL

Most Chevy II and Nova models prior to 1972 are designed to operate on regular grades of fuel commonly sold in the U.S. and Canada.

On 1972–74 models, unleaded or lowlead fuels of approximately 91 octane (Research Octane) or higher are recommended. General Motors recommends the use of unleaded fuels to reduce particulate and hydrocarbon pollutants. In states using the Gasoline Performance and Information system of fuel designation, unleaded or low-lead fuels with an anti-knock designation of "2" or higher are recommended.

Use of a fuel which is too low in anti-knock quality will result in "spark knock." Since many factors affect operating efficiency, such as altitude, terrain and air temperature, knocking may result even though you are using the recommended fuel. If persistent knocking occurs, it may be necessary to switch to a slightly higher grade of gasoline to correct the problem. In the case of late model engines (1972–74), switching to a premium fuel would be an unnecessary expense. In these engines, a slightly higher grade of gasoline (regular) should be used only when persistent knocking occurs. If this will not cure the problem, consult a dealer.

Due to the use of catalytic converters on all 1975 and later Nova models, fuel usage is restricted to unleaded gasoline only.

1975 and later Novas carry the notation "Unleaded Fuel Only" in the center of the speedometer face and near the fuel tank filler. They also have a new fuel tank filler neck that accepts only the small diameter fuel nozzle which is on all unleaded fuel pumps and a threaded gas cap to ensure proper tank sealing.

ENGINE OIL

The SAE grade number indicates the viscosity of the engine oil, or its ability to lubricate under a given temperature. The lower

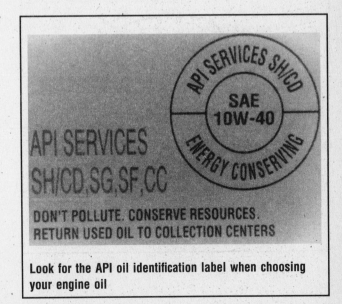

Look for the API oil identification label when choosing your engine oil

1962–68 Engine Oil Viscosity Recommendations

Ambient Temperature	SAE Multigrade	SAE Single Grade
When temperatures are consistently above 32° F	SAE 20W-40, SAE 10W-40, or SAE 10W-30	SAE 30
For year long operation where temperatures occasionally drop to —10° F	SAE 10W-30 or SAE 10W-40	
Where temperatures range between +32° F and —10° F		SAE 10W

1969–71 Recommended SAE Viscosity Number

1972–77 Recommended SAE Viscosity Number

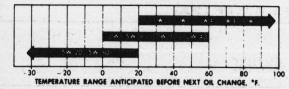

NOTES: 1. SAE 5W and 5W-20 are not recommended for sustained high-speed driving.
2. SAE 30 and 20W-40 may be used at temperatures above 90° F.
3. SAE 5W-30 may be used at temperatures below 32° F.
4. SAE 10W-40 may be used at temperatures between 0° and 90° F.

1978–79 Recommended SAE Viscosity Number

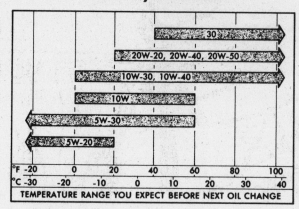

NOTE: *Do not use SAE 5W-20 oils for high speed driving.*

SAE grade number, the lighter the oil; the lower the viscosity, the easier it is to crank the engine in cold weather.

The API (American Petroleum Institute) designation indicates the classification of engine oil for use under given operating conditions. Only oils designated for "Service SH" (old designation MS) should be used. These oils provide maximum engine protection. Both the SAE grade number and the API designation can be found on the label on a quart of oil.

➡ **Non-detergent or straight mineral oils should not be used.**

Oil viscosities should be chosen from those oils recommended for the lowest anticipated temperatures during the oil change interval.

➡ **Do not use SAE 5W-20 oils for high speed driving.**

Engine

OIL LEVEL CHECK

◆ **See Figure 10f and 10g**

Always maintain the engine oil at its proper level in the crankcase. Check the oil level when the engine is cold. If this is not possible, switch off the engine and wait a few minutes before checking the oil level. This will allow the engine oil time to drain into the crankcase.

To check the oil level, remove the dipstick, wipe it clean, and reinsert it. Withdraw the dipstick and observe the oil level marking. The dipstick is marked "add" and "full." The oil level should be kept between the two marks, neither below the "add" mark nor above the "full" mark. If necessary, add oil. When replacing the dipstick, be sure that it is seated firmly in its tube.

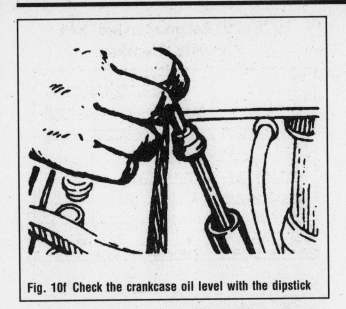

Fig. 10f Check the crankcase oil level with the dipstick

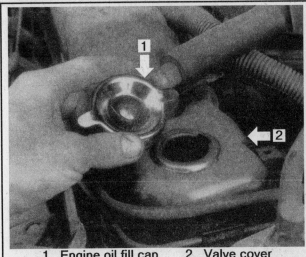

1. Engine oil fill cap   2. Valve cover

If necessary, remove the oil fill cap from the valve cover

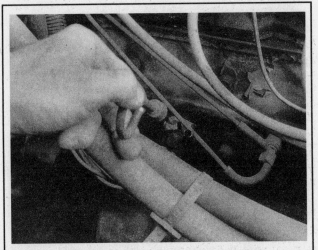

Remove the dipstick, wipe with a clean rag, then reinsert it

Add the proper amount of engine oil, using a clean funnel to prevent a mess

Fig. 10g Withdraw the stick again and read the level while holding it horizontally—the oil should appear between the ADD and FULL marks on the dipstick

OIL CHANGE

▶ **See Figure 10h**

For maximum engine protection during normal operation, the crankcase oil should be drained and refilled every four months or 6,000 miles. (6 months or 7,500 miles on 1975–77 cars, 1 year or 7,500 miles on later cars). If the vehicle is driven frequently in dusty or sandy areas, is used for trailer towing, or is required to idle extensively in heavy traffic, more frequent oil changes are required. In these situations, oil change intervals should not exceed two months (3 months on 1978 and later cars) or 3,000 miles.

Drain the oil when the engine is at normal operating temperature so the warm oil can carry any foreign matter with it that might otherwise cling to the sides of the crankcase. To drain the oil, place a suitable container under the oil pan below the drain plug. Remove the drain plug and allow the warm oil to drain into the container. Remove and replace the oil filter, as discussed below.

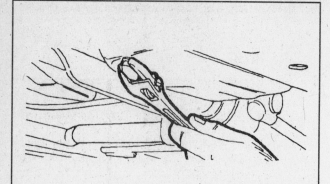

Fig. 10h The oil drain plug is located at the lowest point of the engine oil pan—if you don't have the proper size wrench or socket, an adjustable can be used to carefully loosen it

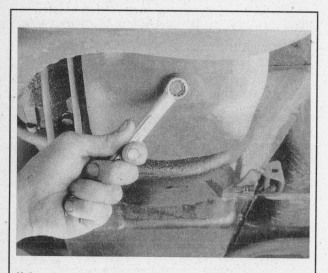

Using a wrench, loosen the oil pan drain plug . . .

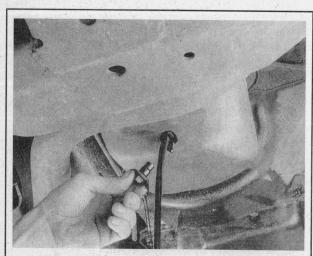

. . . then quickly withdraw the plug and allow the oil to drain into a pan

Be sure that the oil pan is drained as completely as possible before refitting the drain plug. Fill the crankcase with oil of the recommended grade. Start the engine and check the oil level. Add sufficient oil to compensate for the oil which has been drawn into the filter.

OIL FILTER CHANGES

All engines are equipped with a full-flow oil filter, of either a cartridge or throw-away type. The filter should be replaced at every oil change.

Cartridge Type Filter

To change the cartridge type filter, first drain the crankcase oil. Replace the drain plug. Place a container under the filter cartridge container to catch any oil which may be spilled. Unscrew the center bolt of the container and remove the container. Withdraw the old filter cartridge and clean out the cartridge container. Remove the old seal from the filter body casting and position the new seal in the casting. Install the new filter cartridge in the container and position the cartridge/container assembly on the filter body casting. Tighten the center bolt. Fill the crankcase with clean oil, start the engine, and check the oil level. Add sufficient oil to compensate for the oil which has been drawn into the filter.

Throwaway Type Filter

To change the throwaway type filter, first drain the crankcase oil. Replace the drain plug. Place a container under the filter to catch any oil which may be spilled. Remove the old filter by unscrewing it by hand or with a special oil filter wrench. Coat the gasket of the new filter with a thin film of clean oil. Prime the filter by pouring some clean oil into it. Place the filter in position on the filter body casting and tighten the filter by hand until the sealing gaskets just make contact. Further tighten the filter by hand about one-half turn. It is not necessary to use the filter wrench to tighten the filter. Fill the crankcase with clean oil, start the engine, and check the oil level. Add oil as necessary to compensate for the oil which has been drawn into the filter.

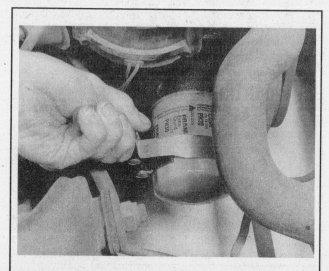

Remove the oil filter using a strap-type wrench

Before installing a new oil filter, lightly coat the rubber gasket with clean oil

Manual Transmission

FLUID RECOMMENDATIONS

The manufacturer recommends SAE 80 or SAE 80W-90 GL-5 Gear Lubricant as the proper lubricant in all three-speed and four-speed manual transmissions.

LEVEL CHECK

▶ **See Figure 10i**

Check the lubricant level when the transmission is warm. Remove the filler plug from the transmission case from underneath

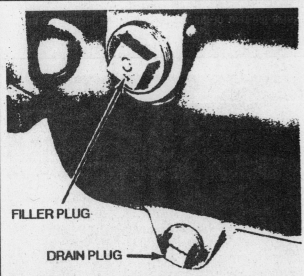

FILLER PLUG

DRAIN PLUG →

Fig. 10i When checking the manual transmission fluid, make sure not to confuse the fill plug with the drain plug

the car. If necessary, add sufficient lubricant to bring its level to the bottom of the filler plug hole. Replace the filler plug.

DRAIN & REFILL

Remove the transmission filler plug. Place a container under the transmission below the transmission drain plug. Remove the drain plug and allow the lubricant to drain into the container. After the lubricant has been drained, install the drain plug. Add sufficient lubricant to bring its level to the lower edge of the filler plug hole and install the filler plug.

Automatic Transmission

FLUID RECOMMENDATIONS

Only Dexron® type automatic transmission fluid is recommended by the manufacturer for use in all Powerglide, Torque Drive, and Turbo-Hydra-matic transmissions. Use Dexron® II type fluid only on 1978–79 cars.

LEVEL CHECK

▶ **See Figure 10j**

Check the fluid level when the transmission is warm. Be sure that the car is parked on a level surface. With transmission in Park and the engine running, withdraw the transmission dipstick at the rear of the engine compartment, wipe it clean, and reinsert it. Withdraw the dipstick again and observe the fluid level reading. If the fluid level is at or below the "add" mark, add Dexron® fluid to bring the transmission fluid to the correct level. When replacing the transmission dipstick, be sure that it is seated firmly in the transmission filler tube.

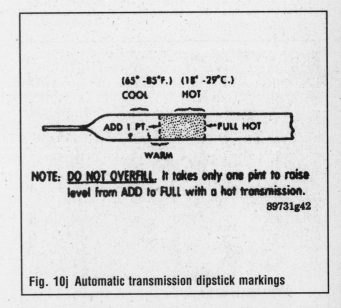

(65°-85°F.) (18°-29°C.)
COOL   HOT

ADD 1 PT.━━ ━FULL HOT

WARM

NOTE: **DO NOT OVERFILL.** It takes only one pint to raise level from ADD to FULL with a hot transmission.

89731g42

Fig. 10j Automatic transmission dipstick markings

Withdraw the A/T dipstick, wipe and reinsert it, then remove it again and check the level

At normal operating temperature, the fluid is extremely hot!

3. Place a container under the transmission below the transmission oil pan. On older models remove the oil pan plug and allow the transmission fluid to drain thoroughly into the container. On models without a drain plug, start removing the pan bolts at the front right corner allowing the fluid to drain. When the fluid has drained, remove the pan and replace the gasket.

4. Replace the drain plug or pan and refill the transmission with approximately two quarts of Dexron® type fluid. Dexron® II type fluid is required on all cars in 1976 and later years. This fluid is compatible with Dexron® fluid and may be used to replenish fluid lost or drained from older cars.

5. Remove the container and lower the car.

6. Start the engine and allow it to idle for a few minutes.

7. With the parking brake engaged, move the selector momentarily to each gear position, ending in the neutral position.

If necessary, add the proper transmission fluid through the dipstick tube

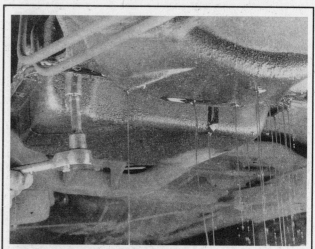

Loosen the automatic transmission pan retaining bolts and allow the fluid to drain

DRAIN & REFILL

For most models in normal service, the automatic transmission fluid should be changed at 24,000 mile intervals on cars built between 1962 and 1974, 30,000 miles on cars built from 1975–1977, and 60,000 miles on cars built in 1978 and 1979. However, for cars which are frequently driven in heavy city traffic or are used for trailer towing, fluid changes should be performed at 12,000 mile intervals for vehicles made before 1975, and 15,000 miles for vehicles made in 1975 and later years. Careful attention to fluid change intervals as established for various types of operating conditions is essential for long transmission life and reliable service.

To drain the transmission fluid, proceed as follows:

1. Run the engine for one minute in neutral.

2. Switch off the ignition. If the car has been raised on a hoist, be sure that it is level. Otherwise, raise the car from the rear only.

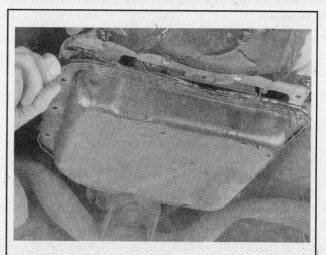

Lower the pan from the transmission, but be careful, there's probably some fluid left in the pan!

8. Run the engine at about 900 revolutions per minute (rpm) until the transmission fluid is warm, then add enough fluid to bring the fluid level to the full mark on the transmission dipstick.

Rear Axle

FLUID RECOMMENDATIONS

The manufacturer recommends that only SAE 80 or 80W-90 GL-5 Gear Lubricants be used in conventional differentials. For cars equipped with Positraction (limited-slip differential), special Positraction lubricant must be used.

LEVEL CHECK

Remove the lubricant filler plug from the differential housing from underneath the car to check the rear axle lubricant level. If necessary, add the proper lubricant to bring the level to the filler plug hole. Replace the filler plug.

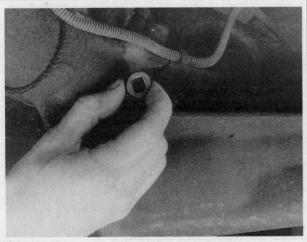
Remove the rear axle fluid filler plug from the differential

DRAIN & REFILL

The rear axle lubricant does not normally require changing for the life of the vehicle. However, if the vehicle is used to pull a trailer, change the rear axle lubricant every 12,000 miles (15,000 miles on 1978 and 1979 models).

If additions are necessary or when refilling the axle after service, proceed as follows:

1. Jack and safely support the rear of the vehicle.
2. If equipped, remove the drain plug and drain off the old lubricant. Remove the fill plug to act as a vent. If only a fill plug is provided, the lubricant will have to be removed with a suction gun, or the cover will have to be removed. If the cover is removed, be sure to use a new gasket on installation.
3. Fill the axle to the bottom of the fill plug hole with SAE 80

If the rear axle has no drain plug, you must remove the cover to drain the fluid

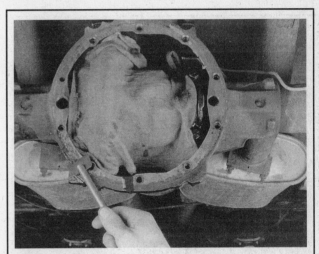
Once removed, clean off all the old gasket material (install a new gasket during installation)

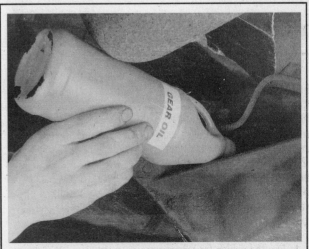
Add gear oil until the level reaches the bottom of the fill plug hole

or SAE 90 GL-5 gear lubricant (use SAE 80 GL-5 gear lubricant in Canadian vehicles).

4. Reinstall the fill plug and check for leaks.
5. Lower the vehicle.

Cooling System

▶ See Figure 11

✴✴ CAUTION

Never remove the radiator cap under any conditions while the engine is running! Failure to follow these instructions could result in damage to the cooling system or engine and/or personal injury. To avoid having scalding hot coolant or steam blow out of the radiator, use extreme care when removing the radiator cap from a hot radiator. Wait until the engine has cooled, then wrap a thick cloth around the radiator cap and turn it slowly to the first stop. Step back while the pressure is released from the cooling system. When you are sure the pressure has been released, press down on the radiator cap (still have the cloth in position) turn and remove the radiator cap.

Dealing with the cooling system can be dangerous matter unless the proper precautions are observed. It is best to check the coolant level in the radiator when the engine is cold. The cooling system may have, as one of its components, a coolant recovery tank. If the coolant level is at or near the FULL COLD line (engine cold) or the FULL HOT line (engine hot), the level is satisfactory. Always be certain that the filler caps on both the radiator and the recovery tank are closed tightly.

In the event that the coolant level must be checked when the engine is hot and the vehicle is not equipped with a coolant recovery tank, place a thick rag over the radiator cap and slowly turn the cap counterclockwise until it reaches the first detent. Allow all hot steam to escape. This will allow the pressure in the system to drop gradually, preventing an explosion of hot coolant. When the hissing noise stops, remove the cap the rest of the way.

If the coolant level is found to be low, add a 50/50 mixture of antifreeze and clean water. If not equipped with a recovery tank, coolant must be added through the radiator filler neck. On most models, which are equipped with a recovery tank, coolant may be added either through the filler neck on the radiator or directly into the recovery tank.

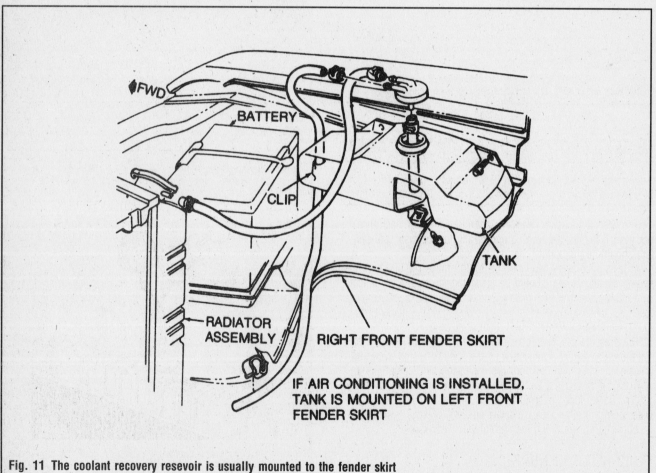

Fig. 11 The coolant recovery resevoir is usually mounted to the fender skirt

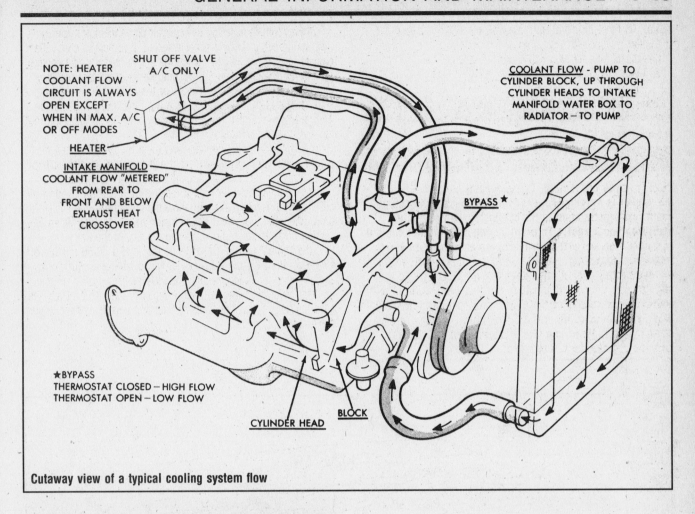

NOTE: HEATER COOLANT FLOW CIRCUIT IS ALWAYS OPEN EXCEPT WHEN IN MAX. A/C OR OFF MODES

SHUT OFF VALVE A/C ONLY

COOLANT FLOW - PUMP TO CYLINDER BLOCK, UP THROUGH CYLINDER HEADS TO INTAKE MANIFOLD WATER BOX TO RADIATOR — TO PUMP

HEATER

INTAKE MANIFOLD COOLANT FLOW "METERED" FROM REAR TO FRONT AND BELOW EXHAUST HEAT CROSSOVER

BYPASS ★

★BYPASS
THERMOSTAT CLOSED — HIGH FLOW
THERMOSTAT OPEN — LOW FLOW

CYLINDER HEAD

BLOCK

Cutaway view of a typical cooling system flow

✳✳ CAUTION

Never add coolant to a hot engine unless it is running. If it is not running you run the risk of cracking the engine block.

It is wise to pressure check the cooling system at least once per year. If the coolant level is chronically low or rusty, the system should be thoroughly checked for leaks.

At least once every two years or 30,000 miles (48,000 km), the engine cooling system should be inspected, flushed, and refilled with fresh coolant. If the coolant is left in the system too long, it loses its ability to prevent rust and corrosion. If the coolant has too much water, it won't protect against freezing.

The pressure cap should be examined for signs of age or deterioration. Fan belt and other drive belts should be inspected and adjusted to the proper tension. (See checking belt tension).

Hose clamps should be tightened, and soft or cracked hoses replaced. Damp spots, or accumulations of rust or dye near hoses, water pump or other areas, indicate possible leakage, which must be corrected before filling the system with fresh coolant.

FLUID RECOMMENDATIONS

Whenever adding or changing fluid, use a good quality ethylene glycol antifreeze (one that will not affect aluminum), mix it with clean water until a 50/50 antifreeze solution is attained.

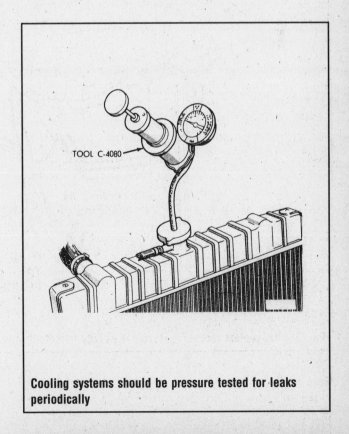

TOOL C-4080

Cooling systems should be pressure tested for leaks periodically

LEVEL CHECK

On most late model vehicles, the fluid level may be checked by observing the fluid level marks of the recovery tank (see through plastic bottle). The level should be near the ADD or FULL COLD mark, as applicable, when the system is cold. At normal operating temperatures, the level should be above the ADD/FULL COLD mark or, if applicable, between the ADD/FULL COLD and the FULL HOT marks. Only add coolant to the recovery tank as necessary to bring the system up to a proper level.

✳✳ CAUTION

Should it be necessary to remove the radiator cap, make sure that the system has had time to cool, reducing the internal pressure.

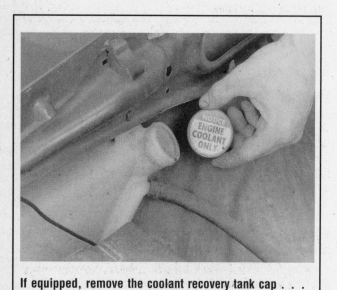

If equipped, remove the coolant recovery tank cap . . .

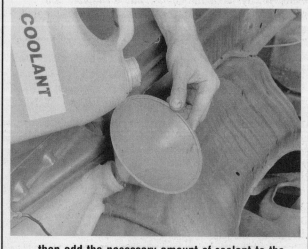

. . . then add the necessary amount of coolant to the tank

On any vehicle that is not equipped with a coolant recovery or overflow tank, the level must be checked by removing the radiator cap. This should only be done when the cooling system has had time to sufficiently cool after the engine has been run. The coolant level should be within 3 in. of the base of the radiator filler neck. If necessary, coolant can then be added directly to the radiator.

COOLING SYSTEM INSPECTION

Checking the Radiator Cap Seal

When you are checking the coolant level, check the radiator cap for a worn or cracked gasket. If the cap doesn't seal properly, fluid will be lost and the engine will overheat.

Worn caps should be replaced with a new one.

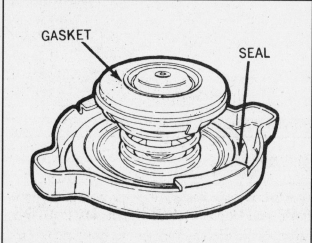

Be sure the rubber gasket on the radiator cap has a tight seal

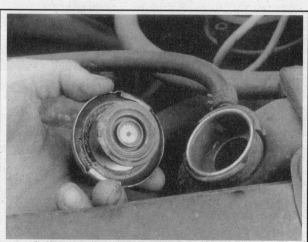

1. If the radiator cap seal is worn or cracked, it must be replaced with a new one.

Remove the cap from the radiator for inspection

Checking the Radiator for Debris

Periodically clean any debris; leaves, paper, insects, etc., from the radiator fins. Pick the large pieces by hand. The smaller pieces can be washed away with water pressure from a hose.

Carefully straighten any bent radiator fins with a pair of needle nose pliers. Be careful, the fins are very soft. Don't wiggle the fins back and forth too much. Straighten them once and try not to move them again.

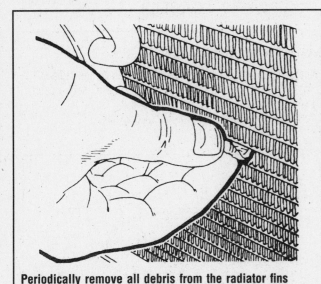

Periodically remove all debris from the radiator fins

DRAIN & REFILL

✳✳ CAUTION

To avoid injuries from scalding fluid and steam, DO NOT remove the radiator cap while the engine and radiator are still HOT.

1. Make sure the engine is cool and the vehicle is parked on a level surface, then remove the radiator neck cap and, if

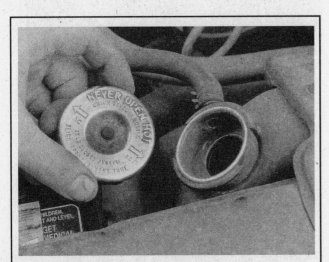

Once cooled, remove the radiator cap to relieve system pressure before draining

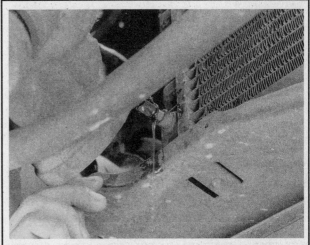

Open the radiator drain valve and allow the coolant to empty into a container

equipped, the recovery tank cap in order to relieve system pressure.

2. Position a large drain pan under the vehicle, then drain the existing coolant by opening the radiator drain valve (petcock). It is sometimes helpful to put a piece of vacuum hose ⅜ inches in diameter and about 12 in. (30 cm) long on the end of the radiator drain cock before opening the drain valve. This will help reduce some of the mess. It is also possible to drain the system by disconnecting the lower radiator hose from the bottom radiator outlet.

✳✳ CAUTION

When draining the coolant, keep in mind that cats and dogs are attracted by ethylene glycol antifreeze, and are quite likely to drink any that is left in an uncovered container or in puddles on the ground. This will prove fatal in sufficient quantity. Always drain the coolant into a sealable container. Coolant should be reused unless it is contaminated or several years old.

3. Close the petcock or reconnect the lower hose. If you used it, don't forget to take the piece of vacuum hose off the valve.

4. If necessary, empty the coolant reservoir and flush it. This is most easily done by removing the reservoir tank from the vehicle.

5. Determine the capacity of your coolant system (see capacities specifications). Though the radiator filler neck, add a 50/50 mix of quality antifreeze (ethylene glycol) and water to provide the desired protection.

6. Leave the radiator pressure cap off, then start and run the engine until the thermostat heats up and opens, this will allow air to bleed from the system and provide room for additional coolant to be added to the radiator.

7. Add additional coolant to the radiator, as necessary, until the level is within 3 in. of the radiator's filler neck base.

8. Stop the engine and check the coolant level.

9. Check the level of protection with an antifreeze tester, then install the radiator pressure cap.

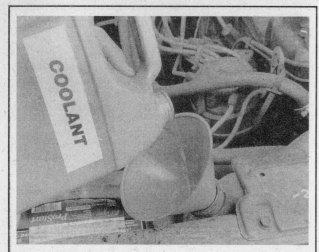

Add a 50/50 mix of coolant and water, until it reaches 2 in. below the radiator neck

10. If equipped with a coolant recovery/overflow tank, add coolant to the tank, as necessary, to achieve the proper level.

11. Start and run the engine to normal operating temperature, then check the system for leaks.

FLUSHING & CLEANING THE SYSTEM

The cooling system should be drained, thoroughly flushed and refilled at least every 30,000 miles (48,000 km) or 24 months. These operations should be done with the engine cold, especially if a backpressure flushing kit is being used. Completely draining and refilling the cooling system every two years will remove accumulated rust, scale and other deposits. Coolant in late model cars is a 50/50 mixture of ethylene glycol and water for year round use. Use a good quality antifreeze with water pump lubricants, rust inhibitors and other corrosion inhibitors along with acid neutralizers.

There are many products available for cooling system flushing. If a backpressure flushing kit is used, it is recommended that the thermostat be temporarily removed in order to allow free flow to the system with cold water. Always follow the kit or cleaner manufacturer's instructions and make sure the product is compatible with your vehicle.

1. Make sure the engine is cool and the vehicle is parked on a level surface, then remove the radiator neck cap and, if equipped, the recovery tank cap in order to relieve system pressure.

2. Position a large drain pan under the vehicle, then drain the existing coolant by opening the radiator drain valve (petcock). It is sometimes helpful to put a piece of vacuum hose ⅜ inches in diameter and about 12 in. (30 cm) long on the end of the radiator drain cock before opening the drain valve. This will help reduce some of the mess. It is also possible to drain the system by disconnecting the lower radiator hose from the bottom radiator outlet.

✳✳ CAUTION

When draining the coolant, keep in mind that cats and dogs are attracted by ethylene glycol antifreeze, and are quite likely to drink any that is left in an uncovered container or in puddles on the ground. This will prove fatal in sufficient quantity. Always drain the coolant into a sealable container. Coolant should be reused unless it is contaminated or several years old.

3. Close the radiator/engine drains or reconnect the lower hose, as applicable. If you used it, don't forget to take the piece of vacuum hose off the valve.

4. Fill the system with water, then add a can of quality radiator flush.

5. Idle the engine until the upper radiator hose gets hot and the thermostat has opened. This will allow the solution to fully circulate through the system.

6. Drain the system again.

7. Repeat this process until the drained water is clear and free of scale.

8. Close all drains and connect all the hoses.

9. If equipped with a coolant recover system, flush the reservoir with water and leave empty.

10. Determine the capacity of your coolant system (see capacities specifications). Add a 50/50 mix of quality antifreeze (ethylene glycol) and water to provide the desired protection.

11. Leave the radiator pressure cap off, then start and run the engine until the thermostat heats up and opens, this will allow air to bleed from the system and provide room for additional coolant to be added to the radiator.

12. Add additional coolant to the radiator, as necessary, until the level is within 2 in. (51mm) of the radiator's filler neck base.

13. Stop the engine and check the coolant level.

14. Check the level of protection with an antifreeze tester, then install the radiator pressure cap.

15. If equipped with a coolant recovery/overflow tank, add coolant to the tank, as necessary, to achieve the proper level.

16. Start and run the engine to normal operating temperature, then check the system for leaks.

Master Cylinder

FLUID RECOMMENDATONS

When adding fluid to the brake master cylinder, always use an approved DOT-3 brake fluid from a clean, sealed container.

LEVEL CHECK

Check the brake fluid level in the master cylinder reservoir at 6,000 mile or four-month intervals. Wipe clean the area around

On some vehicles, you must pry the retaining bail from the master cylinder reservoir lid

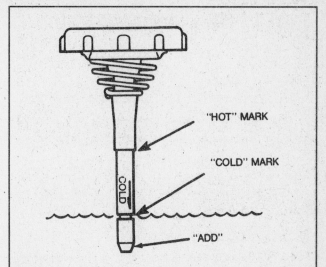

Fig. 12 The power steering pump fluid cap is also the dipstick

the master cylinder and the reservoir cap. Remove the reservoir cap and, if necessary, add brake fluid to maintain the fluid level ¼ inch (in.) below the lowest edge of the filler opening. Replace the reservoir cap.

Manual Steering Gear

FLUID RECOMMENDATION

Periodic change of manual steering gear lubricant should not be performed and the housing should not be drained. During its service life, the steering gear requires no lubrication.

If a seal is replaced or the gear overhauled, refill the gear housing with 13 oz. of GM Steering Gear Lubricant (Part No. 1051052) or its equivalent. Do not use EP chassis lubricant and do not overfill the gear housing.

Power Steering Pump

FLUID RECOMMENDATION & LEVEL CHECK

▶ **See Figure 12**

The fluid level of the power steering pump reservoir should be checked every 6,000 miles or four months. The fluid should be at operating temperature and the front wheels should be in the straight-ahead position before checking. Remove the reservoir cap, to which the reservoir dipstick is attached, wipe the dipstick clean, and reinsert the dipstick. Withdraw the dipstick and note the fluid level reading. If necessary, add power steering fluid or Dexron® type automatic transmission fluid to correct the fluid level. Replace the reservoir cap/dipstick.

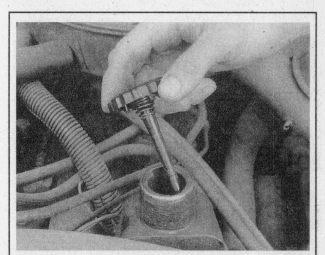

Remove the power steering pump cap/dipstick from the pump to check or add fluid

If necessary, add the proper fluid to bring the pump to the full level

Chassis Greasing

◆ See Figure 13

Refer to the "Lubrication and Maintenance Schedule" chart and the diagrams for chassis locations requiring lubrications. Use EP chassis lubricant which meets GM specification GM 6031M.

Body Lubrication

HOOD LATCH

Every four months or 6,000 miles, lubricate the hood latch assembly and hood hinge assemblies as follows:

1. Remove any accumulated dirt on latch parts.
2. Apply Lubriplate® or its equivalent to the latch pilot bolts and the latch locking plate.
3. Apply light engine oil to all pivot points in the release mechanism as well as the primary and secondary latch mechanisms.
4. Lubricate the hood hinges.
5. Check the operation of the hood hinges and the latch mechanism.

Wheel Bearings

See Chapter 9 for wheel bearing service and adjustment.

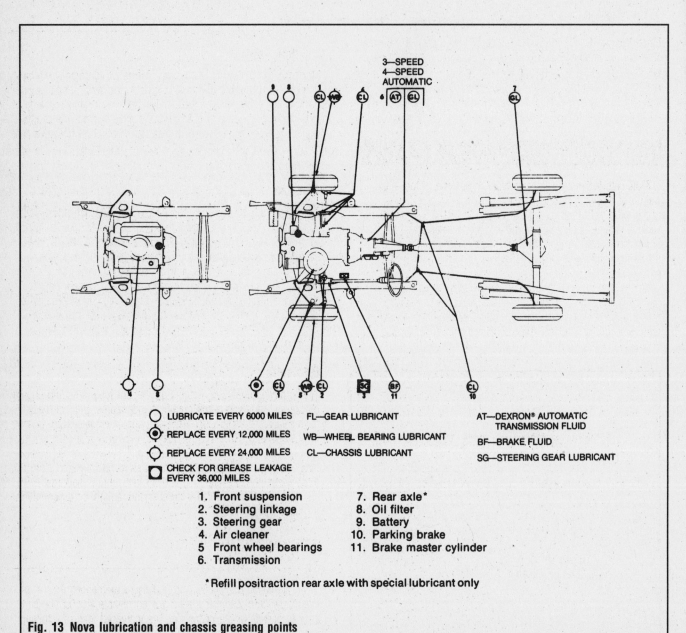

○ LUBRICATE EVERY 6000 MILES
◉ REPLACE EVERY 12,000 MILES
◇ REPLACE EVERY 24,000 MILES
▢ CHECK FOR GREASE LEAKAGE EVERY 36,000 MILES

FL—GEAR LUBRICANT
WB—WHEEL BEARING LUBRICANT
CL—CHASSIS LUBRICANT

AT—DEXRON® AUTOMATIC TRANSMISSION FLUID
BF—BRAKE FLUID
SG—STEERING GEAR LUBRICANT

1. Front suspension
2. Steering linkage
3. Steering gear
4. Air cleaner
5. Front wheel bearings
6. Transmission
7. Rear axle*
8. Oil filter
9. Battery
10. Parking brake
11. Brake master cylinder

*Refill positraction rear axle with special lubricant only

Fig. 13 Nova lubrication and chassis greasing points

TRAILER TOWING

General Recommendations

Your vehicle was primarily designed to carry passengers and cargo. It is important to remember that towing a trailer will place additional loads on your vehicles engine, drivetrain, steering, braking and other systems. However, if you decide to tow a trailer, using the prior equipment is a must.

Local laws may require specific equipment such as trailer brakes or fender mounted mirrors. Check your local laws.

Trailer Weight

The weight of the trailer is the most important factor. A good weight-to-horsepower ratio is about 35:1, 35 lbs. of Gross Combined Weight (GCW) for every horsepower your engine develops. Multiply the engine's rated horsepower by 35 and subtract the weight of the vehicle passengers and luggage. The number remaining is the approximate ideal maximum weight you should tow, although a numerically higher axle ratio can help compensate for heavier weight.

Hitch (Tongue) Weight

Calculate the hitch weight in order to select a proper hitch. The weight of the hitch is usually 9–11% of the trailer gross weight and should be measured with the trailer loaded. Hitches fall into various categories: those that mount on the frame and rear bumper, the bolt-on type, or the weld-on distribution type used for larger trailers. Axle mounted or clamp-on bumper hitches should never be used.

Check the gross weight rating of your trailer. Tongue weight is usually figured as 10% of gross trailer weight. Therefore, a trailer with a maximum gross weight of 2000 lbs. will have a maximum tongue weight of 200 lbs. Class I trailers fall into this category.

$$\frac{\text{TONGUE LOAD}}{\text{TOTAL TRAILER WEIGHT}} \times 100 = 9 \text{ to } 11 \%$$

Calculating proper tongue weight for your trailer

Class II trailers are those with a gross weight rating of 2000–3000 lbs., while Class III trailers fall into the 3500–6000 lbs. category. Class IV trailers are those over 6000 lbs. and are for use with fifth wheel trucks, only.

When you've determined the hitch that you'll need, follow the manufacturer's installation instructions, exactly, especially when it comes to fastener torques. The hitch will subjected to a lot of stress and good hitches come with hardened bolts. Never substitute an inferior bolt for a hardened bolt.

Cooling

ENGINE

Overflow Tank

One of the most common, if not THE most common, problems associated with trailer towing is engine overheating. If you have a cooling system without an expansion tank, you'll definitely need to get an aftermarket expansion tank kit, preferably one with at least a 2 quart capacity. These kits are easily installed on the radiator's overflow hose, and come with a pressure cap designed for expansion tanks.

Flex Fan

Another helpful accessory for vehicles using a belt-driven radiator fan is a flex fan. These fans are large diameter units designed to provide more airflow at low speeds, by using fan blades that have deeply cupped surfaces. The blades then flex, or flatten out, at high speed, when less cooling air is needed. These fans are far lighter in weight than stock fans, requiring less horsepower to drive them. Also, they are far quieter than stock fans. If you do decide to replace your stock fan with a flex fan, note that if your vehicle has a fan clutch, a spacer will be needed between the flex fan and water pump hub.

Oil Cooler

Aftermarket engine oil coolers are helpful for prolonging engine oil life and reducing overall engine temperatures. Both of these factors increase engine life. While not absolutely necessary in towing Class I and some Class II trailers, they are recommended for heavier Class II and all Class III towing. Engine oil cooler systems usually consist of an adapter, screwed on in place of the oil filter, a remote filter mounting and a multi-tube, finned heat exchanger, which is mounted in front of the radiator or air conditioning condenser.

TRANSMISSION

An automatic transmission is usually recommended for trailer towing. Modern automatics have proven reliable and, of course, easy to operate, in trailer towing. The increased load of a trailer, however, causes an increase in the temperature of the automatic transmission fluid. Heat is the worst enemy of an automatic transmission. As the temperature of the fluid increases, the life of the fluid decreases.

It is essential, therefore, that you install an automatic transmission cooler. The cooler, which consists of a multi-tube, finned heat exchanger, is usually installed in front of the radiator or air conditioning compressor, and hooked in-line with the transmission cooler tank inlet line. Follow the cooler manufacturer's installation instructions.

Select a cooler of at least adequate capacity, based upon the combined gross weights of the vehicle and trailer.

Cooler manufacturers recommend that you use an aftermarket cooler in addition to, and not instead of, the present cooling tank in your radiator. If you do want to use it in place of the radiator cooling tank, get a cooler at least two sizes larger than normally necessary.

→**A transmission cooler can, sometimes, cause slow or harsh shifting in the transmission during cold weather, until the fluid has a chance to come up to normal operating temperature. Some coolers can be purchased with or retrofitted with a temperature bypass valve which will allow fluid flow through the cooler only when the fluid has reached above a certain operating temperature.**

Handling A Trailer

Towing a trailer with ease and safety requires a certain amount of experience. It's a good idea to learn the feel of a trailer by practicing turning, stopping and backing in an open area such as an empty parking lot.

TOWING THE VEHICLE

Chevy II and Nova models may be towed safely on all four wheels with the transmission in Neutral at maximum speed of 35 mph for distances under 50 miles, providing that the axle, driveline, and transmission are operating properly.

Disconnect and secure the driveshaft or raise the rear wheels if tow speeds in excess of 35 mph are necessary, vehicle must

be towed over 50 miles, or the transmission or driveline is damaged.

When towing a vehicle on its front wheels, the steering wheel must be secured in the straight-ahead position. On 1969 and later models, DO NOT rely on the steering column lock to accomplish this as it was not designed for that purpose.

JUMP STARTING A DEAD BATTERY

Whenever a vehicle is jump started, precautions must be followed in order to prevent the possibility of personal injury. Remember that batteries contain a small amount of explosive hydrogen gas which is a by-product of battery charging. Sparks should always be avoided when working around batteries, especially when attaching jumper cables. To minimize the possibility of accidental sparks, follow the procedure carefully.

✳✳ CAUTION

NEVER hook the batteries up in a series circuit or the entire electrical system will go up in smoke, including the starter!

Vehicles equipped with a diesel engine may utilize two 12 volt batteries. If so, the batteries are connected in a parallel circuit (positive terminal to positive terminal, negative terminal to negative terminal). Hooking the batteries up in parallel circuit increases battery cranking power without increasing total battery voltage output. Output remains at 12 volts. On the other hand, hooking two 12 volt batteries up in a series circuit (positive terminal to negative terminal, positive terminal to negative terminal) increases total battery output to 24 volts (12 volts plus 12 volts).

Jump Starting Precautions

• Be sure that both batteries are of the same voltage. Vehicles covered by this manual and most vehicles on the road today utilize a 12 volt charging system.

• Be sure that both batteries are of the same polarity (have the same terminal, in most cases NEGATIVE grounded).

• Be sure that the vehicles are not touching or a short could occur.

• On serviceable batteries, be sure the vent cap holes are not obstructed.

• Do not smoke or allow sparks anywhere near the batteries.

• In cold weather, make sure the battery electrolyte is not frozen. This can occur more readily in a battery that has been in a state of discharge.

• Do not allow electrolyte to contact your skin or clothing.

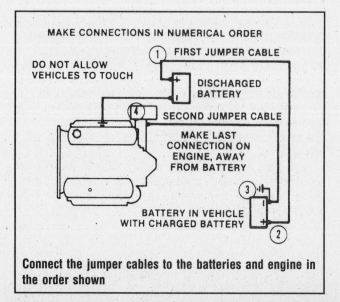

Connect the jumper cables to the batteries and engine in the order shown

Jump Starting Procedure

1. Make sure that the voltages of the 2 batteries are the same. Most batteries and charging systems are of the 12 volt variety.

2. Pull the jumping vehicle (with the good battery) into a position so the jumper cables can reach the dead battery and that vehicle's engine. Make sure that the vehicles do NOT touch.

3. Place the transmissions/transaxles of both vehicles in **Neutral** (MT) or **P** (AT), as applicable, then firmly set their parking brakes.

➡**If necessary for safety reasons, the hazard lights on both vehicles may be operated throughout the entire procedure without significantly increasing the difficulty of jumping the dead battery.**

4. Turn all lights and accessories OFF on both vehicles. Make sure the ignition switches on both vehicles are turned to the **OFF** position.

5. Cover the battery cell caps with a rag, but do not cover the terminals.

6. Make sure the terminals on both batteries are clean and free of corrosion or proper electrical connection will be impeded. If necessary, clean the battery terminals before proceeding.

7. Identify the positive (+) and negative (−) terminals on both batteries.

8. Connect the first jumper cable to the positive (+) terminal of the dead battery, then connect the other end of that cable to the positive (+) terminal of the booster (good) battery.

9. Connect one end of the other jumper cable to the negative (−) terminal on the booster battery and the final cable clamp to an engine bolt head, alternator bracket or other solid, metallic point on the engine with the dead battery. Try to pick a ground on the engine that is positioned away from the battery in order to minimize the possibility of the 2 clamps touching should one loosen during the procedure. DO NOT connect this clamp to the negative (−) terminal of the bad battery.

✳✳ CAUTION

Be very careful to keep the jumper cables away from moving parts (cooling fan, belts, etc.) on both engines.

10. Check to make sure that the cables are routed away from any moving parts, then start the donor vehicle's engine. Run the engine at moderate speed for several minutes to allow the dead battery a chance to receive some initial charge.

11. With the donor vehicle's engine still running slightly above idle, try to start the vehicle with the dead battery. Crank the engine for no more than 10 seconds at a time and let the starter cool for at least 20 seconds between tries. If the vehicle does not start in 3 tries, it is likely that something else is also wrong or that the battery needs additional time to charge.

12. Once the vehicle is started, allow it to run at idle for a few seconds to make sure that it is operating properly.

13. Turn ON the headlights, heater blower and, if equipped, the rear defroster of both vehicles in order to reduce the severity of voltage spikes and subsequent risk of damage to the vehicles' electrical systems when the cables are disconnected. This step is especially important to any vehicle equipped with computer control modules.

14. Carefully disconnect the cables in the reverse order of connection. Start with the negative cable that is attached to the engine ground, then the negative cable on the donor battery. Disconnect the positive cable from the donor battery and finally, disconnect the positive cable from the formerly dead battery. Be careful when disconnecting the cables from the positive terminals not to allow the alligator clips to touch any metal on either vehicle or a short and sparks will occur.

JACKING

◆ **See Figures 14 and 15**

Your vehicle was supplied with a jack for emergency road repairs. This jack is fine for changing a flat tire or other short term procedures not requiring you to go beneath the vehicle. If it is used in an emergency situation, carefully follow the instructions provided either with the jack or in your owner's manual. Do not attempt to use the jack on any portions of the vehicle other than specified by the vehicle manufacturer. Always block the diagonally opposite wheel when using a jack.

A more convenient way of jacking is the use of a garage or floor jack.

Never place the jack under the radiator, engine or transmission components. Severe and expensive damage will result when the jack is raised. Additionally, never jack under the floorpan or bodywork; the metal will deform.

Whenever you plan to work under the vehicle, you must support it on jackstands or ramps. Never use cinder blocks or stacks of wood to support the vehicle, even if you're only going to be under it for a few minutes. Never crawl under the vehicle when it is supported only by the tire-changing jack or other floor jack.

➡**Always position a block of wood or small rubber pad on top of the jack or jackstand to protect the lifting point's finish when lifting or supporting the vehicle.**

Small hydraulic, screw, or scissors jacks are satisfactory for raising the vehicle. Drive-on trestles or ramps are also a handy and safe way to both raise and support the vehicle. Be careful though, some ramps may be too steep to drive your vehicle onto without scraping the front bottom panels. Never support the vehicle on any suspension member (unless specifically instructed to do so by a repair manual) or by an underbody panel.

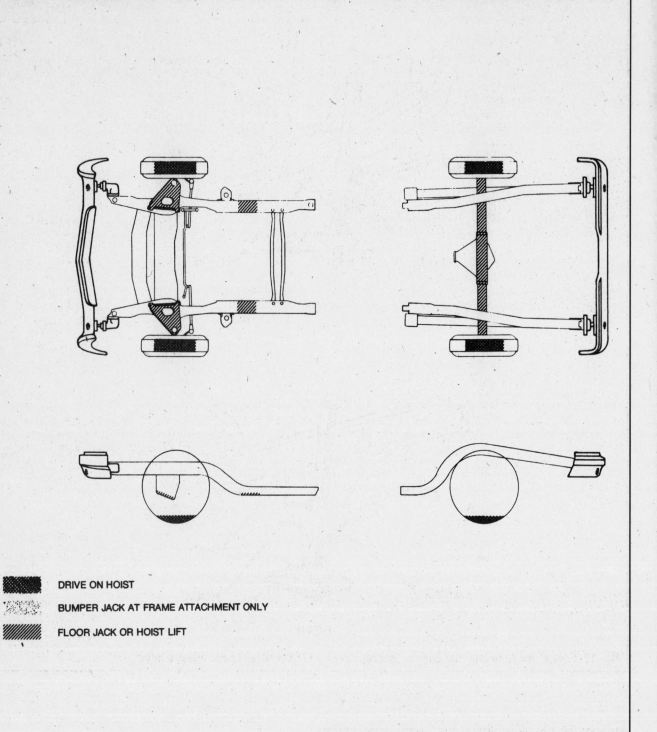

DRIVE ON HOIST

BUMPER JACK AT FRAME ATTACHMENT ONLY

FLOOR JACK OR HOIST LIFT

Fig. 14 Typical lifting points—1974–79 vehicles shown, other years similar. See your owners manual for specific applications

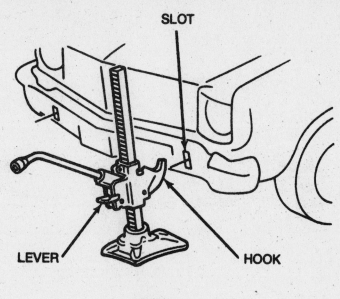

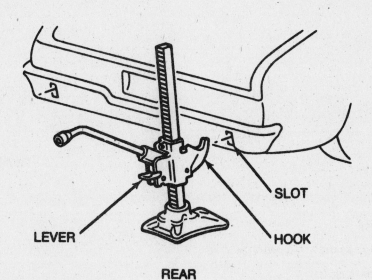

Fig. 15 View of the front and rear bumper jacking points—1973 vehicle shown, others similar

Jacking Precautions

The following safety points cannot be overemphasized:
• Always block the opposite wheel or wheels to keep the vehicle from rolling off the jack.
• When raising the front of the vehicle, firmly apply the parking brake.

• When the drive wheels are to remain on the ground, leave the vehicle in gear to help prevent it from rolling.
• Always use jackstands to support the vehicle when you are working underneath. Place the stands beneath the vehicle's jacking brackets. Before climbing underneath, rock the vehicle a bit to make sure it is firmly supported.

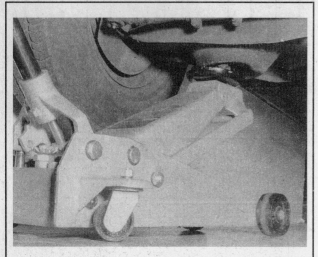

A good quality floor jack is the safe way to raise the front of your vehicle

Make sure to use a proper capacity jack to raise the rear end of the vehicle

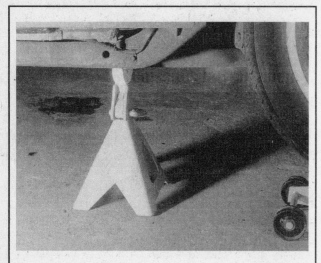

If you plan to work underneath the vehicle, ALWAYS use jackstands to support it

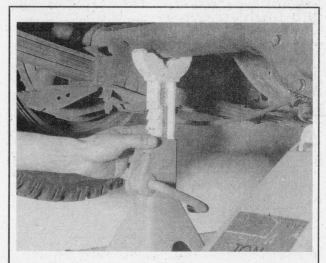

Raise the rear of the vehicle and place jackstands under the rear axle to support it

HOW TO BUY A USED VEHICLE

Many people believe that a two or three year old used car or truck is a better buy than a new vehicle. This may be true as most new vehicles suffer the heaviest depreciation in the first two years and, at three years old, a vehicle is usually not old enough to present a lot of costly repair problems. But keep in mind, when buying a non-warranted automobile, there are no guarantees. Whatever the age of the used vehicle you might want to purchase, this section and a little patience should increase your chances of selecting one that is safe and dependable.

Tips

1. First decide what model you want, and how much you want to spend.
2. Check the used car lots and your local newspaper ads. Privately owned vehicles are usually less expensive, however, you may not get a warranty that, in many cases, comes with a used vehicle purchased from a lot. Of course, some aftermarket warranties

may not be worth the extra money, so this is a point you will have to debate and consider based on your priorities.

3. Never shop at night. The glare of the lights make it easy to miss faults on the body caused by accident or rust repair.

4. Try to get the name and phone number of the previous owner. Contact him/her and ask about the vehicle. If the owner of a lot refuses this information, look for a vehicle somewhere else.

A private seller can tell you about the vehicle and maintenance. But remember, there's no law requiring honesty from private citizens selling used vehicles. There is a law that forbids tampering with or turning back the odometer mileage. This includes both the private citizen and the lot owner. The law also requires that the seller or anyone transferring ownership of the vehicle must provide the buyer with a signed statement indicating the mileage on the odometer at the time of transfer.

5. You may wish to contact the National Highway Traffic Safety Administration (NHTSA) to find out if the vehicle has ever been included in a manufacturer's recall. Write down the year, model and serial number before you buy the vehicle, then contact NHTSA (there should be a 1-800 number that your phone company's information line can supply). If the vehicle was listed for a recall, make sure the needed repairs were made.

6. Refer to the Used Vehicle Checklist in this section and check all the items on the vehicle you are considering. Some items are more important than others. Only you know how much money you can afford for repairs, and depending on the price of the vehicle, may consider performing any needed work yourself. Beware, however, of trouble in areas that will affect operation, safety or emission. Problems in the Used Vehicle Checklist break down as follows:

• Numbers 1–8: Two or more problems in these areas indicate a lack of maintenance. You should beware.

• Numbers 9–13: Problems here tend to indicate a lack of proper care, however, these can usually be corrected with a tune-up or relatively simple parts replacement.

• Numbers 14–17: Problems in the engine or transmission can be very expensive. Unless you are looking for a project, walk away from any vehicle with problems in 2 or more of these areas.

7. If you are satisfied with the apparent condition of the vehicle, take it to an independent diagnostic center or mechanic for a complete check. If you have a state inspection program, have it inspected immediately before purchase, or specify on the bill of sale that the sale is conditional on passing state inspection.

8. Road test the vehicle—refer to the Road Test Checklist in this section. If your original evaluation and the road test agree—the rest is up to you.

USED VEHICLE CHECKLIST

➡**The numbers on the illustrations refer to the numbers on this checklist.**

1. Mileage: Average mileage is about 12,000–15,000 miles per year. More than average mileage may indicate hard usage or could indicate many highway miles (which could be less detrimental than half as many tough around town miles).

2. Paint: Check around the tailpipe, molding and windows for overspray indicating that the vehicle has been repainted.

3. Rust: Check fenders, doors, rocker panels, window moldings, wheelwells, floorboards, under floormats, and in the trunk for signs of rust. Any rust at all will be a problem. There is no way to permanently stop the spread of rust, except to replace the part or panel.

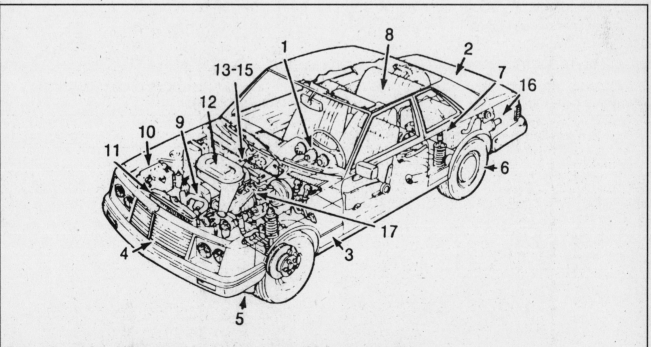

Each of the numbered items should be checked when purchasing a used vehicle

➡️**If rust repair is suspected, try using a magnet to check for body filler. A magnet should stick to the sheet metal parts of the body, but will not adhere to areas with large amounts of filler.**

4. Body appearance: Check the moldings, bumpers, grille, vinyl roof, glass, doors, trunk lid and body panels for general overall condition. Check for misalignment, loose hold-down clips, ripples, scratches in glass, welding in the trunk, severe misalignment of body panels or ripples, any of which may indicate crash work.

5. Leaks: Get down and look under the vehicle. There are no normal leaks, other than water from the air conditioner evaporator.

6. Tires: Check the tire air pressure. One old trick is to pump the tire pressure up to make the vehicle roll easier. Check the tread wear, then open the trunk and check the spare too. Uneven wear is a clue that the front end may need an alignment.

7. Shock absorbers: Check the shock absorbers by forcing downward sharply on each corner of the vehicle. Good shocks will not allow the vehicle to bounce more than once after you let go.

8. Interior: Check the entire interior. You're looking for an interior condition that agrees with the overall condition of the vehicle. Reasonable wear is expected, but be suspicious of new seat covers on sagging seats, new pedal pads, and worn armrests. These indicate an attempt to cover up hard use. Pull back the carpets and look for evidence of water leaks or flooding. Look for missing hardware, door handles, control knobs, etc. Check lights and signal operations. Make sure all accessories (air conditioner, heater, radio, etc.) work. Check windshield wiper operation.

9. Belts and Hoses: Open the hood, then check all belts and hoses for wear, cracks or weak spots.

10. Battery: Low electrolyte level, corroded terminals and/or cracked case indicate a lack of maintenance.

11. Radiator: Look for corrosion or rust in the coolant indicating a lack of maintenance.

12. Air filter: A severely dirty air filter would indicate a lack of maintenance.

13. Ignition wires: Check the ignition wires for cracks, burned spots, or wear. Worn wires will have to be replaced.

14. Oil level: If the oil level is low, chances are the engine uses oil or leaks. Beware of water in the oil (there is probably a cracked block or bad head gasket), excessively thick oil (which is often used to quiet a noisy engine), or thin, dirty oil with a distinct gasoline smell (this may indicate internal engine problems).

15. Automatic Transmission: Pull the transmission dipstick out when the engine is running. The level should read FULL, and the fluid should be clear or bright red. Dark brown or black fluid that has distinct burnt odor, indicates a transmission in need of repair or overhaul.

16. Exhaust: Check the color of the exhaust smoke. Blue smoke indicates, among other problems, worn rings. Black smoke can indicate burnt valves or carburetor problems. Check the exhaust system for leaks; it can be expensive to replace.

17. Spark Plugs: Remove one or all of the spark plugs (the most accessible will do, though all are preferable). An engine in good condition will show plugs with a light tan or gray deposit on the firing tip.

ROAD TEST CHECKLIST

1. Engine Performance: The vehicle should be peppy whether cold or warm, with adequate power and good pickup. It should respond smoothly through the gears.

2. Brakes: They should provide quick, firm stops with no noise, pulling or brake fade.

3. Steering: Sure control with no binding harshness, or looseness and no shimmy in the wheel should be expected. Noise or vibration from the steering wheel when turning the vehicle means trouble.

4. Clutch (Manual Transmission/Transaxle): Clutch action should give quick, smooth response with easy shifting. The clutch pedal should have free-play before it disengages the clutch. Start the engine, set the parking brake, put the transmission in first gear and slowly release the clutch pedal. The engine should begin to stall when the pedal is ½–¾ of the way up.

5. Automatic Transmission/Transaxle: The transmission should shift rapidly and smoothly, with no noise, hesitation, or slipping.

6. Differential: No noise or thumps should be present. Differentials have no normal leaks.

7. Driveshaft/Universal Joints: Vibration and noise could mean driveshaft problems. Clicking at low speed or coast conditions means worn U-joints.

8. Suspension: Try hitting bumps at different speeds. A vehicle that bounces excessively has weak shock absorbers or struts. Clunks mean worn bushings or ball joints.

9. Frame/Body: Wet the tires and drive in a straight line. Tracks should show two straight lines, not four. Four tire tracks indicate a frame/body bent by collision damage. If the tires can't be wet for this purpose, have a friend drive along behind you and see if the vehicle appears to be traveling in a straight line.

Lubrication and Maintenance Schedule

Year	Interval	Service
1962–74	Every 6,000 miles or 4 months, whichever occurs first	• Change engine oil (normal passenger car service). Not to exceed 6,000 miles.
1975–77	Every 7,500 miles or 6 months, which ever occurs first	• Check and lubricate front suspension and steering linkage. Check rear suspension.
1978–79	Every 7,500 miles or 1 year, which ever occurs first	• Check brake lines and hoses. • Check all lubricant and fluid levels (power steering pump, brake master cylinder, transmission, rear axle, radiator, battery). • Check power steering lines and hoses. • Check manifold heat control valve. • Lubricate parking brake pulley, cables, and linkage. • Check emission control items at first oil change (adjust engine idle speed, dwell, ignition timing). • Check exhaust system for proper mounting, leaks, and missing or damaged parts. • Check air conditioning system hose connections, refrigerant charge, and for refrigerant leaks. • Tire and wheel condition inspection. • Inspect accessory drive belts. • Inspect crankcase ventilation filter (located in air cleaner) and replace if necessary. • Lubricate hood latch and hood hinges. **At first oil change** • Set idle speed, ignition timing, and dwell to specifications. **At every oil change** • Change engine oil filter.①
1962–74	Every 6,000 miles	Rotate tires.
1975–79	Every 7,500 miles	
1962–74	First 12,000 miles	• Inspect air cleaner element, if satisfactory rotate 180° from original position and reinstall. See 24,000, 30,000 mile recommendation.
1975–79	First 15,000 miles	• Rotate distributor cam lubricator. See 24,000 30,000 mile recommendation.
1962–74	Every 12 months or 12,000 miles	• Inspect brake linings and check system for leaks.
1975–79	Every 12 months or 15,000 miles	• Check throttle and parking brake linkage and body parts. • Engine tune-up (cars with standard ignition). • Replace carburetor inlet fuel filter element. • Check emission control items. • Evaporation control system—replace filter in base of canister and inspect canister (1970–71 cars only). • Inspect AIR drive belt. • Check headlamp aiming. • Lubricate accelerator linkage.

Lubrication and Maintenance Schedule (cont.)

Year	Interval	Service
1962–74 1975–79	Every 24,000 miles Every 30,000 miles	• Repack front wheel bearings. • Replace air cleaner element. • Replace distributor cam lubricator (conventional ignition systems only). • Drain automatic transmission sump and add fresh fluid (normal passenger car service).② Adjust Powerglide or Torque Drive low band at *first* fluid change. • Replace Turbo Hydra-Matic sump filter.② • Replace carburetor inline filter if so equipped.
1962–74 1975–79	Every 24 months or 24,000 miles Every 24 months or 30,000 miles	• Drain radiator coolant, flush and refill system • Replace PCV valve. Inspect all hoses and fittings. • Replace crankcase ventilation filter (located within air cleaner).
All Years	Every 30,000 Miles	• Check steering gear for seal leakage (actual solid grease—not just oily film. • Lubricate clutch cross-shaft (sooner if necessary), remove plug, and install lube fitting.
	During winter months	• Check operation of air conditioning system.
	Perinodically	• Check battery liquid level. • Inspect seat belt, buckles, retractors, and anchors. • Check all lights for proper operation.
	As required	• Check wheel alignment and balancing.

① If oil is changed once a year, change the filter at every oil change.
② On 1978–79 cars, perform every 60,000 miles

Capacities

Year	Engine No. Cyl Displacement (cu in.)	Engine ° Crankcase Add 1 Qt for New Filter	Transmission Pts. to Refill after Draining			Drive Axle (Pts)	Gasoline Tank (Gals)	Cooling System (Qts)	
			Manual		•			with Heater	with A/C
			3 Speed	4 Speed	Automatic				
'62–'63	4—153	3.5	2	—	15.2	3.5	16	9	9
	6—194	4	2	—	15.2	3.5	16	12	12
'64	4—153	3.5	3	—	15.2	3.5	16	9	9
	6—194	4	3	—	15.2	3.5	16	12	12
	8—283	4	3	3	15.2	4	16	16	16
'65	4—153	3.5	2	—	15.2	4	16	9	9
	6—194, 230	4	2	—	15.2	4	16	12	12
	8—283	4	2	2.5	15.2	4	16	17	17
	8—327	4	2	2.5	15.2	4	16	16②	17②
'66	4—153	3.5	2	—	3	3.5	16	9	9
	6—194	4	2	—	3	3.5	16	12	12
	6—230	4	2	2	3	3.5	16	12	12
	8—283	4	2	2	3	3.5	16	16	17
	8—327	4	3③	3	6.5	3.5④	16	15	17⑤
'67	4—153	3.5	3	—	6	3.5	16	9	9
	6—194	4	3③	3③	6	3.5	16	12	12
	6—230	4	3③	3③	6	3.5	16	14	14
	6—250	4	3③	3③	6	3.5	16	13	14
	8—283	4	3③	3③	6	3.5	16	16	17
	8—327	4	3③	3③	6	3.5	16	15	18
'68	4—153	3.5	3	—	6	3.5	18	9	9
	6—230	4	3	3	6	3.5	18	12	12

Capacities (cont.)

Year	Engine No. Cyl Displacement (cu in.)	Engine • Crankcase Add 1 Qt for New Filter	Transmission Pts. to Refill after Draining			Drive Axle (Pts)	Gasoline Tank (Gals)	Cooling System (Qts)	
			Manual		• Automatic			with Heater	with A/C
			3 Speed	4 Speed					
	6—250	4	3	3	6	3.5	18	12	12
	8—307	4	3	3	6	3.5	18	17	17
	8—327	4	3	3	6	3.5	18	16	16
'69	4—153	3.5	3	—	6	3.5	18	9	9
	6—230	4	3③	—	6⑬	3.5④	18	13	13
	6—250	4	3③	—	6⑬	3.5④	18	13	13
	8—307	4	3③	3	6⑬	3.5④	18	17	17
	8—350	4	3③	3	6⑬	3.5④	18	16	16
	8—396	4	3③	3	8	3.5④	18	23	24
'70	4—153	3.5	3	—	6	3.75⑧	18	9	9
	6—230	4	3	—	6⑬	3.75⑧	18	12	13
	6—250	4	3	—	6⑬	3.75⑧	18	12	13
	8—307	4	3	—	6⑬	3.75⑧	18	15	16
	8—350	4	3	3	6.5⑨⑬	3.75⑧	18	16	16
	8—396	4	3	3	8	3.75⑧	18	23	24
'71	6—250	4	3	—	6	3.75	16	12	—
	8—307	4	3	—	6⑬	3.75	16	15	16
	8—350	4	3	3	6.5⑬	3.75	16	16	16
'72	6—250	4	3	—	6⑬	4.25	16	12	—
	8—307	4	3	—	6⑬	4.25	16	15	16
	8—350	4	3	3	6.5⑬	4.25	16	16	16
'73	6—250	4	3	—	6⑬	4.25	21	12.5	—

Capacities (cont.)

| Year | Engine No. Cyl Displacement (cu in.) | Engine ° Crankcase Add 1 Qt for New Filter | Transmission Pts. to Refill after Draining | | | Drive Axle (Pts) | Gasoline Tank (Gals) | Cooling System (Qts) | |
| | | | Manual | | • | | | | |
			3 Speed	4 Speed	Automatic			with Heater	with A/C
	8—307	4	3	—	5	4.25	21	15.5	16.5
	8—350	4	3	3	5	4.25	21	15.5	16.5
'74	6—250	4	3	—	8	4.25	21	12.5	—
	8—350	4	3	3	8	4.25	21	15.5	16.5
'75–'77	6—250	4	3⑭	—	8	4.25	21	14	15
	8—262, 305	4	3	—	8	4.25	21	17	18
	8—350	4	3	3	8	4.25	21	17	17⑫
'78–'79	6—250	4	3	—	8	3.25	21	14	15
	8—305	4	3	—	8	4.0	21	16	17
	8—350	4	—	3	8	4.0	21	16	17

* Add ½ qt with filter change on 4 cyl engine
• Specifications do not include torque converter
① Not used
② 300 HP, 18 Qts; 350 HP, 19 Qts.
③ 3.5 pts with heavy duty transmission
④ 4 pts with 8.875 in. ring gear
⑤ 16 qts with 350 hp option
⑥ Not used
⑦ Not used
⑧ 4.25 pts with 8.875 in. ring gear
⑨ 8 pts with 360 hp engine
⑩ Not used
⑪ Not used
⑫ 18—1976–77
⑬ 5 pts with Turbo Hydra–matic 350
⑭ Not available—Calif.
— Not applicable

ENGLISH TO METRIC CONVERSION: MASS (WEIGHT)

Current **mass** measurement is expressed in pounds and ounces (lbs. & ozs.). The metric unit of mass (or weight) is the kilogram (kg). Even although this table does not show conversion of masses (weights) larger than 15 lbs, it is easy to calculate larger units by following the data immediately below.

To convert ounces (oz.) to grams (g): multiply th number of ozs. by 28
To convert grams (g) to ounces (oz.): multiply the number of grams by .035

To convert pounds (lbs.) to kilograms (kg): multiply the number of lbs. by .45
To convert kilograms (kg) to pounds (lbs.): multiply the number of kilograms by 2.2

lbs	kg	lbs	kg	oz	kg	oz	kg
0.1	0.04	0.9	0.41	0.1	0.003	0.9	0.024
0.2	0.09	1	0.4	0.2	0.005	1	0.03
0.3	0.14	2	0.9	0.3	0.008	2	0.06
0.4	0.18	3	1.4	0.4	0.011	3	0.08
0.5	0.23	4	1.8	0.5	0.014	4	0.11
0.6	0.27	5	2.3	0.6	0.017	5	0.14
0.7	0.32	10	4.5	0.7	0.020	10	0.28
0.8	0.36	15	6.8	0.8	0.023	15	0.42

ENGLISH TO METRIC CONVERSION: TEMPERATURE

To convert Fahrenheit (°F) to Celsius (°C): take number of °F and subtract 32; multiply result by 5; divide result by 9

To convert Celsius (°C) to Fahrenheit (°F): take number of °C and multiply by 9; divide result by 5; add 32 to total

Fahrenheit (F)		Celsius (C)		Fahrenheit (F)		Celsius (C)		Fahrenheit (F)		Celsius (C)	
°F	°C	°C	°F	°F	°C	°C	°F	°F	°C	°C	°F
−40	−40	−38	−36.4	80	26.7	18	64.4	215	101.7	80	176
−35	−37.2	−36	−32.8	85	29.4	20	68	220	104.4	85	185
−30	−34.4	−34	−29.2	90	32.2	22	71.6	225	107.2	90	194
−25	−31.7	−32	−25.6	95	35.0	24	75.2	230	110.0	95	202
−20	−28.9	−30	−22	100	37.8	26	78.8	235	112.8	100	212
−15	−26.1	−28	−18.4	105	40.6	28	82.4	240	115.6	105	221
−10	−23.3	−26	−14.8	110	43.3	30	86	245	118.3	110	230
−5	−20.6	−24	−11.2	115	46.1	32	89.6	250	121.1	115	239
0	−17.8	−22	−7.6	120	48.9	34	93.2	255	123.9	120	248
1	−17.2	−20	−4	125	51.7	36	96.8	260	126.6	125	257
2	−16.7	−18	−0.4	130	54.4	38	100.4	265	129.4	130	266
3	−16.1	−16	3.2	135	57.2	40	104	270	132.2	135	275
4	−15.6	−14	6.8	140	60.0	42	107.6	275	135.0	140	284
5	−15.0	−12	10.4	145	62.8	44	112.2	280	137.8	145	293
10	−12.2	−10	14	150	65.6	46	114.8	285	140.6	150	302
15	−9.4	−8	17.6	155	68.3	48	118.4	290	143.3	155	311
20	−6.7	−6	21.2	160	71.1	50	122	295	146.1	160	320
25	−3.9	−4	24.8	165	73.9	52	125.6	300	148.9	165	329
30	−1.1	−2	28.4	170	76.7	54	129.2	305	151.7	170	338
35	1.7	0	32	175	79.4	56	132.8	310	154.4	175	347
40	4.4	2	35.6	180	82.2	58	136.4	315	157.2	180	356
45	7.2	4	39.2	185	85.0	60	140	320	160.0	185	365
50	10.0	6	42.8	190	87.8	62	143.6	325	162.8	190	374
55	12.8	8	46.4	195	90.6	64	147.2	330	165.6	195	383
60	15.6	10	50	200	93.3	66	150.8	335	168.3	200	392
65	18.3	12	53.6	205	96.1	68	154.4	340	171.1	205	401
70	21.1	14	57.2	210	98.9	70	158	345	173.9	210	410
75	23.9	16	60.8	212	100.0	75	167	350	176.7	215	414

ENGLISH TO METRIC CONVERSION: LENGTH

To convert inches (ins.) to millimeters (mm): multiply number of inches by 25.4

To convert millimeters (mm) to inches (ins.): multiply number of millimeters by .04

Inches		Decimals	Milli-meters	Inches to millimeters inches	mm	Inches		Decimals	Milli-meters	Inches to millimeters inches	mm
	1/64	0.051625	0.3969	0.0001	0.00254		33/64	0.515625	13.0969	0.6	15.24
1/32		0.03125	0.7937	0.0002	0.00508	17/32		0.53125	13.4937	0.7	17.78
	3/64	0.046875	1.1906	0.0003	0.00762		35/64	0.546875	13.8906	0.8	20.32
1/16		0.0625	1.5875	0.0004	0.01016	9/16		0.5625	14.2875	0.9	22.86
	5/64	0.078125	1.9844	0.0005	0.01270		37/64	0.578125	14.6844	1	25.4
3/32		0.09375	2.3812	0.0006	0.01524	19/32		0.59375	15.0812	2	50.8
	7/64	0.109375	2.7781	0.0007	0.01778		39/64	0.609375	15.4781	3	76.2
1/8		0.125	3.1750	0.0008	0.02032	5/8		0.625	15.8750	4	101.6
	9/64	0.140625	3.5719	0.0009	0.02286		41/64	0.640625	16.2719	5	127.0
5/32		0.15625	3.9687	0.001	0.0254	21/32		0.65625	16.6687	6	152.4
	11/64	0.171875	4.3656	0.002	0.0508		43/64	0.671875	17.0656	7	177.8
3/16		0.1875	4.7625	0.003	0.0762	11/16		0.6875	17.4625	8	203.2
	13/64	0.203125	5.1594	0.004	0.1016		45/64	0.703125	17.8594	9	228.6
7/32		0.21875	5.5562	0.005	0.1270	23/32		0.71875	18.2562	10	254.0
	15/64	0.234375	5.9531	0.006	0.1524		47/64	0.734375	18.6531	11	279.4
1/4		0.25	6.3500	0.007	0.1778	3/4		0.75	19.0500	12	304.8
	17/64	0.265625	6.7469	0.008	0.2032		49/64	0.765625	19.4469	13	330.2
9/32		0.28125	7.1437	0.009	0.2286	25/32		0.78125	19.8437	14	355.6
	19/64	0.296875	7.5406	0.01	0.254		51/64	0.796875	20.2406	15	381.0
5/16		0.3125	7.9375	0.02	0.508	13/16		0.8125	20.6375	16	406.4
	21/64	0.328125	8.3344	0.03	0.762		53/64	0.828125	21.0344	17	431.8
11/32		0.34375	8.7312	0.04	1.016	27/32		0.84375	21.4312	18	457.2
	23/64	0.359375	9.1281	0.05	1.270		55/64	0.859375	21.8281	19	482.6
3/8		0.375	9.5250	0.06	1.524	7/8		0.875	22.2250	20	508.0
	25/64	0.390625	9.9219	0.07	1.778		57/64	0.890625	22.6219	21	533.4
13/32		0.40625	10.3187	0.08	2.032	29/32		0.90625	23.0187	22	558.8
	27/64	0.421875	10.7156	0.09	2.286		59/64	0.921875	23.4156	23	584.2
7/16		0.4375	11.1125	0.1	2.54	15/16		0.9375	23.8125	24	609.6
	29/64	0.453125	11.5094	0.2	5.08		61/64	0.953125	24.2094	25	635.0
15/32		0.46875	11.9062	0.3	7.62	31/32		0.96875	24.6062	26	660.4
	31/64	0.484375	12.3031	0.4	10.16		63/64	0.984375	25.0031	27	690.6
1/2		0.5	12.7000	0.5	12.70						

ENGLISH TO METRIC CONVERSION: TORQUE

To convert foot-pounds (ft. lbs.) to Newton-meters: multiply the number of ft. lbs. by 1.3

To convert inch-pounds (in. lbs.) to Newton-meters: multiply the number of in. lbs. by .11

in lbs	N-m	in lbs	N-m	in lbs	N-m	in lbs	N-m	in lbs	N-m
0.1	0.01	1	0.11	10	1.13	19	2.15	28	3.16
0.2	0.02	2	0.23	11	1.24	20	2.26	29	3.28
0.3	0.03	3	0.34	12	1.36	21	2.37	30	3.39
0.4	0.04	4	0.45	13	1.47	22	2.49	31	3.50
0.5	0.06	5	0.56	14	1.58	23	2.60	32	3.62
0.6	0.07	6	0.68	15	1.70	24	2.71	33	3.73
0.7	0.08	7	0.78	16	1.81	25	2.82	34	3.84
0.8	0.09	8	0.90	17	1.92	26	2.94	35	3.95
0.9	0.10	9	1.02	18	2.03	27	3.05	36	4.0

ENGLISH TO METRIC CONVERSION: TORQUE

Torque is now expressed as either foot-pounds (ft./lbs.) or inch-pounds (in./lbs.). The metric measurement unit for torque is the Newton-meter (Nm). This unit—the Nm—will be used for all SI metric torque references, both the present ft./lbs. and in./lbs.

ft lbs	N-m	ft lbs	N-m	ft lbs	N-m	ft lbs	N-m
0.1	0.1	33	44.7	74	100.3	115	155.9
0.2	0.3	34	46.1	75	101.7	116	157.3
0.3	0.4	35	47.4	76	103.0	117	158.6
0.4	0.5	36	48.8	77	104.4	118	160.0
0.5	0.7	37	50.7	78	105.8	119	161.3
0.6	0.8	38	51.5	79	107.1	120	162.7
0.7	1.0	39	52.9	80	108.5	121	164.0
0.8	1.1	40	54.2	81	109.8	122	165.4
0.9	1.2	41	55.6	82	111.2	123	166.8
1	1.3	42	56.9	83	112.5	124	168.1
2	2.7	43	58.3	84	113.9	125	169.5
3	4.1	44	59.7	85	115.2	126	170.8
4	5.4	45	61.0	86	116.6	127	172.2
5	6.8	46	62.4	87	118.0	128	173.5
6	8.1	47	63.7	88	119.3	129	174.9
7	9.5	48	65.1	89	120.7	130	176.2
8	10.8	49	66.4	90	122.0	131	177.6
9	12.2	50	67.8	91	123.4	132	179.0
10	13.6	51	69.2	92	124.7	133	180.3
11	14.9	52	70.5	93	126.1	134	181.7
12	16.3	53	71.9	94	127.4	135	183.0
13	17.6	54	73.2	95	128.8	136	184.4
14	18.9	55	74.6	96	130.2	137	185.7
15	20.3	56	75.9	97	131.5	138	187.1
16	21.7	57	77.3	98	132.9	139	188.5
17	23.0	58	78.6	99	134.2	140	189.8
18	24.4	59	80.0	100	135.6	141	191.2
19	25.8	60	81.4	101	136.9	142	192.5
20	27.1	61	82.7	102	138.3	143	193.9
21	28.5	62	84.1	103	139.6	144	195.2
22	29.8	63	85.4	104	141.0	145	196.6
23	31.2	64	86.8	105	142.4	146	198.0
24	32.5	65	88.1	106	143.7	147	199.3
25	33.9	66	89.5	107	145.1	148	200.7
26	35.2	67	90.8	108	146.4	149	202.0
27	36.6	68	92.2	109	147.8	150	203.4
28	38.0	69	93.6	110	149.1	151	204.7
29	39.3	70	94.9	111	150.5	152	206.1
30	40.7	71	96.3	112	151.8	153	207.4
31	42.0	72	97.6	113	153.2	154	208.8
32	43.4	73	99.0	114	154.6	155	210.2

ENGLISH TO METRIC CONVERSION: FORCE

Force is presently measured in pounds (lbs.). This type of measurement is used to measure spring pressure, specifically how many pounds it takes to compress a spring. Our present force unit (the pound) will be replaced in SI metric measurements by the Newton (N). This term will eventually see use in specifications for electric motor brush spring pressures, valve spring pressures, etc.

To convert pounds (lbs.) to Newton (N): multiply the number of lbs. by 4.45

lbs	N	lbs	N	lbs	N	oz	N
0.01	0.04	21	93.4	59	262.4	1	0.3
0.02	0.09	22	97.9	60	266.9	2	0.6
0.03	0.13	23	102.3	61	271.3	3	0.8
0.04	0.18	24	106.8	62	275.8	4	1.1
0.05	0.22	25	111.2	63	280.2	5	1.4
0.06	0.27	26	115.6	64	284.6	6	1.7
0.07	0.31	27	120.1	65	289.1	7	2.0
0.08	0.36	28	124.6	66	293.6	8	2.2
0.09	0.40	29	129.0	67	298.0	9	2.5
0.1	0.4	30	133.4	68	302.5	10	2.8
0.2	0.9	31	137.9	69	306.9	11	3.1
0.3	1.3	32	142.3	70	311.4	12	3.3
0.4	1.8	33	146.8	71	315.8	13	3.6
0.5	2.2	34	151.2	72	320.3	14	3.9
0.6	2.7	35	155.7	73	324.7	15	4.2
0.7	3.1	36	160.1	74	329.2	16	4.4
0.8	3.6	37	164.6	75	333.6	17	4.7
0.9	4.0	38	169.0	76	338.1	18	5.0
1	4.4	39	173.5	77	342.5	19	5.3
2	8.9	40	177.9	78	347.0	20	5.6
3	13.4	41	182.4	79	351.4	21	5.8
4	17.8	42	186.8	80	355.9	22	6.1
5	22.2	43	191.3	81	360.3	23	6.4
6	26.7	44	195.7	82	364.8	24	6.7
7	31.1	45	200.2	83	369.2	25	7.0
8	35.6	46	204.6	84	373.6	26	7.2
9	40.0	47	209.1	85	378.1	27	7.5
10	44.5	48	213.5	86	382.6	28	7.8
11	48.9	49	218.0	87	387.0	29	8.1
12	53.4	50	224.4	88	391.4	30	8.3
13	57.8	51	226.9	89	395.9	31	8.6
14	62.3	52	231.3	90	400.3	32	8.9
15	66.7	53	235.8	91	404.8	33	9.2
16	71.2	54	240.2	92	409.2	34	9.4
17	75.6	55	244.6	93	413.7	35	9.7
18	80.1	56	249.1	94	418.1	36	10.0
19	84.5	57	253.6	95	422.6	37	10.3
20	89.0	58	258.0	96	427.0	38	10.6

ENGLISH TO METRIC CONVERSION: LIQUID CAPACITY

Liquid or fluid capacity is presently expressed as pints, quarts or gallons, or a combination of all of these. In the metric system the liter (l) will become the basic unit. Fractions of a liter would be expressed as deciliters, centiliters, or most frequently (and commonly) as milliliters.

To convert pints (pts.) to liters (l): multiply the number of pints by .47
To convert liters (l) to pints (pts.): multiply the number of liters by 2.1
To convert quarts (qts.) to liters (l): multiply the number of quarts by .95

To convert liters (l) to quarts (qts.): multiply the number of liters by 1.06
To convert gallons (gals.) to liters (l): multiply the number of gallons by 3.8
To convert liters (l) to gallons (gals.): multiply the number of liters by .26

gals	liters	qts	liters	pts	liters
0.1	0.38	0.1	0.10	0.1	0.05
0.2	0.76	0.2	0.19	0.2	0.10
0.3	1.1	0.3	0.28	0.3	0.14
0.4	1.5	0.4	0.38	0.4	0.19
0.5	1.9	0.5	0.47	0.5	0.24
0.6	2.3	0.6	0.57	0.6	0.28
0.7	2.6	0.7	0.66	0.7	0.33
0.8	3.0	0.8	0.76	0.8	0.38
0.9	3.4	0.9	0.85	0.9	0.43
1	3.8	1	1.0	1	0.5
2	7.6	2	1.9	2	1.0
3	11.4	3	2.8	3	1.4
4	15.1	4	3.8	4	1.9
5	18.9	5	4.7	5	2.4
6	22.7	6	5.7	6	2.8
7	26.5	7	6.6	7	3.3
8	30.3	8	7.6	8	3.8
9	34.1	9	8.5	9	4.3
10	37.8	10	9.5	10	4.7
11	41.6	11	10.4	11	5.2
12	45.4	12	11.4	12	5.7
13	49.2	13	12.3	13	6.2
14	53.0	14	13.2	14	6.6
15	56.8	15	14.2	15	7.1
16	60.6	16	15.1	16	7.6
17	64.3	17	16.1	17	8.0
18	68.1	18	17.0	18	8.5
19	71.9	19	18.0	19	9.0
20	75.7	20	18.9	20	9.5
21	79.5	21	19.9	21	9.9
22	83.2	22	20.8	22	10.4
23	87.0	23	21.8	23	10.9
24	90.8	24	22.7	24	11.4
25	94.6	25	23.6	25	11.8
26	98.4	26	24.6	26	12.3
27	102.2	27	25.5	27	12.8
28	106.0	28	26.5	28	13.2
29	110.0	29	27.4	29	13.7
30	113.5	30	28.4	30	14.2

ENGLISH TO METRIC CONVERSION: PRESSURE

The basic unit of pressure measurement used today is expressed as pounds per square inch (psi). The metric unit for psi will be the kilopascal (kPa). This will apply to either fluid pressure or air pressure, and will be frequently seen in tire pressure readings, oil pressure specifications, fuel pump pressure, etc.

To convert pounds per square inch (psi) to kilopascals (kPa): multiply the number of psi by 6.89

Psi	kPa	Psi	kPa	Psi	kPa	Psi	kPa
0.1	0.7	37	255.1	82	565.4	127	875.6
0.2	1.4	38	262.0	83	572.3	128	882.5
0.3	2.1	39	268.9	84	579.2	129	889.4
0.4	2.8	40	275.8	85	586.0	130	896.3
0.5	3.4	41	282.7	86	592.9	131	903.2
0.6	4.1	42	289.6	87	599.8	132	910.1
0.7	4.8	43	296.5	88	606.7	133	917.0
0.8	5.5	44	303.4	89	613.6	134	923.9
0.9	6.2	45	310.3	90	620.5	135	930.8
1	6.9	46	317.2	91	627.4	136	937.7
2	13.8	47	324.0	92	634.3	137	944.6
3	20.7	48	331.0	93	641.2	138	951.5
4	27.6	49	337.8	94	648.1	139	958.4
5	34.5	50	344.7	95	655.0	140	965.2
6	41.4	51	351.6	96	661.9	141	972.2
7	48.3	52	358.5	97	668.8	142	979.0
8	55.2	53	365.4	98	675.7	143	985.9
9	62.1	54	372.3	99	682.6	144	992.8
10	69.0	55	379.2	100	689.5	145	999.7
11	75.8	56	386.1	101	696.4	146	1006.6
12	82.7	57	393.0	102	703.3	147	1013.5
13	89.6	58	399.9	103	710.2	148	1020.4
14	96.5	59	406.8	104	717.0	149	1027.3
15	103.4	60	413.7	105	723.9	150	1034.2
16	110.3	61	420.6	106	730.8	151	1041.1
17	117.2	62	427.5	107	737.7	152	1048.0
18	124.1	63	434.4	108	744.6	153	1054.9
19	131.0	64	441.3	109	751.5	154	1061.8
20	137.9	65	448.2	110	758.4	155	1068.7
21	144.8	66	455.0	111	765.3	156	1075.6
22	151.7	67	461.9	112	772.2	157	1082.5
23	158.6	68	468.8	113	779.1	158	1089.4
24	165.5	69	475.7	114	786.0	159	1096.3
25	172.4	70	482.6	115	792.9	160	1103.2
26	179.3	71	489.5	116	799.8	161	1110.0
27	186.2	72	496.4	117	806.7	162	1116.9
28	193.0	73	503.3	118	813.6	163	1123.8
29	200.0	74	510.2	119	820.5	164	1130.7
30	206.8	75	517.1	120	827.4	165	1137.6
31	213.7	76	524.0	121	834.3	166	1144.5
32	220.6	77	530.9	122	841.2	167	1151.4
33	227.5	78	537.8	123	848.0	168	1158.3
34	234.4	79	544.7	124	854.9	169	1165.2
35	241.3	80	551.6	125	861.8	170	1172.1
36	248.2	81	558.5	126	868.7	171	1179.0

ENGLISH TO METRIC CONVERSION: PRESSURE

The basic unit of pressure measurement used today is expressed as pounds per square inch (psi). The metric unit for psi will be the kilopascal (kPa). This will apply to either fluid pressure or air pressure, and will be frequently seen in tire pressure readings, oil pressure specifications, fuel pump pressure, etc.

To convert pounds per square inch (psi) to kilopascals (kPa): multiply the number of psi by 6.89

Psi	kPa	Psi	kPa	Psi	kPa	Psi	kPa
172	1185.9	216	1489.3	260	1792.6	304	2096.0
173	1192.8	217	1496.2	261	1799.5	305	2102.9
174	1199.7	218	1503.1	262	1806.4	306	2109.8
175	1206.6	219	1510.0	263	1813.3	307	2116.7
176	1213.5	220	1516.8	264	1820.2	308	2123.6
177	1220.4	221	1523.7	265	1827.1	309	2130.5
178	1227.3	222	1530.6	266	1834.0	310	2137.4
179	1234.2	223	1537.5	267	1840.9	311	2144.3
180	1241.0	224	1544.4	268	1847.8	312	2151.2
181	1247.9	225	1551.3	269	1854.7	313	2158.1
182	1254.8	226	1558.2	270	1861.6	314	2164.9
183	1261.7	227	1565.1	271	1868.5	315	2171.8
184	1268.6	228	1572.0	272	1875.4	316	2178.7
185	1275.5	229	1578.9	273	1882.3	317	2185.6
186	1282.4	230	1585.8	274	1889.2	318	2192.5
187	1289.3	231	1592.7	275	1896.1	319	2199.4
188	1296.2	232	1599.6	276	1903.0	320	2206.3
189	1303.1	233	1606.5	277	1909.8	321	2213.2
190	1310.0	234	1613.4	278	1916.7	322	2220.1
191	1316.9	235	1620.3	279	1923.6	323	2227.0
192	1323.8	236	1627.2	280	1930.5	324	2233.9
193	1330.7	237	1634.1	281	1937.4	325	2240.8
194	1337.6	238	1641.0	282	1944.3	326	2247.7
195	1344.5	239	1647.8	283	1951.2	327	2254.6
196	1351.4	240	1654.7	284	1958.1	328	2261.5
197	1358.3	241	1661.6	285	1965.0	329	2268.4
198	1365.2	242	1668.5	286	1971.9	330	2275.3
199	1372.0	243	1675.4	287	1978.8	331	2282.2
200	1378.9	244	1682.3	288	1985.7	332	2289.1
201	1385.8	245	1689.2	289	1992.6	333	2295.9
202	1392.7	246	1696.1	290	1999.5	334	2302.8
203	1399.6	247	1703.0	291	2006.4	335	2309.7
204	1406.5	248	1709.9	292	2013.3	336	2316.6
205	1413.4	249	1716.8	293	2020.2	337	2323.5
206	1420.3	250	1723.7	294	2027.1	338	2330.4
207	1427.2	251	1730.6	295	2034.0	339	2337.3
208	1434.1	252	1737.5	296	2040.8	240	2344.2
209	1441.0	253	1744.4	297	2047.7	341	2351.1
210	1447.9	254	1751.3	298	2054.6	342	2358.0
211	1454.8	255	1758.2	299	2061.5	343	2364.9
212	1461.7	256	1765.1	300	2068.4	344	2371.8
213	1468.7	257	1772.0	301	2075.3	345	2378.7
214	1475.5	258	1778.8	302	2082.2	346	2385.6
215	1482.4	259	1785.7	303	2089.1	347	2392.5

SPARK PLUGS AND WIRING 2-2
SPARK PLUGS 2-2
  SPARK PLUG HEAT RANGE 2-2
  REMOVAL & INSTALLATION 2-3
  INSPECTION & GAPPING 2-4
SPARK PLUG WIRES 2-7
  TESTING 2-7
  REMOVAL & INSTALLATION 2-8
FIRING ORDERS 2-8
**BREAKER POINT IGNITION
  SYSTEM 2-9**
BREAKER POINTS AND
  CONDENSER 2-9
  REMOVAL & INSTALLATION 2-9
DWELL ANGLE 2-10
  ADJUSTMENT 2-10
  DWELL VARIATION TEST 2-11
MAGNETIC PULSE DISTRIBUTOR 2-11
HIGH ENERGY IGNITION 2-13
GENERAL INFORMATION 2-13
IGNITION TIMING 2-13
TIMING 2-13
  INSPECTION & ADJUSTMENT 2-13
VALVE LASH 2-13
HYDRAULIC TAPPETS 2-13
  ADJUSTMENT 2-13
MECHANICAL TAPPETS 2-14
  ADJUSTMENT 2-14
**IDLE SPEED AND MIXTURE
  ADJUSTMENTS 2-15**
1962–67 VEHICLES WITHOUT AIR 2-15
1967 VEHICLES WITH AIR 2-15
1968–69 VEHICLES 2-15
1970 VEHICLES 2-15
  4-153 ENGINES 2-16
  6-230/250 ENGINES 2-16
  8-307 ENGINES 2-16
  8-350 (300 HP) ENGINES 2-16
1971–72 VEHICLES 2-16
  6-250 ENGINES 2-16
  8-307 (200 HP) AND 350 (245 HP)
  ENGINES 2-16
  8-350 (270 HP) ENGINES 2-16
1973 VEHICLES 2-16
  6-250 ENGINES 2-17
  8-307, 350 (2 BBL) ENGINES 2-17
  8-350 (4 BBL) ENGINES 2-17
1974 VEHICLES 2-17
  6-250 ENGINES 2-17
  8-350 (2 BBL) ENGINES 2-17
  8-350 (4 BBL) ENGINES 2-17
1975 VEHICLES 2-17
1976–77 VEHICLES 2-17
  1 BBL CARBURETORS 2-17
  2 BBL & 4 BBL
    CARBURETORS 2-17
1978–79 VEHICLES 2-18
SPECIFICATION CHARTS
  TUNE-UP SPECIFICATIONS 2-19

2

TUNE-UP

SPARK PLUGS AND WIRING 2-2
FIRING ORDERS 2-8
BREAKER POINT IGNITION SYSTEM 2-9
HIGH ENERGY IGNITION 2-13
IGNITION TIMING 2-13
VALVE LASH 2-13
IDLE SPEED AND MIXTURE
ADJUSTMENTS 2-15

SPARK PLUGS AND WIRING

Spark Plugs

♦ See Figure 1

A typical spark plug consists of a metal shell surrounding a ceramic insulator. A metal electrode extends downward through the center of the insulator and protrudes a small distance. Located at the end of the plug and attached to the side of the outer metal shell is the side electrode. The side electrode bends in at a 90° angle so that its tip is just past and parallel to the tip of the center electrode. The distance between these two electrodes (measured in thousandths of an inch or hundredths of a millimeter) is called the spark plug gap.

The spark plug does not produce a spark but instead provides a gap across which the current can arc. The coil produces anywhere from 20,000 to 50,000 volts (depending on the type and application) which travels through the wires to the spark plugs. The current passes along the center electrode and jumps the gap to the side electrode, and in doing so, ignites the air/fuel mixture in the combustion chamber.

SPARK PLUG HEAT RANGE

Spark plug heat range is the ability of the plug to dissipate heat. The longer the insulator (or the farther it extends into the engine), the hotter the plug will operate; the shorter the insulator (the closer the electrode is to the block's cooling passages) the cooler it will operate. A plug that absorbs little heat and remains too cool will quickly accumulate deposits of oil and carbon since it is not hot enough to burn them off. This leads to plug fouling and consequently to misfiring. A plug that absorbs too much heat will have no deposits but, due to the excessive heat, the electrodes will burn away quickly and might possibly lead to preignition or other ignition problems. Preignition takes place when plug tips get so hot that they glow sufficiently to ignite the air/fuel mixture before the actual spark occurs. This early ignition will usually cause a pinging during low speeds and heavy loads.

The general rule of thumb for choosing the correct heat range

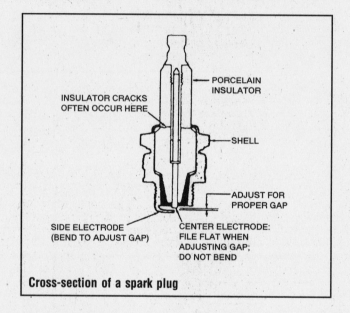

Cross-section of a spark plug

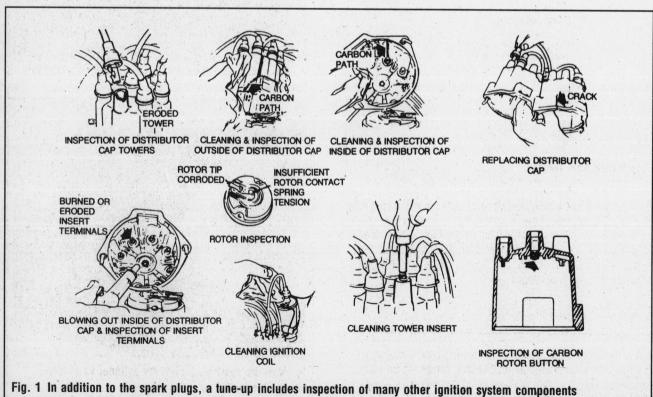

Fig. 1 In addition to the spark plugs, a tune-up includes inspection of many other ignition system components

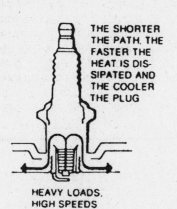

THE SHORTER THE PATH. THE FASTER THE HEAT IS DIS-SIPATED AND THE COOLER THE PLUG

HEAVY LOADS. HIGH SPEEDS

SHORT Insulator Tip
Fast Heat Transfer
LOWER Heat Range
COLD PLUG

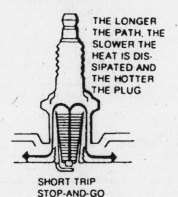

THE LONGER THE PATH. THE SLOWER THE HEAT IS DIS-SIPATED AND THE HOTTER THE PLUG

SHORT TRIP
STOP-AND-GO

LONG Insulator Tip
Slow Heat Transfer
HIGHER Heat Range
HOT PLUG

Spark plug heat range

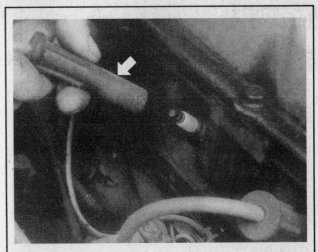

Disconnect the spark plug wire by pulling on the boot (see arrow). Tag the wires, unless you remove the plugs one at a time

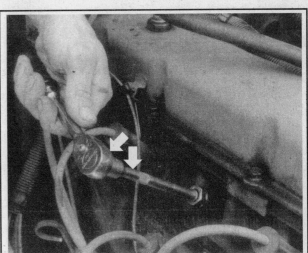

Access to the plug is easier using a suitable socket and extension

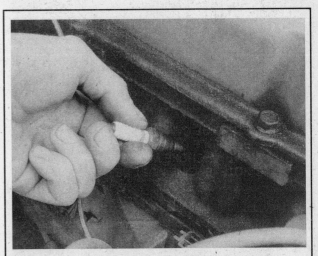

Remove the spark plug from the cylinder head and inspect for fouling or wear

when picking a spark plug is: if most of your driving is long distance, high speed travel, use a colder plug; if most of your driving is stop and go, use a hotter plug. Original equipment plugs are generally a good compromise between the 2 styles and most people never have the need to change their plugs from the factory-recommended heat range.

REMOVAL & INSTALLATION

A set of spark plugs usually requires replacement after about 20,000–30,000 miles (32,000–48,000 km), depending on your style of driving. In normal operation plug gap increases about 0.001 in. (0.025mm) for every 2500 miles (4000 km). As the gap increases, the plug's voltage requirement also increases. It requires a greater voltage to jump the wider gap and about two to three times as much voltage to fire the plug at high speeds than at idle. The improved air/fuel ratio control of modern fuel injection combined with the higher voltage output of modern ignition systems will often allow an engine to run significantly longer on a set of standard spark plugs, but keep in mind that efficiency will drop as the gap widdens (along with fuel economy and power).

When you're removing spark plugs, work on one at a time. Don't start by removing the plug wires all at once, because, unless you number them, they may become mixed up. Take a minute before you begin and number the wires with tape.

1. Disconnect the negative battery cable, and if the vehicle has been run recently, allow the engine to thoroughly cool.

2. Carefully twist the spark plug wire boot to loosen it, then pull upward and remove the boot from the plug. Be sure to pull on the boot and not on the wire, otherwise the connector located inside the boot may become separated.

3. Using compressed air, blow any water or debris from the spark plug well to assure that no harmful contaminants are allowed to enter the combustion chamber when the spark plug is removed. If compressed air is not available, use a rag or a brush to clean the area.

➡**Remove the spark plugs when the engine is cold, if possible, to prevent damage to the threads. If removal of the plugs is difficult, apply a few drops of penetrating oil or silicone spray to the area around the base of the plug, and allow it a few minutes to work.**

4. Using a spark plug socket that is equipped with a rubber insert to properly hold the plug, turn the spark plug counterclockwise to loosen and remove the spark plug from the bore.

✳✳ WARNING

Be sure not to use a flexible extension on the socket. Use of a flexible extension may allow a shear force to be applied to the plug. A shear force could break the plug off in the cylinder head, leading to costly and frustrating repairs.

To install:

5. Inspect the spark plug boot for tears or damage. If a damaged boot is found, the spark plug wire must be replaced.

6. Using a wire feeler gauge, check and adjust the spark plug gap. When using a gauge, the proper size should pass between the electrodes with a slight drag. The next larger size should not be able to pass while the next smaller size should pass freely.

7. Carefully thread the plug into the bore by hand. If resistance is felt before the plug is almost completely threaded, back the plug out and begin threading again. In small, hard to reach areas, an old spark plug wire and boot could be used as a threading tool. The boot will hold the plug while you twist the end of the wire and the wire is supple enough to twist before it would allow the plug to crossthread.

✳✳ WARNING

Do not use the spark plug socket to thread the plugs. Always carefully thread the plug by hand or using an old plug wire to prevent the possibility of crossthreading and damaging the cylinder head bore.

8. Carefully tighten the spark plug. If the plug you are installing is equipped with a crush washer, seat the plug, then tighten about ¼ turn to crush the washer. If you are installing a tapered seat plug, tighten the plug to specifications provided by the vehicle or plug manufacturer.

9. Apply a small amount of silicone dielectric compound to the end of the spark plug lead or inside the spark plug boot to prevent sticking, then install the boot to the spark plug and push until it clicks into place. The click may be felt or heard, then gently pull back on the boot to assure proper contact.

INSPECTION & GAPPING

Check the plugs for deposits and wear. If they are not going to be replaced, clean the plugs thoroughly. Remember that any kind of deposit will decrease the efficiency of the plug. Plugs can be cleaned on a spark plug cleaning machine, which can sometimes be found in service stations, or you can do an acceptable job of cleaning with a stiff brush. If the plugs are cleaned, the electrodes

A normally worn spark plug should have light tan or gray deposits on the firing tip

A carbon fouled plug, identified by soft, sooty, black deposits, may indicate an improperly tuned vehicle. Check the air cleaner, ignition components and engine control system

A physically damaged spark plug may be evidence of severe detonation in that cylinder. Watch that cylinder carefully between services, as a continued detonation will not only damage the plug, but could also damage the engine

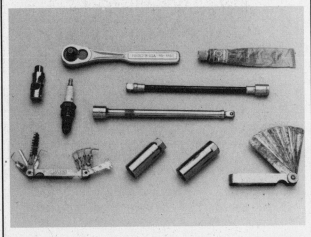

A variety of tools and gauges are needed for spark plug service

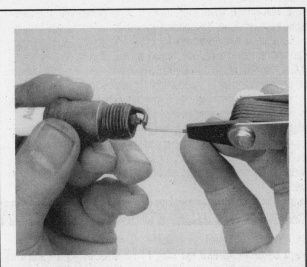

Checking the spark plug gap with a feeler gauge

An oil fouled spark plug indicates an engine with worn piston rings and/or bad valve seals allowing excessive oil to enter the chamber

This spark plug has been left in the engine too long, as evidenced by the extreme gap—Plugs with such an extreme gap can cause misfiring and stumbling accompanied by a noticeable lack of power

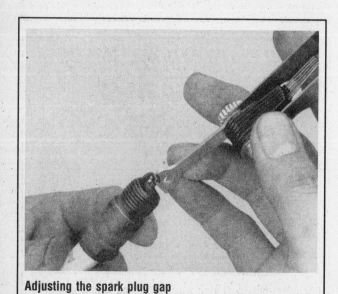

Adjusting the spark plug gap

If the standard plug is in good condition, the electrode may be filed flat—CAUTION: do not file platinum plugs

A bridged or almost bridged spark plug, identified by a build-up between the electrodes caused by excessive carbon or oil build-up on the plug

must be filed flat. Use an ignition points file, not an emery board or the like, which will leave deposits. The electrodes must be filed perfectly flat with sharp edges; rounded edges reduce the spark plug voltage by as much as 50%.

Check spark plug gap before installation. The ground electrode (the L-shaped one connected to the body of the plug) must be parallel to the center electrode and the specified size wire gauge (please refer to the Tune-Up Specifications chart for details) must pass between the electrodes with a slight drag.

➡**NEVER adjust the gap on a used platinum type spark plug.**

Always check the gap on new plugs as they are not always set correctly at the factory. Do not use a flat feeler gauge when measuring the gap on a used plug, because the reading may be inaccurate. A round-wire type gapping tool is the best way to check the gap. The correct gauge should pass through the electrode gap with a slight drag. If you're in doubt, try one size smaller and one larger. The smaller gauge should go through easily, while the larger one shouldn't go through at all. Wire gapping tools usually

have a bending tool attached. Use that to adjust the side electrode until the proper distance is obtained. Absolutely never attempt to bend the center electrode. Also, be careful not to bend the side electrode too far or too often as it may weaken and break off within the engine, requiring removal of the cylinder head to retrieve it.

Spark Plug Wires

TESTING

At every tune-up/inspection, visually check the spark plug cables for burns, cuts, or breaks in the insulation. Check the boots and the nipples on the distributor cap and/or coil. Replace any damaged wiring.

Every 50,000 miles (80,000 Km) or 60 months, the resistance of the wires should be checked with an ohmmeter. Wires with excessive resistance will cause misfiring, and may make the engine difficult to start in damp weather.

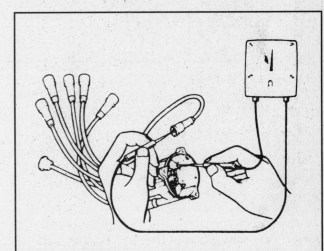

Checking plug wire resistance through the distributor cap with an ohmmeter

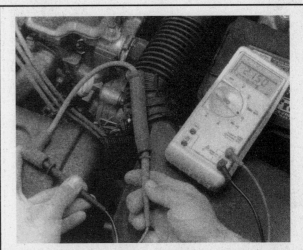

Checking individual plug wire resistance with a digital ohmmeter

To check resistance, remove the distributor cap, leaving the wires attached. Connect one lead of an ohmmeter to an electrode within the cap; connect the other leak to the corresponding spark plug terminal (remove it from the plug for this test). Replace any wire which shows a resistance over 30,000 ohms. Test the high tension leak from the coil by connecting the ohmmeter between the center contact in the distributor cap and either of the primary terminals of the coil. If resistance is more than 25,000 ohms, remove the cable from the coil and check the resistance of the cable alone. Anything over 15,000 ohms is cause for replacement. It should be remembered that resistance is also a function of length; the longer the cable, then greater the resistance. Thus, if the cables on your vehicles are longer than the factory originals, resistance will be higher, and quite possibly outside these limits.

Wire length can therefore be used to determine appropriate resistance values:
- 0–15 in.—3,00–10,000 ohms
- 15–25 in.—4,000–15,000 ohms
- 25–35 in.—6,000–20,000 ohms
- Wire over 35 in.—6,000–25,000 ohms

REMOVAL & INSTALLATION

➡**If all the wires must be disconnected from the spark plugs or from the distributor at the same time, be sure to tag the wires to assure proper reconnection.**

When installing a new set of spark plug wires, replace the wires one at a time so there will be no mix-up. Start by replacing the longest cable first. Install the boot firmly over the spark plug. Route the wire exactly the same as the original. Connect the wire tower connector to the distributor. Repeat the process for each wire. Be sure to apply silicone dielectric compound to the spark plug wire boots and tower connectors prior to installation.

FIRING ORDERS

▶ **See Figures 2, 3, 4, 5 and 6**

➡**To avoid confusion, remove and tag the spark plug wires one at a time, for replacement.**

If a distributor is not keyed for installation with only one orientation, it could have been removed previously and rewired. The resultant wiring would hold the correct firing order, but could change the relative placement of the plug towers in relation to the engine. For this reason it is imperative that you label all wires before disconnecting any of them. Also, before removal, compare the current wiring with the accompanying illustrations. If the current wiring does not match, make notes in your book to reflect how your engine is wired.

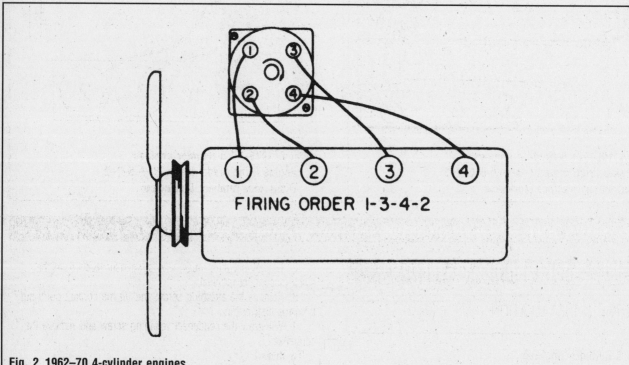

Fig. 2 1962–70 4-cylinder engines
Engine firing order: 1–3–4–2
Distributor rotation: Clockwise

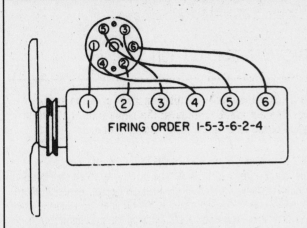

Fig. 3 1962–74 inline 6-cylinder engines
Engine firing order: 1–5–3–6–2–4
Distributor rotation: Clockwise

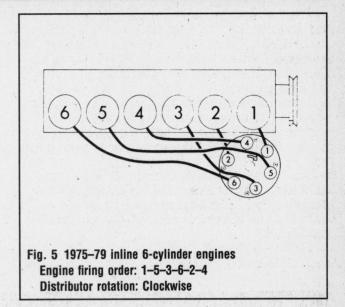

Fig. 5 1975–79 inline 6-cylinder engines
Engine firing order: 1–5–3–6–2–4
Distributor rotation: Clockwise

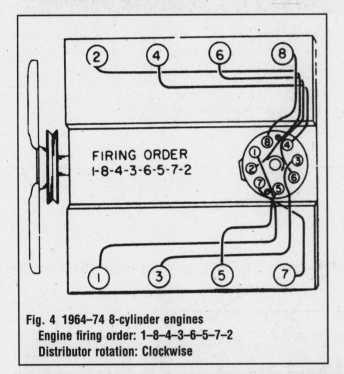

Fig. 4 1964–74 8-cylinder engines
Engine firing order: 1–8–4–3–6–5–7–2
Distributor rotation: Clockwise

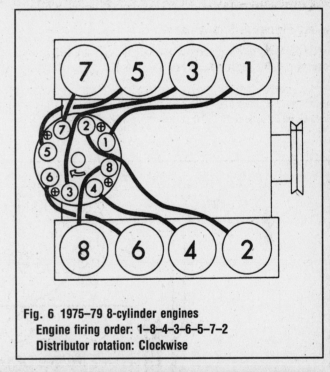

Fig. 6 1975–79 8-cylinder engines
Engine firing order: 1–8–4–3–6–5–7–2
Distributor rotation: Clockwise

BREAKER POINT IGNITION SYSTEM

Breaker Points and Condenser

REMOVAL & INSTALLATION

4 and 6 Cylinder Engines

♦ See Figure 7

Use the procedure described below to remove, install, and gap the contact point set.

1. Unfasten the distributor cap retaining screws and lift off the distributor cap. Remove the rotor.

2. Disconnect the primary and condenser leads from the quick-disconnect terminal.

3. Remove the attaching screw and lift the contact point set from the distributor.

4. Withdraw the condenser retaining screw and remove the condenser.

To install:

5. Install the new condenser and tighten its retaining screw.

6. Install the new point set, but do not fully tighten its attaching screw.

7. Connect the condenser and primary leads to the quick-disconnect terminal.

8. If necessary, align the contacts by bending the stationary

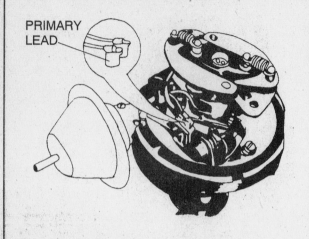

Fig. 7 (90672g02) Location of the breaker points and condenser—4 and 6-cylinder engines

contact bracket only. *Never bend the movable contact arm to correct alignment.*

9. Attach a remote starter switch to the electrical system according to the switch manufacturer's instructions. Use this switch to crank the engine, rotating the distributor cam until the rubbing block of the movable contact arm rests on a peak of the cam lobe. It is also possible to turn the engine manually.

10. Insert the proper thickness feeler gauge between the contact points. If necessary, increase or decrease the gap by inserting a screwdriver in the "V" notch of the stationary contact base and using the screwdriver to move the stationary contact.

11. Tighten the point set attaching screw and recheck the gap setting.

12. Install the new rotor and replace the distributor cap. Check the point dwell and the ignition timing.

8 Cylinder Engines
▶ See Figure 8

Use the procedure described below to remove and install the contact point set. It is not necessary to gap the points with a feeler gauge if a dwell meter is used.

1. Remove the rotor. Using a screwdriver, push in and rotate the cap hold-down screws so that the cap may be removed.

2. Disconnect the primary and condenser leads from the insulated connector in the contact set.

3. Withdraw the two screws which secure the base of the contact set. Remove the contact set.

4. Withdraw the condenser retaining screw and remove the condenser.

To install:

5. Install the new condenser and tighten its retaining screw.

6. Install the new contact set and tighten its securing screws.

7. Connect the condenser and primary leads.

8. Install the new rotor and replace the distributor cap. Check and adjust the point dwell and the ignition timing.

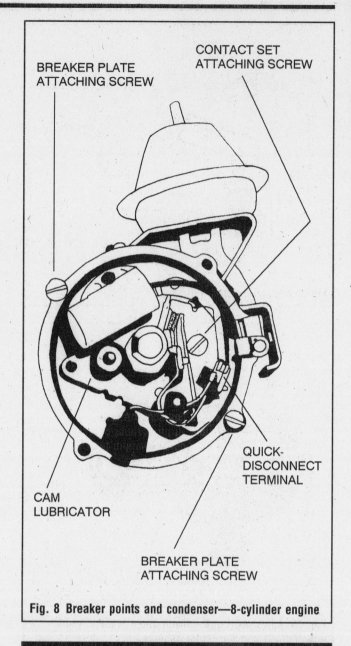

Fig. 8 Breaker points and condenser—8-cylinder engine

Dwell Angle

ADJUSTMENT

4 and 6 Cylinder Engines
▶ See Figures 9 and 10

If the contact points have been installed and gapped correctly, the dwell angle should be within specifications.

1. Connect the dwell meter leads to the distributor terminal of the coil and ground.

2. Start the engine and run it at idle speed.

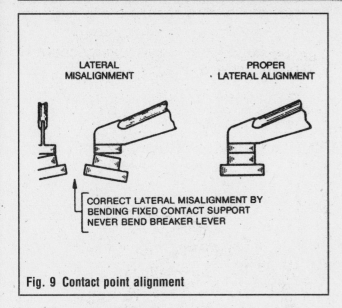

Fig. 9 Contact point alignment

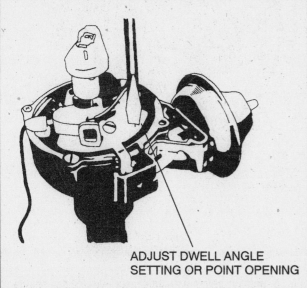

Fig. 10 Adjustment of the dwell angle (contact point opening)—4 and 6-cylinder engines

3. Note the dwell meter reading. If it is not within specifications, the point gap may be incorrect or the movable contact arm may be distorted. Readjust the contact points and recheck the dwell. Be sure that the correct point set has been installed.

➡Dwell and point gap must both be within their specification limits at the same time. If this cannot be accomplished, probably the wrong contacts are installed, the rubbing block or cam lobes are badly worn, or the movable contact is distorted. A dwell variation test (see below) may be performed.

8 Cylinder Engines
◆ See Figure 11

Because the contact points are preset, it is not necessary to gap them with a feeler gauge. The dwell angle can be adjusted by

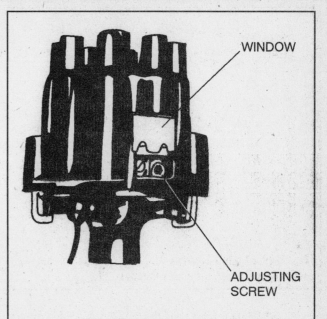

Fig. 11 On 8-cylinder engines, adjust the dwell angle using the proper sized hex wrench

turning the adjusting screw located behind the small window of the distributor cap.
1. Disconnect and plug the vacuum line from the distributor.
2. Connect the dwell meter leads to the distributor terminal of the coil and ground.
3. Start the engine and run it at idle speed.
4. Note the dwell meter reading. If it is not within specifications, raise the window of the distributor cap and insert the proper size hex wrench in the adjusting screw head. Observe the dwell meter and turn the adjusting screw until the dwell angle is within specifications.

DWELL VARIATION TEST

Excessive wear of the distributor mechanical parts may cause variations in dwell that affect ignition timing. The following is the procedure for a dwell variation test.
1. Disconnect the vacuum line at the distributor, connect the dwell meter, and run the engine at its idle speed.
2. Slowly increase engine speed to 1,500 rpm and then slowly reduce to idle speed while noting the dwell meter reading.

If the dwell reading varies more than two degrees, wear in the distributor shaft, bushings, or breaker plate is probably excessive. The distributor will have to be removed for a complete inspection and test.

➡Dwell variation at speeds above 1,500 rpm does not necessarily indicate distributor wear.

Magnetic Pulse Distributor

◆ See Figures 12 and 13

The ignition timing can be checked and adjusted in the normal manner but, because there are no ignition breaker points, there is no point gap or dwell angle to measure and adjust.

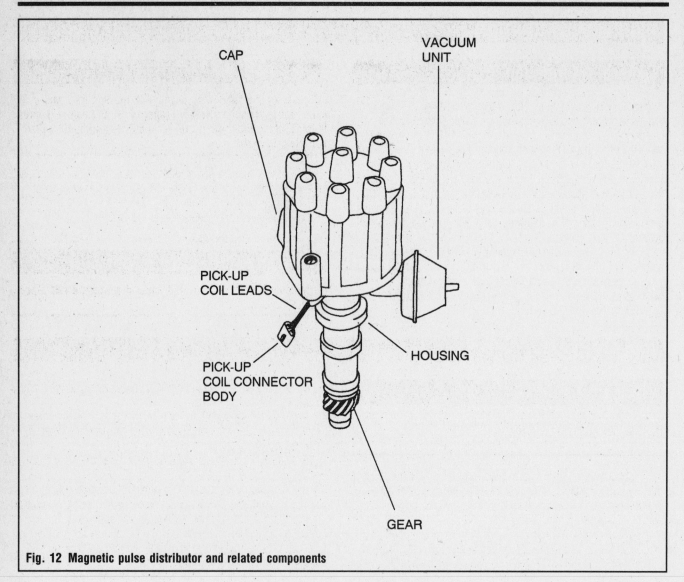

CAP

VACUUM
UNIT

PICK-UP
COIL LEADS

PICK-UP
COIL CONNECTOR
BODY

HOUSING

GEAR

Fig. 12 Magnetic pulse distributor and related components

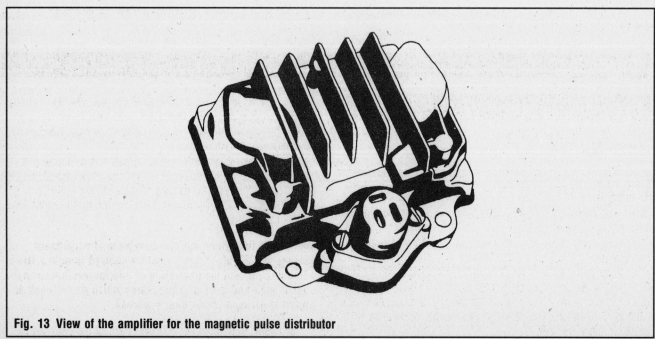

Fig. 13 View of the amplifier for the magnetic pulse distributor

HIGH ENERGY IGNITION

General Information

The High Energy Ignition (HEI) system, found on 1975–79 vehicles, is a pulse-triggered, transistor-controlled, inductive discharge ignition system which does not use contact breaker points. V8 distributors have all ignition components internally. Six-cylinder distributors have an externally-mounted ignition coil. The centrifugal and vacuum advance units are basically the same as those used to provide spark advance in breaker point distributors.

Engine ignition timing is adjusted the same as previous models, however observe the following items when working with HEI systems:

1. Timing light connections should be made in parallel using an adapter at the distributor No. 1 terminal.

2. Larger diameter (8 mm) spark plug wiring is used. Carefully twist the boots about a half turn in either direction to break the seal on the spark plugs.

✳✳ CAUTION

Do not remove spark plug wires with the engine running. The higher secondary voltage (approx. 35,000 volts) is capable of jumping an arc of greater distance and could cause an electric shock.

3. Connect dwell/tachometers to the "tach" terminal in the distributor cap connector and to ground. Some tachometers must connect from the "tach" terminal to the battery positive terminal. Follow the tachometer manufacturer's instructions.

✳✳ CAUTION

Grounding the "tach" terminal could damage the HEI electronic module.

IGNITION TIMING

Timing

INSPECTION & ADJUSTMENT

To obtain maximum engine performance, the distributor must be correctly positioned on the engine to give proper ignition timing. Ignition timing must be checked only when the engine is hot and running at its correct idle speed.

1. Clean the timing indicator and the circumference of the crankshaft vibration damper. Paint the correct timing mark on the indicator and the timing mark on the damper with white or luminescent (dayglo) paint.

2. If the engine compartment sticker so specifies, disconnect and plug the vacuum line to the distributor.

3. Connect a stroboscopic timing light according to the manufacturer's instructions.

4. Start the engine and adjust the idle speed to specification with the *transmission in neutral or drive, as specified on the engine compartment sticker.*

5. Loosen the distributor hold-down bolt so the housing can be rotated.

6. Check the ignition timing by aiming the strobe light at the timing indicator and the vibration damper. If the timing is correct, the painted mark on the damper will appear opposite to the timing indicator painted mark. If necessary, advance or retard the timing by loosening the hold-down and rotating the distributor housing, until the correct timing is obtained.

7. Tighten the distributor hold-down bolt and connect the vacuum line. Stop the engine and disconnect the timing light.

VALVE LASH

Hydraulic Tappets

ADJUSTMENT

▶ **See Figure 14**

The valve lash adjustment should be performed only when the engine is hot and running.

1. Warm up the engine until it reaches its normal operating temperature.

2. Remove the valve cover (two on V8) by withdrawing its securing bolts. Be careful of the hot oil which will splash off the rocker assembly when the cover is removed. It is advisable to use commercially available oil deflector clips on the rocker arms when adjusting the valve lash.

3. With the engine idling, loosen the rocker arm nut until the rocker arm begins to clatter.

4. Turn the rocker arm nut down slowly until the valve clatter just stops (zero lash position).

5. Turn the rocker arm nut down a quarter turn further and pause 10 seconds until the engine runs smoothly. Repeat this procedure three more times, pausing 10 seconds each time, until the rocker arm nut has been turned down one full turn from the zero lash position.

➡**Be sure to perform the one turn preload adjustment slowly as the valve tappet must be allowed to adjust itself. This will prevent the possibility of interference between the valve head and the top of the piston which could result in internal damage and/or bent pushrods.**

6. Repeat steps three through five to adjust the other valves.

Fig. 14 To help prevent mess when adjusting the hydraulic tappets, install oil deflector clips on the rocker arms

7. After all of the valves have been adjusted, stop the engine, remove the oil deflector clips, and replace the valve cover, using a new gasket between the cover and the cylinder head. If much oil was lost during the valve adjustment procedure, check the oil level in the crankcase.

Mechanical Tappets

ADJUSTMENT

♦ **See Figure 15**

The valve lash adjustment should be performed only when the engine is hot and running.

1. Warm up the engine until it reaches its normal operating temperature.

2. Remove the valve covers by withdrawing the securing bolts. Be careful of the hot oil which will splash off the rocker assembly when the cover is removed. It is advisable to use commercially available oil deflector clips on the rocker arms when adjusting the valve lash.

3. With the engine idling, insert the proper thickness feeler gauge (refer to the "Tune-Up Specifications" chart) between the valve stem tip and the rocker arm to measure the clearance between them. If necessary, turn the self-locking rocker arm stud nut to obtain the correct valve clearance.

4. Repeat step three to adjust each of the other valves.

5. After all of the valves have been adjusted, stop the engine, remove the oil deflector clips and replace the valve covers, using new gaskets between the covers and the cylinder heads. If much oil was lost during the valve adjustment procedure, check the oil level in the crankcase.

Fig. 15 Valve lash adjustment—engine equipped with mechanical valve tappets

IDLE SPEED AND MIXTURE ADJUSTMENTS

Refer to Chapter 5 for illustrations which show the locations of idle speed and mixture adjustment screws for each type of carburetor, and for other carburetor adjustments.

The Vehicle Emission Control Information (VECI) sticker contains adjustment information and specifications

1962–67 Vehicles Without Air

Adjustments should be performed with the air cleaner removed and, on models so equipped, with the air conditioning turned off.

1. Remove the air cleaner.
2. Connect a tachometer and vacuum gauge to the engine, set the parking brake, and place the transmission in neutral.
3. Turn in the idle mixture screws until they seat gently, then back them out 1½ turns.
4. Start the engine and allow it to reach normal operating temperature. Make sure that the choke is fully open, then adjust the idle speed (automatic in Drive, manual in neutral).
5. Adjust the idle mixture screw(s) to obtain the highest steady vacuum at the specified idle speed, except for the Rochester BV. For this carburetor, adjust the idle mixture screw out ¼ turn from the lean "drop off," the point where a 20–30 rpm drop is achieved by leaning the mixture.

➡**On carburetors having a hot idle compensator valve (air-conditioned models), hold the brass valve down with a pencil while making the mixture adjustment.**

6. Repeat steps four and five if necessary.
7. Turn off the engine, remove the gauges, and install the air cleaner.

1967 Vehicles With Air

Adjustments should be performed with the air cleaner removed and, on models so equipped, with the air conditioning turned off.

1. Remove the air cleaner.
2. Connect a tachometer and a vacuum gauge to the engine, set the parking brake, and place the transmission in neutral.

3. Turn in the idle mixture screw(s) until they gently seat, then back them out three turns.
4. Start the engine and allow it to reach normal operating temperature. Make sure the choke is fully open, then adjust the idle speed screw(s) to obtain the specified idle speed (automatic transmission in Drive, manual transmission in Neutral).
5. Turn the idle mixture screw(s) clockwise (in) to the point where a 20–30 rpm drop in speed is achieved—this is the lean "drop off" point. Back out the screws ¼ turn from this point.
6. Repeat steps four and five if necessary.
7. Turn off the engine, remove the gauges, and install the air cleaner.

1968–69 Vehicles

Adjustments should be performed on all models with the air cleaner installed. On air-conditioned models, the idle speed and air/fuel mixture should be set with the air conditioning unit turned off, except for those models equipped with four- or six-cylinder engines, or the 325 hp/327 cu in. V8. On these engines, adjustments should be performed with the air conditioner turned on.

1. Turn in the idle mixture screw(s) until they seat gently, then back them out three turns.
2. Start the engine and allow it to reach operating temperature. Make sure the choke is fully open and the preheater valve is open, then adjust the idle speed screw to obtain the specified idle speed (automatic in Drive, manual in neutral).
3. Adjust the idle mixture screw(s) to obtain the highest steady idle speed, then readjust the idle speed screw to obtain the specified speed. On cars having an idle stop solenoid, adjust as follows:

   a. Adjust idle speed to 500 rpm (L-6) or 600 rpm (V8) by turning the hex on the solenoid plunger;

   b. Disconnect the wire at the solenoid. This allows the throttle lever to seat against the idle screw;

   c. Adjust the idle screw to obtain 400 rpm, then reconnect the wire.
4. Adjust one mixture screw to obtain a 20 rpm drop in idle speed, then back out the screw ¼ turn from this point.
5. Repeat steps three and four for the second mixture screw, if so equipped.
6. Readjust the idle speed to obtain the specified idle speed.

1970 Vehicles

Adjustments should be performed on all models with the air cleaner installed.

1. Disconnect the "fuel tank" line from the vapor canister (EEC).
2. Connect a tachometer to the engine, start the engine, and allow it to reach operating temperature. Make sure the choke and preheater valves are fully open.
3. Turn off the air conditioner and set the parking brake. Disconnect and plug the distributor vacuum line.
4. Make the following adjustments:

4-153 ENGINES

a. Set the mixture screw to obtain the maximum idle rpm;

b. Adjust the idle speed screw to obtain 750 rpm for manual transmissions (in neutral), 650 rpm for automatics (in Drive);

c. Adjust the mixture screw to obtain a 20 rpm drop in idle speed, then back it out ¼ turn from this point;

d. Readjust the idle speed to obtain the specified rpm, then reconnect the vacuum line.

6-230/250 ENGINES

a. Turn in the mixture screw until it gently seats, then back out the screw four turns.

b. Adjust the solenoid screw to obtain 830 rpm for manual transmissions (in neutral) or 630 rpm for automatics (in Drive).

c. Adjust the mixture screw to obtain 750 rpm for manual transmission (in neutral) or 600 rpm for automatics (in Drive).

d. Disconnect the solenoid wire and set the idle speed to 400 rpm, then reconnect the wire).

e. Reconnect the distributor vacuum line.

8-307 ENGINES

a. Turn in the mixture screws until they seat gently, then back them out four turns.

b. Adjust the carburetor idle speed screw to obtain 800 rpm for manual transmissions (in neutral), or adjust the solenoid screw to obtain 630 rpm for automatic transmissions (in Drive).

c. Adjust both mixture screws equally, inward, to obtain 700 rpm for manual transmissions; 600 rpm for automatics (in Drive).

d. On cars with automatic transmissions, disconnect the solenoid wire, set the carburetor idle screw to obtain 450 rpm, and reconnect the solenoid.

e. Reconnect the distributor vacuum line.

8-350 (300 HP) ENGINES

a. Turn in both mixture screws until they gently seat, then back them out four turns.

b. Adjust the carburetor idle screw to obtain 775 rpm for manual transmissions; 630 rpm for automatics (in Drive).

c. Adjust the mixture screws equally to obtain 700 rpm for manual transmissions; 600 rpm for automatics (in Drive).

d. Reconnect the distributor vacuum line.

5. Disconnect the tachometer and reconnect the fuel vapor line.

1971–72 Vehicles

Adjustments should be performed on all models with the air cleaner installed.

The idle stop solenoid is no longer used, having been replaced by the combination emission control valve. This valve is energized through the transmission to increase idle speed under conditions of high-gear deceleration and to provide full vacuum spark advance during high-gear operation. The valve is deenergized at curb idle and in the lower gears to provide a retarded spark under these conditions, the result of which is lower hydrocarbon emission. *The valve need not be adjusted unless the solenoid or throttle body is removed, or the carburetor is overhauled.*

Idle limiter caps are installed on the mixture screws of the carburetors of all 1971 cars. Chevrolet does not recommend removing these caps and does not recommend adjusting the mixture. Adjusting the mixture without the proper test gear will result in hydrocarbon emission levels in excess of the specified minimum.

1. Follow steps 1–3 of the 1970 procedure.
2. Make the following adjustments:

6-250 ENGINES

a. Adjust the carburetor idle speed screw to obtain 550 rpm for manual transmissions (in Neutral) or 500 rpm for automatics (in Drive). *Do not adjust the solenoid screw.*

b. Reconnect the vapor line and the distributor vacuum advance line.

8-307 (200 HP) AND 350 (245 HP) ENGINES

a. Adjust the carburetor idle speed screw to obtain 600 rpm for manual transmissions (in Neutral) with the air conditioner turned off or 550 rpm for automatics (in Drive) with the air conditioner turned on. *Do not adjust the solenoid screw.*

b. Reconnect the vapor line and the distributor vacuum advance line.

8-350 (270 HP) ENGINES

a. Adjust the carburetor idle speed screw to obtain 600 rpm for manual transmissions (in neutral) with the air conditioning turned off, or 550 rpm for automatics (in Drive) with the air conditioning turned on. *Do not adjust the solenoid screw.*

b. Place the fast idle cam follower on the second step of the fast idle cam, turn the air conditioner off and adjust the fast idle to 1,350 rpm for manual transmissions (in Neutral) or 1,500 rpm for automatics (in Park).

c. Reconnect the vapor line and the distributor vacuum advance line.

1973 Vehicles

All models are equipped with idle limiter caps and idle solenoids. Disconnect the fuel tank line from the evaporative canister. The engine must be running at operating temperature, choke off, parking brake on, and rear wheels blocked. Connect a tachometer to the engine. Disconnect and plug the distributor vacuum hose. After adjustment, reconnect the vacuum and evaporative hoses.

6-250 ENGINES

Adjust the idle stop solenoid for 700 rpm on manual transmission models or 600 rpm on automatics. On manual models, make no attempt to adjust the CEC solenoid (the larger of the two carburetor solenoids) or a decrease in engine braking could result.

8-307, 350 (2 BBL) ENGINES

1. With air conditioning off, if so equipped, adjust the idle stop solenoid screw for 900 rpm on manual transmission models or 600 on automatics.
2. De-energize the idle stop solenoid and adjust the idle speed screw (screw resting on the lower step of the cam) for 450 rpm.

8-350 (4 BBL) ENGINES

1. Adjust the idle stop solenoid screw for 900 rpm on manual transmission models or 600 rpm on automatics.
2. Connect the distributor vacuum hose and position the fast idle cam follower on the top step of the fast idle cam (air conditioning off if so equipped) and adjust the fast idle to 1,300 rpm on manual transmission models or 1,600 rpm on automatics (in Park).

1974 Vehicles

Refer to the opening notes under the previous "1973" section; they also apply here.

6-250 ENGINES

Adjust the idle stop solenoid hex nut for 800 rpm on manual transmission models or 600 rpm on automatics (in Drive).

8-350 (2 BBL) ENGINES

1. Turn air conditioning off, if so equipped. Adjust the idle stop solenoid screw for 900 rpm on manual transmission models or 600 rpm on automatics (in Drive).
2. De-energize the solenoid and adjust the carburetor idle cam screw (on low step of cam) for 450 rpm.

8-350 (4 BBL) ENGINES

1. Turn air conditioning off, if so equipped. Adjust the idle stop solenoid screw for 900 rpm on manual transmission models or 600 rpm on automatics (in Drive).
2. Connect the distributor vacuum hose. Position the fast idle cam follower on the top step of the fast idle cam and adjust the fast idle speed to 1,300 rpm on manual transmission models or 1,600 rpm on automatics (in Park).

1975 Vehicles

Refer to the preliminary adjustment conditions in the previous "1973" section. Make sure that air conditioning is turned off, if so equipped.

1. Disconnect and plug the distributor vacuum hose.
2. Start engine, check ignition timing, and adjust as necessary.
3. Reconnect vacuum advance hose to the distributor.
4. Turn the idle stop solenoid in or out to set curb idle speed to specified rpm with automatic transmissions in Drive or manual transmissions in Neutral. Refer to the "Tune-Up Specifications" chart.
5. Disconnect the electrical connector at the idle stop solenoid.
6. With automatic transmissions in Drive or manual transmissions in Neutral, turn the 1/8 in. hex screw in the end of the solenoid to set the low idle speed to the specified rpm.
7. Reconnect the electrical connector to the solenoid.

1976–77 Vehicles

The engine must be at normal operating temperature with the air cleaner on, the choke open, the air conditioner off, and the timing correctly set.

1. Set the brake and block the wheels.
2. Set the automatic transmission in Drive and the manual in neutral. Disconnect the fuel tank hose from the vapor canister in the engine compartment.
3. Use needle nose pliers to break off the mixture screw cap or caps.

1 BBL CARBURETORS

4. Adjust the idle speed by turning the solenoid in or out to obtain the higher of the two speeds listed on the sticker. Disconnect the electrical connector from the solenoid and turn the 1/8 in. allen screw in the end of the solenoid body to lower the idle speed to the second figure on the sticker.

2 BBL & 4 BBL CARBURETORS

Adjust the idle speed with the idle speed screw to obtain the higher idle speed shown on the sticker. On the 1977 4-bbl, detach the electrical connector at the idle solenoid, and adjust the idle speed to the lower of the two figures given on the sticker. Reconnect the electrical connector, open the throttle to extend the solenoid plunger, then turn the solenoid plunger screw to obtain the higher of the two idle speed figures. If the procedure listed here for the 1977 4-bbl differs from the one on the engine tune-up sticker, use the sticker procedure.

5. On all but the 2 bbl, turn out the mixture screws until the highest possible idle speed is reached. If the idle speed becomes excessive (more than that set in Step 4), reset the idle speed to that set in Step 4. On the 2 bbl, turn out the mixture screws to obtain the highest idle and then, turn in the mixture screws to obtain the lower of the two figures listed on the sticker.
6. Turn in the mixture screws equally until the normal idle speed is reached.
7. Replace the vapor canister hose.

1978–79 Vehicles

♦ **See Figure 16**

All 1978 and 1979 GM cars employ a redesigned carburetor which requires special equipment for adjustment of the idle mixture. The mixture screws themselves do not provide for significant enrichment, making it impossible to adjust mixture by the ordinary lean drop method. If you suspect an idle mixture adjustment problem, we suggest you take it to a dealer or repair shop where the specialized equipment required is available.

To set idle speed, follow the procedure below:

1. Make sure engine is fully warmed up. Block wheels, set parking brake, and put automatic transmission cars in Drive. Set ignition timing, and reconnect all vacuum hoses.

2. If the car uses an idle solenoid, open the throttle slightly to ensure that the solenoid plunger has extended. If the car uses an idle speed screw which bears directly on the fast idle cam (2GC), make sure the speed screw rests on the low step of the fast idle cam (cam turned fully clockwise).

3. Connect your tachometer as described above.

4. Adjust the idle screw or solenoid plunger to provide the specified idle speed. On V8 carburetors the plunger may be turned with an ordinary open end wrench. On six cylinder engines, use an open end wrench to turn the entire solenoid assembly. On cars equipped with M4MC (four barrel) carburetors and air conditioning, first adjust idle speed screw with A/C off. Then, turn on A/C and unplug A/C compressor. Then adjust solenoid to rpm shown on engine compartment sticker. See Chapter 5 for fast idle adjustment instructions.

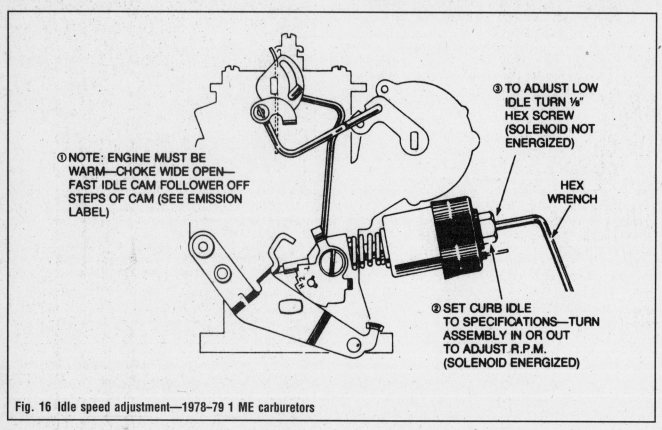

③ TO ADJUST LOW IDLE TURN ⅛" HEX SCREW (SOLENOID NOT ENERGIZED)

HEX WRENCH

① NOTE: ENGINE MUST BE WARM—CHOKE WIDE OPEN—FAST IDLE CAM FOLLOWER OFF STEPS OF CAM (SEE EMISSION LABEL)

② SET CURB IDLE TO SPECIFICATIONS—TURN ASSEMBLY IN OR OUT TO ADJUST R.P.M. (SOLENOID ENERGIZED)

Fig. 16 Idle speed adjustment—1978–79 1 ME carburetors

Tune-Up Specifications

Year	No. Cyl Displacement (cu in.)	hp	Spark Plugs Type	Gap (in.)	Distributor Point Dwell (deg)	Point Gap (in.)	Ignition Timing (deg) ▲ ● Man Trans	Auto Trans	Intake Valve Opens ■ (deg) ●	Fuel Pump Pressure (psi)	▲ Idle Speed (rpm) Man Trans	Auto Trans ●
'62–'63	4—153	90	46N	0.035	31–34	0.019	4B	4B	33½	3–4½	575	575
	6—194	120	46N	0.035	31–34	0.019	8B	8B	62	3–4½	500	500
'64	4—153	90	46N	0.035	31–34	0.019	4B	4B	33½	3–4½	500	500
	6—194	120	46N	0.035	31–35	0.019	8B	8B	62	3–4½	500	500
	8—283	195	45	0.035	28–32	0.019	4B	4B	32½	5–6½	500	500
'65	4—153	90	46N	0.035	31–34	0.019	4B	4B	34	3–4½	500	500
	6—194	120	46N	0.035	31–34	0.019	8B	8B	34	3–4½	500	500
	6—230	140	46N	0.035	31–34	0.019	4B	4B	49	5–6½	500	500
	8—283	195	45	0.035	28–32	0.019	4B	4B	34	5–6½	500	500
	8—327	250	44	0.035	28–32	0.019	4B	4B	32	5–6½	550	550
	8—327	300	44	0.035	28–32	0.019	8B	8B	32	5–6½	550	550
	8—327	350	44	0.035	28–32	0.019	8B	8B	35	5–6½	750	750
'66	4—153	90	46N	0.035	31–34	0.019	4B	4B	33½	5¼–6½	450–500②	450–500②
	4—153①	90	46N	0.035	31–34	0.019	4B	4B	33½	5¼–6½	700	600
	6—194	120	46N	0.035	31–34	0.019	8B	8B	62	3½–4½	450–500②	450–500②
	6—194①	120	46N	0.035	31–34	0.019	3B	8B	62	3½–4½	700	600
	6—230	140	46N	0.035	31–34	0.019	4B	4B	62	3½–4½	450–500②	450–500②
	6—230①	140	46N	0.035	31–34	0.019	4B	4B	62	3½–4½	700	600
	8—283	195	45	0.035	28–32	0.019	4B	4B	32½	5¼–6½	450–500②	450–500②
	8—283①	195	45	0.035	28–32	0.019	4B	4B	32½	5¼–6½	700	600
	8—283	220	45	0.035	28–32	0.019	4B	4B	32½	5¼–6½	450–500②	450–500②
	8—283①	220	45	0.035	28–32	0.019	4B	4B	32½	5¼–6½	700	600
	8—327	275	44	0.035	28–32	0.019	8B	8B	32½	5¼–6½	450–500②	450–500②
	8—327①	275	44	0.035	28–32	0.019	8B	2A	32½	5¼–6½	700	600
	8—327	350	44	0.035	28–32	0.019	10B	—	32½	5–6½	450–500②	—
	8—327①	350	44	0.035	28–32	0.019	10B	—	32½	5–6½	650–750③	—
'67	4—153	90	46N	0.035	31–34	0.019	4B	4B	33½	3½–4½	500②	500②
	6—194	120	46N	0.035	31–34	0.019	4B	4B	62	3½–4½	500②	500②
	6—194①	120	46N	0.035	31–34	0.019	2B	4B	62	3½–4½	700	600

Tune-Up Specifications (cont.)

Year	ENGINE No. Cyl Displacement (cu in.)	hp	SPARK PLUGS Type	Gap (in.)	DISTRIBUTOR Point Dwell (deg)	Point Gap (in.)	IGNITION TIMING (deg) ▲ ● Man Trans	Auto Trans	Intake Valve Opens ■ (deg) ●	Fuel Pump Pressure (psi)	▲ IDLE SPEED (rpm) Man Trans ●	Auto Trans
'67	6—250	155	46N	0.035	31–34	0.019	4B	4B	62	3½–4½	500③	500③
	6—250①	155	46N	0.035	31–34	0.019	4B	4B	62	3½–4½	700	500
	8—283	195	46N	0.035	28–32	0.019	4B	4B	36	5¼–6½	500③	500③
	8—283①	195	46N	0.035	28–32	0.019	TDC	4B	36	5¼–6½	700	600
	8—327	275	44	0.035	28–32	0.019	8B	8B	38	5¼–6½	500③	500③
	8—327①	275	44	0.035	28–32	0.019	6B	6B	38	5¼–6½	700	600
'68	4—153	90	46N	0.035	31–34	0.019	TDC	4B	17½	3½–4½	750	600
	6—230	140	46N	0.035	31–34	0.019	TDC	4B	48	3½–4½	700②	600②/400③
	6—250	155	46N	0.035	31–34	0.019	TDC	4B	16	3½–4½	700②	500②/400③
	8—307	200	45S	0.035	28–32	0.019	2B	2B	28	5–6½	700	600
	8—327	275	44	0.035	28–32	0.019	TDC	4B	28	5–6½	700②	500
	8—350	295	44	0.035	28–32	0.019	TDC	4B	28	5–6½	700	500
'69	4—153	90	R-46N	0.035	31–34	0.019	TDC	4B	28	4–5	750	600
	6—230	140	R-46N	0.035	31–34	0.019	TDC	4B	16	4–5	700	550/400③
	6—250	155	R-46N	0.035	31–34	0.019	TDC	4B	16	4–5	700	550/400③
	8—307	200	R-45S	0.035	31–34	0.019	2B	2B	28	5½–7½	700	600
	8—350	250	R-45S	0.035	29–31	0.019	TDC	4B	28	5½–7½	700	600
	8—350	300	R-44S	0.035	29–31	0.019	TDC	4B	28	7½–9	700	600
	8—396	350	R-43N	0.035	28–32	0.019	TDC	4B	56	5–8½	800	600
	8—396④	375	R-43N	0.035	28–32	0.019	4B	4B	44	5–8½	750	750–400
'70	4—153	90	R-46N	0.035	31–34	0.019	TDC	4B	17½	4–5	750	650
	6—230	140	R-46N	0.035	31–34	0.019	TDC	4B	16	4–5	700	550/400③
	6—250	155	R-46N	0.035	31–34	0.019	TDC	4B	16	4–5	700	550/400③
	8—307	200	R-45	0.035	29–31	0.019	2B	8B	28	5½–7½	700	600/450③
	8—350	250	R-44	0.035	29–31	0.019	TDC	4B	28	5½–7½	750	600/450③
	8—350	300	R-44	0.035	29–31	0.019	TDC	4B	28	7½–9	700	600
'71	6—250	145	R-46TS	0.035	31–34	0.019	4B	4B	16	4–5	550	500
	8—307	200	R-45TS	0.035	29–31	0.019	4B	8B	28	5½–7½	600	550②

Tune-Up Specifications (cont.)

Year	ENGINE No. Cyl Displacement (cu in.)	hp	SPARK PLUGS Type	Gap (in.)	DISTRIBUTOR Point Dwell (deg)	Point Gap (in.)	IGNITION TIMING (deg) ▲ ● Man Trans	Auto Trans	Intake Valve Opens ■ (deg) ●	Fuel Pump Pressure (psi)	▲ IDLE SPEED (rpm) Man Trans ●	Auto Trans
	8—350	245	R-45TS	0.035	29–31	0.019	2B	6B	28	7½–9	600	550②
	8—350	270	R-44TS	0.035	29–31	0.019	4B	8B	28	7½–9	600	550②
'72	6—250	110	R-46T	0.035	31–34	0.019	4B	4B	16	4–5	700	600
	8—307	130	R-44T	0.035	29–31	0.019	4B	8B	28	5½–7½	900	600
	8—350	165	R-44T	0.035	29–31	0.019	6B	6B	28(44)	7½–9	900	600
	8—350	200	R-44T	0.035	29–31	0.019	4B	8B	28(44)	7½–9	800	600
'73	6—250	100	R-46T	0.035	31–34	0.019	6B	6B	16	3½–4½	700/450③	600/450
	8—307	115	R-44T	0.035	29–31	0.019	4B	8B	28	5–6½	900/450③	600/450
	8—350	145	R-44T	0.035	29–31	0.019	8B	8B	28	7–8½	900/450③	600/450
	8—350	175	R-44T	0.035	29–31	0.019	8B	12B	28	7–8½	900/450③	600/450
'74	6—250	100	R-46T	0.035	31–34	0.019	6B	6B	16	4–5	800/450③	600/450
	8—350	145	R-44T	0.035	29–31	0.019	4B	8B	28	7½–9	900/450③	600/450
	8—350	160	R-44T	0.035	29–31	0.019	4B	8B	28	7½–9	900/450③	600/450
	8—350	185	R-44T	0.035	29–31	0.019	4B	8B	28	7½–9	900/450③	600/450
'75	6—250	105	R-46TX	0.060	⑤	⑤	10B	10B	16	4–5	850	550(600)
	8—262	110	R-44TX	0.060	⑤	⑤	8B	8B	26	7½–9	800	600
	8—350	145	R-44TX	0.060	⑤	⑤	6B	6B	28	7½–9	800	600
	8—350	155	R-44TX	0.060	⑤	⑤	6B	6B	28	7½–9	800(600)	600
'76	6—250	105	R-46TS	0.035	⑤	⑤	6B	6B	16	3½–4½	850	550(600)
	6—250⑥	105	R-46TS	0.035	⑤	⑤	6B	8B	16	3½–4½	850	600
	8—305	140	R-45TS	0.045	⑤	⑤	6B	8B (TDC)	28	7–8½	800	600
	8—350	165	R-45TS	0.045	⑤	⑤	8B (6B)	8B (6B)	28	7–8½	800	600
'77	6—250	105	R-46TX	0.035	③	⑤	6B	8B	16	4–5	750 800 with A/C	550 600 with A/C
	8—305	140	R-45TS	0.045	⑤	⑤	8B	8B	28	7½–8½	600 700 with A/C	500 650 with A/C
	8—350	165	R-45TS	0.045	⑤	⑤	NA	NA	28	7½–8½	NA	NA
'78	6—250	110	R-46TS	0.035	⑤	⑤	6B	10B⑦ (6B)	16	4½–6	800	550(600)

Tune-Up Specifications (cont.)

Year	ENGINE No. Cyl Displacement (cu in.)	hp	SPARK PLUGS Type	Gap (in.)	DISTRIBUTOR Point Dwell (deg)	Point Gap (in.)	IGNITION TIMING (deg) ▲ ● Man Trans	Auto Trans	Intake Valve Opens ■ (deg) ●	Fuel Pump Pressure (psi)	▲ IDLE SPEED (rpm) Man Trans	● Auto Trans
'78	8—305	145	R-45TS	0.045	⑤	⑤	4B	4B	28	7½–9	600	500
	8—350	160	R-45TS	0.045	⑤	⑤	6B	6B (8B)⑦⑧	28	7½–9	700	500
'79	6—250	115	R-46TS	0.035	⑤	⑤	8B	10B (6B)	16	4½–6	800	500
	8—305	130	R-45TS	0.045	⑤	⑤	4B	4B	28	7½–9	600	500
	8—350	165	R-45TS	0.045	⑤	⑤	—	8B	28	7½–9	—	500

▲ See text for procedure
● Figures in parentheses indicates California engine
■ All figures Before Top Dead Center
① Equipped with Air Injection Reactor System
② A/C on
③ Lower figure with idle solenoid disconnected
④ Adjust mechanical valve lifter clearance to 0.024 in. for intake with engine hot, and to 0.028 in. for exhaust with engine hot

⑤ Electronic ignition
⑥ With integral intake manifold head
⑦ 8B with A/C
⑧ Also applies to High Altitude models
A After Top Dead Center
B Before Top Dead Center
TDC Top Dead Center
— Not applicable
NA Not available

NOTE: The underhood specifications sticker often reflects tune-up specification changes made in production. Sticker figures must be used if they disagree with those in this chart.

ENGINE ELECTRICAL 3-2
UNDERSTANDING ELECTRICITY 3-2
  BASIC CIRCUITS 3-2
  TROUBLESHOOTING 3-3
BATTERY, STARTING AND CHARGING
  SYSTEMS 3-4
  BASIC OPERATING PRINCIPLES 3-4
HEI ELECTRONIC IGNITION
  SYSTEM 3-5
  TROUBLESHOOTING 3-5
  REMOVAL & INSTALLATION 3-6
CONVENTIONAL IGNITION
  SYSTEM 3-10
  REMOVAL & INSTALLATION 3-10
DC GENERATOR 3-10
  REMOVAL & INSTALLATION 3-10
ALTERNATOR 3-10
  ALTERNATOR PRECAUTIONS 3-10
  REMOVAL & INSTALLATION 3-11
VOLTAGE REGULATOR 3-11
  REMOVAL & INSTALLATION 3-11
STARTER 3-12
  REMOVAL & INSTALLATION 3-12
BATTERY 3-13
  REMOVAL & INSTALLATION 3-13
ENGINE MECHANICAL 3-18
UNDERSTANDING THE ENGINE 3-18
DESIGN 3-18
ENGINE 3-31
  REMOVAL & INSTALLATION 3-31
  SEPARATING THE TRANSMISSION
    FROM THE ENGINE 3-32
CYLINDER HEAD 3-32
  REMOVAL AND INSTALLATION 3-32
VALVE GUIDES 3-36
ROCKER ARMS 3-36
  REMOVAL & INSTALLATION 3-36
INTAKE MANIFOLD 3-37
  REMOVAL & INSTALLATION 3-37
EXHAUST MANIFOLD 3-37
  REMOVAL & INSTALLATION 3-37
TIMING GEAR/CHAIN COVER 3-38
  REMOVAL & INSTALLATION 3-38
  OIL SEAL REPLACEMENT 3-39
TIMING CHAIN 3-39
  REMOVAL & INSTALLATION 3-39
CAMSHAFT 3-40
  REMOVAL & INSTALLATION 3-40
VALVE LASH ADJUSTMENT 3-41
  HYDRAULIC LIFTERS 3-41
  MECHANICAL LIFTERS 3-41
VALVE LIFTERS 3-41
  REMOVAL & INSTALLATION 3-41
PISTONS AND CONNECTING
  RODS 3-43
  REMOVAL 3-43
  INSPECTION 3-43
  INSTALLATION 3-43
OIL PAN 3-44
  REMOVAL & INSTALLATION 3-44
REAR MAIN OIL SEAL 3-45

  REMOVAL & INSTALLATION 3-45
OIL PUMP 3-45
  REMOVAL & INSTALLATION 3-45
RADIATOR 3-46
  REMOVAL & INSTALLATION 3-46
WATER PUMP 3-48
  REMOVAL & INSTALLATION 3-48
THERMOSTAT 3-49
  REMOVAL & INSTALLATION 3-49
EXHAUST SYSTEM 3-50
GENERAL INFORMATION 3-50
  SPECIAL TOOLS 3-51
  COMPONENT REPLACEMENT 3-51
ENGINE REBUILDING 3-52
ENGINE OVERHAUL TIPS 3-52
  TOOLS 3-52
  INSPECTION TECHNIQUES 3-52
  OVERHAUL TIPS 3-52
  REPAIRING DAMAGED
    THREADS 3-52
COMPLETING THE REBUILDING
  PROCESS 3-54
BREAK-IN PROCEDURE 3-54
CYLINDER HEAD 3-54
  RECONDITIONING 3-54
CYLINDER BLOCK 3-65
  RECONDITIONING 3-65
COMPONENT LOCATIONS
HEI DISTRIBUTOR COMPONENTS 3-9
SPECIFICATION CHARTS
GENERATOR AND REGULATOR
  SPECIFICATIONS 3-14
ALTERNATOR AND REGULATOR
  SPECIFICATIONS 3-15
BATTERY AND STARTER
  SPECIFICATIONS 3-17
GENERAL ENGINE
  SPECIFICATIONS 3-19
VALVE SPECIFICATIONS 3-23
CRANKSHAFT AND CONNECTING ROD
  SPECIFICATIONS 3-25
CYLINDER BORE, PISTON, AND RING
  SPECIFICATIONS 1962–77 3-28
PISTON CLEARANCE
  SPECIFICATIONS 3-29
RING SIDE CLEARANCE 3-29
RING GAP SPECIFICATIONS 3-30
TORQUE SPECIFICATIONS 3-31

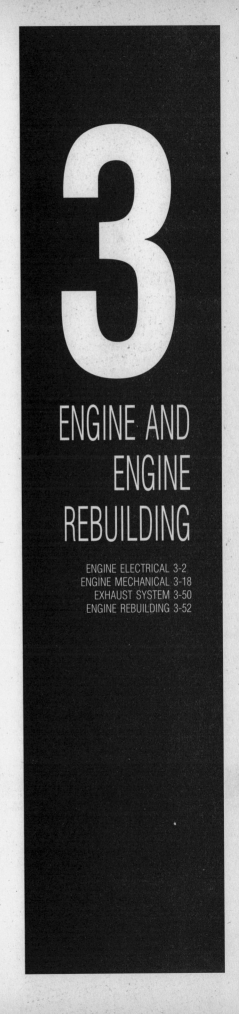

3

ENGINE AND ENGINE REBUILDING

ENGINE ELECTRICAL 3-2
ENGINE MECHANICAL 3-18
EXHAUST SYSTEM 3-50
ENGINE REBUILDING 3-52

ENGINE ELECTRICAL

Understanding Electricity

For any electrical system to operate, there must be a complete circuit. This simply means that the power flow from the battery must make a full circle. When an electrical component is operating, power flows from the battery to the components, passes through the component (load) causing it to function, and returns to the battery through the ground path of the circuit. This ground may be either another wire or a metal part of the vehicle (depending upon how the component is designed).

BASIC CIRCUITS

Perhaps the easiest way to visualize a circuit is to think of connecting a light bulb (with two wires attached to it) to the battery. If one of the two wires was attached to the negative post (−) of the battery and the other wire to the positive post (+), the circuit would be complete and the light bulb would illuminate. Electricity could follow a path from the battery to the bulb and back to the battery. It's not hard to see that with longer wires on our light bulb, it could be mounted anywhere on the vehicle. Further, one wire could be fitted with a switch so that the light could be turned on and off. Various other items could be added to our primitive circuit to make the light flash, become brighter or dimmer under certain conditions, or advise the user that it's burned out.

Ground

Some automotive components are grounded through their mounting points. The electrical current runs through the chassis of the vehicle and returns to the battery through the ground (−) cable; if you look, you'll see that the battery ground cable connects between the battery and the body of the vehicle.

Load

Every complete circuit must include a "load" (something to use the electricity coming from the source). If you were to connect a wire between the two terminals of the battery (DON'T do this, but take our word for it) without the light bulb, the battery would attempt to deliver its entire power supply from one pole to another almost instantly. This is a short circuit. The electricity is taking a short cut to get to ground and is not being used by any load in the circuit. This sudden and uncontrolled electrical flow can cause great damage to other components in the circuit and can develop a tremendous amount of heat. A short in an automotive wiring harness can develop sufficient heat to melt the insulation on all the surrounding wires and reduce a multiple wire cable to one sad lump of plastic and copper. Two common causes of shorts are

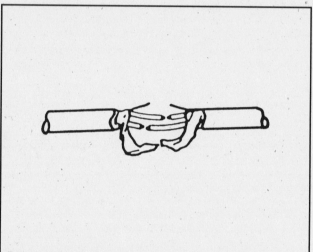

Damaged insulation can allow wires to break (causing an open circuit) or touch (causing a short circuit)

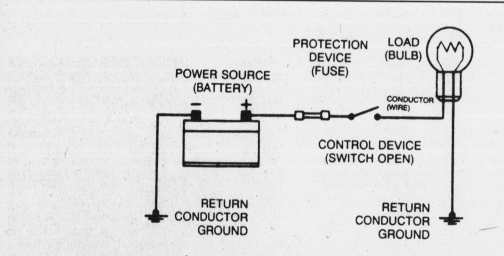

Here is an example of a simple automotive circuit. When the switch is closed, power from the positive battery terminal flows through the fuse, the switch and then the load (light bulb). The light illuminates and the circuit is completed through the return conductor and the vehicle ground. If the light did not work, the tests could be made with a voltmeter or test light at the battery, fuse, switch or bulb socket

broken insulation (thereby exposing the wire to contact with surrounding metal surfaces or other wires) or a failed switch (the pins inside the switch come out of place and touch each other).

Switches and Relays

Some electrical components which require a large amount of current to operate also have a relay in their circuit. Since these circuits carry a large amount of current (amperage or amps), the thickness of the wire in the circuit (wire gauge) is also greater. If this large wire were connected from the load to the control switch on the dash, the switch would have to carry the high amperage load and the dash would be twice as large to accommodate wiring harnesses as thick as your wrist. To prevent these problems, a relay is used. The large wires in the circuit are connected from the battery to one side of the relay and from the opposite side of the relay to the load. The relay is normally open, preventing current from passing through the circuit. An additional, smaller wire is connected from the relay to the control switch for the circuit. When the control switch is turned on, it grounds the smaller wire to the relay and completes its circuit. The main switch inside the relay closes, sending power to the component without routing the main power through the inside of the vehicle. Some common circuits which may use relays are the horn, headlights, starter and rear window defogger systems.

Protective Devices

It is possible for larger surges of current to pass through the electrical system of your vehicle. If this surge of current were to reach the load in the circuit, it could burn it out or severely damage it. To prevent this, fuses, circuit breakers and/or fusible links are connected into the supply wires of the electrical system. These items are nothing more than a built-in weak spot in the system. It's much easier to go to a known location (the fusebox) to see why a circuit is inoperative than to dissect 15 feet of wiring under the dashboard, looking for what happened.

When an electrical current of excessive power passes through the fuse, the fuse blows (the conductor melts) and breaks the circuit, preventing the passage of current and protecting the components.

A circuit breaker is basically a self repairing fuse. It will open the circuit in the same fashion as a fuse, but when either the short is removed or the surge subsides, the circuit breaker resets itself and does not need replacement.

A fuse link (fusible link or main link) is a wire that acts as a fuse. One of these is normally connected between the starter relay and the main wiring harness under the hood. Since the starter is usually the highest electrical draw on the vehicle, an internal short during starting could direct about 130 amps into the wrong places. Consider the damage potential of introducing this current into a system whose wiring is rated at 15 amps and you'll understand the need for protection. Since this link is very early in the electrical path, it's the first place to look if nothing on the vehicle works, but the battery seems to be charged and is properly connected.

TROUBLESHOOTING

Electrical problems generally fall into one of three areas:
• The component that is not functioning is not receiving current.

• The component is receiving power but is not using it or is using it incorrectly (component failure).
• The component is improperly grounded.

The circuit can be can be checked with a test light and a jumper wire. The test light is a device that looks like a pointed screwdriver with a wire on one end and a bulb in its handle. A jumper wire is simply a piece of wire with alligator clips or special terminals on each end. If a component is not working, you must follow a systematic plan to determine which of the three causes is the villain.

1. Turn ON the switch that controls the item not working.

➡**Some items only work when the ignition switch is turned ON.**

2. Disconnect the power supply wire from the component.

3. Attach the ground wire of a test light or a voltmeter to a good metal ground.

4. Touch the end probe of the test light (or the positive lead of the voltmeter) to the power wire; if there is current in the wire, the light in the test light will come on (or the voltmeter will indicate

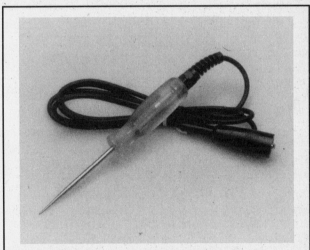

A 12 volt test light is useful when checking parts of a circuit for power

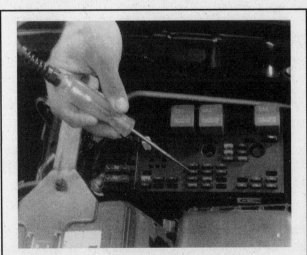

Here, someone is checking a circuit by making sure there is power to the component's fuse

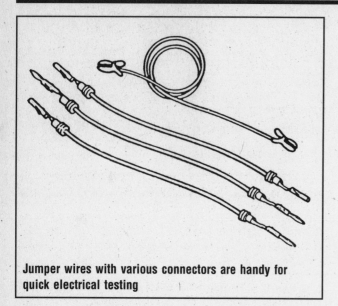

Jumper wires with various connectors are handy for quick electrical testing

the amount of voltage). You have now established that current is getting to the component.

5. Turn the ignition or dash switch **OFF** and reconnect the wire to the component.

If there was no power, then the problem is between the battery and the component. This includes all the switches, fuses, relays and the battery itself. The next place to look is the fusebox; check carefully either by eye or by using the test light across the fuse clips. The easiest way to check is to simply replace the fuse. If the fuse is blown, and upon replacement, immediately blows again, there is a short between the fuse and the component. This is generally (not always) a sign of an internal short in the component. Disconnect the power wire at the component again and replace the fuse; if the fuse holds, the component is the problem.

✳✳ WARNING

DO NOT test a component by running a jumper wire from the battery UNLESS you are certain that it operates on 12 volts. Many electronic components are designed to operate with less voltage and connecting them to 12 volts could destroy them. Jumper wires are best used to bypass a portion of the circuit (such as a stretch of wire or a switch) that DOES NOT contain a resistor and is suspected to be bad.

If all the fuses are good and the component is not receiving power, find the switch for the circuit. Bypass the switch with the jumper wire. This is done by connecting one end of the jumper to the power wire coming into the switch and the other end to the wire leaving the switch. If the component comes to life, the switch has failed.

✳✳ WARNING

Never substitute the jumper for the component. The circuit needs the electrical load of the component. If you bypass it, you will cause a short circuit.

Checking the ground for any circuit can mean tracing wires to the body, cleaning connections or tightening mounting bolts for the component itself. If the jumper wire can be connected to the

case of the component or the ground connector, you can ground the other end to a piece of clean, solid metal on the vehicle. Again, if the component starts working, you've found the problem.

A systematic search through the fuse, connectors, switches and the component itself will almost always yield an answer. Loose and/or corroded connectors, particularly in ground circuits, are becoming a larger problem in modern vehicles. The computers and on-board electronic (solid state) systems are highly sensitive to improper grounds and will change their function drastically if one occurs.

Remember that for any electrical circuit to work, ALL the connections must be clean and tight.

➡**For more information on Understanding and Troubleshooting Electrical Systems, please refer to Section 6 of this manual.**

Battery, Starting and Charging Systems

BASIC OPERATING PRINCIPLES

Battery

The battery is the first link in the chain of mechanisms which work together to provide cranking of the automobile engine. In most modern vehicles, the battery is a lead/acid electrochemical device consisting of six 2v subsections (cells) connected in series so the unit is capable of producing approximately 12v of electrical pressure. Each subsection consists of a series of positive and negative plates held a short distance apart in a solution of sulfuric acid and water.

The two types of plates are of dissimilar metals. This sets-up a chemical reaction, and it is this reaction which produces current flow from the battery when its positive and negative terminals are connected to an electrical accessory such as a lamp or motor. The continued transfer of electrons would eventually convert the sulfuric acid to water, and make the two plates identical in chemical composition. As electrical energy is removed from the battery, its voltage output tends to drop. Thus, measuring battery voltage and battery electrolyte composition are two ways of checking the ability of the unit to supply power. During engine cranking, electrical energy is removed from the battery. However, if the charging circuit is in good condition and the operating conditions are normal, the power removed from the battery will be replaced by the alternator which will force electrons back through the battery, reversing the normal flow, and restoring the battery to its original chemical state.

Starting System

The battery and starting motor are linked by very heavy electrical cables designed to minimize resistance to the flow of current. Generally, the major power supply cable that leaves the battery goes directly to the starter, while other electrical system needs are supplied by a smaller cable. During starter operation, power flows from the battery to the starter and is grounded through the vehicle's frame/body or engine and the battery's negative ground strap.

The starter is a specially designed, direct current electric motor capable of producing a great amount of power for its size. One thing that allows the motor to produce a great deal of power is its tremendous rotating speed. It drives the engine through a tiny pinion gear (attached to the starter's armature), which drives the very large flywheel ring gear at a greatly reduced speed. Another factor allowing it to produce so much power is that only intermittent operation is required of it. Thus, little allowance for air circulation is necessary, and the windings can be built into a very small space.

The starter solenoid is a magnetic device which employs the small current supplied by the start circuit of the ignition switch. This magnetic action moves a plunger which mechanically engages the starter and closes the heavy switch connecting it to the battery. The starting switch circuit usually consists of the starting switch contained within the ignition switch, a neutral safety switch or clutch pedal switch, and the wiring necessary to connect these in series with the starter solenoid or relay.

The pinion, a small gear, is mounted to a one way drive clutch. This clutch is splined to the starter armature shaft. When the ignition switch is moved to the **START** position, the solenoid plunger slides the pinion toward the flywheel ring gear via a collar and spring. If the teeth on the pinion and flywheel match properly, the pinion will engage the flywheel immediately. If the gear teeth butt one another, the spring will be compressed and will force the gears to mesh as soon as the starter turns far enough to allow them to do so. As the solenoid plunger reaches the end of its travel, it closes the contacts that connect the battery and starter, then the engine is cranked.

As soon as the engine starts, the flywheel ring gear begins turning fast enough to drive the pinion at an extremely high rate of speed. At this point, the one-way clutch begins allowing the pinion to spin faster than the starter shaft so that the starter will not operate at excessive speed. When the ignition switch is released from the starter position, the solenoid is de-energized, and a spring pulls the gear out of mesh interrupting the current flow to the starter.

Some starters employ a separate relay, mounted away from the starter, to switch the motor and solenoid current on and off. The relay replaces the solenoid electrical switch, but does not eliminate the need for a solenoid mounted on the starter used to mechanically engage the starter drive gears. The relay is used to reduce the amount of current the starting switch must carry.

Charging System

The automobile charging system provides electrical power for operation of the vehicle's ignition system, starting system and all electrical accessories. The battery serves as an electrical surge or storage tank, storing (in chemical form) the energy originally produced by the engine driven generator. The system also provides a means of regulating output to protect the battery from being overcharged and to avoid excessive voltage to the accessories.

The storage battery is a chemical device incorporating parallel lead plates in a tank containing a sulfuric acid/water solution. Adjacent plates are slightly dissimilar, and the chemical reaction of the two dissimilar plates produces electrical energy when the battery is connected to a load such as the starter motor. The chemical reaction is reversible, so that when the generator is producing a voltage (electrical pressure) greater than that produced by the battery, electricity is forced into the battery, and the battery is returned to its fully charged state.

Newer automobiles use alternating current generators or alternators, because they are more efficient, can be rotated at higher speeds, and have fewer brush problems. In an alternator, the field usually rotates while all the current produced passes only through the stator winding. The brushes bear against continuous slip rings. This causes the current produced to periodically reverse the direction of its flow. Diodes (electrical one way valves) block the flow of current from traveling in the wrong direction. A series of diodes is wired together to permit the alternating flow of the stator to be rectified back to 12 volts DC for use by the vehicle's electrical system.

The voltage regulating function is performed by a regulator. The regulator is often built in to the alternator; this system is termed an integrated or internal regulator.

HEI Electronic Ignition System

TROUBLESHOOTING

▶ **See Figure 1**

1. With transmission lever or selector in Neutral or Park, and ignition switch on, connect a test light between the lead labeled "BAT" on the distributor and a good ground. If the lamp lights, proceed; otherwise, repair the wiring or replace the ignition switch, as necessary.

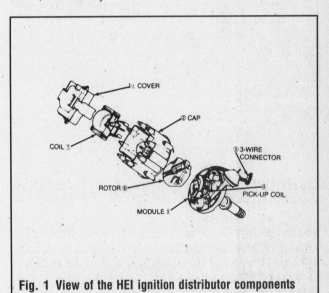

Fig. 1 View of the HEI ignition distributor components

2. Perform the same procedure as in step 1, but with the test light connected to the terminal on the distributor cap labeled B+. If the lamp operates, proceed; otherwise, repair the lead or connector.

3. Disconnect a plug wire, insert a conductor into the open end of the wire, and hold the conductor 1/4 in. from the block. Crank the engine, checking for spark. If there is spark, check the fuel system, spark plugs, and for flooding. Otherwise, proceed.

✸✸ CAUTION

Hold the plug wire with insulated pliers to avoid electric shock!

4. Turn the ignition switch OFF, disconnect the three wire connector, and remove the cap. Visually inspect all parts for moisture, dust, cracks, etc. and dry out/clean up/replace components

as necessary. If there are no visible problems, or repair still fails to produce spark, proceed.

5. Invert the distributor cap and connect an ohmmeter between the two primary terminals. Resistance should read less than 1 ohm, but above zero. If the resistance is above 1 ohm, or absolutely zero, replace the coil. If the resistance is within range, proceed.

6. Test the resistance between each primary connector and the body of the coil. If either test shows 6,000–30,000 ohms, proceed. Otherwise, replace the coil.

7. Remove green and white leads from the module. Connect the ohmmeter between either lead and ground with the meter set on the X1000 scale. Resistance should read infinity. If reading is less than infinity, replace the pick-up coil. If reading is ok, leave the meter hooked up and check the reading while moving the vacuum advance linkage back and forth with a screwdriver. The reading under these conditions should be 500–1,500 ohms. If the resistance is not within this range, replace the pick-up coil. Otherwise, proceed.

8. If these checks have proved out, remove the switching module and take it to a dealer to have it tested. Replace the module if the test shows it is bad. If you have to replace the module, make sure to apply silicone grease included in the kit as described in the enclosed instructions for proper module cooling and long life.

REMOVAL & INSTALLATION

Ignition Coil

REMOTE MOUNTED COIL

1. Disconnect the negative battery cable.
2. Remove the coil wire clip.
3. Disconnect the ignition coil wire.
4. Detach the electrical connector(s) from the ignition coil.
5. Unfasten the retaining bolts/nuts; then remove the ignition coil from the vehicle.

To remove the ignition coil, first disengage the clip securing the high tension lead (noted by arrow)

Unplug the high tension lead by pulling on the boot

Detach the ignition coil primary electrical connector

Unfasten the ignition coil or coil bracket retaining bolts

. . . then remove the ignition coil from the vehicle

To install:

6. Position the ignition coil and secure with the retaining screws or bolts.

7. Attach the ignition coil electrical connector(s).

8. Connect the ignition coil wire and install the retaining clip.

9. Connect the negative battery cable.

INTEGRAL COIL

1. Disconnect the negative battery cable.

2. Detach the feed and module wire terminal connectors from the distributor cap.

3. Remove the ignition set retainer.

4. Remove the 4 coil cover-to-distributor cap screws and the coil cover.

5. Using a blunt drift, carefully press the coil wire spade terminals up out of the distributor cap.

6. Lift the coil up and out of the distributor cap.

7. Remove and clean the coil spring, rubber seal washer and coil cavity of the distributor cap.

8. Coat the rubber seal with the dielectric lubricant that comes with the replacement ignition coil kit.

9. Installation is the reverse of the removal procedure.

Distributor

1. Disengage the wiring harness connectors at the side of the cap. Then, remove the cap and position it out of the way.

2. Disconnect the vacuum advance hose.

3. Scribe a mark on the engine in line with the distributor rotor. Also, scribe a line marking the position of the distributor housing in relation to the block.

➡ **Do not disturb the position of the engine's crankshaft while the distributor is out, or the timing relationship between the distributor shaft and camshaft will be lost!**

4. Remove the distributor hold-down nut and clamp, and remove the distributor. Note the position of the rotor as the drive gear disengages.

To install:

5. Position the distributor rotor slightly counterclockwise of its installed position—that is, in the position noted in the last step

of the removal procedure. With the body of the distributor at its normal angle in relation to the block, slide the lower body straight into the block, being careful not to damage the rubber oil seal. Make sure the rotor matches up with the marks drawn in the removal procedure. If not, pull the distributor up until the drive gear disengages, and try again with the rotor turned in the appropriate direction. You may have to rotate the rotor back and forth while gently pressing downward on the distributor to get the distributor drive gear teeth to engage.

6. Once the drive gear teeth are properly timed (rotor match marks lined up with distributor seated against the block), line up the match marks for the distributor body and block. Then, install the hold-down clamp and loosely install the nut.

7. Position the cap onto the top of the distributor body with the tab in the base of the cap aligned with the notch in the housing. Then, secure the cap with the four latches.

8. Connect the writing harness connector to the terminals on the side of the cap (if connector won't go on reverse it—it will install only one way).

9. Adjust ignition timing as described above.

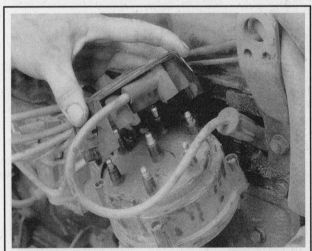

To remove the distributor, first remove the spark plug wires from the distributor cap

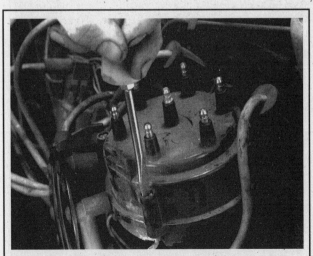

Push down, then turn to disengage the retainers securing the distributor cap

The cap can now be removed from distributor

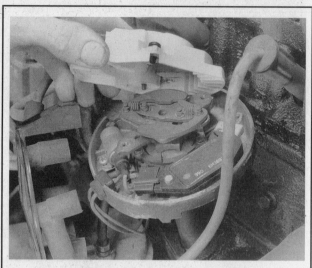

. . . then remove the rotor from the distributor

View of the distributor with the cap removed—1977 inline 6-cylinder shown

Disconnect the vacuum line from the vacuum advance unit

If rotor replacement is necessary, unfasten the retaining screws . . .

Unfasten the hold-down bolt, then lift the distributor up and out of the engine

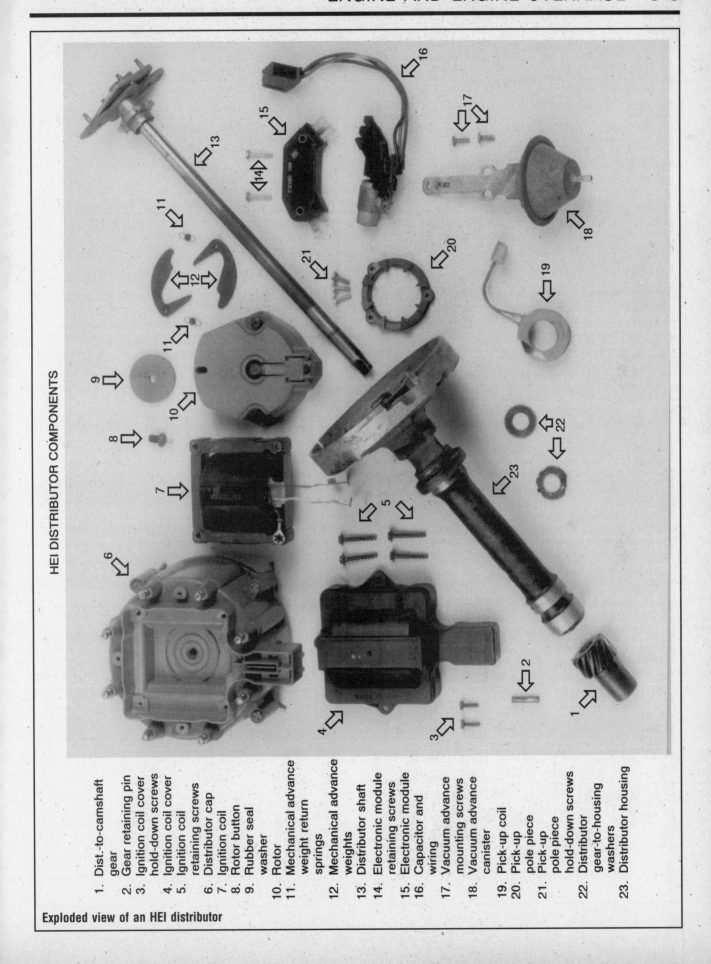

HEI DISTRIBUTOR COMPONENTS

1. Dist.-to-camshaft gear
2. Gear retaining pin
3. Ignition coil cover hold-down screws
4. Ignition coil cover
5. Ignition coil retaining screws
6. Distributor cap
7. Ignition coil
8. Rotor button
9. Rubber seal washer
10. Rotor
11. Mechanical advance weight return springs
12. Mechanical advance weights
13. Distributor shaft
14. Electronic module retaining screws
15. Electronic module
16. Capacitor and wiring
17. Vacuum advance mounting screws
18. Vacuum advance canister
19. Pick-up coil
20. Pick-up pole piece
21. Pick-up pole piece hold-down screws
22. Distributor gear-to-housing washers
23. Distributor housing

Exploded view of an HEI distributor

Conventional Ignition System

REMOVAL & INSTALLATION

Distributor

1. Disconnect the vacuum advance line at the distributor.
2. Disconnect the primary wire at the coil.
3. Unfasten the distributor cap retaining clips and lift off the cap. If it is necessary to disconnect any wires, mark them first.
4. Mark the distributor body and the engine block to indicate the position of the body in the block. Scribe a mark on the edge of the distributor housing to indicate the position of the rotor on the distributor. These marks can be used as guides when installing the distributor in a correctly timed engine.
5. Remove the distributor hold-down clamp screw and clamp.
6. Carefully lift the distributor out of the block.

To install:

If the crankshaft has not been rotated while the distributor was removed from the engine, installation is the reverse of the removal procedure. (See steps two, three, and four of the procedure below.) Use the reference marks that were made before removal to correctly position the distributor in the block. Check the point gap and, before connecting the vacuum advance line, adjust the ignition timing. (See the "Tune-Up Procedures" section.)

If the crankshaft has been rotated or otherwise disturbed (as during engine rebuilding) after the distributor was removed, proceed as follows to install the distributor.

1. Bring the No. 1 piston to top dead center (TDC). By removing the No. 1 spark plug and inserting a finger into the hole, while rotating the crankshaft, the compression pressure can be felt as the No. 1 piston approaches TDC. The TDC timing mark on the crankshaft vibration damper should now be opposite the indicator on the timing chain case.
2. Position the distributor to the block so that the vacuum control unit is in its normal position.
3. Position the rotor to point toward the front of the engine (with the distributor held out of the block, but in the installed attitude). Turn the rotor counterclockwise about one-eighth turn and push the distributor down to engage the camshaft drive. It may be necessary to move the rotor one way or the other to mesh the drive and driven gears properly.
4. While holding the distributor down in place, engage the starter a few times to make sure the oil pump shaft is engaged. Install the hold-down clamp and bolt and snug up the bolt.
5. Once again, rotate the crankshaft until No. 1 cylinder is on the compression stroke and the harmonic balancer mark is on 0°.
6. Turn the distributor body slightly until the points open. Tighten the distributor clamp bolt.
7. Place the distributor cap in position and see that the rotor lines up with the terminal for the No. 1 spark plug.
8. Install the cap and distributor primary wire, and double check the plug wires in the cap towers.
9. Start the engine and set the timing according to the "Tune-Up Specifications" chart.
10. Reconnect the vacuum hose-to-vacuum control assembly.

DC Generator

A DC (direct current) generator was used as standard equipment only on the 1962 Chevy II.

REMOVAL & INSTALLATION

1. Disconnect the armature, field terminal, and ground electrical leads from the generator.
2. Withdraw the bolt from the generator brace. Detach the fan belt from the generator pulley and lower the generator.
3. Withdraw the two generator-to-support bolts and nuts and remove the generator.

To install:

4. Install the generator by placing it in position and installing the support bracket bolts, lockwashers, and nuts. Tighten the bolts and nuts.
5. Position the fan belt on the generator drive pulley. Install the generator brace bolt, but do not fully tighten the bolt.
6. While holding the generator away from the engine, measure the deflection of the fan belt at a point midway between the generator and the fan. When the fan belt deflection is 5/16 in., tighten the generator brace bolt securely.
7. Connect the electrical leads to the generator. Polarize the generator by momentarily connecting a jumper lead between the "gen" and "bat" terminals of the voltage regulator.

Alternator

A Delcotron alternator was introduced as an option on the 1962 Chevy II and became standard equipment on 1963 models.

ALTERNATOR PRECAUTIONS

▶ **See Figure 2**

Because alternator design is unique, special care must be taken when servicing the charging system.

1. Battery polarity should be checked before any connections, such as jumper cables or battery charger leads, are made. Reversed battery connections will damage the diode rectifiers. It is recommended that the battery cables be disconnected before connecting a battery charger.
2. The battery must *never* be disconnected while the alternator is running because the regulator will be destroyed.
3. Always disconnect the battery ground lead before replacing the alternator.
4. Do not attempt to polarize an alternator.
5. Do not short across or ground any alternator terminals.
6. Always disconnect the battery ground lead before removing the alternator output cable, whether the engine is running or not.
7. If electric arc welding has to be done on the car, first dis-

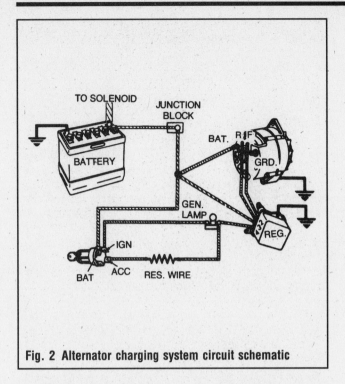

Fig. 2 Alternator charging system circuit schematic

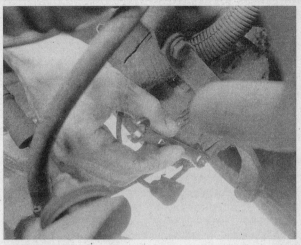

To remove the alternator, first unfasten the BAT terminal retaining nut . . .

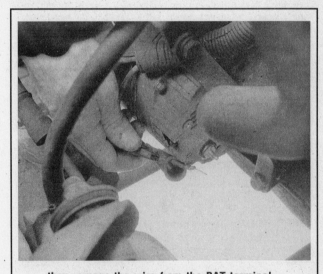

. . . then remove the wire from the BAT terminal

Loosen and remove the alternator brace bolt

connect the battery and alternator cables. Never start the car with the welding unit attached.

REMOVAL & INSTALLATION

1. Disconnect the battery ground cable to prevent diode damage.
2. Disconnect the Delcotron wiring.
3. Remove the generator brace bolt. If the car is equipped with power steering, loosen the pump brace and mount nuts. Detach the drive belt(s).
4. Support the generator and remove the mount bolt(s). Remove the unit from the vehicle.
5. Reverse the procedure to install. Adjust the drive belt to have ¼–½ in. play on the longest run of the belt.

Voltage Regulator

Since 1973 all GM cars have been equipped with alternators which have built-in solid state voltage regulators. The regulator is in the end frame (inside) of the alternator and requires no adjustment. The following procedure applies only to pre-1973 units.

REMOVAL & INSTALLATION

All external voltage regulators can be removed and installed by using the same procedure.
1. Disconnect the cables from the battery posts.
2. Label and disconnect each electrical lead from the voltage regulator.
3. Remove the regulator by withdrawing its securing screws.

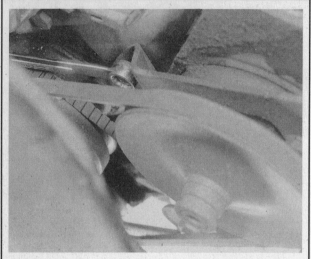

If equipped with power steering, loosen the pump brace nuts . . .

. . . then loosen the tension and remove the drive belt

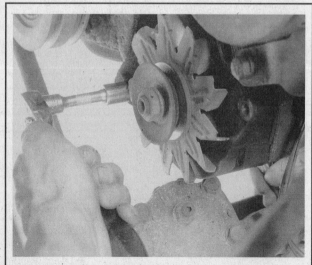

Loosen the alternator mounting bolt(s)

. . . then remove them from the alternator

The alternator can now be removed from the vehicle

4. Installation is the reverse of the above. Be sure that the electrical leads are connected to the correct terminals and that all connections are clean and tight.

Starter

REMOVAL & INSTALLATION

1. Disconnect the battery ground cable.
2. If accessible from the engine compartment, disconnect the starter wiring and unfasten the top mounting bolt.
3. Raise and support the vehicle.
4. If not already done, disconnect all wires at the solenoid terminals. Note the color coding of the wires for reinstallation.
5. Remove the starter front bracket and the two mount bolts. On engines with a solenoid heat shield, remove the front bracket upper bolt and detach the bracket from the starter motor.
6. Remove the front bracket bolt or nut. Rotate the bracket clear. Lower the starter, front end first. Remove the starter.

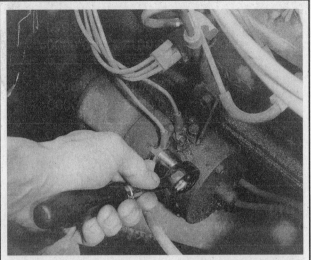

To remove the starter, first detach the battery cable and fusible link(s)

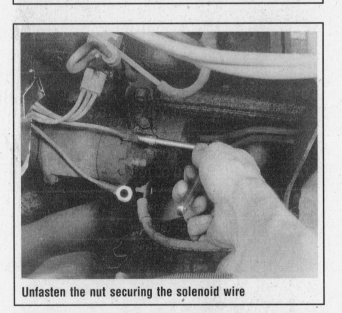

Unfasten the nut securing the solenoid wire

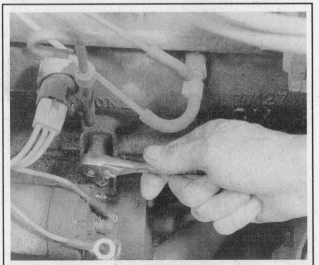

Remove the top starter mounting bolt

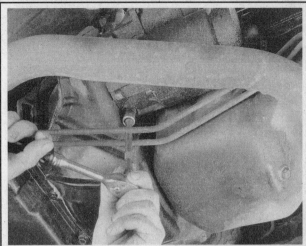

From under the vehicle, unfasten the remaining starter mounting bolts . . .

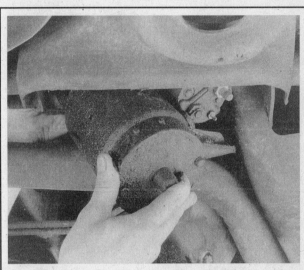

. . . then lower the starter from the vehicle, rear end first

7. Reverse this procedure for installation. Torque the mount bolts to 25–35 ft lbs.

Battery

REMOVAL & INSTALLATION

1. Protect the paint finish with fender covers.
2. Disconnect the battery cables at the battery terminal posts.
3. Remove the battery hold-down clamp and remove the battery from the vehicle.
4. Inspect the battery carrier and fender side panel for damage caused by loss of acid from the battery.
5. If the battery is to be reinstalled, clean the top of the battery with a solution of clean, warm water and baking soda. Scrub heavily deposited areas with a stiff-bristled brush, being careful not to scatter corrosion residue. Finally, wipe off the top of the battery

with a cloth that has been moistened with a solution of baking soda in water. *Keep the cleaning solution out of the battery cells.* Examine the battery case and cover for cracks.

6. Clean the battery posts and cable connectors with wire brush or special cleaning tool. Replace any damaged or frayed cables.

7. Install the battery in the car and tighten the hold-down clamp nuts. Connect the cables to their battery posts and, after tightening the cable connectors, coat all connectors with petroleum jelly to prevent corrosion. If the electrolyte level is low, fill to the recommended level with distilled or de-ionized water.

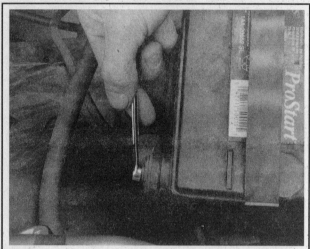

To remove the battery, first loosen the negative battery cable bolt . . .

Use an extension to reach the battery hold-down bolt

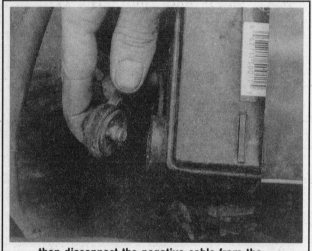

. . . then disconnect the negative cable from the battery. Detach the positive cable in the same manner

Lift the battery up and out of the battery tray

Generator and Regulator Specifications

| | Generator | | | | Regulator | | | | | |
| | | | | | | Cutout Relay | | | Regulator | |
Year	Part No.	Field Current @ 12V	Output (amps)	Brush Spring Tension (oz)	Part No.	Air Gap (in.)	Point Gap (in.)	Volts to Close	Air Gap (in.)	Volts @ 125° F
'62	1100326	1.50–1.62	25	28	1119000	0.020	0.020	11.8–13.5	0.060	13.8–14.7
	1102096	1.69–1.79	30	28	1119001	0.020	0.020	11.8–13.5	0.060	13.8–14.7

Alternator and Regulator Specifications

Year	Alternator Part No.	Field Current @ 12V	Output (amps)	Part No. or Manufacturer	Air Gap (in.)	Point Gap (in.)	Volts to Close	Air Gap (in.)	Point Gap (in.)	Volts @ 125° F
		Alternator				Field Relay			Regulator	
'62	1100600	1.9–2.2	42	1119502	0.015	0.015	6.5–8.5	0.067	0.014	13.5–14.3
	1100601	1.9–2.2	52	1119502	0.015	0.015	6.5–8.5	0.067	0.014	13.5–14.3
	1117765	4.1–4.5	62	9000567	0.014	0.027	5.0–9.5	0.075	0.014	13.3–13.9
'63	1100630	1.9–2.3	32	1119512	0.015	0.030	2.3–3.7	0.067	0.014	13.5–14.4
	1100628	1.9–2.3	37	1119512	0.015	0.030	2.3–3.7	0.067	0.014	13.5–14.4
	1100629	1.9–2.3	42	1119512	0.015	0.030	2.3–3.7	0.067	0.014	13.5–14.4
	1100633	1.9–2.3	52	1119512	0.015	0.030	2.3–3.7	0.067	0.014	13.5–14.4
	1117765	3.7–4.4	62	9000595	0.015	0.030	2.3–3.7	0.067	0.014	①
'64	1100670	1.9–2.3	32	1119515	0.015	0.030	2.3–3.7	0.067	0.014	13.5–14.4
	1100668	1.9–2.3	37	1119515	0.015	0.030	2.3–3.7	0.067	0.014	13.5–14.4
	1100669	1.9–2.3	42	1119515	0.015	0.030	2.3–3.7	0.067	0.014	13.5–14.4
	1117765	3.7–4.4	62	9000595	0.015	0.030	2.3–3.7	0.067	0.014	①
'65	1100695	2.2–2.6	32	1119515	0.015	0.030	1.5–3.2	0.067	0.014	②
	1100693	2.2–2.6	37	1119515	0.015	0.030	1.5–3.2	0.067	0.014	②
	1100696	2.2–2.6	42	1119515	0.015	0.030	1.5–3.2	0.067	0.014	②
	1100694	2.2–2.6	55	1119515	0.015	0.030	1.5–3.2	0.067	0.014	②
	1100697	2.8–3.2	60	1116368	0.011–0.018	0.020–0.030	2.5–3.5	—	—	②
	1117765	3.7–4.4	62	1116368	0.011–0.018	0.020–0.030	2.5–3.5	—	—	③
'66–'67	1100693	2.2–2.6	37	1119515	0.015	0.030	2.3–3.7	0.067	0.014	13.5–14.4
	1100695	2.2–2.6	32	1119515	0.015	0.030	2.3–3.7	0.067	0.014	13.5–14.4
	1100794	2.2–2.6	37	1119515	0.015	0.030	2.3–3.7	0.067	0.014	13.5–14.4
'68	1100813	2.2–2.6	37	1119515	0.015	0.030	2.3–3.7	0.067	0.014	13.5–14.4
	1100693	2.2–2.6	37	1119515	0.015	0.030	2.3–3.7	0.067	0.014	13.5–14.4
'69	1100834	2.2–2.6	37	1119515	0.015	0.030	2.3–3.7	0.067	0.014	13.5–14.4
	1100836	2.2–2.6	37	1119515	0.015	0.030	2.3–3.7	0.067	0.014	13.5–14.4

Alternator and Regulator Specifications

Year	Alternator Part No.	Field Current @ 12V	Output (amps)	Part No. or Manufacturer	Field Relay Air Gap (in.)	Point Gap (in.)	Volts to Close	Regulator Air Gap (in.)	Point Gap (in.)	Volts @ 125° F
'70	1100834	2.2–2.6	37	1119515	0.015	0.030	2.3–3.7	0.067	0.014	13.5–14.4
	1100837	2.2–2.6	37	1119515	0.015	0.030	2.3–3.7	0.067	0.014	13.5–14.4
'71	1100838	2.2–2.6	37	1119515	0.015	0.030	2.3–3.7	0.067	0.014	13.5–14.4
	1100839	2.2–2.6	37	1119515	0.015	0.030	2.3–3.7	0.067	0.014	13.5–14.4
'72	1100566	2.2–2.6	35	1119515	0.015	0.030	1.5–3.2	0.067	0.014	13.8–14.8
	1100917	2.8–3.2	59	1119519	0.030	0.030	1.5–3.2	0.067	0.014	13.8–14.8
	1100843	2.8–3.2	58	Integrated with alternator						13.8–14.8
'73	1100497	2.8–3.2	36	Integrated with alternator						13.8–14.8④
	1100934	2.8–3.2	37	Integrated with alternator						13.8–14.8④
'74	1100934	4–4.5	37	Integrated with alternator						13.8–14.8④
	1102347	4–4.5	61	Integrated with alternator						13.8–14.8④
	1100497	4–4.5	37	Integrated with alternator						13.8–14.8④
	1100573	4–4.5	42	Integrated with alternator						13.8–14.8④
	1100597	4–4.5	61	Integrated with alternator						13.8–14.8④
	1100560, 1100575	4–4.5	55	Integrated with alternator						13.8–14.8④
'75	1100497, 1102397, 1102483	4–4.5	37	Integrated with alternator						13.8–14.8④
	1100560, 1100575	4–4.5	55	Integrated with alternator						13.8–14.8④
'76–'77	1102941, 1102394, 1102491	4–4.5	37	Integrated with alternator						13.8–14.8④
'78–'79	1102491	4–4.5	33	Integrated with alternator						13.8–14.8④
	1102478	4–4.5	51	Integrated with alternator						13.8–14.8④
	1102479	4–4.5	51	Integrated with alternator						13.8–14.8④
	1102394	4–4.5	33	Integrated with alternator						13.8–14.8④

① 13.0–13.6 @ 80° F   ③ 13.7–14.4 @ 85° F
② 13.8–14.8 @ 85° F   ④ @ 85° F

Battery and Starter Specifications

Year	Engine No. Cyl Displacement (cu in.)	BATTERY Ampere Hour Capacity	Volts	Terminal Grounded	STARTER Lock Test Amps	Volts	Torque (ft lbs)	No-Load Test Amps	Volts	RPM	Brush Spring Tension (oz)
'62–'65	All	44	12	Neg	Not Recommended			49–76	10.6	7,800	35
'66–'67	4 & 6, 8—283	44	12	Neg	Not Recommended			49–76	10.6	7,800	35
	8—372	61	12	Neg	Not Recommended			65–100	10.6	4,200	35
'66–'69	4 & 6, 8—307	45	12	Neg	Not Recommended			—	10.6	—	35
	8—302, 327, 350, 396	61	12	Neg	Not Recommended			—	9	—	35
'70–'71	4 & 6, 8—307	45	12	Neg	Not Recommended			50–80	9	5,500–10,500	35
	8—350	61	12	Neg	Not Recommended			55–80	9	3,500–6,000	35
'72	6	45	12	Neg	Not Recommended			50–80	9	5,500–10,500	35
	8—307	61	12	Neg	Not Recommended			50–80	9	5,500–10,500	35
	8—350	76	12	Neg	Not Recommended			65–95	9	7,500–10,500	35
'73–'77	6	45	12	Neg	Not Recommended			50–80	9	5,500–10,500	35
	8—307	61	12	Neg	Not Recommended			50–80	9	5,500–10,500	35
	8—262, 350	76	12	Neg	Not Recommended			65–95①	9	7,500–10,500②	35
'78–'79	6—250	2500③	12	Neg	Not Recommended			50–80	9	5,500–10,500	35
	8—305	3200③	12	Neg	Not Recommended			50–80	9	5,500–10,500	35
	8—350	3200③	12	Neg	Not Recommended			65–95	9	7,500–10,500	35

① 1975 8-262—55–80   ③ Rated in watts
② 1975 8-262—3,500–6,000

ENGINE MECHANICAL

Understanding the Engine

The basic piston engine is a metal block containing a series of chambers. The upper engine block is usually an iron or aluminum alloy casting, consisting of outer walls, which form hollow jackets around the cylinder walls. The lower block provides a number of rigid mounting points for the bearings which hold the crankshaft in place, and is known as the crankcase. The hollow jackets of the upper block add to the rigidity of the engine and contain the liquid coolant which carries the heat away from the cylinders and other engine parts. The block of an air cooled engine consists of a crankcase which provides for the rigid mounting of the crankshaft and for studs which hold the cylinders in place. The cylinders are individual, single-wall castings, finned for cooling, and are usually bolted to the crankcase, rather than cast integrally with the block. In a water-cooled engine, only the cylinder head is bolted to the top of the block. The water pump is mounted directly to the block.

The crankshaft is a long, iron or steel shaft mounted rigidly in the bottom of the crankcase, at a number of points (usually 4–7). The crankshaft is free to turn and contains a number of counter-weighted crankpins (one for each cylinder) that are offset several inches from the center of the crankshaft and turn in a circle as the crankshaft turns. The crankpins are centered under each cylinder. Pistons with circular rings to seal the small space between the pistons and wall of the cylinders are connected to the crankpins by steel connecting rods. The rods connect the pistons at their upper ends with the crankpins at their lower ends.

When the crankshaft spins, the pistons move up and down in the cylinders, varying the volume of each cylinder, depending on the position of the piston. Two openings in each cylinder head (above the cylinders) allow the intake of the air/fuel mixture and the exhaust of burned gasses. The volume of the combustion chamber must be variable for the engine to compress the fuel charge before combustion, to make use of the expansion of the burning gasses and to exhaust the burned gasses and take in a fresh fuel mixture. As the pistons are forced downward by the expansion of burning fuel, the connecting rods convert the reciprocating (up and down) motion of the pistons into rotary (turning) motion of the crankshaft. A round flywheel at the rear of the crankshaft provides a large, stable mass to smooth out the rotation.

The cylinder heads form tight covers for the tops of the cylinders and contain machined chambers into which the fuel mixture is forced as it is compressed by the pistons reaching the upper limit of their travel. Each combustion chamber contains one intake valve, one exhaust valve and one spark plug per cylinder. The spark plugs are screwed into holes in the cylinder head so that the tips protrude into the combustion chambers. The valve in each opening in the cylinder head is opened and closed by the action of the camshaft. The camshaft is driven by the crankshaft through a chain or belt at ½ crankshaft speed (the camshaft gear is twice the size of the crankshaft gear). The valves are operated either through rocker arms and pushrods (overhead valve engine) or directly by the camshaft (overhead cam engine).

Lubricating oil is stored in a pan at the bottom of the engine and is force fed to all parts of the engine by a gear type pump, driven from the crankshaft. The oil lubricates the entire engine and also seals the piston rings, giving good compression.

Design

Four, six, and eight-cylinder engines are used in Chevy II and Nova models. The four-cylinder engine is an inline, overhead valve design having five main bearings and displacing 153 cu in. The 194, 230, and 250 cu in. six-cylinder engines are also inline, overhead valve units, but they have seven main bearings. The V8 engines are of two types: "small block" or "large block." The "small block" series of V8 engines includes the 262, 283, 305, 307, 327, and 350 cu in. engines. They are similar in design and have some interchangeability of parts. The "large block" V8 series applies here to the 396 cu in. engine.

General Engine Specifications

Year	Engine No. Cyl Displacement (cu in.)	Carburetor Type	Advertised Horsepower @ rpm ■	Advertised Torque @ rpm (ft lbs) ■	Bore & Stroke (in.)	Advertised Compression Ratio	Normal Oil Pressure (psi)
'62–'63	4—153	1 bbl	90 @ 4000	152 @ 2400	3.875 x 3.25	8.5 : 1	35
	6—194	1 bbl	120 @ 4400	177 @ 2400	3.563 x 3.25	8.5 : 1	35
'64	4—153	1 bbl	90 @ 4000	152 @ 2400	3.875 x 3.25	8.5 : 1	35
	6—194	1 bbl	120 @ 4400	177 @ 2400	3.563 x 3.25	8.5 : 1	35
	8—283	2 bbl	195 @ 4800	285 @ 2800	3.875 x 3.00	9.25 : 1	45
'65	4—153	1 bbl	90 @ 4000	152 @ 2400	3.875 x 3.25	8.5 : 1	35
	6—194	1 bbl	120 @ 4400	177 @ 2400	3.563 x 3.25	8.5 : 1	35
	6—230	1 bbl	140 @ 4400	215 @ 2000	3.875 x 3.25	8.5 : 1	35
	8—283	2 bbl	195 @ 4800	285 @ 2400	3.875 x 3.00	9.25 : 1	35
	8—327	4 bbl	250 @ 4400	350 @ 2800	4.000 x 3.25	10.5 : 1	35
	8—327	4 bbl	300 @ 5000	360 @ 3200	4.000 x 3.25	10.5 : 1	35
	8—327	4 bbl	350 @ 6000	360 @ 3200	4.000 x 3.25	11.0 : 1	35
'66	4—153	1 bbl	90 @ 4000	152 @ 4200	3.875 x 3.25	8.5 : 1	38①
	6—194	2 bbl	120 @ 4400	177 @ 2400	3.563 x 3.25	8.5 : 1	38①
	6—230	1 bbl	140 @ 4400	220 @ 1600	3.875 x 3.25	8.5 : 1	38①
	8—283	2 bbl	195 @ 4800	285 @ 2800	3.875 x 3.00	9.25 : 1	38①
	8—283	4 bbl	220 @ 4800	295 @ 3200	3.875 x 3.00	9.25 : 1	38①
	8—327	4 bbl	275 @ 4800	335 @ 2800	4.001 x 3.25	10.5 : 1	38①
	8—327	4 bbl	350 @ 5800	360 @ 3600	4.001 x 3.25	11.0 : 1	38①
	8—396	4 bbl	325 @ 4800	410 @ 3200	4.094 x 3.76	10.25 : 1	62
'67	4—153	1 bbl	90 @ 4000	152 @ 2400	3.875 x 3.25	8.5 : 1	38
	6—194	1 bbl	120 @ 4000	177 @ 2400	3.563 x 3.25	8.5 : 1	38

General Engine Specifications (cont.)

Year	Engine No. Cyl Displacement (cu in.)	Carburetor Type	Advertised Horsepower @ rpm ▪	Advertised Torque @ rpm ▪ (ft lbs)	Bore & Stroke (in.)	Advertised Compression Ratio	Normal Oil Pressure (psi)
'67	6—230	1 bbl	140 @ 4400	220 @ 1600	3.875 x 3.25	8.5 : 1	38
	6—250	1 bbl	155 @ 4200	235 @ 1600	3.875 x 3.53	8.5 : 1	38①
	8—283	2 bbl	195 @ 4600	285 @ 2400	3.875 x 3.00	9.25 : 1	38①
	8—327	2 bbl	210 @ 4600	320 @ 2400	4.001 x 3.25	8.75 : 1	38①
	8—327	4 bbl	275 @ 4800	355 @ 3200	4.001 x 3.25	10.0 : 1	38①
'68	4—153	1 bbl	90 @ 4000	152 @ 2400	3.875 x 3.25	8.5 : 1	58
	6—230	1 bbl	145 @ 4400	220 @ 1600	3.875 x 3.25	8.5 : 1	58
	6—250	1 bbl	155 @ 4200	325 @ 1600	3.875 x 3.53	8.5 : 1	58
	8—307	2 bbl	200 @ 4600	300 @ 2400	3.875 x 3.25	9.0 : 1	58
	8—327	2 bbl	210 @ 4600	320 @ 2400	4.001 x 3.25	8.75 : 1	58
	8—327	4 bbl	275 @ 4800	355 @ 3200	4.001 x 3.25	10.0 : 1	58
'69	4—153	1 bbl	90 @ 4000	152 @ 2400	3.875 x 3.25	8.5 : 1	58
	6—230	1 bbl	140 @ 4400	220 @ 1600	3.875 x 3.25	8.5 : 1	58
	6—250	1 bbl	155 @ 4200	235 @ 1600	3.875 x 3.53	8.5 : 1	58
	8—307	2 bbl	200 @ 4600	300 @ 2400	3.875 x 3.25	9.0 : 1	58
	8—350	2 bbl	250 @ 4800	345 @ 2800	4.000 x 3.48	9.0 : 1	62
	8—350	4 bbl	300 @ 4800	380 @ 3200	4.000 x 3.48	10.25 : 1	62
	8—396	4 bbl	325 @ 4800	410 @ 3200	4.094 x 3.76	10.25 : 1	62
	8—396	4 bbl	350 @ 5200	415 @ 3400	4.094 x 3.76	10.25 : 1	62
	8—396	4 bbl	375 @ 5600	415 @ 3600	4.094 x 3.76	11.0 : 1	62
'70	4—153	1 bbl	90 @ 4000	152 @ 2400	3.875 x 3.25	8.5 : 1	40
	6—230	1 bbl	140 @ 4400	220 @ 1600	3.875 x 3.25	8.5 : 1	40

General Engine Specifications (cont.)

Year	Engine No. Cyl Displacement (cu in.)	Carburetor Type	Advertised Horsepower @ rpm ■	Advertised Torque @ rpm (ft lbs) ■	Bore & Stroke (in.)	Advertised Compression Ratio	Normal Oil Pressure (psi)
'70	6—250	1 bbl	155 @ 4200	235 @ 1600	3.875 x 3.53	8.5 : 1	40
	8—307	2 bbl	200 @ 4600	300 @ 2400	3.875 x 3.25	9.0 : 1	40
	8—350	2 bbl	250 @ 4800	345 @ 2800	4.000 x 3.48	9.0 : 1	40
	8—350	4 bbl	300 @ 4800	380 @ 3200	4.000 x 3.48	10.25 : 1	40
'71	6—250	1 bbl	145 @ 4200	230 @ 1600	3.875 x 3.53	8.5 : 1	40
	8—307	2 bbl	200 @ 4600	300 @ 2400	3.875 x 3.25	8.5 : 1	40
	8—350	2 bbl	245 @ 4800	350 @ 2800	4.000 x 3.48	8.5 : 1	40
	8—350	4 bbl	270 @ 4800	360 @ 3200	4.000 x 3.48	8.5 : 1	40
	8—350	4 bbl	330 @ 5000	275 @ 5600	4.000 x 3.48	9.0 : 1	40
'72	6—250	1 bbl	110 @ 3800	185 @ 1600	3.875 x 3.53	8.5 : 1	40
	8—307	2 bbl	130 @ 4000	230 @ 2400	3.875 x 3.25	8.5 : 1	40
	8—350	2 bbl	165 @ 4000	280 @ 2400	4.000 x 3.48	8.5 : 1	40
	8—350	4 bbl	200 @ 4400	300 @ 2800	4.000 x 3.48	8.5 : 1	40
	8—350	4 bbl	255 @ 5600	280 @ 4000	4.000 x 3.48	9.0 : 1	40
'73	6—250	1 bbl	100 @ 3800	175 @ 1600	3.875 x 3.53	8.25 : 1	40
	8—307	2 bbl	115 @ 4000	205 @ 2000	3.875 x 3.25	8.5 : 1	40
	8—350	2 bbl	145 @ 4000	255 @ 2400	4.000 x 3.48	8.5 : 1	40
	8—350	4 bbl	175 @ 4400	270 @ 2400	4.000 x 3.48	8.5 : 1	40
'74	6—250	1 bbl	100 @ 3600	175 @ 1800	3.875 x 3.53	8.25 : 1	40
	8—350②	2 bbl	145 @ 3600	250 @ 2200	4.000 x 3.48	8.5 : 1	40
	8—350	4 bbl	160 @ 3800	245 @ 2400	4.000 x 3.48	8.5 : 1	40
	8—350	4 bbl	185 @ 4000	270 @ 2600	4.000 x 3.48	8.5 : 1	40

General Engine Specifications (cont.)

Year	Engine No. Cyl Displacement (cu in.)	Carburetor Type	Advertised Horsepower @ rpm ■	Advertised Torque @ rpm ■ (ft lbs)	Bore & Stroke (in.)	Advertised Compression Ratio	Normal Oil Pressure (psi)
'75	6—250	1 bbl	105 @ 3800	185 @ 1200	3.875 x 3.53	8.25 : 1	40
	8—262②	2 bbl	110 @ 3600	200 @ 2000	3.671 x 3.10	8.5 : 1	40
	8—350②	2 bbl	145 @ 3800	250 @ 2200	4.000 x 3.48	8.5 : 1	40
	8—350	4 bbl	155 @ 3800	250 @ 2400	4.000 x 3.48	8.5 : 1	40
'76–'77	6—250	1 bbl	105 @ 3800	185 @ 1200	3.875 x 3.53	8.25 : 1	40
	8—305	2 bbl	140 @ 3800	245 @ 2000	3.736 x 3.48	8.5 : 1	40
	8—350	4 bbl	165 @ 3800	260 @ 2400	4.000 x 3.48	8.5 : 1	40
'78	6—250	1 bbl	105 @ 3800	185 @ 1200	3.875 x 3.53	8.1 : 1	40
	8—305	2 bbl	140 @ 3800	245 @ 2000	3.736 x 3.48	8,0 : 1	40
	8—350	4 bbl	165 @ 3800	260 @ 2400	4.000 x 3.48	8.0 : 1	40
'79	6—250	1 bbl	115 @ 3800	190 @ 1300	3.875 x 3.53	8.0 : 1③	40
	8—305	2 bbl	130 @ 3200	230 @ 2000	3.736 x 3.48	8.4 : 1	45
	8—350	4 bbl	165 @ 3800	260 @ 2400	4.000 x 3.48	8.2 : 1	45

■ Beginning 1972, horsepower and torque are SAE net figures. They are measured at the rear of the transmission with all accessories installed and operating. Since the figures vary when a given engine is installed in different models, some are representative rather than exact.
① Oil pressure at 1500 rpm
② Not available—California
③ 8.2 : 1—California

Valve Specifications

Year	Engine No. Cyl Displacement (cu in.)	Seat Angle (deg)	Face Angle (deg)	Spring Test Pressure (lbs @ in.)	Spring Installed Height (in.)	STEM TO GUIDE Clearance (in.)		STEM Diameter (in.)	
						Intake	Exhaust	Intake	Exhaust
'62-'65	4—153	46	45	175 @ 1.26	$1\frac{21}{32}$	0.0010–0.0027	0.0015–0.0033	0.3407–0.3417	0.3410–0.3417
	6—194	46	45	170 @ 1.33	$1\frac{21}{32}$	0.0010–0.0027	0.0015–0.0033	0.3407–0.3417	0.3410–0.3417
	6—230	46	45	175 @ 1.26	$1\frac{21}{32}$	0.0010–0.0027	0.0015–0.0033	0.3407–0.3417	0.3410–0.3417
	8—283	46	45	175 @ 1.26	$1\frac{21}{32}$	0.0010–0.0027	0.0015–0.0033	0.3407–0.3417	0.3410–0.3417
	8—327	46	45	175 @ 1.26	$1\frac{21}{32}$	0.0010–0.0027	0.0010–0.0027	0.3407–0.3417	0.3410–0.3417
'66	4—153	46	45	82 @ 1.66	$1\frac{21}{32}$	0.0010–0.0037	0.0010–0.0047	0.3414	0.3414
	6—194	46	45	60 @ 1.66	$1\frac{21}{32}$	0.0010–0.0037	0.0010–0.0047	0.3414	0.3414
	6—230	46	45	60 @ 1.66	$1\frac{21}{32}$	0.0010–0.0037	0.0010–0.0047	0.3414	0.3414
	8—283	46	45	82 @ 1.66	$1\frac{21}{32}$	0.0010–0.0037	0.0010–0.0047	0.3414	0.3414
	8—327	46	45	82 @ 1.66	$1\frac{21}{32}$	0.0010–0.0037	0.0010–0.0047	0.3414	0.3414
'67	4—153	46③	45	82 @ 1.66	$1\frac{21}{32}$	0.0010–0.0037	0.0010–0.0047	0.3414	0.3414
	6—194	46③	45	60 @ 1.66	$1\frac{21}{32}$	0.0010–0.0037	0.0015–0.0052	0.3414	0.3414
	6—230	46③	45	60 @ 1.66	$1\frac{21}{32}$	0.0010–0.0037	0.0015–0.0052	0.3414	0.3414
'67	6—250	46③	45	60 @ 1.66	$1\frac{21}{32}$	0.0010–0.0047	0.0015–0.0052	0.3414	0.3414
	8—283	46③	45	80 @ 1.70	$1\frac{5}{32}$	0.0010–0.0037	0.0010–0.0047	0.3414	0.3414
	8—327	46③	45	80 @ 1.70	$1\frac{5}{32}$	0.0010–0.0037	0.0010–0.0047	0.3414	0.3414
'68	4—153	46③	45	81 @ 1.66	$1\frac{21}{32}$	0.0010–0.0037	0.0015–0.0052	0.3414	0.3414
	6—230	46③	45	59 @ 1.66	$1\frac{21}{32}$	0.0010–0.0037	0.0015–0.0052	0.3414	0.3414
	6—250	46③	45	59 @ 1.66	$1\frac{21}{32}$	0.0010–0.0037	0.0015–0.0052	0.3414	0.3414
	8—307	46③	45	80 @ 1.70	$1\frac{5}{32}$	0.0010–0.0037	0.0010–0.0047	0.3414	0.3414
	8—327	46③	45	80 @ 1.70	$1\frac{5}{32}$	0.0010–0.0037	0.0010–0.0047	0.3414	0.3414
'69	4—153	46③	45	81 @ 1.66	$1\frac{21}{32}$	0.0010–0.0037	0.0015–0.0052	0.3414	0.3414
	6—230	46③	45	59 @ 1.66	$1\frac{21}{32}$	0.0010–0.0037	0.0015–0.0052	0.3414	0.3414
	6—250	46③	45	59 @ 1.66	$1\frac{21}{32}$	0.0010–0.0037	0.0015–0.0052	0.3414	0.3414
	8—307	46③	45	80 @ 1.70	$1\frac{5}{32}$	0.0010–0.0037	0.0010–0.0047	0.3414	0.3414
	8—350	46③	45	80 @ 1.70	$1\frac{5}{32}$	0.0010–0.0037	0.0010–0.0047	0.3414	0.3414

Valve Specifications

Year	Engine No. Cyl Displacement (cu in.)	Seat Angle (deg)	Face Angle (deg)	Spring Test Pressure (lbs @ in.)	Spring Installed Height (in.)	STEM TO GUIDE Clearance (in.)		STEM Diameter (in.)	
						Intake	Exhaust	Intake	Exhaust
'69	8—396①	46③	45	90 @ 1.88	1⅞	0.0010–0.0035	0.0012–0.0047	0.3719	0.3719
	8—396④	46③	45	100 @ 1.88	1⅞	0.0010–0.0035	0.0012–0.0047	0.3719	0.3719
'70	4—153	46③	45	81 @ 1.66	1 21/32	0.0010–0.0037	0.0015–0.0052	0.3414	0.3414
	6—230	46③	45	59 @ 1.66	1 21/32	0.0010–0.0037	0.0015–0.0052	0.3414	0.3414
	6—250	46③	45	59 @ 1.66	1 21/32	0.0010–0.0037	0.0015–0.0052	0.3414	0.3414
	8—307	46③	45	80 @ 1.70	1 23/32	0.0010–0.0037	0.0012–0.0049	0.3414	0.3414
	8—350	46③	45	80 @ 1.70	1 23/32	0.0010–0.0037	0.0012–0.0049	0.3414	0.3414
'71	6—250	46	45	60 @ 1.66	1 21/32	0.0010–0.0037	0.0015–0.0052	0.3414	0.3414
	8—307	46	45	80 @ 1.70	1 23/32	0.0010–0.0037	0.0012–0.0049	0.3414	0.3414
	8—350	46	45	80 @ 1.70	1 23/32	0.0010–0.0037	0.0012–0.0049	0.3414	0.3414
'72	6—250	46	45	60 @ 1.66	1 21/32	0.0010–0.0037	0.0015–0.0052	0.3414	0.3414
	8—307	46	45	80 @ 1.70	1 23/32	0.0010–0.0037	0.0012–0.0049	0.3414	0.3414
	8—350	46	45	80 @ 1.70	1 23/32	0.0010–0.0037	0.0012–0.0049	0.3414	0.3414
'73	6—250	46	45	60 @ 1.66	1 21/32	0.0010–0.0027	0.0015–0.0032	0.3414	0.3414
	8—307	46	45	80 @ 1.61	1⅝	0.0010–0.0027	0.0012–0.0029	0.3414	0.3414
	8—350	46	45	80 @ 1.70	1 23/32	0.0010–0.0027	0.0012–0.0027	0.3414	0.3414
'74	6—250	46	45	60 @ 1.66	1 21/32	0.0010–0.0027	0.0010–0.0027	0.3414	0.3414
	8—350	46	45	80 @ 1.70	1 23/32	0.0010–0.0027	0.0010–0.0027	0.3414	0.3414
'75–'77	6—250	46	45	60 @ 1.66	1 21/32	0.0010–0.0027	0.0010–0.0027	0.3414	0.3414
	8—262	46	45	80 @ 1.70⑤	1 23/32	0.0010–0.0027	0.0010–0.0027	0.3414	0.3414
	8—305	46	45	80 @ 1.70	1 23/32	0.0010–0.0027	0.0010–0.0027	0.3414	0.3414
	8—350	46	45	80 @ 1.70⑤	1 23/32	0.0010–0.0027	0.0010–0.0027	0.3414	0.3414
'78	6—250	46	45	80 @ 1.66	1 23/32	0.0010–0.0027	0.0015–0.0032	0.3414	0.3414
	8—305	46	45	80 @ 1.70⑤	1 23/32	0.0010–0.0027	0.0010–0.0027	0.3414	0.3414
	8—350	46	45	80 @ 1.70⑤	1 23/32	0.0010–0.0027	0.0010–0.0027	0.3414	0.3414
'79	6—250	46	45	80 @ 1.66	1 21/32	0.0010–0.0027	0.0010–0.0027	0.3414	0.3414
	8—305	46	45	80 @ 1.7⑤	1 23/32	0.0010–0.0027	0.0010–0.0027	0.3414	0.3414
	8—350	46	45	80 @ 1.7⑤	1 23/32	0.0010–0.0027	0.0010–0.0027	0.3414	0.3414

① 325 hp   ③ 45° on aluminum heads   ④ 350 hp   ⑤ 80 @ 1.61 for exhaust

Crankshaft and Connecting Rod Specifications

All measurements are given in in.

Year	Engine No. Cyl Displacement (cu in.)	Crankshaft				Connecting Rod		
		Main Brg Journal Dia	Main Brg Oil Clearance	Shaft End-Play	Thrust on No.	Journal Diameter	Oil Clearance	Side Clearance
'62–'63	4—153	2.2983–2.2993	0.0003–0.0029	0.002–0.006	5	1.999–2.000	0.0007–0.0027	0.009–0.013
	6—194	2.2983–2.2993	0.0003–0.0029	0.002–0.006	7	1.999–2.000	0.0007–0.0027	0.009–0.013
'64	4—153	2.2983–2.2993	0.0003–0.0029	0.002–0.006	5	1.999–2.000	0.0007–0.0027	0.009–0.013
	6—194	2.2983–2.2993	0.0003–0.0029	0.002–0.006	7	1.999–2.000	0.0007–0.0027	0.009–0.013
	8—283	2.2978–2.2988	0.0003–0.0029①	0.003–0.011	5	1.999–2.000	0.0007–0.0027	0.009–0.013
'65	4—153	2.2983–2.2993	0.0003–0.0029	0.002–0.006	5	1.999–2.000	0.0007–0.0027	0.009–0.013
	6—194	2.2983–2.2993	0.0003–0.0029	0.002–0.006	7	1.999–2.000	0.0007–0.0027	0.009–0.013
	6—230	2.2983–2.2993	0.0003–0.0029	0.002–0.006	7	1.999–2.000	0.0007–0.0027	0.009–0.013
	8—283	2.2978–2.2988	0.0003–0.0029①	0.002–0.006	5	1.999–2.000	0.0007–0.0027	0.009–0.013
	8—327	2.2978–2.2988	0.0008–0.0034①	0.002–0.006	5	1.999–2.000	0.0007–0.0028	0.009–0.013
'66	4—153	2.2983–2.2993	0.0003–0.0029	0.002–0.006	5	1.999–2.000	0.0007–0.0027	0.009–0.013
	6—194	2.2983–2.2993	0.0003–0.0029	0.002–0.006	7	1.999–2.000	0.0007–0.0027	0.009–0.013
	6—230	2.2983–2.2993	0.0003–0.0029	0.002–0.006	7	1.999–2.000	0.0007–0.0027	0.009–0.013
'66	8—283	②	0.0003–0.0029①	0.003–0.011	5	1.999–2.000	0.0007–0.0027	0.009–0.013
	8—327	②	0.0003–0.0034①	0.003–0.011	5	1.999–2.000	0.0007–0.0028	0.009–0.013
'67	4—153	2.2983–2.2993	0.0003–0.0029	0.002–0.006	5	1.999–2.000	0.0007–0.0027	0.009–0.013
	6—194	2.2983–2.2993	0.0003–0.0029	0.002–0.006	7	1.999–2.000	0.0007–0.0027	0.009–0.013
	6—230	2.2983–2.2993	0.0003–0.0028	0.002–0.006	7	1.999–2.000	0.0007–0.0027	0.009–0.013
	6—250	2.2983–2.2993	0.0003–0.0029	0.002–0.006	7	1.999–2.000	0.0007–0.0027	0.009–0.013
	8—283	⑤	⑦	0.003–0.011	5	1.999–2.000	0.0007–0.0027	0.009–0.013
	8—327	⑤	⑦	0.003–0.011	5	1.999–2.000	0.0007–0.0028	0.009–0.013

Crankshaft and Connecting Rod Specifications
All measurements are given in in.

Year	Engine No. Cyl Displacement (cu in.)	Crankshaft				Connecting Rod		
		Main Brg Journal Dia	Main Brg Oil Clearance	Shaft End-Play	Thrust on No.	Journal Diameter	Oil Clearance	Side Clearance
'68	4—153	2.2983–2.2993	0.0003–0.0029	0.002–0.006	5	1.999–2.000	0.0007–0.0027	0.009–0.013
	6—230	2.2983–2.2993	0.0003–0.0029	0.002–0.006	7	1.999–2.000	0.0007–0.0027	0.009–0.013
	6—250	2.2983–2.2993	0.0003–0.0029	0.002–0.006	7	1.999–2.000	0.0007–0.0027	0.009–0.013
	8—307	2.4484–2.4493[6]	0.0008–0.002[8]	0.003–0.011	5	2.099–2.100	0.0007–0.0027	0.009–0.013
	8—327	2.4484–2.4493[6]	0.0008–0.002[8]	0.003–0.011	5	2.099–2.100	0.0007–0.0028	0.009–0.013
	8—350	2.4484–2.4493[6]	0.0008–0.002[8]	0.003–0.011	5	2.099–2.100	0.0007–0.0028	0.009–0.013
	8—396	[9]	[11]	0.006–0.010	5	2.199–2.200	0.0009–0.0025	0.015–0.021
	8—396 (375 HP)	[10]	0.0013–0.0025[12]	0.006–0.010	5	2.1985–2.1995	0.0014–0.0030	0.019–0.025
'69	4—153	2.2983–2.2993	0.0003–0.0029	0.002–0.006	5	1.999–2.000	0.0007–0.0027	0.009–0.013
	6—230	2.2983–2.2993	0.0003–0.0029	0.002–0.006	7	1.999–2.000	0.0007–0.0027	0.009–0.013
	6—250	2.2983–2.2993	0.0003–0.0029	0.002–0.006	7	1.999–2.000	0.0007–0.0027	0.009–0.013
	8—307	2.4479–2.4488	0.0008–0.002[8]	0.003–0.011	5	2.099–2.100	0.0007–0.0027	0.009–0.013
	8—327	2.4479–2.4488	0.0008–0.002[8]	0.003–0.011	5	2.099–2.100	0.0007–0.0028	0.009–0.013
	8—350	2.4479–2.4488	0.0008–0.002[8]	0.003–0.011	5	2.099–2.100	0.0007–0.0028	0.009–0.013
	8—396	[9]	[11]	0.006–0.010	5	2.199–2.200	0.0009–0.0025	0.015–0.021
	8—396 (375 HP)	[10]	0.0013–0.0025[12]	0.006–0.010	5	2.1985–2.1995	0.0014–0.0030	0.019–0.025
'70	4—153	2.2983–2.2993	0.0003–0.0029	0.002–0.006	5	1.999–2.000	0.0007–0.0027	0.009–0.013
	6—230	2.2983–2.2993	0.0003–0.0029	0.002–0.006	7	1.999–2.000	0.0007–0.0027	0.009–0.013
	6—250	2.2983–2.2993	0.0003–0.0029	0.002–0.006	7	1.999–2.000	0.0007–0.0027	0.009–0.013
	8—307, 350	2.4484–2.4493[6]	0.000–0.0015[13]	0.002–0.006	5	2.099–2.100	0.0007–0.0028	0.008–0.014
'71	6—250	2.2983–2.2993	0.0003–0.0029	0.002–0.006	7	1.999–2.000	0.0007–0.0027	0.009–0.014
	8—307, 350	2.4484–2.4493[20]	0.0008–0.0020[21]	0.002–0.006	5	2.099–2.100	0.0013–0.0035	0.008–0.014
'72	6—250	2.2983–2.2993	0.0003–0.0029	0.002–0.006	7	1.999–2.000	0.0007–0.0027	0.009–0.014
	8—307, 350	2.4484–2.4493[20]	0.0008–0.0020[21]	0.002–0.006	5	2.099–2.100	0.0013–0.0035	0.008–0.014

Crankshaft and Connecting Rod Specifications

All measurements are given in in.

Year	Engine No. Cyl Displacement (cu in.)	Crankshaft				Connecting Rod		
		Main Brg Journal Dia	Main Brg Oil Clearance	Shaft End-Play	Thrust on No.	Journal Diameter	Oil Clearance	Side Clearance
'73	6—250	2.3004	0.0003–0.0029	0.002–0.006	7	1.999–2.000	0.0007–0.0027	0.009–0.014
	8—307, 350	2.4502[22]	0.0008–0.0020[21]	0.002–0.007	5	2.099–2.100	0.0013–0.0035	0.008–0.014
'74–'77	6—250	2.2988	0.0003–0.0029	0.002–0.006	7	1.9928–2.000	0.0007–0.0027	0.007–0.016
	8—262	2.4489[20]	[23]	0.002–0.006	5	2.099–2.100	0.0012–0.0035	0.008–0.014
	8—305	2.4489[20]	[23]	0.002–0.006	5	2.099–2.100	0.0013–0.0035	0.008–0.014
	8—350	2.4489[20]	[23]	0.002–0.006	5	2.099–2.100	0.0035–0.0035	0.008–0.014
'78	6—250	2.2979–2.2994	0.0010–0.0024[24]	0.002–0.006	7	1.9928–2.000	0.0010–0.0026	0.006–0.017
	8—305, 350	[24]	[25]	0.002–0.006	5	2.0986–2.0998	0.0013–0.0035	0.008–0.014
'79	6—250	2.2999	0.0003–0.0029	0.002–0.006	7	1.999–2.000	0.0007–0.0027	0.007–0.016
	8—305, 350	[26]	[27]	0.002–0.007	5	2.099–2.100	0.0013–0.0035	0.006–0.016

[1] No. 5—0.0010–0.0036
[2] No. 1—2.2987–2.2997
  Nos. 2–4—2.2983–2.2993
  No. 5—2.2978–2.2988
[5] No. 1—2.2984–2.2993
  Nos. 2–4—2.2983–2.2993
  No. 5—2.2978–2.2988
[6] No. 5—2.4478–2.4488
[7] No. 1—0.0008–0.002
  Nos. 2–4—0.0018–0.002
  No. 5—0.0010–0.0036
[8] No. 5—0.0018–0.0034

[9] Nos. 1–2—2.7484–2.7493
  Nos. 3–4—2.7481–2.7490
  No. 5—2.7478–2.7488
[10] No. 1—2.7484–2.7493
  Nos. 2–4—2.7481–2.7490
  No. 5—2.7478–2.7488
[11] Nos. 1–2—0.0010–0.0022
  Nos. 3–4—0.0013–0.0025
  No. 5—0.0015–0.0031
[12] No. 5—0.0015–0.0031
[13] Nos. 2–4—0.0006–0.0018
  No. 5—0.0008–0.0023

[20] Nos. 2–4—2.4481–2.4490
  No. 5—2.4479–2.4488
[21] Nos. 2–4—0.0011–0.0023
  No. 5—0.0017–0.0033
[22] No. 5—2.4508
[23] w/Man trans—
  No. 5—0.0023–0.0033
  w/Auto trans—
  No. 1—.0019–.0031
  Nos. 2–4—0.0013–0.0025
  No. 5—0.0023–0.0033

[24] No. 1—2.4484–2.4493
  Nos. 2, 3, 4—2.4481–2.4490
  No. 5—2.4479–2.4488
[25] No. 1—0.0008–0.0020
  Nos. 2, 3, 4—0.0011–0.0023
  No. 5—0.0017–0.0032
[26] Nos. 1–4—2.4489
  No. 5—2.4484
[27] No. 1—0.0008–0.0020
  Nos. 2, 3, 4—0.0011–0.0023
  No. 5—0.0017–0.0033

Cylinder Bore, Piston, and Ring Specifications 1962–77

Engine No. Cyl Displacement (cu in.)	Cylinders (in.)		Pistons (in.)	Rings (in.)		
	Standard Bore Diameter	Maximum Bore Oversize	Oversizes Available	Side Clearance		
				Top	Second	Oil
4—153	3.8750	0.040	0.010, 0.020, 0.030, 0.040	0.0012–0.0027	0.0012–0.0032	0.0000–0.0050
6—194	3.5625	0.040	0.010, 0.020, 0.030, 0.040	0.0012–0.0027	0.0012–0.0032	0.0000–0.0050
6—230	3.8745–3.8775	0.040	0.010, 0.020, 0.030, 0.040	0.0012–0.0027	0.0012–0.0032	0.0000–0.0050
6—250	3.8745–3.8775	0.040	0.010, 0.020, 0.030, 0.040	0.0012–0.0027	0.0012–0.0032	0.0000–0.0050
8—262	3.6710	0.040	0.010, 0.020, 0.030, 0.040	0.0012–0.0032	0.0012–0.0027	0.0000–0.0050
8—283	3.8745–3.8775	0.040	0.010, 0.020, 0.030, 0.040	0.0012–0.0027	0.0012–0.0032	0.0000–0.0050
8—307	3.8745–3.8775	0.040	0.010, 0.020, 0.030, 0.040	0.0012–0.0027	0.0012–0.0032	0.0000–0.0050
8—327 (275 hp)	3.9995–4.0025	0.040	0.010, 0.020, 0.030, 0.040	0.0012–0.0027	0.0012–0.0032	0.0000–0.0050
8—327 (300, 325, 350 hp)	3.9995–4.0025	0.040	0.010, 0.020, 0.030, 0.040	0.0012–0.0032	0.0012–0.0027	0.0000–0.0050
8—262, 305, 350	3.9995–4.0025	0.040	0.010, 0.020, 0.030, 0.040	0.0012–0.0032	0.0012–0.0027	0.0000–0.0050
8—396	4.0925–4.0995	0.040	0.010, 0.020, 0.030, 0.040	0.0017–0.0032	0.0017–0.0032	0.0050–0.0065

Piston Clearance

Year	Engine No. Cyl Displacement (cu in.)	Piston to Bore Clearance (in.)
'78–'79	6—250	0.0010–0.0020
	8—305, 350①	0.0007–0.0017

① 1979 305: 0.0017–0.0042

Ring Side Clearance
(All measurements are given in in.)

Year	Engine	Top Compression	Bottom Compression	Oil Control
'78–'79	6—250	0.0012–0.0027	0.0012–0.0032	0.000–0.005
'78–'79	8—305, 350	0.0012–0.0032	0.0012–0.0032	0.002–0.007

Ring Gap

Year	Engine	Top Compression	Bottom Compression	Year	Engine	Oil Control
'62–'64	All engines	0.010–0.020	0.010–0.020	'64–'65	All engines	0.015–0.055
'65	4—153, 6—194, 230	0.010–0.020	0.010–0.020	'66–'69	8—396)	0.010–0.030
'65	8—283, 327	0.013–0.023	0.013–0.028	'66–'79 (Except 8—396	All engines	0.015–0.055④
'66–'79	4—153, 6—194, 230, 250 8—283, 307, 396 400, 402, 454	0.010–0.020	0.010–0.020			
'66–'69	8—327	0.013–0.023①	0.013–0.025①			
'68	8—350	0.010–0.020	0.013–0.023			
'69	8—350	0.013–0.023②	0.013–0.025②			
'70–'72	8—350	0.010–0.020②	0.013–0.025②			
'73–'75	8—350, 262	0.010–0.020	0.013–0.025			
'76–'77	8—305	0.010–0.020	0.010–0.025			
	8—350 2 bbl	0.010–0.020	0.010–0.020			
	8—350 4 bbl	0.010–0.020	0.013–0.025			
'78–'79	8—305	0.010–0.020	0.010–0.025③			
'78–'79	8—350	0.010–0.025	0.013–0.025			

① 325, 350 hp Top 0.010–0.020
      2nd 0.013–0.023

② 225, 330, 350, 370 hp Top 0.010–0.020
      2nd 0.013–0.023

③ 1979—0.013–0.025

④ 1979–305—0.010–0.035

Torque Specifications
(All readings in ft lbs)

Year	Engine No. Cyl Displacement (cu in.)	Cylinder Head Bolts	Rod Bearing Bolts	Main Bearing Bolts	Crankshaft Pulley Bolt	Flywheel to Crankshaft Bolts	Manifold	
							Intake	Exhaust
'62–'63	4—153, 6—194	90–95	30–35	45–55	—	50–65	25	25
'64	4—153, 6—194	90–95	30–35	45–55	—	50–65	25	25
	8—283	60–70	30–35	60–70	—	55–65	25–35	18–22
'65	4—153, 6—194, 230	90–100	30–35	60–70	—	55–70	25	25
	8—283, 327	60–70	30–35	60–70	—	55–65	25–35	18–22
'66–'79	6—230, 250	95⑩	35	65	—	60	30⑧	25⑦⑨
'66–'67	8—283, 327	60–70	35	80	60⑥	60	30	20
'68–'77	8—262, 305, 307, 350	60–70	45	75②	60⑥	60	30	⑤
'66–'69	8—396	80①	50	105③	85⑥	65	30	30
'78–'79	8—305, 350	65	45	70	60	60	30	20

① Aluminum Heads—Short bolts 65, Long bolts 75
② Engines with 4-bolt mains—Outer bolts 65
③ 1966–68 2-bolt mains 95
   1966–67 4-bolt mains 115
⑤ Center bolts—25–30, end bolts 15–20
⑥ Where applicable
⑦ Exhaust-to-intake
⑧ With intake manifold integral with head—
   30 center, 20 on four end bolts
⑨ Outer bolts (integral head)—20
⑩ 78–79—L.H. front head bolt—85

Engine

→Unless otherwise stated, the following operations cover the four-cylinder, six-cylinder and V8 engines.

REMOVAL & INSTALLATION

1. Raise car and place it on jackstands.
2. Drain the cooling system, transmission, and crankcase. Carefully lower the vehicle.
3. Scribe alignment marks on the underside of the hood and around the hood hinges, then remove the hood from the hinges.
4. Disconnect the coolant and heater hoses at the engine attachment.
5. Disconnect the battery cables from the battery.
6. Remove the radiator and shroud assembly. Remove the fan and pulley.
7. Remove the air cleaner.

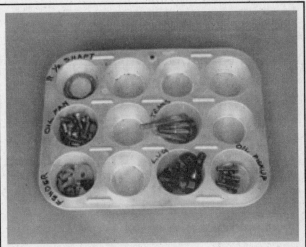

When removing nuts, bolts and other parts, place them in a tray or other container

8. Disconnect the coil, starter, and Delcotron wires, engine-to-body ground strap, oil pressure and engine temperature sender wires, and the CEC wire.

9. Disconnect the gas tank line from the fuel pump.

10. Disconnect the accelerator control linkage from the firewall.

11. Disconnect the hand choke linkage (four-cylinder) and the power brake vacuum line.

12. Disconnect the exhaust pipe from the manifold. On V8 engines, disconnect the crossover pipe.

13. Disconnect the clutch shaft bracket at the frame and disconnect the clutch linkage. On automatic transmission models, remove the transmission oil filler tube and plug the opening.

14. Attach an engine lifting tool. Attach it to a hoist and secure the engine.

15. Remove the driveshaft.

16. Remove the set aside the power steering pump and air conditioning compressor. *Do not disconnect the hoses.*

17. Remove the engine rear mounting bolts.

18. Disconnect the speedometer cable, transmission control rod linkage lower ends, TCS switch, and transmission oil cooler lines.

19. Loosen the front engine mounting bolts.

20. Raise the engine slightly and remove the bolts.

21. Remove the transmission crossmember and free the transmission rear mounting.

22. Remove the engine and transmission as a unit from the car.

To install:

23. Bolt the engine lifting tool to the engine and lower the engine and transmission into the chassis as a unit. Guide the engine to align the front engine mounts with the mounts on the frame.

24. Install one rear transmission crossmember side bolt, swing the crossmember up under the transmission mount, and install the bolt in the opposite side rail.

25. Align and install the rear mount bolts.

26. Install the engine front mount bolts and remove the lifting tool from the engine.

27. Install and connect all items in the reverse order from the engine removal procedure.

SEPARATING THE TRANSMISSION FROM THE ENGINE

Manual Transmission

1. Remove the clutch housing cover plate screws.

2. Remove the bolts holding the clutch housing to the engine block. Remove the clutch housing and transmission assembly.

3. Remove the starter and clutch housing cover plate.

4. Loosen the clutch-to-flywheel bolts, alternately, until the spring pressure is released. Remove all bolts, the clutch disc, and the pressure plate assembly.

5. Reattach the transmission by reversing the above procedure.

Automatic Transmission

1. Lower the engine and support it on suitable blocks.

2. Remove the starter and converter housing underpan.

3. Remove the flywheel-to-converter assembly attaching bolts.

4. Support the transmission on blocks.

5. Remove the transmission-to-engine mounting bolts.

6. With the engine hoist attached, remove the blocks from the engine only and slowly guide the engine from the transmission.

7. Reattach the automatic transmission by reversing the above process.

Cylinder Head

REMOVAL AND INSTALLATION

4 and 6-Cylinder Engines

◆ See Figures 3 and 4

1962–77 VEHICLES

1. Drain the cooling system and remove the air cleaner. Disconnect the PCV hose.

2. Disconnect the choke cable (four-cylinder), the accelerator pedal rod at the bellcrank on the manifold, and the fuel and vacuum lines at the carburetor.

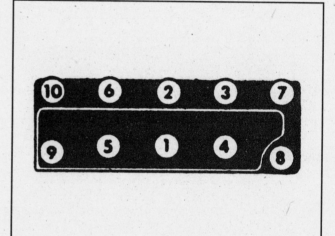

Fig. 3 Cylinder head bolt torque sequence—4-cylinder engines

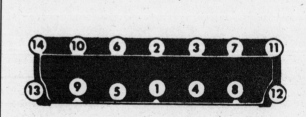

Fig. 4 Cylinder head bolt torque sequence—6-cylinder engines

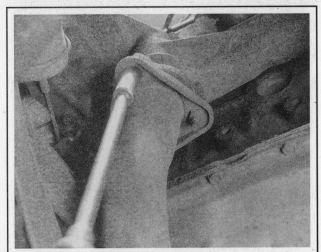

To remove the cylinder head, disconnect the exhaust pipe from the manifold flange

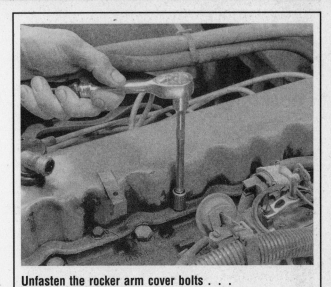

Unfasten the rocker arm cover bolts . . .

Unfasten the exhaust manifold retaining bolts . . .

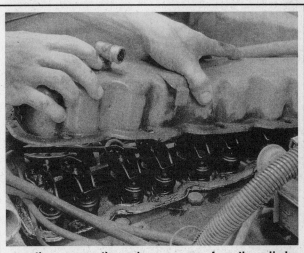

. . . then remove the rocker arm cover from the cylinder head

. . . then remove the manifold and carburetor as as assembly

Scrape off all the old gasket material

Loosen the rocker arm nuts . . .

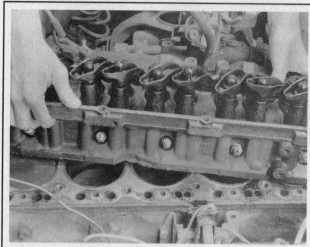

After unfastening the cylinder head bolts, remove the head from the engine block

. . . then pivot the rocker arms to clear the pushrods for removal

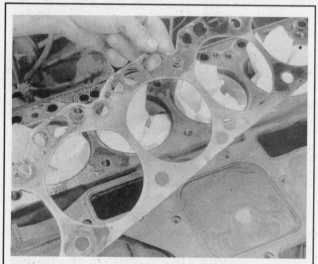

Remove and discard the cylinder head gasket

When removing the pushrods, keep them in order so they can be reinstalled in their original positions

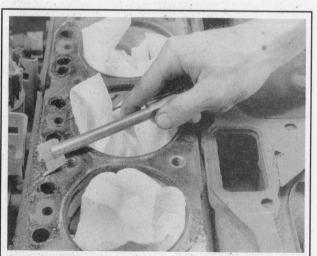

Cover the cylinder bores and carefully scrape off any remaining gasket material

Always tighten the cylinder head bolts to the proper torque using the correct sequence

3. Disconnect the exhaust pipe at the manifold flange, then remove the manifold bolts and clamps and remove the manifolds and carburetor as an assembly.

4. Remove the fuel and vacuum line retaining clip from the water outlet. Disconnect the wire harness from the heat-sending unit and coil, leaving the harness clear of the clips on the rocker arm cover.

5. Disconnect the radiator hose from the water outlet housing and the battery ground strap at the cylinder head.

6. Tag and disconnect the wires and remove the spark plugs. On the six-cylinder engine, disconnect the coil-to-distributor primary wire lead at the coil and remove the coil.

7. Remove the rocker arm cover. Back off the rocker arm nuts, pivot the rocker arms to clear the pushrods, and remove the pushrods.

8. Remove the cylinder head bolts, cylinder head, and gasket.

To install:

1. Place a new cylinder head gasket over the dowel pins in the cylinder block.

2. Guide and lower the cylinder head into place over the dowels and gasket.

3. Oil the cylinder head bolts, install, and run them down snugly.

4. Tighten the cylinder head bolts a little at a time with a torque wrench in the correct sequence. Final torque should be 90–95 ft lbs.

5. Install the valve pushrods down through the cylinder head openings and seat them in their lifter sockets.

6. Install the rocker arms, balls, and nuts, and tighten the rocker arm nuts until all pushrod play is taken up.

7. Install the thermostat, thermostat housing, and water outlet, using new gaskets. Connect the radiator hose.

8. Install the heat-sending switch and torque to 15–20 ft lbs.

9. Clean the spark plugs or install new ones. Set the gaps.

10. Torque $^{13}/_{16}$ in. hex plugs to 20 ft lbs. and $^{5}/_{8}$ in. hex plugs to 15 ft lbs. Tapered seat plugs are used on some engines starting in 1970 and all engines beginning in 1971.

11. Install the coil (on six-cylinder engines) then connect the heat-sending unit and coil primary wires, and connect the battery ground cable at the cylinder head.

12. Clean the surfaces and install a new gasket over the mani-

fold studs. Install the manifold. Install the bolts and clamps and torque as specified.

13. Connect the throttle linkage and the choke wire (on the four-cylinder engine).

14. Connect the PCV, fuel, and vacuum lines and secure the lines the clip at the water outlet.

15. Fill the cooling system and check for leaks.

16. Adjust the valve lash.

17. Install the rocker arm cover and position the wiring harness in the clips.

18. Clean and install the air cleaner.

1978–79 VEHICLES

1. Remove the intake manifold as described in the appropriate procedure in this section.

2. Remove the rocker cover. Loosen rocker arm nuts, and then rotate rocker arms to disengage them from the pushrods. Mark pushrod locations, and then remove them.

3. Drain the cooling system into a suitable container.

4. Remove fuel and vacuum lines from the clip at the thermostat housing, and disconnect all wiring from temperature sending units. Where engine has an air pump, disconnect the air injection hose at the check valve.

5. Disconnect battery ground strap. Disconnect upper radiator hose from the thermostat housing.

6. Remove cylinder head bolts, and then remove head and gasket. Inspect the head for warpage and cracks, as described below in the rebuilding section.

➡**Make sure gasket surfaces on both head and block are clean of foreign matter, and free of any nicks or heavy scratches. Bolt threads and female thread in the block must be clean. Do not use gasket sealer with a composition steel and asbestos gasket.**

7. Coat gasket with sealer, unless it's a composition gasket. Position the gasket over the dowel pins.

8. Carefully guide the head into position over the dowel pins and gasket.

9. Coat threads of all cylinder head bolts with sealing compound and install hand-tight. Then, going in the sequence shown above, tighten to 95 ft lbs. torque *in several stages*. Note that the torque for the left-hand front bolt is *85 ft lbs.* on 1978 and later engines, *not 95 ft lbs.*

10. Connect the upper radiator hose and battery ground. Connect temperature sending unit wiring, and reposition fuel and vacuum lines under the clip on the thermostat housing. Fill the cooling system.

11. Install the manifold assembly as described in the appropriate procedure in this section.

12. Install the pushrods in their former positions and adjust valve mechanism as described in the appropriate procedure.

13. Install the rocker cover with a new gasket, and tighten the bolts evenly to the required torque. Reconnect the air injection hose.

V8 Engines

♦ **See Figures 5 and 6**

1. Drain the coolant. Remove the air cleaner.

2. Disconnect the following components:

   a. Battery.

   b. Radiator and heater hose from manifold.

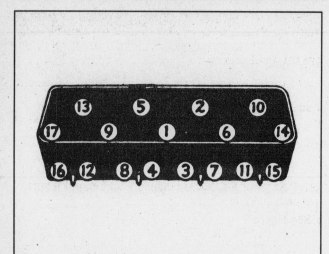

Fig. 5 Cylinder head bolt torque sequence—262, 283, 305, 307, 327 and 350 V8 engines

Fig. 6 Cylinder head bolt torque sequence—396 V8 engine

c. Throttle linkage
d. Fuel line
e. Coil wires
f. Temperature sending unit
g. Power brake hose, distributor vacuum hose, and crankcase vent hoses.
3. Remove the following components:
a. Distributor, marking position
b. Alternator upper bracket
c. Coil and bracket (where so equipped)
4. On 1977 and later engines, remove the following components, as applicable:
a. Air cleaner bracket
b. Air pump and bracket
c. Accelerator return spring and bracket
d. Accelerator bellcrank
5. Remove all manifold attaching bolts, and remove the intake manifold.
6. Disconnect the air manifold and tubes, and spark plug

wires, remove the air cleaner preheater and spark plug heat shields, loosen and remove the exhaust manifold flange nuts, then lower the exhaust pipe assembly and hang it from the frame with wire.
7. Remove the manifold end bolts, then the center ones and remove the manifold from the engine.
8. Remove rocker cover(s). Loosen rocker nuts and pivot rockers 90° to permit removal of pushrods. Remove pushrods, marking the locating of each.
9. Remove the cylinder head bolts, cylinder head, and gasket.
10. Inspect the gasket surfaces on the head(s). All surface must be clean and free of nicks and burrs. The threads on bolts and inside the boltholes in the block must be clean. Inspect the head for warpage as described in the engine rebuilding section below.
To install:
Install, reversing the removal procedures, keeping the following important points in mind:
11. Tighten the head bolts in several stages, going in the pattern specified in the illustration.
12. Coat new gaskets (both sides) and headbolts with sealer, unless a composition steel-asbestos gasket is used; in that case, put sealer on head bolts only, and leave the gasket dry.
13. Make sure to relocate pushrods according to their markings. Adjust the valves according to the procedure labeled "Engine Not Running" before running the engine. Then, readjust the valves with the engine hot and running.
14. Coat *new* rocker cover gaskets with sealer, and tighten cover bolts to specified torque evenly in several stages.

Valve Guides

Valve guides are integral with the cylinder head on all engines. Valve guide bores may be reamed to accommodate oversize valves. If wear permits, valve guides can be knurled to allow the retention of standard valves. Maximum allowable valve stem-to-guide bore clearances are listed under "Valve Specifications."

Rocker Arms

REMOVAL & INSTALLATION

Rocker arms are removed by removing the adjusting nut. Be sure to adjust the valve lash after replacing the rocker arms. Coat the replacement rocker arm and ball with SAE 90 gear oil before installation.

➡**When replacing an exhaust rocker, move an old intake rocker to the exhaust rocker arm stud and install the new rocker arm on the intake stud. This will prevent burning of the new rocker arm on the exhaust position.**

Rocker arm studs that have damaged threads or are loose in the cylinder heads may be replaced by reaming the bore and installing oversize studs. Oversizes available are .003 and .013 in. The bores may also be tapped and screw-in studs installed. Several aftermarket companies produce complete rocker arm stud kits with installation tools. Late model high-performance small-block engines use screw-in studs and pushrod guide plates.

Intake Manifold

REMOVAL & INSTALLATION

4 and 6 Cylinder Engines

Follow steps one through three of the cylinder head removal and installation procedure for these engines.

Starting with some 1975 and all later six cylinder engines, the intake manifold is cast integrally with the cylinder head.

V8 Engines

◗ **See Figures 7 and 8**

Follow steps one through five of the cylinder head removal and installation procedure for these engines.

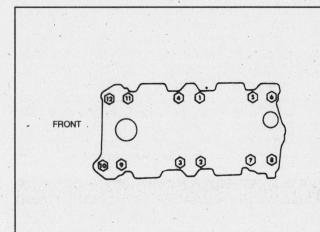

Fig. 7 Intake manifold bolt torque sequence—262, 283, 305, 307, 327 and 350 V8 engines

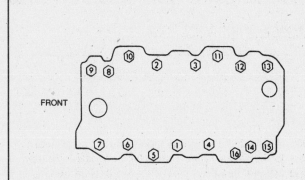

Fig. 8 Intake manifold bolt torque sequence—396 V8 engine

Exhaust Manifold

REMOVAL & INSTALLATION

4 and 6 Cylinder Engines

Follow steps one through three of the cylinder head removal and installation procedure for these engines.

1975 and Later 6 Cylinder Engines With Integral Intake Manifold/Cylinder Head

◗ **See Figure 9**

1. Remove the air cleaner.
2. Remove the power steering pump and/or AIR pump brackets, if so equipped.
3. Remove the early fuel evaporation (EFE) valve bracket.
4. Disconnect the throttle control and the throttle return spring.

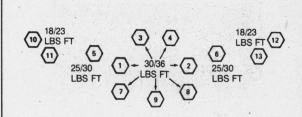

Fig. 9 Exhaust manifold bolt torque sequence—1975–79 6-cylinder engines with the integral intake manifold/cylinder head

5. Disconnect the exhaust pipe at the manifold flange.
6. Remove the manifold attaching bolts. Remove the manifold and discard the gasket.
7. Check the manifold for cracks.
   To install:
8. Clean the gasket surfaces on the cylinder head and the manifold.
9. Use a new gasket and install the exhaust manifold. Make sure to clean, oil, and torque all exhaust manifold-to-cylinder head bolts and nuts to the proper specifications (see the illustration).
10. Connect the exhaust pipe to the manifold.
11. Connect the throttle control and throttle return spring.
12. Install the air cleaner, start the engine, and check for leaks.

V8 Engines

Follow steps one through three of the cylinder head removal and installation procedure for these engines.

Timing Gear/Chain Cover

All 4 and 6 cylinder engines have gear driven camshafts, while all V8 camshafts are driven by a timing chain. 4 or 6 cylinder timing gear replacement requires camshaft removal.

➡ **The six-cylinder engine uses a harmonic balancer that closely resembles the V8 type. The removal procedure for this damper will be the same as that used for the V8. Driving the damper back onto the crankshaft without supporting the pulley can cause damage. A replacing tool must be used during the reassembly operation.**

REMOVAL & INSTALLATION

1. Drain and remove the radiator.
2. If necessary for access, remove the water pump as outlined later in this section.
3. Remove the harmonic balancer (six- and eight-cylinder) or crankshaft pulley (four-cylinder) using a puller.
4. Drain the engine oil and remove the oil pan on all engines through 1972, and on small block V8s through 1974. Remove the V8 water pump. If the oil pan isn't to be removed, cut the pan seal off flush with the block.
5. Remove the timing cover attaching screws, cover, and gasket.
6. Reverse this procedure for installation for all engines except 1975–79 V8 engines.

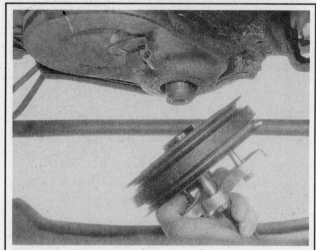

Turn the pushing screw, then remove the harmonic balancer from the crankshaft

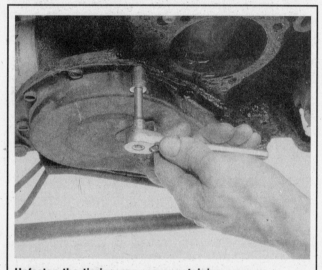

Unfasten the timing gear cover retaining screws

To access the timing cover, the harmonic balancer must be removed. Attach a puller as shown

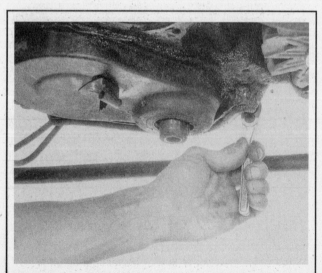

Make sure to remove the oil pan-to-timing cover bolts

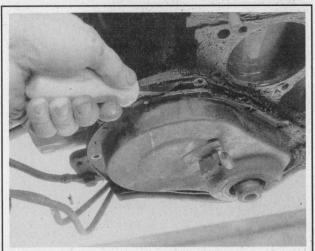

Carefully separate the timing gear cover from the engine block . . .

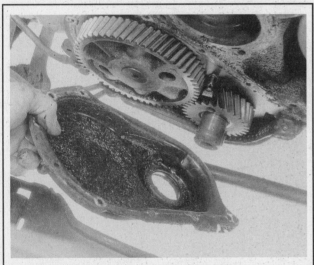

. . . then remove the cover from the vehicle

With the timing cover removed, inspect the gears or chain for wear and damage

✱✱ WARNING

The six- and eight-cylinder engines use a harmonic balancer. Breakage may occur if the balancer is hammered onto the crankshaft.
This balancer must be drawn back into place.

Cover Installation
1975–79 V8 Engines

The installation procedure for these engines has been revised. Use the following procedure.

1. Clean the block and timing cover gasket surfaces.

2. Use a sharp knife to remove any excess oil pan gasket material which may be protruding at the oil pan-to-engine block junction.

3. Apply a ⅛ in. bead of silicone rubber sealer to the joint formed at the oil pan and cylinder block, as well as the entire oil pan front lip.

4. Coat the cover gasket with gasket sealer and place it in position on the timing cover.

5. Place the timing cover on the block. Loosely install the top four bolts (approximately three turns). Install two ¼-20 × ½ in. screws one on each side at the lower hole in the front cover. Apply a bead of silicone sealer on the bottom of the seal and install the cover.

6. Tighten the cover screws alternately and evenly while using a drift to align the dowel pins in the block to the corresponding holes in the cover.

7. Remove the two screws which were used in Step 5 to draw up the cover and install the rest of the cover screws, torquing them to 80 in. lbs.

OIL SEAL REPLACEMENT

1. After removing the gear cover, carefully pry the oil seal out of the front of the cover with a large prytool.

2. Install a new lip seal with the lip (open side of seal) inside, then drive or press the seal into place.

Timing Chain

REMOVAL & INSTALLATION

V8 Engines

♦ See Figure 10

V8 models are equipped with a timing chain. To replace the chain, remove the radiator core, water pump harmonic balancer, and crankcase front cover. This will allow access to the timing chain. Crank the engine until the zero marks punched on both sprockets are closest to one another and in line between the shaft centers. Take out the three bolts that hold the camshaft gear to the camshaft. This gear is a light press fit on the camshaft and will come off readily. It is located by a dowel.

The chain comes off with the camshaft gear.

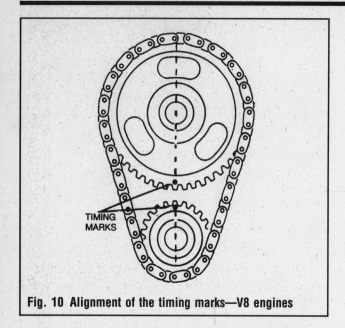

Fig. 10 Alignment of the timing marks—V8 engines

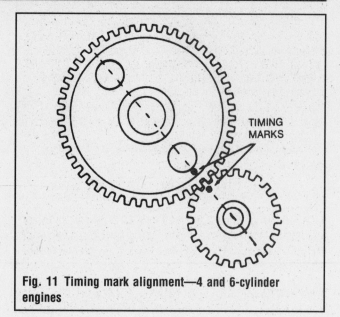

Fig. 11 Timing mark alignment—4 and 6-cylinder engines

A gear puller will be required to remove the crankshaft gear.

Without disturbing the position of the engine, mount the new crank gear on the shaft, then mount the chain over the camshaft gear. Arrange the camshaft gear in such a way that the timing marks will line up between the shaft centers and the camshaft locating dowel will enter the dowel hole in the cam sprocket.

Place the cam sprocket, with its chain mounted over it, in position on the front of the camshaft and pull up with the three bolts that hold it to the camshaft.

After the gears are in place, turn the engine two full revolutions to make certain that the timing marks are in correct alignment between the shaft centers.

Camshaft

REMOVAL & INSTALLATION

4 and 6 Cylinder Engines

▶ **See Figure 11**

1962–69 VEHICLES

1. In addition to removing the timing gear cover, remove the grille assembly.

2. Remove the valve cover and gasket, loosen all the valve rocker arm nuts, and pivot the arms clear of the pushrods.

3. Remove the distributor and fuel pump.

4. Remove the coil, side cover, and gasket. Remove the pushrods and valve lifters.

5. Remove the two camshaft thrust plate retaining screws by working through the holes in the camshaft gear.

6. Remove the camshaft and gear assembly by pulling it out through the front of the block.

➡**If renewing either the camshaft or camshaft gear, the gear must be pressed off the camshaft. The replacement parts must be assembled in the same manner (under pressure). In placing the gear on the camshaft, press the gear onto the shaft until it bottoms against the gear spacer ring.**

The end-clearance of the thrust plate should be 0.001–0.005 in.

To install:

7. Install the camshaft assembly in the engine.

8. Turn the crankshaft and camshaft to align and bring the timing marks together. Push the camshaft into this aligned position. Install the camshaft thrust plate-to-block screws and torque them to 6–7½ ft lbs.

9. Run-out on either crankshaft or camshaft gear should not exceed 0.003 in.

10. Backlash between the two gears should be 0.004–0.006 in.

11. Install the timing gear cover and gasket.

12. Install the oil pan and gaskets.

13. Install the harmonic balancer.

14. Line up the keyway in the balancer with the key on the crankshaft and the drive balancer onto the shaft until it bottoms against the crankshaft gear.

15. Install the valve lifters and pushrods. Install the side cover with a new gasket. Attach the coil wires; install the fuel pump.

16. Install the distributor and set the timing as described under "Distributor" at the beginning of this chapter.

17. Pivot the rocker arms over the pushrods and adjust the valves.

18. Add oil to the engine. Install and adjust the fan belt.

19. Install the radiator or shroud.

20. Install the grille assembly.

21. Fill the cooling system, start the engine, and check for leaks.

22. Check and adjust the timing.

1970–79 VEHICLES

The manufacturer recommends that the engine be removed from the car to remove the camshaft. However, in most cases the preceeding procedure can be used. You may also have to raise the front of the engine for clearance.

V8 Engines

1. Remove the intake manifold, valve lifters, and timing chain cover (requires oil pan removal), as described in this section.

2. Remove the grille, except on 1969 and later Novas. On these models, remove both front motor mount bolts and the right motor mount, then lower the engine until it rests on the frame.

3. On 1969 and later Novas, remove the two center bolts and the one lower bolt that secure the hood latch support. This will give adequate clearance for the cam.

4. Remove the camshaft sprocket bolts, sprocket, and timing chain. A light blow to the lower edge of a tight sprocket with a plastic mallet, should free it.

5. Install two ⁵⁄₁₆—18 × 4 in. bolts in the cam bolt holes and carefully pull the cam from the block.

6. To install, reverse the removal procedure, aligning the timing marks as illustrated.

➡ **Cam lobes must be lubricated with Molykote or equivalent before installation. All cam journals are the same diameter, so make sure cam bearings are not dislodged during installation.**

Valve Lash Adjustment

✳✳ WARNING

Final valve adjustment must be accomplished with the engine warm. However, an accurate preliminary setting is required if the engine valve train has been disturbed for mechanical work; otherwise, damage to various engine parts could occur when the engine is started. If you are checking valve adjustment on an engine which has not had any work done on it, simply perform the adjustment with the engine hot and running. If you are adjusting the valves because of cylinder head or valve work, perform the cold, "Engine Not Running" procedure first, then warm the engine and make final adjustments using the "Engine Running" procedure in Section 2.

HYDRAULIC LIFTERS

1. Adjust the rocker arm nuts to eliminate lash. This must be done when the lifter is on the base of the circle of the cam.

2. Remove the distributor cap and crank the engine until the distributor rotor points to no. 1 cylinder terminal, with the points open.

The following valves can be adjusted with the engine in the no. 1 firing position:

OHV 6—Intake no. 1, 2, 4, Exhaust no. 1, 3, 5
V8—Intake no. 1, 2, 5, 7, Exhaust no. 1, 3, 4, 8

3. Turn the adjusting nut until all lash is removed from this particular valve train. This can be determined by checking pushrod side-play while turning the adjustment. When all play has been removed, turn the adjusting nut one more turn except on 1976–77 engines. On these, turn the nut ¾ turn. This will place the lifter plunger in the center of its travel.

4. Follow steps two and three to adjust the remaining valves.

The following valves can be adjusted with the engine in the no. 6 firing position:

OHV 6—Intake no. 3, 5, 6, Exhaust no. 2, 4, 6
V8—Intake no. 3, 4, 6, 8, Exhaust no. 2, 5, 6, 7

5. Readjust using "Engine Running" procedure in section 2.

MECHANICAL LIFTERS

1. Set the engine to the no. 1 firing position.

2. Adjust the clearance between the valve stems and the rocker arms with a feeler gauge. Check the Mechanical Valve Lifter Clearance chart for the proper clearance. Adjust the following valves in the no. 1 firing position: Intake no. 2, 7, Exhaust no. 4, 8.

3. Turn the crankshaft one-half revolution clockwise. Adjust the following valves: Intake no. 1, 8, Exhaust no. 3, 6.

4. Turn the crankshaft one-half revolution clockwise to no. 6 firing position. Adjust the following valves in the no. 6 firing position: Intake no. 3, 4, Exhaust no. 5, 7.

5. Turn the crankshaft one-half revolution clockwise. Adjust the following valves: Intake no. 5, 6, Exhaust no. 1, 2.

6. Reset all clearances using the procedure in section 2.

Valve Lifters

REMOVAL & INSTALLATION

Inline Engines

1. Remove the rocker arm cover.
2. Remove the pushrod covers.

➡ **Keep all components in order. If reusing components, install them into their original positions. If a new hydraulic lifter is being installed, all sealer coating inside the lifter must be removed.**

3. Remove the pushrods.
4. Remove the lifters.

5. Inspect the lifter and lifter bore for wear and scuffing. Examine the roller for freedom of movement and/or flat spots on the roller surface.

6. Installation is the reverse of removal, be sure to lubricate the lifter and lifter body using clean engine oil. If installing new lifters, all sealer coating inside the lifter must first be removed.

7. When installing the pushrod cover, use a thin coating of

On inline engines, access the lifters through the pushrod cover

After removing the retaining bolts, separate the cover from the block

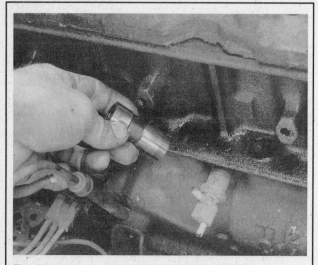

The lifters can now be withdrawn from their bores

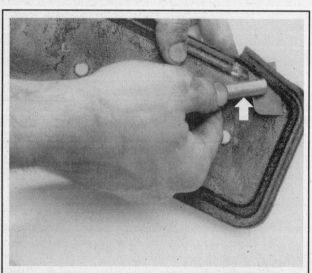

Use a suitable tool to scrape off the old gasket material

On V-type engines, the lifters can be accessed after removing the intake manifold

RTV sealant around the entire cover flange. Install the cover retaining nuts.

➡ **Use of a Hydraulic Lifter Remover tool J-9290-1 (slide hammer type) or J-3049-A (plier type) will greatly ease the removal of stuck lifters.**

1. Remove the rocker arm covers.
2. Remove the intake manifold.
3. Remove the rocker arm nuts and balls.
4. Remove the rocker arms and pushrods.

➡ **If any valve train components (lifters, pushrods, rocker arms) are to be reused, they must be tagged or arranged during removal to assure installation in their original locations.**

5. Remove the lifters from the bores.

To install:

6. For proper rotation during engine operation, the lifter bottom must be convex. Check the lifter bottom for proper shape using a straight edge. If the lifter bottom is not convex, replace the

lifter. Chances are if lifters are in need of replacement, so is the camshaft.

7. Lubricate and install the lifters. If installing new lifters, coat the lifter body and foot using Molykote® or an equivalent pre-lue, then add 1051396 or an equivalent engine oil supplement to the crankcase.

8. Install the pushrods, rocker arms, rocker arm nuts and balls, then properly adjust the valve lash.

9. Install the intake manifold.

10. Install the rocker arm covers.

Pistons and Connecting Rods

REMOVAL

▶ **See Figures 12, 13 and 14**

1. Drain the crankcase and remove the oil pan.
2. Drain the cooling system and remove the cylinder heads.

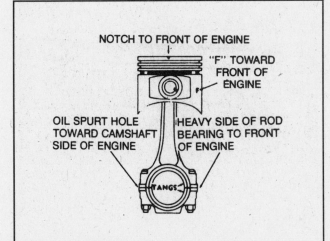

Fig. 12 Piston and connecting rod assembly—4 and 6-cylinder engines

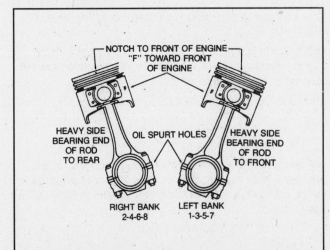

Fig. 13 Piston and connecting rod assembly—small block V8 engines

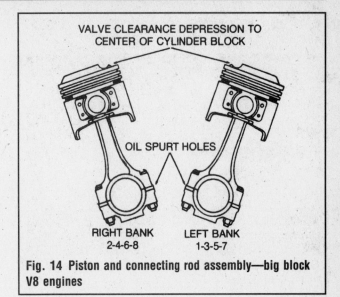

Fig. 14 Piston and connecting rod assembly—big block V8 engines

3. Remove any ridge or deposits from the upper end of the cylinder bores with a ridge reamer.

4. Check the rods and pistons for identification numbers and, if necessary, number them.

5. Remove the connecting rod cap nuts and caps. Push the rods away from the crankshaft and install the caps and nuts loosely to their respective rods.

6. Push the piston and rod assemblies up and out of the cylinders.

INSPECTION

1. Before replacing rings, inspect the cylinder bores. If the cylinder bore is in satisfactory condition, place each ring in its bore in turn and square it in the bore with the head of the piston. Measure the ring end-gap. If the gap is greater than the limit, get a new ring. If the gap is less than the limit, file the end of the ring to obtain the correct gap.

2. Check the ring side-clearance by installing rings on the piston and inserting a feeler gauge of the correct dimension between the ring and the lower land. The gauge should slide freely around the circumference of the ring without binding. Any wear will form a step on the lower land. Replace any pistons having high steps. Before checking ring side-clearance, be sure the ring grooves are clean and free of carbon, sludge, or grit.

3. Space the ring gaps at equal intervals around the circumference of the piston. Be sure to install the piston in its original bore.

INSTALLATION

Install the piston and rod assembly with the connecting rod bearing tang slots on the side opposite the camshaft, on V8 engines. Inline engine pistons must have the piston notch facing the front of the engine. Install short lengths of rubber tubing over the connecting rod bolts to prevent damage to the rod journals. Install a ring compressor over the rings on the piston. Lower the piston and rod assembly into the bore until the ring compressor contacts the block. Using the wooden handle of a hammer, push the piston into the bore while guiding the rod onto the journal.

Oil Pan

REMOVAL & INSTALLATION

4 and 6 Cylinder Engines

1962–67 VEHICLES

1. Disconnect the battery ground strap at the battery.
2. Drain the oil from the engine.
3. Disconnect all wires from the starter. Remove the starter.
4. Disconnect the steering idler arm bracket at the right-hand frame rail. Swing the linkage down for pan clearance.
5. Remove the front crossmember from six-cylinder engines only.

➡On a station wagon, let the stabilizer bar hang while removing the crossmember.

6. Remove the oil pan bolts, drop the pan, and clean off the gaskets and end seals.
7. Reverse the above to install the oil pan.

1968–79 VEHICLES

1. Disconnect the battery ground cable.
2. Remove the front engine mount bolts.

➡Remove the upper radiator panel or side mount bolts from post-1969 cars.

3. Drain the coolant. Remove the radiator hoses.
4. Remove the fan.
5. Drain the engine oil.
6. On all pre-1974 models, and 1975 and later models with manual transmission, disconnect and remove the starter.
7. Disconnect the oil cooler lines and remove the converter housing underpan.
8. Disconnect the steering rod at the idler lever. Swing the linkage to one side for pan clearance.
9. Rotate the crankshaft until the timing mark on the torsional damper is at the six o'clock position.
10. Raise the engine enough to insert 2×4 in. blocks under the engine mounts.
11. Unbolt oil pan. On some models it may be necessary to remove the oil pump and intake pipe for clearance. On Nova, remove the left engine mount and frame bracket. Lower the pan slightly and roll it into the area where the mount was. Then tilt the front of the pan up and pull it down and to the rear. Lower the pan.
12. Reverse the above to install the oil pan.

V8 Engines

1964–67 VEHICLES

1. Disconnect the battery ground cable.
2. Drain the engine oil into a suitable container.
3. Disconnect and remove the starter.
4. Disconnect the steering idler arm bracket at the right frame rail. Swing the linkage down for clearance.
5. Disconnect the exhaust pipes from the manifolds.

6. Remove the oil pan.
7. Installation is the reverse of the above.

1968 AND 1970–79 VEHICLES

1. Disconnect the battery ground cable.
2. Remove the distributor cap.
3. Remove the radiator upper mounting panel.
4. Remove the fan. On Mark IV (big block) engine models, place a piece of heavy cardboard between the radiator and fan.
5. Drain the engine oil.
6. Disconnect the exhaust or crossover pipes.
7. Remove the converter housing underpan and splash shield.
8. Disconnect the steering idler lever at the frame. Swing the linkage down.
9. Rotate the crankshaft until the timing mark on the torsional damper is at the six o'clock position.
10. Remove the starter.
11. On small block V8s through 1970, remove the fuel pump.
12. Remove the front engine mount thru-bolts.
13. Raise the engine and insert blocks under the engine mounts. Block thickness should be 2 in.
14. Remove the oil pan.
15. Installation is the reverse of the above.

1969 VEHICLES

1. Disconnect battery positive cable. Remove the distributor cap and set it aside.
2. Remove the upper radiator mounting panel. On cars with 396 engines, put a piece of heavy cardboard between the fan and radiator.
3. Drain the engine oil. Disconnect the exhaust pipes (dual exhaust) or crossover pipe. On vehicles with automatic transmissions, remove the pan located under the converter housing and the splash shield.
4. Disconnect the steering idler lever at the frame and swing the linkage down and out of the way.
5. Rotate the crankshaft until the timing mark on the vibration damper is at 6 o'clock position.
6. Disconnect the starter brace at the starter. Then, remove the inboard starter bolt, but just loosen the outboard bolt slightly. Swing the starter outward using the outboard bolt as a hinge.
7. Remove the through bolts from the two front engine mounts.
8. Raise the engine far enough to place a 2″ long wooden block between the mounts and the crossmember on either side. Use a suitable jack (with a block of wood to protect the oil pan) on 396 engines. On smaller V8s a special tool such as Chevrolet Tool J-8105 is required. To raise the engine with the special device shown:
   A. Punch out pin, remove tip, and then remove the yoke from the bolt portion of the tool.
   B. Insert the bolt portion of the tool upward through the hole in the crossmember, and screw the yoke onto the bolt.
   C. Place the tip on the end of the bolt. Then turn the bolt with the tip centered under the vibration damper. Continue to turn the bolt until the engine has been raised 2″ for installation of support blocks.
9. Remove the oil pan bolts, and remove the oil pan.
10. To install, reverse the removal procedure, bearing the following in mind:
    A. Clean all gasket surfaces thoroughly. Use all new gaskets.

B. Install front and rear seals snugly in appropriate grooves so they will butt up against side gaskets.

C. Install side gaskets on block using gasket sealer as a retainer.

Rear Main Oil Seal

REMOVAL & INSTALLATION

▶ **See Figures 15 and 16**

The rear main bearing seal may be replaced without removing the crankshaft. Seals should only be replaced as a pair. Fabrication of a seal installation tool as shown in the figure will prevent damaging the bead on the cylinder block. The seal lips should face the front of the engine when properly installed.

1. Remove the oil pan and the oil pump.
2. Remove the rear main bearing cap.
3. Pry the lower half of the old seal from the rear main bearing cap.
4. Position a brass punch at one end of the upper seal half. Using a small hammer, tap the punch until the other end of the seal protrudes far enough to be grasped with a pair of pliers. Pull out the old seal.
5. Clean all sealant and foreign matter from the engine block bearing cap and the crankshaft.

To install:

6. Coat the lips and bead of the new upper seal half with light engine oil, but do not oil the mating ends of the seal.
7. Insert the tip of the installation tool between the crankshaft and the seal seat of the cylinder block. Place the seal between the tip of the tool and the crankshaft, so that the bead contacts the tip of the tool. Be sure that the seal lip is facing the front of the engine, and work the seal around the crankshaft, using the installation tool to protect the seal from the corner of the cylinder block.

➡**Do not remove the tool until the opposite end of the seal is flush with the cylinder block surface.**

8. Remove the installation tool, being careful not to pull the seal out at the same time.
9. Using the same procedure, install the lower seal into the

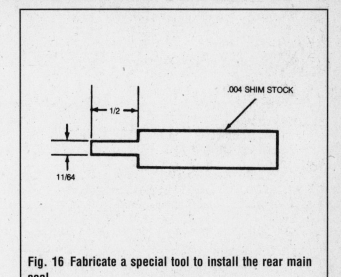

Fig. 16 Fabricate a special tool to install the rear main seal

bearing cap. Using your finger and thumb to lever the seal into the cap.

10. Apply a suitable sealant to the mating faces of the engine block and the bearing cap. (See illustration.) Be careful to keep sealant off the seal split line. Fit the bearing cap to the engine block and torque the cap bolts to specifications.

11. Install the oil pump and the oil pan.

Oil Pump

REMOVAL & INSTALLATION

▶ **See Figure 17**

4 and 6 Cylinder Engines

1. Remove the oil pan.
2. Withdraw the two oil pump flange bolts. Withdraw the pump pick-up pipe bolt (if so equipped).
3. Remove the oil pump and screen as an assembly.

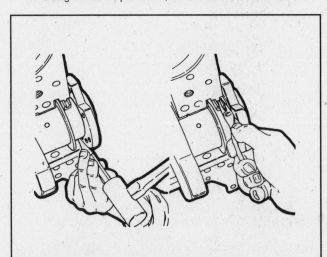

Fig. 15 Removing the upper half of the rear main bearing oil seal

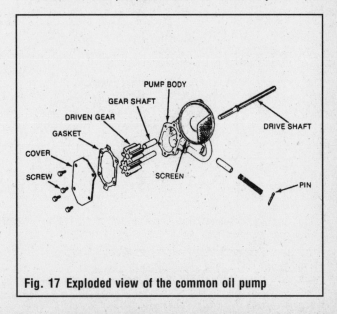

Fig. 17 Exploded view of the common oil pump

To install:

4. Align the oil pump driveshaft with the distributor tang. Fit the oil pump to the engine block so that the pump flange is over the distributor lower bushing. Do not use any gaskets.

5. Install the oil pan.

V8 Engines

1. Remove the oil pan.

2. Withdraw the oil pump-to-rear main bearing cap bolt and remove the pump and extension shaft.

To install:

3. Fit the pump and extension shaft to the rear main bearing cap. Align the slot on the top of the extension shaft with the drive tang at the lower end of the distributor driveshaft. Install the oil pump-to-rear main bearing cap bolt.

4. Install the oil pan.

Radiator

A standard pressure cooling system is used on all models. The radiator cap is designed to maintain a cooling system pressure of about 13 or 15 pounds per square inch (psi) above atmospheric. The water pump requires no attention other than making certain the air vent at the top of the housing and the drain holes in the bottom do not become clogged.

1973 and later models are equipped with a coolant recovery system. The plastic reservoir prevents loss of coolant if the engine overheats by allowing for coolant expansion.

REMOVAL & INSTALLATION

▶ **See Figure 18**

1. Drain the radiator.

2. Disconnect the hoses and oil cooler lines.

3. Remove the radiator upper panel and shroud (if so equipped).

4. Remove the radiator attaching bolts and lift the radiator from the car.

Before removing the radiator, drain the coolant into a suitable container

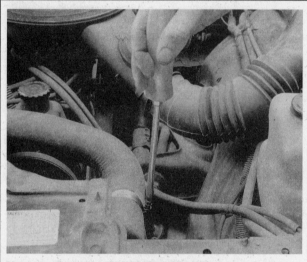

Unfasten the upper radiator hose clamp screw . . .

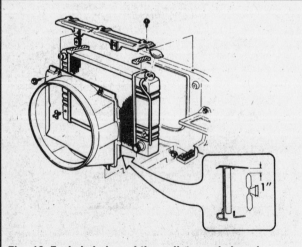

Fig. 18 Exploded view of the radiator and shroud mounting—1968–79 6 and 8-cylinder engines

. . . then disconnect the upper hose from the radiator

Use pliers to unfasten the overflow hose clip . . .

Disconnect the automatic transmission oil cooler lines, then plug them to prevent contamination

. . . then disconnect the overflow hose from the radiator

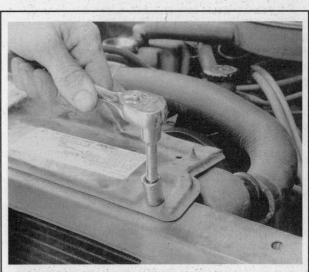

Unfasten the radiator shroud mounting bolts . . .

Use a flare-nut wrench to loosen the automatic transmission oil cooler lines

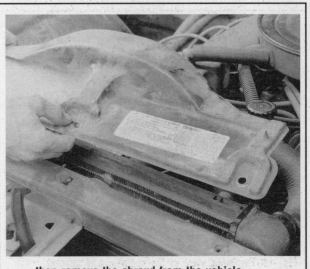

. . . then remove the shroud from the vehicle

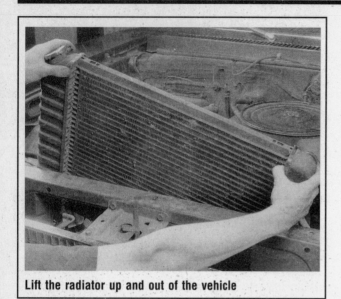

Lift the radiator up and out of the vehicle

. . . then remove the fan and the spacer

To install:
5. Slide the radiator into position.
6. Install the attaching bolts, shroud, and upper panel.
7. Install the hoses and close the drain.
8. Fill the cooling system and run the engine until the operating temperature has been reached. Again fill the cooling system and check for leaks.

Water Pump

REMOVAL & INSTALLATION

1. Drain the radiator. Loosen the fan pulley bolts.
2. Disconnect the heater hose, lower radiator hose, and bypass hose (as required) at the water pump, if accessible at this time.
3. Remove the Delcotron upper brace (V8 only), loosen the swivel bolt, and remove the fan belt.

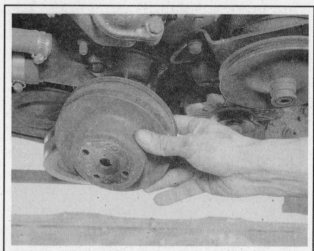

With the fan removed, simply slide the pulley off of the pump hub

Remove the fan to access the water pump. Unfasten the retaining bolts . . .

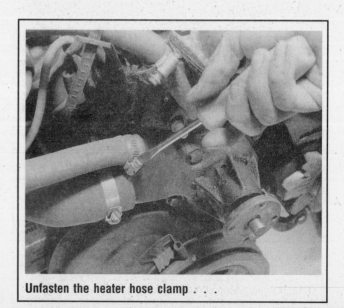

Unfasten the heater hose clamp . . .

. . . then disconnect the heater hose from the water pump

After loosening the lower radiator hose clamp, disconnect the hose from the water pump

Unfasten the water pump retaining bolts . . .

➡On Mark IV (big block) engines, disconnect the power steering and air conditioning belts and pivot the power steering pump to one side.

4. Remove the fan blade assembly bolts, fan, and pulley. Thermostatic fan clutches must not be tilted on removal or the silicone fluid will leak out.

5. If not already done, disconnect the heater hose, lower radiator hose and bypass hose (as required) from the water pump.

6. Remove the pump bolts, pump, and gasket. On inline engines, pull the pump straight out to avoid impeller damage.

7. Installation is the reverse of the removal procedure.

Thermostat

REMOVAL & INSTALLATION

The thermostat is mounted in the housing at the cylinder head water outlet above the water pump. When replacing the thermo-

. . . then remove the water pump from the engine

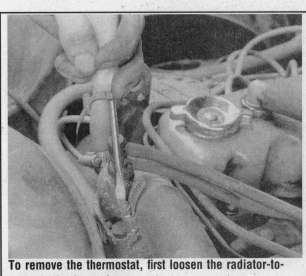

To remove the thermostat, first loosen the radiator-to-water outlet hose clamp

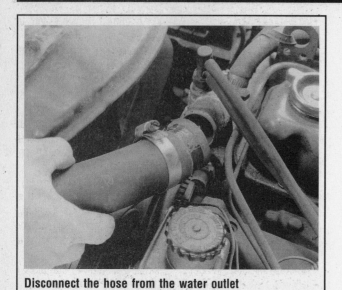

Disconnect the hose from the water outlet

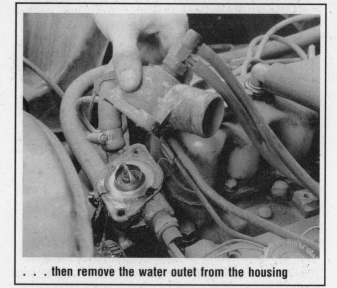

. . . then remove the water outet from the housing

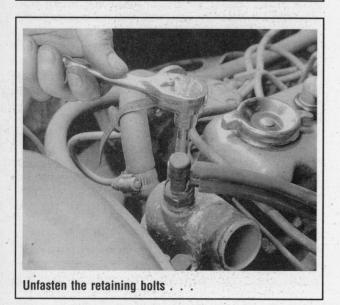

Unfasten the retaining bolts . . .

To remove the thermostat, simply lift it from the housing

stat, be sure that the new thermostat is the correct unit for the engine in which it will be installed.

1. Remove the radiator-to-water outlet hose.
2. Withdraw the thermostat housing bolts.
3. Remove the water outlet and the thermostat from the housing.

To install:

4. Install the new thermostat with a new gasket in the housing.
5. Install the water outlet and the radiator hose.
6. Start the engine and check for leaks around the thermostat housing and the radiator hose. Check the coolant level and add if necessary.

EXHAUST SYSTEM

General Information

➡ **Safety glasses should be worn at all times when working on or near the exhaust system. Older exhaust systems will almost always be covered with loose rust particles which will shower you when disturbed. These particles are more than a nuisance and could injure your eye.**

Whenever working on the exhaust system always keep the following in mind:

• Check the complete exhaust system for open seams, holes loose connections, or other deterioration which could permit exhaust fumes to seep into the passenger compartment.

• The exhaust system is usually supported by free-hanging rubber mountings which permit some movement of the exhaust system, but does not permit transfer of noise and vibration into the passenger compartment. Do not replace the rubber mounts with solid ones.

• Before removing any component of the exhaust system, ALWAYS squirt a liquid rust dissolving agent onto the fasteners for ease of removal. A lot of knuckle skin will be saved by following this rule. It may even be wise to spray the fasteners and allow them to sit overnight.

✸✸ CAUTION

Allow the exhaust system to cool sufficiently before spraying a solvent exhaust fasteners. Some solvents are highly flammable and could ignite when sprayed on hot exhaust components.

• Annoying rattles and noise vibrations in the exhaust system are usually caused by misalignment of the parts. When aligning the system, leave all bolts and nuts loose until all parts are properly aligned, then tighten, working from front to rear.

• When installing exhaust system parts, make sure there is enough clearance between the hot exhaust parts and pipes and hoses that would be adversely affected by excessive heat. Also make sure there is adequate clearance from the floor pan to avoid possible overheating of the floor.

SPECIAL TOOLS

A number of special exhaust system tools can be rented from auto supply houses or local stores that rent special equipment. A common one is a tail pipe expander, designed to enable you to join pipes of identical diameter.

It may also be quite helpful to use solvents designed to loosen rusted bolts or flanges. Soaking rusted parts the night before you do the job can speed the work of freeing rusted parts considerably. Remember that these solvents are often flammable. Apply only to parts after they are cool!

COMPONENT REPLACEMENT

System components may be welded or clamped together. The system consists of a head pipe, catalytic converter (depending upon vehicle year), intermediate pipe, muffler and tail pipe, in that order from the engine to the back of the car.

The head pipe is bolted to the exhaust manifold. Various hangers suspend the system from the floor pan. When assembling exhaust system parts, the relative clearances around all system parts is extremely critical. Observe all clearances during assembly. In the event that the system is welded, the various parts will have to be cut apart for removal. In these cases, the cut parts may not be reused. To cut the parts, a hacksaw is the best choice. An oxyacetylene cutting torch may be faster but the sparks are DANGEROUS near the fuel tank, and, at the very least, accidents could happen, resulting in damage to other under-car parts, not to mention yourself!

The following replacement steps relate to clamped parts:

1. Raise and support the car on jackstands. It's much easier on you if you can get the car up on 4 stands. Some pipes need lots of clearance for removal and installation. If the system has been in the car for a long time, spray the clamped joints with a rust dissolving solutions such as WD-40® or Liquid Wrench®, and let it set according to the instructions on the can.

2. Remove the nuts from the U-bolts; don't be surprised if the U-bolts break while removing the nuts. Age and rust account for this. Besides, you shouldn't reuse old U-bolts. When unbolting the headpipe from the exhaust manifold, make sure that the bolts are free before trying to remove them. If you snap a stud in the exhaust manifold, the stud will have to be removed with a bolt extractor, which often necessitates the removal of the manifold itself.

3. After the clamps are removed from the joints, first twist the parts at the joints to break loose rust and scale, then pull the components apart with a twisting motion. If the parts twist freely but won't pull apart, check the joint. The clamp may have been installed so tightly that it has caused a slight crushing of the joint. In this event, the best thing to do is secure a chisel designed for the purpose and, using the chisel and a hammer, peel back the female pipe end until the parts are freed.

4. Once the parts are freed, check the condition of the pipes which you had intended keeping. If their condition is at all in doubt, replace them too. You went to a lot of work to get one or more components out. You don't want to have to go through that again in the near future. If you are retaining a pipe, check the pipe end. If it was crushed by a clamp, it can be restored to its original diameter using a pipe expander, which can be rented at most good auto parts stores. Check, also, the condition of the exhaust system hangers. If ANY deterioration is noted, replace them. Oh, and one note about parts: use only parts designed for your car. Don't use fits-all parts or flex pipes. The fits-all parts never fit and the flex pipes don't last very long.

5. When installing the new parts, coat the pipe ends with exhaust system lubricant. It makes fitting the parts much easier. It's also a good idea to assemble all the parts in position before clamping them. This will ensure a good fit, detect any problems and allow you to check all clearances between the parts and surrounding frame and floor members.

6. When you are satisfied with all fits and clearances, install the clamps. If the studs were rusty, wire-brush them clean and spray them with WD-40® or Liquid Wrench®. This will ensure a proper torque reading. Position the clamps on the slip points as illustrated. The slits in the female pipe ends should be under the U-bolts, not under the clamp end. Tighten the U-bolt nuts securely, without crushing the pipe. The pipe fit should be tight, so that you can't swivel the pipe by hand. Don't forget: always use new clamps. When the system is tight, recheck all clearances. Start the engine and check the joints for leaks. A leak can be felt by hand. MAKE CERTAIN THAT THE CAR IS SECURE ON THE JACKSTANDS BEFORE GETTING UNDER IT WITH THE ENGINE RUNNING!! If any leaks are detected, tighten the clamp until the leak stops. If the pipe starts to deform before the leak stops, reposition the clamp and tighten it. If that still doesn't stop the leak, it may be that you don't have enough overlap on the pipe fit. Shut off the engine, let it cool, and try pushing the pipe together further. Be careful, the pipe gets hot quickly.

7. When everything is tight and secure, lower the car and take it for a road test. Make sure there are no unusual sounds or vibration. Most new pipes are coated with a preservative, so the system will be pretty smelly for a day or two while the coating burns off.

ENGINE REBUILDING

Engine Overhaul Tips

Most engine overhaul procedures are fairly standard. In addition to specific parts replacement procedures and specifications for your individual engine, this section is also a guide to acceptable rebuilding procedures. Examples of standard rebuilding practice are given and should be used along with specific details concerning your particular engine.

Competent and accurate machine shop services will ensure maximum performance, reliability and engine life. In most instances it is more profitable for the do-it-yourself mechanic to remove, clean and inspect the component, buy the necessary parts and deliver these to a shop for actual machine work.

On the other hand, much of the rebuilding work (crankshaft, block, bearings, piston rods, and other components) is well within the scope of the do-it-yourself mechanic's tools and abilities. You will have to decide for yourself the depth of involvement you desire in an engine repair or rebuild.

TOOLS

The tools required for an engine overhaul or parts replacement will depend on the depth of your involvement. With a few exceptions, they will be the tools found in a mechanic's tool kit (see Section 1 of this manual). More in-depth work will require some or all of the following:
• A dial indicator (reading in thousandths) mounted on a universal base
• Micrometers and telescope gauges
• Jaw and screw-type pullers
• Scraper
• Valve spring compressor
• Ring groove cleaner
• Piston ring expander and compressor
• Ridge reamer
• Cylinder hone or glaze breaker
• Plastigage®
• Engine stand

The use of most of these tools is illustrated in this chapter. Many can be rented for a one-time use from a local parts jobber or tool supply house specializing in automotive work.

Occasionally, the use of special tools is called for. See the information on Special Tools and the Safety Notice in the front of this book before substituting another tool.

INSPECTION TECHNIQUES

Procedures and specifications are given in this chapter for inspecting, cleaning and assessing the wear limits of most major components. Other procedures such as Magnaflux® and Zyglo® can be used to locate material flaws and stress cracks. Magnaflux® is a magnetic process applicable only to ferrous materials. The Zyglo® process coats the material with a fluorescent dye penetrant and can be used on any material.

Checking for suspected surface cracks can be more readily made using spot check dye. The dye is sprayed onto the sus-

pected area, wiped off and the area sprayed with a developer. Cracks will show up brightly.

OVERHAUL TIPS

Aluminum has become extremely popular for use in engines, due to its low weight. Observe the following precautions when handling aluminum parts:
• Never hot tank aluminum parts (the caustic hot tank solution will eat the aluminum.
• Remove all aluminum parts (identification tag, etc.) from engine parts prior to the tanking.
• Always coat threads lightly with engine oil or anti-seize compounds before installation, to prevent seizure.
• Never overtorque bolts or spark plugs especially in aluminum threads.

Stripped threads in any component can be repaired using any of several commercial repair kits (Heli-Coil®, Microdot®, Keenserts®, etc.).

When assembling the engine, any parts that will be exposed to frictional contact must be prelubed to provide lubrication at initial start-up. Any product specifically formulated for this purpose can be used, but engine oil is not recommended as a prelube in most cases.

When semi-permanent (locked, but removable) installation of bolts or nuts is desired, threads should be cleaned and coated with Loctite® or another similar, commercial non-hardening sealant.

REPAIRING DAMAGED THREADS

Several methods of repairing damaged threads are available. Heli-Coil® (shown here), Keenserts® and Microdot® are among the most widely used. All involve basically the same principle—drilling out stripped threads, tapping the hole and installing a pre-

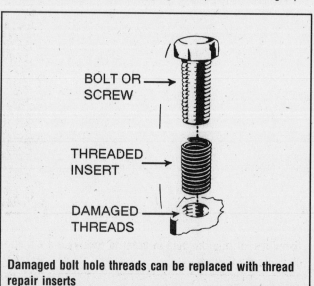

Damaged bolt hole threads can be replaced with thread repair inserts

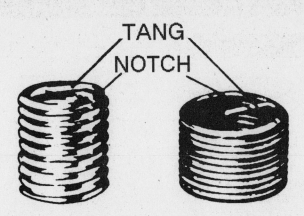

Standard thread repair insert (left), and spark plug thread insert

Drill out the damaged threads with the specified size bit. Be sure to drill completely through the hole or to the bottom of a blind hole

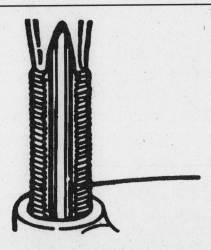

Using the kit, tap the hole in order to receive the thread insert. Keep the tap well oiled and back it out frequently to avoid clogging the threads

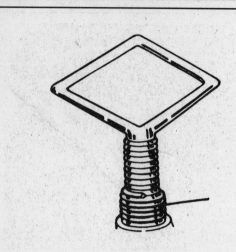

Screw the insert onto the installer tool until the tang engages the slot. Thread the insert into the hole until it is ¼–½ turn below the top surface, then remove the tool and break off the tang using a punch

wound insert—making welding, plugging and oversize fasteners unnecessary.

Two types of thread repair inserts are usually supplied: a standard type for most inch coarse, inch fine, metric course and metric fine thread sizes and a spark lug type to fit most spark plug port sizes. Consult the individual tool manufacturer's catalog to determine exact applications. Typical thread repair kits will contain a selection of prewound threaded inserts, a tap (corresponding to the outside diameter threads of the insert) and an installation tool. Spark plug inserts usually differ because they require a tap equipped with pilot threads and a combined reamer/tap section. Most manufacturers also supply blister-packed thread repair inserts separately in addition to a master kit containing a variety of taps and inserts plus installation tools.

Before attempting to repair a threaded hole, remove any snapped, broken or damaged bolts or studs. Penetrating oil can be used to free frozen threads. The offending item can usually be removed with locking pliers or using a screw/stud extractor. After the hole is clear, the thread can be repaired, as shown in the series of accompanying illustrations and in the kit manufacturer's instructions.

Completing the Rebuilding Process

Follow the above procedures, complete the rebuilding process as follows:

Fill the oil pump with oil, to prevent cavitating (sucking air) on initial engine start up. Install the oil pump and the pickup tube on the engine. Coat the oil pan gasket as necessary, and install the gasket and the oil pan. Mount the flywheel and the crankshaft vibration damper or pulley on the crankshaft.

➤**Always use new bolts when installing the flywheel.**

Inspect the clutch shaft pilot bushing in the crankshaft. If the bushing is excessively worn, remove it with an expanding puller and a slide hammer, and tap a new bushing into place.

Position the engine, cylinder head side up. Lubricate the lifters, and install them into their bores. Install the cylinder head, and torque it as specified. Insert the pushrods and install the rocker shaft(s) or position the rocker arms on the pushrods. Adjust the valves.

Install the intake and exhaust manifolds, the carburetor(s), the distributor and spark plugs. Adjust the point gap and the static ignition timing. Mount all accessories and install the engine in the car. Fill the radiator with coolant, and the crankcase with high quality engine oil.

Break-in Procedure

Start the engine, and allow it to run at low speed for a few minutes, while checking for leaks. Stop the engine, check the oil level, and fill as necessary. Restart the engine, and fill the cooling system to capacity. Check the point dwell angle and adjust the ignition timing and the valves. Run the engine at low to medium speed (800–2500 rpm) for approximately ½ hour, and retorque the cylinder head bolts. Road test the car, and check again for leaks.

Follow the manufacturer's recommended engine break-in procedure and maintenance schedule for new engines.

Cylinder Head

RECONDITIONING

Removing the Cylinder Head

See the engine service procedures earlier in this chapter for details concerning specific engines.

Identifying the Valves

Invert the cylinder head, and number the valve faces front to rear, using a permanent felt-tip marker.

Removing the Rocker Arms

Remove the rocker arms with shaft(s) or balls and nuts. Wire the sets of rockers, balls and nuts together, and identify according to the corresponding valve.

Removing the Valves and Springs

Using an appropriate valve spring compressor (depending on the configuration of the cylinder head), compress the valve springs. Lift out the keepers with needlenose pliers, release the compressor, and remove the valve, spring, and spring retainer. See the engine service procedures earlier in this chapter for details concerning specific engines.

Use a valve spring compressor tool to relieve spring tension from the valve caps

Once the spring has been removed, the O-ring may be removed from the valve stem

A small magnet will help in removal of the valve keepers

Be careful not to lose the valve keepers

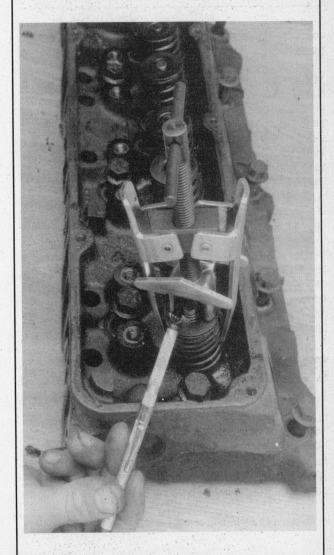

A magnet may be helpful in removing the valve keepers

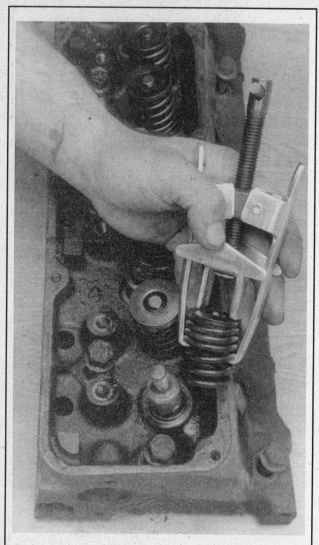

Remove the spring from the valve stem in order to access the seal

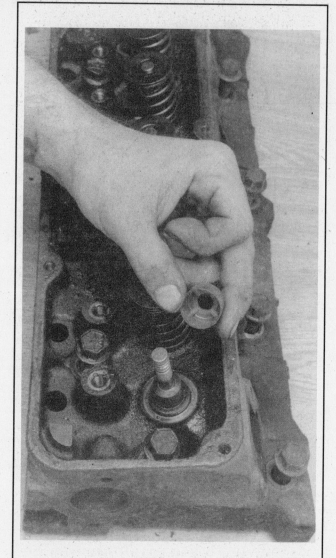

Remove the valve stem seal from the cylinder head

Invert the cylinder head and withdraw the valve from the cylinder head bore

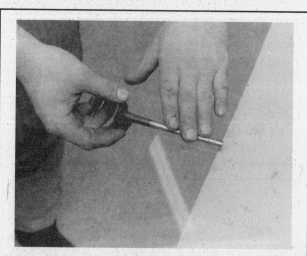

Valve stems may be rolled on a flat surface to check for bends

With the valve spring out of the way, the valve stem seals may now be replaced

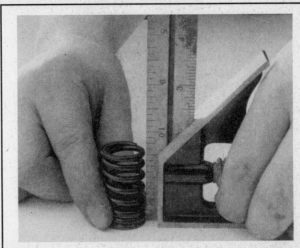

The valve spring should be straight up and down when placed like this

Use a caliper gauge to check the valve spring free-length

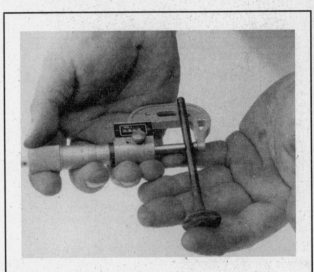

Use a micrometer to check the valve stem diameter

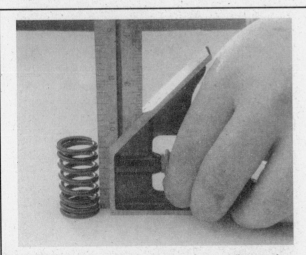

Check the valve spring for squareness on a flat service; a carpenter's square can be used

Checking the Valve Stem-to-Guide Clearance

Clean the valve stem with lacquer thinner or a similar solvent to remove all gum and varnish. Clean the valve guides using solvent and an expanding wire-type valve guide cleaner. Mount a dial indicator so that the stem is at 90° to the valve stem, as close to the valve guide as possible. Move the valve off its seat, and measure the valve guide-to-stem clearance by rocking the stem back and forth to actuate the dial indicator. Measure the valve stems using a micrometer, and compare to specifications, to determine whether stem or guide wear is responsible for excessive clearance.

➡Consult the Specifications tables earlier in this chapter.

A dial gauge may be used to check valve stem-to-guide clearance

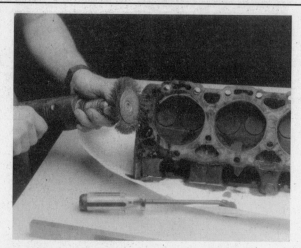

An electric drill equipped with a wire wheel will expedite complete gasket removal

De-carboning the Cylinder Head and Valves

Chip carbon away from the valve heads, combustion chambers, and ports, using a chisel made of hardwood. Remove the remaining deposits with a stiff wire brush.

➡ Be sure that the deposits are actually removed, rather than burnished.

Hot-Tanking the Cylinder Head

✳✳ CAUTION

Do not hot-tank aluminum parts.

Have the cylinder head hot-tanked to remove grease, corrosion, and scale from the water passages.

➡ In the case of overhead cam cylinder heads, consult the operator to determine whether the camshaft bearings will be damaged by the caustic solution.

Degreasing the Remaining Cylinder Head Parts

Clean the remaining cylinder head parts in an engine cleaning solvent. Do not remove the protective coating from the springs.

Checking the Cylinder Head

Place a straight-edge across the gasket surface of the cylinder head. Using feeler gauges, determine the clearance at the center of the straight-edge. If warpage exceeds .003″ in a 6″ span, or .006″ over the total length, the cylinder head must be resurfaced.

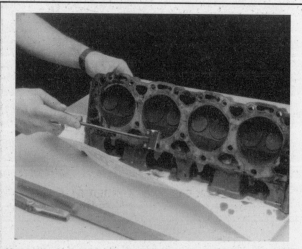

Use a gasket scraper to remove the bulk of the old head gasket from the mating surface

Check the cylinder head for warpage along the center using a straightedge and a feeler gauge

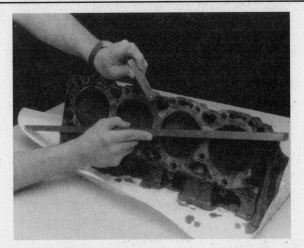

Be sure to check for warpage across the cylinder head at both diagonals

→If warpage exceeds the manufacturer's maximum tolerance for material removal, the cylinder head must be replaced.

When milling the cylinder heads of V-type engines, the intake manifold mounting position is altered, and must be corrected by milling the manifold flange a proportionate amount.

Knurling the Valve Guides
▶ See Figure 19

Valve guides which are not excessively worn or distorted may, in some cases, be knurled rather than replaced. Knurling is a process in which metal is displaced and raised, thereby reducing clearance. Knurling also provides excellent oil control. The possibility of knurling rather than replacing valve guides should be discussed with a machinist.

Replacing the Valve Guides
▶ See Figure 20

→Valve guides should only be replaced if damaged or if an oversize valve stem is not available.

See the engine service procedures earlier in this chapter for details concerning specific engines. Depending on the type of cylinder head, valve guides may be pressed, hammered, or shrunk in. In cases where the guides are shrunk into the head, replacement should be left to an equipped machine shop. In other cases, the guides are replaced using a stepped drift (see illustration). Determine the height above the boss that the guide must extend, and obtain a stack of washers, their I.D. similar to the guide's O.D., of that height. Place the stack of washers on the guide, and insert the guide into the boss.

→Valve guides are often tapered or beveled for installation.

Using the stepped installation tool, press or tap the guides into position. Ream the guides according to the size of the valve stem.

Replacing Valve Seat Inserts

Replacement of valve seat inserts which are worn beyond resurfacing or broken, if feasible, must be done by a machine shop.

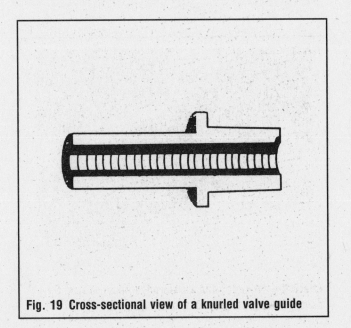

Fig. 19 Cross-sectional view of a knurled valve guide

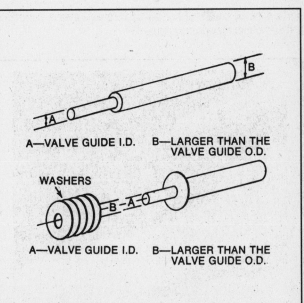

A—VALVE GUIDE I.D.   B—LARGER THAN THE VALVE GUIDE O.D.

WASHERS

A—VALVE GUIDE I.D.   B—LARGER THAN THE VALVE GUIDE O.D.

Fig. 20 Using washers and the special tool for valve guide installation

Resurfacing (Grinding) the Valve Face

▶ See Figures 21 and 22

Using a valve grinder, resurface the valves according to specifications given earlier in this chapter.

✳✳ CAUTION

Valve face angle is not always identical to valve seat angle.

A minimum margin of 1/32 inch should remain after grinding the valve. The valve stem top should also be squared and resurfaced, by placing the stem in the V-block of the grinder, and turning it while pressing lightly against the grinding wheel.

➡**Do not grind sodium filled exhaust valves on a machine. These should be hand lapped.**

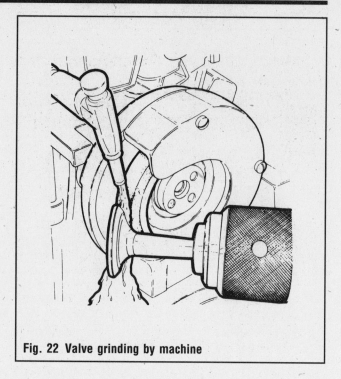

Fig. 22 Valve grinding by machine

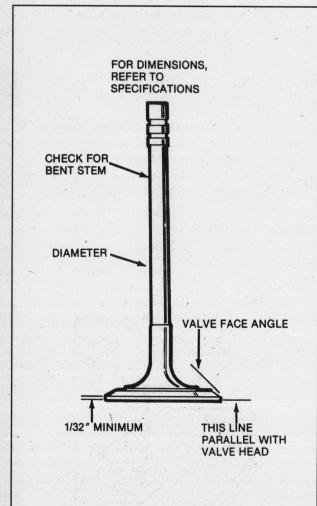

Fig. 21 Check the valve dimensions to see if replacment is necessary

Resurfacing the Valve Seats

▶ See Figures 23 and 24

Select a reamer of the correct seat angle, slightly larger than the diameter of the valve seat, and assemble it with a pilot of the correct size. Install the pilot into the valve guide, and using steady pressure, turn the reamer clockwise.

✳✳ CAUTION

Do not turn the reamer counterclockwise.

Remove only as much material as necessary to clean the seat. Check the concentricity of the seat (following). If the dye method is not used, coat the valve face with Prussian blue dye, install and rotate it on the valve seat. Using the dye marked area as a centering guide, center and narrow the valve seat to specifications with correction cutters.

➡**When no specifications are available, minimum seat width for exhaust valves should be 5/64 inch, intake valves 1/16 inch.**

After making correction cuts, check the position of the valve seat on the valve face using Prussian blue dye.

To resurface the seat with a power grinder, select a pilot of the correct size and coarse stone of the proper angle. Lubricate the pilot and move the stone on and off the valve seat at 2 cycles per second, until all flaws are gone. Finish the seat with a fine stone. If necessary the seat can be corrected or narrowed using correction stones.

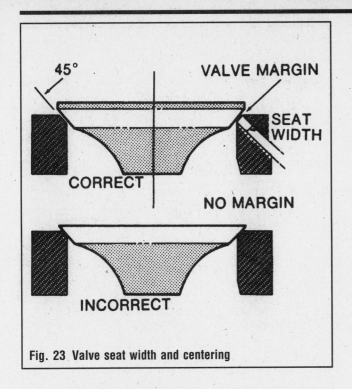

Fig. 23 Valve seat width and centering

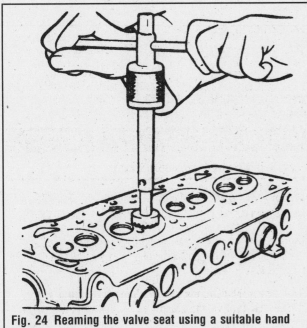

Fig. 24 Reaming the valve seat using a suitable hand reamer

Fig. 25 Check the valve seat concentricity using a dial gauge

Checking the Valve Seat Concentricity

♦ See Figure 25

Coat the valve face with Prussian blue dye, install the valve, and rotate it on the valve seat. If the entire seat becomes coated, and the valve is known to be concentric, the seat is concentric.

Install the dial gauge pilot into the guide, and rest of the arm on the valve seat. Zero the gauge, and rotate the arm around the seat. Run-out should not exceed .002″.

Lapping the Valves

♦ See Figures 26 and 27

➡Valve lapping is done to ensure efficient sealing of resurfaced valves and seats.

Invert the cylinder head, lightly lubricate the valve stems, and install the valves in the head as numbered. Coat valve seats with fine grinding compound, and attach the lapping tool suction cup to a valve head.

➡Moisten the suction cup.

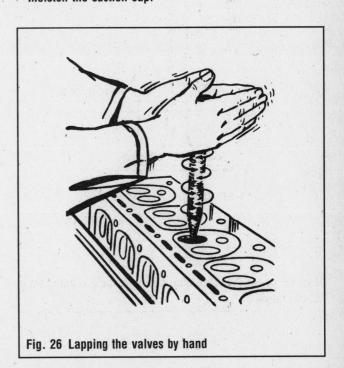

Fig. 26 Lapping the valves by hand

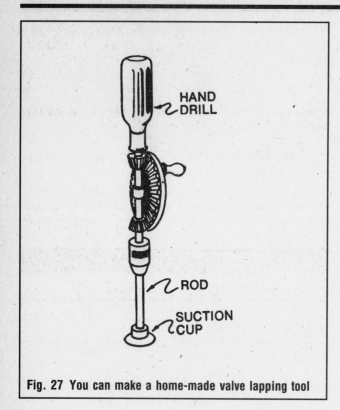

Fig. 27 You can make a home-made valve lapping tool

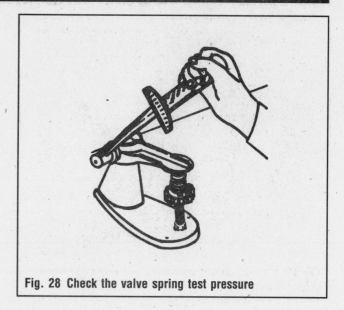

Fig. 28 Check the valve spring test pressure

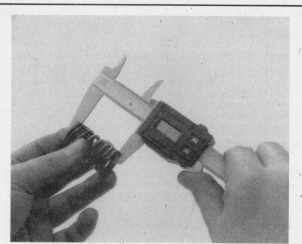

Use a caliper gauge to check the valve spring free-length

Check the valve spring for squareness on a flat service; a carpenter's square can be used

Rotate the tool between the palms, changing position and lifting the tool often to prevent grooving. Lap the valve until a smooth, polished seat is evident. Remove the valve and tool, and rinse away all traces of grinding compound.

Fasten a suction cup to a piece of drill rod, and mount the rod in a hand drill. Proceed as above, using the hand drill as a lapping tool.

✱✱ CAUTION

Due to the higher speeds involved when using the hand drill, care must be exercised to avoid grooving the seat.

Lift the tool and change direction of rotation often.

Checking the Valve Springs
▶ See Figure 28

Place the spring on a flat surface next to a square. Measure the height of the spring, and rotate it against the edge of the square to measure distortion. If spring height varies (by comparison) by more than 1/16" or if distortion exceeds 1/16", replace the spring.

In addition to evaluating the spring as above, test the spring pressure at the installed and compressed (installed height minus valve lift) height using a valve spring tester. Springs used on small displacement engines (up to 3 liters) should be ∓ 1 lb of all other springs in either position. A tolerance of ∓ 5 lbs is permissible on larger engines.

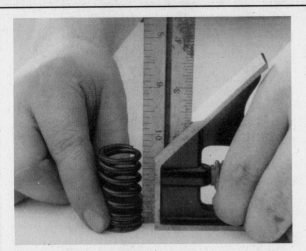

The valve spring should be straight up and down when placed like this

Installing Valve Stem Seals
◆ See Figure 29

Due to the pressure differential that exists at the ends of the intake valve guides (atmospheric pressure above, manifold vacuum below), oil is drawn through the valve guides into the intake port. This has been alleviated somewhat since the addition of positive crankcase ventilation, which lowers the pressure above the guides. Several types of valve stem seals are available to reduce blow-by. Certain seals simply slip over the stem and guide boss, while others require that the boss be machined. Recently, Teflon guide seals have become popular. Consult a parts supplier or machinist concerning availability and suggested usages.

➡When installing seals, ensure that a small amount of oil is able to pass the seal to lubricate the valve guides; otherwise, excessive wear may result.

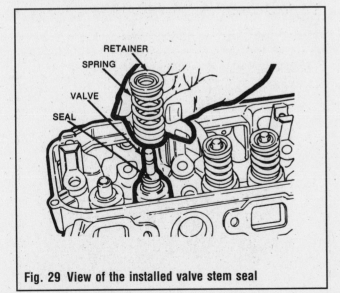

Fig. 29 View of the installed valve stem seal

Installing the Valves

See the engine service procedures earlier in this chapter for details concerning specific engines.

Lubricate the valve stems, and install the valves in the cylinder head as numbered. Lubricate and position the seals (if used) and the valve springs. Install the spring retainers, compress the springs, and insert the keys using needlenose pliers or a tool designed for this purpose.

➡Retain the keys with wheel bearing grease during installation.

Checking Valve Spring Installed Height
◆ See Figures 30 and 31

Measure the distance between the spring pad and the lower edge of the spring retainer, and compare to specifications. If the installed height is incorrect, add shim washers between the spring pad and the spring.

✳✳ CAUTION

Use only washers designed for this purpose.

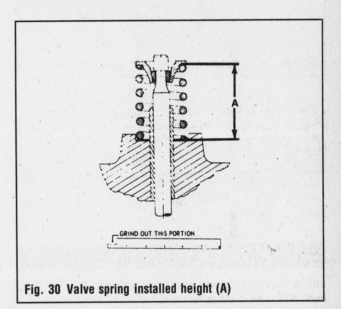

Fig. 30 Valve spring installed height (A)

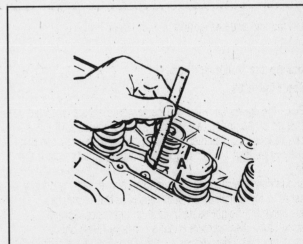

Fig. 31 Measure the valve spring installed height (A) with a modified steel ruler

Inspecting the Rocker Arms, Balls, Studs, and Nuts
◗ See Figure 32

Visually inspect the rocker arms, balls, studs, and nuts for cracks, galling, burning, scoring, or wear. If all parts are intact, liberally lubricate the rocker arms and balls, and install them on the cylinder head. If wear is noted on a rocker arm at the point of valve contact, grind it smooth and square, removing as little material as possible. Replace the rocker arm if excessively worn. If a rocker stud shows signs of wear, it must be replaced (see below). If a rocker nut shows stress cracks, replace it. If an exhaust ball is galled or burned, substitute the intake ball from the same cylinder (if it is intact), and install a new intake ball.

➡ Avoid using new rocker balls on exhaust valves.

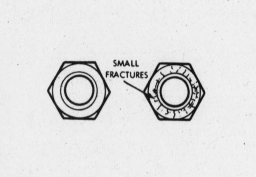

Fig. 32 Replace the rocker arm nuts if they have small fractures or "stress cracks"

Replacing Rocker Studs
◗ See Figures 33 and 34

In order to remove a threaded stud, lock two nuts on the stud, and unscrew the stud using the lower nut. Coat the lower threads of the new stud with Loctite, and install.

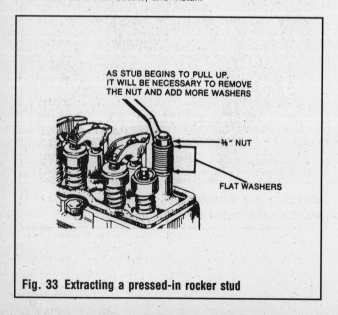

Fig. 33 Extracting a pressed-in rocker stud

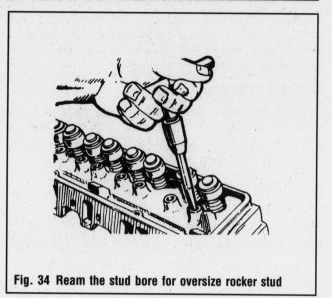

Fig. 34 Ream the stud bore for oversize rocker stud

Two alternative methods are available for replacing pressed in studs. Remove the damaged stud using a stack of washers and a nut (see illustration). In the first, the boss is reamed .005–.006″ oversize, and an oversize stud pressed in. Control the stud extension over the boss using washers, in the same manner as valve guides. Before installing the stud, coat it with white lead and grease. To retain the stud more positively drill a hole through the stud and boss, and install a roll pin. In the second method, the boss is tapped, and a threaded stud installed.

Inspecting the Rocker Shaft(s) and Rocker Arms
◗ See Figure 34a

Remove rocker arms, springs and washers from rocker shaft.

➡ Lay out parts in the order as they are removed.

Inspect rocker arms for pitting or wear on the valve contact point, or excessive bushing wear. Bushings need only be replaced if wear is excessive, because the rocker arm normally contacts the shaft at one point only. Grind the valve contact point of rocker arm smooth if necessary, removing as little material as possible.

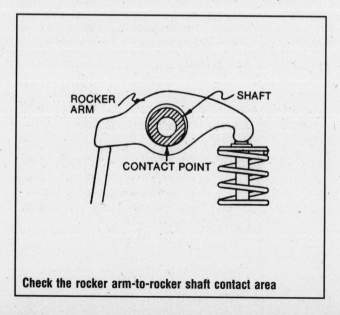

Check the rocker arm-to-rocker shaft contact area

If excessive material must be removed to smooth and square the arm, it should be replaced. Clean out all oil holes and passages in rocker shaft. If shaft is grooved or worn, replace it. Lubricate and assemble the rocker shaft.

Inspecting the Pushrods

Remove the pushrods, and, if hollow, clean out the oil passages using fine wire. Roll each pushrod over a piece of clean glass. If a distinct clicking sound is heard as the pushrod rolls, the rod is bent, and must be replaced.

The length of all pushrods must be equal. Measure the length of the pushrods, compare to specifications, and replace as necessary.

Inspecting the Valve Lifters
♦ See Figure 35

Remove lifters from their bores, and remove gum and varnish, using solvent. Clean walls of lifter bores. Check lifters for concave wear as illustrated. If face is worn concave, replace lifter, and carefully inspect the camshaft. Lightly lubricate lifter and insert it into its bore. If play is excessive, an oversize lifter must be installed (where possible). Consult a machinist concerning feasibility. If play is satisfactory, remove, lubricate, and reinstall the lifter.

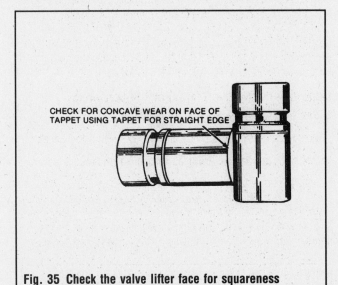

Fig. 35 Check the valve lifter face for squareness

Testing Hydraulic Lifter Leak Down

Submerge lifter in a container of kerosene. Chuck a used pushrod or its equivalent into a drill press. Position container of kerosene so pushrod acts on the lifter plunger. Pump lifter with the drill press, until resistance increases. Pump several more times to bleed any air out of lifter. Apply very firm, constant pressure to the lifter, and observe rate at which fluid bleeds out of lifter. If the fluid bleeds very quickly (less than 15 seconds), lifter is defective. If the time exceeds 60 seconds, lifter is sticking. In either case, recondition or replace lifter. If lifter is operating properly (leak down time 15–60 seconds), lubricate and install it.

Cylinder Block

RECONDITIONING

Checking the Main Bearing Clearance
♦ See Figure 36

Invert engine, and remove cap from the bearing to be checked. Using a clean, dry rag, thoroughly clean all oil from crankshaft journal and bearing insert.

➡ Plastigage® is soluble in oil; therefore, oil on the journal or bearing could result in erroneous readings.

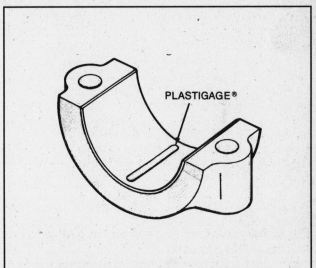

Fig. 36 Plastigage® installed on the lower bearing shell

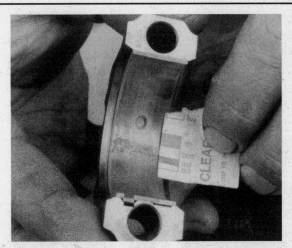

After the cap is removed again, use the scale supplied with the gauge material to check clearances

Place a piece of Plastigage along the full length of journal, reinstall cap, and torque to specifications.

➡**Specifications are given in the engine specifications earlier in this chapter.**

Remove bearing cap, and determine bearing clearance by comparing width of Plastigage to the scale on Plastigage envelope. Journal taper is determined by comparing width of the Plastigage strip near its ends. Rotate crankshaft 90° and retest, to determine journal eccentricity.

➡**Do not rotate crankshaft with Plastigage installed.**

If bearing insert and journal appear intact, and are within tolerances, no further main bearing service is required. If bearing or journal appear defective, cause of failure should be determined before replacement.

Remove crankshaft from block (see below). Measure the main bearing journals at each end twice (90° apart) using a micrometer, to determine diameter, journal taper and eccentricity. If journals are within tolerances, reinstall bearing caps at their specified torque. Using a telescope gauge and micrometer, measure bearing I.D. parallel to piston axis and at 30° on each side of piston axis. Subtract journal O.D. from bearing I.D. to determine oil clearance. If crankshaft journals appear defective, or do not meet tolerances, there is no need to measure bearings; for the crankshaft will require grinding and/or undersize bearings will be required. If bearing appears defective, cause for failure should be determined prior to replacement.

Checking the Connecting Rod Bearing Clearance

Connecting rod bearing clearance is checked in the same manner as main bearing clearance, using Plastigage. Before removing the crankshaft, connecting rod side clearance also should be measured and recorded.

Checking connecting rod bearing clearance, using a micrometer, is identical to checking main bearing clearance. If no other service is required, the piston and rod assemblies need not be removed.

Removing the Crankshaft
◆ **See Figures 37 and 38**

Using a punch, mark the corresponding main bearing caps and saddles according to position (i.e., one punch on the front main cap and saddle, two on the second, three on the third, etc.). Using number stamps, identify the corresponding connecting rods and caps, according to cylinder (if no numbers are present). Remove the main and connecting rod caps, and place sleeves of plastic tubing or vacuum hose over the connecting rod bolts, to protect the journals as the crankshaft is removed. Lift the crankshaft out of the block.

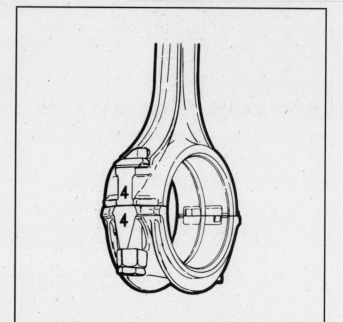

Fig. 37 Match the connecting rod to the cylinder it corresponds with using a number stamp

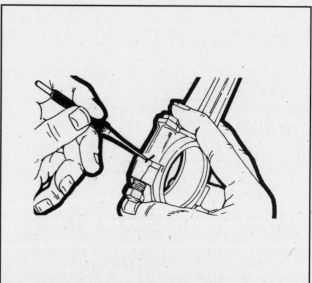

Fig. 38 Matchmark the connecting rod and cap with scribe marks

Removing the Cylinder Ridge
◆ **See Figure 39**

In order to facilitate removal of the piston and connecting rod, the ridge at the top of the cylinder (unworn area; see illustration) must be removed. Place the piston at the bottom of the bore, and cover it with a rag. Cut the ridge away using a ridge reamer, exercising extreme care to avoid cutting too deeply. Remove the rag, and remove cuttings that remain on the piston.

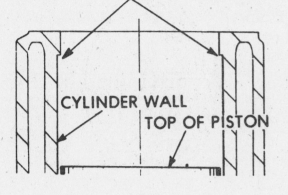

RIDGE CAUSED BY CYLINDER WEAR

CYLINDER WALL

TOP OF PISTON

Fig. 39 View of the cylinder bore ridge

Place rubber hose over the connecting rod studs to protect the crank and bores from damage

As with a ball hone, work the hone carefully up and down the bore to achieve the desired results

✳✳ CAUTION

If the ridge is not removed, and new rings are installed, damage to rings will result.

Removing the Piston and Connecting Rod

Invert the engine, and push the pistons and connecting rods out of the cylinders. If necessary, tap the connecting rod boss with a wooden hammer handle, to force the piston out.

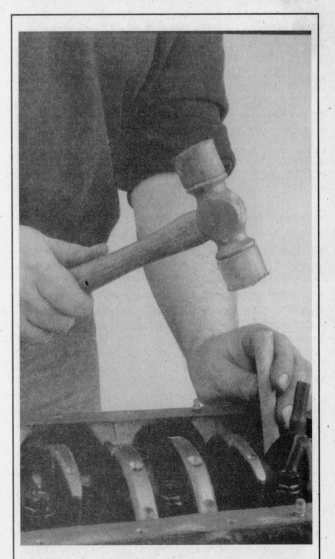

Carefully tap the piston out of the bore using a wooden dowel

✳✳ CAUTION

Do not attempt to force the piston past the cylinder ridge (see above).

Servicing the Crankshaft

Ensure that all oil holes and passages in the crankshaft are open and free of sludge. If necessary, have the crankshaft ground to the largest possible undersize.

Have the crankshaft Magnafluxed, to locate stress cracks. Consult a machinist concerning additional service procedures, such as surface hardening (e.g., nitriding, Tuftriding) to improve wear characteristics, cross drilling and chamfering the oil holes to improve lubrication, and balancing.

Removing the Freeze Plugs

Drill a small hole in the middle of the freeze plugs. Thread a large sheet metal screw into the hole and remove the plug with a slide hammer.

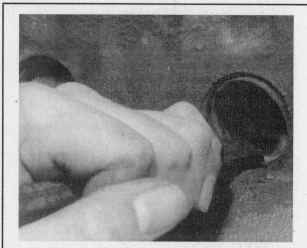

Using a punch and hammer, the freeze plug can be loosened in the block

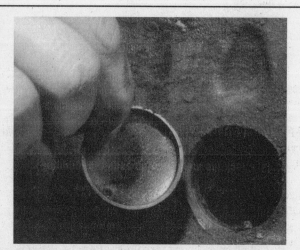

Once the freeze plug has been loosened, it can be removed from the block

Removing the Oil Gallery Plugs

Threaded plugs should be removed using an appropriate (usually square) wrench. To remove soft, pressed in plugs, drill a hole in the plug, and thread in a sheet metal screw. Pull the plug out by the screw using pliers.

Hot-Tanking the Cylinder Block

➡ **Do not hot-tank aluminum parts.**

Have the block hot-tanked to remove grease, corrosion, and scale from the water jackets.

➡ **Consult the operator to determine whether the camshaft bearings will be damaged during the hot-tank process.**

Checking the Block

Visually inspect the block for cracks or chips. The most common locations are as follows:
Adjacent to freeze plugs.
Between the cylinders and water jackets.
Adjacent to the main bearing saddles.
At the extreme bottom of the cylinders.
Check only suspected cracks using spot check dye (see introduction). If a crack is located, consult a machinist concerning possible repairs.

Magnaflux the block to locate hidden cracks. If cracks are located, consult a machinist about feasibility of repair.

Installing the Oil Gallery Plugs and Freeze Plugs

Coat freeze plugs with sealer and tap into position using a piece of pipe, slightly smaller than the plug, as a driver. To ensure retention, stake the edges of the plugs. Coat threaded oil gallery plugs with sealer and install. Drive replacement soft plugs into block using a large drift as a driver.

Rather than reinstalling lead plugs, drill and tap the holes, and install threaded plugs.

Checking the Bore Diameter and Surface
▶ **See Figures 40 and 41**

Visually inspect the cylinder bores for roughness, scoring, or scuffing. If evident, the cylinder bore must be bored or honed oversize to eliminate imperfections, and the smallest possible oversize piston used. The new pistons should be given to the machinist with the block, so that the cylinders can be bored or honed exactly to the piston size (plus clearance). If no flaws are evident, measure the bore diameter using a telescope gauge and micrometer, or dial gauge, parallel and perpendicular to the engine centerline, at the top (below the ridge) and bottom of the bore. Subtract the bottom measurements from the top to determine taper, and the parallel to the centerline measurements from the perpendicular measurements to determine eccentricity. If the measurements are not within specifications, the cylinder must be bored or honed, and an oversize piston installed. If the measurements are within specifications the cylinder may be used as is, with only finish honing (see below).

➡ **Prior to submitting the block for boring, perform the following operation(s).**

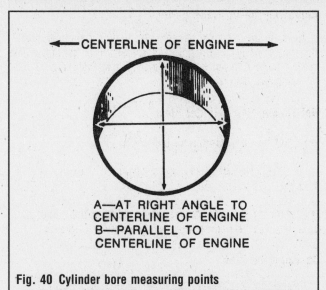

Fig. 40 Cylinder bore measuring points

A—AT RIGHT ANGLE TO CENTERLINE OF ENGINE
B—PARALLEL TO CENTERLINE OF ENGINE

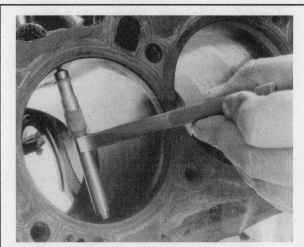

A telescoping gauge may be used to measure the cylinder bore diameter

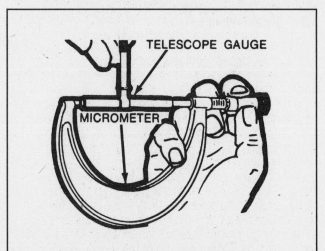

Fig. 41 Measure the telescoping gauge with a micrometer to determine the cylinder bore

Checking the Cylinder Block Bearing Alignment
▶ See Figure 42

Remove the upper bearing inserts. Place a straightedge in the bearing saddles along the centerline of the crankshaft. If clearance exists between the straightedge and the center saddle, the block must be alignbored.

Fig. 42 Check the main bearing saddle alignment

Checking the Deck Height

The deck height is the distance from the crankshaft centerline to the block deck. To measure, invert the engine, and install the crankshaft, retaining it with the center main cap. Measure the distance from the crankshaft journal to the block deck, parallel to the cylinder centerline. Measure the diameter of the end (front and rear) main journals, parallel to the centerline of the cylinders, divide the diameter in half, and subtract it from the previous measurement. The results of the front and rear measurements should be identical. If the difference exceeds .005″, the deck height should be corrected.

➡ Block deck height and warpage should be corrected at the same time.

Checking the Block Deck for Warpage

Using a straightedge and feeler gauges, check the block deck for warpage in the same manner that the cylinder head is checked (see Cylinder Head Reconditioning). If warpage exceeds specifications, have the deck resurfaced.

➡ In certain cases a specification for total material removal (cylinder head and block deck) is provided. This specification must not be exceeded.

Cleaning and Inspection of the Pistons and Connecting Rods
▶ See Figure 43

Using a ring expander, remove the rings from the piston. Remove the retaining rings (if so equipped) and remove piston pin.

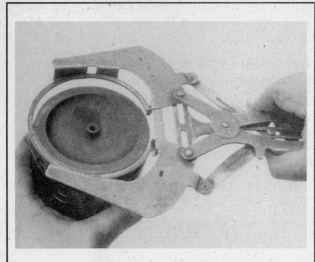

Use a ring expander tool to remove the piston rings

Clean the piston grooves using a ring groove cleaner

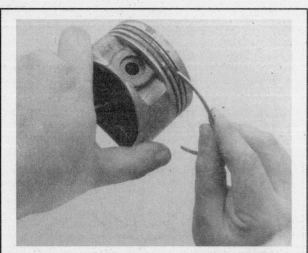

You can use a piece of an old ring to clean the piston grooves, BUT be careful, the ring is sharp

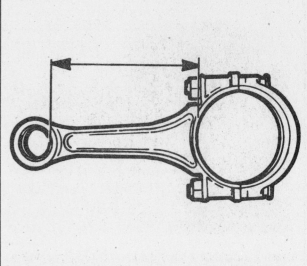

Fig. 43 Measure the connecting rod length designated by the arrow

➡If the piston pin must be pressed out, determine the proper method and use the proper tools; otherwise the piston will distort.

Clean the ring grooves using an appropriate tool, exercising care to avoid cutting too deeply. Thoroughly clean all carbon and varnish from the piston with solvent.

✳✳ CAUTION

Do not use a wire brush or caustic solvent on pistons.

Inspect the pistons for scuffing, scoring, cracks, pitting, or excessive ring groove wear. If wear is evident, the piston must be replaced. Check the connecting rod length by measuring the rod from the inside of the large end to the inside of the small end using calipers (see illustration). All connecting rods should be equal length. Replace any rod that differs from the others in the engine.

Have the connecting rod alignment checked in an alignment fixture by a machinist. Replace any twisted or bent rods.

Magnaflux the connecting rods to locate stress cracks. If cracks are found, replace the connecting rod.

Fitting the Pistons to the Cylinder

Using a telescope gauge and micrometer, or a dial gauge, measure the cylinder bore diameter perpendicular to the piston pin, 2½″ below the deck. Measure the piston perpendicular to its pin on the skirt. The difference between the two measurements is the piston clearance. If the clearance is within specifications or slightly below (after boring or honing), finish honing is all that is required. If the clearance is excessive, try to obtain a slightly larger piston to bring clearance within specifications. Where this is not possible, obtain the first oversize piston, and hone (or if necessary, bore) the cylinder to size.

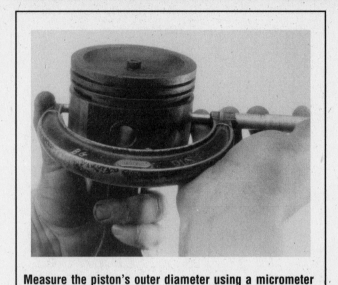

Measure the piston's outer diameter using a micrometer

Assembling the Pistons and Connecting Rods
♦ See Figure 44

Inspect piston pin, connecting rod small end bushing, and piston bore for galling, scoring, or excessive wear. If evident, replace defective part(s). Measure the I.D. of the piston boss and connecting rod small end, and the O.D. of the piston pin. If within specifications, assemble piston pin and rod.

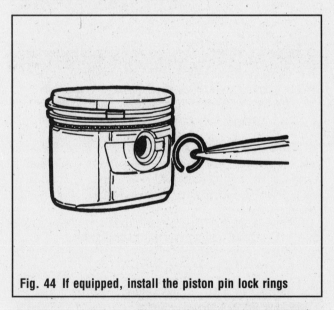

Fig. 44 If equipped, install the piston pin lock rings

※※ CAUTION

If piston pin must be pressed in, determine the proper method and use the proper tools; otherwise the piston will distort.

Install the lock rings; ensure that they seat properly. If the parts are not within specifications, determine the service method for the type of engine. In some cases, piston and pin are serviced as an assembly when either is defective. Others specify reaming the piston and connecting rods for an oversize pin. If the connecting rod

bushing is worn, it may in many cases be replaced. Reaming the piston and replacing the rod bushing are machine shop operations.

Cleaning and Inspection of the Camshaft
♦ See Figures 45 and 46

Degrease the camshaft, using solvent, and clean out all oil holes. Visually inspect cam lobes and bearing journals for excessive wear. If a lobe is questionable, check all lobes as indicated below. If a journal or lobe is worn, the camshaft must be reground or replaced.

➡ If a journal is worn, there is a good chance that the bushings are worn.

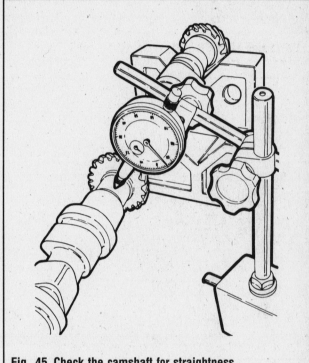

Fig. 45 Check the camshaft for straightness

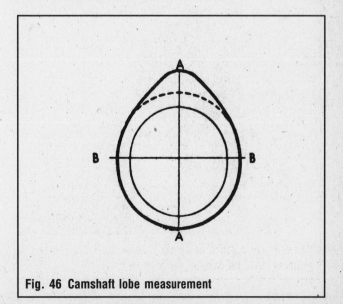

Fig. 46 Camshaft lobe measurement

If lobes and journals appear intact, place the front and rear journals in V-blocks, and rest a dial indicator on the center journal. Rotate the camshaft to check straightness. If deviation exceeds .001″, replace the camshaft.

Check the camshaft lobes with a micrometer, by measuring the lobes from the nose to base and again at 90° (see illustration). The lift is determined by subtracting the second measurement from the first. If all exhaust lobes and all intake lobes are not identical, the camshaft must be reground or replaced.

Replacing the Camshaft Bearings
▶ **See Figure 47**

If excessive wear is indicated, or if the engine is being completely rebuilt, camshaft bearings should be replaced as follows: Drive the camshaft rear plug from the block. Assemble the removal puller with its shoulder on the bearing to be removed. Gradually tighten the puller nut until bearing is removed. Remove remaining bearings, leaving the front and rear for last. To remove front and rear bearings, reverse position of the tool, so as to pull the bearings in toward the center of the block. Leave the tool in this position, pilot the new front and rear bearings on the installer, and pull them into position. Return the tool to its original position and pull remaining bearings into position.

➡ **Ensure that oil holes align when installing bearings.**

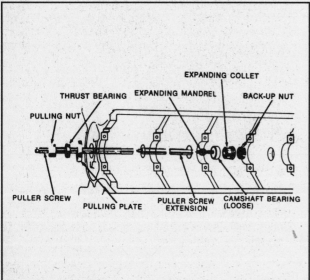

Fig. 47 Using the special tool to remove and install the camshaft bearings

Replace camshaft rear plug, and stake it into position to aid retention.

Final Honing the Cylinders

Chuck a flexible drive hone into a power drill, and insert it into the cylinder. Start the hone, and move it up and down in the cylin-

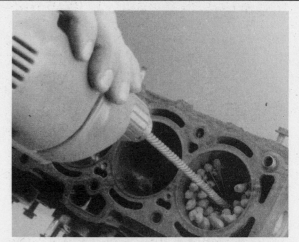

Using a ball type cylinder hone is an easy way to hone the cylinder bore

A properly cross-hatched cylinder bore

der at a rate which will produce approximately a 60° cross-hatch pattern.

➡ **Do not extend the hone below the cylinder bore.**

After developing the pattern, remove the hone and recheck piston fit. Wash the cylinders with a detergent and water solution to remove abrasive dust, dry, and wipe several times with a rag soaked in engine oil.

Checking Piston Ring End-Gap
▶ **See Figure 48**

Compress the piston rings to be used in a cylinder, one at a time, into that cylinder, and press them approximately 1″ below the deck with an inverted piston. Using feeler gauges, measure the ring end-gap, and compare to specifications. Pull the ring out

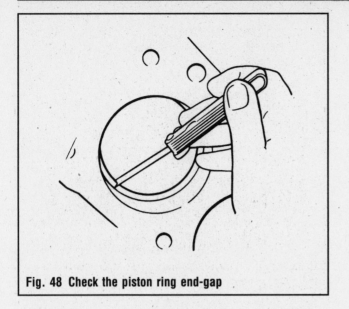

Fig. 48 Check the piston ring end-gap

of the cylinder and file the ends with a fine file to obtain proper clearance.

❋❋ CAUTION

If inadequate ring end-gap is utilized, ring breakage will result.

Installing the Piston Rings

Inspect the ring grooves in the piston for excessive wear or taper. If necessary, recut the grooves(s) for use with an overwidth ring or a standard ring and spacer. If the groove is worn uniformly, overwidth rings, or standard rings and spacers may be installed without recutting. Roll the outside of the ring around the groove to check for burrs or deposits. If any are found, remove with a fine file. Hold the ring in the groove, and measure side clearance. If necessary, correct as indicated above.

➡**Always install any additional spacers above the piston ring.**

The ring groove must be deep enough to allow the ring to seat below the lands (see illustration). In many cases, a "go-no-go" depth gauge will be provided with the piston rings. Shallow grooves may be corrected by recutting, while deep grooves require some type of filler or expander behind the piston. Consult the piston ring supplier concerning the suggested method. Install the rings on the piston, lowest ring first, using a ring expander.

➡**Position the rings as specified by the manufacturer.**

Consult the engine service procedures earlier in this chapter for details concerning specific engines.

Installing the Camshaft

Liberally lubricate the camshaft lobes and journals, and install the camshaft.

❋❋ CAUTION

Exercise extreme care to avoid damaging the bearings when inserting the camshaft.

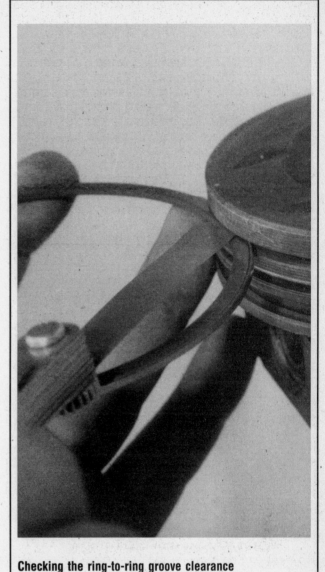

Checking the ring-to-ring groove clearance

Install and tighten the camshaft thrust plate retaining bolts.

See the engine service procedures earlier in this chapter for details concerning specific engines.

Checking Camshaft End-Play
◢ **See Figures 49 and 50**

Using feeler gauges, determine whether the clearance between the camshaft boss (or gear) and backing plate is within specifications. Install shims behind the thrust plate, or reposition the camshaft gear and retest endplay. In some cases, adjustment is by replacing the thrust plate.

See the engine service procedures earlier in this chapter for details concerning specific engines.

Mount a dial indicator stand so that the stem of the dial indicator rests on the nose of the camshaft, parallel to the camshaft axis. Push the camshaft as far in as possible and zero the gauge. Move the camshaft outward to determine the amount of camshaft endplay. If the endplay is not within tolerance, install shims behind the thrust plate, or reposition the camshaft gear and retest.

Fig. 49 Check the camshaft end-play with a feeler gauge

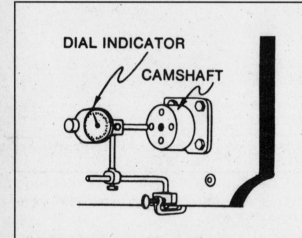

Fig. 50 Check the camshaft end-play with a dial indicator

position. Place a strip of Plastigage on each of the crankshaft journals, install the main caps, and torque to specifications. Remove the main caps, and compare the Plastigage to the scale on the Plastigage envelope. If clearances are within tolerances, remove the Plastigage, turn the crankshaft 90°, wipe off all oil and retest. If all clearances are correct, remove all Plastigage, thoroughly lubricate the main caps and bearing journals, and install the main caps. If clearances are not within tolerance, the upper bearing inserts may be removed, without removing the crankshaft, using a bearing roll out pin (see illustration). Roll in a bearing that will provide proper clearance, and retest. Torque all main caps, excluding the thrust bearing cap, to specifications. Tighten the thrust bearing cap finger-tight. To properly align the thrust bearing, pry the crankshaft the extent of its axial travel several times, the last movement held toward the front of the engine, and torque the thrust bearing cap to specifications. Determine the crankshaft end-play (see below), and bring within tolerance with thrust washers.

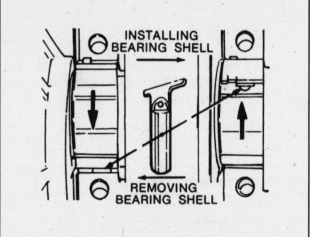

Fig. 51 Remove or install the upper bearing insert using a roll-out pin

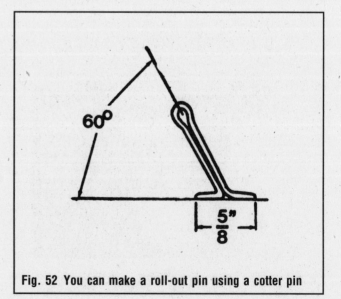

Fig. 52 You can make a roll-out pin using a cotter pin

See the engine service procedures earlier in this chapter for details concerning specific engines.

Installing the Rear Main Seal

See the engine service procedures earlier in this chapter for details concerning specific engines.

Installing the Crankshaft
▶ **See Figures 51, 52 and 53**

Thoroughly clean the main bearing saddles and caps. Place the upper halves of the bearing inserts on the saddles and press into position.

➡**Ensure that the oil holes align.**

Press the corresponding bearing inserts into the main bearing caps. Lubricate the upper main bearings, and lay the crankshaft in

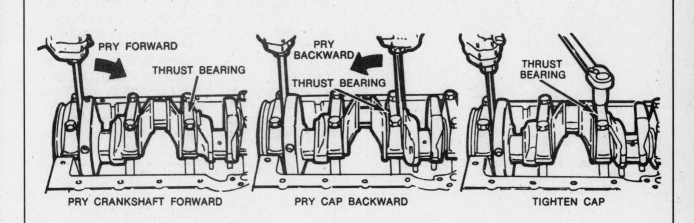

Fig. 53 Aligning the thrust bearing

Measuring Crankshaft End-Play

Mount a dial indicator stand on the front of the block, with the dial indicator stem resting on the nose of the crankshaft, parallel to the crankshaft axis. Pry the crankshaft the extent of its travel rearward, and zero the indicator. Pry the crankshaft forward and record crankshaft end-play.

➡**Crankshaft end-play also may be measured at the thrust bearing, using feeler gauges (see illustration).**

A dial gauge may be used to check crankshaft end-play

Carefully pry the shaft back and forth while reading the dial gauge for play

Installing the Pistons
♦ **See Figure 54**

Press the upper connecting rod bearing halves into the connecting rods, and the lower halves into the connecting rod caps. Position the piston ring gaps according to specifications (see car section), and lubricate the pistons. Install a ring compressor on a piston, and press two long (8″) pieces of plastic tubing over the rod bolts. Using the tubes as a guide, press the pistons into the bores and onto the crankshaft with a wooden hammer handle. After seating the rod on the crankshaft journal, remove the tubes and install the cap finger tight. Install the remaining pistons in the same manner. Invert the engine and check the bearing clearance at two points (90° apart) on each journal with Plastigage.

➡**Do not turn the crankshaft with Plastigage installed.**

If clearance is within tolerances, remove *all* Plastigage, thoroughly lubricate the journals, and torque the rod caps to specifications. If clearance is not within specifications, install different thickness bearing inserts and recheck.

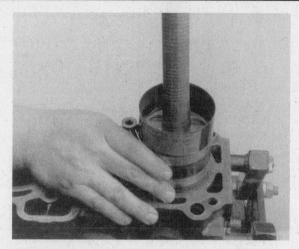

Installing the piston into the block using a ring compressor and the handle of a hammer

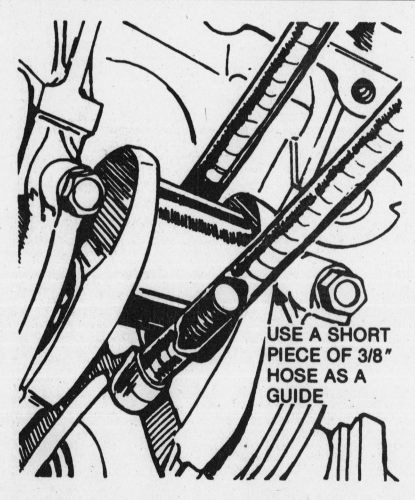

USE A SHORT PIECE OF 3/8″ HOSE AS A GUIDE

Fig. 54 Use lengths of vacuum hose or rubber tubing to protect the crankshaft journals and cylinder walls during piston installation

Never shim or file the connecting rods or caps.

Always install plastic tube sleeves over the rod bolts when the caps are not installed, to protect the crankshaft journals.

Checking Connecting Rod Side Clearance
▶ **See Figure 55**

Determine the clearance between the sides of the connecting rods and the crankshaft, using feeler gauges. If clearance is below the minimum tolerance, the rod may be machined to provide adequate clearance. If clearance is excessive, substitute an unworn rod, and recheck. If clearance is still outside specifications, the crankshaft must be welded and reground, or replaced.

Inspecting the Timing Chain

Visually inspect the timing chain for broken or loose links, and replace the chain if any are found. If the chain will flex sideways, it must be replaced. Install the timing chain as specified.

➡ **If the original timing chain is to be reused, install it in its original position.**

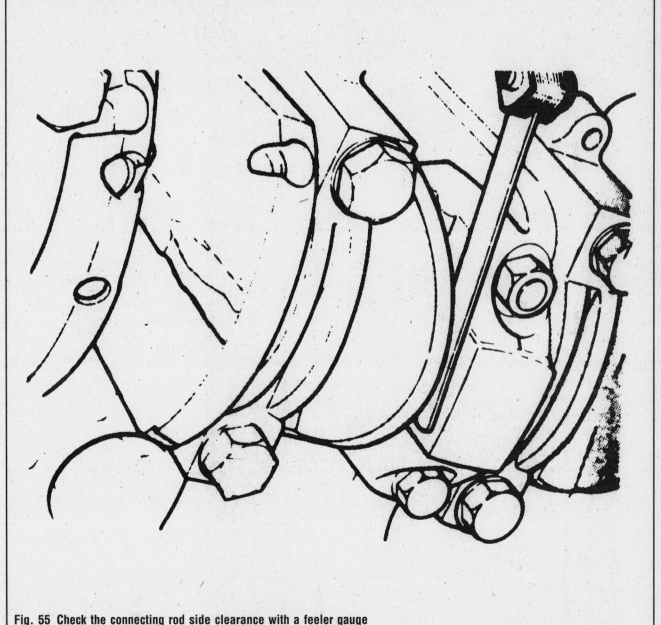

Fig. 55 Check the connecting rod side clearance with a feeler gauge

Checking Timing Gear Backlash and Runout

♦ **See Figures 56 and 57**

Mount a dial indicator with its stem resting on a tooth of the camshaft gear (as illustrated). Rotate the gear until all slack is removed, and zero the indicator. Rotate the gear in the opposite direction until slack is removed, and record gear backlash. Mount the indicator with its stem resting on the edge of the camshaft gear, parallel to the axis of the camshaft. Zero the indicator, and turn the camshaft gear one full turn, recording the runout. If either backlash or runout exceed specifications, replace the worn gear(s).

Fig. 56 Use a dial indicator to check the camshaft gear backlash

Fig. 57 Check the camshaft gear run-out

USING A VACUUM GAUGE

White needle = steady needle   *Dark needle = drifting needle*

The vacuum gauge is one of the most useful and easy-to-use diagnostic tools. It is inexpensive, easy to hook up, and provides valuable information about the condition of your engine.

Indication: Normal engine in good condition

Gauge reading: Steady, from 17–22 in./Hg.

Indication: Sticking valve or ignition miss

Gauge reading: Needle fluctuates from 15–20 in./Hg. at idle

Indication: Late ignition or valve timing, low compression, stuck throttle valve, leaking carburetor or manifold gasket.

Gauge reading: Low (15–20 in./Hg.) but steady

Indication: Improper carburetor adjustment, or minor intake leak at carburetor or manifold

NOTE: Bad fuel injector O-rings may also cause this reading.

Gauge reading: Drifting needle

Indication: Weak valve springs, worn valve stem guides, or leaky cylinder head gasket (vibrating excessively at all speeds).

NOTE: A plugged catalytic converter may also cause this reading.

Gauge reading: Needle fluctuates as engine speed increases

Indication: Burnt valve or improper valve clearance. The needle will drop when the defective valve operates.

Gauge reading: Steady needle, but drops regularly

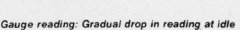

Indication: Choked muffler or obstruction in system. Speed up the engine. Choked muffler will exhibit a slow drop of vacuum to zero.

Gauge reading: Gradual drop in reading at idle

Indication: Worn valve guides

Gauge reading: Needle vibrates excessively at idle, but steadies as engine speed increases

Troubleshooting Engine Mechanical Problems

Problem	Cause	Solution
External oil leaks	• Cylinder head cover RTV sealant broken or improperly seated	• Replace sealant; inspect cylinder head cover sealant flange and cylinder head sealant surface for distortion and cracks
	• Oil filler cap leaking or missing	• Replace cap
	• Oil filter gasket broken or improperly seated	• Replace oil filter
	• Oil pan side gasket broken, improperly seated or opening in RTV sealant	• Replace gasket or repair opening in sealant; inspect oil pan gasket flange for distortion
	• Oil pan front oil seal broken or improperly seated	• Replace seal; inspect timing case cover and oil pan seal flange for distortion
	• Oil pan rear oil seal broken or improperly seated	• Replace seal; inspect oil pan rear oil seal flange; inspect rear main bearing cap for cracks, plugged oil return channels, or distortion in seal groove
	• Timing case cover oil seal broken or improperly seated	• Replace seal
	• Excess oil pressure because of restricted PCV valve	• Replace PCV valve
	• Oil pan drain plug loose or has stripped threads	• Repair as necessary and tighten
	• Rear oil gallery plug loose	• Use appropriate sealant on gallery plug and tighten
	• Rear camshaft plug loose or improperly seated	• Seat camshaft plug or replace and seal, as necessary
Excessive oil consumption	• Oil level too high	• Drain oil to specified level
	• Oil with wrong viscosity being used	• Replace with specified oil
	• PCV valve stuck closed	• Replace PCV valve
	• Valve stem oil deflectors (or seals) are damaged, missing, or incorrect type	• Replace valve stem oil deflectors
	• Valve stems or valve guides worn	• Measure stem-to-guide clearance and repair as necessary
	• Poorly fitted or missing valve cover baffles	• Replace valve cover
	• Piston rings broken or missing	• Replace broken or missing rings
	• Scuffed piston	• Replace piston
	• Incorrect piston ring gap	• Measure ring gap, repair as necessary
	• Piston rings sticking or excessively loose in grooves	• Measure ring side clearance, repair as necessary
	• Compression rings installed upside down	• Repair as necessary
	• Cylinder walls worn, scored, or glazed	• Repair as necessary

Troubleshooting Engine Mechanical Problems

Problem	Cause	Solution
Excessive oil consumption (cont.)	• Piston ring gaps not properly staggered	• Repair as necessary
	• Excessive main or connecting rod bearing clearance	• Measure bearing clearance, repair as necessary
No oil pressure	• Low oil level	• Add oil to correct level
	• Oil pressure gauge, warning lamp or sending unit inaccurate	• Replace oil pressure gauge or warning lamp
	• Oil pump malfunction	• Replace oil pump
	• Oil pressure relief valve sticking	• Remove and inspect oil pressure relief valve assembly
	• Oil passages on pressure side of pump obstructed	• Inspect oil passages for obstruction
	• Oil pickup screen or tube obstructed	• Inspect oil pickup for obstruction
	• Loose oil inlet tube	• Tighten or seal inlet tube
Low oil pressure	• Low oil level	• Add oil to correct level
	• Inaccurate gauge, warning lamp or sending unit	• Replace oil pressure gauge or warning lamp
	• Oil excessively thin because of dilution, poor quality, or improper grade	• Drain and refill crankcase with recommended oil
	• Excessive oil temperature	• Correct cause of overheating engine
	• Oil pressure relief spring weak or sticking	• Remove and inspect oil pressure relief valve assembly
	• Oil inlet tube and screen assembly has restriction or air leak	• Remove and inspect oil inlet tube and screen assembly. (Fill inlet tube with lacquer thinner to locate leaks.)
	• Excessive oil pump clearance	• Measure clearances
	• Excessive main, rod, or camshaft bearing clearance	• Measure bearing clearances, repair as necessary
High oil pressure	• Improper oil viscosity	• Drain and refill crankcase with correct viscosity oil
	• Oil pressure gauge or sending unit inaccurate	• Replace oil pressure gauge
	• Oil pressure relief valve sticking closed	• Remove and inspect oil pressure relief valve assembly
Main bearing noise	• Insufficient oil supply	• Inspect for low oil level and low oil pressure
	• Main bearing clearance excessive	• Measure main bearing clearance, repair as necessary
	• Bearing insert missing	• Replace missing insert
	• Crankshaft end-play excessive	• Measure end-play, repair as necessary
	• Improperly tightened main bearing cap bolts	• Tighten bolts with specified torque
	• Loose flywheel or drive plate	• Tighten flywheel or drive plate attaching bolts
	• Loose or damaged vibration damper	• Repair as necessary

Troubleshooting Engine Mechanical Problems

Problem	Cause	Solution
Connecting rod bearing noise	• Insufficient oil supply	• Inspect for low oil level and low oil pressure
	• Carbon build-up on piston	• Remove carbon from piston crown
	• Bearing clearance excessive or bearing missing	• Measure clearance, repair as necessary
	• Crankshaft connecting rod journal out-of-round	• Measure journal dimensions, repair or replace as necessary
	• Misaligned connecting rod or cap	• Repair as necessary
	• Connecting rod bolts tightened improperly	• Tighten bolts with specified torque
Piston noise	• Piston-to-cylinder wall clearance excessive (scuffed piston)	• Measure clearance and examine piston
	• Cylinder walls excessively tapered or out-of-round	• Measure cylinder wall dimensions, rebore cylinder
	• Piston ring broken	• Replace all rings on piston
	• Loose or seized piston pin	• Measure piston-to-pin clearance, repair as necessary
	• Connecting rods misaligned	• Measure rod alignment, straighten or replace
	• Piston ring side clearance excessively loose or tight	• Measure ring side clearance, repair as necessary
	• Carbon build-up on piston is excessive	• Remove carbon from piston
Valve actuating component noise	• Insufficient oil supply	• Check for: (a) Low oil level (b) Low oil pressure (c) Wrong hydraulic tappets (d) Restricted oil gallery (e) Excessive tappet to bore clearance
	• Rocker arms or pivots worn	• Replace worn rocker arms or pivots
	• Foreign objects or chips in hydraulic tappets	• Clean tappets
	• Excessive tappet leak-down	• Replace valve tappet
	• Tappet face worn	• Replace tappet; inspect corresponding cam lobe for wear
	• Broken or cocked valve springs	• Properly seat cocked springs; replace broken springs
	• Stem-to-guide clearance excessive	• Measure stem-to-guide clearance, repair as required
	• Valve bent	• Replace valve
	• Loose rocker arms	• Check and repair as necessary
	• Valve seat runout excessive	• Regrind valve seat/valves
	• Missing valve lock	• Install valve lock
	• Excessive engine oil	• Correct oil level

Troubleshooting Engine Performance

Problem	Cause	Solution
Hard starting (engine cranks normally)	• Faulty engine control system component	• Repair or replace as necessary
	• Faulty fuel pump	• Replace fuel pump
	• Faulty fuel system component	• Repair or replace as necessary
	• Faulty ignition coil	• Test and replace as necessary
	• Improper spark plug gap	• Adjust gap
	• Incorrect ignition timing	• Adjust timing
	• Incorrect valve timing	• Check valve timing; repair as necessary
Rough idle or stalling	• Incorrect curb or fast idle speed	• Adjust curb or fast idle speed (If possible)
	• Incorrect ignition timing	• Adjust timing to specification
	• Improper feedback system operation	• Refer to Chapter 4
	• Faulty EGR valve operation	• Test EGR system and replace as necessary
	• Faulty PCV valve air flow	• Test PCV valve and replace as necessary
	• Faulty TAC vacuum motor or valve	• Repair as necessary
	• Air leak into manifold vacuum	• Inspect manifold vacuum connections and repair as necessary
	• Faulty distributor rotor or cap	• Replace rotor or cap (Distributor systems only)
	• Improperly seated valves	• Test cylinder compression, repair as necessary
	• Incorrect ignition wiring	• Inspect wiring and correct as necessary
	• Faulty ignition coil	• Test coil and replace as necessary
	• Restricted air vent or idle passages	• Clean passages
	• Restricted air cleaner	• Clean or replace air cleaner filter element
Faulty low-speed operation	• Restricted idle air vents and passages	• Clean air vents and passages
	• Restricted air cleaner	• Clean or replace air cleaner filter element
	• Faulty spark plugs	• Clean or replace spark plugs
	• Dirty, corroded, or loose ignition secondary circuit wire connections	• Clean or tighten secondary circuit wire connections
	• Improper feedback system operation	• Refer to Chapter 4
	• Faulty ignition coil high voltage wire	• Replace ignition coil high voltage wire (Distributor systems only)
	• Faulty distributor cap	• Replace cap (Distributor systems only)
Faulty acceleration	• Incorrect ignition timing	• Adjust timing
	• Faulty fuel system component	• Repair or replace as necessary
	• Faulty spark plug(s)	• Clean or replace spark plug(s)
	• Improperly seated valves	• Test cylinder compression, repair as necessary
	• Faulty ignition coil	• Test coil and replace as necessary

Troubleshooting Engine Performance

Problem	Cause	Solution
Faulty acceleration (cont.)	• Improper feedback system operation	• Refer to Chapter 4
Faulty high speed operation	• Incorrect ignition timing • Faulty advance mechanism	• Adjust timing (if possible) • Check advance mechanism and repair as necessary (Distributor systems only)
	• Low fuel pump volume • Wrong spark plug air gap or wrong plug • Partially restricted exhaust manifold, exhaust pipe, catalytic converter, muffler, or tailpipe • Restricted vacuum passages • Restricted air cleaner	• Replace fuel pump • Adjust air gap or install correct plug • Eliminate restriction • Clean passages • Cleaner or replace filter element as necessary
	• Faulty distributor rotor or cap • Faulty ignition coil • Improperly seated valve(s) • Faulty valve spring(s) • Incorrect valve timing • Intake manifold restricted • Worn distributor shaft • Improper feedback system operation	• Replace rotor or cap (Distributor systems only) • Test coil and replace as necessary • Test cylinder compression, repair as necessary • Inspect and test valve spring tension, replace as necessary • Check valve timing and repair as necessary • Remove restriction or replace manifold • Replace shaft (Distributor systems only) • Refer to Chapter 4
Misfire at all speeds	• Faulty spark plug(s) • Faulty spark plug wire(s) • Faulty distributor cap or rotor • Faulty ignition coil • Primary ignition circuit shorted or open intermittently • Improperly seated valve(s) • Faulty hydraulic tappet(s) • Improper feedback system operation • Faulty valve spring(s) • Worn camshaft lobes • Air leak into manifold • Fuel pump volume or pressure low • Blown cylinder head gasket • Intake or exhaust manifold passage(s) restricted	• Clean or relace spark plug(s) • Replace as necessary • Replace cap or rotor (Distributor systems only) • Test coil and replace as necessary • Troubleshoot primary circuit and repair as necessary • Test cylinder compression, repair as necessary • Clean or replace tappet(s) • Refer to Chapter 4 • Inspect and test valve spring tension, repair as necessary • Replace camshaft • Check manifold vacuum and repair as necessary • Replace fuel pump • Replace gasket • Pass chain through passage(s) and repair as necessary
Power not up to normal	• Incorrect ignition timing • Faulty distributor rotor	• Adjust timing • Replace rotor (Distributor systems only)

Troubleshooting Engine Performance

Problem	Cause	Solution
Power not up to normal (cont.)	• Incorrect spark plug gap • Faulty fuel pump • Faulty fuel pump • Incorrect valve timing • Faulty ignition coil • Faulty ignition wires • Improperly seated valves • Blown cylinder head gasket • Leaking piston rings • Improper feedback system operation	• Adjust gap • Replace fuel pump • Replace fuel pump • Check valve timing and repair as necessary • Test coil and replace as necessary • Test wires and replace as necessary • Test cylinder compression and repair as necessary • Replace gasket • Test compression and repair as necessary • Refer to Chapter 4
Intake backfire	• Improper ignition timing • Defective EGR component • Defective TAC vacuum motor or valve	• Adjust timing • Repair as necessary • Repair as necessary
Exhaust backfire	• Air leak into manifold vacuum • Faulty air injection diverter valve • Exhaust leak	• Check manifold vacuum and repair as necessary • Test diverter valve and replace as necessary • Locate and eliminate leak
Ping or spark knock	• Incorrect ignition timing • Distributor advance malfunction • Excessive combustion chamber deposits • Air leak into manifold vacuum • Excessively high compression • Fuel octane rating excessively low • Sharp edges in combustion chamber • EGR valve not functioning properly	• Adjust timing • Inspect advance mechanism and repair as necessary (Distributor systems only) • Remove with combustion chamber cleaner • Check manifold vacuum and repair as necessary • Test compression and repair as necessary • Try alternate fuel source • Grind smooth • Test EGR system and replace as necessary
Surging (at cruising to top speeds)	• Low fuel pump pressure or volume • Improper PCV valve air flow • Air leak into manifold vacuum • Incorrect spark advance • Restricted fuel filter • Restricted air cleaner • EGR valve not functioning properly • Improper feedback system operation	• Replace fuel pump • Test PCV valve and replace as necessary • Check manifold vacuum and repair as necessary • Test and replace as necessary • Replace fuel filter • Clean or replace air cleaner filter element • Test EGR system and replace as necessary • Refer to Chapter 4

Troubleshooting the Serpentine Drive Belt

Problem	Cause	Solution
Tension sheeting fabric failure (woven fabric on outside circumference of belt has cracked or separated from body of belt)	• Grooved or backside idler pulley diameters are less than minimum recommended • Tension sheeting contacting (rubbing) stationary object • Excessive heat causing woven fabric to age • Tension sheeting splice has fractured	• Replace pulley(s) not conforming to specification • Correct rubbing condition • Replace belt • Replace belt
Noise (objectional squeal, squeak, or rumble is heard or felt while drive belt is in operation)	• Belt slippage • Bearing noise • Belt misalignment • Belt-to-pulley mismatch • Driven component inducing vibration • System resonant frequency inducing vibration	• Adjust belt • Locate and repair • Align belt/pulley(s) • Install correct belt • Locate defective driven component and repair • Vary belt tension within specifications. Replace belt.
Rib chunking (one or more ribs has separated from belt body)	• Foreign objects imbedded in pulley grooves • Installation damage • Drive loads in excess of design specifications • Insufficient internal belt adhesion	• Remove foreign objects from pulley grooves • Replace belt • Adjust belt tension • Replace belt
Rib or belt wear (belt ribs contact bottom of pulley grooves)	• Pulley(s) misaligned • Mismatch of belt and pulley groove widths • Abrasive environment • Rusted pulley(s) • Sharp or jagged pulley groove tips • Rubber deteriorated	• Align pulley(s) • Replace belt • Replace belt • Clean rust from pulley(s) • Replace pulley • Replace belt
Longitudinal belt cracking (cracks between two ribs)	• Belt has mistracked from pulley groove • Pulley groove tip has worn away rubber-to-tensile member	• Replace belt • Replace belt
Belt slips	• Belt slipping because of insufficient tension • Belt or pulley subjected to substance (belt dressing, oil, ethylene glycol) that has reduced friction • Driven component bearing failure • Belt glazed and hardened from heat and excessive slippage	• Adjust tension • Replace belt and clean pulleys • Replace faulty component bearing • Replace belt
"Groove jumping" (belt does not maintain correct position on pulley, or turns over and/or runs off pulleys)	• Insufficient belt tension • Pulley(s) not within design tolerance • Foreign object(s) in grooves	• Adjust belt tension • Replace pulley(s) • Remove foreign objects from grooves

AIR POLLUTION 4-2
NATURAL POLLUTANTS 4-2
INDUSTRIAL POLLUTANTS 4-2
AUTOMOTIVE POLLUTANTS 4-2
  TEMPERATURE INVERSION 4-2
  HEAT TRANSFER 4-3
AUTOMOTIVE EMISSIONS 4-3
EXHAUST GASES 4-3
  HYDROCARBONS 4-3
  CARBON MONOXIDE 4-4
  NITROGEN 4-4
  OXIDES OF SULFUR 4-4
  PARTICULATE MATTER 4-4
CRANKCASE EMISSIONS 4-5
EVAPORATIVE EMISSIONS 4-5
EMISSION CONTROLS 4-6
POSITIVE CRANKCASE VENTILATION
 SYSTEM 4-6
  OPERATION 4-6
  SERVICE 4-6
CONTROLLED COMBUSTION SYSTEM
 (CCS) 4-6
  OPERATION 4-6
  SERVICE 4-6
EVAPORATIVE EMISSION CONTROL
 SYSTEM 4-7
  OPERATION 4-7
  SERVICE 4-7
TRANSMISSION CONTROLLED SPARK
 SYSTEM 4-8
  OPERATION 4-8
AIR INJECTION REACTOR
 SYSTEM 4-10
  OPERATION 4-10
  SERVICE 4-11
  REMOVAL & INSTALLATION 4-11
EXHAUST GAS RECIRCULATION
 SYSTEM 4-13
  OPERATION 4-13
  REMOVAL & INSTALLATION 4-14
EARLY FUEL EVAPORATION
 SYSTEM 4-14
  OPERATION 4-14
CATALYTIC CONVERTER 4-15
  OPERATION 4-15
VACUUM DIAGRAMS 4-16

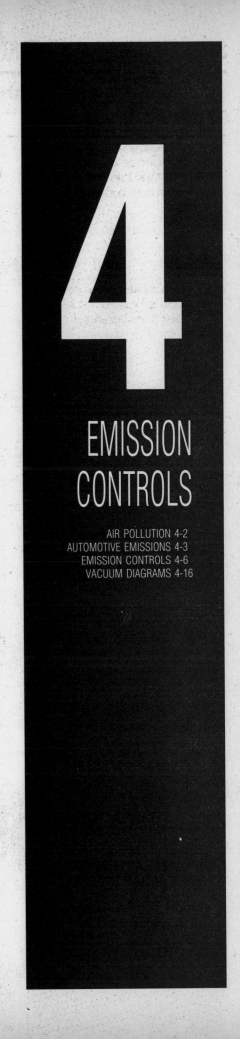

4

EMISSION CONTROLS

AIR POLLUTION 4-2
AUTOMOTIVE EMISSIONS 4-3
EMISSION CONTROLS 4-6
VACUUM DIAGRAMS 4-16

AIR POLLUTION

The earth's atmosphere, at or near sea level, consists approximately of 78 percent nitrogen, 21 percent oxygen and 1 percent other gases. If it were possible to remain in this state, 100 percent clean air would result. However, many varied sources allow other gases and particulates to mix with the clean air, causing our atmosphere to become unclean or polluted.

Some of these pollutants are visible while others are invisible, with each having the capability of causing distress to the eyes, ears, throat, skin and respiratory system. Should these pollutants become concentrated in a specific area and under certain conditions, death could result due to the displacement or chemical change of the oxygen content in the air. These pollutants can also cause great damage to the environment and to the many man made objects that are exposed to the elements.

To better understand the causes of air pollution, the pollutants can be categorized into 3 separate types, natural, industrial and automotive.

Natural Pollutants

Natural pollution has been present on earth since before man appeared and continues to be a factor when discussing air pollution, although it causes only a small percentage of the overall pollution problem. It is the direct result of decaying organic matter, wind born smoke and particulates from such natural events as plain and forest fires (ignited by heat or lightning), volcanic ash, sand and dust which can spread over a large area of the countryside.

Such a phenomenon of natural pollution has been seen in the form of volcanic eruptions, with the resulting plume of smoke, steam and volcanic ash blotting out the sun's rays as it spreads and rises higher into the atmosphere. As it travels into the atmosphere the upper air currents catch and carry the smoke and ash, while condensing the steam back into water vapor. As the water vapor, smoke and ash travel on their journey, the smoke dissipates into the atmosphere while the ash and moisture settle back to earth in a trail hundreds of miles long. In some cases, lives are lost and millions of dollars of property damage result.

Industrial Pollutants

Industrial pollution is caused primarily by industrial processes, the burning of coal, oil and natural gas, which in turn produce smoke and fumes. Because the burning fuels contain large amounts of sulfur, the principal ingredients of smoke and fumes are sulfur dioxide and particulate matter. This type of pollutant occurs most severely during still, damp and cool weather, such as at night. Even in its less severe form, this pollutant is not confined to just cities. Because of air movements, the pollutants move for miles over the surrounding countryside, leaving in its path a barren and unhealthy environment for all living things.

Working with Federal, State and Local mandated regulations and by carefully monitoring emissions, big business has greatly reduced the amount of pollutant introduced from its industrial sources, striving to obtain an acceptable level. Because of the mandated industrial emission clean up, many land areas and streams in and around the cities that were formerly barren of vegetation and life, have now begun to move back in the direction of nature's intended balance.

Automotive Pollutants

The third major source of air pollution is automotive emissions. The emissions from the internal combustion engines were not an appreciable problem years ago because of the small number of registered vehicles and the nation's small highway system. However, during the early 1950's, the trend of the American people was to move from the cities to the surrounding suburbs. This caused an immediate problem in transportation because the majority of suburbs were not afforded mass transit conveniences. This lack of transportation created an attractive market for the automobile manufacturers, which resulted in a dramatic increase in the number of vehicles produced and sold, along with a marked increase in highway construction between cities and the suburbs. Multi-vehicle families emerged with a growing emphasis placed on an individual vehicle per family member. As the increase in vehicle ownership and usage occurred, so did pollutant levels in and around the cities, as suburbanites drove daily to their businesses and employment, returning at the end of the day to their homes in the suburbs.

It was noted that a smoke and fog type haze was being formed and at times, remained in suspension over the cities, taking time to dissipate. At first this "smog," derived from the words "smoke" and "fog," was thought to result from industrial pollution but it was determined that automobile emissions shared the blame. It was discovered that when normal automobile emissions were exposed to sunlight for a period of time, complex chemical reactions would take place.

It is now known that smog is a photo chemical layer which develops when certain oxides of nitrogen (NOx) and unburned hydrocarbons (HC) from automobile emissions are exposed to sunlight. Pollution was more severe when smog would become stagnant over an area in which a warm layer of air settled over the top of the cooler air mass, trapping and holding the cooler mass at ground level. The trapped cooler air would keep the emissions from being dispersed and diluted through normal air flows. This type of air stagnation was given the name "Temperature Inversion."

TEMPERATURE INVERSION

In normal weather situations, surface air is warmed by heat radiating from the earth's surface and the sun's rays. This causes it to rise upward, into the atmosphere. Upon rising it will cool through a convection type heat exchange with the cooler upper air. As warm air rises, the surface pollutants are carried upward and dissipated into the atmosphere.

When a temperature inversion occurs, we find the higher air is no longer cooler, but is warmer than the surface air, causing the cooler surface air to become trapped. This warm air blanket can extend from above ground level to a few hundred or even a few thousand feet into the air. As the surface air is trapped, so are the pollutants, causing a severe smog condition. Should this stagnant air mass extend to a few thousand feet high, enough air movement with the inversion takes place to allow the smog layer to rise above ground level but the pollutants still cannot dissipate. This inversion can remain for days over an area, with the smog level only rising or lowering from ground level to a few hundred feet high. Meanwhile, the pollutant levels increase, causing eye irritation, respiratory problems, reduced visibility, plant damage and in some cases, even disease.

This inversion phenomenon was first noted in the Los Angeles, California area. The city lies in terrain resembling a basin and with certain weather conditions, a cold air mass is held in the basin while a warmer air mass covers it like a lid.

Because this type of condition was first documented as prevalent in the Los Angeles area, this type of trapped pollution was named Los Angeles Smog, although it occurs in other areas where a large concentration of automobiles are used and the air remains stagnant for any length of time.

HEAT TRANSFER

Consider the internal combustion engine as a machine in which raw materials must be placed so a finished product comes out. As in any machine operation, a certain amount of wasted material is formed. When we relate this to the internal combustion engine, we find that through the input of air and fuel, we obtain power during the combustion process to drive the vehicle. The by-product or waste of this power is, in part, heat and exhaust gases with which we must dispose.

The heat from the combustion process can rise to over 4000°F (2204°C). The dissipation of this heat is controlled by a ram air effect, the use of cooling fans to cause air flow and a liquid coolant solution surrounding the combustion area to transfer the heat of combustion through the cylinder walls and into the coolant. The coolant is then directed to a thin-finned, multi-tubed radiator, from which the excess heat is transferred to the atmosphere by 1 of the 3 heat transfer methods, conduction, convection or radiation.

The cooling of the combustion area is an important part in the control of exhaust emissions. To understand the behavior of the combustion and transfer of its heat, consider the air/fuel charge. It is ignited and the flame front burns progressively across the combustion chamber until the burning charge reaches the cylinder walls. Some of the fuel in contact with the walls is not hot enough to burn, thereby snuffing out or quenching the combustion process. This leaves unburned fuel in the combustion chamber. This unburned fuel is then forced out of the cylinder and into the exhaust system, along with the exhaust gases.

Many attempts have been made to minimize the amount of unburned fuel in the combustion chambers due to quenching, by increasing the coolant temperature and lessening the contact area of the coolant around the combustion area. However, design limitations within the combustion chambers prevent the complete burning of the air/fuel charge, so a certain amount of the unburned fuel is still expelled into the exhaust system, regardless of modifications to the engine.

AUTOMOTIVE EMISSIONS

Before emission controls were mandated on internal combustion engines, other sources of engine pollutants were discovered along with the exhaust emissions. It was determined that engine combustion exhaust produced approximately 60 percent of the total emission pollutants, fuel evaporation from the fuel tank and carburetor vents produced 20 percent, with the final 20 percent being produced through the crankcase as a by-product of the combustion process.

Exhaust Gases

The exhaust gases emitted into the atmosphere are a combination of burned and unburned fuel. To understand the exhaust emission and its composition, we must review some basic chemistry.

When the air/fuel mixture is introduced into the engine, we are mixing air, composed of nitrogen (78 percent), oxygen (21 percent) and other gases (1 percent) with the fuel, which is 100 percent hydrocarbons (HC), in a semi-controlled ratio. As the combustion process is accomplished, power is produced to move the vehicle while the heat of combustion is transferred to the cooling system. The exhaust gases are then composed of nitrogen, a diatomic gas (N_2), the same as was introduced in the engine, carbon dioxide (CO_2), the same gas that is used in beverage carbonation, and water vapor (H_2O). The nitrogen (N_2), for the most part, passes through the engine unchanged, while the oxygen (O_2) reacts (burns) with the hydrocarbons (HC) and produces the carbon dioxide (CO_2) and the water vapors (H_2O). If this chemical process would be the only process to take place, the exhaust emissions would be harmless. However, during the combustion process, other compounds are formed which are considered dangerous. These pollutants are hydrocarbons (HC), carbon monoxide (CO), oxides of nitrogen (NOx) oxides of sulfur (SOx) and engine particulates.

HYDROCARBONS

Hydrocarbons (HC) are essentially fuel which was not burned during the combustion process or which has escaped into the atmosphere through fuel evaporation. The main sources of incomplete combustion are rich air/fuel mixtures, low engine temperatures and improper spark timing. The main sources of hydrocarbon emission through fuel evaporation on most vehicles used to be the vehicle's fuel tank and carburetor float bowl.

To reduce combustion hydrocarbon emission, engine modifications were made to minimize dead space and surface area in the combustion chamber. In addition, the air/fuel mixture was made more lean through the improved control which feedback carburetion and fuel injection offers and by the addition of external controls to aid in further combustion of the hydrocarbons outside the engine. Two such methods were the addition of air injection systems, to inject fresh air into the exhaust manifolds and the installation of catalytic converters, units that are able to burn traces of hydrocarbons without affecting the internal combustion process or fuel economy.

To control hydrocarbon emissions through fuel evaporation, modifications were made to the fuel tank to allow storage of the fuel vapors during periods of engine shut-down. Modifications were also made to the air intake system so that at specific times during engine operation, these vapors may be purged and burned by blending them with the air/fuel mixture.

CARBON MONOXIDE

Carbon monoxide is formed when not enough oxygen is present during the combustion process to convert carbon (C) to carbon dioxide (CO_2). An increase in the carbon monoxide (CO) emission is normally accompanied by an increase in the hydrocarbon (HC) emission because of the lack of oxygen to completely burn all of the fuel mixture.

Carbon monoxide (CO) also increases the rate at which the photo chemical smog is formed by speeding up the conversion of nitric oxide (NO) to nitrogen dioxide (NO_2). To accomplish this, carbon monoxide (CO) combines with oxygen (O_2) and nitric oxide (NO) to produce carbon dioxide (CO_2) and nitrogen dioxide (NO_2). ($CO + O_2 + NO$ $CO_2 + NO_2$).

The dangers of carbon monoxide, which is an odorless and colorless toxic gas are many. When carbon monoxide is inhaled into the lungs and passed into the blood stream, oxygen is replaced by the carbon monoxide in the red blood cells, causing a reduction in the amount of oxygen supplied to the many parts of the body. This lack of oxygen causes headaches, lack of coordination, reduced mental alertness and, should the carbon monoxide concentration be high enough, death could result.

NITROGEN

Normally, nitrogen is an inert gas. When heated to approximately 2500°F (1371°C) through the combustion process, this gas becomes active and causes an increase in the nitric oxide (NO) emission.

Oxides of nitrogen (NOx) are composed of approximately 97–98 percent nitric oxide (NO). Nitric oxide is a colorless gas but when it is passed into the atmosphere, it combines with oxygen and forms nitrogen dioxide (NO_2). The nitrogen dioxide then combines with chemically active hydrocarbons (HC) and when in the presence of sunlight, causes the formation of photo-chemical smog.

Ozone

To further complicate matters, some of the nitrogen dioxide (NO_2) is broken apart by the sunlight to form nitric oxide and oxygen. (NO_2 + sunlight $NO + O$). This single atom of oxygen then combines with diatomic (meaning 2 atoms) oxygen (O_2) to form ozone (O_3). Ozone is one of the smells associated with smog. It

has a pungent and offensive odor, irritates the eyes and lung tissues, affects the growth of plant life and causes rapid deterioration of rubber products. Ozone can be formed by sunlight as well as electrical discharge into the air.

The most common discharge area on the automobile engine is the secondary ignition electrical system, especially when inferior quality spark plug cables are used. As the surge of high voltage is routed through the secondary cable, the circuit builds up an electrical field around the wire, which acts upon the oxygen in the surrounding air to form the ozone. The faint glow along the cable with the engine running that may be visible on a dark night, is called the "corona discharge." It is the result of the electrical field passing from a high along the cable, to a low in the surrounding air, which forms the ozone gas. The combination of corona and ozone has been a major cause of cable deterioration. Recently, different and better quality insulating materials have lengthened the life of the electrical cables.

Although ozone at ground level can be harmful, ozone is beneficial to the earth's inhabitants. By having a concentrated ozone layer called the "ozonosphere," between 10 and 20 miles (16–32 km) up in the atmosphere, much of the ultra violet radiation from the sun's rays are absorbed and screened. If this ozone layer were not present, much of the earth's surface would be burned, dried and unfit for human life.

OXIDES OF SULFUR

Oxides of sulfur (SOx) were initially ignored in the exhaust system emissions, since the sulfur content of gasoline as a fuel is less than $\frac{1}{10}$ of 1 percent. Because of this small amount, it was felt that it contributed very little to the overall pollution problem. However, because of the difficulty in solving the sulfur emissions in industrial pollutions and the introduction of catalytic converter to the automobile exhaust systems, a change was mandated. The automobile exhaust system, when equipped with a catalytic converter, changes the sulfur dioxide (SO_2) into sulfur trioxide (SO_3).

When this combines with water vapors (H_2O), a sulfuric acid mist (H_2SO_4) is formed and is a very difficult pollutant to handle since it is extremely corrosive. This sulfuric acid mist that is formed, is the same mist that rises from the vents of an automobile battery when an active chemical reaction takes place within the battery cells.

When a large concentration of vehicles equipped with catalytic converters are operating in an area, this acid mist may rise and be distributed over a large ground area causing land, plant, crop, paint and building damage.

PARTICULATE MATTER

A certain amount of particulate matter is present in the burning of any fuel, with carbon constituting the largest percentage of the particulates. In gasoline, the remaining particulates are the burned remains of the various other compounds used in its manufacture. When a gasoline engine is in good internal condition, the particulate emissions are low but as the engine wears internally, the particulate emissions increase. By visually inspecting the tail pipe emissions, a determination can be made as to where an engine defect may exist. An engine with light gray or blue smoke emitting from the tail pipe normally indicates an increase in the oil consumption through burning due to internal engine wear. Black smoke would indicate a defective fuel delivery system, causing the engine to operate in a rich mode. Regardless of the color of the smoke, the internal part of the engine or the fuel delivery system should be repaired to prevent excess particulate emissions.

Diesel and turbine engines emit a darkened plume of smoke from the exhaust system because of the type of fuel used. Emission control regulations are mandated for this type of emission and more stringent measures are being used to prevent excess emission of the particulate matter. Electronic components are being introduced to control the injection of the fuel at precisely the proper time of piston travel, to achieve the optimum in fuel ignition and fuel usage. Other particulate after-burning components are being tested to achieve a cleaner emission.

Good grades of engine lubricating oils should be used, which meet the manufacturers specification. Cut-rate oils can contribute to the particulate emission problem because of their low flash or ignition temperature point. Such oils burn prematurely during the combustion process causing emission of particulate matter.

The cooling system is an important factor in the reduction of particulate matter. The optimum combustion will occur, with the cooling system operating at a temperature specified by the manufacturer. The cooling system must be maintained in the same manner as the engine oiling system, as each system is required to perform properly in order for the engine to operate efficiently for a long time.

Crankcase Emissions

Crankcase emissions are made up of water, acids, unburned fuel, oil fumes and particulates. These emissions are classified as hydrocarbons (HC) and are formed by the small amount of unburned, compressed air/fuel mixture entering the crankcase from the combustion area (between the cylinder walls and piston rings) during the compression and power strokes. The head of the compression and combustion help to form the remaining crankcase emissions.

Since the first engines, crankcase emissions were allowed into the atmosphere through a road draft tube, mounted on the lower side of the engine block. Fresh air came in through an open oil filler cap or breather. The air passed through the crankcase mixing with blow-by gases. The motion of the vehicle and the air blowing past the open end of the road draft tube caused a low pressure area (vacuum) at the end of the tube. Crankcase emissions were simply drawn out of the road draft tube into the air.

To control the crankcase emission, the road draft tube was deleted. A hose and/or tubing was routed from the crankcase to the intake manifold so the blow-by emission could be burned with the air/fuel mixture. However, it was found that intake manifold vacuum, used to draw the crankcase emissions into the manifold,

would vary in strength at the wrong time and not allow the proper emission flow. A regulating valve was needed to control the flow of air through the crankcase.

Testing, showed the removal of the blow-by gases from the crankcase as quickly as possible, was most important to the longevity of the engine. Should large accumulations of blow-by gases remain and condense, dilution of the engine oil would occur to form water, soots, resins, acids and lead salts, resulting in the formation of sludge and varnishes. This condensation of the blow-by gases occurs more frequently on vehicles used in numerous starting and stopping conditions, excessive idling and when the engine is not allowed to attain normal operating temperature through short runs.

Evaporative Emissions

Gasoline fuel is a major source of pollution, before and after it is burned in the automobile engine. From the time the fuel is refined, stored, pumped and transported, again stored until it is pumped into the fuel tank of the vehicle, the gasoline gives off unburned hydrocarbons (HC) into the atmosphere. Through the redesign of storage areas and venting systems, the pollution factor was diminished, but not eliminated, from the refinery standpoint. However, the automobile still remained the primary source of vaporized, unburned hydrocarbon (HC) emissions.

Fuel pumped from an underground storage tank is cool but when exposed to a warmer ambient temperature, will expand. Before controls were mandated, an owner might fill the fuel tank with fuel from an underground storage tank and park the vehicle for some time in warm area, such as a parking lot. As the fuel would warm, it would expand and should no provisions or area be provided for the expansion, the fuel would spill out of the filler neck and onto the ground, causing hydrocarbon (HC) pollution and creating a severe fire hazard. To correct this condition, the vehicle manufacturers added overflow plumbing and/or gasoline tanks with built in expansion areas or domes.

However, this did not control the fuel vapor emission from the fuel tank. It was determined that most of the fuel evaporation occurred when the vehicle was stationary and the engine not operating. Most vehicles carry 5–25 gallons (19–95 liters) of gasoline. Should a large concentration of vehicles be parked in one area, such as a large parking lot, excessive fuel vapor emissions would take place, increasing as the temperature increases.

To prevent the vapor emission from escaping into the atmosphere, the fuel systems were designed to trap the vapors while the vehicle is stationary, by sealing the system from the atmosphere. A storage system is used to collect and hold the fuel vapors from the carburetor (if equipped) and the fuel tank when the engine is not operating. When the engine is started, the storage system is then purged of the fuel vapors, which are drawn into the engine and burned with the air/fuel mixture.

EMISSION CONTROLS

Positive Crankcase Ventilation System

OPERATION

▶ See Figure 1

This system draws crankcase vapors that are formed through normal combustion into the intake manifold and subsequently into the combustion chamber to be burned. Fresh air is introduced to the crankcase by a hose connected to the carburetor air cleaner or a vented oil filler cap, on older models. Manifold vacuum is used to draw the vapors from the crankcase through a PCV valve and into the intake manifold. Vented and nonvented filler caps were used on various models until 1968, after which only nonvented caps were used.

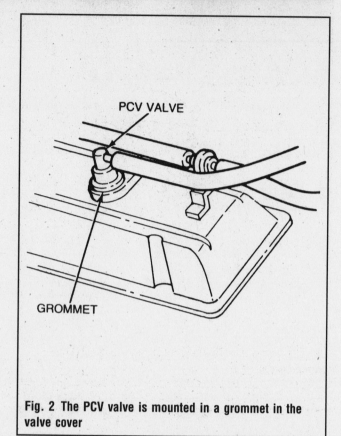

Fig. 2 The PCV valve is mounted in a grommet in the valve cover

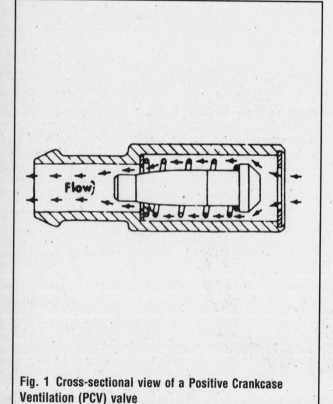

Fig. 1 Cross-sectional view of a Positive Crankcase Ventilation (PCV) valve

SERVICE

▶ See Figure 2

Inspect the PCV system hose and connections at each tune-up and replace any deteriorated hoses. Check the PCV valve at every tune-up and replace it every 24,000 miles. For details on PCV valve replacement, refer to Section 1.

Controlled Combustion System (CCS)

OPERATION

CCS relies upon leaner air/fuel mixtures and altered ignition timing to improve combustion efficiency. A special air cleaner with a thermostatically controlled opening is used on most models equipped with CCS to make sure that air entering the carburetor is kept at 100°F. This allows leaner carburetor settings and improves engine warm-up. A higher temperature thermostat (15°F higher) is employed on CCS cars to further improve emission control.

SERVICE

▶ See Figure 3

Since the only extra component added to CCS vehicles is the thermostatically controlled air cleaner, there is no additional maintenance required; however, tune-up adjustments such as idle speed, ignition timing, and dwell become much more critical. Care must be taken to make sure that these settings are correct, both for trouble-free operation and a low emission level.

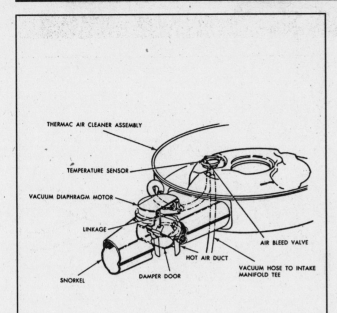

Fig. 3 View of the Thermac air cleaner and related components

Evaporative Emission Control System

OPERATION

◆ **See Figure 4**

Introduced on California cars in 1970, and nationwide in 1971, this system reduces the amount of escaping gasoline vapors. Float bowl emissions are controlled by internal carburetor modifications. Redesigned bowl vents, reduced bowl capacity, heat shields, and improved intake manifold-to-carburetor insulation serve to reduce vapor loss into the atmosphere. The venting of fuel tank vapors into the air has been stopped. Fuel vapors are now directed through lines to a canister containing an activated charcoal filter. Unburned vapors are trapped here until the engine is started. When the engine is running, the canister is purged by air drawn in by manifold vacuum. The air and fuel vapors are directed into the engine to be burned.

SERVICE

◆ **See Figure 5**

Replace the canister filter every 12 months or 12,000 miles on 1971 models; on 1972 and later models, it is replaced every 24 months or 24,000 miles. If the fuel tank cap requires replacement, make sure that the new cap is the correct part for your car.

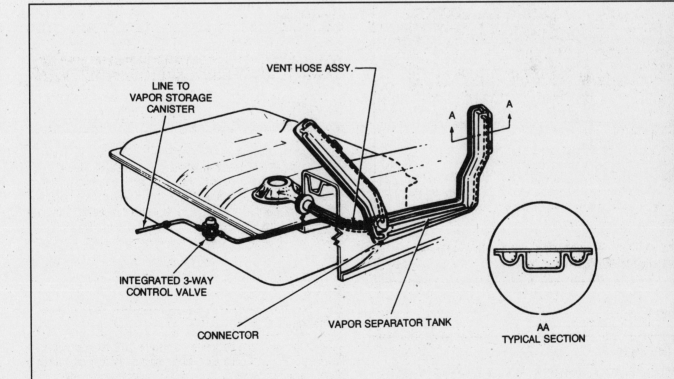

Fig. 4 Evaporative emission control vapor separator system

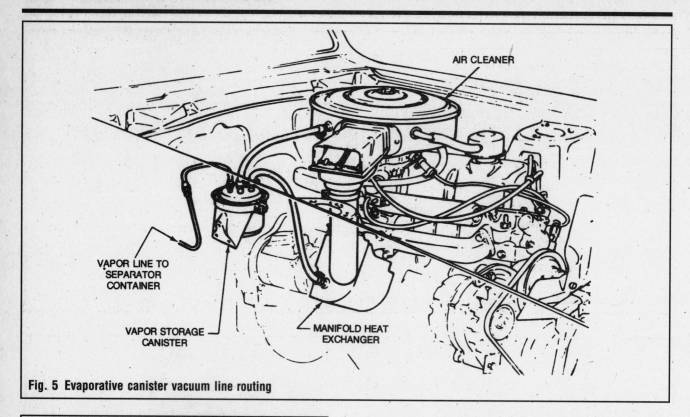

Fig. 5 Evaporative canister vacuum line routing

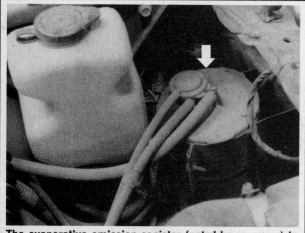

The evaporative emission canister (noted by an arrow) is located in the front driver's side of the engine compartment

Transmission Controlled Spark System

OPERATION

♦ See Figures 6, 7 and 8

This system, introduced in 1970, controls exhaust emissions by eliminating vacuum advance in the lower forward gears.

The 1970 system consists of a transmission switch, solenoid vacuum switch, time delay relay, and a thermostatic water temperature switch. The solenoid vacuum switch is de-energized in the lower gears via the transmission switch and closes off distributor vacuum. The transmission switch is activated by the shifter shaft,

on manual transmissions, or by oil pressure, on automatic transmissions. The switch energizes the solenoid in high gear, the plunger extends and uncovers the vacuum port, and the distributor receives full vacuum. The temperature switch overrides the system until the engine temperature reaches 82°F. This allows vacuum advance in all gears, thereby preventing stalling after starting. A time delay relay opens 15 seconds after the ignition is switched on. Full vacuum advance during this delay eliminates the possibility of stalling.

The 1971 system is similar, except that the vacuum solenoid, now called a Combination Emissions Control solenoid, (CEC) serves two functions. One function is to control distributor vacuum; the added function is to act as a deceleration throttle stop in high gear. This cuts down on emissions when the vehicle is coming to a stop in high gear. Two throttle settings are necessary; one for curb idle and one for emission control on coast. Both settings are described in the tune-up section.

The 1972 6-cylinder system is similar to that used in 1971, except that an idle stop solenoid has been added to the system. In the energized position, the solenoid maintains engine speed at a predetermined fast idle. When de-energized, the solenoid allows the throttle plates to close beyond the normal idle position; thus cutting off the air supply and preventing engine run-on. The six is the only 1972 engine with a CEC valve, which serves the same deceleration function as in 1971. The time delay relay delays full vacuum 20 seconds after the transmission is shifted into high gear. A vacuum advance solenoid, similar to that used in 1970, is used on V8 engines. The solenoid controls distributor vacuum advance and performs no throttle positioning function. The idle stop solenoid used operates in the same manner as the one on 6-cylinder engines. All air-conditioned cars have an additional anti-diesel (run-on) solenoid which engages the compressor clutch for three seconds after the ignition is switched off. The 1973 TCS system differs from the 1972 system in three ways. The 23 second up-shift delay has been replaced by a 20 second starting relay. This

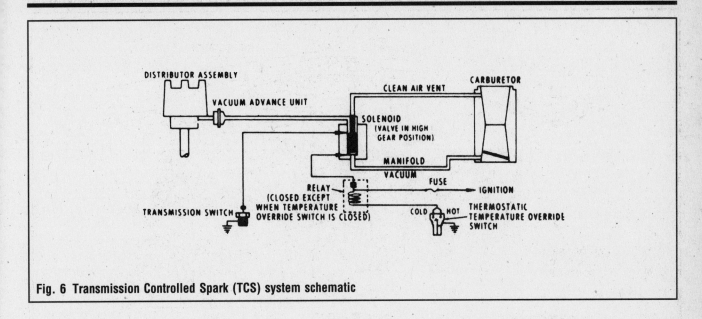

Fig. 6 Transmission Controlled Spark (TCS) system schematic

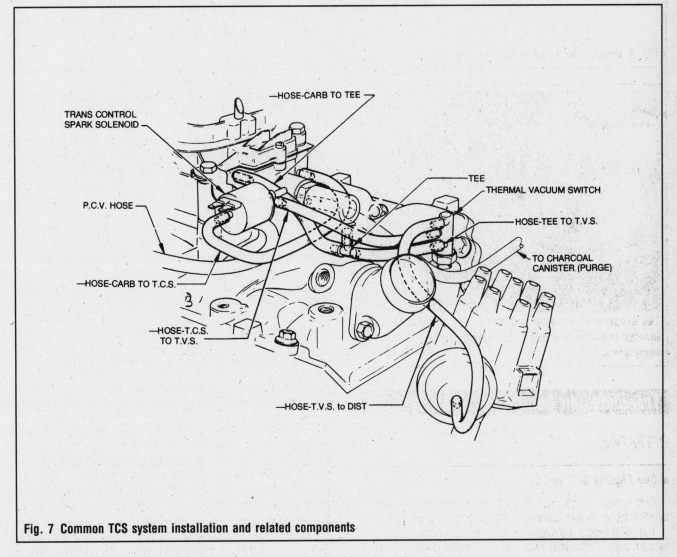

Fig. 7 Common TCS system installation and related components

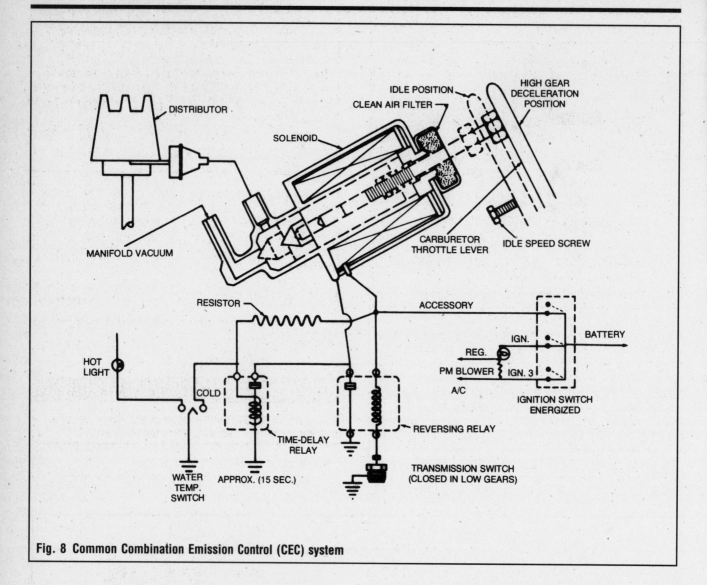

Fig. 8 Common Combination Emission Control (CEC) system

relay closes to complete the TCS circuit and open the TCS sole-noid, allowing vacuum advance, for 20 seconds after the key is turned to the **ON** position. The operating temperature of the tem-perature override switch has been raised to 93°F, and the switch which was used to engage the A/C compressor when the key was turned **OFF** has been eliminated. All models are equipped with an electric throttle control solenoid to prevent run-on. The 1973 TCS system is used on all models equipped with a 307 cu in. V8 en-gine and all V8 models equipped with a manual transmission.

The 1974 TCS system is used only on manual transmission models. System components remain unchanged from 1973. The vacuum advance solenoid is located on the coil bracket. The TCS system is not used on 1975 and later models.

Air Injection Reactor System

OPERATION

▶ **See Figures 9 and 10**

This system was first introduced on California cars in 1966. The Air Injection Reactor (AIR) system injects compressed air into

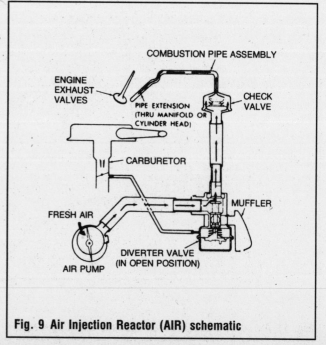

Fig. 9 Air Injection Reactor (AIR) schematic

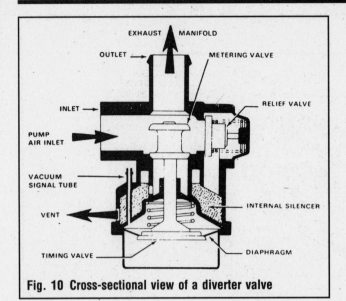

Fig. 10 Cross-sectional view of a diverter valve

the exhaust system, close enough to the exhaust valves to continue the burning of the normally unburned segment of the exhaust gases. To do this, it employs an air injection pump and a system of hoses, valves, tubes, etc., necessary to carry the compressed air from the pump to the exhaust manifolds. Carburetors and distributors for AIR engines have specific modifications to adapt them to the air injection system; these components should not be interchanged with those intended for use on engines that do not have the system.

A diverter valve is used to prevent backfiring. The valve senses sudden increases in manifold vacuum and ceases the injection of air during fuel-rich periods. During coasting, this valve diverts the entire air flow through a muffler and during high engine speeds, expels it through a relief valve. Check valves in the system prevent exhaust gases from entering the pump.

The 1975 and later AIR system remains basically the same in some engine applications. However, some engines use a converter AIR system in which air is injected into the exhaust system ahead of the catalytic converter.

SERVICE

The AIR system's effectiveness depends on correct engine idle speed, ignition timing, and dwell. These settings should be strictly adhered to and checked frequently. All hoses and fittings should be inspected for condition and the tightness of connections. Check the drive belt for wear and tension every 12 months or 12,000 miles.

REMOVAL & INSTALLATION

Air Pump

▶ **See Figures 11, 12, 13 and 14**

❈❈ WARNING

Do not pry on the pump housing or clamp the pump in a vise; the housing is soft and may become distorted.

1. Disconnect the air hoses at the pump.
2. Hold the pump pulley from turning and loosen the pulley bolts.

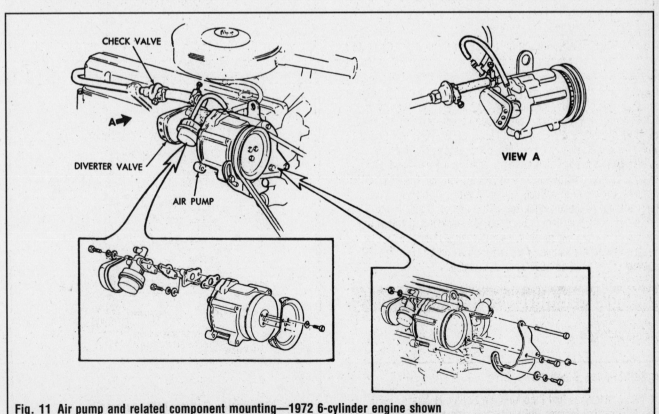

Fig. 11 Air pump and related component mounting—1972 6-cylinder engine shown

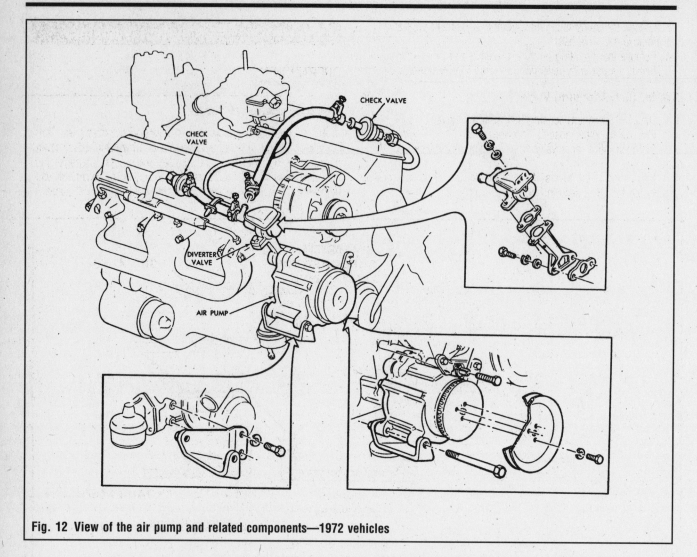

Fig. 12 View of the air pump and related components—1972 vehicles

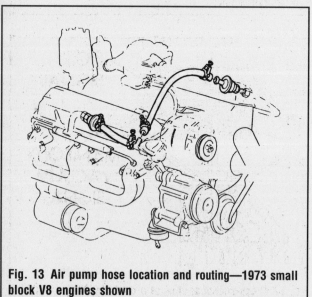

Fig. 13 Air pump hose location and routing—1973 small block V8 engines shown

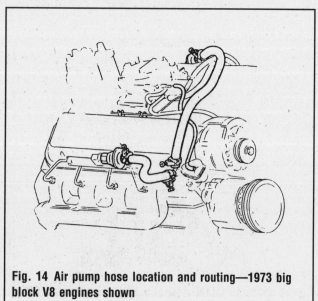

Fig. 14 Air pump hose location and routing—1973 big block V8 engines shown

3. Loosen the pump mounting bolt and adjustment bracket bolt. Remove the drive belt.

4. Remove the mounting bolts, and then remove the pump.

5. Install the pump by reversing the removal procedure.

Diverter (Anti-Afterburn) Valve

1. Detach the vacuum sensing line from the valve.

2. Remove the other hose(s) from the valve.

3. Unfasten the diverter valve from the elbow or the pump body.

4. Installation is the reverse of removal. Always use a new gasket. Tighten the valve securing bolts to 85 inch lbs.

Exhaust Gas Recirculation System

OPERATION

▶ **See Figures 15, 16 and 17**

All 1973 and later engines are equipped with Exhaust Gas Recirculation (EGR). This system consists of a metering valve, a vacuum line to the carburetor, and internal exhaust gas passages in the intake manifold. The EGR valve is controlled by carburetor vacuum, and accordingly opens and closes to admit exhaust gases

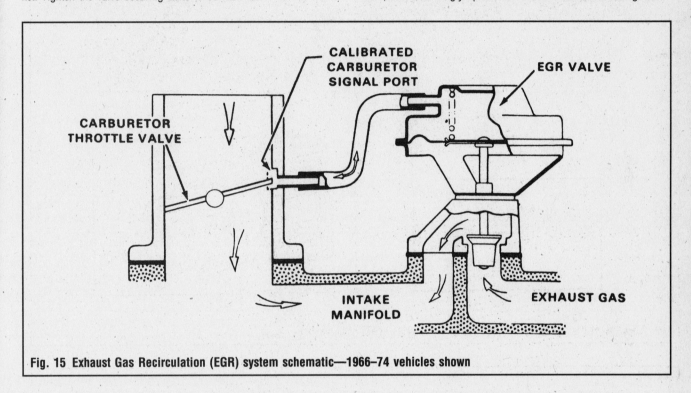

Fig. 15 Exhaust Gas Recirculation (EGR) system schematic—1966–74 vehicles shown

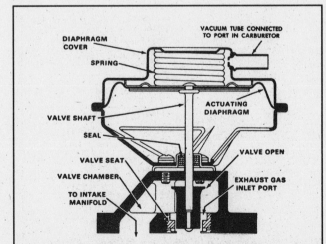

Fig. 16 Cross-sectional view of a single diaphragm EGR valve

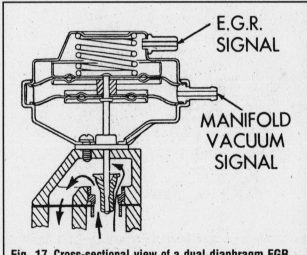

Fig. 17 Cross-sectional view of a dual diaphragm EGR valve

into the fuel/air mixture. The exhaust gases lower the combustion temperature and reduce the amount of oxides of nitrogen (NO_x) produced. The valve is closed at idle and wide open throttle, but is open between the two extreme throttle positions.

Some California engines are equipped with a dual diaphragm EGR valve. This valve further limits the exhaust gas opening (compared to the single diaphragm EGR valve) during high intake manifold vacuum periods, such as high-speed cruising, and provides more exhaust gas recirculation during acceleration when manifold vacuum is low. In addition to the hose running to the thermal vacuum switch, a second hose is connected directly to the intake manifold.

REMOVAL & INSTALLATION

EGR Valve

▶ **See Figure 18**

1. Pull the vacuum sensing line from the fitting on top of the EGR valve.
2. Unfasten the bolt which secures the valve clamp to the manifold, or carburetor, as applicable.
3. Remove the clamp and the EGR valve from the manifold, or carburetor, as applicable.
4. Installation is the reverse of removal. Use a new valve gasket. Tighten the clamp bolt to 25 ft. lbs. and lock it with its tab, if equipped.

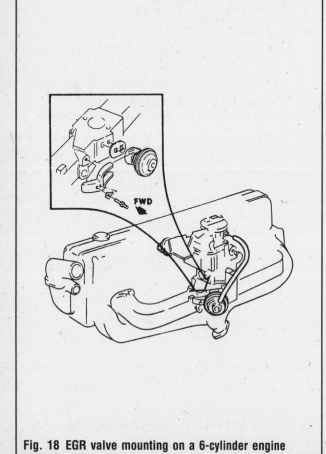

Fig. 18 EGR valve mounting on a 6-cylinder engine

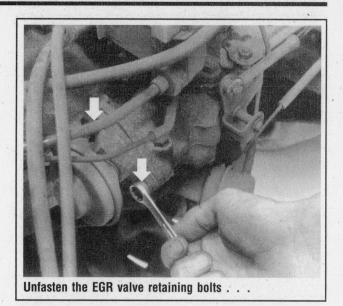

Unfasten the EGR valve retaining bolts . . .

. . . then remove the EGR valve. Note that on in-line 6-cylinder engines, the EGR valve is mounted to the carburetor

Early Fuel Evaporation System

OPERATION

▶ **See Figure 19**

This system is used on all 1975 and later engines to provide quicker warmups and improved driveability while reducing exhaust emissions.

Six-cylinder EFE systems consist of an EFE valve at the flange of the exhaust manifold, an actuator, a Thermal Vacuum Switch (TVS) and a vacuum solenoid. The TVS is a normally closed switch which is sensitive to oil temperature. It is located on the rightside of the cylinder block, forward of the oil pressure switch. With oil temperature below 150°F, the TVS is closed which energizes the vacuum solenoid and allows manifold vacuum to the actuator valve. The actuator in turn closes the EFE valve which causes hot exhaust gases to be routed up to the base of the carburetor. When oil temperature reaches 150°F, the TVS opens. This

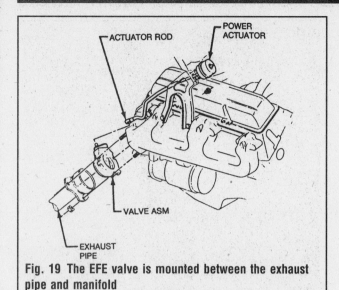

Fig. 19 The EFE valve is mounted between the exhaust pipe and manifold

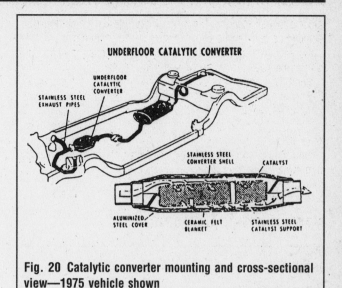

Fig. 20 Catalytic converter mounting and cross-sectional view—1975 vehicle shown

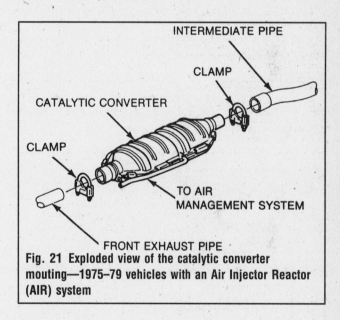

Fig. 21 Exploded view of the catalytic converter mouting—1975–79 vehicles with an Air Injector Reactor (AIR) system

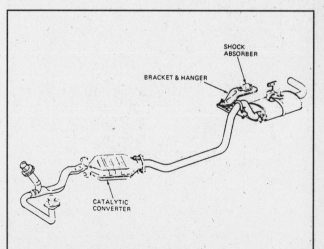

Fig. 22 View of the catalytic converter mounting—1975–79 vehicles without an AIR system

deenergizes the vacuum solenoid, blocking vacuum to the actuator. Without vacuum, an internal spring in the actuator opens the EFE valve, terminating carburetor heat.

The V8 EFE system differs by not using a vacuum solenoid and by using a TVS which is mounted in the coolant outlet housing. The TVS is coolant temperature sensitive and directly controls vacuum. With coolant temperature below 180°F, manifold vacuum is applied to the actuator which closes the EFE valve. When coolant temperature reaches 180°F, vacuum is cut off to the actuator and an internal spring opens the EFE valve, ending carburetor heat.

Catalytic Converter

OPERATION

▶ See Figures 20, 21 and 22

All 1975 and later Novas are equipped with an underfloor catalytic converter. This mufflerlike appearing device is attached to the exhaust pipe(s) coming from the exhaust manifold(s). The converter housing is of a three-layer construction. The outer layer is an aluminized steel cover with a ceramic felt insulating blanket beneath. The main structure (converter shell) is below the blanket and is made of stainless steel as are the exhaust pipes forward of the converter.

Inside the housing are pellets which contain the catalyst agent. The pellets are made of a ceramic material and are impregnated with platinum and palladium. These "noble" metals contain the catalyst agent. The total amount of catalyst agent in the converter is 0.05 Troy ounces (0.36 grams).

The catalyst agent remains effective in converting exhaust gases (hydrocarbons and carbon monoxide) into carbon dioxide and water only as long as it is exposed to the gases. It is for this reason that unleaded fuel only must be used. Lead in leaded fuel is not consumed in the combustion process and enters the converter where it attaches itself to the ceramic pellets. When the catalyst agent becomes coated, the converter becomes useless for emission control. If necessary, the catalyst in a converter can be replaced.

VACUUM DIAGRAMS

Following are vacuum diagrams for most of the engine and emissions package combinations covered by this manual. Because vacuum circuits will vary based on various engine and vehicle options, always refer first to the vehicle emission control information label, if present. Should the label be missing, or should vehicle be equipped with a different engine from the vehicle's original equipment, refer to the diagrams below for the same or similar configuration.

If you wish to obtain a replacement emissions label, most manufacturers make the labels available for purchase. The labels can usually be ordered from a local dealer.

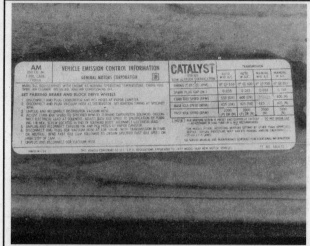

The Vehicle Emission Control Information (VECI) sticker is usually affixed to the radiator shroud

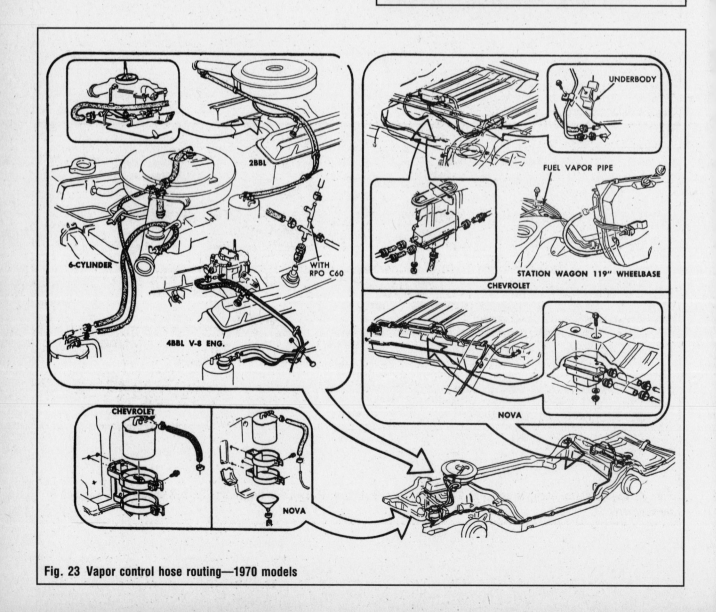

Fig. 23 Vapor control hose routing—1970 models

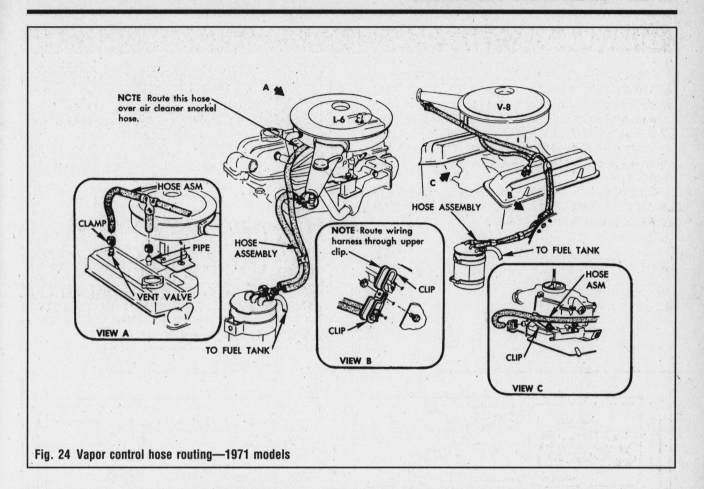

Fig. 24 Vapor control hose routing—1971 models

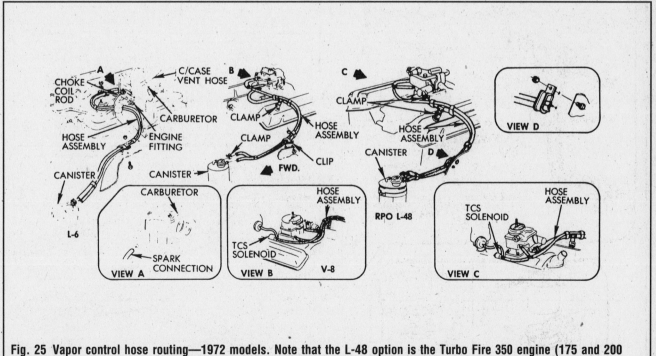

Fig. 25 Vapor control hose routing—1972 models. Note that the L-48 option is the Turbo Fire 350 engine (175 and 200 horsepower)

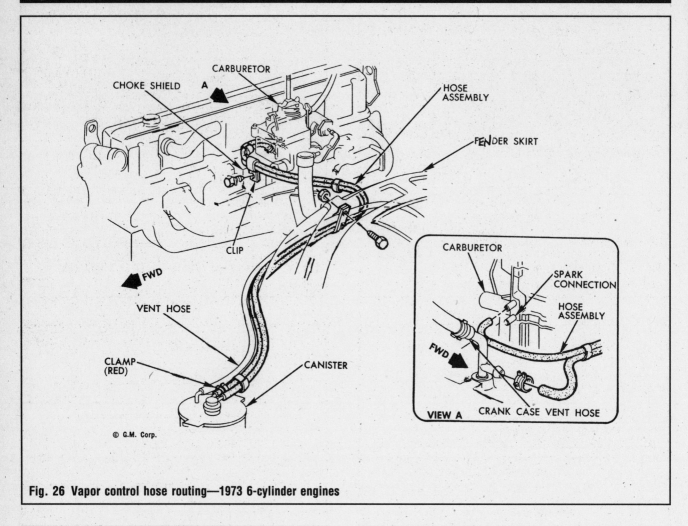

Fig. 26 Vapor control hose routing—1973 6-cylinder engines

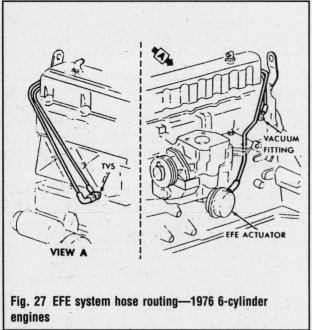

Fig. 27 EFE system hose routing—1976 6-cylinder engines

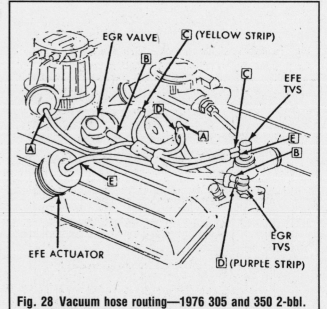

Fig. 28 Vacuum hose routing—1976 305 and 350 2-bbl. carbureted engines

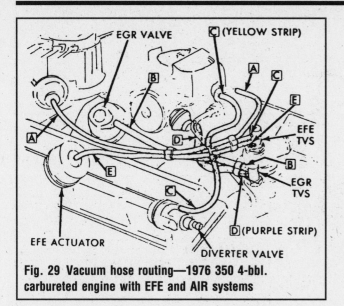

Fig. 29 Vacuum hose routing—1976 350 4-bbl. carbureted engine with EFE and AIR systems

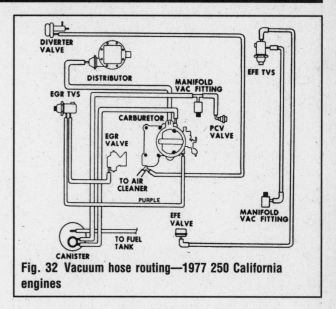

Fig. 32 Vacuum hose routing—1977 250 California engines

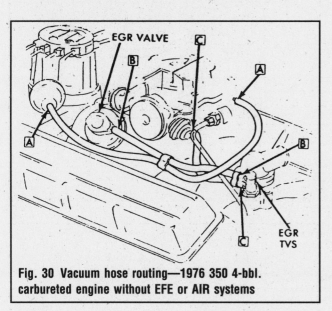

Fig. 30 Vacuum hose routing—1976 350 4-bbl. carbureted engine without EFE or AIR systems

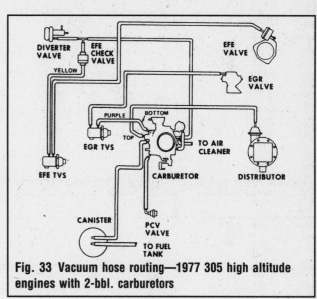

Fig. 33 Vacuum hose routing—1977 305 high altitude engines with 2-bbl. carburetors

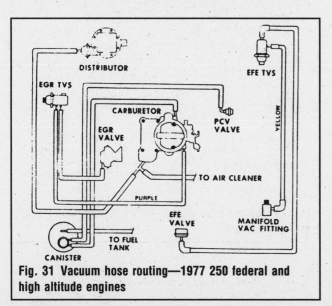

Fig. 31 Vacuum hose routing—1977 250 federal and high altitude engines

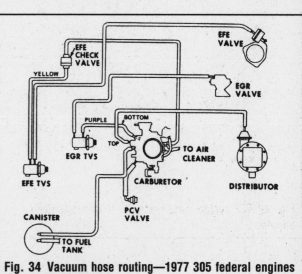

Fig. 34 Vacuum hose routing—1977 305 federal engines with 2-bbl. carburetors

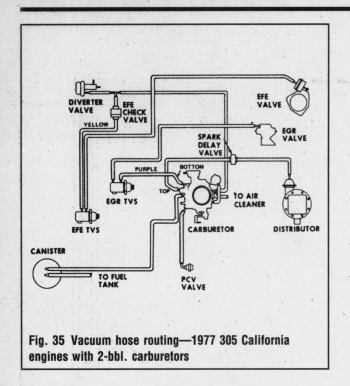

Fig. 35 Vacuum hose routing—1977 305 California engines with 2-bbl. carburetors

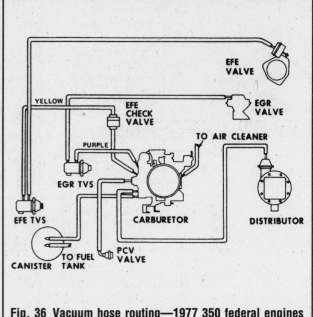

Fig. 36 Vacuum hose routing—1977 350 federal engines with 4-bbl. carburetors

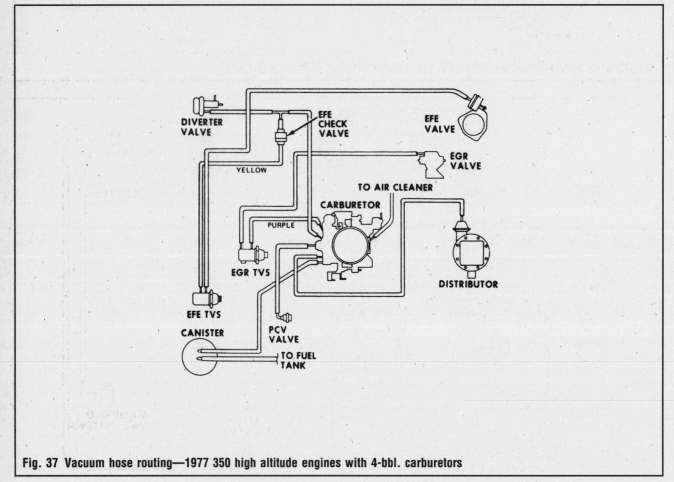

Fig. 37 Vacuum hose routing—1977 350 high altitude engines with 4-bbl. carburetors

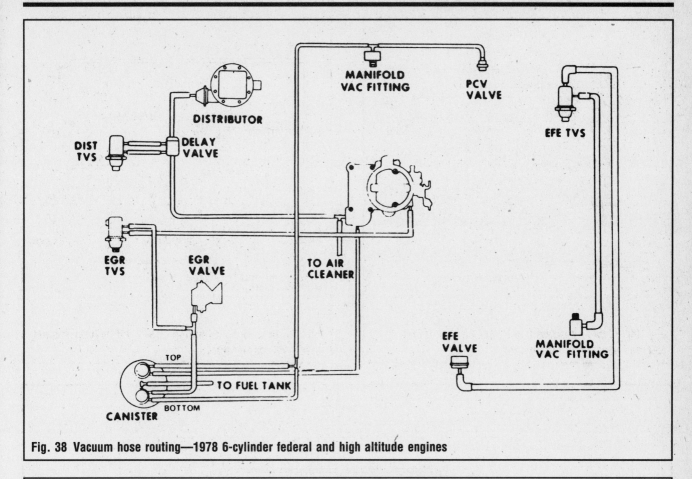

Fig. 38 Vacuum hose routing—1978 6-cylinder federal and high altitude engines

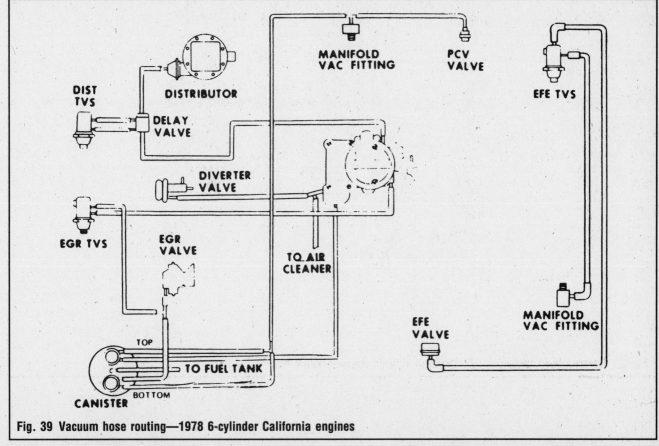

Fig. 39 Vacuum hose routing—1978 6-cylinder California engines

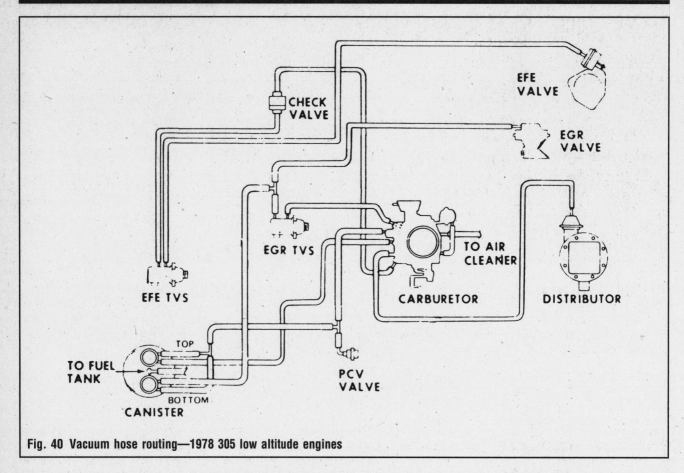

Fig. 40 Vacuum hose routing—1978 305 low altitude engines

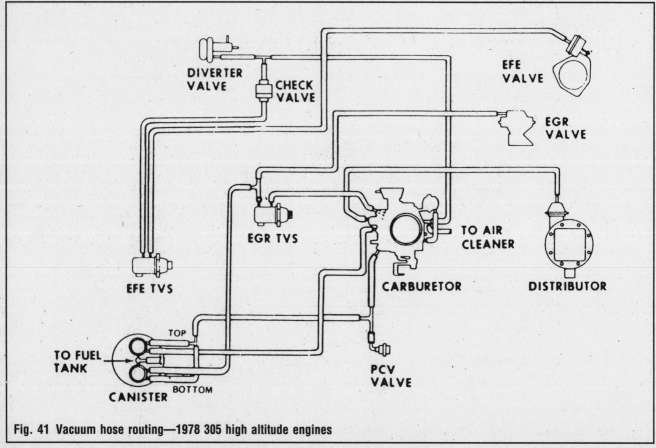

Fig. 41 Vacuum hose routing—1978 305 high altitude engines

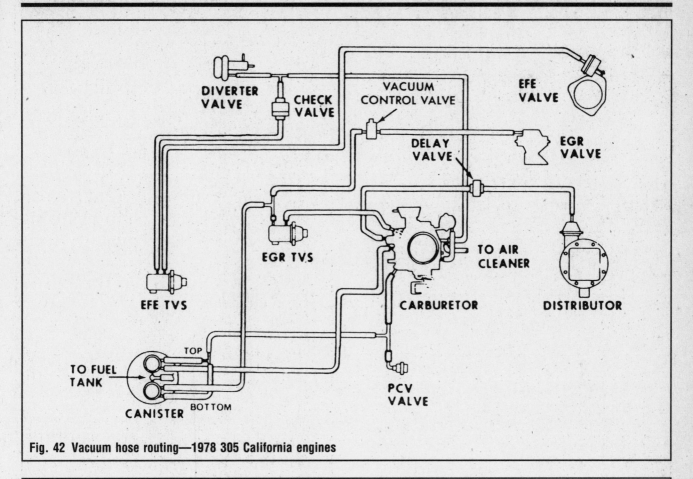

Fig. 42 Vacuum hose routing—1978 305 California engines

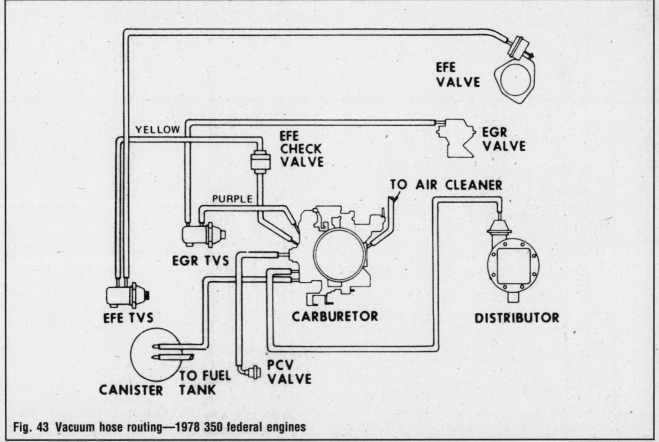

Fig. 43 Vacuum hose routing—1978 350 federal engines

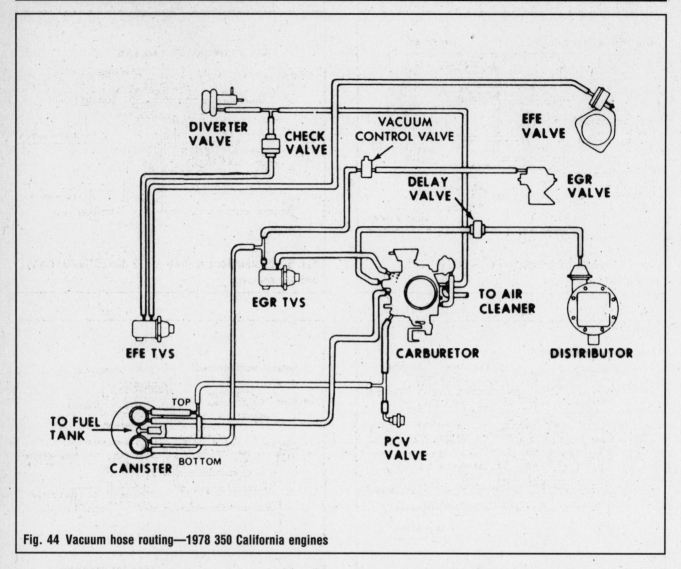

Fig. 44 Vacuum hose routing—1978 350 California engines

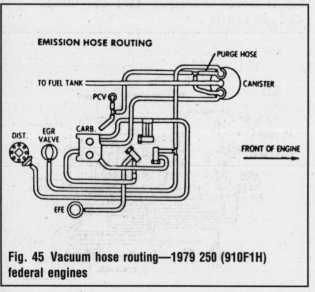

Fig. 45 Vacuum hose routing—1979 250 (910F1H) federal engines

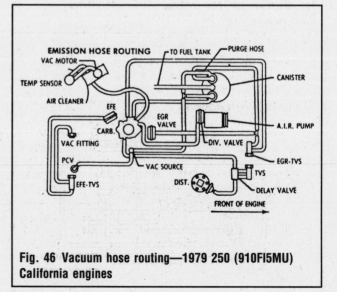

Fig. 46 Vacuum hose routing—1979 250 (910FI5MU) California engines

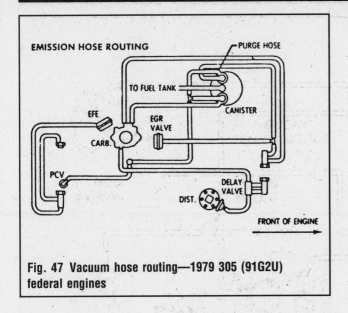

Fig. 47 Vacuum hose routing—1979 305 (91G2U) federal engines

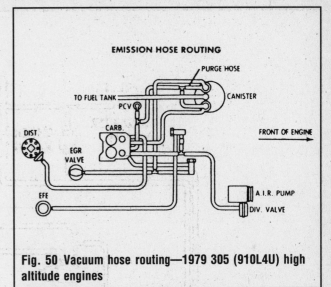

Fig. 50 Vacuum hose routing—1979 305 (910L4U) high altitude engines

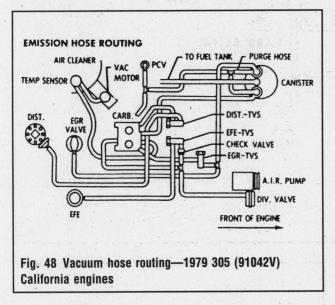

Fig. 48 Vacuum hose routing—1979 305 (91042V) California engines

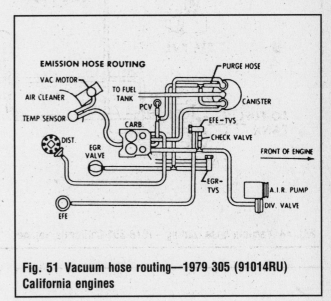

Fig. 51 Vacuum hose routing—1979 305 (91014RU) California engines

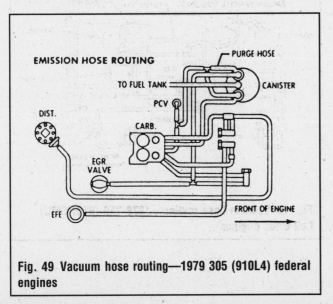

Fig. 49 Vacuum hose routing—1979 305 (910L4) federal engines

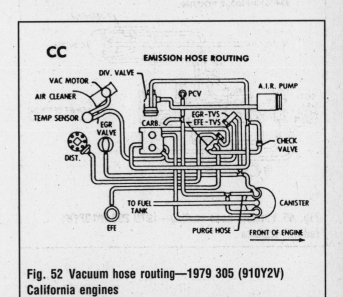

Fig. 52 Vacuum hose routing—1979 305 (910Y2V) California engines

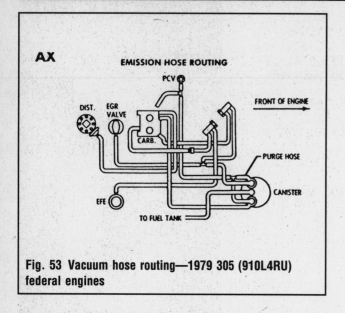

Fig. 53 Vacuum hose routing—1979 305 (910L4RU) federal engines

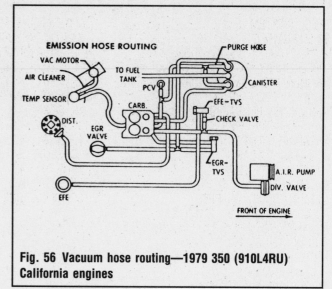

Fig. 56 Vacuum hose routing—1979 350 (910L4RU) California engines

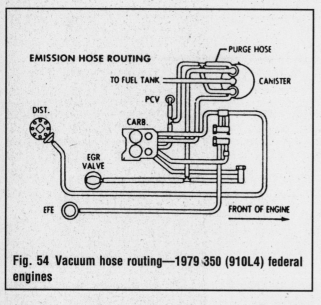

Fig. 54 Vacuum hose routing—1979 350 (910L4) federal engines

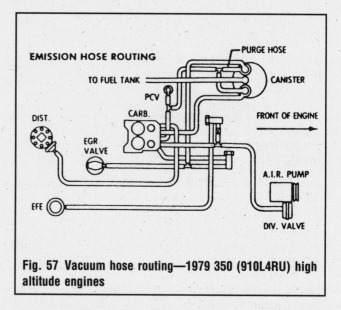

Fig. 57 Vacuum hose routing—1979 350 (910L4RU) high altitude engines

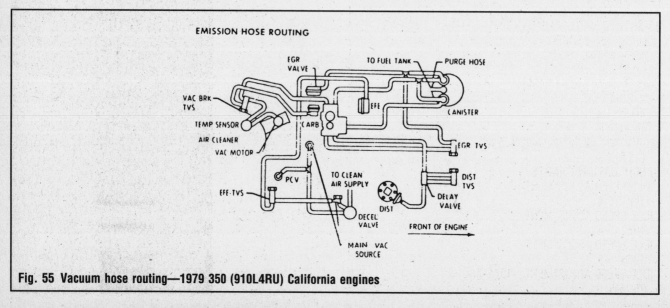

Fig. 55 Vacuum hose routing—1979 350 (910L4RU) California engines

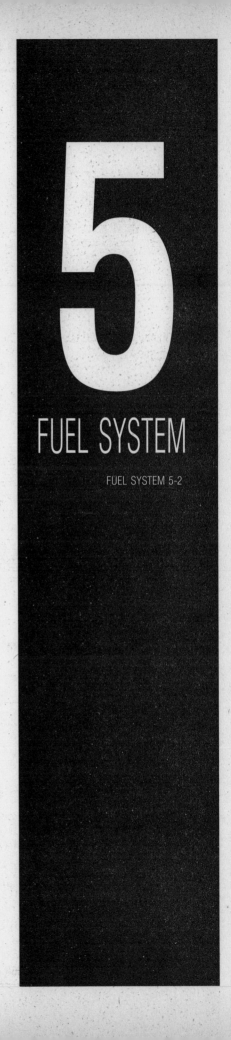

FUEL SYSTEM

FUEL SYSTEM 5-2

FUEL SYSTEM 5-2
FUEL PUMP 5-2
  REMOVAL & INSTALLATION 5-2
PRELIMINARY ADJUSTMENTS 5-3
  IDLE SPEED AND MIXTURE 5-3
  IDLE SOLENOID 5-6
ROCHESTER B-1 BARREL
  CARBURETOR 5-6
  ADJUSTMENTS 5-6
CARTER YF-1 BARREL
  CARBURETOR 5-7
  ADJUSTMENTS 5-7
ROCHESTER BC-1 BARREL
  CARBURETOR 5-8
  ADJUSTMENTS 5-8
ROCHESTER BV-1 BARREL
  CARBURETOR 5-9
  ADJUSTMENTS 5-9
ROCHESTER MV-1 BARREL
  CARBURETOR 5-10
  ADJUSTMENTS 5-10
ROCHESTER 1ME-1 BARREL
  CARBURETORS 5-11
  ADJUSTMENTS 5-11
ROCHESTER 2GV-2 BARREL
  CARBURETOR 5-12
  ADJUSTMENTS 5-12
ROCHESTER 2GC-2 BARREL
  CARBURETOR 5-13
  ADJUSTMENT 5-13
ROCHESTER 4GC-4 BARREL
  CARBURETOR 5-15
  ADJUSTMENTS 5-15
CARTER AFB-4 BARREL
  CARBURETOR 5-18
  ADJUSTMENTS 5-18
CARTER AVS-4 BARREL
  CARBURETOR 5-19
  ADJUSTMENTS 5-19
ROCHESTER 4MV QUADRAJET-4
  BARREL CARBURETOR 5-21
  ADJUSTMENTS 5-21
ROCHESTER M4MC, M4MCA
  QUADRAJET-4 BARREL
  CARBURETORS 5-24
  ADJUSTMENTS 5-24
HOLLEY 4150, 4160-4 BARREL
  CARBURETORS 5-29
  ADJUSTMENTS 5-29
CARBURETOR 5-32
  REMOVAL & INSTALLATION 5-32
  OVERHAUL 5-32
SPECIFICATION CHARTS
  IDLE SPEED ADJUSTMENT—
    1971 5-4
  IDLE SPEED ADJUSTMENT—
    1972 5-4
  IDLE SPEED ADJUSTMENT—
    1973 5-5
  IDLE SPEED ADJUSTMENT—1974–
    75 5-5

CARBURETOR SPECIFICATIONS—
  CARTER CARBURETORS 5-34
HOLLEY CARBURETORS 5-34
ROCHESTER CARBURETORS—1962–
  76 5-35
ROCHESTER CARBURETORS—1967–
  76 5-38
ROCHESTER ME SPECIFICATIONS—
  1977–79 5-43
ROCHESTER 2GC SPECIFICATIONS—
  1977–79 5-43
ROCHESTER 4MV, 4MC, M4MC
  SPECIFICATIONS—1977–79 5-44

FUEL SYSTEM

Fuel Pump

The fuel pump is the single-action, diaphragm type. Two types of fuel pump are used; serviceable and nonserviceable. The serviceable type is used on all 1962–65 engines, 1966 inline engines without the AIR emission control system, and 1966 283 and 327 cu in. V8s. The nonserviceable type is used on all other engines.

The pump is actuated by an eccentric located on the engine camshaft. On inline engines, the eccentric actuates the pump rocker arm. On V8 engines, a pushrod between the camshaft eccentric and the fuel pump activates the pump rocker arm.

REMOVAL & INSTALLATION

1. Disconnect the fuel inlet and outlet lines at the pump and plug the pump inlet lines.
2. On small-block V8 engines, remove the upper bolt from the right front mounting boss. Insert a longer bolt (⅜–16 x 2 in.) in this hole to hold the fuel pump pushrod.
3. Remove the two pump mounting bolts and lockwashers; remove the pump and its gasket.
4. On all small-block engines: if the rocker arm pushrod is to be removed, remove the two adaptor bolts and lock-washers and remove the adaptor and its gasket.
5. On all big-block engines: remove the pipe plug if the rocker arm pushrod is to be removed.

➡**The pump pushrod may be retained on big-block engines by inserting nonfibrous grease in the pump opening.**

6. Install the fuel pump with a new gasket. Coat the mating surfaces with sealer.
7. Connect the fuel lines and check for leaks.

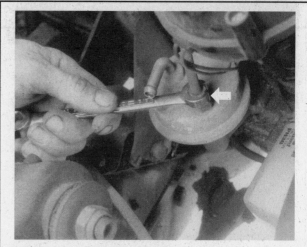

Use a flare nut wrench to loosen . . .

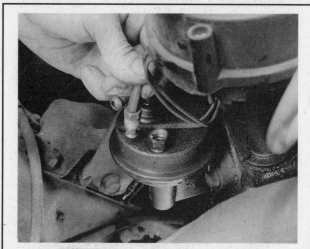

. . . then remove the fuel inlet line

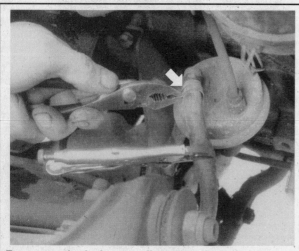

To remove the fuel pump, disconnect the fuel outlet hose from the pump

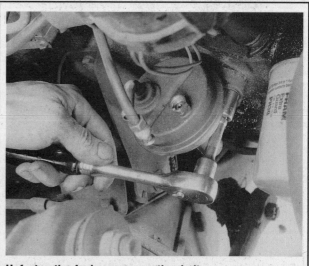

Unfasten the fuel pump mounting bolts . . .

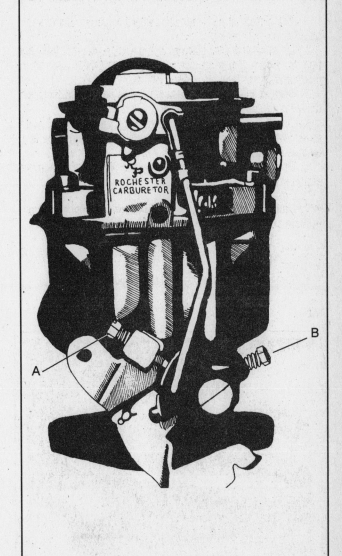

. . . then remove the fuel pump from the vehicle

Preliminary Adjustments

IDLE SPEED AND MIXTURE

▶ **See Figures 1 and 2**

For idle speed and mixture adjustment procedures, please refer to Section 2 of this manual. If necessary, you can use the accompanying illustrations, along with the procedures in Section 2, to assist with adjustment screw locations.

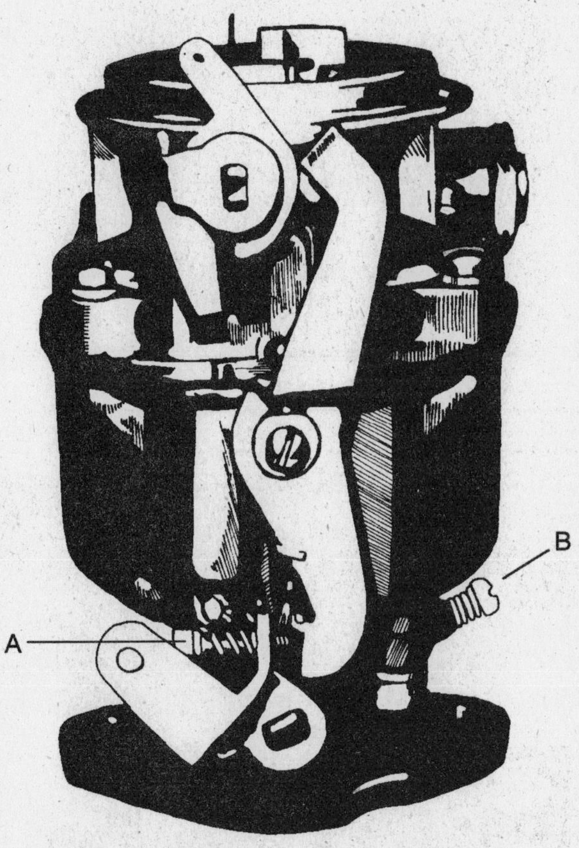

Fig. 1 Idle speed (A) and mixture (B) adjustment screw locations—Rochester B carburetor shown

Fig. 2 Idle speed (A) and mixture (B) adjustment screw locations—Rochester BC carburetor shown

Idle Speed Adjustment—1971

Transmission	Engine	Initial Idle Speed (rpm)	Final Idle Speed (rpm)	Percent CO @ Idle	CEC Valve Engine Speed (rpm)
Manual (In Neutral)	L6	625	550	1.0	850
	V8—307 V8—350	700	600	0.5	900
Automatic (In Drive)	L6	530	500	1.0	650
	V8—307 V8—350	580	550	0.5	650

Idle Speed Adjustment—1972

Transmission	Engine	Initial Idle Speed (rpm)	Final Idle Speed (rpm)	CEC Valve Engine Speed (rpm)
Manual (In Neutral) ②	6	800①	700③	850
	V8—307	1000①	900③	
	V8—350	1050①	900③	
Automatic (In Drive) ②	6	630①	600③	650
	V8—307	650①	600③	
	V8—350			

① Idle adjustment with AIR is ¼ turn rich from lean roll (20 rpm drop).
② AIR operating, if so equipped.
③ Set the low idle with the idle speed screw or the idle solenoid allen screw adjustment (solenoid de-energized) at 450 rpm.

Idle Speed Adjustment—1973

Transmission	Engine	Initial Idle Speed (rpm)	Final Idle Speed (rpm)	CEC Valve Engine Speed (rpm)
Manual (In Neutral) ②	6	750	700③	850
	V8—307	950	900③	
	V8—350 (2 bbl)	1000	900④	
	V8—350 (4 bbl)	920①	900③	
Automatic (In Drive) ②	6	630	600③	
	V8—307	630	600③	
	V8—350 (2 bbl)	630	600④	
	V8—350 (4 bbl)	620①	600③	

① ¼ turn rich from lean roll (20 rpm drop).
② AIR operating.
③ Set low idle with the idle speed screw or the idle solenoid allen screw adjustment (solenoid de-energized) at 500 rpm.
④ Set low idle with the idle speed screw or the idle solenoid allen screw adjustment (solenoid de-energized) at 400 rpm.

Idle Speed Adjustment—1974–75

Transmission	Engine	Curb Idle① (rpm)	Lean Drop Idle Mixture (rpm)	Low Idle② (rpm)
1974 Manual (In Neutral)	6—250	850	950/850	450
	8—350 (2 bbl)	900	1000/900	500
	8—350 (4 bbl)	900	950/900	500
1974 Automatic (In Drive)	6—250	600	650/600③	450
	8—350 (2 bbl)	600	650/600	500
	8—350 (4 bbl)	600	650/600④	500
1975 Manual (In Neutral)	6—250	850	—	⑥
	8—262	800	—	⑥
	8—350 (2 bbl)	800	—	⑥
	8—350 (4 bbl)	800	—	⑥
1975 Automatic (In Drive)	6—250	550⑤	—	⑥
	8—262	600	—	⑥
	8—350 (2 bbl)	600	—	⑥
	8—350 (4 bbl)	600	—	⑥

① Solenoid energized
② Solenoid de-energized
③ Calif. 6-250—630/600 rpm
④ Calif. 8-350 (4 bbl)—630/600 rpm
⑤ Calif.—600 rpm
⑥ Refer to underhood tune-up specifications sticker

1971 Vehicles and 1972–73 6-Cylinder Vehicles

◆ **See Figure 3**

This adjustment is made only after: 1) replacement of the sole-noid; 2) major overhaul of the carburetor; or 3) after the throttle body is removed and replaced.

Perform the initial adjustments and tune-up as described on the tune-up decal before proceeding with the CEC valve adjustment. Warm up the engine and leave it running while making the adjustment, leaving the manual transmission in Neutral or the automatic transmission in Drive. Turn off the air conditioner, disconnect the fuel tank vapor line from the canister, and disconnect the distributor vacuum hose from the distributor and plug the house.

1. Manually extend the CEC valve plunger to contact the throttle lever.

2. Adjust the plunger length to obtain the idle speed specified in the "Idle Speed Adjustment" tables.

3. Reconnect the fuel tank vapor hose and the distributor vacuum hose.

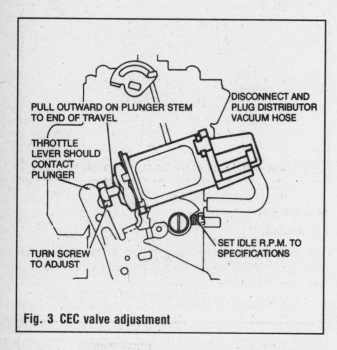

Fig. 3 CEC valve adjustment

(Labels in figure: PULL OUTWARD ON PLUNGER STEM TO END OF TRAVEL; THROTTLE LEVER SHOULD CONTACT PLUNGER; TURN SCREW TO ADJUST; DISCONNECT AND PLUG DISTRIBUTOR VACUUM HOSE; SET IDLE R.P.M. TO SPECIFICATIONS)

IDLE SOLENOID

1972–79 Vehicles

Most 1972 and later models are equipped with an idle solenoid on the carburetor. The solenoid should allow the throttle plate to close further when the ignition is turned **OFF**. If it does not, the solenoid must be replaced. The following adjustment should be performed when the carburetor is overhauled or a new solenoid is installed. The preconditions necessary for the idle adjustment procedure also apply here. On 1976–79 models, after replacing the idle solenoid, adjust the idle speed as shown in Section 2.

❋❋ WARNING

Do not turn the solenoid more than one complete turn unless the electrical wire is disconnected.

1 BARREL CARBURETORS

The solenoid is turned clockwise for an increase of rpm and counterclockwise for a decrease.

1. Set the final idle speed, with the idle solenoid energized, to the specification in the chart.

2. Adjust the low idle speed, with the solenoid de-energized, to 450 rpm. Use an allen wrench in the end of the solenoid for this adjustment.

2 AND 4 BARREL CARBURETORS

1. Disconnect the idle solenoid wire.

2. Set the low idle to 450 rpm with the adjustment screw on the low step of the cam.

3. Adjust the dwell angle and timing, and again check the low idle speed.

4. Reconnect the solenoid wire.

5. Open the throttle for a moment and adjust the solenoid plunger screw to the specified idle in the chart.

Rochester B-1 Barrel Carburetor

ADJUSTMENTS

Manual Choke

1. Be sure that the choke control knob is pushed all the way in at the instrument panel.

2. Loosen the manual choke cable clip at the carburetor bracket and adjust the cable as necessary so that the choke valve is in the wide open position. Allow ⅛ in. clearance at the instrument panel for the choke control knob. Tighten the choke cable clip.

3. Check the choke operation by pulling the hand choke control knob out from the instrument panel. The choke valve should then be fully closed.

Float Level

◆ **See Figures 4 and 5**

1. Remove the air cleaner.

2. Disconnect the choke cable and the fuel line from the carburetor.

3. Withdraw the bowl cover screws and carefully lift the cover off the carburetor.

4. Install a new gasket on the cover before making any adjustments.

5. Invert the cover assembly and measure the float level with a float gauge. The level should be ¹⁹⁄₃₂ in.

➡**Rebuilding kits include a float level gauge.**

6. Check float centering while holding the cover sideways. Use the same gauge as in step five. The floats should not touch the gauge.

7. Hold the cover upright and measure the float drop. If the drop is more or less than 1¾ in., bend the step tang until the drop is correct.

8. Install the cover and reconnect the fuel line and the choke cable.

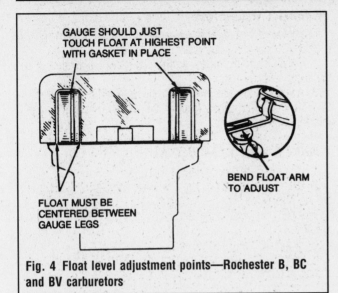

Fig. 4 Float level adjustment points—Rochester B, BC and BV carburetors

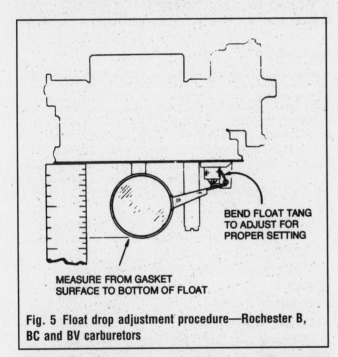

Fig. 5 Float drop adjustment procedure—Rochester B, BC and BV carburetors

Carter YF-1 Barrel Carburetor

ADJUSTMENTS

Manual Choke

1. Be sure that the choke control knob is pushed all the way in at the instrument panel.

2. Loosen the manual choke cable clip at the carburetor bracket and adjust the cable as necessary so the choke valve is in the wide open position. Allow ⅛ in. clearance at the instrument panel for the choke control knob. Tighten the choke cable clip.

3. Check the choke operation by pulling the hand choke control knob out from the instrument panel. The choke valve should then be fully closed.

Idle Vent
♦ See Figure 6

1. Back the idle speed screw out until it is free of the fast idle cam.

2. Using a 0.030 in. wire gauge, check the clearance between the cover and the vent valve. If necessary, adjust by turning the vent valve with a screwdriver.

3. Adjust the engine idle speed.

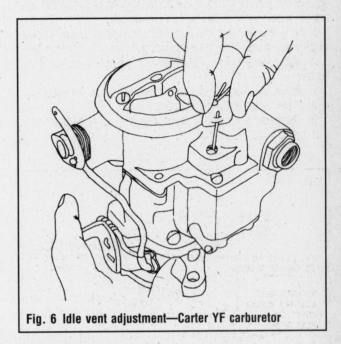

Fig. 6 Idle vent adjustment—Carter YF carburetor

Fast Idle Rod
♦ See Figure 7

1. With the choke valve in the wide open position, the fast idle lever tang should just contact the stop boss on the carburetor body.

2. If necessary, bend the fast idle rod at its offset to adjust.

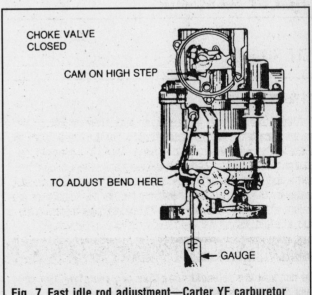

Fig. 7 Fast idle rod adjustment—Carter YF carburetor

Float Level

◆ **See Figures 8 and 9**

1. Remove the carburetor from the engine.
2. Disconnect the fast idle rod at the choke lever.
3. Withdraw the bowl cover screws and carefully remove the bowl cover.
4. Invert the bowl cover and measure the distance between the float and cover at the free end of the float. This measurement should be ⅜ in. If necessary, adjust by bending the float lip, not the float arm, which rests on the needle.
5. Hold the cover in its upright position and measure the float drop from the cover to the end of the float opposite the hinge. This measurement should be 1¹³⁄₁₆ in. If necessary, adjust by bending the stop tab on the float arm.
6. Refit the bowl cover, connect the fast idle rod, and install the carburetor on the engine.

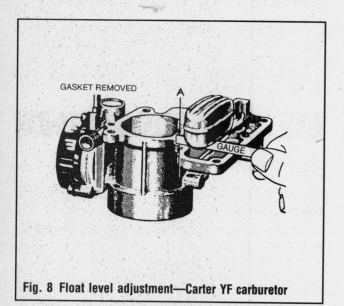

Fig. 8 Float level adjustment—Carter YF carburetor

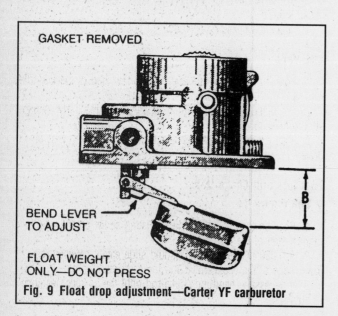

Fig. 9 Float drop adjustment—Carter YF carburetor

Rochester BC-1 Barrel Carburetor

ADJUSTMENTS

Automatic Choke

◆ **See Figure 10**

1. Loosen the three small screws which secure the choke cover.
2. Using a screwdriver to rotate the choke cover, align the scribe mark on the cover with the index mark on the choke housing for automatic transmission models, or set the cover one notch lean for manual transmission models.
3. Tighten the three cover screws.

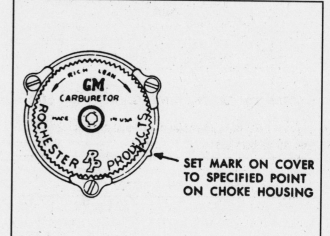

Fig. 10 Automatic choke adjustment—Rochester BC carburetor

Fast Idle and Choke Valve

◆ **See Figure 11**

1. Position the end of the idle adjusting screw on the next to the highest step of the fast idle cam.
2. A 0.050 in. feeler gauge should slide easily between the lower edge of the choke valve and the carburetor bore.
3. If necessary, bend the choke rod until the correct clearance is obtained.

Unloader

◆ **See Figure 12**

1. Open the throttle to the wide open position.
2. A 0.350 gauge should slide freely between the lower edge of the choke valve and the bore of the carburetor.
3. If necessary, bend the throttle tang to obtain the proper clearance.

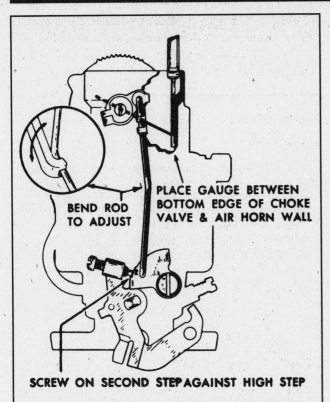

BEND ROD TO ADJUST

PLACE GAUGE BETWEEN BOTTOM EDGE OF CHOKE VALVE & AIR HORN WALL

SCREW ON SECOND STEP AGAINST HIGH STEP

Fig. 11 Fast idle and choke adjustmenet—Rochester BC and BV carburetors

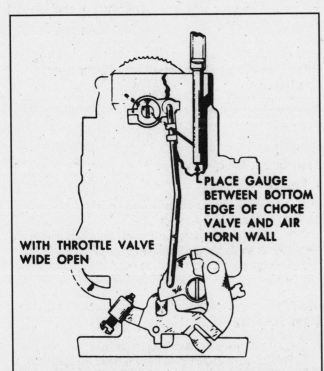

WITH THROTTLE VALVE WIDE OPEN

PLACE GAUGE BETWEEN BOTTOM EDGE OF CHOKE VALVE AND AIR HORN WALL

Fig. 12 Unloader adjustment—Rochester BC, BV and MV carburetors

Float Level

▶ **See Figure 4 and 5**

1. Remove the air cleaner.

2. Disconnect the fuel line, fast idle rod, cam-to-choke kick lever, vacuum hose at the diaphragm, and the choke rod at the choke lever.

3. Withdraw the bowl cover screws and carefully lift the cover off the carburetor.

4. Install a new gasket on the cover before making any adjustments.

5. Invert the cover assembly and measure the float level with a float gauge. The level should be $19/32$ in.

➡ **Rebuilding kits include a float level gauge.**

6. Check float centering while holding the cover sideways. Use the same gauge as in step five. The floats should not touch the gauge.

7. Hold the cover upright and measure the float drop. If the drop is more or less than $1\frac{3}{4}$ in., bend the step tang until the drop is correct.

8. Install the cover and reconnect the lines and linkage in the reverse order of removal.

Rochester BV-1 Barrel Carburetor

ADJUSTMENTS

Automatic Choke

1. Disconnect the choke rod from the choke lever at the carburetor.

2. While holding the choke valve shut, pull the choke rod up against the stop in the thermostat housing.

3. Adjust the length of the choke rod so that the bottom edge of the choke rod is even with the top edge of the hole in the choke lever.

4. Check the linkage for freedom of operation.

Idle Vent

1. Position the carburetor lever on the low step of the fast idle cam.

2. The distance between the choke valve and the body casting should be 0.050 in.

3. If an adjustment is necessary, turn the valve with a screwdriver.

Fast Idle and Choke Valve

▶ **See Figure 11**

1. Position the end of the idle adjusting screw on the next to highest step of the fast idle cam.

2. A 0.050 in. feeler gauge should slide easily between the lower edge of the choke valve and the carburetor bore.

3. If necessary, bend the choke rod until the correct clearance is obtained.

Unloader

◆ See Figure 12

1. Open the throttle to the wide open position.
2. A 0.350 in. feeler gauge should slide freely between the lower edge of the choke valve and the bore of the carburetor.
3. If necessary, bend the throttle tang to obtain the proper clearance.

Vacuum Break

◆ See Figure 13

1. Hold the diaphragm lever against the diaphragm body.
2. The clearance between the lower edge of the choke valve and the air horn wall should be 0.136–0.154 in. on Powerglide cars and 0.154–0.173 in. on manual cars.
3. Bend the diaphragm link, if necessary.

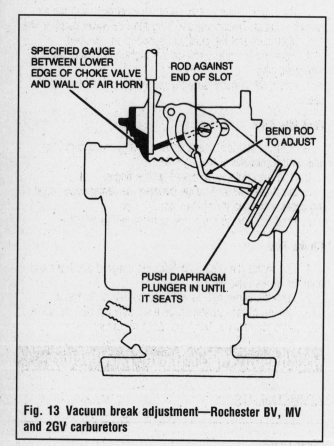

Fig. 13 Vacuum break adjustment—Rochester BV, MV and 2GV carburetors

Float Level

◆ See Figures 4 and 5

1. Remove the air cleaner.
2. Disconnect the fuel line, fast idle rod, cam-to-choke kick lever, vacuum hose at the diaphragm, and the choke rod at the choke lever.
3. Remove the bowl cover screws and carefully lift the cover off the carburetor.
4. Install a new gasket on the cover before making any adjustments.
5. Invert the cover assembly and measure the float level with a float gauge. The level should be 19/32 in.

➡Rebuilding kits include a float level gauge.

6. Check float centering while holding the cover sideways. Use the same gauge as in step five. The floats should not touch the gauge.
7. Hold the cover upright and measure the float drop. If the drop is more or less than 1¾ in., bend the step tang until the drop is correct.
8. Install the cover and reconnect lines and linkage in the reverse order of removal.

Rochester MV-1 Barrel Carburetor

ADJUSTMENTS

Choke Rod

◆ See Figure 14

1. Position the fast idle cam follower on the second step of the fast idle cam and hold it against the foot of the top step.
2. Turn the choke valve in the direction of the closed choke by moving the choke coil lever.
3. Bend the choke rod where it angles to give an opening of 0.125 in. (automatic) or 0.150 in. (manual) between the lower edge of the choke valve and the inside of the air horn.

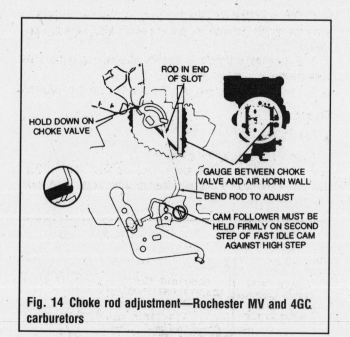

Fig. 14 Choke rod adjustment—Rochester MV and 4GC carburetors

Vacuum Break

◆ See Figure 13

1. Place the fast idle speed screw on the highest cam step.
2. Tape over the bleed hole in the diaphragm unit. Apply suction by mouth to seat the diaphragm.
3. Push down on the choke valve with a finger.
4. Insert the gauge between the upper edge of the choke valve and the airhorn wall.
5. Bend the link to adjust.

Choke Unloader

♦ **See Figure 12**

1. Hold the throttle valve wide open.
2. Hold-down the choke valve with a finger and insert the specified gauge between the upper edge of the choke valve and the airhorn wall.
3. Bend the linkage tang to adjust.

Choke Coil Lever

1. Place the fast idle speed screw on the highest cam step.
2. Hold the choke valve closed.
3. Insert a 0.120 in. gauge through the hole in the arm on the choke housing and into the hole in the casting.
4. Bend the link to adjust.

Electric Choke

1. Place the fast idle cam follower on the high step.
2. Loosen the three retaining screws and rotate the cover counterclockwise until the choke valve just closes.
3. Align the index mark on the cover with the specified housing mark.
4. Tighten the three screws.

Fast Idle

➡ **The fast idle adjustment must be made with the transmission in Neutral.**

1. Disconnect and plug the distributor vacuum line on 1976 and later models. Position the fast idle lever on the high step of the fast idle cam.
2. Be sure that the choke is properly adjusted and in the wide open position with the engine warm.
3. Bend the fast idle lever until the specified speed is obtained.

Float Level

♦ **See Figure 15**

1. Remove the top of the carburetor.
2. Hold the float retaining pin in place and push down on the float arm at the outer end against the top of the float needle valve.

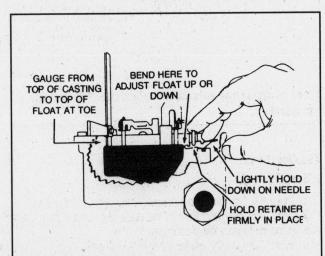

GAUGE FROM TOP OF CASTING TO TOP OF FLOAT AT TOE

BEND HERE TO ADJUST FLOAT UP OR DOWN

LIGHTLY HOLD DOWN ON NEEDLE

HOLD RETAINER FIRMLY IN PLACE

Fig. 15 Float level adjustment—Rochester MV carburetors

3. Measure the distance from the bump on the top of the float at the end of the bowl gasket surface, without the gasket.
4. To adjust, bend the float arm at the point where it joins the float.

Metering Rod

1. Remove the top of the carburetor.
2. Back out the idle stop solenoid and rotate the fast idle cam so that the fast idle screw does not contact the cam.
3. With the throttle valve completely closed, make sure the power piston is all the way up.
4. Insert the specified size gauge (.070–.078 in.) between the bowl gasket surface with no gasket and the lower surface of the metering rod holder, next to the metering rod.
5. To adjust, carefully bend the metering rod holder.

Fast Idle Speed

1. The engine should be at normal temperature with the air cleaner in place. Disconnect and plug the EGR valve vacuum line.
2. Make sure that the curb idle speed is as specified.
3. Place the fast idle screw on the highest cam step with the engine running.
4. Adjust the fast idle speed screw to the correct fast idle speed.

Fast Idle Cam

1. Hold the fast idle speed screw on the second cam step against the shoulder of the high step.
2. Hold the choke valve closed with a finger.
3. Insert the specified gauge between the center upper edge of the choke valve and the airhorn wall.
4. Bend the linkage rod at the upper angle to adjust.

Choke Rod

1. Disconnect the choke rod from the upper choke lever and hold the choke valve closed.
2. Push the choke rod down to the bottom of its travel.
3. The top of the rod should be even with the bottom of the hole in the choke lever; bend the rod if necessary.

Rochester 1ME-1 Barrel Carburetors

ADJUSTMENTS

Float Level

1. Push down on the end of the float arm and against the top of the float needle to hold the retaining pin firmly in place.
2. While holding the position of the retaining pin, gauge from the top of the casting to the top of the index point at the toe of the float.
3. If float level needs to be changed do it by bending the float arm just on the float side of the float needle.

Fast Idle

1. If the carburetor has a stepped fast idle cam, put the cam follower on the high step of the cam. If the cam has a smooth contour, open the throttle slightly and rotate the cam to its highest position, then release throttle.

2. Support the lever with a pair of pliers, and bend the tang in or out to achieve specified rpm. Perform the adjustment with engine hot and choke open.

Choke Coil Lever

➡This adjustment requires a plug gauge or other metal rod of 0.120 in. diameter.

1. Place the fast idle cam follower on the highest step of the cam or rotate the cam to its highest possible position. Close the choke all the way and hold.

2. Insert the plug gauge through the small hole in the outer end of the choke lever. Bend the link at the lowest point of the curved portion until the gauge will enter the hole in the carburetor casting.

Choke

1. Place the fast idle cam follower on the high step of the cam or rotate the cam until it is at the highest position.

2. Slightly loosen the three screws which retain the choke cover just enough to turn the cover—don't loosen them more than necessary, or the lever may slip out of the tang inside.

3. Turn the cover until the mark on the cover lines up with the appropriate mark on the choke housing—see specifications.

Metering Rod

1. Hold throttle wide open. Push downward on metering rod until it can be slid out of slot in holder. Slide the rod out of the holder and remove it from the main metering jet.

2. Back the solenoid hex screw out until the throttle can be closed all the way.

3. Remove float bowl gasket.

4. Holding the power piston down and the throttle closed, swing the metering rod holder over the flat surface of the bowl casting next to the throttle bore. Measure the distance from the flat surface to the outer end of the rod holder with the specified gauge (see specifications), or a metal rod of equivalent diameter.

5. Bend the horizontal portion of the rod holder where it joins the vertical portion until the gauge just passes between the holder and surface of the bowl casting with the power piston bottomed.

Rochester 2GV-2 Barrel Carburetor

ADJUSTMENTS

These procedures are for both the 1¼ and 1½ models; where there are differences these are noted. The 1½ model has larger throttle bores and an additional fuel feed circuit to make it suitable for use on the 350 and 400 cu in. V8s.

Fast Idle Cam

◆ See Figure 16

1. Turn the idle screw onto the second step of the fast idle cam, abutting against the top side.

2. Hold the choke valve toward the closed position and check

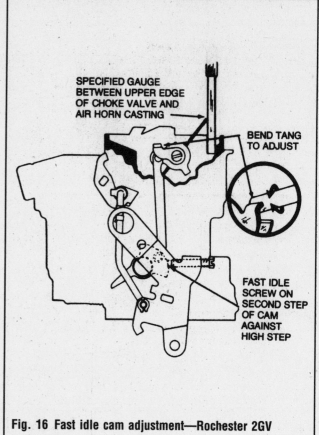

Fig. 16 Fast idle cam adjustment—Rochester 2GV carburetor

the clearance between the upper edge of the choke valve and the air horn wall.

3. If this measurement varies from specifications, bend the tang on the choke lever.

Choke Vacuum Break

◆ See Figure 13

1. Apply vacuum to the diaphragm to fully seat the plunger.

2. Push the choke valve in toward the closed position and hold it there.

3. Check the distance between the lower edge of the choke valve and the air horn wall.

4. If this dimension is not within specifications, bend the vacuum break rod to adjust.

Choke Unloader

◆ See Figure 17

1. Hold the throttle valves wide open and use a rubber band to hold the choke valve toward the closed position.

2. Measure the distance between the upper edge of the choke valve and the air horn wall.

3. If this measurement is not within specifications, bend the unloader tang on the throttle lever to correct it.

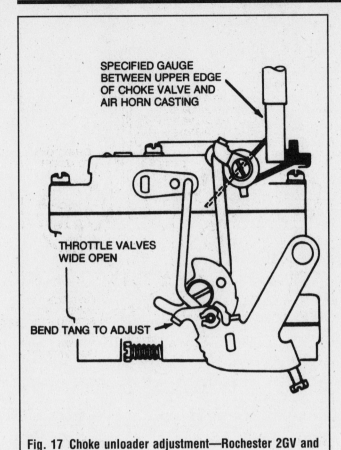

Fig. 17 Choke unloader adjustment—Rochester 2GV and 4GC carburetors

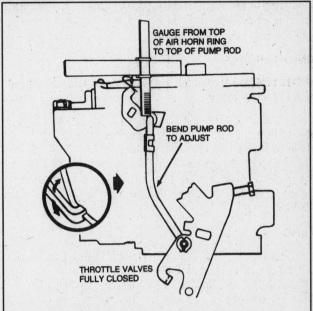

Fig. 18 Accelerator pump rod adjustment—Rochester 2GV carburetors

Rochester 2GC-2 Barrel Carburetor

ADJUSTMENT

Accelerator Pump Rod
▶ See Figure 19

1. Back out the idle speed adjusting screw.
2. Hold the throttle valve completely closed.

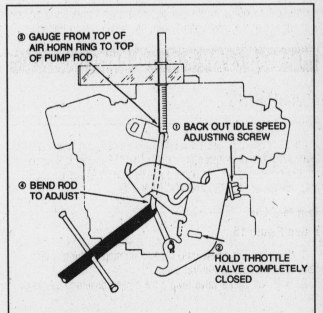

Fig. 19 Accelerator pump rod adjustment—Rochester 2GC carburetor

Accelerator Pump Rod
▶ See Figure 18

1. Back the idle stop screw out and close the throttle valves in their bores.
2. Measure the distance from the top of the air horn to the top of the pump rod.
3. Bend the pump rod at a lower angle to correct this dimension.

Float Level

Invert the air horn and, with the gasket in place and the needle seated, measure the level as follows:
On nitrophyl floats, measure from the air horn gasket to the lip on the toe of the float.
On brass floats, measure from the air horn gasket to the lower edge of the float seam.
Bend the float tang to adjust the level.

Float Drop

Holding the air horn right side up, measure float drop as follows:
On nitrophyl floats, measure from the air horn gasket to the lip at the toe of the float.
On brass floats, measure from the air horn gasket to the bottom of the float.
Bend the float tang to adjust either type of float.

3. Measure the clearance from the top of the air horn ring to the top of the pump rod.

4. Bend the rod to adjust.

Fast Idle Cam
▶ See Figure 20

1. Turn the idle speed screw in until it just contacts the low step of the fast idle cam. Turn the screw in one full turn.

2. Place the idle speed screw on the second step of the fast idle cam against the highest step.

3. Place the specified gauge between the upper edge of the choke and the air horn wall.

4. Bend the choke lever tang to adjust.

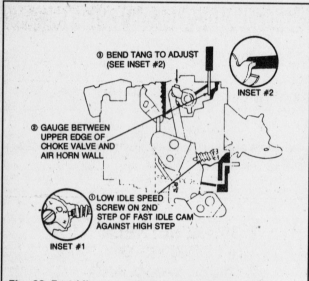

③ BEND TANG TO ADJUST (SEE INSET #2)

INSET #2

② GAUGE BETWEEN UPPER EDGE OF CHOKE VALVE AND AIR HORN WALL

① LOW IDLE SPEED SCREW ON 2ND STEP OF FAST IDLE CAM AGAINST HIGH STEP

INSET #1

Fig. 20 Fast idle cam adjustment—Rochester 2GC carburetor

Choke Unloader
▶ See Figure 21

1. With the throttle valves held in the wide open position, place the choke toward the closed position.

2. Place the specified gauge between the upper edge of the choke and the air horn casting.

3. Bend the tang on the throttle lever to adjust.

Intermediate Choke Rod
▶ See Figure 22

1. Remove the thermostatic cover, coil, gasket, and the inside baffle plate assembly by removing the three attaching screws and retainers.

2. Place the idle speed screw on the highest step of the fast idle cam.

3. Close the choke by pushing up on the intermediate choke lever.

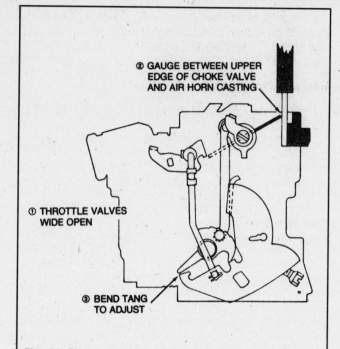

② GAUGE BETWEEN UPPER EDGE OF CHOKE VALVE AND AIR HORN CASTING

① THROTTLE VALVES WIDE OPEN

③ BEND TANG TO ADJUST

Fig. 21 Choke unloader adjustment—Rochester 2GC carburetor

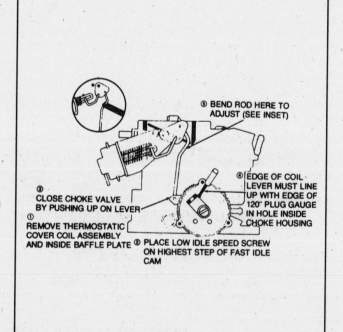

⑤ BEND ROD HERE TO ADJUST (SEE INSET)

③ CLOSE CHOKE VALVE BY PUSHING UP ON LEVER

① REMOVE THERMOSTATIC COVER COIL ASSEMBLY AND INSIDE BAFFLE PLATE

② PLACE LOW IDLE SPEED SCREW ON HIGHEST STEP OF FAST IDLE CAM

④ EDGE OF COIL LEVER MUST LINE UP WITH EDGE OF 120" PLUG GAUGE IN HOLE INSIDE CHOKE HOUSING

Fig. 22 Intermediate choke rod adjustment—Rochester 2GC carburetor

4. The edge of the coil lever inside the choke housing must align with the edge of the specified plug gauge.

5. Bend the intermediate choke rod at the point shown in the illustration to adjust.

Automatic Choke Coil

1. Place the idle speed screw on the highest step of the fast idle cam.

2. Loosen the thermostatic choke coil cover retaining screws.

3. Turn the choke cover against the coil tension until the choke begins to close. Keep turning until the index mark aligns with the specified point on the choke housing.

4. Tighten the thermostatic coil cover retaining screws.

Vacuum Break

▶ See Figure 23

1. Using a vacuum source, seat the vacuum break diaphragm.

2. Cover the vacuum break bleed hole with a small piece of tape, so that the diaphragm unit will hold inward and not bleed down. Refer to the illustration.

3. Place the idle speed screw on the high step of the fast idle cam.

4. Hold the choke coil lever inside the choke housing toward the closed choke position.

5. Place the specified gauge between the upper edge of the choke and the air horn wall.

6. Adjust by bending the vacuum break rod at the point shown in the illustration.

7. Remove the piece of tape covering the bleed hole at the rear of the diaphragm unit. Reconnect the vacuum hose.

Float Level

With the air horn assembly upside down, measure the distance from the air horn gasket to the lip at the toe of the float. Adjust by bending the float arm.

Float Drop

While holding the air horn assembly upright, measure the distance from the gasket to the lip at the toe of the float. To adjust, bend the float tang at the rear, next to the needle and seat.

Rochester 4GC-4 Barrel Carburetor

ADJUSTMENTS

▶ See Figure 24

Automatic Choke

Set the cover index mark on the one notch lean mark on the housing.

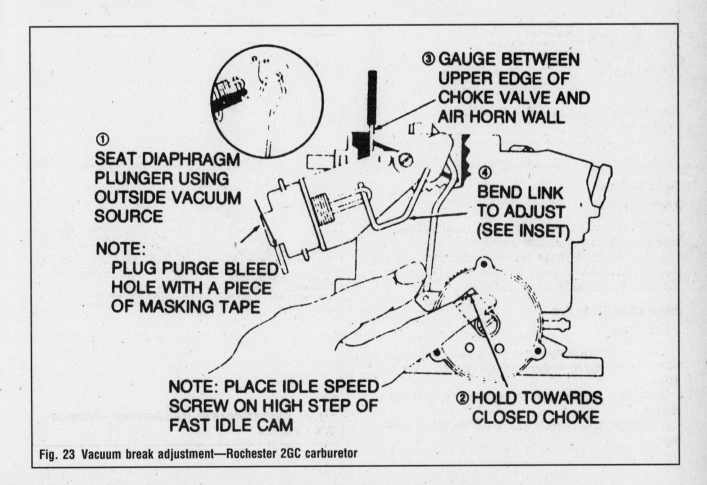

Fig. 23 Vacuum break adjustment—Rochester 2GC carburetor

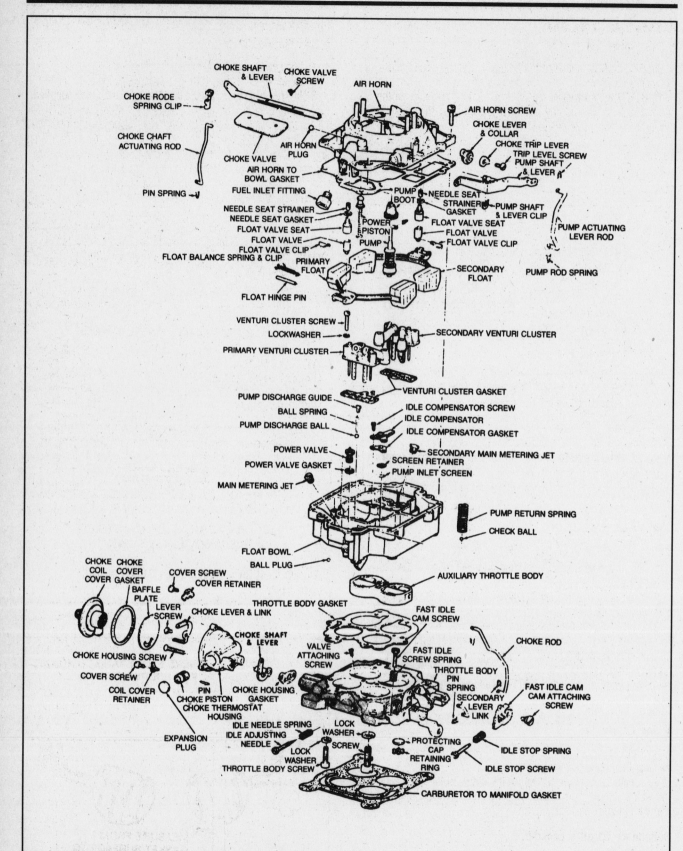

Fig. 24 Exploded view of the Rochester 4GC 4-barrel carburetor

Intermediate Choke Rod
▶ See Figure 25

The intermediate choke rod is adjusted with the choke cover and baffle removed.

1. Hold the choke valve closed; exert a light pressure on the choke piston to take up any lash and note whether the choke piston is at the end of its sleeve.

2. If necessary, bend the intermediate choke rod for correct piston positioning.

3. Install the choke baffle and cover.

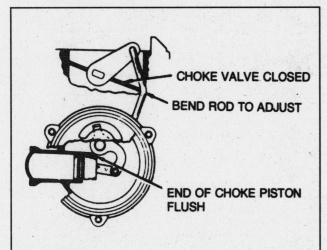

Fig. 25 Intermediate choke rod adjustment—Rochester 4GC carburetor

Choke Rod
▶ See Figure 14

1. Turn the idle speed screw in until it just touches the second step of the fast idle cam.

2. Make sure that the choke trip lever is touching the choke counterweight lever.

3. While holding the idle speed screw on the second cam step and against the shoulder of the high step, there should be 0.043 in. clearance between the edge of the choke valve and the air horn dividing wall.

4. Bend the choke rod at the lower angle, if necessary.

Choke Unloader
▶ See Figure 17

1. Hold the throttle valve wide open, while the choke trip lever touches the choke counterweight.

2. Clearance between the top of the choke valve and the dividing wall of the air horn should now be 0.235 in. Bend the fast idle cam tang, if necessary.

Secondary Throttle Lockout

1. Close the choke valve so that the secondary lockout tang is in the fast idle cam slot. Clearance between the fast idle cam and the tang should be 0.015 in.

2. Bend the tang horizontally as necessary to obtain the correct clearance.

Float Level and Drop
▶ See Figures 26 and 27

1. Remove the bowl cover.

2. Install a new gasket on the bowl cover surface.

3. Invert the cover and install the float level gauges supplied with the rebuilding kit over the primary and secondary floats. The floats should just touch the gauges. The height from the bottom of the float to the bowl cover gasket is $1^{33}/_{64}$ in. for the primaries and $1^{37}/_{64}$ in. for the secondaries. Bend the float arms as necessary to obtain the correct level.

4. Center the floats in the level gauge, bending them to the left or right as necessary.

5. While holding the bowl cover in an upright position, measure the distance from the bowl cover gasket to the bottom of the float. This distance, float drop, should be $2^{1}/_{4}$ in. Bend the float tang on the end of the hinge arm to correct the drop.

6. Install the bowl cover.

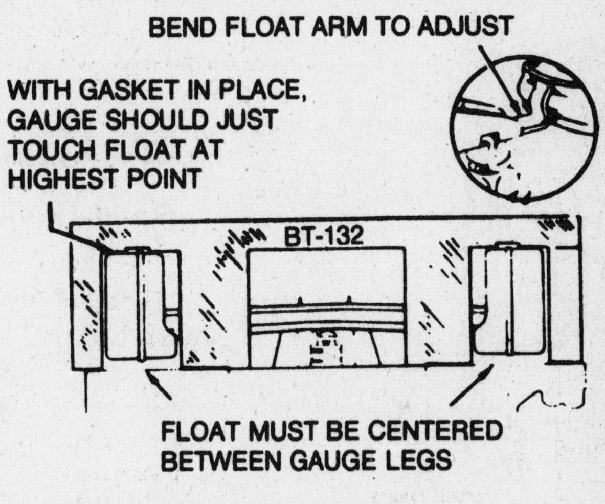

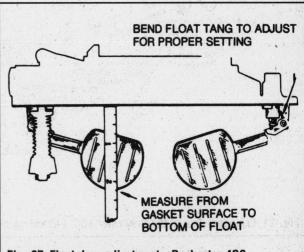

Fig. 26 Float level adjustment—Rochester 4GC carburetor

Fig. 27 Float drop adjustment—Rochester 4GC carburetor

Carter AFB-4 Barrel Carburetor

ADJUSTMENTS

Automatic Choke

The automatic choke is correctly adjusted when the scribe mark on the coil housing is aligned with the center notch in the choke housing for automatic transmission cars and one notch lean for manual transmission cars.

Float
♦ **See Figure 28**

Remove the metering rods and the bowl cover. Align the float by sighting down its side to determine whether it is parallel with the outer edge of the air horn. Bend the float to adjust. Float level is adjusted with the air horn inverted and the air horn gasket in place. Clearance between each float (at the outer end) and the air horn gasket should be 5/16 in. Bend to adjust.

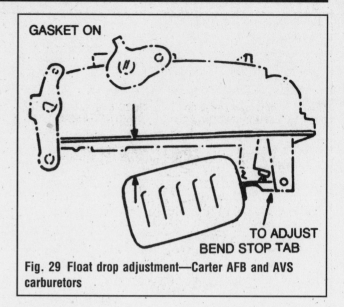
Fig. 29 Float drop adjustment—Carter AFB and AVS carburetors

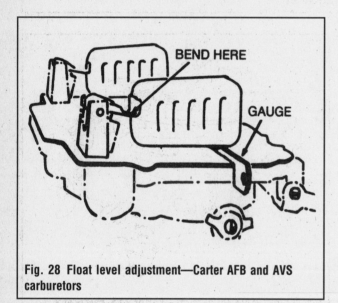
Fig. 28 Float level adjustment—Carter AFB and AVS carburetors

Float Drop
♦ **See Figure 29**

Float drop is adjusted by holding the air horn in an upright position and bending the float arm until the vertical distance from the air horn gasket to the outer end of each float measures 3/4 in.

Intermediate Choke Rod

Remove the choke coil housing assembly, gasket, and baffle plate. Position a 0.026 in. wire gauge between the bottom of the slot in the piston and the top of the slot in the choke piston housing. Close the choke piston against the gauge and secure it with a rubber band. Bend the intermediate choke rod so that the distance between the top edge of the choke valve and the air horn divider measures 0.070 in.

Accelerator Pump

The first step in adjusting the accelerator pump is to push aside the fast idle cam and firmly seat the throttle valves. Bend the pump rod at the lower angle to obtain a 1/2 in. clearance between the air horn and the top of the plunger shaft.

Unloader, Closing Shoe, and Secondary Throttle
♦ **See Figures 30 and 31**

To adjust the unloader, hold the throttle wide open and bend the unloader tang to obtain a 3/16 in. clearance between the upper edge of the choke valve and the inner wall of the air horn.

The clearance between the positive closing shoes on the primary and secondary throttle valves is checked with the valves

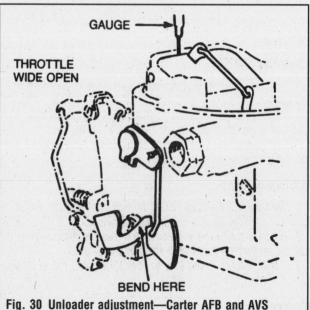
Fig. 30 Unloader adjustment—Carter AFB and AVS carburetors

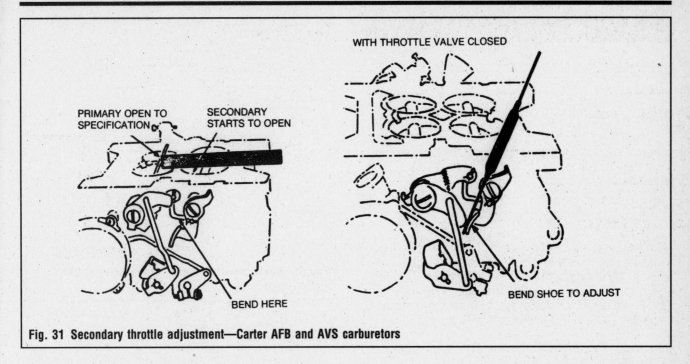

Fig. 31 Secondary throttle adjustment—Carter AFB and AVS carburetors

closed. Bend the secondary closing shoe as required to obtain a clearance of 0.020 in.

The secondary throttle opening is governed by the pick-up lever on the primary throttle shaft. It has two points of contact with the loose lever on the primary shaft. If the contact points do not simultaneously engage, bend the pick-up lever to obtain proper engagement. The primary and secondary throttle valve opening must be synchronized.

Carter AVS-4 Barrel Carburetor

ADJUSTMENTS

Air Valve

▶ **See Figure 32**

1. Turn the air valve bearing retainer until the air valve freely falls open.
2. Wind the air valve bearing counterclockwise until the air valve just starts to close.
3. Continue to wind the bearing an additional 2⅛ turns, and then tighten the retainer.

Accelerator Pump

1. With the fast idle cam out of the way, back the idle speed screw out until the throttle valves seat in their bores.
2. Hold the throttle valves closed and measure the distance from the air horn to the bottom of the pump S-link.
3. If this distance is not $1\frac{1}{32}$ in., bend the pump rod to obtain it.

Idle Vent

While holding the choke valve open and the throttle valve closed, the clearance at the idle valve should be 0.030 in. Bend the vent valve lever to adjust.

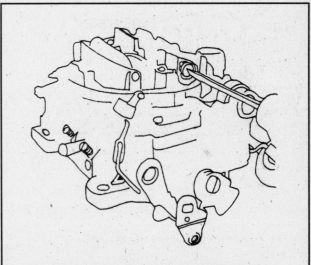

Fig. 32 Air valve adjustment—Carter AVS carburetor

Fast Idle Choke Rod

▶ **See Figure 33**

Bend the fast idle rod at a lower angle until the fast idle cam index mark lines up with the fast idle adjustment screw. Perform this adjustment while holding the choke valve closed.

Float Level and Drop

These adjustments are made in the same manner as was used for the Carter AFB.

Choke Unloader

▶ **See Figure 30**

1. Hold the throttle wide open and the choke valve toward the closed position with a rubber band.
2. Bend the unloader tang on the throttle shaft lever to obtain

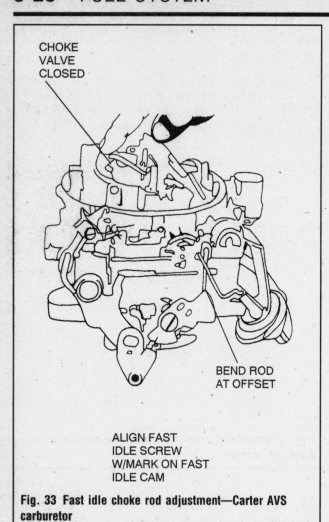

CHOKE
VALVE
CLOSED

BEND ROD
AT OFFSET

ALIGN FAST
IDLE SCREW
W/MARK ON FAST
IDLE CAM

Fig. 33 Fast idle choke rod adjustment—Carter AVS carburetor

a clearance of 0.170 in. between the upper edge of the choke valve and the dividing wall of the air horn.

Choke Vacuum Break

1. Hold the vacuum break in against its stop and the choke valve toward the closed position with a rubber band.
2. Bend the vacuum break link at an offset to obtain 0.020 in. clearance between the upper edge of the choke valve and the air horn wall.

Closing Shoe

1. Hold the primary and secondary throttle valves closed.
2. Bend the secondary closing shoe to obtain 0.020 in. clearance between the positive closing shoes on the primary and secondary throttle levers.

Secondary Throttle Opening
◆ See Figure 31

1. Check to see that the pick-up lever contacts the loose lever on the primary shaft at both points simultaneously. Bend the pick-up lever to obtain proper contact, if necessary.
2. If the primary and secondary throttle valves do not come to the wide open position simultaneously, bend the connecting link until they do.

Secondary Lock-Out
◆ See Figure 34

1. When the choke valve is closed, the lock-out tang on the secondary throttle lever should engage the lock-out dog. When the valve is open, the lock-out dog should swing free of the tang.
2. Bend the lock-out tang on the secondary throttle lever, if an adjustment is necessary.

SECONDARY
THROTTLE SHAFT

LOCK-OUT DOG

BEND TANG AS REQUIRED

Fig. 34 Secondary lock-out adjustment—Carter AVS carburetor

Auxiliary Vacuum Break

1975–79 VEHICLES

1. Seat the auxiliary vacuum diaphragm by applying an outside source of vacuum. Tape over the vacuum bleed hole so the vacuum will not bleed down.

2. Place the idle speed screw on the high step of the fast idle cam.

3. Hold the choke coil lever inside the choke housing towards the closed choke position.

4. Rotate the inside choke coil lever until the spring in the diaphragm plunger is seated. Measure the distance between the upper edge of the choke valve and the air horn wall.

5. Adjust by bending the auxiliary vacuum break rod at the bottom of the U-shaped bend. Remove the piece of tape from the auxiliary vacuum diaphragm.

Bowl Vent Valve

➡ Check and adjust, if necessary, the pump rod clearance and curb idle speed before adjusting the bowl vent valve.

1. Remove the two bowl vent valve cover attaching screws in the top of the air horn and remove the cover and gasket. Remove the bowl vent valve spring.

2. Place the idle speed screw on the second step of the fast idle cam next to the highest step. In this position, the bowl vent valve should just be closed.

3. If the vent valve is just closed with the idle speed screw on the second step of the fast idle cam, rotate the fast idle cam so that the idle speed screw is on the next lower step. In this position, the vent valve should just begin to open.

4. If it is necessary to adjust the bowl vent valve, turn the adjustment screw in the top of the valve, to obtain the conditions mentioned in Steps 2 and 3.

Rochester 4MV Quadrajet-4 Barrel Carburetor

ADJUSTMENTS

The Rochester Quadrajet carburetor is a two stage, four-barrel downdraft carburetor. The designation MC, MV, or ME refers to the type of choke system the carburetor is designed for. The MV model is equipped with a manifold mounted thermostatic choke coil. The MC model has a choke housing and coil mounted on the side of the float bowl. ME models have an electric choke.

The primary side of the carburetor is equipped with 1⅜ diameter bores and a triple venturi with plain tube nozzles. During off idle and part throttle operation, the fuel is metered through tapered metering rods operating in specifically designed jets positioned by a manifold vacuum responsive piston.

The secondary side of the carburetor contains two 2¼ bores. An air valve is used on the secondary side for metering control and supplements the primary bores.

The secondary air valve operates tapered metering rods which regulate the fuel in constant proportion to the air being supplied.

Accelerator Pump
▶ See Figure 35

Close the throttle valves and position the pump rod in the specified hole of the pump lever. Use an adjustable T-scale to measure from the top of the choke valve wall, nearest the vent stack, to the top of the pump stem. Bend the pump lever to obtain the specified distance.

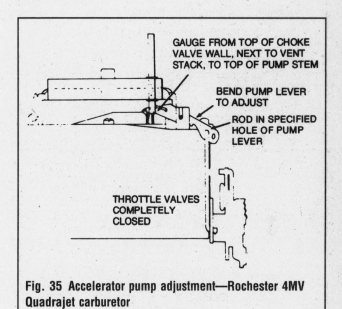

Fig. 35 Accelerator pump adjustment—Rochester 4MV Quadrajet carburetor

Float
▶ See Figure 36

Remove the top cover and gasket, and use an adjustable T-scale to measure the distance from the top of the float bowl gasket surface to the top of the float at a point ³⁄₁₆ in. back from the toe of the float. Bend the float tang to specifications.

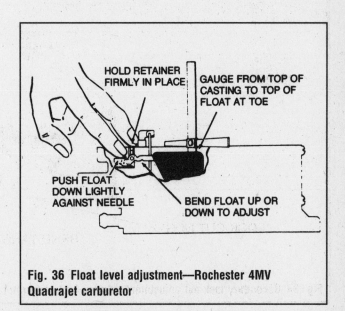

Fig. 36 Float level adjustment—Rochester 4MV Quadrajet carburetor

Idle Vent

After adjusting the accelerator pump rod as specified above, open the primary throttle valve enough to just close the idle vent. Measure from the top of the choke valve wall to the top of the pump plunger stem. If adjustment is necessary, bend the wire tang on the pump lever.

Fast Idle

♦ **See Figure 37**

1. Position the fast idle lever on the high step of the fast idle cam.
2. Be sure that the choke is wide open and the engine warm. Plug the EGR vacuum hose. Disconnect the vacuum hose to the front vacuum break unit, if there are two.
3. Turn the fast idle screw to gain the proper fast idle rpm.

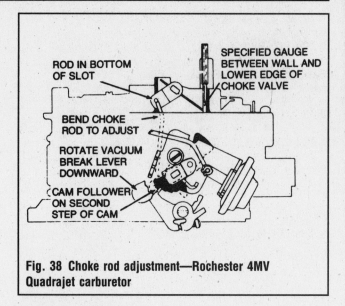

Fig. 38 Choke rod adjustment—Rochester 4MV Quadrajet carburetor

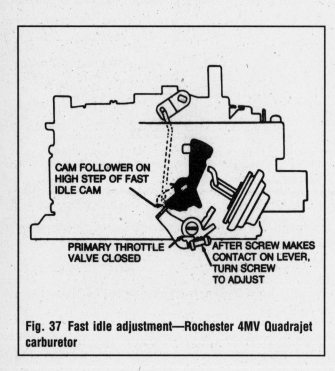

Fig. 37 Fast idle adjustment—Rochester 4MV Quadrajet carburetor

Choke Rod (Fast Idle Cam)

♦ **See Figure 38**

1. Adjust the fast idle and place the cam follower on the second step of the fast idle cam.
2. Close the choke valve by exerting counterclockwise pressure on the external choke lever. On 1975 and later models, remove the coil assembly from the choke housing and push upon the choke coil lever.
3. Insert a gauge of the proper size between the lower (upper beginning 1975) edge of the choke valve and the inside air horn wall.
4. To adjust models through 1974, bend the choke rod. To adjust 1975 and later models, bend the tang on the fast idle cam. Be sure that the tang rests against the cam after bending.

Air Valve Dashpot

♦ **See Figure 39**

Seat the vacuum break diaphragm and gauge the clearance between the dashpot rod and the end of the slot in the air valve lever. Bend the rod to adjust.

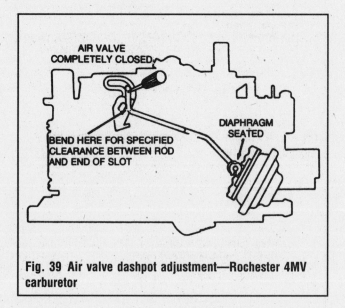

Fig. 39 Air valve dashpot adjustment—Rochester 4MV carburetor

Primary Vacuum Break

♦ **See Figure 40**

1. Fully seat the vacuum break diaphragm using an outside vacuum source.
2. Open the throttle valve enough to allow the fast idle cam follower to clear the fast idle cam.
3. The end of the vacuum break rod should be at the outer end of the slot in the vacuum break diaphragm plunger.

4. The specified clearance should register from the lower end of the choke valve to the inside air horn wall.

5. If the clearance is not correct, bend the vacuum break link.

Secondary Vacuum Break

1. Using an outside vacuum source, seat the auxiliary vacuum break diaphragm plunger.

2. Rotate the choke lever in the closed position until the spring loaded diaphragm plunger is fully extended.

3. Holding the choke valve closed, check the distance between the lower edge of the choke valve and the air horn wall.

4. To adjust to specifications, bend the vacuum break link.

Unloader

▶ **See Figure 41**

Close the choke valve and secure it with a rubber band placed on the vacuum break lever. Completely open the primary throttle

and measure the distance between the air horn and the lower edge of the throttle valve. Bend the fast idle lever tang to achieve the correct specification.

Secondary Lock-Out

▶ **See Figure 42**

Completely open the choke valve and rotate the vacuum break lever clockwise. Bend the lever if the measurement between the lever and the secondary throttle shaft exceed specifications. Close the choke and gauge the distance between the lever and the secondary throttle shaft pin. Bend the lever to adjust.

Air Valve Spring

Remove all spring tension by loosening the locking screw and backing out the spring adjusting screw. Close the air valve and turn the adjusting screw until the torsion spring touches the pin on the shaft, and then turn it the additional number of turns specified. Secure the locking screw.

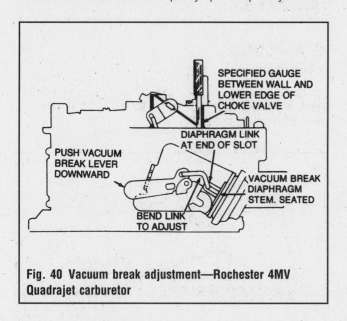

Fig. 40 Vacuum break adjustment—Rochester 4MV Quadrajet carburetor

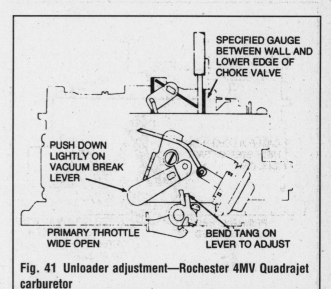

Fig. 41 Unloader adjustment—Rochester 4MV Quadrajet carburetor

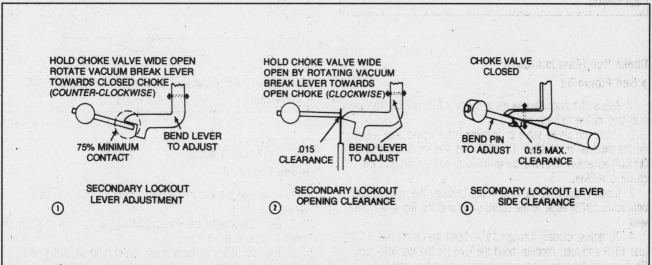

Fig. 42 Secondary lock-out adjustment—Rochester 4MV Quadrajet carburetor

Secondary Opening

With the primary throttle valves open and the actuating link touching the secondary lever, the bottom of the link should be in the center of the secondary lever slot and the clearance between the tang and the link should be 0.070 in.

Secondary Closing

With the curb idle speed set to the specified rpm and the cam follower free of the fast idle cam, there should be 0.020 in. clearance between the actuation link and the front of the secondary lever slot. The tang must touch the tang on the primary shaft actuating lever. Bend to adjust.

Rochester M4MC, M4MCA Quadrajet-4 Barrel Carburetors

ADJUSTMENTS

Accelerator Pump Rod

◆ **See Figure 43**

1. With the fast idle cam follower off the steps of the fast idle cam, back the carburetor idle speed screw out until the throttle plates are completely closed.

➡**Make sure that the secondary actuating rod is not keeping the primary throttle plates from closing. If the primary throttle plates do not close completely, bend the secondary closing tang out of position, then readjust after adjustment.**

2. Place the pump rod in the specified hole in the pump lever.
3. Measure the distance from the top of the choke valve wall (next to the vent stack) to the top of the pump stem with the specified gauge.
4. If adjustment is necessary, support the pump lever with a screwdriver and bend the pump lever.
5. Adjust the idle speed.

Fast Idle Speed Adjustment

◆ **See Figures 44 and 45**

1. Put the cam follower on the highest step of the fast idle cam.
2. Turn the fast idle screw out until the primary throttle plates are closed.
3. Turn the fast idle screw in to contact the lever, then turn the screw three turns in to adjust.
4. Recheck the fast idle speed on the car. Check as follows:
   A. Position the fast idle lever on the high step of the fast idle cam. Disconnect and plug the vacuum hose at the EGR valve.
   B. Be sure that the choke is wide open and the engine warm.
   C. Turn the fast idle screw to gain the proper fast idle rpm.

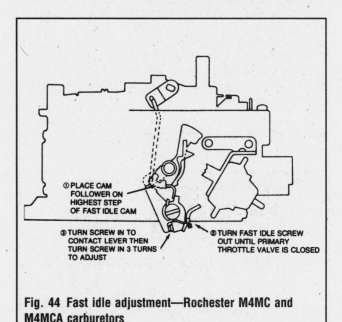

Fig. 44 Fast idle adjustment—Rochester M4MC and M4MCA carburetors

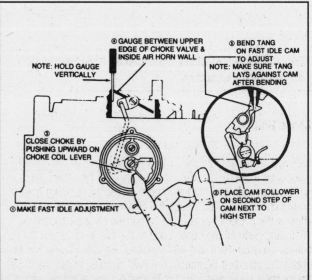

Fig. 43 Accelerator pump rod adjustment—Rochester M4MC and M4MCA carburetors

Fig. 45 Fast idle cam adjustment—Rochester M4MC and M4MCA carburetors

Choke Coil Lever and Choke Thermostatic Coil

1977–79 VEHICLES

▶ **See Figure 46**

1. Remove the three mounting screws and retainers, and pull the thermostatic coil cover assembly off the choke housing and set it aside.

2. Place the fast idle cam follower on the high step of the cam and then push up on the thermostatic coil tang in the choke housing until the choke is closed.

3. Insert a 0.120″ plug gauge or rod of that diameter into the hole in the housing located just below the lever. With the choke closed, the lever should just touch the gauge.

4. Adjust the choke rod by changing the angle of the bend it makes just below the choke itself, if necessary. See illustration.

5. Then, install the coil cover back on the choke housing, making sure that the thermostatic coil engages the tang. Install the three retainers and screws, but do not tighten. With the fast idle cam follower still on the high step of the cam, rotate the cover assembly counterclockwise until the choke closes. Set all models 2 notches lean except 1977 models with manual transmission; set these three notches lean. Hold the position of the housing while tightening screws evenly.

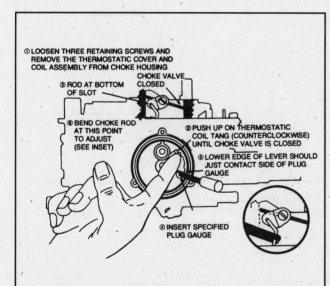

Fig. 46 Choke coil lever adjustment—Rochester M4MC and M4MCA carburetors

Choke Rod

Position the cam follower on the second step of the fast idle cam, touching the high step. Close the choke valve directly on models up to 1976. On 1977 models, remove the choke thermostatic cover, and then hold the choke closed by pushing upward on the choke coil lever. Gauge the clearance between the lower edge of the choke valve and the carburetor body on models to 1975, and between the upper edge of the choke valve and the carburetor body on 1976 and 1977 models. Bend the choke rod to obtain the specified clearance. On 1977 models, install the choke thermostatic cover and adjust it to specification when the adjustment is complete. This adjustment requires sophisticated special tools on 1978 and later models, and so is not included here.

Air Valve Dashpot

▶ **See Figure 47**

Seat the vacuum break diaphragm. On 1977–79 models, this requires plugging the bleed purge hole on the back of the diaphragm with tape, and the use of an external vacuum source. Hold the air valve tightly closed on all models. Gauge the clearance between the dashpot rod and the end of the slot in the air valve lever. Bend the rod to adjust. Remove the tape from the bleed purge hole.

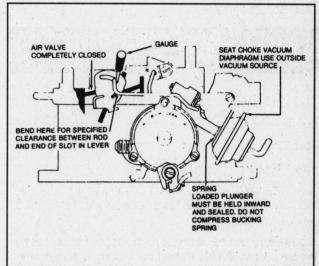

Fig. 47 Air valve dashpot adjustment—Rochester M4MC and M4MCA carburetors

Idle Vent

➡ **This adjustment is not required on 1977–79 carburetors.**

After adjusting the accelerator pump rod as specified above, open the primary throttle valve enough to just close the idle vent. Measure from the top of the choke valve wall to the top of the pump plunger stem. If adjustment is necessary, bend the wire tang on the pump lever.

Front Vacuum Break

▶ **See Figure 48**

1967–76 VEHICLES

1. Loosen the three retaining screws and remove the thermostatic cover and coil assembly from the choke housing.

2. Put the cam follower lever on the highest step of the fast idle cam.

3. Using a vacuum source, seat the front vacuum diaphragm.

4. Push up on the inside choke coil lever until the tang on the vacuum break lever contacts the tang on the vacuum break plunger.

5. Measure the distance between the upper edge of the choke and the inside of the air horn wall with the specified gauge.

6. To adjust, turn the adjustment screw on the vacuum break plunger lever.

7. After adjustment, install the vacuum hose to the vacuum break unit.

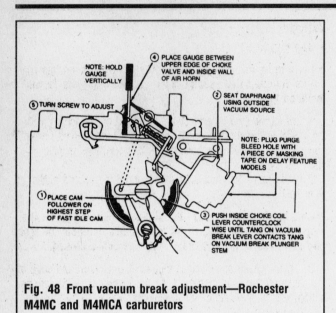

Fig. 48 Front vacuum break adjustment—Rochester M4MC and M4MCA carburetors

Rear Vacuum Break
▶ See Figure 49

1967–76 VEHICLES

1. Loosen the three-retaining screws and remove the thermostatic cover and coil assembly from the choke housing.

2. Put the cam follower lever on the highest step of the fast idle cam.

3. Plug the bleed hole in the end of the cover of the vacuum break unit using a small piece of tape.

4. Using a vacuum source, seat the rear vacuum diaphragm.

5. Push up on the choke coil lever inside the choke housing toward closed choke.

6. With the choke rod in the bottom of the slot in the choke lever, measure the distance between the upper edge of the choke plate and the air horn wall with the specified gauge.

7. If adjustment is necessary, bend the vacuum break rod at the point shown in the illustration.

8. After adjustment, remove the tape from over the bleed hole in the end cover of the vacuum break unit. Install the vacuum hose onto the vacuum break unit.

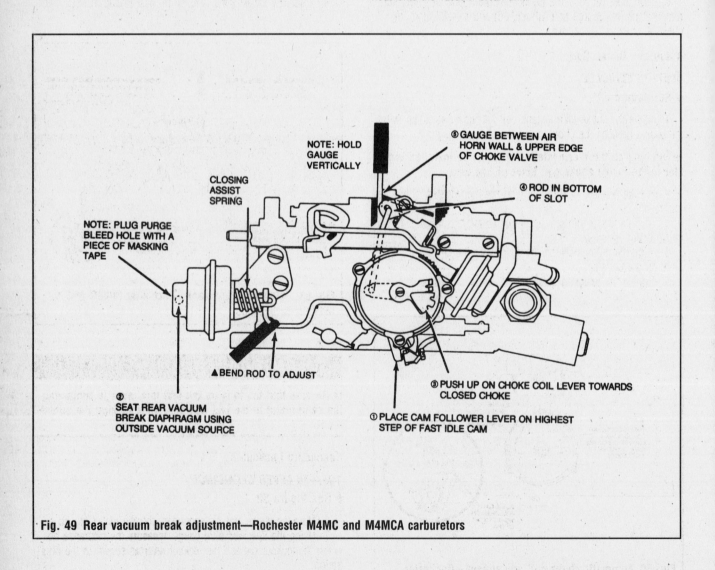

Fig. 49 Rear vacuum break adjustment—Rochester M4MC and M4MCA carburetors

1977 VEHICLES

➡Adjustment procedures for 1978 and later models require the use of an expensive and sophisticated special tool, so procedures are not included here.

1. Remove the choke thermostatic cover. Place fast idle cam follower on high step of cam.
2. Where there is a purge bleed hole on the back of the choke vacuum break, put tape over the hole. Then, seat the diaphragm using an outside vacuum source.
3. Push the inside choke coil lever counter-clockwise until the tang on the vacuum break lever touches the tang on the vacuum break plunger stem.
4. Place a gauge of the following diameter between the upper edge of the choke butterfly and the inside wall of the air horn: California Engines: 0.165 in. All Other Engines: 0.160 in.
5. If the dimension is incorrect, adjust the screw on the vacuum break plunger stem until all play is taken up nd choke butterfly just touches the gauge when its held vertically.
6. Reconnect vacuum line to vacuum break port of carburetor, remove tape from purge hole (if applied) and reinstall and adjust choke thermostat (see above).

Automatic Choke Coil

1967–76 VEHICLES

♦ See Figure 50

1. Install the choke thermostatic coil and cover assembly with the gasket between the choke cover the choke housing.

➡The tang on the thermostatic coil must be installed in the slot in the inside choke coil lever pickup arm

2. Put the fast idle cam follower on the highest step of the fast idle cam.
3. Turn the cover and coil assembly counterclockwise until the choke plate just closes.
4. Align the index mark on the cover with the specified index mark on the housing.
5. Tighten the retaining screws.

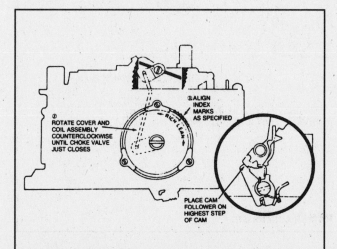

Fig. 50 Automatic choke coil adjustment—Rochester M4MC and M4MCA carburetors

Unloader

♦ See Figure 51

➡Performing this adjustment on 1978 and later models requires sophisticated special tools, so the procedure is not included here.

1. Install the choke thermostatic cover and coil assembly with the gasket in the choke housing and align the index mark on the housing. On 1977 models, make sure the choke thermostatic spring is properly adjusted (see above).
2. With the choke completely closed, hold the throttle plates wide open.

➡On a warm engine, close the choke by pushing up on the tang of the intermediate choke lever which contacts the fast idle cam; use a rubber band to hold the choke closed.

3. Then measure the distance between the air horn and edge of the choke butterfly. On models up to and including 1976, use the bottom side of the butterfly for this measurement; on 1977 models, use the top side.
4. Adjust by bending the tang on the fast idle lever.

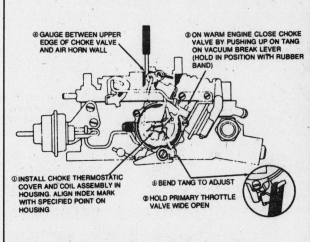

Fig. 51 Unloader adjustment—Rochester M4MC and M4MCA carburetors

✳✳ CAUTION

Make sure that the tang on the fast idle lever is contacting the centerpoint of the fast idle cam after making the adjustment.

Secondary Lockout

1967–76 LEVER CLEARANCE

♦ See Figure 52

1. Hold the choke and the secondary throttle plates closed.
2. Using the specified plug gauge, measure the clearance between the lockout pin and the lockout lever as shown in the illustration.
3. If adjustment is necessary, bend the lockout pin at the point shown.

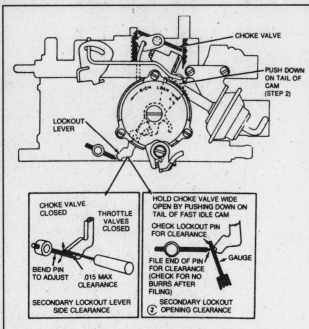

Fig. 52 Secondary lock-out adjustment—1967–76 Rochester M4MC and M4MCA carburetors

1967–76 OPENING CLEARANCE

1. Hold the choke wide open by pushing down on the tail of the fast idle cam.

2. Hold the secondary throttle plates slightly open.

3. Using the specified plug gauge, measure the clearance between the end of the lockout pin and the toe of the lockout lever as shown.

4. If adjustment is necessary, file off the end of the lockout pin to obtain the specified clearance.

1977–79 VEHICLES

◗ See Figure 53

1. See accompanying illustration.

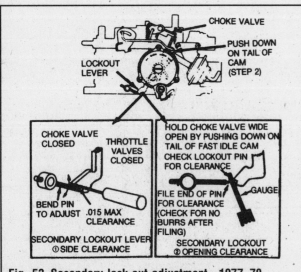

Fig. 53 Secondary lock-out adjustment—1977–79 Rochester M4MC and M4MCA carburetors

Secondary Opening

◗ See Figure 54

1. Open the primary throttle valves until the actuating link contacts the upper tang on the secondary lever slot.

2. With two point linkage, the bottom of the link should be in the center of the secondary lever slot.

3. With three point linkage, there should be 0.070 in. clearance between the link and the middle tang.

4. Bend the upper tang on the secondary lever to adjust as necessary.

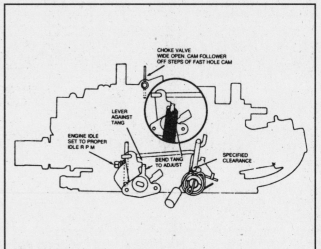

Fig. 54 Secondary opening adjustment—Rochester M4MC and M4MCA carburetors

Secondary Closing

◗ See Figure 55

1. Preset the carburetor idle speed screw to specification.

2. Hold the choke wide open with the cam follower lever off the steps of the fast idle cam.

3. Using the specified gauge (0.020 in.), measure the clearance between the slot in the secondary throttle valve pickup lever and the secondary actuating rod.

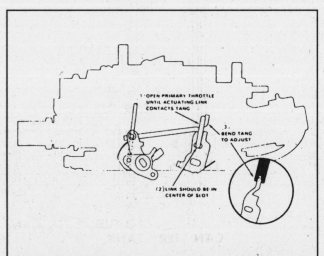

Fig. 55 Secondary closing adjustment—Rochester M4MC and M4MCA carburetors

4. To adjust, bend the secondary closing tang on the primary throttle lever as shown.

Air Valve Spring

▶ **See Figure 56**

1. Remove the front vacuum break diaphragm unit and air valve dashpot rod.
2. Loosen the lockscrew using the special hex wrench (required on 1977 and later carburetors).
3. Turn the tension adjusting screw counterclockwise until the air valve opens part way.
4. Manually hold the air valve closed.
5. Turn the tension adjusting screw clockwise the specified number of turns after the spring contacts the pin.
6. Tighten the lockscrew and replace the air valve dashpot rod and the front vacuum break diaphragm unit and bracket.

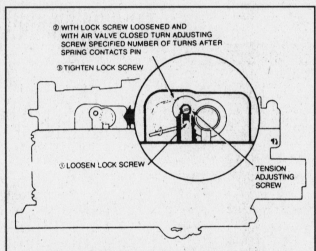

Fig. 56 Air valve spring adjustment—Rochester M4MC and M4MCA carburetors

Deceleration Throttle Stop

▶ **See Figure 57**

1. Adjust the carburetor idle speed screw to specification.
2. Push the hex end of the throttle stop plunger in (toward the throttle lever) until the plunger stem hits the stop inside the diaphragm unit.
3. With the plunger held inward against the stop, turn the plunger adjusting screw in or out to obtain the specified deceleration rpm.

Float Level

With the air horn assembly upside down, measure the distance from the air horn gasket surface (gasket removed) to the top of the float at the toe.

➡ **Make sure that the retaining pin is firmly held in place and that the tang of the float is firmly against the needle and seat assembly.**

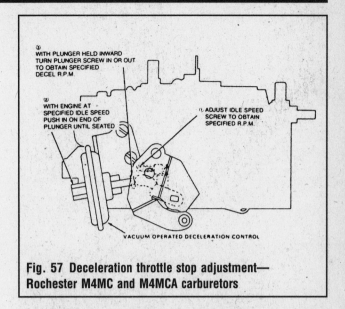

Fig. 57 Deceleration throttle stop adjustment— Rochester M4MC and M4MCA carburetors

Holley 4150, 4160-4 Barrel Carburetors

ADJUSTMENTS

▶ **See Figure 58**

These carburetors are basically similar in design. The 4160 is an end-inlet carburetor, while the 4150 carburetor may be either an end or center inlet type.

Choke

The 1965 model 4150 uses a bimetallic choke that is mounted on the carburetor. It is correctly set when the cover scribe mark aligns with the specified notch mark. The later model 4150s and 4160s employ a remotely located choke. To adjust, disconnect the choke rod at the choke lever and secure the choke lever shut. Bend the rod so that when the rod is depressed to the contact stop, the top is even with the bottom of the hole in the choke lever.

Float Level

Position the car on a flat, level surface and start the engine. Remove the sight plugs and check to see that the fuel level reaches the bottom threads of the sight plug port. A positive or negative tolerance of $1/32$ in. is acceptable. To change the level, loosen the fuel inlet needle locking screw and adjust the nut. Turning it clockwise lowers the fuel level; counterclockwise raises it. Turn the nut $1/6$ of a turn for each $1/16$ in. desired change. Open the primary throttle slightly to assure a stabilized adjusting condition on the secondaries. There is no required float drop adjustment.

Fast Idle

1965 4150 CARBURETORS

Bring the engine to the normal operating temperature with the air cleaner off. Open the throttle. Place the fast idle cam on its

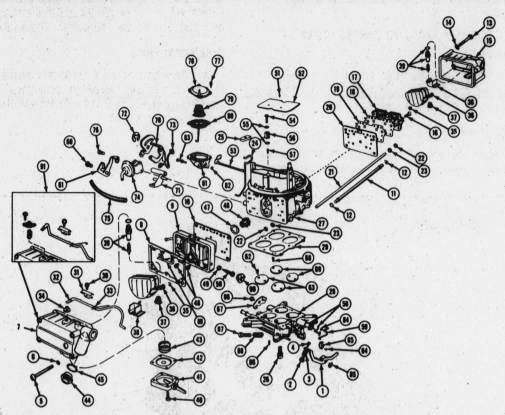

1. Lever, pump operating
2. Locknut
3. Spring, override
4. Screw, pump adjusting
5. Screw, fuel bowl (primary)
6. Gasket, bowl screw
7. Fuel bowl (primary)
8. Gasket, fuel bowl
9. Metering body (primary side)
10. Gasket, metering body
11. Fuel tube (float bowl connecting)
12. O-ring, fuel tube
13. Screw, fuel bowl (secondary)
14. Gasket, bowl screw
15. Fuel bowl (secondary)
16. Screw, metering body (secondary)
17. Metering body (secondary)
18. Gasket, metering body (secondary)
19. Plate, metering body (secondary)
20. Gasket, metering body plate
21. Balance tube
22. Washers, balance tube
23. O-rings, balance tube
24. Choke link
25. Seals, choke rod
26. Throttle body screws
27. Main body
28. Throttle body
29. Gasket, main-to-throttle body
30. Screw, bowl vent valve rod clamp
31. Clamp, valve rod

32. Rod, bowl vent valve
33. Spring vent valve rod
34. Valve, bowl vent
35. Retainer, clip, float
36. Float
37. Spring, float
38. Baffle, float
39. Needle valve and seat
40. Screws, fuel pump cover
41. Cover assembly, fuel pump
42. Diaphragm, fuel pump
43. Spring, fuel pump diaphragm
44. Fitting, fuel inlet
45. Gasket, fuel inlet, fitting
46. Valve assembly, power
47. Gasket, power valve
48. Primary jets
49. Needle, idle adjusting mixture
50. Gasket, idle mixture needle
51. Screws, choke valve
52. Choke valve
53. Choke shaft and lever assembly
54. Discharge nozzle screw, pump
55. Gasket, nozzle screw
56. Nozzle, pump discharge
57. Needle, pump discharge jet
58. Cotter pins, connecting rods
59. Rod, secondary connecting
60. Screw and lockwasher, fast idl cam lever
61. Lever, fast idle cam
62. Screws, primary throttle valve
63. Throttle valves, primary
64. Screw, pump cam

65. Pump cam
66. Screw and lockwasher, secondary stop lever
67. Lever, secondary stop
68. Screws, secondary throttle valves
69. Throttle valves, secondary
70. Fast idle cam lever
71. Fast idle cam
72. Retainer (E-clip)
73. Choke diaphragm link
74. Choke diaphragm assembly
75. Choke vacuum hose
76. Choke diaphragm bracket screw
77. Secondary diaphragm cover screw
78. Diaphragm cover (machine)
79. Secondary diaphragm return spring
80. Secondary diaphragm assembly
81. Secondary diaphragm housing (machine)
82. Secondary diaphragm housing gasket
83. Secondary diaphragm assembly screw
84. Throttle connecting rod retainer washer
85. Pump operating lever (E-clip)
86. Secondary stopscrew
87. Throttle stopscrew
88. Throttle stopscrew spring
89. Baffle
90. Limiter cap
91. Bowl vent valve ass'y. (ECS)

Fig. 58 Exploded view of the Holley 4160 carburetor

high step and close the throttle. Adjust the fast idle screw to reach the specified idle speed.

1966 AND LATER 4150 AND 4160 CARBURETORS
▶ **See Figure 59**

Open the throttle and place the choke plate fast idle lever against the top step of the fast idle cam. Bend the fast idle lever to obtain the specified throttle plate opening.

Choke Unloader

Adjustment should be made with the engine not running. Fully open and secure the throttle plate. Force the choke valve toward a closed position, so that contact is made with the unloader tang. Bend the choke rod to gain the specified clearance between the main body and the lower edge of the choke valve.

Accelerator Pump

With the engine off, block the throttle open and push the pump lever down. Clearance between the pump lever arm and the spring adjusting nut should be 0.015 in., minimum. Turn the screw or nut to adjust this clearance.

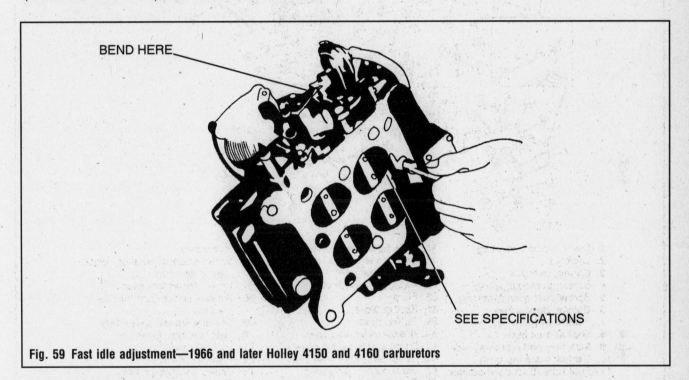

BEND HERE

SEE SPECIFICATIONS

Fig. 59 Fast idle adjustment—1966 and later Holley 4150 and 4160 carburetors

Secondary Throttle Valve

LATER 4150 AND 4160
▶ **See Figure 60**

Close the throttle plates, and then turn the adjustment screw until it contacts the throttle lever. Advance the screw ½ turn more.

Air Vent Valve

LATER 4150 AND 4160

Close the throttle valves and open the choke valve so the throttle arm is free of the idle screw. Bend the air vent valve rod to obtain the specified clearance between the choke valve and seat. Advance the idle speed screw until it touches the throttle lever and then advance it 1½ turns.

Vacuum Break

LATER 4150 AND 4160

Secure the choke valve closed and the vacuum break against the stop. Bend the vacuum break link to gain the specified clearance between the main body and the lower edge of the choke valve.

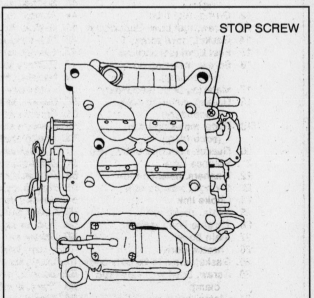

STOP SCREW

Fig. 60 Secondary throttle valve adjustment—Holley 4150 and 4160 carburetors

Carburetor

REMOVAL & INSTALLATION

1. Remove the air cleaner and its gasket.
2. Disconnect the fuel and vacuum lines from the carburetor.
3. Disconnect the choke coil rod or heated air line tube.
4. Disconnect the throttle linkage.
5. On cars with automatic transmissions, disconnect the throttle valve linkage.
6. Remove the CEC valve vacuum hose and electrical connector.
7. Remove the idle stop electrical wiring from the idle stop solenoid, if so equipped.
8. Remove the carburetor attaching nuts and/or bolts, gasket or insulator, and remove the carburetor.

Remove the carburetor mounting bolts . . .

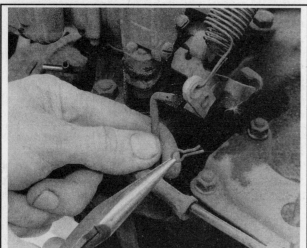

To remove the carburetor, first disconnect the linkages from the carburetor

. . . then remove the carburetor from the manifold

9. Install the carburetor using a reverse of the removal procedure. Use a new gasket and fill the float bowl with gasoline to ease starting of the engine.

OVERHAUL

Efficient carburetion depends greatly on careful cleaning and inspection during overhaul since dirt, gum, water, or varnish in or on the carburetor parts are often responsible for poor performance.

Overhaul your carburetor in a clean, dust-free area. Carefully disassemble the carburetor, referring often to the exploded views. Keep all similar and look-alike parts segregated during disassembly and cleaning to avoid accidental interchange during assembly. Make a note of all jet sizes.

After labeling and unplugging the vacuum lines, detach the electrical connectors

When the carburetor is disassembled, wash all parts (except diaphragms, electric choke units, pump plunger, and any other plastic, leather, fiber, or rubber parts) in clean carburetor solvent. Do not leave parts in the solvent any longer than is necessary to sufficiently loosen the deposits. Excessive cleaning may remove the special finish from the float bowl and choke valve bodies, leaving these parts unfit for service. Rinse all parts in clean solvent and blow them dry with compressed air or allow them to air dry. Wipe clean all cork, plastic, leather, and fiber parts with a clean, lint-free cloth.

Blow out all passages and jets with compressed air and be sure that there are no restrictions or blockages. Never use wire or similar tools to clean jets, fuel passages, or air bleeds. Clean all jets and valves separately to avoid accidental interchange.

Check all parts for wear or damage. If wear or damage is found, replace the defective parts. Especially check the following:

1. Check the float needle and seat for wear. If wear is found, replace the complete assembly.

2. Check the float hinge pin for wear and the float(s) for dents or distortion. Replace the float if fuel has leaked into it.

3. Check the throttle and choke shaft bores for wear or an out-of-round condition. Damage or wear to the throttle arm, shaft, or shaft bore will often require replacement of the throttle body. These parts require a close tolerance of fit; wear may allow air leakage, which could affect starting and idling.

→**Throttle shafts and bushings are not included in overhaul kits. They can be purchased separately.**

4. Inspect the idle mixture adjusting needles for burrs or grooves. Any such condition requires replacement of the needle, since you will not be able to obtain a satisfactory idle.

5. Test the accelerator pump check valves. They should pass air one way but not the other. Test for proper seating by blowing and sucking on the valve. Replace the valve if necessary. If the valve is satisfactory, wash the valve again to remove breath moisture.

6. Check the bowl cover for warped surfaces with a straight-edge.

7. Closely inspect the valves and seats for wear and damage, replacing as necessary.

8. After the carburetor is assembled, check the choke valve for freedom of operation.

Carburetor overhaul kits are recommended for each overhaul. These kits contain all gaskets and new parts to replace those that deteriorate most rapidly. Failure to replace all parts supplied with the kit (especially gaskets) can result in poor performance later.

Some carburetor manufacturers supply overhaul kits of three basic types; minor repair; major repair; and gasket kits. Basically, they contain the following:

Minor Repair Kits:
• All gaskets
• Float needle valve
• Volume control screw
• All diaphragms
• Spring for the pump diaphragm

Major Repair Kits:
• All jets and gaskets
• All diaphragms
• Float needle valve
• Volume control screw
• Pump ball valve
• Main jet carrier
• Float
• Complete intermediate rod

Gasket Kits:
• All gaskets

After cleaning and checking all components, reassemble the carburetor, using new parts and referring to the exploded view. When reassembling, make sure that all screws and jets are tight in their seats, but do not overtighten, as the tips will be distorted. Tighten all screws gradually, in rotation. Do not tighten needle valves into their seats; uneven jetting will result. Always use new gaskets. Be sure to adjust the float level when reassembling.

Carburetor Specifications
Carter Carburetors

Year	Model or Type	Float Level (in.) Prim	Float Level (in.) Sec	Float Drop (in.) Prim	Float Drop (in.) Sec	Pump Travel Setting (in.)	Choke Setting Unloader (in.)	Choke Setting Housing	Secondary Lockout Adj	Throttle Bore Diam Prim	Throttle Bore Diam Sec	Venturi Diam Prim	Venturi Diam Sec
1963	YF	$\frac{3}{8}$	—	$1\frac{3}{16}$	—	—	—	—	—	$1\frac{11}{16}$	—	$1\frac{5}{16}$	—
1964	YF	$\frac{7}{16}$	—	$1\frac{3}{16}$	—	—	—	—	—	$1\frac{11}{16}$	—	$1\frac{5}{16}$	—
1965	YF	$\frac{7}{16}$	—	$1\frac{3}{16}$	—	—	—	—	—	$1\frac{11}{16}$	—	$1\frac{5}{16}$	—
	AFB	$\frac{7}{32}$	$\frac{7}{32}$	$\frac{3}{4}$	$\frac{3}{4}$	—	$\frac{1}{4}$	1 Lean	0.020	$1\frac{9}{16}$	$1\frac{11}{16}$	$1\frac{1}{4}$	$1\frac{9}{16}$
1966	YF	$\frac{1}{2}$	—	$1\frac{3}{16}$	—	—	$\frac{1}{4}$	—	—	$1\frac{11}{16}$	—	$1\frac{5}{16}$	—
	AVS	$1\frac{15}{32}$	$1\frac{15}{32}$	2	2	$\frac{11}{32}$	$\frac{1}{6}$	—	—	$1\frac{9}{16}$	$1\frac{11}{16}$	$1\frac{1}{4}$	$1\frac{9}{16}$
1967	YF	$\frac{7}{32}$	—	$1\frac{3}{16}$	—	—	$\frac{1}{4}$	—	—	$1\frac{11}{16}$	—	$1\frac{5}{16}$	—

Holley Carburetors

Year	Model	Float Level (in.)	Fuel Level (in.)	Bowl Vent Valve (in.)	Pump Travel Setting (in.)	CHOKE SETTING Unloader (in.)	CHOKE SETTING Housing	Secondary Lockout Adj	Throttle Bore Diam Prim	Throttle Bore Diam Sec	Venturi Diam Prim	Venturi Diam Sec
1965	327 (4150)	①	①	—	0.015	0.375	—	—	$1\frac{9}{16}$	$1\frac{9}{16}$	$1\frac{1}{4}$	$1\frac{5}{16}$
1966	327-350 hp (4150)	①	①	0.065	0.015	0.260	—	—	$1\frac{9}{16}$	$1\frac{9}{16}$	$1\frac{1}{4}$	$1\frac{5}{16}$
1967	327 (4160)	①	①	0.065	0.015	0.260	—	—	$1\frac{9}{16}$	$1\frac{9}{16}$	$1\frac{1}{4}$	$1\frac{5}{16}$
	327-325 hp-4 bbl (4150)	A①	A①	.065	0.015	0.265	—	—	$1\frac{9}{16}$	$1\frac{9}{16}$	$1\frac{1}{4}$	$1\frac{5}{16}$
	327, 396, 427-4 bbl (4160)	A①	A①	0.065	0.015	0.265	—	—	$1\frac{9}{16}$	$1\frac{9}{16}$	$1\frac{1}{4}$	$1\frac{5}{16}$
1968–1969	V8-396 (4150)	B①	B①	0.065	0.015	0.350	—	—	$1\frac{11}{16}$	$1\frac{11}{16}$	$1\frac{3}{8}$	$1\frac{7}{16}$

A—Primary 0.170, Secondary 0.300.
B—Primary 0.350, Secondary 0.500.
①—Float adjustment; Fuel level should be plus or minus $\frac{1}{32}$ in. with threads at bottom of sight holes. To adjust turn adjusting nut on top of bowl clockwise, to lower, counterclockwise to raise.

Rochester Carburetors—1962–76

Year	Model or Type	FLOAT LEVEL (in.)		FLOAT DROP (in.)		Pump Travel Setting (in.)	CHOKE SETTING		Secondary Lockout Adj (in.)	Throttle Bore Diam (in.)		Venturi Diam (in.)	
		Prim	Sec	Prim	Sec		Unloader (in.)	Housing		Prim	Sec	Prim	Sec
1962	B	1 9/32	—	1 3/4	—	—	—	—	—	1 9/16	—	1 11/32	—
	BC	1 9/32	—	1 3/4	—	—	0.230	—	—	1 9/16	—	1 11/32	—
1963	BC	1 9/32	—	1 3/4	—	—	0.350	—	—	1 9/16	—	1 11/32	—
1964	BC	1 9/32	—	1 3/4	—	—	0.350	—	—	1 9/16	—	1 11/32	—
	2CV	1 27/64	—	1 29/32	—	0.203	—	—	—	1 7/16	—	1 3/32	—
1965	6 Cyl-BV	1 9/32	—	1 3/4	—	—	0.350	—	—	1 9/16	—	1 11/32	—
	V8-2GV	1 23/64	—	1 29/32	—	57/64	0.203	—	—	1 7/16	—	1 3/32	—
	V8-4GC	1 33/64	1 37/64	2 1/4	2 1/4	1 1/16	0.235	Index	—	1 7/16	1 7/16	1 1/8	1 1/4
1966	6 Cyl-BV	1 9/32	—	1 3/4	—	—	0.350	—	—	1 9/16	—	1 11/32	—
	V8-2GV	3/4	—	1 3/4	—	1 1/8	0.215	—	—	1 7/16	—	1 3/32	—
	V8-4GC	1 17/32	1 19/32	2 1/4	2 1/4	1 1/16	0.250	Index	0.015	1 7/16	1 7/16	1 1/8	1 1/4
1967	BV	1 9/32	—	1 3/4	—	—	0.350	—	—	1 9/16	—	1 11/32	—
	2GV	3/4	—	1 3/4	—	1 1/8	0.215	—	—	1 7/16	—	1 3/32	—
	4MV-Aut	9/32	—	—	—	13/32	0.260	—	0.010	1 3/8	2 1/4	1 3/32	—
	4MV-Std	9/32	—	—	—	13/32	0.300	—	0.010	1 3/8	2 1/4	1 3/32	—
1968	M	9/32	—	—	—	—	—	—	—	1 11/16	—	—	—
	MV-Aut	9/32	—	—	—	—	0.350	—	—	1 11/16	—	—	—
	MV-Std	9/32	—	—	—	—	0.350	—	—	1 11/16	—	—	—
	2GV	3/4	—	1 3/4	—	1 1/8	0.200	—	—	1 7/16	—	1 3/32	—
	4MV	9/32	—	—	—	9/32	0.300	—	0.010	1 3/8	2 1/4	1 3/32	—
1969	M	1/4	—	—	—	—	—	—	—	1 11/16	—	—	—
	MV-Aut	1/4	—	—	—	0.350	—	—	—	1 11/16	—	—	—
	MV-Std	1/4	—	—	—	0.350	—	—	—	1 11/16	—	—	—
	2GV-Std	27/32	—	1 3/4	—	1 1/8	0.215	—	—	1 7/16	—	1 3/16	—
	2GV-Aut	27/32	—	1 3/4	—	1 1/8	0.215	—	—	1 7/16	—	1 3/16	—
	4MV-Std 350	7/32	—	—	—	5/16	0.450	—	0.015	1 3/8	2 1/4	1 3/32	—

Rochester Carburetors—1962–76 (cont.)

Year	Model or Type	FLOAT LEVEL (in.)		FLOAT DROP (in.)		Pump Travel Setting (in.)	CHOKE SETTING		Secondary Lockout Adj (in.)	Throttle Bore Diam (in.)		Venturi Diam (in.)	
		Prim	Sec	Prim	Sec		Unloader (in.)	Housing		Prim	Sec	Prim	Sec
1969	4MV-Aut 350	7/32	—	—	—	5/16	0.450	—	0.015	1 3/8	2 1/4	1 3/32	—
	4MV-Std 396	1/4	—	—	—	5/16	0.450	—	0.015	1 3/8	2 1/4	1 3/32	—
	4MV-Aut 396	1/4	—	—	—	5/16	0.450	—	0.015	1 3/8	2 1/4	1 3/32	—
1970	M-153 (4 Cyl)	1/4	—	—	—	—	—	—	—	1 11/16	—	—	—
	MV-230, Auto	1/4	—	—	—	—	0.350	—	—	1 11/16	—	—	—
	MV-230, Std	1/4	—	—	—	—	0.350	—	—	1 11/16	—	—	—
	MV-250 Auto	1/4	—	—	—	—	0.350	—	—	1 11/16	—	—	—
1970	MV-250, Std	1/4	—	—	—	—	0.350	—	—	1 11/16	—	—	—
	2GV-1.25—307, Auto	27/32	—	1 3/4	—	1 1/8	0.215	—	—	1 7/16	—	1 3/16	—
	2GV-1.25—307, Auto w AC	27/32	—	1 3/4	—	1 1/8	0.215	—	—	1 7/16	—	1 3/16	—
	2GV-1.25—307, Std	27/32	—	1 3/4	—	1 1/8	0.160	—	—	1 7/16	—	1 3/16	—
	2GV-1.25—307, Std w AC	27/32	—	1 3/4	—	1 1/8	0.225	—	—	1 7/16	—	1 3/16	—
	2GV-1.50—350, Auto	23/32	—	1 3/8	—	1 17/32	0.325	—	—	1 11/16	—	1 1/4	—
	2GV-1.50—350, Auto w AC	23/32	—	1 3/8	—	1 17/32	0.325	—	—	1 11/16	—	1 1/4	—
	2GV-1.50—350, Std	23/32	—	1 3/8	—	1 17/32	0.275	—	—	1 11/16	—	1 1/4	—
	2GV-1.50—350, Std w AC	23/32	—	1 3/8	—	1 17/32	0.275	—	—	1 11/16	—	1 1/4	—
	4MV-All	1/4	—	—	—	5/16	0.450	—	—	1 3/8	2 1/4	1 3/32	—
1971	MV-250 Auto	1/4	—	—	—	—	0.350	—	—	1 11/16	—	—	—
	MV-250 Std	1/4	—	—	—	—	0.350	—	—	1 11/16	—	—	—
	2GV-307 Auto	27/32	—	1 3/4	—	1 5/16	0.215	—	—	1 7/16	—	1 3/16	—
	2GV-307 Std	27/32	—	1 3/4	—	1 5/16	0.215	—	—	1 7/16	—	1 3/16	—
	2GV-350 Auto	25/32	—	1 3/8	—	1 17/32	0.325	—	—	1 11/16	—	1 1/4	—
	2GV-350 Std	23/32	—	1 3/8	—	1 17/32	0.325	—	—	1 11/16	—	1 1/4	—
1972	MV, 250	1/4	—	—	—	—	0.350	—	—	1 11/16	—	—	—
	2GV, 307	27/32	—	1 3/4	—	1 5/16	0.215	—	—	1 7/16	—	1 3/16	—
	2GV, 350	25/32	—	1 3/8	—	1 17/32	0.325	—	—	1 11/16	—	1 1/4	—
	4MV, 350	1/4	—	—	—	—	0.100	—	—	1 3/8	2 1/4	1 7/32	—
1973	MV, 250	1/4	—	—	—	—	0.500	—	—	1 11/16	—	—	—
	2GV, 307	21/32	—	1 9/32	—	1 5/16	0.215	—	—	1 7/16	—	1 3/16	—

Rochester Carburetors—1962–76 (cont.)

| Year | Model or Type | FLOAT LEVEL (in.) | | FLOAT DROP (in.) | | Pump Travel Setting (in.) | CHOKE SETTING | | Secondary Lockout Adj (in.) | Throttle Bore Diam (in.) | | Venturi Diam (in.) | |
		Prim	Sec	Prim	Sec		Unloader (in.)	Housing		Prim	Sec	Prim	Sec
1973	2GV, 350	$1\frac{9}{32}$	—	$1\frac{9}{32}$	—	$1\frac{7}{16}$	0.250①	—	—	$1\frac{11}{16}$	—	$1\frac{1}{4}$	—
	4MV, 350	$\frac{7}{32}$	—	—	—	$1\frac{3}{32}$*	0.450	—	—	$1\frac{3}{8}$	$2\frac{1}{4}$	$1\frac{7}{32}$	—
1974	MV, 250	0.295	—	—	—	—	0.500	—	—	$1\frac{11}{16}$	—	—	—
	2GV, 350 (Auto)	$1\frac{9}{32}$	—	$1\frac{9}{32}$	—	$1\frac{3}{16}$	0.325	—	—	$1\frac{11}{16}$	—	$1\frac{1}{4}$	—
	2GV, 350 (Std)	$1\frac{9}{32}$	—	$1\frac{9}{32}$	—	$1\frac{9}{32}$	0.250	—	—	$1\frac{11}{16}$	—	$1\frac{1}{4}$	—
	4MV, 350	$\frac{1}{4}$	—	—	—	$1\frac{3}{32}$*	0.450	—	—	$1\frac{3}{8}$	$2\frac{1}{4}$	$1\frac{7}{32}$	—
1975	MV, 250	$1\frac{1}{32}$	—	—	—	—	0.275②	—	—	$1\frac{11}{16}$	—	—	—
	2GC, 262	$1\frac{9}{32}$	—	$1\frac{7}{32}$	—	$1\frac{19}{32}$	0.350	—	—	$1\frac{11}{16}$	—	$1\frac{1}{4}$	—
	2GC, 350	$\frac{21}{32}$	—	$\frac{31}{32}$	—	$1\frac{5}{8}$	0.350	—	—	$1\frac{11}{16}$	—	$1\frac{1}{4}$	—
	M4MC, 350	$1\frac{5}{32}$	—	—	—	0.275*	0.325	—	—	$1\frac{3}{8}$	$2\frac{1}{4}$	$1\frac{7}{32}$	—
	M4MCA, 350	$\frac{15}{32}$	—	—	—	0.275*	0.325	—	—	$1\frac{3}{8}$	$2\frac{1}{4}$	$1\frac{7}{32}$	—
1976	MV-250, Std	$1\frac{1}{32}$	—	—	—	—	0.265	—	—	—	—	—	—
	MV-250, Auto	$1\frac{1}{32}$	—	—	—	—	0.265	—	—	—	—	—	—
	MV-250, Auto	$1\frac{1}{32}$	—	—	—	—	0.265	—	—	—	—	—	—
	2GC-305, Auto	$\frac{9}{16}$	—	$1\frac{9}{32}$	—	$1\frac{21}{32}$	0.325	Index	—	—	—	—	—
	2GC-350, Auto	$\frac{21}{32}$	—	$\frac{31}{32}$	—	$\frac{31}{32}$	0.325	1NR	—	—	—	—	—
	M4MC-350, Auto	$1\frac{3}{32}$	—	—	—	$\frac{9}{32}$	0.325	2NL	—	—	—	—	—
	M4MC-400, Auto	$1\frac{3}{32}$	—	—	—	$\frac{9}{32}$	0.325	2NL	—	—	—	—	—
	M4MC-400, Auto	$1\frac{3}{32}$	—	—	—	$\frac{9}{32}$	0.325	2NL	—	—	—	—	—

① Carburetor No. 7043114—0.325
② Carburetor No. 7045012—0.215
* Pump rod location—inner

Rochester Carburetors—1967–76

Year	Model	Number (A) Automatic Trans (M) Manual Trans	Choke Rod (Fast Idle Cam 2nd Step) (in.)	Air Valve Dashpot (in.)	Choke Vacuum Break (in.)	Idle Vent (in.)	Air Valve Spring	Secondary Lockout (in.)
1967	2GV	7027110 (A)	0.060	—	0.110	1.00	—	—
	2GV	7027101 (M)	0.060	—	0.120	1.00	—	—
	2GV	7027112 (A)	0.060	—	0.110	1.00	—	—
	2GV	7027103 (M)	0.060	—	0.120	1.00	—	—
	2GV	7037101 (M)	0.060	—	0.130	1.00	—	—
	2GV	7037110 (A)	0.060	—	0.110	1.00	—	—
	2GV	7037112 (A)	0.060	—	0.110	1.00	—	—
	2GV	7037103 (M)	0.060	—	0.130	1.00	—	—
	4MV	7027202 (A)	0.100	0.015	0.160	3/8	7/8 turn	0.100
	4MV	7027203 (M)	0.100	0.015	0.200	3/8	7/8 turn	0.100
	4MV	7027200 (A)	0.100	0.015	0.160	3/8	7/8 turn	0.100
	4MV	7027201 (M)	0.100	0.015	0.240	3/8	7/8 turn	0.100
	4MV	7037202 (A)	0.100	0.015	0.160	3/8	7/8 turn	0.100
	4MV	7037203 (M)	0.100	0.015	0.200	3/8	7/8 turn	0.100
	4MV	7037200 (A)	0.100	0.015	0.160	3/8	7/8 turn	0.100
	4MV	7037201 (M)	0.100	0.015	0.240	3/8	7/8 turn	0.100
1968	2GV	7028110 (A)	0.060	—	0.100	1.00	—	—
	2GV	7028101 (M)	0.060	—	0.100	1.00	—	—
	2GV	7028112 (A)	0.060	—	0.100	1.00	—	—
	2GV	7028103 (M)	0.060	—	0.100	1.00	—	—
	4MV	7028212 (A)	0.100	0.015	0.160	3/8	3/8 turn	0.010
	4MV	7028213 (M)	0.100	0.015	0.245	3/8	3/8 turn	0.010
	4MV	7028229 (M)	0.100	0.015	0.245	3/8	7/8 turn	0.010
	4MV	7028207 (M)	0.100	0.015	0.245	3/8	3/8 turn	0.010
	4MV	7028219 (M)	0.100	0.015	0.245	3/8	7/8 turn	0.010
	4MV	7028218 (A)	0.100	0.015	0.160	3/8	7/8 turn	0.010

Rochester Carburetors—1967–76 (cont.)

Year	Model	Number (A) Automatic Trans (M) Manual Trans	Choke Rod (Fast Idle Cam 2nd Step) (in.)	Air Valve Dashpot (in.)	Choke Vacuum Break (in.)	Idle Vent (in.)	Air Valve Spring	Secondary Lockout (in.)
1968	4MV	7028217 (M)	0.100	0.015	0.245	$\frac{3}{8}$	$\frac{7}{8}$ turn	0.010
	4MV	7028210 (A)	0.100	0.015	0.160	$\frac{3}{8}$	$\frac{7}{8}$ turn	0.010
	4MV	7028211 (M)	0.100	0.015	0.245	$\frac{3}{8}$	$\frac{7}{8}$ turn	0.010
	4MV	7028216 (A)	0.100	0.015	0.160	$\frac{3}{8}$	$\frac{7}{8}$ turn	0.010
	4MV	7028209 (M)	0.100	0.015	0.245	$\frac{3}{8}$	$\frac{7}{8}$ turn	0.010
1969	2GV	7029101 (M)	0.060	—	0.100	0.020	—	—
	2GV	7029103 (M)	0.060	—	0.100	0.020	—	—
	2GV	7029110 (A)	0.060	—	0.100	0.020	—	—
	2GV	7029112 (A)	0.060	—	0.100	0.020	—	—
	2GV	7029102 (A)	0.085	—	0.215	0.020	—	—
	2GV	7029104 (A)	0.085	—	0.215	0.020	—	—
	2GV	7029127 (M)	0.085	—	0.215	0.020	—	—
	2GV	7029129 (M)	0.085	—	0.215	0.020	—	—
	2GV	7029117 (M)	0.085	—	0.215	0.020	—	—
	2GV	7029118 (A)	0.085	—	0.215	0.020	—	—
	2GV	7029119 (M)	0.085	—	0.215	0.020	—	—
	2GV	7029120 (A)	0.085	—	0.215	0.020	—	—
	4MV	7029203 (M)	0.100	0.015	0.245	$\frac{3}{8}$	$\frac{7}{16}$ turn	0.015
	4MV	7029202 (A)	0.100	0.015	0.180	$\frac{3}{8}$	$\frac{7}{16}$ turn	0.015
	4MV	7029207 (M)	0.100	0.015	0.245	$\frac{3}{8}$	$1\frac{3}{16}$ turn	0.015
	4MV	7029215 (M)	0.100	0.015	0.245	$\frac{3}{8}$	$1\frac{3}{16}$ turn	0.015
	4MV	7029204 (A)	0.100	0.015	0.180	$\frac{3}{8}$	$1\frac{3}{16}$ turn	0.015
1970	2GV	7040110 (A)	0.060	—	0.100	0.020	—	—
	2GV	7040112 (A)	0.060	—	0.100	0.020	—	—
	2GV	7040101 (M)	0.060	—	0.125	0.020	—	—
	2GV	7040103 (M)	0.060	—	0.125	0.020	—	—
	2GV	7040114 (A)	0.085	—	0.200	0.020	—	—
	2GV	7040116 (A)	0.085	—	0.200	0.020	—	—
	2GV	7040113 (M)	0.085	—	0.215	0.020	—	—

Rochester Carburetors—1967–76 (cont.)

Year	Model	Number (A) Automatic Trans (M) Manual Trans	Choke Rod (Fast Idle Cam 2nd Step) (in.)	Air Valve Dashpot (in.)	Choke Vacuum Break (in.)	Idle Vent (in.)	Air Valve Spring	Secondary Lockout (in.)
1970	2GV	7040115 (M)	0.085	—	0.215	0.020	—	—
	2GV	7040118 (A)	0.085	—	0.215	0.020	—	—
	2GV	7040120 (A)	0.085	—	0.215	0.020	—	—
	2GV	7040117 (M)	0.085	—	0.215	0.020	—	—
	2GV	7040119 (M)	0.085	—	0.215	0.020	—	—
	4MV	7040202 (A)	0.100	0.020	0.245	—	$\frac{7}{16}$ turn	—
	4MV	7040203 (M)	0.100	0.020	0.275	—	$\frac{7}{16}$ turn	—
	4MV	7040207 (M)	0.100	0.020	0.275	—	$1\frac{3}{16}$ turn	—
	4MV	7040200 (A)	0.100	0.020	0.245	—	$1\frac{3}{16}$ turn	—
	4MV	7040201 (M)	0.100	0.020	0.275	—	$1\frac{3}{16}$ turn	—
	4MV	7040204 (A)	0.100	0.020	0.245	—	$1\frac{3}{16}$ turn	—
	4MV	7040205 (M)	0.100	0.020	0.275	—	$1\frac{3}{16}$ turn	—
1971	2GV	7041024 (A)	0.080	—	0.140	—	—	—
	2GV	7041101 (M)	0.075	—	0.110	—	—	—
	2GV	7041110 (A)	0.040	—	0.080	—	—	—
	2GV	7041114 (A)	0.100	—	0.170	—	—	—
	2GV	7041113 (M)	0.100	—	0.180	—	—	—
	2GV	7041127 (M)	0.100	—	0.180	—	—	—
	2GV	7041118 (A)	0.100	—	0.170	—	—	—
	2GV	7041181 (M)	0.080	—	0.120	—	—	—
	2GV	7041182 (A)	0.080	—	0.120	—	—	—
	4MV	7041200 (A)	0.100	0.020	0.260	—	—	—
	4MV	7041202 (A)	0.100	0.020	0.260	—	—	—
	4MV	7041204 (A)	0.100	0.020	0.260	—	—	—
	4MV	7041212 (A)	0.100	0.020	0.260	—	—	—
	4MV	7041201 (M)	0.100	0.020	0.275	—	—	—
	4MV	7041203 (M)	0.100	0.020	0.275	—	—	—
	4MV	7041205 (M)	0.100	0.020	0.275	—	—	—
	4MV	7041213 (M)	0.100	0.020	0.275	—	—	—

Rochester Carburetors—1967–76 (cont.)

Year	Model	Number (A) Automatic Trans (M) Manual Trans	Choke Rod (Fast Idle Cam 2nd Step) (in.)	Air Valve Dashpot (in.)	Choke Vacuum Break (in.)	Idle Vent (in.)	Air Valve Spring	Secondary Lockout (in.)
1972	2GV	7042102 (A)	0.040	—	0.080	—	—	—
	2GV	7042104 (A)	0.040	—	0.080	—	—	—
	2GV	7042822 (A)	0.040	—	0.080	—	—	—
	2GV	7042824 (A)	0.040	—	0.080	—	—	—
	2GV	7042103 (M)	0.075	—	0.110	—	—	—
	2GV	7042105 (M)	0.075	—	0.110	—	—	—
	2GV	7042823 (M)	0.075	—	0.110	—	—	—
	2GV	7042825 (M)	0.075	—	0.110	—	—	—
	2GV	7042108 (A) (M)	0.100	—	0.170	—	—	—
	4MV	7042206 (A)	0.100	0.020	0.250	—	—	—
	4MV	7042207 (M)	0.100	0.020	0.250	—	—	—
	4MV	7042208 (A) (M)	0.100	0.020	0.215	—	—	—
	4MV	7042219 (M)	0.100	0.020	0.250	—	—	—
	4MV	7042210 (A)	0.100	0.020	0.215	—	—	—
	4MV	7042218 (A)	0.100	0.020	0.250	—	—	—
	4MV	7042211 (M)	0.100	0.020	0.215	—	—	—
	4MV	7042910 (A)	0.100	0.020	0.215	—	—	—
	4MV	7042911 (M)	0.100	0.020	0.215	—	—	—
1973	MV	7043017 (M)	0.275	—	0.350	—	—	—
	MV	7043014 (A)	0.245	—	0.300	—	—	—
	2GV	7043101 (M)	0.150	—	0.080	—	—	—
	2GV	7043100 (A)	0.150	—	0.080	—	—	—
	2GV	7043113 (M)	0.200	—	0.140	—	—	—
	2GV	7043114 (A)	0.245	—	0.130	—	—	—
	4MV	7043203 (M)	0.430	—	0.250	—	½ turn	—
	4MV	7043202 (A)	0.430	—	0.250	—	½ turn	—
1974	MV	7044017 (M)	0.275	—	0.350	—	—	—
	MV	7044014 (A)	0.230	—	0.275	—	—	—
	MV	7044314 (A)	0.245	—	0.300	—	—	—

Rochester Carburetors—1967–76 (cont.)

Year	Model	Number (A) Automatic Trans (M) Manual Trans	Choke Rod (Fast Idle Cam 2nd Step) (in.)	Air Valve Dashpot (in.)	Choke Vacuum Break (in.)	Idle Vent (in.)	Air Valve Spring	Secondary Lockout (in.)
1974	2GV	7044115 (M)	0.200	—	0.140	—	—	—
	2GV	7044116 (A)	0.245	—	0.130	—	—	—
	4MV	7044207 (M)	0.430	—	0.230	—	7/8 turn	—
	4MV	7044206 (A)	0.430	—	0.230	—	7/8 turn	—
	4MV	7044507 (M)	0.430	—	0.230	—	7/8 turn	—
	4MV	7044506 (A)	0.430	—	0.230	—	7/8 turn	—
1975	MV	7045013 (M)	0.275	—	0.350①	—	—	—
	MV	7045012 (A)	0.160	—	0.200②	—	—	—
	MV	7045314 (A)	0.230	—	0.275①	—	—	—
	2GC	7045105 (M)	0.375	—	0.130	—	—	—
	2GC	7045106 (A)	0.380	—	0.130	—	—	—
	2GC	7045123 (M)	0.400	—	0.130	—	—	—
	2GC	7045124 (A)	0.400	—	0.130	—	—	—
	M4MC	7045207 (M)	0.300	0.015	0.180 (F) 0.170 (R)	—	7/8 turn	—
	M4MC	7045206 (A)	0.300	0.015	0.180 (F) 0.170 (R)	—	7/8 turn	—
	M4MCA	7045507 (M)	0.300	0.015	0.180 (F) 0.170 (R)	—	7/8 turn	—
	M4MCA	7045506 (A)	0.300	0.015	0.180 (F) 0.170 (R)	—	7/8 turn	—
1976	MV	17056018 (A)	0.084	—	0.110②	—	—	—
	MV	17056012 (M)	0.090	—	0.110②	—	—	—
	MV	17060013 (A)	0.082	—	0.110②	—	—	—
	MV	17056314 (A)	0.083	—	0.150②	—	—	—
	2GC	17056108 (A)	0.260	—	0.140	—	—	—
	2GC	17056114 (A)	0.260	—	0.140	—	—	—
	4MC	17056228 (A)	0.325	0.015	0.185	0.185	3/4 turn	—
	4MC	17056502 (A)	0.325	0.015	0.185	0.185	7/8 turn	—
	4MC	17056528 (A)	0.325	0.015	0.185	0.185	3/4 turn	—

① Auxiliary vacuum break—0.312   (F) Front vacuum break
② Auxiliary vacuum break—0.215   (R) Rear vacuum break

Rochester ME Specifications—1977–79

Year	Carburetor Identifi- cation	Float Level (in.)	Metering Rod (in.)	Pump Rod	Idle Vent (in.)	Vacuum Break (in.)	Auxiliary Vacuum Break (in.)	Fast Idle Off Car (in.)	Choke① Rod (in.)	Choke Unloader (in.)	Fast Idle Speed (rpm)②
1977	17057013	3/8	.070	—	—	.125	—	—	1 CCW	.375	2000
	17057014	3/8	.070	—	—	.120	—	—	2 CCW	.325	2000
	17057316	3/8	.070	—	—	—	—	—	Index	—	1800
1978	17058013	3/8	.080	—	—	.200	—	—	Index	.200	2000
	17058014	5/16	.160	—	—	.200	—	—	Index	.200	2100
	17058314	3/8	.160	—	—	.243	—	—	Index	.245	2000
1979	17059013	—	—	Information not available
	17059014	—	—	Information not available
	17059314	—	—	Information not available

① Choke adjustment—Index, CCW—counterclockwise in notches, or CW—clockwise in notches
② Transmission in Neutral

Rochester 2GC Specifications—1977–79

Year	Carburetor Identifi- cation①	Float Level (in.)	Float Drop (in.)	Pump Rod (in.)	Idle Vent (in.)	Vacuum Break (in.)	Auto- matic② Choke	Choke Rod (in.)	Choke Unloader (in.)	Fast Idle Speed
1977	17057111	19/32	19/32	1 21/32	—	0.130③	Index	—	0.325	—
	17057108	19/32	19/32	1 21/32	—	0.130③	Index	—	0.325	—
	17057412	21/32	19/32	1 21/32	—	0.140③	1/2 CCW	—	0.325	—
1978	17058102	15/32	19/32	1 17/32	0	0.130④	Index	—	0.325	—
	17058103	15/32	19/32	1 17/32	0	0.130④	Index	—	0.325	—
	17058104	15/32	19/32	1 21/32	0	0.130③	Index	—	0.325	—
	17058105	15/32	19/32	1 21/32	0	0.130③	Index	—	0.325	—
	17058107	15/32	19/32	1 17/32	0	0.130③	Index	—	0.325	—
	17058109	15/32	19/32	1 17/32	0	0.130③	Index	—	0.325	—
	17058404	1/2	19/32	1 21/32	0	0.140③	1/2 CCW	—	0.325	—
	17058405	1/2	19/32	1 21/32	0	0.140③	1/2 CCW	—	0.325	—
1979	17059135	—	—	Information not available
	17059134	—	—	Information not available
	17059434	—	—	Information not available

① The carburetor identification tag is located at the rear of the carburetor on one of the air horn screws
② Index or notches clockwise (CW) or counterclockwise (CCW)
③ .160 after 22,500 miles or first tune-up   ④ .150 after 22,500 miles or first tune-up

Rochester 4MV, 4MC, M4MC Specifications—1977–79

Year	Carburetor Identifi-cation①	Float Level (in.)	Air Valve Spring	Pump Rod (in.)	Idle Vent (in.)	Vacuum Break (in.)	Secondary Opening (in.)	Choke Rod (in.)	Choke Unloader (rpm)	Fast Idle Speed
1977	17057203	$\frac{15}{32}$	$\frac{7}{8}$	$\frac{9}{32}$②	—	0.160	—	0.325	0.280	1300
	17057202	$\frac{15}{32}$	—	$\frac{9}{32}$②	—	0.160	—	0.325	—	1600②
	17057502	$\frac{15}{32}$	$\frac{7}{8}$	$\frac{9}{32}$②	—	0.165	—	0.325	0.280	1600②
1978	17058203	$\frac{15}{32}$	$\frac{7}{8}$	$\frac{9}{32}$	—	—	—	—	—	③
	17058202	$\frac{15}{32}$	$\frac{7}{8}$	$\frac{9}{32}$	—	—	—	—	—	③
	17058502	$\frac{15}{32}$	$\frac{7}{8}$	$\frac{9}{32}$	—	—	—	—	—	③
1979	17059502	—	—	Information not available						
	17059582	—	—	Information not available						

① The carburetor identification tag is located at the rear of the carburetor on one of the air horn screws

③ See engine compartment sticker

② Inner pump rod location

**UNDERSTANDING AND
  TROUBLESHOOTING ELECTRICAL
  SYSTEMS 6-2**
SAFETY PRECAUTIONS 6-2
UNDERSTANDING BASIC
  ELECTRICITY 6-2
    THE WATER ANALOGY 6-2
    CIRCUITS 6-2
    AUTOMOTIVE CIRCUITS 6-3
    SHORT CIRCUITS 6-3
TROUBLESHOOTING 6-3
    BASIC TROUBLESHOOTING
      THEORY 6-4
    TEST EQUIPMENT 6-4
    TESTING 6-6
WIRING HARNESSES 6-8
    WIRING REPAIR 6-8
ADD-ON ELECTRICAL EQUIPMENT 6-12
HEATER 6-12
BLOWER MOTOR 6-12
    REMOVAL & INSTALLATION 6-12
HEATER CORE 6-12
    REMOVAL & INSTALLATION 6-12
RADIO 6-13
RADIO RECEIVER 6-13
    REMOVAL & INSTALLATION 6-13
WINDSHIELD WIPERS 6-15
WINDSHIELD WIPER MOTOR 6-15
    REMOVAL & INSTALLATION 6-15
WIPER TRANSMISSION 6-16
    REMOVAL & INSTALLATION 6-16
INSTRUMENT PANEL 6-17
IGNITION SWITCH (DASH-
  MOUNTED) 6-17
    REMOVAL & INSTALLATION 6-17
SEATBELT SYSTEM 6-17
WARNING BUZZER AND LIGHT 6-17
    GENERAL INFORMATION 6-17
SEAT BELT/STARTER INTERLOCK
  SYSTEM 6-18
    GENERAL INFORMATION 6-18
    DISABLING THE SEATBELT
      INTERLOCK SYSTEM 6-18
LIGHTING 6-19
HEADLIGHTS 6-19
    REMOVAL & INSTALLATION 6-19
    AIMING 6-21
SIGNAL AND MARKER LIGHTS 6-21
    REMOVAL & INSTALLATION 6-21
TRAILER WIRING 6-24
CIRCUIT PROTECTION 6-25
FUSES 6-25
FUSIBLE LINKS 6-25
    REPLACEMENT 6-25
CIRCUIT BREAKERS 6-25
FLASHERS 6-25
    REPLACEMENT 6-25
WIRING DIAGRAMS 6-30
SPECIFICATION CHARTS
    FUSES AND CIRCUIT BREAKERS 6-26
    FUSIBLE LINKS—1962–77 6-28

FUSIBLE LINKS—1978–79 6-28
LIGHT BULB SPECIFICATIONS 1978–
  79 6-28
LIGHT BULB SPECIFICATIONS 1962–
  77 6-29

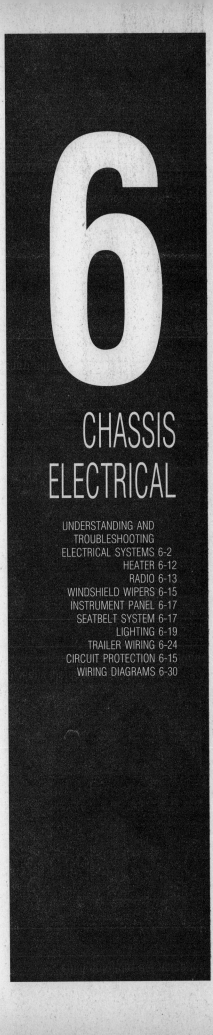

6

CHASSIS ELECTRICAL

UNDERSTANDING AND
  TROUBLESHOOTING
ELECTRICAL SYSTEMS 6-2
HEATER 6-12
RADIO 6-13
WINDSHIELD WIPERS 6-15
INSTRUMENT PANEL 6-17
SEATBELT SYSTEM 6-17
LIGHTING 6-19
TRAILER WIRING 6-24
CIRCUIT PROTECTION 6-15
WIRING DIAGRAMS 6-30

UNDERSTANDING AND TROUBLESHOOTING ELECTRICAL SYSTEMS

Over the years import and domestic manufacturers have incorporated electronic control systems into their production lines. In fact, electronic control systems are so prevalent that all new cars and trucks built today are equipped with at least one on-board computer. These electronic components (with no moving parts) should theoretically last the life of the vehicle, provided that nothing external happens to damage the circuits or memory chips.

While it is true that electronic components should never wear out, in the real world malfunctions do occur. It is also true that any computer-based system is extremely sensitive to electrical voltages and cannot tolerate careless or haphazard testing/service procedures. An inexperienced individual can literally cause major damage looking for a minor problem by using the wrong kind of test equipment or connecting test leads/connectors with the ignition switch **ON**. When selecting test equipment, make sure the manufacturer's instructions state that the tester is compatible with whatever type of system is being serviced. Read all instructions carefully and double check all test points before installing probes or making any test connections.

The following section outlines basic diagnosis techniques for dealing with automotive electrical systems. Along with a general explanation of the various types of test equipment available to aid in servicing modern automotive systems, basic repair techniques for wiring harnesses and connectors are also given. Read the basic information before attempting any repairs or testing. This will provide the background of information necessary to avoid the most common and obvious mistakes that can cost both time and money. Although the replacement and testing procedures are simple in themselves, the systems are not, and unless one has a thorough understanding of all components and their function within a particular system, the logical test sequence these systems demand cannot be followed. Minor malfunctions can make a big difference, so it is important to know how each component affects the operation of the overall system in order to find the ultimate cause of a problem without replacing good components unnecessarily. It is not enough to use the correct test equipment; the test equipment must be used correctly.

Safety Precautions

✳✳ CAUTION

Whenever working on or around any electrical or electronic systems, always observe these general precautions to prevent the possibility of personal injury or damage to electronic components.

• Never install or remove battery cables with the key **ON** or the engine running. Jumper cables should be connected with the key **OFF** to avoid power surges that can damage electronic control units. Engines equipped with computer controlled systems should avoid both giving and getting jump starts due to the possibility of serious damage to components from arcing in the engine compartment if connections are made with the ignition **ON**.

• Always remove the battery cables before charging the battery. Never use a high output charger on an installed battery or attempt to use any type of "hot shot" (24 volt) starting aid.

• Exercise care when inserting test probes into connectors to in-sure good contact without damaging the connector or spreading the pins. Always probe connectors from the rear (wire) side, NOT the pin side, to avoid accidental shorting of terminals during test procedures.

• Never remove or attach wiring harness connectors with the ignition switch **ON**, especially to an electronic control unit.

• Do not drop any components during service procedures and never apply 12 volts directly to any component (like a solenoid or relay) unless instructed specifically to do so. Some component electrical windings are designed to safely handle only 4 or 5 volts and can be destroyed in seconds if 12 volts are applied directly to the connector.

• Remove the electronic control unit if the vehicle is to be placed in an environment where temperatures exceed approximately 176°F (80°C), such as a paint spray booth or when arc/gas welding near the control unit location.

Understanding Basic Electricity

Understanding the basic theory of electricity makes electrical troubleshooting much easier. Several gauges are used in electrical troubleshooting to see inside the circuit being tested. Without a basic understanding, it will be difficult to understand testing procedures.

THE WATER ANALOGY

Electricity is the flow of electrons—hypothetical particles thought to constitute the basic stuff of electricity. Many people have been taught electrical theory using an analogy with water. In a comparison with water flowing in a pipe, the electrons would be the water. As the flow of water can be measured, the flow of electricity can be measured. The unit of measurement is amperes, frequently abbreviated amps. An ammeter will measure the actual amount of current flowing in the circuit.

Just as the water pressure is measured in units such as pounds per square inch, electrical pressure is measured in volts. When a voltmeter's two probes are placed on two live portions of an electrical circuit with different electrical pressures, current will flow through the voltmeter and produce a reading which indicates the difference in electrical pressure between the two parts of the circuit.

While increasing the voltage in a circuit will increase the flow of current, the actual flow depends not only on voltage, but on the resistance of the circuit. The standard unit for measuring circuit resistance is an ohm, measured by an ohmmeter. The ohmmeter is somewhat similar to an ammeter, but incorporates its own source of power so that a standard voltage is always present.

CIRCUITS

An actual electric circuit consists of four basic parts. These are: the power source, such as a generator or battery; a hot wire, which conducts the electricity under a relatively high voltage to the component supplied by the circuit; the load, such as a lamp, motor, resistor or relay coil; and the ground wire, which carries the current back to the source under very low voltage. In such a circuit the bulk of the resistance exists between the point where the hot wire is connected to the load, and the point where the load is grounded. In an automobile, the vehicle's frame or body, which is made of steel, is used as a part of the ground circuit for many of the electrical devices.

Remember that, in electrical testing, the voltmeter is connected in parallel with the circuit being tested (without disconnecting any wires) and measures the difference in voltage between the locations of the two probes; that the ammeter is connected in series with the load (the circuit is separated at one point and the ammeter inserted so it becomes a part of the circuit); and the ohmmeter is self-powered, so that all the power in the circuit should be off and the portion of the circuit to be measured contacted at either end by one of the probes of the meter.

For any electrical system to operate, it must make a complete circuit. This simply means that the power flow from the battery must make a complete circle. When an electrical component is operating, power flows from the battery to the component, passes through the component causing it to perform it to function (such as lighting a light bulb) and then returns to the battery through the ground of the circuit. This ground is usually (but not always) the metal part of the vehicle on which the electrical component is mounted.

Perhaps the easiest way to visualize this is to think of connecting a light bulb with two wires attached to it to your vehicle's battery. The battery in your vehicle has two posts (negative and positive). If one of the two wires attached to the light bulb was attached to the negative post of the battery and the other wire was attached to the positive post of the battery, you would have a complete circuit. Current from the battery would flow out one post, through the wire attached to it and then to the light bulb, where it would pass through causing it to light. It would then leave the light bulb, travel through the other wire, and return to the other post of the battery.

AUTOMOTIVE CIRCUITS

The normal automotive circuit differs from this simple example in two ways. First, instead of having a return wire from the bulb to the battery, the light bulb return the current to the battery through the chassis of the vehicle. Since the negative battery cable is attached to the chassis and the chassis is made of electrically conductive metal, the chassis of the vehicle can serve as a ground wire to complete the circuit. Secondly, most automotive circuits contain switches to turn components on and off.

Some electrical components which require a large amount of current to operate also have a relay in their circuit. Since these circuits carry a large amount of current, the thickness of the wire in the circuit (gauge size) is also greater. If this large wire were connected from the component to the control switch on the instrument panel, and then back to the component, a voltage drop would occur in the circuit. To prevent this potential drop in voltage, an electromagnetic switch (relay) is used. The large wires in the circuit are connected from the vehicle battery to one side of the relay, and from the opposite side of the relay to the component. The relay is normally open, preventing current from passing through the circuit. An additional, smaller wire is connected from the relay to the control switch for the circuit. When the control switch is turned on, it grounds the smaller wire from the relay and completes the circuit.

SHORT CIRCUITS

If you were to disconnect the light bulb (from the previous example of a light-bulb being connected to the battery by two wires) from the wires and touch the two wires together (please take our word for this; don't try it), the result will be a shower of sparks. A similar thing happens (on a smaller scale) when the power supply wire to a component or the electrical component itself becomes grounded before the normal ground connection for the circuit. To prevent damage to the system, the fuse for the circuit blows to interrupt the circuit—protecting the components from damage. Because grounding a wire from a power source makes a complete circuit—less the required component to use the power—the phenomenon is called a short circuit. The most common causes of short circuits are: the rubber insulation on a wire breaking or rubbing through to expose the current carrying core of the wire to a metal part of the car, or a shorted switch.

Some electrical systems on the vehicle are protected by a circuit breaker which is, basically, a self-repairing fuse. When either of the described events takes place in a system which is protected by a circuit breaker, the circuit breaker opens the circuit the same way a fuse does. However, when either the short is removed from the circuit or the surge subsides, the circuit breaker resets itself and does not have to be replaced as a fuse does.

Troubleshooting

When diagnosing a specific problem, organized troubleshooting is a must. The complexity of a modern automobile demands that you approach any problem in a logical, organized manner. There are certain troubleshooting techniques that are standard:

1. Establish when the problem occurs. Does the problem appear only under certain conditions? Were there any noises, odors, or other unusual symptoms?

2. Isolate the problem area. To do this, make some simple tests and observations; then eliminate the systems that are working properly. Check for obvious problems such as broken wires, dirty connections or split/disconnected vacuum hoses. Always check the obvious before assuming something complicated is the cause.

3. Test for problems systematically to determine the cause once the problem area is isolated. Are all the components functioning properly? Is there power going to electrical switches and motors? Is there vacuum at vacuum switches and/or actuators? Is there a mechanical problem such as bent linkage or loose mounting screws? Performing careful, systematic checks will often turn up most causes on the first inspection without wasting time checking components that have little or no relationship to the problem.

4. Test all repairs after the work is done to make sure that the problem is fixed. Some causes can be traced to more than one component, so a careful verification of repair work is important in order to pick up additional malfunctions that may cause a problem to reappear or a different problem to arise. A blown fuse, for example, is a simple problem that may require more than another fuse to repair. If you don't look for a problem that caused a fuse to blow, a shorted wire (for example) may go undetected.

Experience has shown that most problems tend to be the result of a fairly simple and obvious cause, such as loose or corroded connectors or air leaks in the intake system. This makes careful inspection of components during testing essential to quick and accurate troubleshooting.

BASIC TROUBLESHOOTING THEORY

Electrical problems generally fall into one of three areas:
• The component that is not functioning is not receiving current.
• The component itself is not functioning.
• The component is not properly grounded.

Problems that fall into the first category are by far the most complicated. It is the current supply system to the component which contains all the switches, relay, fuses, etc.

The electrical system can be checked with a test light and a jumper wire. A test light is a device that looks like a pointed screwdriver with a wire attached to it. It has a light bulb in its handle. A jumper wire is a piece of insulated wire with an alligator clip attached to each end.

If a light bulb is not working, you must follow a systematic plan to determine which of the three causes is the villain.

1. Turn on the switch that controls the inoperable bulb.
2. Disconnect the power supply wire from the bulb.
3. Attach the ground wire to the test light to a good metal ground.
4. Touch the probe end of the test light to the end of the power supply wire that was disconnected from the bulb. If the bulb is receiving current, the test light will go on.

➡ **If the bulb is one which works only when the ignition key is turned on (turn signal), make sure the key is turned on.**

If the test light does not go on, then the problem is in the circuit between the battery and the bulb. As mentioned before, this includes all the switches, fuses, and relays in the system. Turn to a wiring diagram and find the bulb on the diagram. Follow the wire that runs back to the battery. The problem is an open circuit between the battery and the bulb. If the fuse is blown and, when replaced, immediately blows again, there is a short circuit in the system which must be located and repaired. If there is a switch in the system, bypass it with a jumper wire. This is done by connecting one end of the jumper wire to the power supply wire into the switch and the other end of the jumper wire to the wire coming out of the switch. If the test light illuminates with the jumper wire installed, the switch or whatever was bypassed is defective.

➡ **Never substitute the jumper wire for the bulb, as the bulb is the component required to use the power from the power source.**

5. If the bulb in the test light goes on, then the current is getting to the bulb that is not working in the car. This eliminates the first of the three possible causes. Connect the power supply wire and connect a jumper wire from the bulb to a good metal ground. Do this with the switch which controls the bulb works with jumper wire installed, then it has a bad ground. This is usually caused by the metal area on which the bulb mounts to the vehicle being coated with some type of foreign matter.
6. If neither test located the source of the trouble, then the light bulb itself is defective.

The above test procedure can be applied to any of the components of the chassis electrical system by substituting the component that is not working for the light bulb. Remember that for any electrical system to work, all connections must be clean and tight.

TEST EQUIPMENT

➡ **Pinpointing the exact cause of trouble in an electrical system can sometimes only be accomplished by the use of special test equipment. The following describes different types of commonly used test equipment and explains how to use them in diagnosis. In addition to the information covered below, the tool manufacturer's instructions booklet (provided with the tester) should be read and clearly understood before attempting any test procedures.**

Jumper Wires

Jumper wires are simple, yet extremely valuable, pieces of test equipment. They are basically test wires which are used to bypass sections of a circuit. The simplest type of jumper wire is a length of multi-strand wire with an alligator clip at each end. Jumper

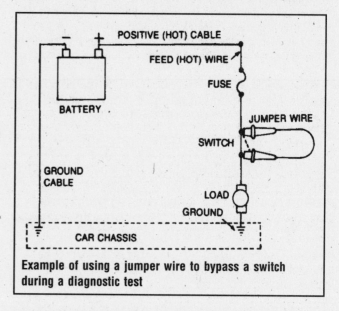

Example of using a jumper wire to bypass a switch during a diagnostic test

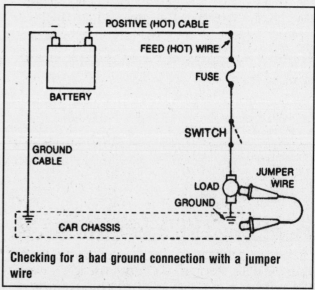

Checking for a bad ground connection with a jumper wire

wires are usually fabricated from lengths of standard automotive wire and whatever type of connector (alligator clip, spade connector or pin connector) that is required for the particular vehicle being tested. The well equipped tool box will have several different styles of jumper wires in several different lengths. Some jumper wires are made with three or more terminals coming from a common splice for special purpose testing. In cramped, hard-to-reach areas it is advisable to have insulated boots over the jumper wire terminals in order to prevent accidental grounding, sparks, and possible fire, especially when testing fuel system components.

Jumper wires are used primarily to locate open electrical circuits, on either the ground (−) side of the circuit or on the hot (+) side. If an electrical component fails to operate, connect the jumper wire between the component and a good ground. If the component operates only with the jumper installed, the ground circuit is open. If the ground circuit is good, but the component does not operate, the circuit between the power feed and component may be open. By moving the jumper wire successively back from the lamp toward the power source, you can isolate the area of the circuit where the open is located. When the component stops functioning, or the power is cut off, the open is in the segment of wire between the jumper and the point previously tested.

You can sometimes connect the jumper wire directly from the battery to the hot terminal of the component, but first make sure the component uses 12 volts in operation. Some electrical components, such as fuel injectors, are designed to operate on about 4 volts and running 12 volts directly to the injector terminals can cause damage.

By inserting an in-line fuse holder between a set of test leads, a fused jumper wire can be used for bypassing open circuits. Use a 5 amp fuse to provide protection against voltage spikes. When in doubt, use a voltmeter to check the voltage input to the component and measure how much voltage is normally being applied.

✳✳ CAUTION

Never use jumpers made from wire that is of lighter gauge than that which is used in the circuit under test. If the jumper wire is of too small a gauge, it may overheat and possibly melt. Never use jumpers to bypass high resistance loads in a circuit. Bypassing resistances, in effect, creates a short circuit. This may, in turn, cause damage and fire. Jumper wires should only be used to bypass lengths of wire.

Unpowered Test Lights

The 12 volt test light is used to check circuits and components while electrical current is flowing through them. It is used for voltage and ground tests. Twelve volt test lights come in different styles but all have three main parts; a ground clip, a probe, and a light. The most commonly used 12 volt test lights have pick-type probes. To use a 12 volt test light, connect the ground clip to a good ground and probe wherever necessary with the pick. The pick should be sharp so that it can be probed into tight spaces.

✳✳ CAUTION

Do not use a test light to probe electronic ignition spark plug or coil wires. Never use a pick-type test light to probe wiring on computer controlled systems unless specifically in-

structed to do so. Any wire insulation that is pierced by the test light probe should be taped and sealed with silicone after testing.

Like the jumper wire, the 12 volt test light is used to isolate opens in circuits. But, whereas the jumper wire is used to bypass the open to operate the load, the 12 volt test light is used to locate the presence of voltage in a circuit. If the test light glows, you know that there is power up to that point; if the 12 volt test light does not glow when its probe is inserted into the wire or connector, you know that there is an open circuit (no power). Move the test light in successive steps back toward the power source until the light in the handle does glow. When it glows, the open is between the probe and point which was probed previously.

➡**The test light does not detect that 12 volts (or any particular amount of voltage) is present; it only detects that some voltage is present. It is advisable before using the test light to touch its terminals across the battery posts to make sure the light is operating properly.**

Self-Powered Test Lights

The self-powered test light usually contains a 1.5 volt penlight battery. One type of self-powered test light is similar in design to the 12 volt unit. This type has both the battery and the light in the handle, along with a pick-type probe tip. The second type has the light toward the open tip, so that the light illuminates the contact point. The self-powered test light is a dual purpose piece of test equipment. It can be used to test for either open or short circuits when power is isolated from the circuit (continuity test). A powered test light should not be used on any computer controlled system or component unless specifically instructed to do so. Many engine sensors can be destroyed by even this small amount of voltage applied directly to the terminals.

Voltmeters

A voltmeter is used to measure voltage at any point in a circuit, or to measure the voltage drop across any part of a circuit. It can also be used to check continuity in a wire or circuit by indicating current flow from one end to the other. Analog voltmeters usually have various scales on the meter dial and a selector switch to allow the selection of different voltages. The voltmeter has a positive and a negative lead. To avoid damage to the meter, always connect the negative lead to the negative (−) side of the circuit (to ground or nearest the ground side of the circuit) and connect the positive lead to the positive (+) side of the circuit (to the power source or the nearest power source). Note that the negative voltmeter lead will always be black and that the positive voltmeter will always be some color other than black (usually red).

Depending on how the voltmeter is connected into the circuit, it has several uses. A voltmeter can be connected either in parallel or in series with a circuit and it has a very high resistance to current flow. When connected in parallel, only a small amount of current will flow through the voltmeter current path; the rest will flow through the normal circuit current path and the circuit will work normally. When the voltmeter is connected in series with a circuit, only a small amount of current can flow through the circuit. The circuit will not work properly, but the voltmeter reading will show if the circuit is complete or not.

Ohmmeters

The ohmmeter is designed to read resistance (which is measured in ohms or Ω) in a circuit or component. Although there are several different styles of ohmmeters, all analog meters will usually have a selector switch which permits the measurement of different ranges of resistance (usually the selector switch allows the multiplication of the meter reading by 10, 100, 1000, and 10,000). A calibration knob allows the meter to be set at zero for accurate measurement. Since all ohmmeters are powered by an internal battery, the ohmmeter can be used as a self-powered test light. When the ohmmeter is connected, current from the ohmmeter flows through the circuit or component being tested. Since the ohmmeter's internal resistance and voltage are known values, the amount of current flow through the meter depends on the resistance of the circuit or component being tested.

The ohmmeter can be used to perform a continuity test for opens or shorts (either by observation of the meter needle or as a self-powered test light), and to read actual resistance in a circuit. It should be noted that the ohmmeter is used to check the resistance of a component or wire while there is no voltage applied to the circuit. Current flow from an outside voltage source (such as the vehicle battery) can damage the ohmmeter, so the circuit or component should be isolated from the vehicle electrical system before any testing is done. Since the ohmmeter uses its own voltage source, either lead can be connected to any test point.

➡When checking diodes or other solid state components, the ohmmeter leads can only be connected one way in order to measure current flow in a single direction. Make sure the positive (+) and negative (−) terminal connections are as described in the test procedures to verify the one-way diode operation.

In using the meter for making continuity checks, do not be concerned with the actual resistance readings. Zero resistance, or any ohm reading, indicates continuity in the circuit. Infinite resistance indicates an open in the circuit. A high resistance reading where there should be none indicates a problem in the circuit. Checks for short circuits are made in the same manner as checks for open circuits except that the circuit must be isolated from both power and normal ground. Infinite resistance indicates no continuity to ground, while zero resistance indicates a dead short to ground.

Ammeters

An ammeter measures the amount of current flowing through a circuit in units called amperes or amps. Amperes are units of electron flow which indicate how fast the electrons are flowing through the circuit. Since Ohms Law dictates that current flow in a circuit is equal to the circuit voltage divided by the total circuit resistance, increasing voltage also increases the current level (amps). Likewise, any decrease in resistance will increase the amount of amps in a circuit. At normal operating voltage, most circuits have a characteristic amount of amperes, called "current draw" which can be measured using an ammeter. By referring to a specified current draw rating, measuring the amperes, and comparing the two values, one can determine what is happening within the circuit to aid in diagnosis. An open circuit, for example, will not allow any current to flow so the ammeter reading will be zero. More current flows through a heavily loaded circuit or when the charging system is operating.

An ammeter is always connected in series with the circuit being tested. All of the current that normally flows through the circuit must also flow through the ammeter; if there is any other path for the current to follow, the ammeter reading will not be accurate. The ammeter itself has very little resistance to current flow and therefore will not affect the circuit, but it will measure current draw only when the circuit is closed and electricity is flowing. Excessive current draw can blow fuses and drain the battery, while a reduced current draw can cause motors to run slowly, lights to dim and other components to not operate properly. The ammeter can help diagnose these conditions by locating the cause of the high or low reading.

Multimeters

Different combinations of test meters can be built into a single unit designed for specific tests. Some of the more common combination test devices are known as Volt/Amp testers, Tach/Dwell meters, or Digital Multimeters. The Volt/Amp tester is used for charging system, starting system or battery tests and consists of a voltmeter, an ammeter and a variable resistance carbon pile. The voltmeter will usually have at least two ranges for use with 6, 12 and/or 24 volt systems. The ammeter also has more than one range for testing various levels of battery loads and starter current draw. The carbon pile can be adjusted to offer different amounts of resistance. The Volt/Amp tester has heavy leads to carry large amounts of current and many later models have an inductive ammeter pickup that clamps around the wire to simplify test connections. On some models, the ammeter also has a zero-center scale to allow testing of charging and starting systems without switching leads or polarity. A digital multimeter is a voltmeter, ammeter and ohmmeter combined in an instrument which gives a digital readout. These are often used when testing solid state circuits because of their high input impedance (usually 10 megohms or more).

The tach/dwell meter that combines a tachometer and a dwell (cam angle) meter is a specialized kind of voltmeter. The tachometer scale is marked to show engine speed in rpm and the dwell scale is marked to show degrees of distributor shaft rotation. In most electronic ignition systems, dwell is determined by the control unit, but the dwell meter can also be used to check the duty cycle (operation) of some electronic engine control systems. Some tach/dwell meters are powered by an internal battery, while others take their power from the vehicle battery in use. The battery powered testers usually require calibration (much like an ohmmeter) before testing.

TESTING

Open Circuits

To use the self-powered test light or a multimeter to check for open circuits, first isolate the circuit from the vehicle's 12 volt power source by disconnecting the battery or wiring harness connector. Connect the test light or ohmmeter ground clip to a good ground and probe sections of the circuit sequentially with the test light. (start from either end of the circuit). If the light is out/or there is infinite resistance, the open is between the probe and the circuit ground. If the light is on/or the meter shows continuity, the open is between the probe and end of the circuit toward the power source.

Short Circuits

By isolating the circuit both from power and from ground, and using a self-powered test light or multimeter, you can check for shorts to ground in the circuit. Isolate the circuit from power and ground. Connect the test light or ohmmeter ground clip to a good ground and probe any easy-to-reach test point in the circuit. If the light comes on or there is continuity, there is a short somewhere in the circuit. To isolate the short, probe a test point at either end of the isolated circuit (the light should be on/there should be continuity). Leave the test light probe engaged and open connectors, switches, remove parts, etc., sequentially, until the light goes out/continuity is broken. When the light goes out, the short is between the last circuit component opened and the previous circuit opened.

➡The battery in the test light and does not provide much current. A weak battery may not provide enough power to illuminate the test light even when a complete circuit is made (especially if there are high resistances in the circuit). Always make sure that the test battery is strong. To check the battery, briefly touch the ground clip to the probe; if the light glows brightly the battery is strong enough for testing. Never use a self-powered test light to perform checks for opens or shorts when power is applied to the electrical system under test. The 12 volt vehicle power will quickly burn out the light bulb in the test light.

Available Voltage Measurement

Set the voltmeter selector switch to the 20V position and connect the meter negative lead to the negative post of the battery. Connect the positive meter lead to the positive post of the battery and turn the ignition switch **ON** to provide a load. Read the voltage on the meter or digital display. A well charged battery should register over 12 volts. If the meter reads below 11.5 volts, the battery power may be insufficient to operate the electrical system properly. This test determines voltage available from the battery and should be the first step in any electrical trouble diagnosis procedure. Many electrical problems, especially on computer controlled systems, can be caused by a low state of charge in the battery. Excessive corrosion at the battery cable terminals can cause a poor contact that will prevent proper charging and full battery current flow.

Normal battery voltage is 12 volts when fully charged. When the battery is supplying current to one or more circuits it is said to be "under load." When everything is off the electrical system is under a "no-load" condition. A fully charged battery may show about 12.5 volts at no load; will drop to 12 volts under medium load; and will drop even lower under heavy load. If the battery is partially discharged the voltage decrease under heavy load may be excessive, even though the battery shows 12 volts or more at no load. When allowed to discharge further, the battery's available voltage under load will decrease more severely. For this reason, it is important that the battery be fully charged during all testing procedures to avoid errors in diagnosis and incorrect test results.

Voltage Drop

When current flows through a resistance, the voltage beyond the resistance is reduced (the larger the current, the greater the reduction in voltage). When no current is flowing, there is no voltage drop because there is no current flow. All points in the circuit which are connected to the power source are at the same voltage as the power source. The total voltage drop always equals the total source voltage. In a long circuit with many connectors, a series of small, unwanted voltage drops due to corrosion at the connectors can add up to a total loss of voltage which impairs the operation of the normal loads in the circuit. The maximum allowable voltage drop under load is critical, especially if there is more than one high resistance problem in a circuit because all voltage drops are cumulative. A small drop is normal due to the resistance of the conductors.

INDIRECT COMPUTATION OF VOLTAGE DROPS

1. Set the voltmeter selector switch to the 20 volt position.
2. Connect the meter negative lead to a good ground.
3. While operating the circuit, probe all loads in the circuit with the positive meter lead and observe the voltage readings. A drop should be noticed after the first load. But, there should be little or no voltage drop before the first load.

DIRECT MEASUREMENT OF VOLTAGE DROPS

1. Set the voltmeter switch to the 20 volt position.
2. Connect the voltmeter negative lead to the ground side of the load to be measured.
3. Connect the positive lead to the positive side of the resistance or load to be measured.
4. Read the voltage drop directly on the 20 volt scale.

Too high a voltage indicates too high a resistance. If, for example, a blower motor runs too slowly, you can determine if perhaps there is too high a resistance in the resistor pack. By taking voltage drop readings in all parts of the circuit, you can isolate the problem. Too low a voltage drop indicates too low a resistance. Take the blower motor for example again. If a blower motor runs too fast in the MED and/or LOW position, the problem might be isolated in the resistor pack by taking voltage drop readings in all parts of the circuit to locate a possibly shorted resistor.

HIGH RESISTANCE TESTING

1. Set the voltmeter selector switch to the 4 volt position.
2. Connect the voltmeter positive lead to the positive post of the battery.
3. Turn on the headlights and heater blower to provide a load.
4. Probe various points in the circuit with the negative voltmeter lead.
5. Read the voltage drop on the 4 volt scale. Some average maximum allowable voltage drops are:

- FUSE PANEL: 0.7 volts
- IGNITION SWITCH: 0.5 volts
- HEADLIGHT SWITCH: 0.7 volts
- IGNITION COIL (+): 0.5 volts
- ANY OTHER LOAD: 1.3 volts

➡Voltage drops are all measured while a load is operating; without current flow, there will be no voltage drop.

Resistance Measurement

The batteries in an ohmmeter will weaken with age and temperature, so the ohmmeter must be calibrated or "zeroed" before taking measurements. To zero the meter, place the selector switch in its lowest range and touch the two ohmmeter leads together. Turn the calibration knob until the meter needle is exactly on zero.

➡All analog (needle) type ohmmeters must be zeroed before use, but some digital ohmmeter models are automatically calibrated when the switch is turned on. Self-calibrating digital ohmmeters do not have an adjusting knob, but its a good idea to check for a zero readout before use by touching the leads together. All computer controlled systems require the use of a digital ohmmeter with at least 10 megohms impedance for testing. Before any test procedures are attempted, make sure the ohmmeter used is compatible with the electrical system or damage to the on-board computer could result.

To measure resistance, first isolate the circuit from the vehicle power source by disconnecting the battery cables or the harness connector. Make sure the key is **OFF** when disconnecting any components or the battery. Where necessary, also isolate at least one side of the circuit to be checked in order to avoid reading parallel resistances. Parallel circuit resistances will always give a lower reading than the actual resistance of either of the branches. When measuring the resistance of parallel circuits, the total resistance will always be lower than the smallest resistance in the circuit. Connect the meter leads to both sides of the circuit (wire or component) and read the actual measured ohms on the meter scale. Make sure the selector switch is set to the proper ohm scale for the circuit being tested to avoid misreading the ohmmeter test value.

✳✳ WARNING

Never use an ohmmeter with power applied to the circuit. Like the self-powered test light, the ohmmeter is designed to operate on its own power supply. The normal 12 volt automotive electrical system current could damage the meter!

Wiring Harnesses

The average automobile contains about ½ mile of wiring, with hundreds of individual connections. To protect the many wires from damage and to keep them from becoming a confusing tangle, they are organized into bundles, enclosed in plastic or taped together and called wiring harnesses. Different harnesses serve different parts of the vehicle. Individual wires are color coded to help trace them through a harness where sections are hidden from view.

Automotive wiring or circuit conductors can be in any one of three forms:

1. Single strand wire
2. Multi-strand wire
3. Printed circuitry

Single strand wire has a solid metal core and is usually used inside such components as alternators, motors, relays and other devices. Multi-strand wire has a core made of many small strands of wire twisted together into a single conductor. Most of the wiring in an automotive electrical system is made up of multi-strand wire, either as a single conductor or grouped together in a harness. All wiring is color coded on the insulator, either as a solid color or as a colored wire with an identification stripe. A printed circuit is a thin film of copper or other conductor that is printed on an insulator backing. Occasionally, a printed circuit is sandwiched between two sheets of plastic for more protection and flex-

ibility. A complete printed circuit, consisting of conductors, insulating material and connectors for lamps or other components is called a printed circuit board. Printed circuitry is used in place of individual wires or harnesses in places where space is limited, such as behind instrument panels.

Since automotive electrical systems are very sensitive to changes in resistance, the selection of properly sized wires is critical when systems are repaired. A loose or corroded connection or a replacement wire that is too small for the circuit will add extra resistance and an additional voltage drop to the circuit. A ten percent voltage drop can result in slow or erratic motor operation, for example, even though the circuit is complete. The wire gauge number is an expression of the cross-section area of the conductor. The most common system for expressing wire size is the American Wire Gauge (AWG) system.

Gauge numbers are assigned to conductors of various cross-section areas. As gauge number increases, area decreases and the conductor becomes smaller. A 5 gauge conductor is smaller than a 1 gauge conductor and a 10 gauge is smaller than a 5 gauge. As the cross-section area of a conductor decreases, resistance increases and so does the gauge number. A conductor with a higher gauge number will carry less current than a conductor with a lower gauge number.

➡Gauge wire size refers to the size of the conductor, not the size of the complete wire. It is possible to have two wires of the same gauge with different diameters because one may have thicker insulation than the other.

12 volt automotive electrical systems generally use 10, 12, 14, 16 and 18 gauge wire. Main power distribution circuits and larger accessories usually use 10 and 12 gauge wire. Battery cables are usually 4 or 6 gauge, although 1 and 2 gauge wires are occasionally used. Wire length must also be considered when making repairs to a circuit. As conductor length increases, so does resistance. An 18 gauge wire, for example, can carry a 10 amp load for 10 feet without excessive voltage drop; however if a 15 foot wire is required for the same 10 amp load, it must be a 16 gauge wire.

An electrical schematic shows the electrical current paths when a circuit is operating properly. It is essential to understand how a circuit works before trying to figure out why it doesn't. Schematics break the entire electrical system down into individual circuits and show only one particular circuit. In a schematic, no attempt is made to represent wiring and components as they physically appear on the vehicle; switches and other components are shown as simply as possible. Face views of harness connectors show the cavity or terminal locations in all multi-pin connectors to help locate test points.

If you need to backprobe a connector while it is on the component, the order of the terminals must be mentally reversed. The wire color code can help in this situation, as well as a keyway, lock tab or other reference mark.

WIRING REPAIR

Soldering is a quick, efficient method of joining metals permanently. Everyone who has the occasion to make wiring repairs should know how to solder. Electrical connections that are soldered are far less likely to come apart and will conduct electricity much better than connections that are only "pig-tailed" together. The most popular (and preferred) method of soldering is with an electrical soldering gun. Soldering irons are available in many sizes and wattage ratings. Irons with higher wattage ratings deliver higher temperatures and recover lost heat faster. A small soldering iron rated for no more than 50 watts is recommended, especially on electrical systems where excess heat can damage the components being soldered.

There are three ingredients necessary for successful soldering; proper flux, good solder and sufficient heat. A soldering flux is necessary to clean the metal of tarnish, prepare it for soldering and to enable the solder to spread into tiny crevices. When soldering, always use a rosin core solder which is non-corrosive and will not attract moisture once the job is finished. Other types of flux (acid core) will leave a residue that will attract moisture and cause the wires to corrode. Tin is a unique metal with a low melting point. In a molten state, it dissolves and alloys easily with many metals. Solder is made by mixing tin with lead. The most common proportions are 40/60, 50/50 and 60/40, with the percentage of tin listed first. Low priced solders usually contain less tin, making them very difficult for a beginner to use because more heat is required to melt the solder. A common solder is 40/60 which is well suited for all-around general use, but 60/40 melts easier and is preferred for electrical work.

Soldering Techniques

Successful soldering requires that the metals to be joined be heated to a temperature that will melt the solder, usually 360–460°F (182–238°C). Contrary to popular belief, the purpose of the soldering iron is not to melt the solder itself, but to heat the parts being soldered to a temperature high enough to melt the solder when it is touched to the work. Melting flux-cored solder on the soldering iron will usually destroy the effectiveness of the flux.

➡**Soldering tips are made of copper for good heat conductivity, but must be "tinned" regularly for quick transference of heat to the project and to prevent the solder from sticking to the iron. To "tin" the iron, simply heat it and touch the flux-cored solder to the tip; the solder will flow over the hot tip. Wipe the excess off with a clean rag, but be careful as the iron will be hot.**

After some use, the tip may become pitted. If so, simply dress the tip smooth with a smooth file and "tin" the tip again. Flux-cored solder will remove oxides but rust, bits of insulation and oil or grease must be removed with a wire brush or emery cloth. For maximum strength in soldered parts, the joint must start off clean and tight. Weak joints will result in gaps too wide for the solder to bridge.

If a separate soldering flux is used, it should be brushed or swabbed on only those areas that are to be soldered. Most solders contain a core of flux and separate fluxing is unnecessary. Hold the work to be soldered firmly. It is best to solder on a wooden board, because a metal vise will only rob the piece to be soldered of heat and make it difficult to melt the solder. Hold the soldering tip with the broadest face against the work to be soldered. Apply solder under the tip close to the work, using enough solder to give a heavy film between the iron and the piece being soldered, while moving slowly and making sure the solder melts properly. Keep the work level or the solder will run to the lowest part and favor the thicker parts, because these require more heat

to melt the solder. If the soldering tip overheats (the solder coating on the face of the tip burns up), it should be retinned. Once the soldering is completed, let the soldered joint stand until cool. Tape and seal all soldered wire splices after the repair has cooled.

Wire Harness Connectors

Most connectors in the engine compartment or that are otherwise exposed to the elements are protected against moisture and dirt which could create oxidation and deposits on the terminals.

These special connectors are weather-proof. All repairs require the use of a special terminal and the tool required to service it. This tool is used to remove the pin and sleeve terminals. If removal is attempted with an ordinary pick, there is a good chance that the terminal will be bent or deformed. Unlike standard blade type terminals, these weather-proof terminals cannot be straightened once they are bent. Make certain that the connectors are properly seated and all of the sealing rings are in place when connecting leads. On some models, a hinge-type flap provides a backup or secondary locking feature for the terminals. Most secondary locks are used to improve connector reliability by retaining the terminals if the small terminal lock tangs are not positioned properly.

Molded-on connectors require complete replacement of the connection. This means splicing a new connector assembly into the harness. All splices should be soldered to insure proper contact. Use care when probing the connections or replacing terminals in them as it is possible to short between opposite terminals. If this happens to the wrong terminal pair, it is possible to damage certain components. Always use jumper wires between connectors for circuit checking and never probe through weatherproof seals.

Open circuits are often difficult to locate by sight because corrosion or terminal misalignment are hidden by the connectors. Merely wiggling a connector on a sensor or in the wiring harness may correct the open circuit condition. This should always be considered when an open circuit or a failed sensor is indicated. Intermittent problems may also be caused by oxidized or loose connections. When using a circuit tester for diagnosis, always probe connections from the wire side. Be careful not to damage sealed connectors with test probes.

All wiring harnesses should be replaced with identical parts, using the same gauge wire and connectors. When signal wires are spliced into a harness, use wire with high temperature insulation only. It is seldom necessary to replace a complete harness. If replacement is necessary, pay close attention to insure proper harness routing. Secure the harness with suitable plastic wire clamps to prevent vibrations from causing the harness to wear in spots or contact any hot components.

➡**Weatherproof connectors cannot be replaced with standard connectors. Instructions are provided with replacement connector and terminal packages. Some wire harnesses have mounting indicators (usually pieces of colored tape) to mark where the harness is to be secured.**

In making wiring repairs, its important that you always replace damaged wires with wiring of the same gauge as the wire being replaced. The heavier the wire, the smaller the gauge number. Wires are color-coded to aid in identification and whenever possible the same color coded wire should be used for replacement. A wire stripping and crimping tool is necessary to install solderless terminal connectors. Test all crimps by pulling on the wires; it should not be possible to pull the wires out of a good crimp.

Wires which are open, exposed or otherwise damaged are repaired by simple splicing. Where possible, if the wiring harness is accessible and the damaged place in the wire can be located, it is best to open the harness and check for all possible damage. In an inaccessible harness, the wire must be bypassed with a new insert, usually taped to the outside of the old harness.

When replacing fusible links, be sure to use fusible link wire, NOT ordinary automotive wire. Make sure the fusible segment is of the same gauge and construction as the one being replaced and double the stripped end when crimping the terminal connector for a good contact. The melted (open) fusible link segment of the wiring harness should be cut off as close to the harness as possible, then a new segment spliced in as described. In the case of a damaged fusible link that feeds two harness wires, the harness connections should be replaced with two fusible link wires so that each circuit will have its own separate protection.

➡ **Most of the problems caused in the wiring harness are due to bad ground connections. Always check all vehicle ground connections for corrosion or looseness before performing any power feed checks to eliminate the chance of a bad ground affecting the circuit.**

Hard-Shell Connectors

Unlike molded connectors, the terminal contacts in hard-shell connectors can be replaced. Weatherproof hard-shell connectors with the leads molded into the shell have non-replaceable terminal ends. Replacement usually involves the use of a special terminal removal tool that depresses the locking tangs (barbs) on the connector terminal and allows the connector to be removed from the rear of the shell. The connector shell should be replaced if it shows any evidence of burning, melting, cracks, or breaks. Replace individual terminals that are burnt, corroded, distorted or loose.

➡ **The insulation crimp must be tight to prevent the insulation from sliding back on the wire when the wire is pulled. The insulation must be visibly compressed under the crimp tabs, and the ends of the crimp should be turned in for a firm grip on the insulation.**

The wire crimp must be made with all wire strands inside the crimp. The terminal must be fully compressed on the wire strands with the ends of the crimp tabs turned in to make a firm grip on the wire. Check all connections with an ohmmeter to insure a good contact. There should be no measurable resistance between the wire and the terminal when connected.

Fusible Links

The fuse link is a short length of special, Hypalon (high temperature) insulated wire, integral with the engine compartment wiring harness and should not be confused with standard wire. It is several wire gauges smaller than the circuit which it protects. Under no circumstances should a fuse link replacement repair be made using a length of standard wire cut from bulk stock or from another wiring harness.

To repair any blown fuse link use the following procedure:
1. Determine which circuit is damaged, its location and the cause of the open fuse link. If the damaged fuse link is one of three fed by a common No. 10 or 12 gauge feed wire, determine the specific affected circuit.

2. Disconnect the negative battery cable.
3. Cut the damaged fuse link from the wiring harness and discard it. If the fuse link is one of three circuits fed by a single feed wire, cut it out of the harness at each splice end and discard it.
4. Identify and procure the proper fuse link with butt connectors for attaching the fuse link to the harness.

➡ **Heat shrink tubing must be slipped over the wire before crimping and soldering the connection.**

5. To repair any fuse link in a 3-link group with one feed:
   a. After cutting the open link out of the harness, cut each of the remaining undamaged fuse links close to the feed wire weld.
   b. Strip approximately ½ in. (13mm) of insulation from the detached ends of the two good fuse links. Insert two wire ends into one end of a butt connector, then carefully push one stripped end of the replacement fuse link into the same end of the butt connector and crimp all three firmly together.

➡ **Care must be taken when fitting the three fuse links into the butt connector as the internal diameter is a snug fit for three wires. Make sure to use a proper crimping tool. Pliers, side cutters, etc. will not apply the proper crimp to retain the wires and withstand a pull test.**

   c. After crimping the butt connector to the three fuse links, cut the weld portion from the feed wire and strip approximately ½ in. (13mm) of insulation from the cut end. Insert the stripped end into the open end of the butt connector and crimp very firmly.
   d. To attach the remaining end of the replacement fuse link, strip approximately ½ in. (13mm) of insulation from the wire end of the circuit from which the blown fuse link was removed, and firmly crimp a butt connector or equivalent to the stripped wire. Then, insert the end of the replacement link into the other end of the butt connector and crimp firmly.
   e. Using rosin core solder with a consistency of 60 percent tin and 40 percent lead, solder the connectors and the wires at the repairs then insulate with electrical tape or heat shrink tubing.
6. To replace any fuse link on a single circuit in a harness, cut out the damaged portion, strip approximately ½ in. (13mm) of insulation from the two wire ends and attach the appropriate replacement fuse link to the stripped wire ends with two proper size butt connectors. Solder the connectors and wires, then insulate.
7. To repair any fuse link which has an eyelet terminal on one end such as the charging circuit, cut off the open fuse link behind the weld, strip approximately ½ in. (13mm) of insulation from the cut end and attach the appropriate new eyelet fuse link to the cut stripped wire with an appropriate size butt connector. Solder the connectors and wires at the repair, then insulate.
8. Connect the negative battery cable to the battery and test the system for proper operation.

➡ **Do not mistake a resistor wire for a fuse link. The resistor wire is generally longer and has print stating, "Resistor-don't cut or splice."**

When attaching a single No. 16, 17, 18 or 20 gauge fuse link to a heavy gauge wire, always double the stripped wire end of the fuse link before inserting and crimping it into the butt connector for positive wire retention.

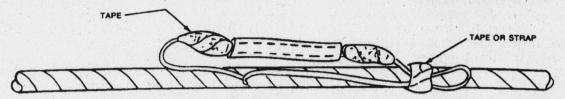

REMOVE EXISTING VINYL TUBE SHIELDING
REINSTALL OVER FUSE LINK BEFORE CRIMPING
FUSE LINK TO WIRE ENDS

TAPE

TAPE OR STRAP

TYPICAL REPAIR USING THE SPECIAL #17 GA. (9.00" LONG-YELLOW) FUSE LINK REQUIRED FOR THE AIR/COND.
CIRCUITS (2) #687E and #261A LOCATED IN THE ENGINE COMPARTMENT

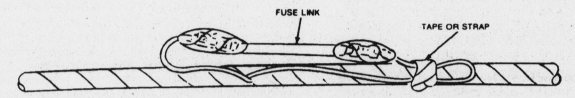

FUSE LINK

TAPE OR STRAP

TYPICAL REPAIR FOR ANY IN-LINE FUSE LINK USING THE SPECIFIED GAUGE FUSE LINK FOR THE SPECIFIC CIRCUIT

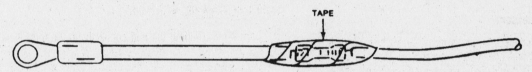

TAPE

TYPICAL REPAIR USING THE EYELET TERMINAL FUSE LINK OF THE SPECIFIED GAUGE FOR ATTACHMENT TO A CIRCUIT WIRE END

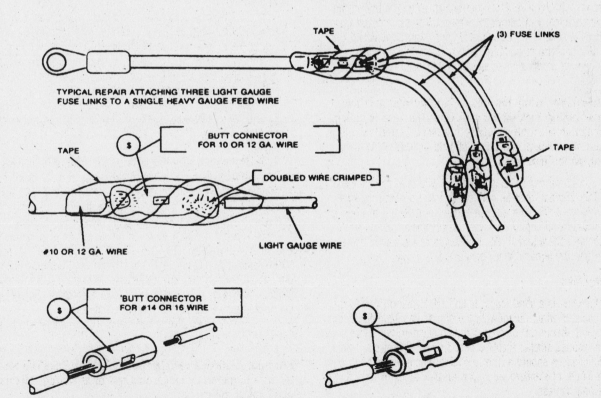

TAPE

(3) FUSE LINKS

TYPICAL REPAIR ATTACHING THREE LIGHT GAUGE
FUSE LINKS TO A SINGLE HEAVY GAUGE FEED WIRE

TAPE

BUTT CONNECTOR
FOR 10 OR 12 GA. WIRE

DOUBLED WIRE CRIMPED

TAPE

#10 OR 12 GA. WIRE

LIGHT GAUGE WIRE

'BUTT CONNECTOR
FOR #14 OR 16 WIRE

FUSIBLE LINK REPAIR PROCEDURE

General fusible link repair—never replace a fusible link with regular wire or a fusible link rated at a higher amperage than the one being replaced

Add-On Electrical Equipment

The electrical system in your vehicle is designed to perform under reasonable operating conditions without interference between components. Before any additional electrical equipment is installed, it is recommended that you consult your dealer or a reputable repair facility that is familiar with the vehicle and its systems.

If the vehicle is equipped with mobile radio equipment and/or mobile telephone, it may have an effect upon the operation of any on-board computer control modules. Radio Frequency Interference (RFI) from the communications system can be picked up by the vehicle's wiring harnesses and conducted into the control module, giving it the wrong messages at the wrong time. Although well shielded against RFI, the computer should be further protected by taking the following measures:

• Install the antenna as far as possible from the control module. For instance, if the module is located behind the center console area, then the antenna should be mounted at the rear of the vehicle.

• Keep the antenna wiring a minimum of eight inches away from any wiring running to control modules and from the module itself. NEVER wind the antenna wire around any other wiring.

• Mount the equipment as far from the control module as possible. Be very careful during installation not to drill through any wires or short a wire harness with a mounting screw.

• Insure that the electrical feed wire(s) to the equipment are properly and tightly connected. Loose connectors can cause interference.

• Make certain that the equipment is properly grounded to the vehicle. Poor grounding can damage expensive equipment.

HEATER

Blower Motor

REMOVAL & INSTALLATION

1962–67 Chevy II

1. Disconnect the negative battery cable.
2. Remove the screws attaching the motor and blower to the heater assembly.
3. Remove the retainer attaching the blower to the motor shaft.
4. Reverse the above to install the blower.

1968 Chevy II and 1969–79 Nova
▶ See Figures 1 and 2

1. Disconnect the battery ground cable.
2. Disconnect the hoses and wiring from the fender skirt.
3. Remove all fender skirt attaching bolts except those attaching the skirt to the radiator support.

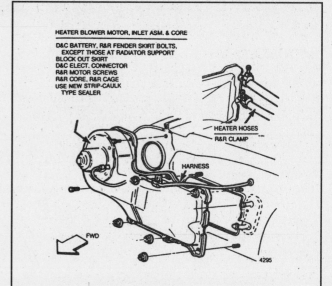

Fig. 2 Heater blower motor and core removal and installation—1978–79 vehicles

4. Pull out, then down, on the skirt. Place a block between the skirt and the fender.
5. Remove the blower-to-case attaching screws. Remove the blower assembly.
6. Remove the blower wheel retaining nut and separate the motor and wheel.
7. Installation is the reverse of the removal procedure. The open end of the blower should be away from the motor.

Heater Core

REMOVAL & INSTALLATION

➡**The first two heater system procedures are applicable to cars without factory air conditioning.**

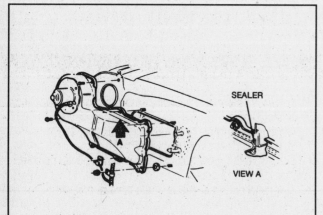

Fig. 1 Heater blower motor and case attachment—1968–78 vehicles

1962–67 Chevy II

1. Drain the radiator.
2. From the engine compartment, remove the hoses from the inlet and outlet connections.
3. Remove the nuts around the blower motor holding the heater to the dash panel.
4. From inside the vehicle, remove the glove compartment and glove compartment door.
5. Remove the screws attaching the heater distributor bracket to the dash.
6. Remove the screw holding the case bracket to the adaptor bracket.
7. Detach the heater assembly from the dash panel and adaptor assembly, then lower it toward the floor.
8. Disconnect all cable connections, wire connector, and defroster hoses.
9. Remove the assembly from the vehicle.
10. Remove the screws attaching the core cover to the heater.
11. Remove the core mounting screws and the core from the heater.
12. Installation is the reverse of the removal procedure.

1968 Chevy II and 1969–79 Nova

WITHOUT A/C

1. Disconnect the battery ground cable.
2. Drain the radiator.
3. Disconnect the heater hoses. Plug the core inlet and outlet.
4. Remove the nuts from the air distributor duct studs on the firewall.
5. Remove the glove compartment and door assembly.
6. From beneath the dash, drill out the lower right-hand distributor duct stud with a ¼ in. drill.
7. Pull the distributor duct from the firewall mounting. Remove the resistor wires. Lay the duct on the floor.
8. Remove the core assembly from the distributor duct.
9. Installation is the reverse of the removal procedure.

WITH A/C

▶ **See Figure 3**

1. Disconnect the battery ground cable and drain the cooling system. It is not necessary to purge the refrigerant from the A/C system.

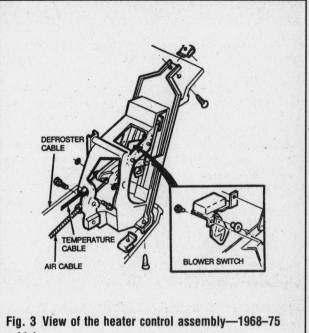

Fig. 3 View of the heater control assembly—1968–75 vehicles

2. Disconnect the heater hose from the upper pipe at the firewall.
3. Remove the nuts from the heater studs in the firewall.
4. Remove the right front inner fender panel screws and lower the panel onto the tire.
5. Remove the remaining stud nut and lower heater hose.
6. Remove the glove compartment.
7. Remove the right kick pad recirculating air valve.
8. Detach the center duct from the selector duct.
9. Remove the floor duct and separate the two selector halves.
10. Remove the selector duct from the firewall.
11. Disconnect the control cables and electrical wires.
12. Scribe the temperature door camming plate-to-selector duct relationship and remove the plate.
13. Place the selector duct on the floor and remove the heater core housing and core.
14. Reverse the removal steps to install the core.

RADIO

Radio Receiver

REMOVAL & INSTALLATION

▶ **See Figure 4**

1. Disconnect the battery ground cable.
2. Remove the ashtray and ashtray housing as necessary.

3. Remove the knobs, controls, washers, trim plate, and nuts from the radio.
4. Remove the hoses from the center A/C duct as necessary.
5. Disconnect all wiring leads.
6. Remove the screw from the radio's rear mounting bracket and then lower the radio.
7. Installation is the reverse of the removal procedure.

Fig. 4 Exploded view of the radio mounting—1973–79 vehicles

Remove the radio control knobs

Remove the retaining washers

Carefully pull the radio out, detach the wiring, then remove it from the vehicle

WINDSHIELD WIPERS

Windshield Wiper Motor

REMOVAL & INSTALLATION

1962–67 Chevy II

1. Make certain that the wiper motor is in the park position.
2. Working under the instrument panel, remove the transmission linkage from the motor crank arm.
3. Disconnect the washer hoses and electrical connectors.
4. Remove the motor retaining bolts and remove the motor.
5. Reverse the procedure to install, checking the sealing gaskets at the motor.

1968 Chevy II and 1969–79 Nova

1. Make sure that the wiper motor is in the park position.
2. Disconnect the washer hoses and electrical connectors.
3. Remove the plenum chamber grille or access cover. Remove the nut retaining the crank arm to the motor assembly.

Detach the wiper motor electrical connectors

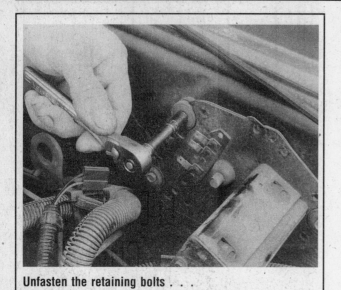

Unfasten the retaining bolts . . .

. . . then remove the windshield wiper motor from the vehicle

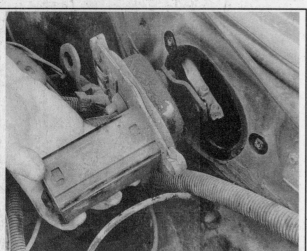

. . . then pull the windshield wiper motor slightly away from the firewall

Unfasten the crank arm from the transmission assembly . . .

4. Remove the retaining screws or nuts and remove the motor.

5. Reverse the procedure to install, checking the sealing gaskets at the motor.

Wiper Transmission

REMOVAL & INSTALLATION

1962–67 Chevy II

▶ See Figure 5

1. Make certain that the wiper motor is in the park position. Remove the wiper arm and blade assemblies from the transmission shaft.

2. Remove the linkage from the wiper crank arm. Remove the left transmission link from the right transmission.

3. Remove the two screws securing the transmission to the

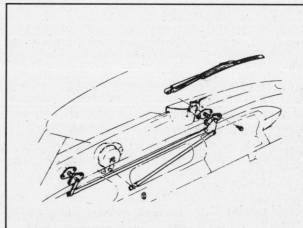

Fig. 5 Windshield wiper transmission location—1962–67 vehicles

cowl on one side. Remove the transmission from beneath the dash.

4. Reverse the procedure to install, checking the gasket.

1968 Chevy II and 1969–79 Nova
▶ See Figure 6

1. Make sure that the wiper motor is in the park position.
2. Disconnect the battery ground cable.
3. Remove the wiper arm and blade assemblies from the transmission. On articulated left arm assemblies, remove the clip retaining the pinned arm to the blade arm.
4. Remove the plenum chamber air intake grille or screen.
5. Loosen the nuts retaining the drive rod ball stud to the crank arm and detach and drive rod from the crank arm.
6. Remove the transmission retaining screws. Lower the transmission and drive rod assemblies into the plenum chamber.
7. Remove the transmission and linkage from the plenum chamber through the cowl opening.
8. Reverse the procedure to install, making sure that the wiper blade assemblies are installed in the park position.

Fig. 6 Windshield wiper motor and transmission mounting—1968–75 vehicles shown

INSTRUMENT PANEL

Ignition Switch (Dash-Mounted)

REMOVAL & INSTALLATION

1968 Chevy II

1. Disconnect the battery negative cable.
2. Remove the lock cylinder by placing it in the off position and inserting a wire in the small hole in the cylinder face. While pushing on the wire, continue to turn the cylinder counter-clockwise. Pull the cylinder from the case.

3. Remove the nut from the passenger side of the dash.
4. From under the dash, reach up and remove the wiring connector from the rear of the switch.
5. To remove the theft-resistant connector, the switch must be removed from under the dash. Use a suitable prytool to depress the locking tangs and separate the connector.
6. Reverse the above procedure to install the switch.

SEATBELT SYSTEM

Warning Buzzer and Light

GENERAL INFORMATION

1972–73 Vehicles

Beginning January 1, 1972, all cars are required to have a warning system which operates a buzzer and a warning light if either the driver's or the right-hand front passenger's seat belts are not fastened when the seats are occupied and the car is in forward motion.

On Chevrolet products, this system consists of seat belt retractor switches, pressure sensitive front seat switches, a parking brake switch (MT), or a transmission switch (AT), a warning light, and a buzzer.

The seat belt warning system is wired through the 20 amp "Gauges" fuse.

The warning light is located in the instrument cluster; and the buzzer, which is shared with the ignition key warning system, is taped to the instrument cluster wiring harness.

The warning system is activated when the ignition switch is **ON,** the front seats are occupied, and the seat belts are left in their retractors. Only when the front seat belts are extended and properly fastened, will the warning light and buzzer stop.

Two different types of switches are used to control the operation of the system, depending upon the type of transmission used:

On manual transmission-equipped cars, the parking brake warning light switch is used to activate the seat belt warning circuit through a relay as soon as the parking brake is released. A diode is used in the circuit to prevent feedback to the brake warning system.

On automatic transmission equipped models, the seat belt warning system is activated by the neutral safety/back-up lamp switch, when the car is placed into any forward gear and the seat belts are not used.

Seat Belt/Starter Interlock System

GENERAL INFORMATION

1974 Vehicles

▶ **See Figure 7**

As previously required by law, all 1974 and some 1975 Chevrolet passenger cars were designed so that they could not be started until the front seat occupants were seated with their seat belts fastened. If the proper sequence is not followed (for example, the occupants fasten the seat belts and then sit on them), the engine cannot be started.

If, after the car is started, the seat belts are unfastened, a warning buzzer and light will be activated in a similar manner to that described previously for 1972–73 models.

The shoulder harness and lap belt are permanently fastened together, so that they both must be worn. The shoulder harness uses an inertia-lock reel to allow freedom of movement under normal driving conditions.

➡**This type of reel locks up when the car decelerates rapidly, as during a crash.**

The lap belts use the same ratchet-type retractors that the 1972–73 models use.

The switches for the interlock system have been removed from the lap belt retractors and placed in the belt buckles. The seat sensors remain the same as those used in 1972–73.

For ease of service, the car may be started from outside, by reaching in and turning the key, but without depressing the seat sensors.

In case of system failure, an override switch is located under the hood. This is a "one start" switch and it must be reset each time it is used.

On Chevrolet products, this system consists of seat belt retractor switches, pressure sensitive front seat switches, a parking brake switch (MT), or a transmission switch (AT), a warning light, and a buzzer.

The seat belt warning system is wired through the 20 amp "Gauges" fuse.

The warning light is located in the instrument cluster; and the buzzer, which is shared with the ignition key warning system, is taped to the instrument cluster wiring harness.

The warning system is activated when the ignition switch is **ON,** the front seats are occupied, and the seat belts are left in their retractors. Only when the front seat belts are extended and properly fastened will the warning light and buzzer stop.

Two different types of switches are used to control the operation of the system, depending upon the type of transmission used:

On manual transmission-equipped cars, the parking brake warning light switch is used to activate the seat belt warning circuit through a relay as soon as the parking brake is released. A diode is used in the circuit to prevent feedback to the brake warning system.

On automatic transmission equipped models, the seat belt warning system is activated by the neutral safety/back-up lamp switch, when the car is placed into any forward gear and the seat belts are not used.

DISABLING THE SEATBELT INTERLOCK SYSTEM

Since the requirement for the interlock system was dropped during the 1975 model year, those systems installed on cars built earlier may now be legally disabled. The seat belt warning light is still required.

1. Disconnect the negative battery cable.
2. Locate the interlock harness connector under the left side of the instrument panel on or near the fuse block. It has orange, yellow, and green leads.
3. Cut and tape the ends of the green wire on the body side of the connector.
4. Remove the buzzer from the fuse block or connector.

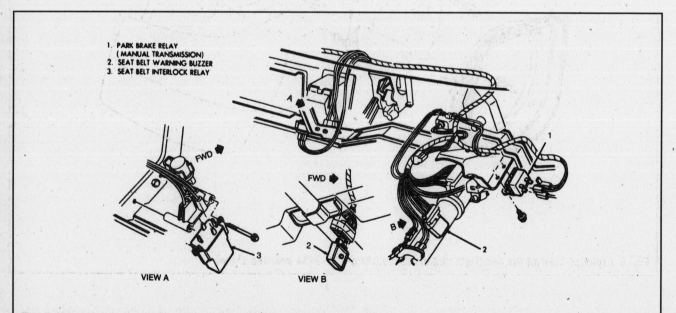

1. PARK BRAKE RELAY (MANUAL TRANSMISSION)
2. SEAT BELT WARNING BUZZER
3. SEAT BELT INTERLOCK RELAY

VIEW A   VIEW B

Fig. 7 Nova seat belt warning and starter interlock system components

LIGHTING

Headlights

REMOVAL & INSTALLATION

◆ **See Figure 8**

1. Disconnect the negative battery cable.
2. Remove the headlight bezel retaining screws and remove the bezel.

3. Disengage the spring from the retaining ring with a cotter pin removal tool and remove the two attaching screws.
4. Remove the retaining ring and disconnect the sealed beam unit at the wiring connector.
5. Attach the wiring connector to the replacement sealed beam unit. Position the unit in place making sure that the number molded into the lens face is at the top.
6. Position the retaining ring in place and install the retaining ring attaching screws and spring.
7. Check the operation of the light and install the headlight bezel.

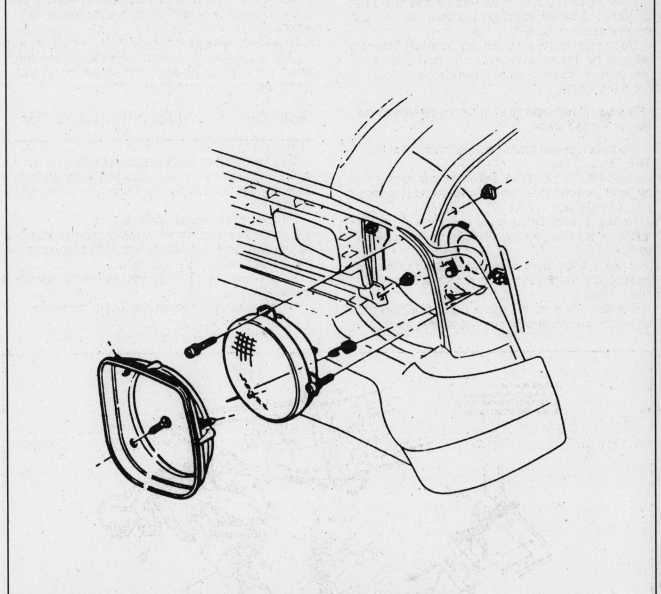

Fig. 8 Exploded view of the headlight and bezel mounting—1973–74 vehicles shown

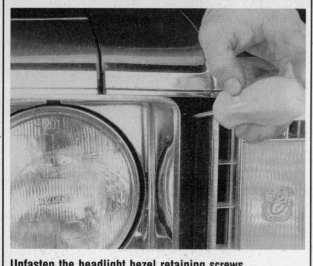

Unfasten the headlight bezel retaining screws . . .

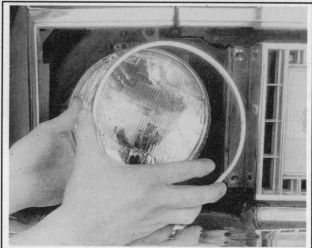

Remove the retaining ring and carefully lift the headlight from the housing

. . . then remove the bezel from the headlight

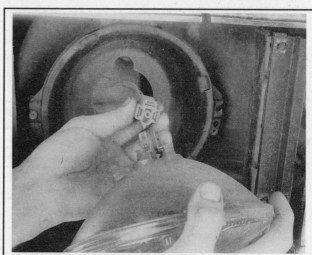

Detach the headlight connector, then remove the light from the vehicle

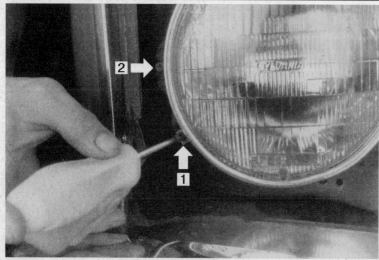

1. Headlight retaining ring screws. Do Not confuse these with the aiming screws.
2. Headlight aiming screws.

Headlight retaining and aiming screw locations

AIMING

The headlights must be properly aimed to provide the best, safest road illumination. The lights should be checked for proper aim, and adjusted if necessary, after installing a new sealed beam unit or if the front end sheet metal has been replaced. The headlamps should be aimed by a professional with a special alignment tool. Certain state and local authorities may require professional adjustment, but use the procedure below for temporary adjustments.

➡**The vehicle's fuel tank should be about half full when adjusting the headlights. Tires should be properly inflated, and if a heavy load is carried in the trunk or in the cargo area of station wagons, it should remain there.**

Horitontal and vertical aiming of each sealed beam unit is provided by two adjusting screws, which move the mounting ring in the body against the tension of the coil spring.

1. Place the car on a level floor with headlamps 25 ft. (7.62m) from a light colored wall.
2. Tape three vertical lines on the wall, one for the vertical center of the car and two for the vertical center of the headlamps. Then, tape one horizontal line for the horizontal and vertical center of the headlamps.
3. Adjust the low beams so the high intensity zone is just below the horizontal line and to the right of the outboard vertical lines.
4. Adjust the high beams so the high intensity zone is centered where the outboard lines intersect with the horizontal line.

Signal and Marker Lights

REMOVAL & INSTALLATION

Front Turn Signal & Parking Lights

➡**This is a general procedure and applies to all models and types covered by this manual. A few steps may need to be slightly altered to comply with your particular vehicle.**

1. Disconnect the negative battery cable.
2. To replace the bulb, reach up and in behind the bumper or access the bulb from the engine compartment in front of the radiator, as applicable.
3. Twist the lamp socket counterclockwise until it can be pulled backward and out from the housing.
4. Either pull the light bulb from the socket or lightly depress the bulb and turn it counterclockwise to release it from the socket, as applicable.
5. Installation is the reverse of the removal procedure. During installation, make sure that the light bulb contacts are clean and free of corrosion.
6. Connect the negative battery cable, then check light operation.

Side Marker Lights

➡**This is a general procedure and applies to all models and types covered by this manual. A few steps may need to be slightly altered to comply with your particular vehicle.**

1. Disconnect the negative battery cable.
2. To replace the bulb, reach up behind the housing and twist the lamp socket counterclockwise until it can be pulled away from the housing.
3. As applicable, carefully pull the light bulb from the socket or lightly depress the bulb and turn it counterclockwise to release it from the socket.
4. Installation is the reverse of the removal procedure. During installation, make sure that the light bulb contacts are clean and free of corrosion.
5. Connect the negative battery cable, then check the light operation.

Rear Turn Signal, Brake and Parking Lights

➡**This is a general procedure and applies to all models covered by this manual. A few steps may need to be slightly altered to comply with your particular vehicle.**

1. Disconnect the negative battery cable.
2. Some vehicles are equipped with lenses that are attached with screws accessible from the rear. To remove these, simple unfasten the screws, then remove the lens.
3. On some vehicles, you must open the trunk lid, then twist the socket to release it from the housing.
4. Once the lens is removed or the socket released, as applicable, the bulb can be replaced by carefully pulling it from the socket, or by depressing it, turning it counterclockwise, and removing it from the socket.
5. Installation is the reverse of the removal procedure. During installation, make sure that the light bulb contacts are clean and free of corrosion.
6. Connect the negative battery cable, then check light operation.

Dome Light

1. Disconnect the negative battery cable.
2. Remove the dome light cover by unfastening the retaining screws, or prying the cover off, as applicable.
3. Remove the bulb and replace with a new one.
4. Installation is the reverse of the removal procedure. During

Use a suitable tool to pry . . . .

. . . then remove the dome light cover

Remove the dome light bulb by pulling it straight down from the socket

installation, make sure that the light bulb contacts are clean and free of corrosion.

5. Connect the negative battery cable, then check light operation.

License Plate Lights

1. Disconnect the negative battery cable.
2. Remove the lamp attaching bolts or screws.
3. Lower the lamp socket, then remove the light bulb.
4. Installation is the reverse of the removal procedure. During installation, make sure that the light bulb contacts are clean and free of corrosion.
5. Connect the negative battery cable, then check light operation.

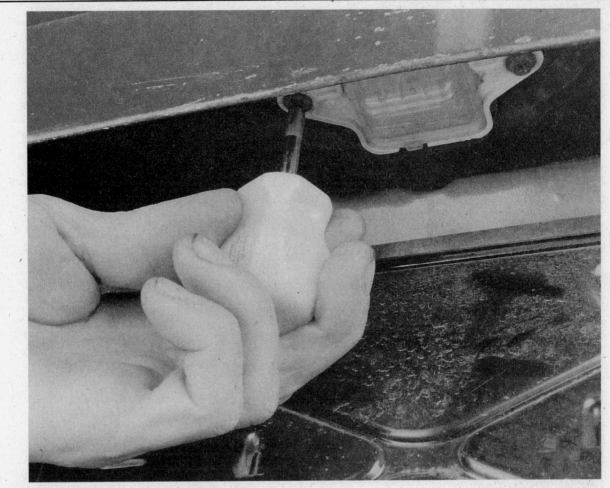

Unfasten the license plate lamp retaining screws

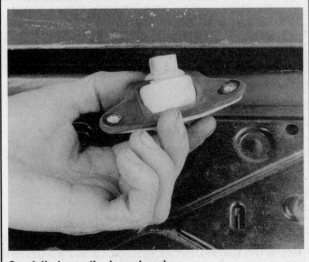

Carefully lower the lamp housing

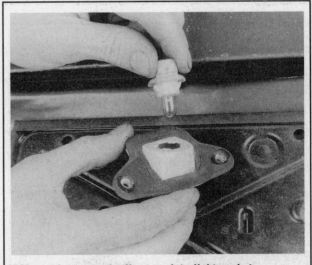

Twist and remove the license plate light socket . . .

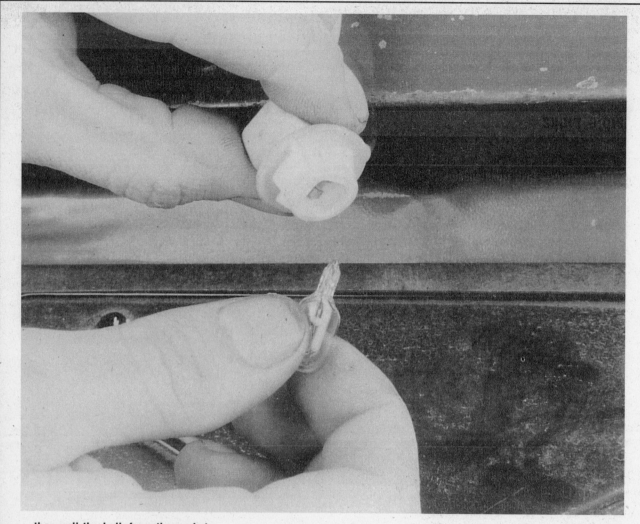

. . . then pull the bulb from the socket

TRAILER WIRING

Wiring the vehicle for towing is fairly easy. There are a number of good wiring kits available and these should be used, rather than trying to design your own.

All trailers will need brake lights and turn signals as well as tail lights and side marker lights. Most areas require extra marker lights for overwide trailers. Also, most areas have recently required back-up lights for trailers, and most trailer manufacturers have been building trailers with back-up lights for several years.

Additionally, some Class I, most Class II and just about all Class III trailers will have electric brakes. Add to this number an accessories wire, to operate trailer internal equipment or to charge the trailer's battery, and you can have as many as seven wires in the harness.

Determine the equipment on your trailer and buy the wiring kit necessary. The kit will contain all the wires needed, plus a plug adapter set which includes the female plug, mounted on the bumper or hitch, and the male plug, wired into, or plugged into the trailer harness.

When installing the kit, follow the manufacturer's instructions.

The color coding of the wires is usually standard throughout the industry. One point to note: some domestic vehicles, and most imported vehicles, have separate turn signals. On most domestic vehicles, the brake lights and rear turn signals operate with the same bulb. For those vehicles with separate turn signals, you can purchase an isolation unit so that the brake lights won't blink whenever the turn signals are operated, or, you can go to your local electronics supply house and buy four diodes to wire in series with the brake and turn signal bulbs. Diodes will isolate the brake and turn signals. The choice is yours. The isolation units are simple and quick to install, but far more expensive than the diodes. The diodes, however, require more work to install properly, since they require the cutting of each bulb's wire and soldering in place of the diode.

One, final point, the best kits are those with a spring loaded cover on the vehicle mounted socket. This cover prevents dirt and moisture from corroding the terminals. Never let the vehicle socket hang loosely; always mount it securely to the bumper or hitch.

CIRCUIT PROTECTION

Fuses

The fuse block on all models is located under the left hand side of the instrument panel. All flashers are mounted on the fuse block. Each fuse is marked on the fuse block as to which circuit it is protecting. Some early models also use an in-line 30 amp fuse for the air conditioning hi-blower, located at the cowl relay and an in-line 10 amp, fuse for power antennas.

To determine whether a fuse is blown, remove the suspect fuse and check to see if the element is broken. If so replace the fuse with one of equal amperage value.

1. The fuse block is located under the left hand side of the instrument panel.

Fuse box location—1977 Nova shown

Fusible Links

All models are equipped with fusible links. These links are attached to the lower ends of the main supply wires and connect to the starter solenoid. One of the main wires is a No. 12 red wire which supplies the headlight circuit and the other is a No. 10 red wire which supplies all electrical units except the headlights. The links consist of wire which is several gauges smaller than the supply wires they are connected to and function as additional protection to the wiring. In the event of an overloaded or short circuited condition they will melt before the wiring is damaged elsewhere in the circuit. A burned out fusible link would be indicated by: all the electrical accessories dead except the headlights or, headlights dead but all other electrical units operative.

REPLACEMENT

1. Disconnect the battery ground cable.
2. Disconnect the fusible link from the junction block or starter solenoid.
3. Cut the harness directly behind the connector to remove the damaged fusible link.
4. Strip the harness wire approximately ½ in.
5. Connect the new fusible link to the harness wire using a crimp on connector. Solder the connection using resin core solder.
6. Tape all exposed wires with plastic electrical tape.
7. Connect the fusible link to the junction block or starter solenoid and reconnect the battery ground cable.

Circuit Breakers

Circuit breakers are also located in the fuse block. A circuit breaker is an electrical switch which breaks the circuit during an electrical overload. The circuit breaker will remain open until the short or overload condition in the circuit is corrected.

To replace the breaker, pull it out from the fuse block.

Flashers

REPLACEMENT

The turn signal flasher is located under the dash either to the left or right of the steering column on most models. The lower dash panel may have to be removed to gain access to the unit. The hazard flasher is located in the fuse block.

Fuses and Circuit Breakers

1962–66 Chevy II

Circuit	Amps
Instrument and clock lamps	3
Tail, stop, and dome lamps	15
Radio	*
Heater	10
Air Conditioning (including heater)	20
Back-up and parking brake indicator lamps	10
Windshield wiper motor	20

* 1962–63, 4 amps; 1964–65, 2.5 amps; 1966, 3 amps.

1967 Chevy II

Circuit	Amps
Instrument lamps	4
Stop and tail lamps	20
Clock, lighter, courtesy, and hazard warning lamps	20
Air conditioning (including heater)	25
Inline air conditioner fuses:	
All weather system—between horn relay and air conditioner relay	20
Universal system—between ignition switch and control switch	10
Windshield wiper motor and radio	20

1968 Chevy II and 1969–70 Nova

Circuit	Amps
Instrument lamps	4
Radio, accessories, and tape player	10
Heater and air conditioning	25
Tail, side marker, and parking lamps	20
Stop and hazard warning lamps	20
Lighter, courtesy, dome, and clock lamps	20
Back-up, turn signal, and cruise control circuits (1968–69)	20

Fuses and Circuit Breakers

1968 Chevy II and
1969–70 Nova

Circuit	Amps
Back-up, turn signal, cruise control, and heater circuits (1970)	25
Gauges and Tell-tale lamps	10
Windshield wiper/washer (1968–69)	20
(1970)	25
Inline air conditioner fuses—located between horn relay and air conditioner relay:	
GM Chevrolet	20
Four Season	30
Air conditioning and transmission controlled spark solenoid (1970 only)	25

1971 Nova

Circuit	Amps
Instrument, dome and console lamps	4
Radio, transmission-controlled spark solenoid, rear window defogger, and glove compartment lamp	10
Windshield wipers	25
Stop and hazard warning lamps	20
Turn signal and back-up lamps	20
Heater and/or air conditioning	25
Inline air conditioner fuse—located between horn relay or junction box and air conditioner relay	30
Gauges, warning lamps, antidiesel relay, and blocking relay	10
Clock, lighter, and courtesy lamps	20
Tail, parking, side marker, luggage, and license plate lamps	20

NOTE: On 1972 and later models, the fuse box, located on the firewall under the left side of the dash, is clearly marked as to fuse amperage ratings and primary accessories serviced by each circuit. Therefore, fuse ratings and circuits are not listed here.

Fusible Links—1962–77

Location	Wire Color/Gauge
Molded splice at solenoid "Bat" terminal	Brown/14
Molded splice at horn relay	Black/16
Molded splice in voltage regulator #3 terminal wire	Orange/20
Molded splice in voltage regulator (both sides of meter)	Orange/20

Fusible Links—1978–79

Location	Wire Color/Gauge
Molded splice at solenoid "Bat" terminal	Red/14
Fusible link at junction block	Red/16
Battery feed to voltage regulator #3 terminal in-line fusible link	Red/20
Ammeter circuit and battery-to-starter circuit, at junction block, both molded splices	Red/20

Light Bulb Specifications 1978–79

Application	Bulb No.
Headlamp	6012
Front park/directional	1157
Side marker lamps	194
Tail/stop/rear directional	1157
License plate lamp	194
Back-up	1156
Courtesy	631
Dome	561
Instrument illumination	168
Auto trans. selector	1445
High beam, generator, oil, temperature, brake warning, turn signal, seat belt warning indicators, and wiper control lamp	194
Heater/AC panel light	194
Glove box	1891
Radio dial	1893
Stereo indicator	DS410
Underhood light	93
Luggage compartment light	1003

Light Bulb Specifications—1962–77

Application	Model Year					
	1962–63	1964–65	1966–67	1968–69	1970–71	1972–77
Headlamp	6012	6012	6012	6012	6012	6014
Parking and front turn signal lamp	1034	1157	1157	1157	1157NA	1157
Tail, stop, and rear turn signal lamp	1034	1157	1157	1157	1157	1157
Front side marker lamp	—	—	—	194A②	194A	194
Rear side marker lamp	—	—	—	194	194	194
Back-up lamp	1073	1156	1156	1156	1156	1156
License plate lamp	67	1155	1155	67	67	67
Instrument lamps	1816	1816	1895	168	168	168
Turn signal indicator lamp	57	1895	1895	194	194	194
Generator, headlamp high-beam, low fuel, oil pressure, and temperature indicator lamps	57	1895	1895	194	194	194
Parking brake indicator lamp	257	257	257①	194	194	194
Heater or air conditioning control panel lamp	—	—	—	1445	1895	1895
Radio dial lamp	1891	1893	1893	1893	④	⑤⑥
Glove compartment lamp	57	1895	1895	1895	1895	1895
Console lamp	—	—	—	1895③	1816	1816
Dome lamp	211	211	211	211	211	211
Courtesy lamp	89	631	—	—	631	631
Engine compartment lamp	—	—	—	93	93	93

① 1967 Chevy II, 1895
② 1969 Nova, 194
③ 1969 Nova, 1445
④ AM only, 216; all except AM, 1893
⑤ AM only, 293; all except AM, 1893; stereo indicator, 2182
⑥ 1973–75—AM only, 293; AM/FM, 1893; AM/FM dial (stereo), 564 or 1893; stereo indicator, Drake 66

WIRING DIAGRAMS

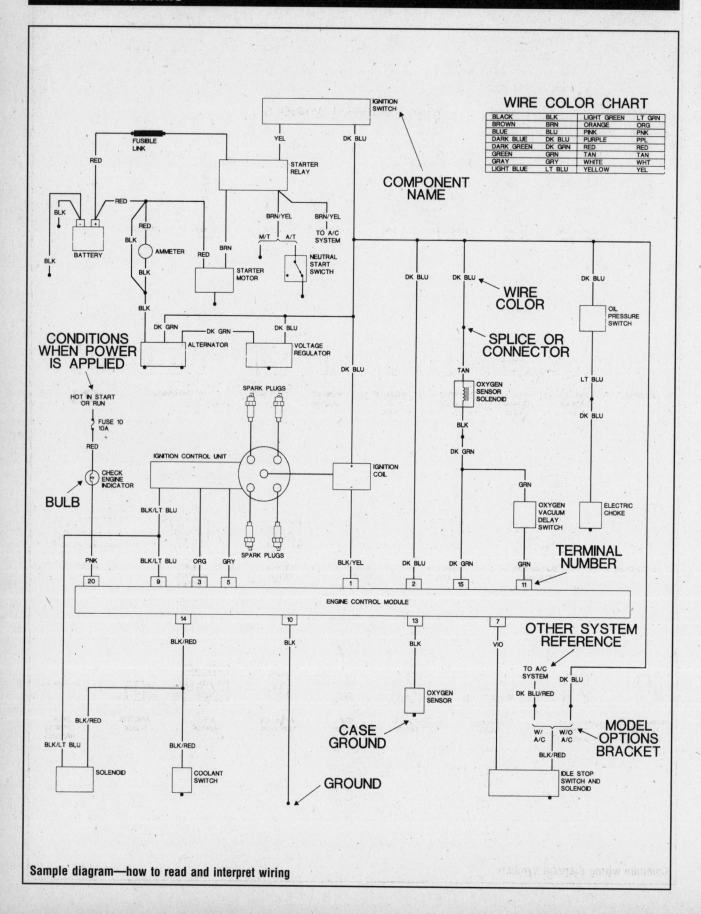

WIRE COLOR CHART			
BLACK	BLK	LIGHT GREEN	LT GRN
BROWN	BRN	ORANGE	ORG
BLUE	BLU	PINK	PNK
DARK BLUE	DK BLU	PURPLE	PPL
DARK GREEN	DK GRN	RED	RED
GREEN	GRN	TAN	TAN
GRAY	GRY	WHITE	WHT
LIGHT BLUE	LT BLU	YELLOW	YEL

Sample diagram—how to read and interpret wiring

WIRING DIAGRAM SYMBOLS

| BATTERY | CONNECTOR OR SPLICE | CIRCUIT BREAKER | CAPACITOR | COIL | DIODE | FUSE | FUSIBLE LINK | GROUND | LED |

| RESISTOR | SINGLE FILAMENT BULB | DUAL FILAMENT BULB | HEATING ELEMENT | SOLENOID OR COIL | VARIABLE RESISTOR | CRYSTAL | POTENTIOMETER | HORN OR SPEAKER |

| ALTERNATOR | DISTRIBUTOR ASSEMBLY | IGNITION COIL | SPARK PLUG | STEPPER MOTOR | HEAT ACTIVATED SWITCH | RELAY |

| NORMALLY OPEN SWITCH | NORMALLY CLOSED SWITCH | GANGED SWITCH | 3-POSITION SWITCH | REED SWITCH | MOTOR OR ACTUATOR | SPEED SENSOR | JUNCTION BLOCK | MODEL OPTIONS BRACKET |

Common wiring diagram symbols

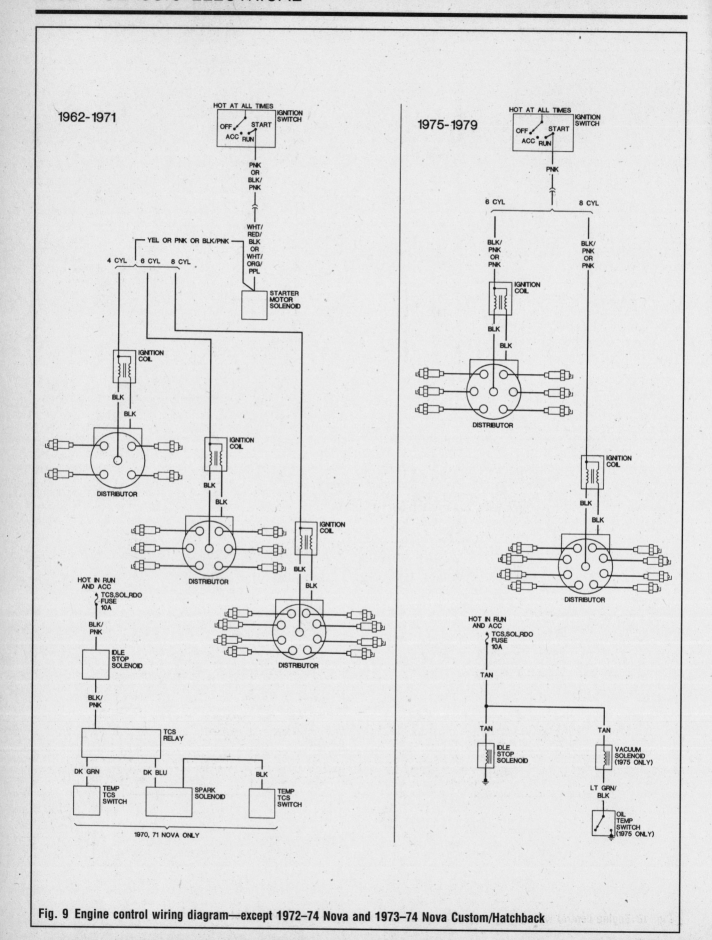

Fig. 9 Engine control wiring diagram—except 1972-74 Nova and 1973-74 Nova Custom/Hatchback

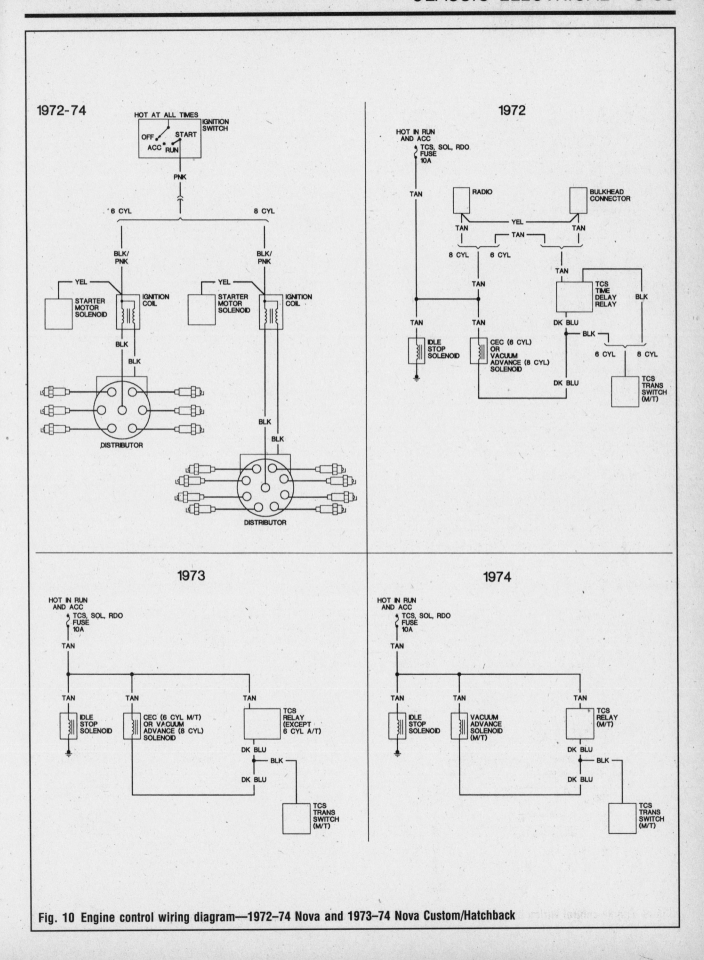

Fig. 10 Engine control wiring diagram—1972–74 Nova and 1973–74 Nova Custom/Hatchback

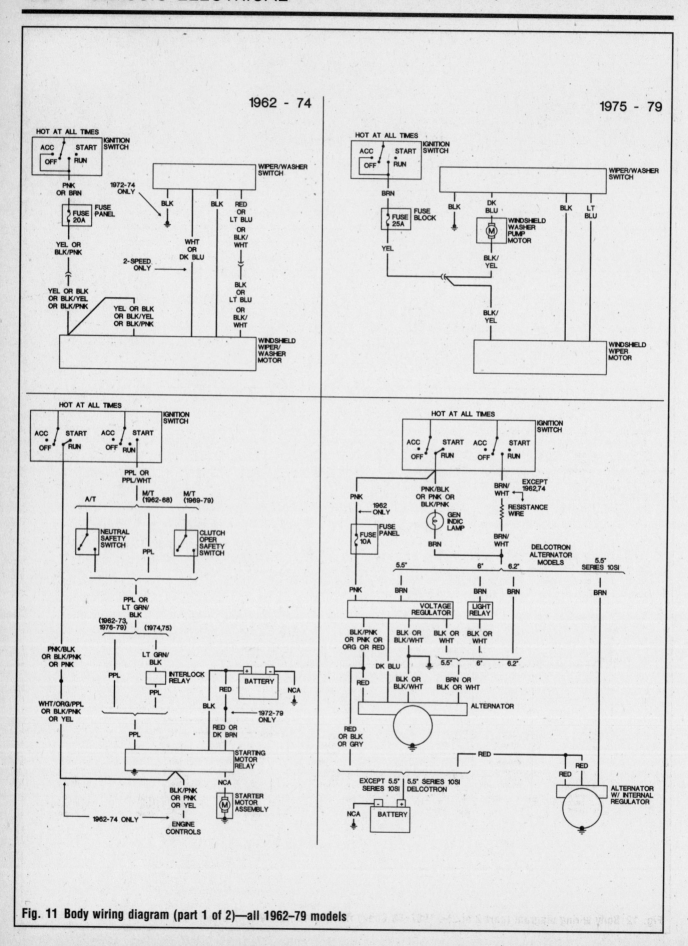

Fig. 11 Body wiring diagram (part 1 of 2)—all 1962–79 models

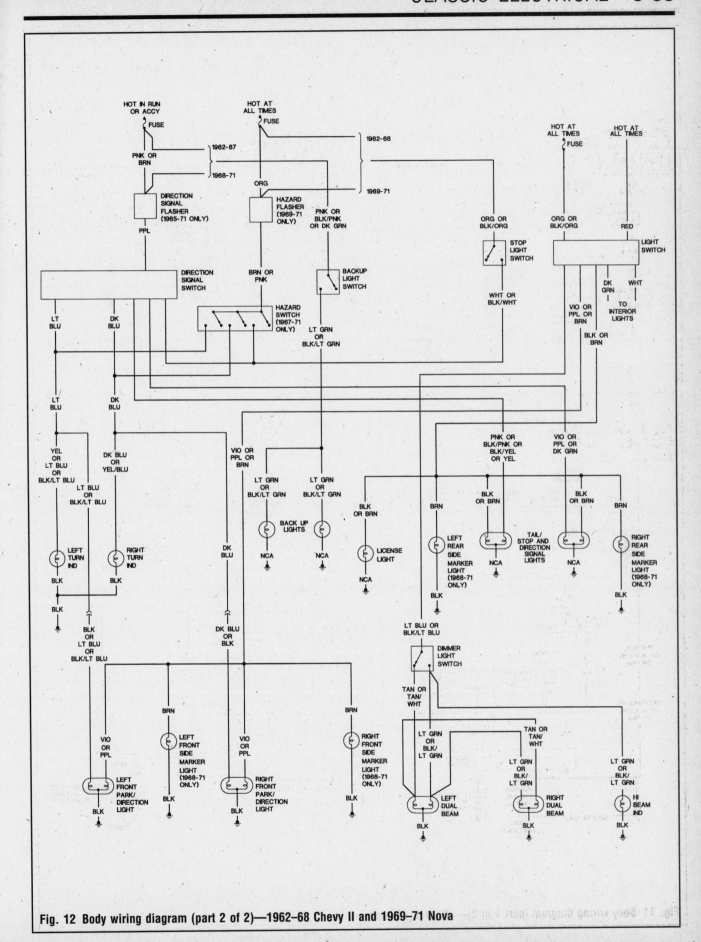

Fig. 12 Body wiring diagram (part 2 of 2)—1962–68 Chevy II and 1969–71 Nova

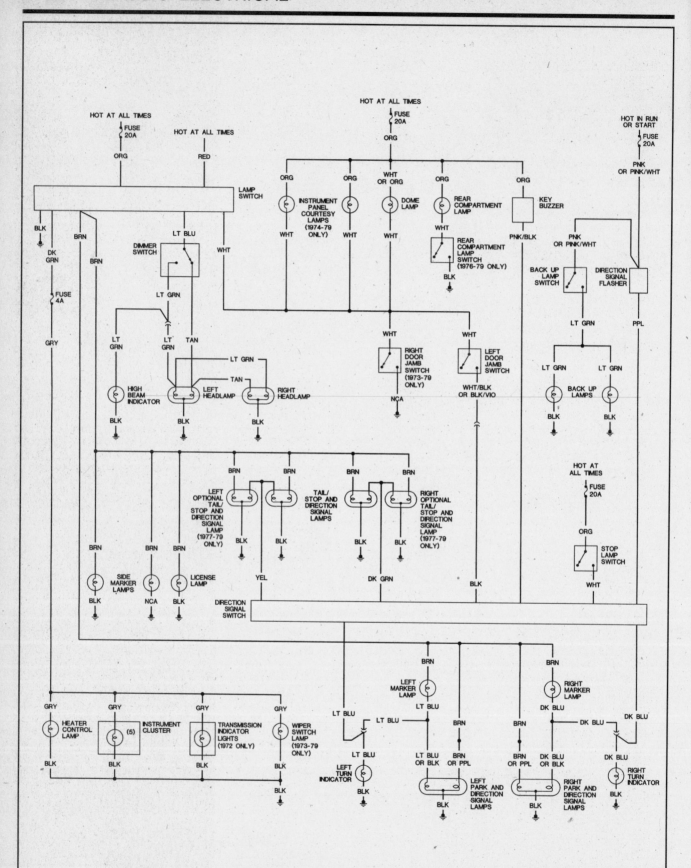

Fig. 13 Body wiring diagram (part 2 of 2)—1972–79 Nova, 1973–79 Nova Custom/Hatchback, 1975 Nova LN and 1976–77 Concours

MANUAL TRANSMISSION 7-2
UNDERSTANDING THE MANUAL
  TRANSMISSION 7-2
ADJUSTMENTS 7-2
  LINKAGE 7-2
TRANSMISSION 7-5
  REMOVAL & INSTALLATION 7-5
CLUTCH 7-5
UNDERSTANDING THE CLUTCH 7-5
DRIVEN DISC AND PRESSURE
  PLATE 7-6
  REMOVAL & INSTALLATION 7-6
ADJUSTMENT 7-10
  LINKAGE & FREE-PLAY 7-10
AUTOMATIC TRANSMISSION 7-12
UNDERSTANDING AUTOMATIC
  TRANSMISSIONS 7-12
  TORQUE CONVERTER 7-12
  PLANETARY GEARBOX 7-12
  SERVOS & ACCUMULATORS 7-13
  HYDRAULIC CONTROL
    SYSTEM 7-13
ADJUSTMENTS 7-14
  SHIFT LINKAGE 7-14
  THROTTLE VALVE LINKAGE 7-16
  DETENT CABLE 7-17
  DETENT SWITCH 7-17
NEUTRAL SAFETY SWITCH 7-18
  REMOVAL & INSTALLATION 7-18
  ADJUSTMENTS 7-18
FLUID PAN 7-19
  REMOVAL & INSTALLATION 7-19
TRANSMISSION 7-20
  REMOVAL & INSTALLATION 7-20
DRIVELINE 7-21
DRIVESHAFT AND U-JOINTS 7-22
  DRIVESHAFT REMOVAL &
    INSTALLATION 7-22
  U-JOINT OVERHAUL 7-24
REAR AXLE 7-25
UNDERSTANDING REAR AXLES 7-25
AXLE SHAFTS AND BEARINGS 7-25
  REMOVAL, OVERHAUL &
    INSTALLATION 7-25
DETERMINING AXLE RATIO 7-28
  1962 VEHICLES 7-28
  1963 VEHICLES 7-28
  1964 VEHICLES 7-28
  1965 VEHICLES 7-28
  1966 VEHICLES 7-29
  1967 VEHICLES 7-29
  1968 VEHICLES 7-29
  1969 VEHICLES 7-29
  1970 VEHICLES 7-29
  1971 VEHICLES 7-30
  1972 VEHICLES 7-30
  1973–74 VEHICLES 7-30
  1975–77 VEHICLES 7-30

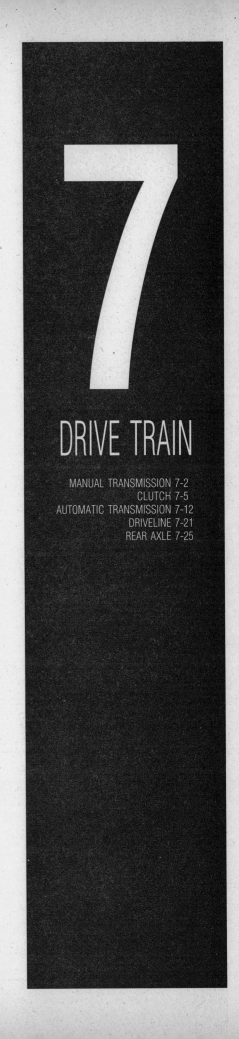

7
DRIVE TRAIN

MANUAL TRANSMISSION 7-2
CLUTCH 7-5
AUTOMATIC TRANSMISSION 7-12
DRIVELINE 7-21
REAR AXLE 7-25

MANUAL TRANSMISSION

Understanding the Manual Transmission

Because of the way an internal combustion engine breathes, it can produce torque (or twisting force) only within a narrow speed range. Most overhead valve pushrod engines must turn at about 2500 rpm to produce their peak torque. Often by 4500 rpm, they are producing so little torque that continued increases in engine speed produce no power increases.

The torque peak on overhead camshaft engines is, generally, much higher, but much narrower.

The manual transmission and clutch are employed to vary the relationship between engine RPM and the speed of the wheels so that adequate power can be produced under all circumstances. The clutch allows engine torque to be applied to the transmission input shaft gradually, due to mechanical slippage. The vehicle can, consequently, be started smoothly from a full stop.

The transmission changes the ratio between the rotating speeds of the engine and the wheels by the use of gears. 4-speed or 5-speed transmissions are most common. The lower gears allow full engine power to be applied to the rear wheels during acceleration at low speeds.

The clutch driveplate is a thin disc, the center of which is splined to the transmission input shaft. Both sides of the disc are covered with a layer of material which is similar to brake lining and which is capable of allowing slippage without roughness or excessive noise.

The clutch cover is bolted to the engine flywheel and incorporates a diaphragm spring which provides the pressure to engage the clutch. The cover also houses the pressure plate. When the clutch pedal is released, the driven disc is sandwiched between the pressure plate and the smooth surface of the flywheel, thus forcing the disc to turn at the same speed as the engine crankshaft.

The transmission contains a mainshaft which passes all the way through the transmission, from the clutch to the driveshaft. This shaft is separated at one point, so that front and rear portions can turn at different speeds.

Power is transmitted by a countershaft in the lower gears and reverse. The gears of the countershaft mesh with gears on the mainshaft, allowing power to be carried from one to the other. Countershaft gears are often integral with that shaft, while several of the mainshaft gears can either rotate independently of the shaft or be locked to it. Shifting from one gear to the next causes one of the gears to be freed from rotating with the shaft and locks another to it. Gears are locked and unlocked by internal dog clutches which slide between the center of the gear and the shaft. The forward gears usually employ synchronizers; friction members which smoothly bring gear and shaft to the same speed before the toothed dog clutches are engaged.

Adjustments

LINKAGE

3-Speed Column Shift

◆ **See Figures 1, 2 and 3**

1962–67 VEHICLES

1. Position both transmission levers in Neutral.
2. Position the column selector in neutral. Align the first/reverse and second/third shifter tube levers on the steering jacket.
3. Install the control rods on the steering jacket levers and secure them with lock clips.
4. Install a swivel on the first/reverse shifter control rod, and adjust until the swivel can freely enter the transmission shift lever hole (rear). Install a retaining clip on the swivel, insert the swivel in the lever hole, and secure it with a nut.
5. Install the second/third lower rod to the frame-mounted idler lever and in the second/third lower rod to the frame-mounted idler

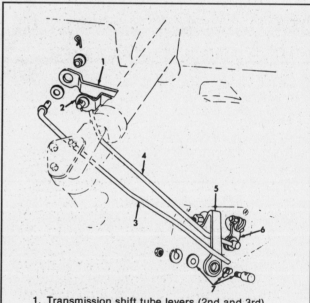

1. Transmission shift tube levers (2nd and 3rd)
2. Transmission shift tube levers (1st and Reverse)
3. Shift control rod (2nd and 3rd)
4. Shift control rod (1st and Reverse)
5. Transmission shift levers (2nd and 3rd)
6. Transmission shift levers (1st and Reverse)
7. Swivel assembly

Fig. 1 3-speed column shift linkage adjustment—1962–67 vehicles

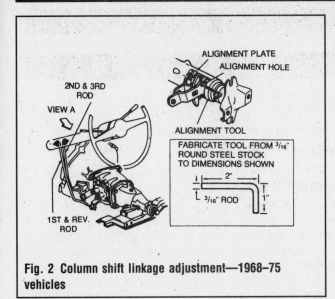

Fig. 2 Column shift linkage adjustment—1968-75 vehicles

ment tool may be fabricated from a ³⁄₁₆ in. rod as shown in the accompanying illustration.

1. Loosen the swivel locking clamps on both shift rods. The shift rods should freely pass through the swivels.

2. Position the shift lever on the column in Neutral. Insert the adjustment tool through the first/reverse lever, the relay lever, and the second/third lever and then into the alignment plate on the steering jacket.

3. Position the shift levers on the transmission into Neutral.

4. Tighten both the swivel locking clamp nuts on the rods while holding the swivel with one hand.

5. Remove the adjustment tool. Shift the transmission through the gears, and then place it into Neutral. Insert the tool through the alignment holes and the bracket.

6. If the tool doesn't freely pass through the holes and bracket, loosen the clamps and readjust the linkage.

1969 VEHICLES

1. Position the ignition switch to the **OFF** position.

2. Loosen the swivel locknuts on both shift rods. The shift rods should pass freely through the swivels.

3. Move both the column shift lever and the transmission first/reverse lever into reverse detent position, and then tighten the swivel locknut.

4. Move the column and transmission levers into Neutral. Insert the adjustment tool into the lever alignment holes and the alignment plate.

5. While holding the second/third control rod and swivel, tighten the swivel locknut.

6. Remove the adjusting tool. Shift the column lever into Reverse, turn the ignition switch to **LOCK** position, and check the interlock control. If the interlock binds, leave the switch in lock and readjust the first/reverse rod at the swivel.

7. Check the shifting pattern of the transmission and then place it in Neutral. Insert the adjusting tool through the levers and the bracket. If it does not go through easily, loosen the swivel locknut and readjust the linkage.

lever and in the second/third transmission lever and secure with retaining clips.

6. Install the upper second/third shifter control rod, in the same manner as the first/reverse shifter control rod (Step 4), to the frame idler and the mast jacket shifter lever.

✳✳ WARNING

Ensure that the shifter tube levers stay in alignment.

7. Check the adjustment by moving the shift lever through all the gear positions.

1968 VEHICLES

Post-1967 column shift cars are equipped with a steering jacket alignment bracket to ease linkage adjustment. An adjust-

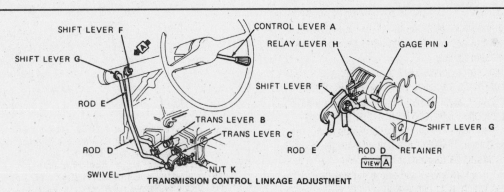

TRANSMISSION CONTROL LINKAGE ADJUSTMENT

1. Set Levers (A) and (C) in "REVERSE" position and turn ignition switch to "LOCK" position. **NOTE** Obtain "REVERSE" position by moving Trans Lever (C) clockwise to forward detent.
2. Attach Rod (D) to Shift Lever (G) with retainer. See View A. Slide swivel onto Rod (D). Insert Swivel with Clamp into Lever (C) and loosely assemble with Nut (K) and washers at this time.
3. Remove column "LASH" by rotating Lever (G) in a downward direction and complete attachment of Rod (D) to Lever (C) by tightening Nut (K) using recommended torque.
4. Turn ignition key to "UNLOCK" position and position Levers (A), (B) and (C) in "NEUTRAL". **NOTE** Obtain "NEUTRAL" position by moving Levers (B) and (C) clockwise to forward detent then counter-clockwise one detent.
5. Align gage holes in Levers (F), (G) and (H) and insert Gage Pin (J). See View A.
6. Repeat steps 2 & 3 for Rod (E) & Levers (B) & (F).
7. Remove Gage Pin (J).

NOTE With shift lever in "REVERSE" the ignition key must move freely to "LOCK" position. It must not be possibly to obtain ignition "LOCK" position in "NEUTRAL" or any gear other than "REVERSE".

Fig. 3 Column shift linkage adjustment procedure—1978-79 vehicles

1970–77 VEHICLES

1. Shift the column lever into Reverse, and turn the ignition into the **LOCK** position.

2. Slacken the shift control rod swivel locknuts. Pull the first/reverse control rod (attached to the column lever) down slightly and then tighten the transmission lever, clevis locknut.

3. Unlock the ignition switch and place the shift lever in Neutral. Place the lower column levers in neutral position, align the lever gauge holes and insert the adjustment tool. (Holes are on the lower side of the levers.)

4. Hold the rod and swivel and tighten the second/third shift control rod locknut.

5. Withdraw the adjustment tool from the levers and check the shift operation. Shift the column lever into reverse and check the interlock operation.

6. When the shift lever is in reverse, the ignition switch should move freely to the **LOCK** position. The ignition switch must not be able to be turned to **LOCK** in any other gear except Reverse.

1978–79 VEHICLES

See the accompanying illustration for the adjustment procedure.

3-Speed Floor Shift

1968–79 VEHICLES

▶ **See Figure 4**

1. Loosen the locknuts on both shift rod swivels. The shift rods should pass freely through the swivels.

2. Move the floor shift to Neutral and install the locating gauge into the shifter bracket assembly.

➡**The locating gauge is a piece of ⅛ in. thick flat stock ⁴¹⁄₆₄ in. wide and 3 in. long.**

3. Position the levers on the transmission in Neutral. Turn the first/reverse shift rod nut down against the swivel, and then tighten the locknut against the swivel.

4. Turn the second/third rod nut down against the swivel, and then tighten the locknut against the swivel.

➡**On 1969 and later cars, skip Step 5 and perform Steps 6–8. Step 5 is the final step for 1968 cars.**

5. Remove the locating gauge, and shift into reverse. Turn the ignition switch to the **LOCK** position.

6. Loosen the swivel locknut on the backdrive control rod. Pull down slightly on the control rod to take up any slack in the column mechanism, and then tighten the clevis jam nut.

7. The ignition switch should move easily in and out of **LOCK.** If there is any binding present keep the switch in lock and readjust the backdrive control rod.

8. Check the shift pattern for correct operation.

4-Speed Floor Shift

▶ **See Figure 5**

1964–68 VEHICLES

1. Remove the control rods from the transmission levers, and position the levers in neutral.

2. Move the floor shift lever into neutral and insert a locating gauge into the bracket assembly. (Use a ⁵⁄₁₆ in. rod on 1964 cars; 1965 and later four-speeds use the same gauge as the three-speed floor shift.)

3. Adjust the length of the control rods, then secure the swivels with the jam nuts and install the clevis pins.

4. Remove the locating gauge and check the shift pattern.

➡**Post-1964 Muncie transmission levers have two control rod holes. Attaching the control rods in the lower holes will result in reduced shift lever travel and allow faster shifting, with increased shifting effort as a drawback.**

1969–79 VEHICLES

1. Turn the ignition switch to the **OFF** position, except on 1970 models which should be turned to lock.

2. Loosen the swivel locknuts on the shift rods and backdrive control rod. Position the transmission side cover levers to their neutral detent positions.

3. Place the floor shift in neutral and insert a locating gauge (same gauge as three-speed floor shift) into the lever bracket assembly.

4. Adjust all control rod swivels for easy entry into their respective levers.

5. Tighten the shift rod locknuts and remove the gauge.

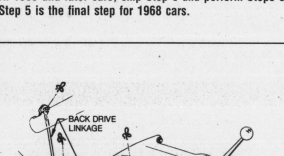

Fig. 4 3-speed floor shift linkage adjustment—1968–75 vehicles

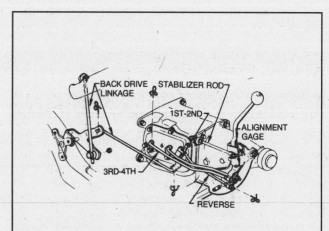

Fig. 5 4-speed floor shift linkage adjustment—1964–79 vehicles

6. Shift the lever into reverse and pull down slightly on the backdrive rod to remove the slack. Tighten the locknut.

7. The ignition switch should now be able to be moved easily into **LOCK,** and it must not be possible to turn the key to lock, when in any other position other than reverse. Readjust the backdrive rod, if necessary.

8. Check the shift pattern for correctness.

Transmission

REMOVAL & INSTALLATION

3-Speed and 4-Speed Transmissions

➡Removal of a three-speed transmission with overdrive is similar to that for a standard transmission, but additionally requires disconnecting the overdrive control cable and electrical connections.

1. On 1977–79 cars, remove the shift lever knob and, if equipped with a four speed, the spring and T-handle. Raise the car high enough for working clearance.

2. Disconnect the speedometer cable and TCS switch connector, if so equipped.

3. Remove the driveshaft as outlined in this section.

4. Support the engine with a jack and remove the crossmember-to-frame bolts.

5. If the car is equipped with a floor shift, remove the crossmember-to-shifter support attaching bolts and the shifter brace-to-crossmember attaching bolts.

6. Remove the transmission mount-to-crossmember bolts.

7. Raise the engine/transmission enough to allow the crossmember to be removed.

8. Remove the linkage from the side cover on column shift cars. It is not necessary to remove the linkage on cars built before 1977 and equipped with floor shifts. Remove the shift lever from the linkage for removal clearance. On 1977–79 cars, remove lever and linkage.

➡The shift lever is attached to the linkage by two bolts on earlier models and a pin and spring clip on later models.

9. On floor shift cars, remove the stabilizer shaft-to-lever assembly retaining nut, and push the bolt to the side until the stabi-

lizer rod can be disconnected. Also, on floor shift cars built in 1977 and later years, remove the bolts attaching the shaft control assembly to the support on the transmission and pull the unit down until the lever clears the boot and remove it.

10. Remove the top two transmission-to-bellhousing bolts and install guide pins in these holes. Remove the bottom two bolts.

➡Use of guide pins will prevent clutch plate damage or displacement during transmission removal. They may be fabricated from two ½ in. × 13 bolts by removing the heads and filing off half the threads.

11. Carefully pull the transmission to the rear, and then down and out of the car.
   To install:
12. To install the transmission, bring it into position with the bellhousing and carefully guide it into the housing.

➡Keep in mind that the input shaft will be going through the throwout bearing, clutch plate, and finally into the crankshaft pilot bearing. The shaft may have to be turned in order for its splines to engage the grooves in the clutch hub.

13. Install the four transmission-to-bell housing bolts and lockwashers and torque them to 55 ft. lbs. on cars built through 1976. On 1977–79 cars, torque 3-speed and 4-speed 76mm bolts to 75 ft. lbs.; 4-speed 83mm bolts to 52 ft. lbs.

14. On 1977–79 cars, slide the shift lever into the rubber boot and position the shift control to the support. Install the bolts retaining the control to the support and torque. Install the shift levers on the transmission of column shift and 1977–79 models. Connect the stabilizer rod to the lever assembly and shift lever on floor shift models.

15. Raise the engine until the crossmember can be reinstalled. Torque the crossmember-to-frame bolts to 25 ft lbs. Remove the engine jack.

16. Install the crossmember-lever support attaching bolts and lever assembly brace-to-crossmember attaching bolts.

17. Install the transmission crossmember-to-mount bolts and torque to 40 ft. lbs.

18. Install the driveshaft as outlined later in this section.

19. Connect the speedometer cable and TCS switch wire, if so equipped.

20. Fill the transmission with SAE 90 gear lubricant and check the operation of the transmission.

CLUTCH

Understanding the Clutch

The purpose of the clutch is to disconnect and connect engine power at the transmission. A vehicle at rest requires a lot of engine torque to get all that weight moving. An internal combustion engine does not develop a high starting torque (unlike steam engines) so it must be allowed to operate without any load until it builds up enough torque to move the vehicle. To a point, torque increases with engine rpm. The clutch allows the engine to build up torque by physically disconnecting the engine from the transmission, relieving the engine of any load or resistance.

The transfer of engine power to the transmission (the load) must be smooth and gradual; if it weren't, drive line components would wear out or break quickly. This gradual power transfer is made possible by gradually releasing the clutch pedal. The clutch disc and pressure plate are the connecting link between the engine and transmission. When the clutch pedal is released, the disc and plate contact each other (the clutch is engaged) physically joining the engine and transmission. When the pedal is pushed in, the disc and plate separate (the clutch is disengaged) disconnecting the engine from the transmission.

Most clutch assemblies consists of the flywheel, the clutch

disc, the clutch pressure plate, the throw out bearing and fork, the actuating linkage and the pedal. The flywheel and clutch pressure plate (driving members) are connected to the engine crankshaft and rotate with it. The clutch disc is located between the flywheel and pressure plate, and is splined to the transmission shaft. A driving member is one that is attached to the engine and transfers engine power to a driven member (clutch disc) on the transmission shaft. A driving member (pressure plate) rotates (drives) a driven member (clutch disc) on contact and, in so doing, turns the transmission shaft.

There is a circular diaphragm spring within the pressure plate cover (transmission side). In a relaxed state (when the clutch pedal is fully released) this spring is convex; that is, it is dished outward toward the transmission. Pushing in the clutch pedal actuates the attached linkage. Connected to the other end of this is the throw out fork, which hold the throw out bearing. When the clutch pedal is depressed, the clutch linkage pushes the fork and bearing forward to contact the diaphragm spring of the pressure plate. The outer edges of the spring are secured to the pressure plate and are pivoted on rings so that when the center of the spring is compressed by the throw out bearing, the outer edges bow outward and, by so doing, pull the pressure plate in the same direction away from the clutch disc. This action separates the disc from the plate, disengaging the clutch and allowing the transmission to be shifted into another gear. A coil type clutchturn spring attached to the clutch pedal arm permits full release of the pedal. Releasing the pedal pulls the throw out bearing away from the diaphragm spring resulting in a reversal of spring position. As bearing pressure is gradually released from the spring center, the outer edges of the spring bow outward, pushing the pressure plate into closer contact with the clutch disc. As the disc and plate move closer together, friction between the two increases and slippage is reduced until, when full spring pressure is applied (by fully releasing the pedal) the speed of the disc and plate are the same. This stops all slipping, creating a direct connection between the plate and disc which results in the transfer of power from the engine to the transmission. The clutch disc is now rotating with the pressure plate at engine speed and, because it is splined to the transmission shaft, the shaft now turns at the same engine speed.

The clutch is operating properly if:

1. It will stall the engine when released with the vehicle held stationary.

2. The shift lever can be moved freely between 1st and reverse gears when the vehicle is stationary and the clutch disengaged.

A diaphragm type clutch assembly is used on all Chevy II and Nova models. A flat-finger diaphragm clutch is used for most engine/transmission combinations except V8s with a four-speed transmission, which use a bent-finger, centrifugal-diaphragm clutch assembly. In this design, the release fingers are bent back to gain a centrifugal boost and to ensure quick reengagement at high engine speeds.

Clutch throwout bearings used with the flat- and bent-finger diaphragms are not interchangeable. The flat-finger throwout bearing measures $1\frac{7}{8}$ in. in height, and the bent-finger $1\frac{1}{4}$ in.

The only service adjustment necessary on the clutch is to maintain the correct pedal free-play. Clutch pedal free-play, or throwout bearing lash, decreases with driven disc wear.

Driven Disc and Pressure Plate

REMOVAL & INSTALLATION

▶ **See Figure 6**

1. Remove the transmission as previously outlined.
2. Disconnect the clutch fork pushrod and spring.
3. Remove the bellhousing.
4. Slide the clutch fork from the ball stud and remove the fork from the dust boot. The ball stud is threaded into the bellhousing, and may be replaced if worn.
5. Install a clutch pilot tool to support the clutch assembly during removal. Mark the flywheel and clutch cover for reinstallation, if the factory "X" marks are not visible.
6. Loosen the clutch-to-flywheel attaching bolts evenly, one turn at a time, until spring pressure is released. Remove the bolts and lift out the clutch assembly.
7. Clean the transmission, clutch fork, and bell housing. Clean the flywheel surface with other than an oil-based solvent. Wash your hands before installing or handling the clutch assembly parts. Hold the clutch disc by the center hub only.

➡**Before assembly, slide the clutch disc up and down on the transmission input shaft to check for any binding. Remove any rough spots with crocus cloth and then coat the shaft lightly with Lubriplate®.**

To install:

8. Support the clutch disc and pressure plate with the pilot tool. The driven disc is installed with the damper springs on the transmission side. The grease slinger is always on the transmission side.
9. Turn the clutch assembly until the previously made mark on the cover lines up with the mark on the flywheel, then install the retaining bolts. Tighten the bolts evenly to avoid distortion. Torque the bolts to 15–20 ft. lbs. (6-cylinder engine), or 30–35 ft. lbs. (V8).
10. Remove the clutch pilot tool.
11. Lubricate the ball socket and fork fingers at the throwout bearing end with a high melting-point grease. Lubricate the inside recess of the throwout bearing and throwout fork groove with a light coat of graphite grease.
12. Install the clutch fork and dust boot into the housing. Install the throwout bearing into the fork.

➡**All three of these parts should be carefully examined for wear or damage. Replacement of these components is cheap insurance for a dependable clutch installation.**

13. Install the bell housing and transmission as outlined in the Transmission removal and installation procedure, earlier in this section.
14. Connect the fork pushrod and spring. Lubricate the spring and pushrod ends.
15. Adjust the shift linkage and clutch pedal free-play.

Typical clutch alignment tool, note how the splines match the transmission's input shaft

Check across the flywheel surface, it should be flat

Loosen and remove the clutch and pressure plate bolts evenly, a little at a time . . .

If necessary, lock the flywheel in place and remove the retaining bolts . . .

. . . then carefully remove the clutch and pressure plate assembly from the flywheel

. . . then remove the flywheel from the crankshaft in order replace it or have it machined

Upon installation, it is usually a good idea to apply a thread-locking compound to the flywheel bolts

Install a clutch alignment arbor, to align the clutch assembly during installation

Check the pressure plate for excessive wear

Clutch plate installed with the arbor in place

Be sure that the flywheel surface is clean, before installing the clutch

Clutch plate and pressure plate installed with the alignment arbor in place

Pressure plate-to-flywheel bolt holes should align

Install the clutch assembly bolts and tighten in steps, using an X pattern

You may want to use a thread locking compound on the clutch assembly bolts

Be sure to use a torque wrench to tighten all bolts

View of the clutch and pressure plate assembly

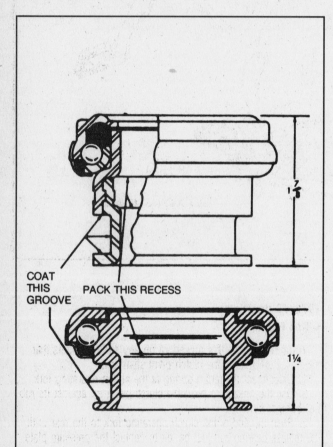

COAT
THIS
GROOVE

PACK THIS RECESS

1⅞

1¼

Fig. 6 Clutch release bearing lubrication—flat finger type shown on the top, bent finger type shown on the bottom

Adjustment

LINKAGE & FREE-PLAY

This adjustment is made from under the car. Free-play is measured at the clutch pedal.

1962–67 Vehicles
▶ **See Figure 7**

4 AND 6-CYLINDER ENGINES

1. Loosen the nut at the forward end of the clutch fork pushrod.
2. Using a wrench on the machined flat at the pedal end of the clutch fork pushrod, lengthen or shorten the rod in the swivel to allow ¾–1 in. free travel at the clutch pedal. Shortening the rod will increase free travel and vice versa.
3. Hold the pushrod at its machined flat and tighten the locknut.

V8 ENGINES

This clutch linkage has a two section clutch fork pushrod.
1. Loosen the locknut.
2. Turn the adjusting rod section of the pushrod until a clearance of ³⁄₁₆ in. is obtained between the clutch fork and the end of the pushrod.
3. Torque the locknut to 8–12 ft lbs. Check the free travel at the clutch pedal, which should be ¾–1⅛ in. for 1964–65 models, or 1–1½ in. for 1966–67 models.

1968–71 Vehicles
▶ **See Figure 8**

4 AND 6-CYLINDER ENGINES

1. Disconnect the return spring at the clutch fork.
2. While holding the clutch pedal against the stop, loosen the locknut enough to allow the adjusting rod to be turned out of its swivel and against the clutch fork until the throwout bearing just touches the clutch fingers.
3. Turn the pushrod three turns and tighten the locknut.
4. Install the return spring and check for the correct pedal free travel, which should be 1–1⅛ in. for 1968–70 models, or 1–1½ in. for 1971–72 models.

V8 ENGINES

The adjustment is the same as for the 1968–71 4 and 6-cylinder models, except that the V8 models have a two-section clutch fork pushrod. In this case, turn the adjusting rod section of the pushrod to obtain the correct clutch pedal free travel.

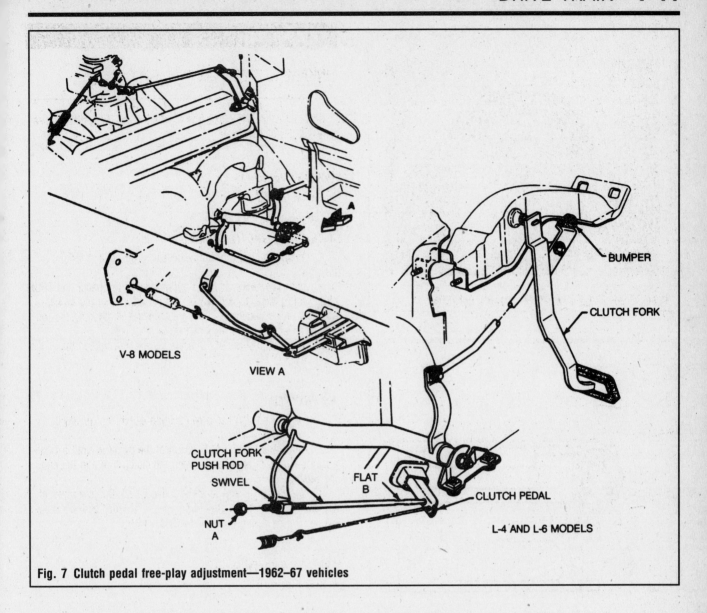

V-8 MODELS

VIEW A

CLUTCH FORK
PUSH ROD

SWIVEL

NUT
A

FLAT
B

BUMPER

CLUTCH FORK

CLUTCH PEDAL

L-4 AND L-6 MODELS

Fig. 7 Clutch pedal free-play adjustment—1962–67 vehicles

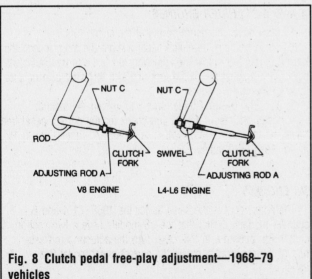

NUT C

ROD

CLUTCH
FORK

ADJUSTING ROD A

V8 ENGINE

NUT C

SWIVEL

CLUTCH
FORK

ADJUSTING ROD A

L4-L6 ENGINE

Fig. 8 Clutch pedal free-play adjustment—1968–79 vehicles

1972–79 Vehicles
♦ **See Figure 8**

You can also use this procedure on any earlier models that have a gauge hole in the clutch pivot shaft arm.

1. Disconnect the return spring at the clutch operating fork.
2. Use the linkage to push the clutch pedal up against its rubber bumper stop.
3. Push the end of the clutch operating fork to the rear until the release bearing can just be felt to contact the pressure plate fingers.
4. Detach the front end of the operating rod from the clutch pivot shaft arm and place it in the gauge hole on the arm.
5. Loosen the locknut and lengthen the rod just enough to take all the play out of the linkage. Tighten the locknut.
6. Replace the operating rod in its original location.
7. Replace the return spring and check the free-play at the pedal pad. It should be about 1 in. or more.

AUTOMATIC TRANSMISSION

Understanding Automatic Transmissions

The automatic transmission allows engine torque and power to be transmitted to the rear wheels within a narrow range of engine operating speeds. It will allow the engine to turn fast enough to produce plenty of power and torque at very low speeds, while keeping it at a sensible rpm at high vehicle speeds (and it does this job without driver assistance). The transmission uses a light fluid as the medium for the transmission of power. This fluid also works in the operation of various hydraulic control circuits and as a lubricant. Because the transmission fluid performs all of these functions, trouble within the unit can easily travel from one part to another. For this reason, and because of the complexity and unusual operating principles of the transmission, a very sound understanding of the basic principles of operation will simplify troubleshooting.

TORQUE CONVERTER

The torque converter replaces the conventional clutch. It has three functions:

1. It allows the engine to idle with the vehicle at a standstill, even with the transmission in gear.

2. It allows the transmission to shift from range-to-range smoothly, without requiring that the driver close the throttle during the shift.

3. It multiplies engine torque to an increasing extent as vehicle speed drops and throttle opening is increased. This has the effect of making the transmission more responsive and reduces the amount of shifting required.

The torque converter is a metal case which is shaped like a sphere that has been flattened on opposite sides. It is bolted to the rear end of the engine's crankshaft. Generally, the entire metal case rotates at engine speed and serves as the engine's flywheel.

The case contains three sets of blades. One set is attached di-

rectly to the case. This set forms the torus or pump. Another set is directly connected to the output shaft, and forms the turbine. The third set is mounted on a hub which, in turn, is mounted on a stationary shaft through a one-way clutch. This third set is known as the stator.

A pump, which is driven by the converter hub at engine speed, keeps the torque converter full of transmission fluid at all times. Fluid flows continuously through the unit to provide cooling.

Under low speed acceleration, the torque converter functions as follows:

The torus is turning faster than the turbine. It picks up fluid at the center of the converter and, through centrifugal force, slings it outward. Since the outer edge of the converter moves faster than the portions at the center, the fluid picks up speed.

The fluid then enters the outer edge of the turbine blades. It then travels back toward the center of the converter case along the turbine blades. In impinging upon the turbine blades, the fluid loses the energy picked up in the torus.

If the fluid was now returned directly into the torus, both halves of the converter would have to turn at approximately the same speed at all times, and torque input and output would both be the same.

In flowing through the torus and turbine, the fluid picks up two types of flow, or flow in two separate directions. It flows through the turbine blades, and it spins with the engine. The stator, whose blades are stationary when the vehicle is being accelerated at low speeds, converts one type of flow into another. Instead of allowing the fluid to flow straight back into the torus, the stator's curved blades turn the fluid almost 90° toward the direction of rotation of the engine. Thus the fluid does not flow as fast toward the torus, but is already spinning when the torus picks it up. This has the effect of allowing the torus to turn much faster than the turbine. This difference in speed may be compared to the difference in speed between the smaller and larger gears in any gear train. The result is that engine power output is higher, and engine torque is multiplied.

As the speed of the turbine increases, the fluid spins faster and faster in the direction of engine rotation. As a result, the ability of the stator to redirect the fluid flow is reduced. Under cruising conditions, the stator is eventually forced to rotate on its one-way clutch in the direction of engine rotation. Under these conditions, the torque converter begins to behave almost like a solid shaft, with the torus and turbine speeds being almost equal.

PLANETARY GEARBOX

The ability of the torque converter to multiply engine torque is limited. Also, the unit tends to be more efficient when the turbine is rotating at relatively high speeds. Therefore, a planetary gearbox is used to carry the power output of the turbine to the driveshaft.

Planetary gears function very similarly to conventional transmission gears. However, their construction is different in that three elements make up one gear system, and, in that all three elements are different from one another. The three elements are: an outer gear that is shaped like a hoop, with teeth cut into the inner surface; a sun gear, mounted on a shaft and located at the very center of the outer gear; and a set of three planet gears, held by pins

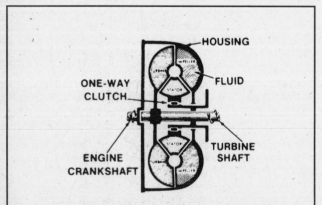

The torque converter housing is rotated by the engine's crankshaft, and turns the impeller—The impeller then spins the turbine, which gives motion to the turbine shaft, driving the gears

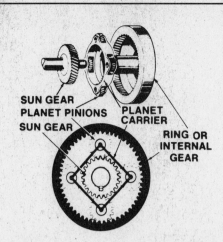

Planetary gears work in a similar fashion to manual transmission gears, but are composed of three parts

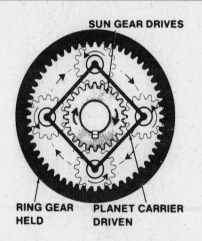

Planetary gears in the maximum reduction (low) range. The ring gear is held and a lower gear ratio is obtained

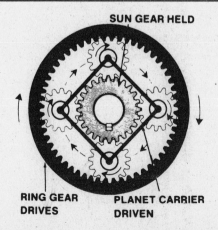

Planetary gears in the minimum reduction (drive) range. The ring gear is allowed to revolve, providing a higher gear ratio

in a ring-like planet carrier, meshing with both the sun gear and the outer gear. Either the outer gear or the sun gear may be held stationary, providing more than one possible torque multiplication factor for each set of gears. Also, if all three gears are forced to rotate at the same speed, the gearset forms, in effect, a solid shaft.

Most automatics use the planetary gears to provide various reductions ratios. Bands and clutches are used to hold various portions of the gearsets to the transmission case or to the shaft on which they are mounted. Shifting is accomplished, then, by changing the portion of each planetary gearset which is held to the transmission case or to the shaft.

SERVOS & ACCUMULATORS

The servos are hydraulic pistons and cylinders. They resemble the hydraulic actuators used on many other machines, such as bulldozers. Hydraulic fluid enters the cylinder, under pressure, and forces the piston to move to engage the band or clutches.

The accumulators are used to cushion the engagement of the servos. The transmission fluid must pass through the accumulator on the way to the servo. The accumulator housing contains a thin piston which is sprung away from the discharge passage of the accumulator. When fluid passes through the accumulator on the way to the servo, it must move the piston against spring pressure, and this action smooths out the action of the servo.

HYDRAULIC CONTROL SYSTEM

The hydraulic pressure used to operate the servos comes from the main transmission oil pump. This fluid is channeled to the various servos through the shift valves. There is generally a manual shift valve which is operated by the transmission selector lever and an automatic shift valve for each automatic upshift the transmission provides.

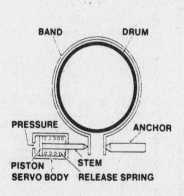

Servos, operated by pressure, are used to apply or release the bands, to either hold the ring gear or allow it to rotate

➡Many new transmissions are electronically controlled. On these models, electrical solenoids are used to better control the hydraulic fluid. Usually, the solenoids are regulated by an electronic control module.

There are two pressures which affect the operation of these valves. One is the governor pressure which is effected by vehicle speed. The other is the modulator pressure which is effected by intake manifold vacuum or throttle position. Governor pressure rises with an increase in vehicle speed, and modulator pressure rises as the throttle is opened wider. By responding to these two pressures, the shift valves cause the upshift points to be delayed with increased throttle opening to make the best use of the engine's power output.

Most transmissions also make use of an auxiliary circuit for downshifting. This circuit may be actuated by the throttle linkage the vacuum line which actuates the modulator, by a cable or by a solenoid. It applies pressure to a special downshift surface on the shift valve or valves.

The transmission modulator also governs the line pressure, used to actuate the servos. In this way, the clutches and bands will be actuated with a force matching the torque output of the engine.

There are two basic automatic transmissions. The first is the two-speed Powerglide which was available until mid-1973. The second type is the three-speed Turbo Hydra-Matic, which is available in four load capacities, Turbo Hydra-Matic 200, 250, 350, and 400.

Adjustments

SHIFT LINKAGE

Powerglide Column Shift

▶ See Figure 9

1. The shift tube and lever assembly must be free in the mast jacket.
2. Lift the selector lever toward the steering wheel and allow the selector lever to be positioned in Drive by the transmission detent.
3. Release the selector lever. The lever should be prevented from engaging low, unless the lever is lifted.
4. Lift the selector lever toward the steering wheel and allow the lever to be positioned in Neutral by the transmission detent.
5. Release the selector lever. The selector lever should now be kept from engaging Reverse unless the lever is lifted. If the linkage is adjusted correctly, the selector lever should be prevented from moving beyond both the neutral detent and the Drive detent unless the lever is lifted to pass over the mechanical stop in the steering column.

If adjustment is necessary, perform the following steps:
6. Adjust the linkage by loosening the adjustment clamp at the cross-shaft. Place the transmission lever in Drive by rotating

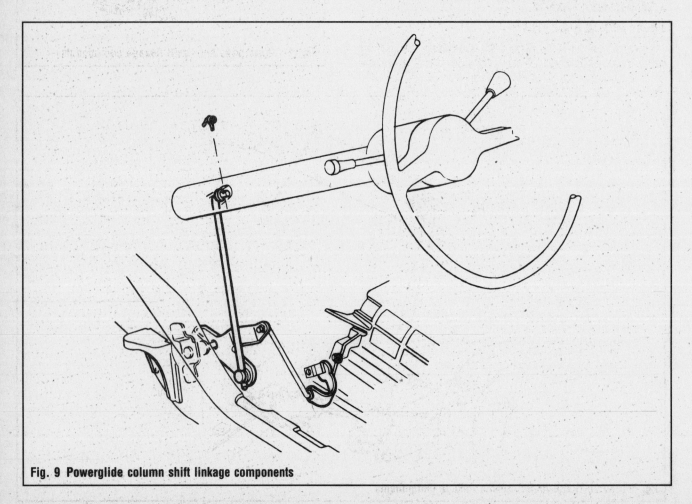

Fig. 9 Powerglide column shift linkage components

the lever counterclockwise to the Low detent, and then clockwise one detent to Drive.

7. Place the selector lever in Drive and remove any free-play by holding the cross-shaft up and pulling the shift rod downward.

8. Tighten the clamp and check the adjustment.

On 1969–73 cars, carry out the following additional steps:

9. Place the shift lever in Park and the ignition switch in **LOCK.** Loosen the back-drive rod clamp nut. Remove any lash in the column and tighten the clamp nut.

10. When the selector lever is in Park, the ignition key should move freely into **LOCK.** The **LOCK** position should be obtainable only when the transmission is in Park.

Powerglide Floor Shift

▶ See Figure 10

1. Loosen the adjustment nuts at the swivel. Place the transmission control actuating lever in the Drive position by moving it counterclockwise to the Low detent, and then clockwise one detent position to Drive.

2. Place the floorshift lever in Drive. Hold the floorshift unit lower operating lever forward against the shift lever detent.

3. Place a 3/32 in. (0.09) spacer between the rear nut and the swivel. Tighten the rear nut against the spacer.

4. Remove the spacer and tighten the front nut against the swivel, locking the swivel between the nuts.

Turbo Hydra-Matic Column and Floor Shift

▶ See Figures 11 and 12

VEHICLES THROUGH 1974

Linkages used on Turbo Hydra-Matic transmissions are similar to those used on Powerglides. Adjustments are the same, except

that the transmission lever is adjusted to Drive by moving the lever clockwise to the Low detent, and then counterclockwise two detent positions to Drive.

Column Shift

EXCEPT TURBO HYDRA-MATIC 200

1. Loosen the swivel at the lower end of the rod that comes from the column.

2. On 1973 and later models, set the transmission lever in the Neutral detent by turning the lever counterclockwise to the L1 detent, then clockwise three positions. On models through 1972, set

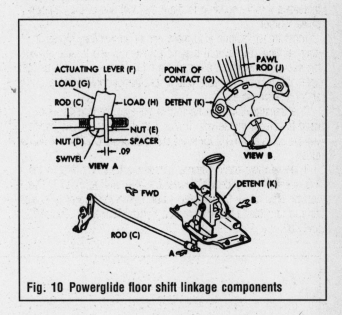

Fig. 10 Powerglide floor shift linkage components

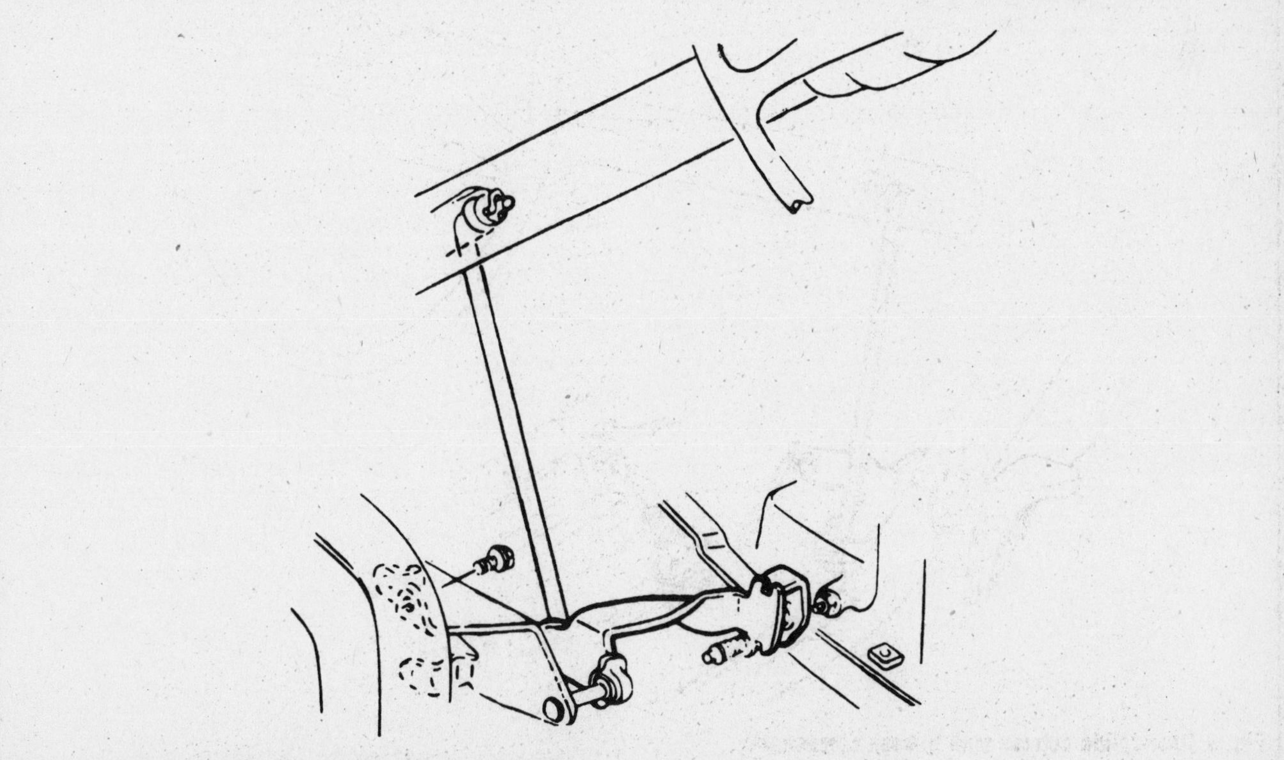

Fig. 11 Turbo Hydra-Matic column linkage components

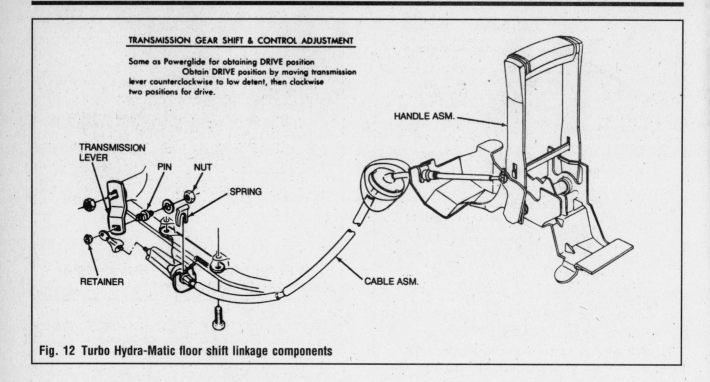

TRANSMISSION GEAR SHIFT & CONTROL ADJUSTMENT

Same as Powerglide for obtaining DRIVE position
          Obtain DRIVE position by moving transmission
lever counterclockwise to low detent, then clockwise
two positions for drive.

HANDLE ASM.

TRANSMISSION LEVER

PIN   NUT

SPRING

RETAINER

CABLE ASM.

Fig. 12 Turbo Hydra-Matic floor shift linkage components

the lever in the Drive detent by turning the lever counterclockwise to the L1 detent, then clockwise two positions.

3. Put the column lever in Neutral for 1973 and later models, and in Drive for models through 1972. The important thing here is not where the indicator points but that the lever be in the correct position.

4. Tighten the swivel. Readjust neutral start switch as necessary.

5. Check that the key cannot be removed and that the wheel is not locked with the key in **RUN.** Check that the key can be removed in **LOCK** with the lever in Park, and that the steering wheel is locked.

TURBO HYDRA-MATIC 200

1. Remove the screw and washer from the swivel assembly on the rod which activates the transmission shift lever.

2. Put the transmission shift lever in neutral by turning it counter-clockwise to L1 detent and then clockwise three detent positions. Put the transmission selector lever in neutral as determined by the mechanical stop in the steering column assembly—do not use indicator pointer.

3. Turn the swivel until it lines up directly with the hole in the shift lever, and install screw and washer. You should not have to force the transmission lever to move in either direction to install the screw.

4. Adjust the transmission indicator pointer and neutral start switch.

5. Check that key cannot be removed from the **RUN** position if the transmission selector is in Reverse and that key can be removed with the selector in Park. Make sure lever will not move from Park position with key out of ignition.

1975–79 Cars With Cable Linkage

1. Loosen the swivel at the lower end of the rod that comes from the steering column.

2. Loosen the pin at the transmission end of the cable.

3. Set the floorshift lever in the Drive detent.

4. Set the transmission lever in the Drive detent by moving it counterclockwise to the L1 detent, then clockwise three detent positions.

5. Tighten the nut on the pin at the transmission end of the cable.

6. Put the floorshift lever in Park and the ignition switch in **LOCK.**

7. Pull down lightly on the rod from the column and tighten its clamp nut.

THROTTLE VALVE LINKAGE

Powerglide Transmissions

1964–66 V8, 1964–73 4 AND 6-CYLINDER ENGINES
♦ See Figure 13

1. Depress the accelerator pedal.

2. The bell crank on 6-cylinder engines and the carburetor lever on V8 engines must be at the wide open throttle position.

3. The dash lever at the firewall must be $1/64$–$1/16$ in. off its lever stop.

4. The transmission lever must be against the transmission internal stop.

5. Adjust the linkage to simultaneously obtain the conditions in Steps 1–4.

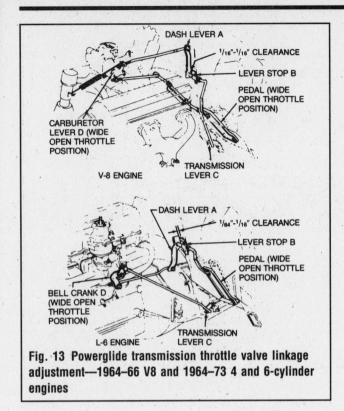

Fig. 13 Powerglide transmission throttle valve linkage adjustment—1964–66 V8 and 1964–73 4 and 6-cylinder engines

1967–73 V8 ENGINES

◆ See Figure 14

1. Remove the air cleaner.
2. Disconnect the accelerator linkage at the carburetor.
3. Disconnect both return springs.
4. Pull the throttle valve upper rod forward until the transmission is through the detent.
5. Open the carburetor to the wide open throttle position. Adjust the swivel on the end of the upper throttle valve rod so that the carburetor reaches wide open throttle position at the same time that the ball stud contacts the end of the slot in the upper throttle valve rod. A tolerance of $1/32$ in. is allowable.

DETENT CABLE

Turbo Hydra-Matic 250 and 350 Transmissions

◆ See Figure 15

These transmissions utilize a downshift cable between the carburetor and the transmission.

1. Pry up on each side of the detent cable snap-lock with a suitable prytool to release the lock. On cars equipped with a retaining screw, loosen the detent cable screw.
2. Squeeze the locking tabs and disconnect the snap-lock assembly from the throttle bracket.
3. Place the carburetor lever in the wide open throttle position. Make sure that the lever is against the wide open stop. On cars

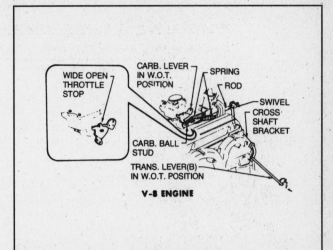

Fig. 14 Powerglide transmission throttle valve linkage adjustment—1967–73 V8 engines

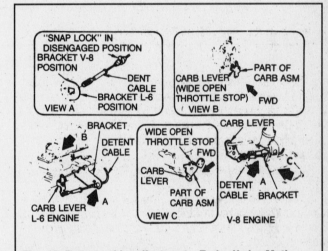

Fig. 15 Detent cable adjustment—Turbo Hydra-Matic 250 and 350 transmissions

with Quadrajet carburetors, disengage the secondary lock-out before placing the lever in the wide open position.

➡ **The detent cable must be pulled through the detent position.**

4. With the carburetor lever in the wide open position, push the snap-lock on the cable or else tighten the retaining screw.

➡ **Do not lubricate the detent cable.**

DETENT SWITCH

Turbo Hydra-Matic 400 transmissions are equipped with an electrical detent, or down-shift switch operated by the throttle linkage.

Turbo Hydra-Matic 400 Transmission
♦ See Figure 16

1968 VEHICLES

1. Place the carburetor lever in the wide open position.
2. Position the automatic choke so that it is off.
3. Fully depress the switch plunger.
4. Adjust the switch mounting to obtain a distance of 0.05 in. between the switch plunger and the throttle lever paddle.

1969–71 VEHICLES

1. Pull the detent switch driver rearward until the hole in the switch body aligns with the hole in the driver. Insert a 0.092 in. diameter pin through the aligned holes to hold the driver in position.
2. Loosen the mounting bolt.

1972–79 VEHICLES

1. Install the detent switch.
2. Press the switch plunger as far forward as possible. This will preset the switch for adjustment, which will occur on the first application of wide open throttle.

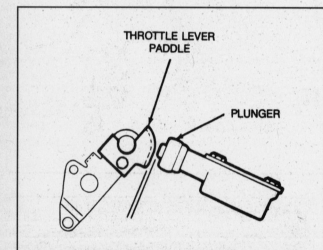

Fig. 16 Detent switch adjustment—Turbo Hydra-Matic 400 transmissions

Neutral Safety Switch

REMOVAL & INSTALLATION

♦ See Figure 17

The neutral safety switch prevents the engine from being started in any transmission position except Neutral or Park. The switch is located on the upper side of the steering column under the instrument panel on column shift cars, and inside the shift console on floor shift models.

1. Remove the console for access on floor shift models.
2. Disconnect the electrical connectors.

3. Remove the neutral switch.
4. Place 1962–70 column shift lever models in Drive, and 1971 and later models in Neutral. Locate the lever tang against the transmission selector plate on column shift models. Place 1962 through early 1972 floor shift models in Drive, and mid-1972 and later models in Park.
5. Align the slot in the contact support with the hole in the switch. Insert a 3/32 in. diameter pin through the aligned slot and hole. The switch is now aligned in Drive position.

➡ **1973 and later neutral safety switches have a shear-pin installed to aid in proper switch alignment so that insertion of a pin is unnecessary. Moving the shift lever from Neutral shears the pin.**

6. Place the contact support drive slot over the drive tang. Install the switch mounting screws.
7. Remove the aligning pin. Connect the electrical wiring, and replace the console.
8. Set the parking brake and hold your foot on the service brake pedal. Check to see that the engine will start only in Park or Neutral.

ADJUSTMENTS

There are no band adjustments possible or required for the Turbo Hydra-Matic 350 or 400.

Low Band

POWERGLIDE

The low band must be adjusted at the first required fluid change or whenever there is slippage.

1. Position the shift lever in Neutral.
2. Remove the protective cap from the adjusting screw on the left side of the transmission.
3. Loosen the locknut ¼ turn and hold it with a wrench during the entire adjusting procedure.
4. Tighten the adjusting nut to 70 inch lbs, using a 7/32 Allen wrench.
5. Back off the adjusting nut *exactly* three turns for a band used less than 6,000 miles. Back off *exactly* four turns for a band used 6,000 miles or more.
6. Torque the locknut to 15 ft lbs and replace the cap.

Intermediate Band

TURBO HYDRA-MATIC 250

The intermediate band must be adjusted with every required fluid change or whenever there is slippage.

1. Position the shift lever in Neutral.
2. Loosen the locknut on the right side of the transmission and tighten the adjusting screw to 30 inch lbs.
3. Back the screw out three turns and then tighten the locknut to 15 ft. lbs.

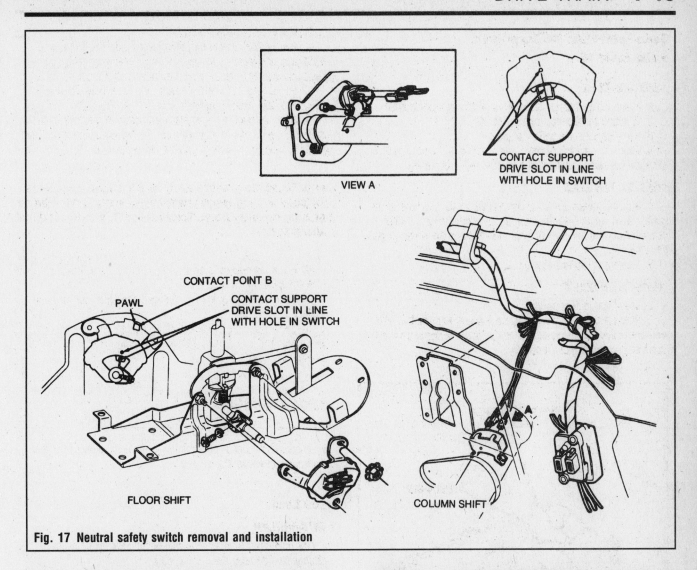

VIEW A

CONTACT SUPPORT
DRIVE SLOT IN LINE
WITH HOLE IN SWITCH

PAWL

CONTACT POINT B

CONTACT SUPPORT
DRIVE SLOT IN LINE
WITH HOLE IN SWITCH

FLOOR SHIFT

COLUMN SHIFT

Fig. 17 Neutral safety switch removal and installation

Fluid Pan

REMOVAL & INSTALLATION

The fluid should be changed with the transmission warm.

1. Raise and support the vehicle, preferably in a level attitude.

2. With Turbo Hydra-Matic 250 or 350, support the transmission and remove the support crossmember.

3. Place a large pan under the transmission pan. Remove all the front and side pan bolts. Loosen the rear bolts about four turns.

4. Pry the pan loose and let it drain.

5. Remove the pan and gasket. Clean the pan thoroughly with solvent and air dry it. Be very careful not to get any lint from rags in the pan.

6. Remove the strainer to valve body screws, the strainer, and the gasket. Most 350 transmissions will have a throw-away filter

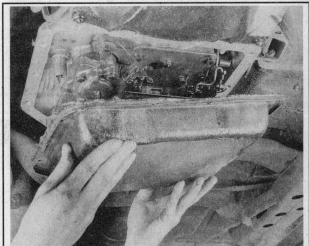

After all the transmission fluid has drained, remove the remaining bolts and lower the pan

instead of a strainer. On the 400 transmission, remove the filter retaining bolt, filter, and intake pipe O-ring.

7. If there is a strainer, clean it in solvent and air dry.

To install:

8. Install the new filter or cleaned strainer with a new gasket. Tighten the screws to 12 ft lbs. On the 400, install a new intake pipe O-ring and a new filter, tightening the retaining bolt to 10 ft lbs.

9. Install the pan with a new gasket. Tighten the bolts evenly to 12 ft. lbs. (8 ft. lbs. for Powerglide).

10. Lower the car and add 5 pts. (3 pts. on Powerglide) of DEXRON® or DEXRON II® automatic transmission fluid through the dipstick tube.

11. Start the engine in Park and let it idle. Do not race the engine. Shift into each shift lever position, shift back into Park, and check the fluid level on the dipstick. The level should be ¼ in.

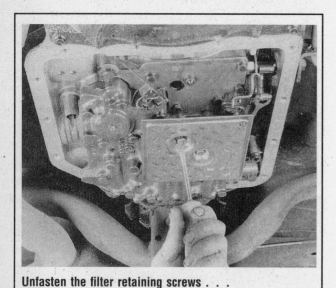

Unfasten the filter retaining screws . . .

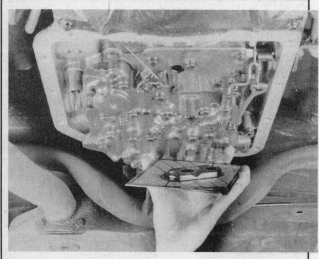

. . . then remove the filter from the transmission

below ADD. Be very careful not to overfill. Recheck the level after the car has been driven long enough to thoroughly warm up the transmission. Add fluid as necessary. The level should then be at FULL.

Transmission

REMOVAL & INSTALLATION

Powerglide

1. Disconnect the negative battery cable.
2. Raise and safely support the vehicle, then drain the engine oil into a suitable container.
3. Disconnect the oil cooler and vacuum modulator lines and the speedometer drive cable from the transmission. Fasten the lines out of the way.
4. Detach the manual and throttle valve control level rods from the transmission.
5. Disconnect the driveshaft.
6. Install a suitable transmission lifting device.
7. Disconnect the engine rear mount from the transmission extension, then remove the transmission support crossmember.
8. Remove the converter underpan, then scribe the flywheel-to-converter position for assembly purposes. Remove the converter-to-flywheel attaching bolts.
9. Support the engine at the oil pan rail with a jack or other suitable brace capable of supporting the engine weight when the transmission is removed.
10. Lower the rear of the transmission slightly so that the upper transmission housing-to-engine attaching bolts can be reached by using a universal socket and a long extension. Remove the upper bolts.

➡**Make sure the distributor does not hit the firewall when lowering the transmission.**

11. Remove the remaining transmission-to-housing bolts.

➡**Watch the converter when moving the transmission rearward. If it does not follow the transmission, pry it free of the flywheel before proceeding.**

12. Separate the transmission from the vehicle by moving it slightly to the rear and downward, then remove it from beneath the car and transfer it to a workbench.

✳✳ WARNING

Use some sort of holding strap to keep the converter from falling out of the transmission during transmission removal and handling.

13. Installation is the reverse of the removal procedure.

Turbo Hydra-Matic 250

1. Disconnect the negative battery cable.
2. Disconnect the detent downshift cable from the carburetor.

3. Make sure the parking brake is off. Raise and safely support the vehicle.

4. Remove the drive shaft from the vehicle.

5. Disconnect the following components from the transmission:

    a. Speedometer cable
    b. Detent downshift cable
    c. Modulator vacuum line
    d. Fluid cooler lines

6. Unfasten the shift control linkage from the transmission.

7. Place a transmission jack underneath the transmission.

8. Unfasten the rear transmission mounting pads at the rear frame crossmember.

9. Remove the two bolts at either end of the crossmember, then remove the crossmember.

10. Remove the converter access plate.

11. Unfasten and remove the bolts securing the converter to the flexplate.

12. Carefully lower the transmission, so that the jack just barely supports it.

13. Remove the bolts which secure the bell housing to the engine.

14. Remove the oil filler tube from the transmission.

15. Bring the transmission back up to its normal position and then support the engine with a jack.

✳✳ WARNING

While the transmission is being lowered, either use a tool to retain the converter in the housing or keep the rear of the transmission below the front. Do NOT allow the converter to fall out.

16. Slide the transmission toward the rear of the car and away from the eingine. Carefully lower, then remove the transmission.

17. Installation is the reverse of the removal procedure. Make sure to keep the following points in mind:

    a. Before installing the flexplate-to-converter bolts, be sure that the attaching lugs on the converter are flush with the flexplate. Try rotating the converter by hand; it should turn freely.

    b. Hand-start all 3 stud bolts and finger-tighten them. Then, final-tighten all bolts.

    c. After installation, adjust the linkage and check the fluid level.

Turbo Hydra-Matic 350 and 400

1. Disconnect the negative battery cable.

2. Make sure the parking brake is off.

3. Raise and safely support the vehicle, then drain the engine oil into a suitable container.

4. Remove the drive shaft from the vehicle.

5. Disconnect the following components from the transmission:

    a. Speedometer cable
    b. Detent downshift cable (Turbo Hydra-Matic 350)
    c. Electrical lead-to-case connector (Turbo Hydra-Matic 400)
    d. Modulator vacuum line
    e. Fluid cooler lines

6. Unfasten the shift control linkage from the transmission.

7. Place a transmission jack underneath the transmission.

8. Remove the following components:

    a. Crossmember
    b. Converter underpan
    c. Converter-to-flywheel bolts

9. Loosen the exhaust pipe-to-manifold bolts.

10. Lower the transmission until the jack is barely supporting it. Be careful that the distributor on the V8 engine is not forced against the firewall.

11. Remove the transmission-to-engine mounting bolts and the oil filler tube.

12. Raise the transmission to its normal position. Support the engine with a jack. Slide the transmission rearward and then down. Use a strap to hold the converter to the transmission or keep the rear of the transmission down to avoid losing the converter.

13. Installation is the reverse of the removal procedure.

DRIVELINE

▶ **See Figure 18**

A one-piece, exposed type, tubular driveshaft is used on all models. The driveshaft has two cross and roller universal joints and a splined slip joint. The cross and roller universal joints may be of two types. The first is the Cleveland type which uses external snaprings for trunnion retention. The second is the Saginaw design in which the trunnions are retained by a nylon material which is injected into a groove in the yoke. A third type of driveshaft, introduced in 1971, employs a constant-velocity joint at the axle end. It should be noted that this last type of joint is not serviceable.

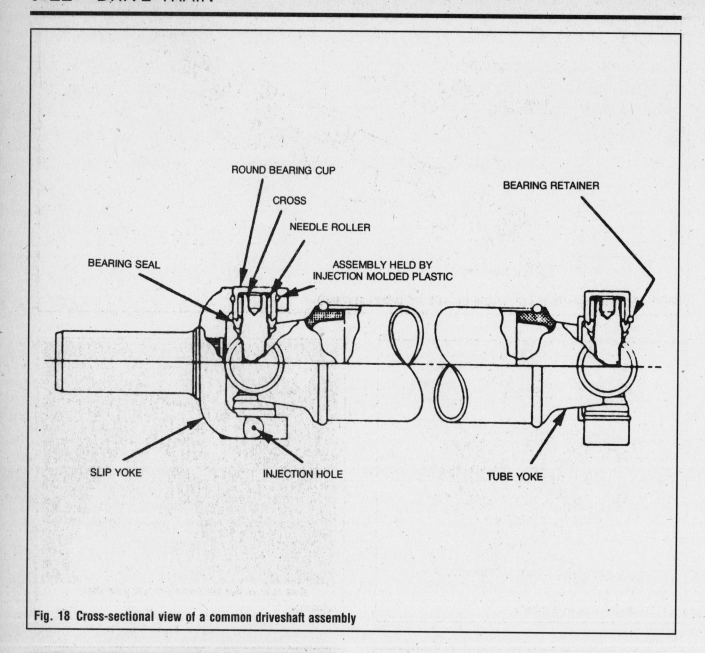

ROUND BEARING CUP

CROSS

NEEDLE ROLLER

BEARING SEAL

ASSEMBLY HELD BY
INJECTION MOLDED PLASTIC

BEARING RETAINER

SLIP YOKE

INJECTION HOLE

TUBE YOKE

Fig. 18 Cross-sectional view of a common driveshaft assembly

Driveshaft and U-Joints

DRIVESHAFT REMOVAL & INSTALLATION

▶ See Figures 19 and 20

1. Raise the vehicle and safely support it on jackstands. Paint a reference line from the rear end of the driveshaft to the companion flange so that they can be reassembled in the same position.
2. Disconnect the rear universal joint by removing the U-bolts or retaining straps.
3. To prevent the loss of the needle bearings, tape the bearing caps to the trunnion.

4. Remove the driveshaft from the transmission by sliding it rearward.

➡Do not be alarmed by oil leakage at the transmission output shaft. This oil is there to lubricate the splines of the front yoke.

To install:
5. Check the yoke seal in the transmission case extension and replace it if necessary.
6. Position the driveshaft and insert the front yoke into the transmission so that the splines mesh with the splines of the transmission shaft.
7. Using the reference marks made during removal, align the driveshaft with the companion flange and secure it with the U-bolts or retaining straps.

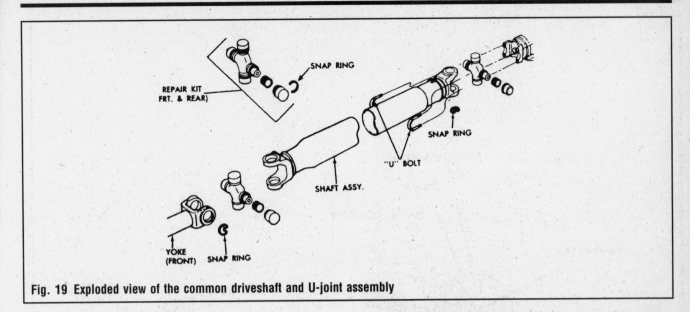

Fig. 19 Exploded view of the common driveshaft and U-joint assembly

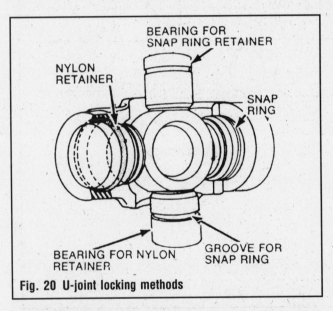

Fig. 20 U-joint locking methods

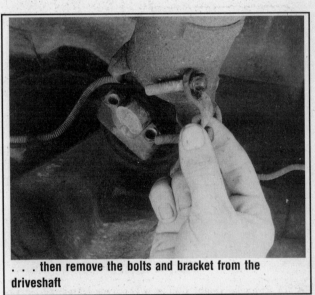

. . . then remove the bolts and bracket from the driveshaft

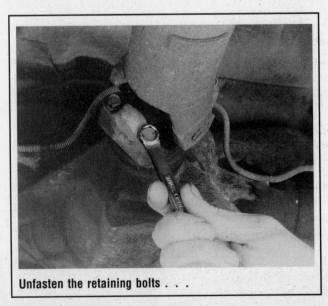

Unfasten the retaining bolts . . .

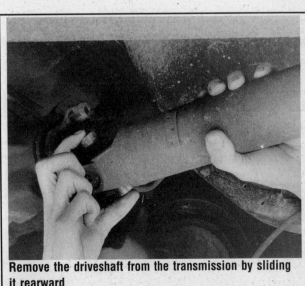

Remove the driveshaft from the transmission by sliding it rearward

U-JOINT OVERHAUL

◆ **See Figures 21, 22, 23 and 24**

1. Remove the driveshaft as explained above and remove the snaprings from the ends of the bearing cup.

2. After removing the snaprings, place the driveshaft on the floor and place a large diameter socket under one of the bearing cups. Using a hammer and a drift, tap on the bearing opposite this one. This will push the trunnion through the yoke enough to force the bearing cup out of the yoke and into the socket. Repeat this procedure for the outer bearing cups. If the hammer fails to loosen the cups, a press may be necessary.

➡**A Saginaw design driveshaft secures its U-joints in a different manner than the conventional snaprings of the Dana and Cleveland designs.**

Nylon material is injected through a small hole in the yoke and flows along a circular groove between the U-joint and the yoke, creating a synthetic snapring. Disassembly of this Saginaw type U-joint requires the joint to be pressed from the yoke. If a press is not available, it may be carefully hammered out using the same procedure (step two) as the Cleveland design although it may require more force to break the nylon ring. Either method, press or hammer, will damage the bearing cups and destroy the nylon rings. Replacement kits include new bearing cups and conventional metal snaprings to replace the original nylon rings.

3. Clean the entire U-joint assembly thoroughly with solvent. Inspect for excessive wear in the yoke bores and on the four ends of the trunnion. The needle bearings should not be scored, broken, or loose in their cups. Bearing cups may suffer slight distortion during removal and should be replaced.

4. Pack the bearings with chassis lube (lithium base) and completely fill each trunnion end with the same lubricant.

5. Place new dust seals on the trunnions with the cavity of the seal toward the end of the trunnion. Care must be taken to avoid distortion of the seal. A suitably sized socket and a vise can be used to press on the seal.

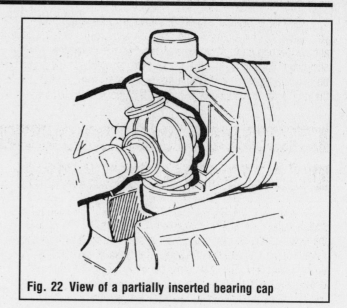

Fig. 22 View of a partially inserted bearing cap

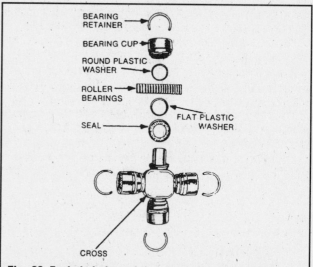

Fig. 23 Exploded view of the plastic retainer U-joint repair kit components

Fig. 21 Remove the bearing using a press, if necessary

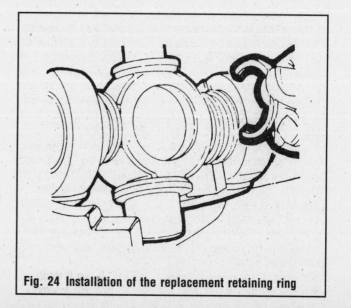

Fig. 24 Installation of the replacement retaining ring

6. Insert one bearing cup about a quarter of the way into the yoke and place the trunnion into the yoke and bearing cup. Install another bearing cup and press both cups in and install the snaprings. Snaprings on the Dana and Cleveland shafts must go on the outside of the yoke while the Saginaw shaft requires that the ring go on the inside of the yoke. The gap in the Saginaw ring must face in toward the yoke. Once installed, the trunnion must move freely in the yoke.

➡ **The Saginaw shaft uses two different size bearing cups at the differential end. The larger cups (the ones with the groove) fit into the driveshaft yoke.**

REAR AXLE

Understanding Rear Axles

The rear axle is a special type of transmission that reduces the speed of the drive from the engine and transmission and divides the power to the rear wheels. Power enters the rear axle from the driveshaft via the companion flange. The flange is mounted on the drive pinion shaft. The drive pinion shaft and gear which carry the power into the differential turn at engine speed. The gear on the end of the pinion shaft drives a large ring gear the axis of rotation of which is 90° away from that of the pinion. The pinion and gear reduce the speed and multiply the power by the gear ratio of the axle, and change the direction of rotation to turn the axle shafts which drive both wheels. The rear axle gear ratio is found by dividing the number of pinion gear teeth into the number of ring gear teeth.

The ring gear drives the differential case. The case provides the two mounting points for the end of a pinion shaft on which are mounted two pinion gears. The pinion gears drive the two side gears, one of which is located on the inner end of each axle shaft.

By driving the axle shafts through this arrangement, the differential allows the outer drive wheel to turn faster than the inner drive wheel in a turn.

The main drive pinion and the side bearings, which bear the weight of the differential case, are shimmed to provide proper bearing preload, and to position the pinion and ring gears properly.

➡ **The proper adjustment of the relationship of the ring and pinion gears is critical. It should be attempted only by those with extensive equipment and/or experience.**

Limited-slip differentials include clutches which tend to link each axle shaft to the differential case. Clutches may be engaged either by spring action or by pressure produced by the torque on the axles during a turn. During turning on a dry pavement, the effects of the clutches are overcome, and each wheel turns at the required speed. When slippage occurs at either wheel, however, the clutches will transmit some of the power to the wheel which has the greater amount of traction. Because of the presence of clutches, limited-slip units require a special lubricant.

Chevy II and Nova models use two different types of rear axle, the "C" type and the non "C" type. Axle shaft in the "C" type are retained by C-shaped locks, which fit grooves at the inner end of the shaft. Axle shafts in the non "C" type are retained by the brake backing plate, which is bolted to the axle housing. Bearings in the "C" type axle consists of an outer race, bearing rollers and a roller cage, retained by snaprings. The non "C" type axle uses a unit roller bearing (inner race, rollers, and outer race), which is pressed onto the shaft.

The non "C" type axle is used on 1962–63 Chevy II models. All post-1963 models are fitted with the "C" type axle assembly.

Axle Shafts and Bearings

REMOVAL, OVERHAUL & INSTALLATION

Non C-Lock Type

◗ **See Figure 25**

1. Raise the car and support it safely on jackstands. Remove the wheel, tire, and brake drum.
2. Remove the nuts holding the retainer plate to the backing plate. Disconnect the brake line.
3. Remove the retainer and install the nuts, finger-tight, to prevent the brake backing plate from being dislodged.
4. Pull out the axle shaft and bearing assembly, using a slide hammer.
5. Using a chisel, nick the bearing retainer in three or four places. The retainer does not have to be cut, merely collapsed sufficiently to allow the bearing retainer to be slid from the shaft.
6. Press off the bearing and install the new one by pressing it into position.
7. Press on the new retainer.

➡ **Do not attempt to press the bearing and the retainer on at the same time.**

8. Assemble the shaft and bearing in the housing, being sure that the bearing is seated properly in the housing.
9. Install the retainer, drum, wheel, and tire. Bleed the brakes.

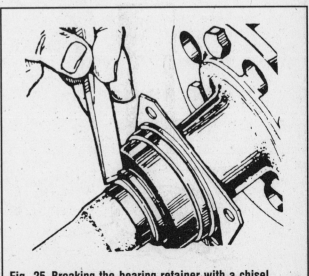

Fig. 25 Breaking the bearing retainer with a chisel

C-Lock Type

▶ **See Figure 26**

1. Raise the car and support it safely on jackstands. Remove the wheel and tire, and the brake drum.

2. Thoroughly clean the area around the differential carrier cover. Place a drain pan under the axle carrier and remove the cover.

3. Remove the differential pinion shaft lockscrew and the differential pinion shaft. Push the flanged end of the axle shaft toward the center of the vehicle and remove the "C" lock from the end of the shaft.

4. Remove the oil seal by inserting the button end of the axle shaft behind the steel case of the oil seal.

5. Remove the oil seal by inserting the button end of the axle shaft behind the steel case of the oil seal. Pry the seal loose from the bore.

6. Seat the legs of the bearing puller behind the bearing. Seat a washer against the bearing and hold it in place with a nut. Use a slide hammer to pull the bearing.

To install:

7. Pack the cavity between the seal lips with wheel bearing lubricant and lubricate a new wheel bearing with the same.

8. Using a suitable driver, install the bearing until it bottoms against the tube. Install the oil seal.

9. Slide the axle shaft into place. Be sure that the splines on the shaft do not damage the oil seal. Make sure that the splines engage the differential side gear.

10. Install the axle shaft "C" lock on the inner end of the axle shaft and push the shaft outward so that the "C" lock seats in the differential side gear counterbore.

11. Position the differential pinion shaft through the case and pinions, aligning the hold in the case with the hole for the lockscrew.

12. Install the pinion shaft lockscrew. Using a new gasket, install the carrier cover. Be sure that the gasket surfaces are clean before installing the gasket and cover.

13. Fill the axle with lubricant to the bottom of the filler hole.

14. Install the brake drum, and the wheel and tire, then lower the car. Check for leaks and road-test the car.

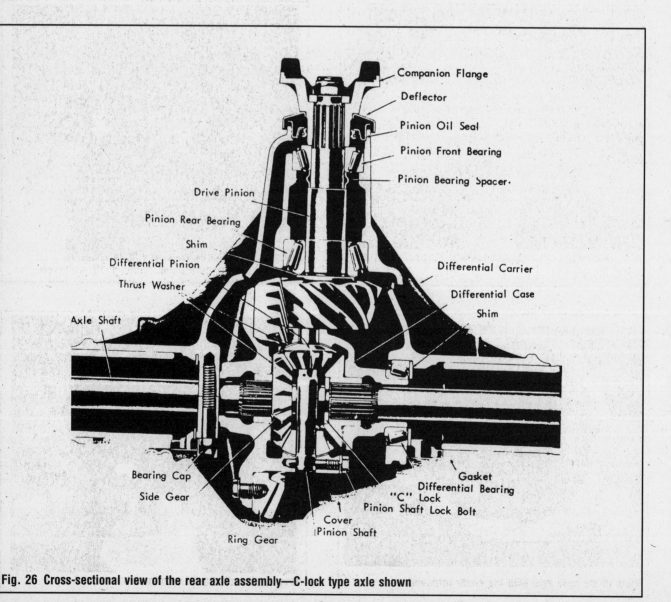

Fig. 26 Cross-sectional view of the rear axle assembly—C-lock type axle shown

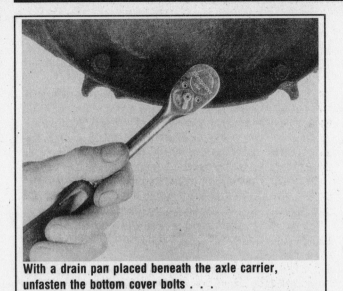

With a drain pan placed beneath the axle carrier, unfasten the bottom cover bolts . . .

Using a suitably sized wrench . . .

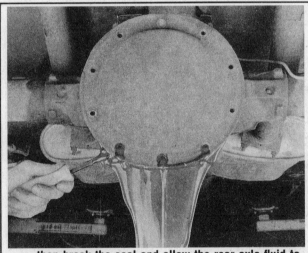

. . . then break the seal and allow the rear axle fluid to drain into the pan

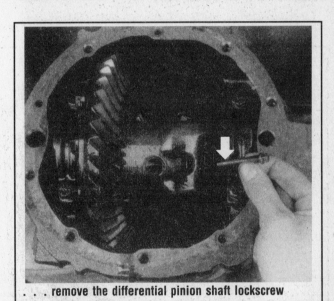

. . . remove the differential pinion shaft lockscrew

View of the rear axle with the cover removed

Remove the differential pinion shaft

Remove the C-lock from the axle shaft

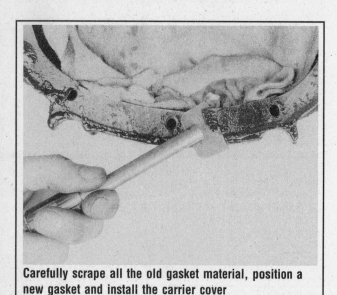

Carefully scrape all the old gasket material, position a new gasket and install the carrier cover

Determining Axle Ratio

The rear axle ratio may be determined by finding the two- or three-letter serial number prefix in the following chart. The 1962–63 serial numbers are located on the front, right side of the differential carrier. The 1964 serial numbers are found on the bottom of the carrier. The 1965–75 numbers are on the left or right of the axle tube.

1962 VEHICLES

3 Speed—Automatic Transmission (3.36 ratio)	DA
(3.08 ratio)	DB
3 Speed (4 cyl) (3.55 ratio)	DC
Positraction (4 cyl) (3.55 ratio)	DD

Positraction (3.36 ratio)	DE
Positraction (3.08 ratio)	DF
Positraction (6 cyl) (3.08 ratio)	DH
w/Metallic Brakes (3.08 ratio)	DJ
Positraction w/Metallic Brakes (3.08 ratio)	DK
w/Metallic Brakes (3.36 ratio)	DL
Positraction w/Metallic Brakes (3.36 ratio)	DM
4 cyl w/Metallic Brakes (3.55 ratio)	DN
4 cyl Positraction w/Metallic Brakes (3.55 ratio)	DP

1963 VEHICLES

3 Speed—Automatic Transmission (3.36 ratio)	DA
(3.08 ratio)	DB
3 Speed (4 cyl) (3.55 ratio)	DC
Positraction (4 cyl) (3.55 ratio)	DD
Positraction (3.36 ratio)	DE
Positraction (3.08 ratio)	DF
Positraction (6 cyl) (3.08 ratio)	DH
w/Metallic Brakes (3.08 ratio)	DJ
Positraction w/Metallic Brakes (3.08 ratio)	DK
w/Metallic Brakes (3.36 ratio)	DL
Positraction w/Metallic Brakes (3.36 ratio)	DM
4 cyl w/Metallic Brakes (3.55 ratio)	DN
4 cyl Positraction w/Metallic Brakes (3.55 ratio)	DP

1964 VEHICLES

3 Speed—Automatic Transmission (3.36 ratio)	DA
(3.08 ratio)	DB
3 Speed (4 cyl) (3.55 ratio)	DC
Positraction (4 cyl) (3.55 ratio)	DD
Positraction (3.36 ratio)	DE
Positraction (3.08 ratio)	DF
Positraction (6 cyl) (3.08 ratio)	DH
w/Metallic Brakes (3.08 ratio)	DJ
Positraction w/Metallic Brakes (3.08 ratio)	DK
w/Metallic Brakes (3.36 ratio)	DL
Positraction w/Metallic Brakes (3.36 ratio)	DM
4 cyl w/Metallic Brakes (3.55 ratio)	DN
4 cyl Positraction w/Metallic Brakes (3.55 ratio)	DP

1965 VEHICLES

(3.08 ratio)	BA
(3.36 ratio)	BC
Positraction (3.08 ratio)	BE
Positraction (3.36 ratio)	BF
Positraction (3.55 ratio)	BG
w/Metallic Brakes (2.73 ratio)	BZ
Positraction w/Metallic Brakes (2.73 ratio)	FD
327 w/Powerglide (2.73 ratio)	BX
Positraction (2.75 ratio)	BY
w/Metallic Brakes (3.08 ratio)	BJ
Positraction w/Metallic Brakes (3.08 ratio)	BK
w/Metallic Brakes (3.36 ratio)	BL
Positraction w/Metallic Brakes (3.36 ratio)	BM
w/Metallic Brakes (3.55 ratio)	BN

1966 VEHICLES

(3.08 ratio)..	BA
(3.36 ratio)..	BC
Positraction (3.08 ratio)	BE
Positraction (3.36 ratio)	BF
Positraction (3.55 ratio) (small ring gear)............	BG
(3.55)	BH
w/Metallic Brakes (3.08 ratio)............................	BJ
Positraction w/Metallic Brakes (3.08 ratio)...........	BK
w/Metallic Brakes (3.36 ratio)............................	BL
Positraction w/Metallic Brakes (3.36 ratio)...........	BM
w/Metallic Brakes (3.55 ratio) (small ring gear)	BN
Positraction w/Metallic Brakes (3.55 ratio)...........	BO
Air Cond. w/Sp Hi Per (3.31 ratio)	BQ
Positraction (3.07 ratio)	BR
Positraction (3.31 ratio)	BS
w/Metallic Brakes (3.07 ratio)............................	BT
Positraction w/Metallic Brakes (3.07 ratio)...........	BU
w/Metallic Brakes (3.31 ratio)............................	BV
Positraction w/Metallic Brakes 93.31 ratio)...........	BW
w/4 Spd Close Ratio (3.55 ratio)........................	FI
w/Metallic Brakes 93.55 ratio) (large ring gear)	FJ
Positraction w/Metallic Brakes (3.55 ratio) (large ring gear)	FK
Positraction (3.55 ratio) (large ring gear)............	FL
(3.73 ratio)..	FM
w/Metallic Brakes (e.73 ratio)	FN
Positraction w/Metallic Brakes (3.73 ratio)...........	FO
Positraction (3.73 ratio)	FP
w/"327" Sp Hi Per (3.07 ratio)...........................	FQ

1967 VEHICLES

(3.08 ratio)..	BA
(3.36 ratio)..	BC
Positraction (3.08 ratio)	BE
Positraction (3.36 ratio)	BF
Positraction (3.55 ratio) (small ring gear)............	BG
(3.55)	BH
Air Cond w/Sp Hi Per (3.31 ratio)	BQ
Positraction (3.07 ratio)	BR
Positraction (3.31 ratio)	BS
w/Metallic Brakes 93.07 ratio)............................	BT
Positraction w/Metallic Brakes (3.07 ratio)...........	BU
w/Metallic Brakes (3.31 ratio)............................	BV
Positraction w/Metallic Brakes (3.31 ratio)...........	BW
w/4 Spd Close Ratio (3.55 ratio)........................	FI
w/Metallic Brakes (3.55 ratio) (large ring gear)	FJ
Positraction w/Metallic Brakes (3.55 ratio) (large ring gear)	FK
Positraction (3.55 ratio) (large ring gear)............	FL
(3.73 ratio)..	FM
w/Metallic Brakes (3.73 ratio)............................	FN
Positraction w/Metallic Brakes (3.73 ratio)...........	FO
Positraction (3.73 ratio)	FP
w/"327" Sp Hi Per (3.07 ratio)...........................	FQ

1968 VEHICLES

(2.56 ratio) (small ring gear)	BA
Positraction (2.56 ratio) (small ring gear)............	BB
(3.36 ratio)..	BC
Positraction (3.36 ratio)	BD
(2.73 ratio)..	BI
(3.07 ratio)..	BL
(3.31 ratio)..	BM
(3.55 ratio)..	BN
(3.73 ratio)..	BO
(2.73 ratio)..	BP
Positraction (2.73 ratio) (large ring gear)............	BQ
Positraction (3.07 ratio)	BR
Positraction (3.31 ratio)	BS
Positraction (3.55 ratio)	BT
Positraction (3.37 ratio)	BU
Positraction (4.10 ratio)	BV
Positraction (4.56 ratio)	BW
Positraction (4.88 ratio)	BX
(3.03 ratio)..	PA
Positraction (3.08 ratio)	PE
Positraction (3.55 ratio) (small ring gear)............	PH
(3.55 ratio)..	PK-PL
Positraction (2.73 ratio) (small ring gear)............	PX
Positraction (2.73 ratio) (large ring gear)............	BQ
(3.55 ratio)..	QE

1969 VEHICLES

(2.56 ratio)..	BA
Positraction (2.56 ratio)	BB
(3.36 ratio)..	BC
Positraction (3.36 ratio)	BD
(2.73 ratio)..	BI
(3.07 ratio)..	BL
(3.31 ratio)..	BM
(3.55 ratio)..	BN
(3.73 ratio)..	BO
(2.73 ratio)..	BP
Positraction (2.73 ratio)	BQ
Positraction (3.07 ratio)	BR
Positraction (3.31 ratio)	BS
Positraction (3.55 ratio)	BT
Positraction (3.73 ratio)	BU
Positraction (4.10 ratio)	BV
Positraction (4.56 ratio)	BW
Positraction (4.88 ratio)	BX
(3.08 ratio)..	PA
(2.56 ratio)..	PB
Positraction (2.56 ratio)	PC
Positraction (3.08 ratio)	PE
Positraction (2.73 ratio)	PX

1970 VEHICLES

Positraction (2.73 ratio)	CPX
Positraction (3.08 ratio)	CPE

Positraction (3.08 ratio) .... CPR
Positraction (3.07 ratio) .... CBR
(2.56 ratio) .... CBA
Positraction (2.56 ratio) .... CBB
(2.73 ratio) .... CBP
(3.08 ratio) .... CPA
(3.36 ratio) .... CBC
Positraction (3.36 ratio) .... CBD
(2.56 ratio) .... CPI
Positraction (2.56 ratio) .... CPJ
(3.08 ratio) .... CPO
(3.07 ratio) .... CBL
(3.31 ratio) .... CBM
Positraction (3.31 ratio) .... CBS
(3.55 ratio) .... CBN
Positraction (3.55 ratio) .... CBT

1971 VEHICLES

Positraction (3.08) .... PR
Positraction (3.07) .... BR
(2.56) .... PI
Positraction (2.56) .... PJ
(3.08) .... PO
(3.07) .... BL
(3.31) .... BM
Positraction (3.31) .... BS
(2.56) .... GJ
(3.08) .... GR
(3.36) .... GT
Positraction (2.56) .... GK
Positraction (3.08) .... GS
Positraction (3.36) .... GW

1972 VEHICLES

Positraction (2.08) (G92) .... JQ
(2.73) .... PW

Positraction (2.73) .... PX
(3.08) (G-92) .... JC
(3.42) (G-58) .... JE
(3.42) (GT6) .... JK
Positraction (3.42) (G58) .... JS
(2.73) (G-97) .... JB
(3.08) (G-52) .... JI
(3.36) .... GT
Positraction (2.73) G-97 .... JN
Positraction (3.08) (G-52) .... JW
Positraction (3.42) (GT6) .... JY

1973–74 VEHICLES

(2.73) .... JA
Positraction (2.73) .... JM
(3.08) .... JB
Positraction (3.08) .... JN
(3.42) .... JC
Positraction (3.42) .... JP

1975–77 VEHICLES

(2.56) ....
  PH or PT
(2.73) ....
  PA, PU, 2PA, 2PU
(3.08) ....
  PC, PW, 2PC, 2PW
(3.42) ....
  PZ or PY

➡ **On 1978 and later axles, the axle numerical ratio is indicated in place of a code.**

WHEELS 8-2
WHEEL ASSEMBLY 8-2
  REMOVAL & INSTALLATION 8-2
  INSPECTION 8-2
WHEEL LUG STUDS 8-2
  REPLACEMENT 8-2
FRONT SUSPENSION 8-4
COIL SPRINGS 8-5
  REMOVAL & INSTALLATION 8-5
SHOCK ABSORBERS 8-6
  REMOVAL & INSTALLATION 8-6
UPPER BALL JOINT 8-7
  INSPECTION 8-7
  REMOVAL & INSTALLATION 8-8
LOWER BALL JOINT 8-9
  INSPECTION 8-9
  REMOVAL & INSTALLATION 8-9
UPPER CONTROL ARM 8-10
  REMOVAL & INSTALLATION 8-10
LOWER CONTROL ARM 8-11
  REMOVAL & INSTALLATION 8-11
FRONT END ALIGNMENT 8-11
  CASTER 8-12
  CAMBER 8-12
  TOE-IN 8-12
REAR SUSPENSION 8-14
LEAF SPRINGS 8-14
  REMOVAL & INSTALLATION 8-14
COIL SPRINGS 8-16
  REMOVAL & INSTALLATION 8-16
SHOCK ABSORBERS 8-16
  REMOVAL & INSTALLATION 8-16
STEERING 8-18
STEERING WHEEL 8-18
  REMOVAL & INSTALLATION 8-18
TURN SIGNAL SWITCH 8-20
  REMOVAL & INSTALLATION 8-20
IGNITION SWITCH (COLUMN-
  MOUNTED) 8-20
  REMOVAL & INSTALLATION 8-20
POWER STEERING PUMP 8-20
  REMOVAL & INSTALLATION 8-20
  BLEEDING 8-22
TIE-ROD ENDS 8-22
  REMOVAL & INSTALLATION 8-22
COMPONENT LOCATIONS
  FRONT SUSPENSION
  COMPONENTS—LATE MODEL
  NOVA 8-4
  REAR SUSPENSION 8-14
SPECIFICATION CHARTS
  WHEEL ALIGNMENT
  SPECIFICATIONS 8-13

8

SUSPENSION AND STEERING

WHEELS 8-2
FRONT SUSPENSION 8-4
REAR SUSPENSION 8-14
STEERING 8-18

WHEELS

Wheel Assembly

REMOVAL & INSTALLATION

◆ **See Figure 1**

1. If equipped, remove the hub cap, wheel cover.
2. Loosen, but do not remove the lug nuts.
3. Raise and safely support the vehicle so the tire is clear of the ground.

➡**Always use a suitable floor jack for raising the vehicle to be serviced. Never use the jacking device supplied with the vehicle for vehicle service. That jacking device is designed for emergency use only to change a flat tire.**

4. Remove the lug nuts, then remove the wheel from the vehicle.

To install:

5. Install the wheel.
6. Install the lug nuts, then hand-tighten in a star pattern.
7. Carefully lower the vehicle.
8. Final tighten the lug nuts in a star pattern.

INSPECTION

Inspect the tread for abnormal wear, check for nails or other foreign material embedded into the tire. To check for leaks, submerse the wheel assembly into a tub of water and watch for air bubbles.

Wheels must be replaced if they are bent, dented, leak air through welds, have elongated bolt holes, if wheel nuts won't stay tight, or if the wheels are heavily rusted. Replacement wheels must be equivalent to the original equipment wheels in load capacity, diameter, rim width, offset and mounting configuration.

A wheel of improper size may affect wheel bearing lift, brake cooling, speedometer/odomter calibration, vehicle ground clearance and tire clearance to the body and/or chassis.

➡**Replacement with used wheels is not recommended as their service history may have included severe treatment or very high mileage and they could fail without warning.**

Wheel Lug Studs

REPLACEMENT

Front Wheels

◆ **See Figure 2**

1. Remove the rotor assembly from the vehicle, as outlined in Section 9 of this manual.
2. Remove the damaged bolt with a press. Do not damage the wheel mounting surface on the hub flange.

To install:

3. Install a new serrated bolt into the hole in the hub. Tap

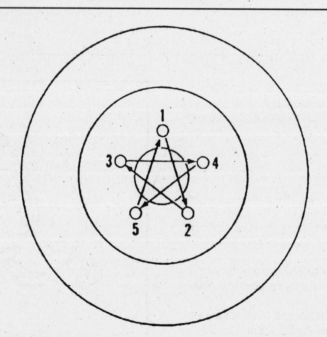

Fig. 1 Wheel lug nut tightening sequence

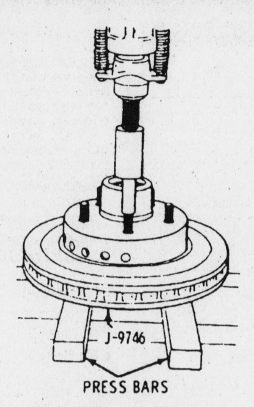

PRESS BARS

TOOL J-9746 IS RESTING
ON PRESS BARS TO PREVENT
DAMAGE TO ROTOR FACE.

Fig. 2 Pressing out the front wheel studs

lightly with a hammer to start the bolt serrations in the hole, make sure the bolt is square with the hub flange.

4. The brake disc must be supported properly before pressing the wheel stud in or out.

Rear Wheels
▶ **See Figure 3**

1. Raise and support the vehicle. Mark the relationship of the wheel assembly to the axle flange and remove the brake drum.

2. Using tool J-6627 or equivalent, press the wheel stud from the axle flange.

To install:

3. Insert a new wheel stud in the axle flange hole. Rotate the bolt slowly to assure the serrations are aligned with those made with the original bolt.

4. Place a flat washer over the outside end of the wheel stud and thread a standard wheel nut with the flat side against the washer. Tighten the wheel nut until the bolt head seats against the axle flange.

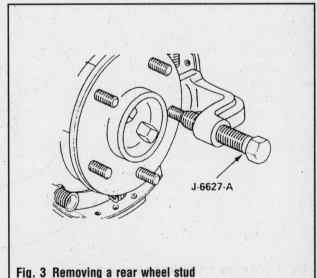

Fig. 3 Removing a rear wheel stud

FRONT SUSPENSION

FRONT SUSPENSION COMPONENTS - LATE MODEL NOVA

1. Lower shock absorber mount
2. Lower control arm
3. Lower ball joint
4. Tie rod end
5. Coil spring
6. Shock absorber
7. Steering linkage
8. Stabilizer bar

1962–67 Chevy II

Front suspension is an independent coil spring, ball-joint type with rubber-brushed, pivoting, upper and lower control arms. The coil springs are positioned at their lower ends on a pivoting spring seat bolted to the upper control arm. The upper end of the spring extends into spring towers formed in the front-end sheet metal. Direct, double-acting shock absorbers are located inside the coil springs and are attached to the lower coil spring seat and to the upper bracket, accessible from the engine compartment.

Each lower control arm has a strut rod running diagonally forward to a brace attached between the frame and radiator support. This strut rod provides for caster angle adjustment. Camber angle is adjusted by means of a cam-shaped lower control arm inner pivot bolt. A stabilizer rod, on station wagons, connects the two lower control arms and is rubber-mounted to the front crossmember. Front wheel bearings are tapered roller bearing.

1968 and Later Chevy II and Nova
▶ **See Figure 4**

In these models, the springs ride on the lower control arms. Ball joints connect the upper and lower arms to the steering knuckle. Tapered roller wheel bearings are used.

Camber angle is adjusted by means of upper control arm inner support shaft shims.

Caster angle is adjusted by means of upper control arm inner support shaft shims.

Periodic maintenance of the front suspension includes lubrication of the four ball joints, spring seat lower pivot shafts and adjustment and lubrication of the front wheel bearings.

Coil Springs

REMOVAL & INSTALLATION

1962–67 Chevy II

1. Raise the car and remove the wheel.
2. Support the lower control arm with an adjustable jackstand and raise it slightly from the full rebound position.
3. Remove the shock absorber.
4. Insert a spring compressor into the upper spring tower so that the lower U-bolt fits into the shock absorber mounting holes in the spring seat. Secure the two lower studs to the spring seat with nuts.
5. Fit the tool upper pilot to the top of the spring and compress the spring by tightening the upper nut. Compress the spring until the screw is bottomed out.
6. Remove the lower spring seat retaining nuts, lift the spring and seat assembly from the control arm, and guide it down and out through the fender skirt.
   To install:
7. Install a new spring into the tool and compress the spring until the screw is bottomed out.

➡**Spring coil ends must be against the spring stops in the upper and lower seats.**

8. Lift the spring and tool assembly into place and position it so that the upper spring stop is inboard.
9. Install the lower spring seat to the control arm. Torque the nuts to 25–35 ft lbs.

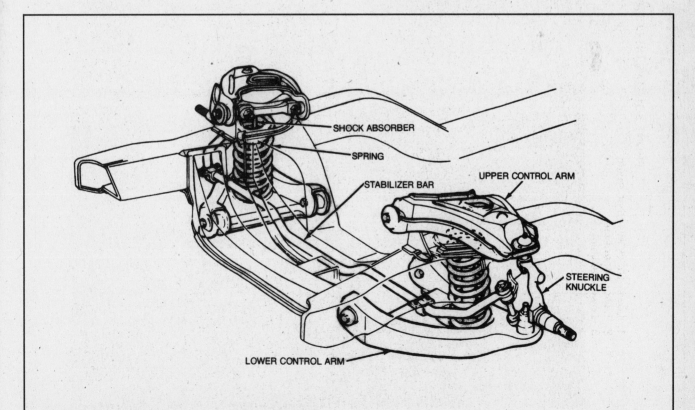

Fig. 4 Front suspension components—1968–79 vehicles

10. Loosen the spring compressor until the spring is properly seated in the upper spring tower and remove the tool.

11. Install the shock absorber.

12. Remove the adjustable jackstand and install the wheel and tire. Lower the car to the floor.

1968–79 Chevy II and Nova

1. Hold the shock absorber upper stem from turning, then disconnect the shock absorber at the top.

2. Support the car by the frame, so the control arms hang free, remove the wheel assembly (replace one wheel nut to hold the brake drum), shock absorber, and the stabilizer bar-to-lower control arm link.

3. Place a steel bar through the shock absorber mounting hole in the lower control arm so that the notch seats over the bottom spring coil and the bar extends outboard beyond the end of the control arm and slightly toward the front of the car.

4. With a suitable jack, raise the end of the bar.

5. Remove the lower ball stud cotter pin and nut, then remove the ball stud from the knuckle.

➡ **Place a chain around the spring and through the lower arm for safety.**

6. Lower the jack supporting the steel bar and control arm until the spring can be removed.

7. Install by reversing the removal procedure. During installation, make sure the new spring matches the position of the old one. Torque for the pivot bolts is 85 ft. lbs. for models through 1974; all others are tightened to 100 ft. lbs.

Shock Absorbers

REMOVAL & INSTALLATION

1962–67 Chevy II

◆ **See Figure 5**

1. Fabricate a support for the upper control arm. With the car weight resting on its wheels, install this support between the upper control arm and the frame side member.

2. Raise the front of the car and remove the wheel and tire.

3. Remove the shock absorber lower mounting nuts, lockwashers, and rubber washers from the lower spring seat.

4. Working under the hood, withdraw the shock absorber upper mounting bracket bolts from the spring tower. Lift the bracket and shock absorber assembly from the car.

5. Disconnect the shock absorber from the upper mounting bracket and remove the rubber bushings and washers.

To install:

6. Begin installation by assembling the upper washer and rubber bushing to the shock absorber. Assemble the upper mounting bracket, bushing, washer, and nut to the shock absorber. Torque the nut to 8–12 ft lbs.

7. Fit the rubber washers to the shock absorber lower seat studs. Insert the shock absorber and upper bracket assembly through the access hole in the spring tower and position it on the lower spring seat. Fit the washers and nuts and torque the nuts to 9–12 ft. lbs. for 1962–64 models, or to 6–9 ft. lbs. for 1965–67 models.

8. Install the upper mounting bracket to the spring tower and

Fig. 5 Front shock absorber mounting—1962–67 vehicles

torque the bracket bolts to 9–12 ft. lbs. for 1962–64 models, or to 6–9 ft. lbs. for 1965–67 models.

9. Install the wheel and tire. Lower the car, remove the upper control arm support, and check the shock absorber action.

1968–79 Chevy II and Nova

◆ **See Figure 6**

1. Use an open-end wrench to secure the upper stem of the shock absorber (in the engine compartment) and then remove the stem retaining nut, retainer, and rubber grommet.

2. Withdraw the two bolts which secure the shock absorber lower pivot to the lower control arm.

3. Pull the shock absorber assembly out from the bottom.

To install:

4. Begin installation by fully extending the shock absorber stem. Fit the retainer and rubber grommet to the shock absorber stem and insert the shock absorber up through the lower control arm and spring so that the upper stem passes through the mounting hole in the upper support arm.

5. Fit the rubber grommet, retainer, and mounting nut over the shock absorber upper stem.

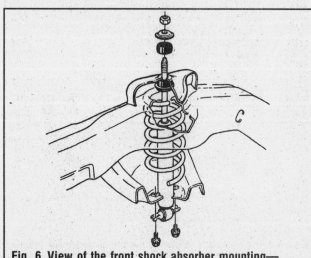

Fig. 6 View of the front shock absorber mounting—1968–79 vehicles

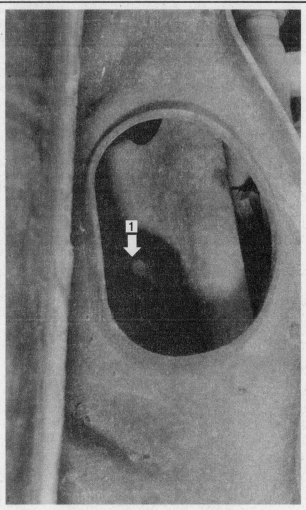

1. Access the upper shock absorber nut through here.

View of the upper shock mounting nut. Start shock removal by unfastening the upper nut—1968-79 only

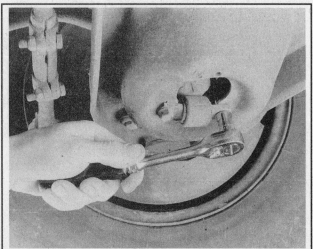

Remove the two bolts securing the shock absorber lower pivot to the lower control arm . . .

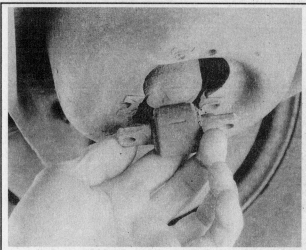

. . . then, on 1968-79 vehicles, pull the shock absorber out through the bottom

6. Use an open-end wrench to secure the upper stem of the shock absorber and torque the stem retaining nut to 8 ft lbs.

7. Fit the two lower mounting bolts to the lower control arm and torque each bolt to 20 ft lbs.

8. Check the shock absorber action.

Upper Ball Joint

INSPECTION

If an inspection of the upper ball joint on one side of the car indicates that replacement is necessary, it is recommended that the upper ball joint on the other side also be replaced.

1962-67 Chevy II

The upper ball joint is a loose fit when it is not connected to the steering knuckle. Wear may be measured without disassembling the ball joint stud as follows:

1. Fabricate a support for the upper control arm. With the car resting on its wheels, install this support between the upper control arm and the frame side member.

2. Raise the front of the car, allowing the wheel and tire to hang freely.

3. Measure and record the distance from the tip of the ball joint stud to the top surface of the control arm.

4. Position a jack under the tire and raise the tire slightly to take up the slack in the ball joint.

5. Repeat the measurement in step three and, if the difference in the measurements exceeds $3/32$ in., the ball joint is excessively worn and should be replaced.

6. Lower the car and remove the upper control arm support.

1968-79 Chevy II and Nova

◆ See Figure 7

➡Before performing this inspection, make sure the wheel bearings are adjusted correctly and that the A-arm bushings are in good condition.

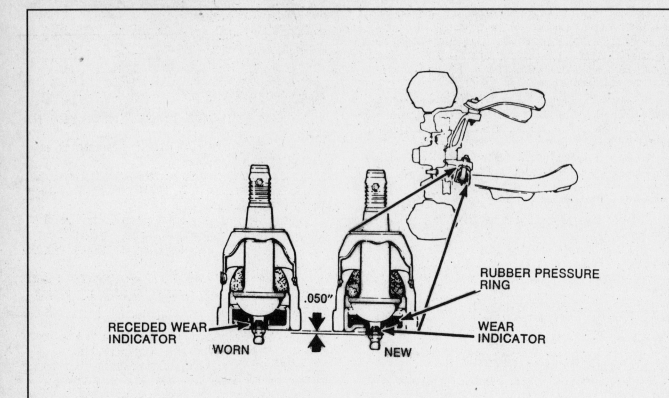

Fig. 7 The lower ball joints on 1975–79 Novas are equipped with wear indicators

1. Jack the car up under the front lower control arm at the spring seat.

2. Raise the car until there is 1–2 in. of clearance under the wheel.

3. Insert a bar under the wheel and pry upward. If the wheel raises more than ⅛ in., the ball joints are worn. Determine if the upper or lower ball joint is worn by visual inspection while prying on the wheel.

4. The upper ball joint can be further inspected after partial suspension disassembly. If the stud has any detectable side-to-side movement or if it can be twisted with your fingers it should be replaced.

➡️**Due to the distribution of forces in the suspension, the lower ball joint is usually the defective joint. Because of this, 1975 and later Nova models are equipped with wear indicators on the lower ball joint. As long as the indicator extends below the ball stud seat, replacement is unnecessary.**

REMOVAL & INSTALLATION

◗ **See Figure 8**

1962–67 Chevy II

1. Perform steps one and two of the "Upper Ball Joint Inspection" procedure and remove the wheel and tire.

2. Disconnect the stabilizer link (if so equipped) and the strut rod at the lower control arm.

3. Remove the cotter pin and nut from the upper ball joint stud. Place a jack under the lower control arm.

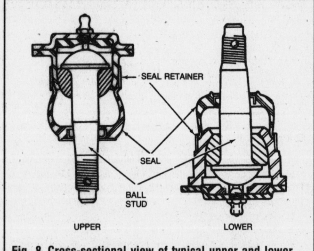

Fig. 8 Cross-sectional view of typical upper and lower ball joints

4. Break the ball joint stud loose. Lower the jack to drop the lower control arm and steering knuckle assembly, thereby gaining easy access to the upper ball joint.

5. Using a large chisel, cut off the three ball joint retaining plate rivet heads. The upper control arm may require additional support while chiseling. If necessary, drill out the rivet heads before chiseling.

6. Clean the ball joint seat in the upper control arm. Inspect the seat for cracks or other evidence of fatigue and, if necessary, replace the control arm.

7. Fit the replacement ball joint assembly to the upper control arm, using the bolts supplied with the replacement kit.

8. Raise the jack to position the lower control arm and steering knuckle assembly, and insert the upper ball joint stud into the upper boss of the steering knuckle. Fit the stud nut and torque to 45 ft. lbs. Install a new cotter pin.

9. Connect the stabilizer link (if so equipped) and the strut rod to the lower control arm.

10. Lubricate the new ball joint. Install the wheel and tire, and remove the jack.

11. Lower the car and remove the control arm support. Check and adjust the front-end alignment as required.

1968 and Later Chevy II and Nova

1. Perform steps one and two of the "Upper Ball Joint Inspection" procedure.

2. Using a chisel, cut off the upper ball joint rivets. Clean the ball joint seat in the upper control arm. Inspect the seat for cracks or other evidence of fatigue and, if necessary, replace the control arm.

3. Increase the diameter of the ball joint stud mounting holes in the control arm to $21/64$ in. so that the $5/16$ in. bolts included in the replacement ball joint kit may be installed.

4. Install the new ball joint and secure it with the special nuts and bolts included in the replacement kit.

5. Reconnect the steering knuckle to the ball joint stud. Fit the stud nut and torque to 50 ft. lbs. Install a new cotter pin.

6. Install the wheel and tire, and lower the car. Check and adjust the front-end alignment as required.

Lower Ball Joint

INSPECTION

If an inspection of the lower ball joint on one side of the car indicates that replacement is necessary, it is recommended that the lower ball joint on the other side also be replaced.

1962–67 Chevy II

1. Fabricate a support for the upper control arm according to the dimensions shown in the illustration. With the car resting on its wheels, install this support between the upper control arm and the frame side member.

2. Remove the cotter pin and nut from the lower ball joint stud. Disconnect the stud from the steering knuckle.

3. Fit the nut to the lower ball joint stud. Using a torque wrench, measure the torque required to rotate the lower ball joint stud. The specified value for a new lower ball joint is 4–8 ft lbs for 1962–65 models, or 9 ft lbs for 1965–67 models. If the torque required is excessively higher or lower than the specified value, the ball joint should be replaced.

4. Reconnect the steering knuckle and remove the upper control arm support.

1968 and Later Chevy II and Nova

See the procedure listed under 1968 and later Upper Ball Joint Inspection.

REMOVAL & INSTALLATION

▶ **See Figure 8**

1962–67 Chevy II

1. Perform step one of the "Lower Ball Joint Inspection" procedure.

2. Raise the front of the car and remove the cotter pin and nut from the lower ball joint stud.

3. Place a jack under the lower control arm. Disconnect the stabilizer at the upper link. Break the ball joint stud loose. Lower the jack to drop the lower control arm.

4. Using a large chisel, cut off the three ball joint retaining plate rivet heads. The lower control arm may require additional support while chiseling. If necessary, drill out the rivet heads before chiseling.

5. Clean the ball joint seat in the lower control arm. Inspect the seat for cracks or other evidence of fatigue and, if necessary, replace the control arm.

To install:

6. Fit the replacement ball joint assembly to the lower control arm, using the bolts supplied with the replacement kit.

7. Raise the jack to position the lower control arm and insert the lower ball joint stud into the lower boss of the steering knuckle. Fit the stud nut and torque to 45 ft lbs. Install a new cotter pin.

8. Connect the stabilizer to the upper link.

9. Lubricate the new ball joint. Remove the jack.

10. Lower the car and remove the control arm support. Check and adjust the front-end alignment as required.

1968 and Later Chevy II and Nova

1. Raise the front of the car and remove the wheel and tire. On cars equipped with disc brakes, remove the brake caliper assembly as described in Section 9.

2. Place a jack under the lower control arm at its outer end.

3. Withdraw the cotter pins from the upper and lower ball joint studs. Remove the upper and lower ball joint stud nuts.

4. Disconnect the ball joint studs from the steering knuckle. Wire the steering knuckle and brake assembly up and out of the way.

5. Using a suitable ball joint removal tool, remove the lower ball joint.

6. Clean the ball joint seat in the lower control arm. Inspect the seat for cracks or other evidence of fatigue and, if necessary, replace the control arm.

7. Fit the replacement ball joint in the control arm and, using the special tool, seat the ball joint in the control arm.

8. Insert the ball joint studs in the steering knuckle. Fit the stud nuts and torque the upper nut to 50 ft. lbs. and the lower nut to 85 ft. lbs. Install new cotter pins. Install the brake caliper (if so equipped).

9. Install the wheel and tire, and lower the car. Check and adjust the front-end alignment as required.

Upper Control Arm

REMOVAL & INSTALLATION

1962–67 Chevy II

1. Remove the front shock absorber and the coil spring as described previously.
2. Place a jack under the lower control arm.
3. Remove the cotter pin and nut from the upper ball joint stud. Break the ball joint and stud loose. Lower the jack to drop the lower control arm and steering knuckle assembly.
4. Remove the upper control arm pivot shaft stud nuts from the fender skirt and remove the upper control arm. Inspect the upper control arm for cracks, bends, or other signs of fatigue. Replace if necessary.

To install:

5. Begin installation by inserting the upper control arm pivot shaft into the fender skirt openings. Fit the lockwasher and nuts and torque the nuts to 60–90 ft. lbs.
6. Raise the jack to position the lower control arm and steering knuckle assembly and insert the upper ball joint stud into the upper boss of the steering knuckle. Fit the stud nut and torque to 45 ft. lbs. Install a new cotter pin.
7. Install the coil spring and shock absorber as described previously.
8. Lubricate the new ball joint. Check and adjust the front-end alignment as required.

1968–74 Chevy II and Nova

▶ **See Figure 9**

1. Place a jack under the outer end of the lower control arm to support the weight of the car. Remove the wheel and tire.
2. Remove the cotter pin and nut from the upper ball joint stud. Disconnect the stud from the steering knuckle.
3. Remove the two nuts which secure the upper control arm shaft to the front crossmember. Note the number of shims at each bolt.

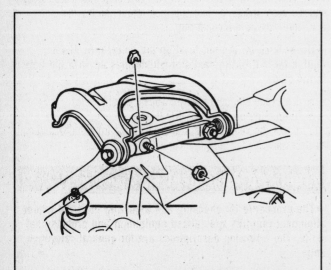

Fig. 9 Upper control arm mounting—1968–74 vehicles

4. If necessary, withdraw the bolts which secure the control arm to the frame to obtain adequate clearance for control arm removal. Inspect the upper control arm for cracks, bends, or other signs of fatigue. Replace if necessary.

To install:

5. Begin installation by positioning the upper control arm in the car. Fit the locknuts and bolts which secure the upper control arm shaft to the frame. Be sure to install the same number of shims as were removed at each bolt. Torque the bolts to 50 ft. lbs.
6. Connect the steering knuckle to the ball joint stud. Fit the stud nut and torque to 50 ft. lbs. Install a new cotter pin.
7. Install the wheel and tire and lower the car. Bounce the front end of the car to centralize the bushings. Torque the bushing collar bolts to 50 ft. lbs. Check and adjust the front-end alignment as required.

1975–79 Nova

1. Raise the vehicle on a hoist.
2. Support the lower control arm with a jackstand.
3. Remove the tire and wheel.
4. Separate the upper control arm ball stud from the steering knuckle.
5. Remove the two nuts which secure the upper control arm shaft to the frame bracket.

➡ **Tape the shims together and mark them for the position from which they were removed.**

In some cases it is necessary to remove the upper control arm attaching bolts to allow clearance to remove the upper control arm. The attaching bolts are splined into the frame. To remove them, proceed as follows:

   a. Tap the bolt down gently with a brass drift;
   b. Gently pry the bolt up with a box wrench;
   c. Remove the nut and, using a suitable prybar and block of wood, pry the bolts from the frame.

6. Remove the upper control arm from the vehicle.

To install:

7. To install the upper control arm, loosen the end shaft retainer bolts and/or nuts.
8. If they were removed, position new upper control arm attaching bolts loosely in the frame and install the control arm crossshaft on the attaching bolts.
9. Using a free running nut instead of the regular locknut, tighten both nuts until the serrated bolts are reseated.
10. Remove the free running nuts and install the regular locknuts.
11. Install the same number of shims to each bolt which were removed and taped together. Torque the nuts to 75 ft. lbs.

➡ **Tighten the nut on the thinner shim pack first for improved shaft-to-frame clamping force and torque retention.**

12. Install the ball joint stud through the steering knuckle, torque the nut to 60 ft. lbs, and install the cotter pin.

➡ **Never back off the nut to align the cotter pin. Always tighten the nut to the next slot which lines up with the hole in the stud.**

13. Install the tire and wheel and lower the vehicle.
14. With the vehicle lowered, torque the shaft retainer bolts and/or nuts to 75 ft. lbs. Check and adjust the front end alignment as necessary.

Lower Control Arm

REMOVAL & INSTALLATION

1962–67 Chevy II

▶ **See Figure 10**

1. Perform steps one, two, and three of the lower ball joint "Removal and Installation" procedure.
2. Mark the lower control arm pivot bolt and adjusting cam to ensure proper alignment during installation.
3. Remove the nut which secures the pivot bolt and cam assembly and withdraw the pivot bolt and cam. Remove the lower control arm.
4. Inspect the lower control arm for cracks, bends, or other signs of fatigue. Replace if necessary.

To install:

5. Begin installation by positioning the lower control arm in its support bracket. Align the pivot bolt assembly and install. Fit the pivot nut and torque to 90–120 ft. lbs. for 1962–64 models, or to 60–75 ft. lbs. for 1965–67 models.
6. Perform steps 7–10 of the corresponding lower ball joint "Removal and Installation" procedure.

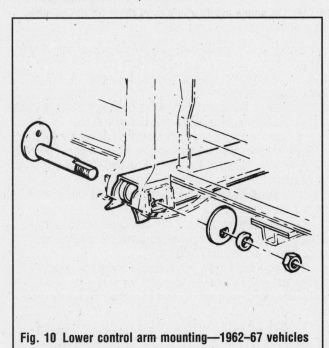

Fig. 10 Lower control arm mounting—1962–67 vehicles

1968–74 Chevy II and Nova

▶ **See Figure 11**

1. Remove the front coil spring as described previously.
2. Disconnect the lower ball joint stud from the steering knuckle as described in steps 1–4 of the corresponding lower ball joint "Removal and Installation" procedure.
3. Remove the pivot bolts and nuts which secure the lower control arm to the frame and withdraw the control arm.
4. Inspect the lower control arm for cracks, bends, or other signs of fatigue. Replace if necessary.

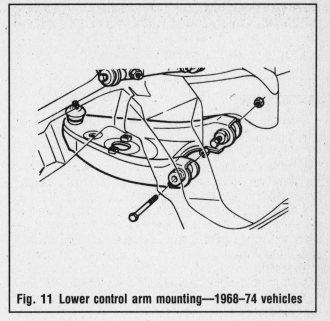

Fig. 11 Lower control arm mounting—1968–74 vehicles

To install:

5. Begin installation by positioning the lower control arm in the frame and fitting the pivot bolts and nuts. Torque the bolts to 80 ft. lbs.
6. Insert the lower ball joint stud into the steering knuckle. Fit the stud nut and torque to 85 ft. lbs. Install new cotter pins and the brake caliper.
7. Install the front coil spring as described previously.
8. Lower the car. Check and adjust the front-end alignment as required.

1975–79 Nova

1. Remove the coil spring as previously described.
2. Remove the ball joint from the steering knuckle as previously described.
3. Remove the pivot bolts and nuts which secure the lower control arm to the frame and remove the control arm.

To install:

4. Insert the lower control arm ball joint stud into the steering knuckle boss. Install the ball stud nut, torque the nut to 83 ft. lbs., and insert a new cotter pin.

➡ **Never back off the nut to align the cotter pin. Always tighten the nut to the next slot which lines up with the hole in the stud.**

5. Install the coil spring as previously described.
6. Torque the pivot nuts to 100 ft. lbs.
7. Lower the vehicle. Check and adjust the front end alignment as necessary.

Front End Alignment

➡ **The procedure for checking and adjusting the front wheel alignment requires specialized equipment and professional skills. The following descriptions are for general reference only.**

Front wheel alignment is the position of the front wheels relative to each other and to the vehicle. It is determined and must be maintained to provide safe, accurate steering with minimum tire wear. Many factors are involved in wheel alignment and adjustments are provided to return those that might change due to normal wear to their original value. The factors which determine wheel alignment are dependent on one another; therefore, when one of the factors is adjusted, the others must be adjusted to compensate. Descriptions of these factors and their effects on the vehicle are provided below.

➡**Do not attempt to check and/or adjust the front wheel alignment without first making a thorough inspection of the front suspension components.**

CASTER

Caster angle is the number of degrees that a line drawn through the steering knuckle pivots is inclined from the vertical, toward the front or rear of the vehicle. Caster improves directional stability and decreases susceptibility to crosswinds or road surface deviations.

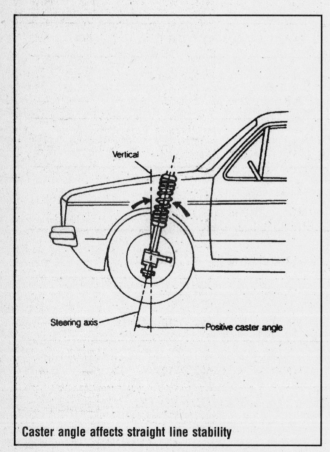

Caster angle affects straight line stability

CAMBER

Camber angle is the number of degrees that the centerline of the wheel is inclined from the vertical. Camber reduces loading of the outer wheel bearing and improves the tire contact patch while cornering.

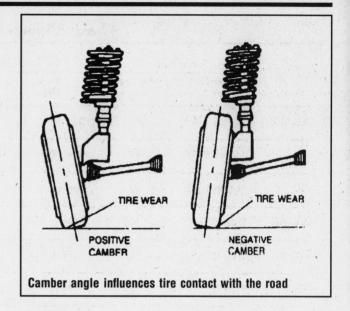

Camber angle influences tire contact with the road

TOE-IN

Toe-in is the difference of the distance between the centers of the front and rear of the front wheels. It is most commonly measured in inches, but is occasionally referred to as an angle between the wheels. Toe-in is necessary to compensate for the tendency of the wheels to deflect rearward while in motion. Due to this tendency, the wheels of a vehicle, with properly adjusted toe-in, are traveling straight forward when the vehicle itself is traveling straight forward, resulting in directional stability and minimum tire wear.

➡**The Do-It-Yourself mechanic should not attempt to perform any wheel alignment procedures. Expensive alignment equipment and tools are needed and it would not be cost efficient to purchase these tools. The wheel alignment should be performed by a certified alignment technician using the proper alignment tools.**

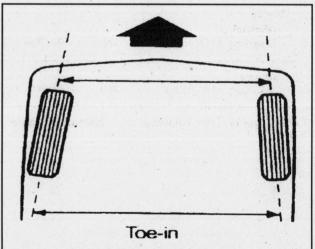

Toe-in means the distance between the wheels is closer at the front than at the rear of the wheels

Wheel Alignment Specifications

Year	CASTER Range (deg)	CASTER Pref Setting (deg)	CAMBER Range (deg)	CAMBER Pref Setting (deg)	Toe-in (in.)	Steering Axis Inclination (deg)	WHEEL PIVOT RATIO (deg) Inner Wheel	WHEEL PIVOT RATIO (deg) Outer Wheel
'62–'65	$\frac{1}{2}$P to $1\frac{1}{2}$P	1P	0 to 1P	$\frac{1}{2}$P	$\frac{1}{4}$ to $\frac{3}{8}$	7	20	$18\frac{3}{4}$
'66	$\frac{1}{2}$P to $1\frac{1}{2}$P	1P	0 to 1P	$\frac{1}{2}$P	$\frac{1}{4}$ to $\frac{3}{8}$	7	20	$18\frac{3}{4}$
'67	$\frac{1}{2}$P to $1\frac{1}{2}$P	1P	0 to 1P	$\frac{1}{2}$P	$\frac{1}{8}$ to $\frac{1}{4}$	7	20	$18\frac{3}{4}$
'68–'69	0 to 1P	$\frac{1}{2}$P	$\frac{1}{4}$N to $\frac{3}{4}$P	$\frac{1}{2}$P	$\frac{1}{8}$ to $\frac{1}{4}$	$8\frac{3}{4}$	20	NA
'70–'71	0 to 1P	$\frac{1}{2}$P	$\frac{1}{4}$N to $\frac{3}{4}$P	$\frac{1}{2}$P	$\frac{1}{8}$ to $\frac{1}{4}$	$8\frac{1}{4}$ to $9\frac{1}{4}$	20	NA
'72	0 to 1P	$\frac{1}{2}$P	$\frac{1}{4}$N to $\frac{3}{4}$P	$\frac{1}{4}$P	$\frac{1}{8}$ to $\frac{1}{4}$	$8\frac{3}{4}$ to $9\frac{1}{4}$	NA	NA
'73	$\frac{1}{2}$N to $1\frac{1}{2}$P	$\frac{1}{2}$P	$\frac{1}{2}$N to 1P	$\frac{3}{4}$P	$\frac{1}{16}$ to $\frac{5}{16}$	9	NA	NA
'74	0 to 1P	$\frac{1}{2}$P	$\frac{1}{4}$ to $\frac{3}{4}$P	$\frac{1}{4}$P	$\frac{1}{8}$ to $\frac{1}{4}$	$8\frac{3}{4}$	NA	NA
'75–'76 (Manual Steering)	$1\frac{1}{2}$N to $\frac{1}{2}$N	1N	$\frac{1}{4}$P to $1\frac{1}{4}$P	$\frac{3}{4}$P	0 to $\frac{1}{8}$	10	—	—
(Power Steering)	$\frac{1}{2}$P to $1\frac{1}{2}$P	1P	$\frac{1}{4}$P to $1\frac{1}{4}$P	$\frac{3}{4}$P	0 to $\frac{1}{8}$	10	—	—
'77 (Manual Steering)	1N to $\frac{1}{2}$P	$\frac{1}{4}$N	$\frac{3}{10}$P to $1\frac{3}{10}$P	$\frac{4}{5}$P	0 to $\frac{1}{8}$	10	—	—
(Power Steering)	$\frac{1}{2}$P to $1\frac{1}{2}$P	$\frac{3}{4}$P	$\frac{3}{10}$P to $1\frac{3}{10}$P	$\frac{4}{5}$P	0 to $\frac{1}{8}$	10	—	—
'78–'79 (Manual Steering)	$1\frac{1}{2}$N to $\frac{1}{2}$N	1N	$\frac{3}{10}$P to $1\frac{3}{10}$P	$\frac{4}{5}$P	$\frac{1}{16}$ to $\frac{3}{16}$	10	—	—
(Power Steering)	$\frac{1}{2}$P to $1\frac{1}{2}$P	$\frac{3}{4}$P	$\frac{3}{10}$P to $1\frac{3}{10}$P	$\frac{4}{5}$P	$\frac{1}{16}$ to $\frac{3}{16}$	10	—	—

N Negative   P Positive   NA Not available

REAR SUSPENSION

1. Leaf spring front mount
2. Lower shock absorber mount
3. Rear shock absorber
4. Leaf spring assembly
5. Leaf spring shackle

Rear suspension component locations

All Chevy II and Nova models built until 1977 have a leaf spring rear suspension. Some light-duty models, and all Chevy II models up to 1967, have single-leaf rear springs. Other models use the more conventional multiple leaf springs.

All leaf spring equipped models, starting in 1968, use staggered shock absorbers to prevent axle hop on hard acceleration. The right shock absorber is mounted forward of the axle and the left shock absorber is mounted behind the axle.

Some 1977 and later Novas are equipped with a coil spring rear suspension for improved ride. The axle is located by means of four rubber bushed control arms—two upper and two lower. The lower arms control primarily for and aft movement of the axle, while the primary duty of the upper control arms is to absorb braking and accelerating torque and, due to their angular mounting, sideways motion of the axle. With coil spring rear suspension, both shock absorbers are mounted in front of the axle.

Leaf Springs

REMOVAL & INSTALLATION

▶ **See Figures 12, 13, 14 and 15**

1. Raise the rear of the vehicle and support it with jackstands at both frame side members, near the front eyes of the springs. Position a jack under the rear axle and raise the axle assembly until all tension is removed from the springs.

2. Separate the handbrake cable from its clamp. Disconnect the cable above the axle banjo housing. Remove the shock absorber lower mounting bolt.

3. Remove the four nuts which secure the lower spring pad mounting bracket to the axle spring seat. Lower the bracket and remove the rubber spring pad.

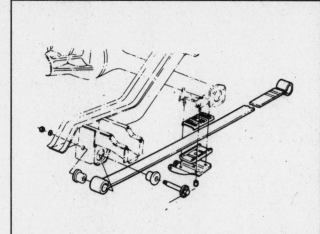

Fig. 12 Exploded view of the single-leaf spring assembly mounting

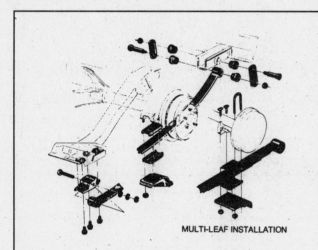

MULTI-LEAF INSTALLATION

Fig. 13 Rear leaf spring assembly—multiple leaf-type shown

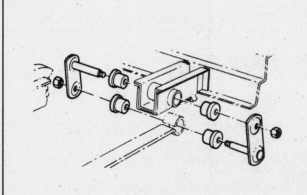

Fig. 14 Exploded view of the rear spring shackle—all models, except station wagons

Fig. 15 Rear spring shackle mounting for station wagons

4. Loosen and drive out the front spring eye bolt. Lower the spring and remove the front rubber eye bushing.

5. Remove the nuts from the rear spring shackle. Note the positions of the shackle nuts. Separate the spring eye and support bracket from the shackle by spreading the shackle and then removing the spring. Withdraw the rear spring eye bushings.

6. Remove the upper spring pad cushion.

To install:

7. Assemble the rear shackle. Insert the inboard rubber spring eye bushings into the spring eye and the outboard shackle bushings into the shackle mounting bracket. Place the rear spring in position and fit the shackle to the spring and mounting bracket.

➡**On all models, except station wagons, the top nut of the shackle should be toward the outside of the car. On station wagons, the top nut should be toward the center of the car.**

8. Position the inboard rubber bushing in the spring front eye.

9. Position the upper spring pad cushion on the spring and raise the spring, being certain that the ribs of the spring cushion align with the spring seat locating ribs.

10. Insert the spring front eye and its bushing in the frame bracket. Fit the spring eye bolt, bushing, retainer, lockwasher, and nut, but do not tighten the nut yet.

11. Position the lower spring pad cushion on the spring. Check to see that the upper and lower spring pads are aligned.

12. Position the lower mounting plate over the locating dowel on the spring pad. Install the four locknuts and torque them to 45–55 ft. lbs. Fit the shock absorber lower eyebolt and torque to 45–55 ft. lbs.

13. Remove the supports and lower the car. Bounce the rear of the car several times and torque the front eyebolt to 60–80 ft. lbs. and the rear shackle nuts to 30–50 ft. lbs.

Coil Springs

REMOVAL & INSTALLATION

➡**Do not attempt to remove both coil springs from the rear suspension at once—replace them one at a time.**

1. Support the car securely on axle stands. Support the rear axle with an adjustable jack.
2. Disconnect both upper control arms from the axle.
3. Disconnect the stabilizer bar (if so equipped) from the side you are working on.
4. Remove brake hose support bolt and support to permit the axle to drop. Do not disconnect any brake lines.
5. Remove the lower attachments from the shock on the side you are working on.
6. Lower the axle *until the spring is no longer under compression,* and remove it. *Be careful not to pull the spring free of the axle and frame while it is still under compression.*

To install:

➡**Use only replacement parts which match Chevrolet Specifications.**

7. Position the insulator on top of the spring with the lip downward so spring coils will locate it.
8. Position the spring between axle and frame with the upper end coil leg pointing outwards and directly perpendicular to the centerline of the vehicle—that is, pointing straight outward.
9. Make sure the spring is properly located—with top and bottom coils surrounding the appropriate parts of frame and axle so compression cannot cause it to spring free. Raise the axle on the jack.
10. Reconnect shock absorbers. Remount brake hose support. Connect stabilizer bar to axle.
11. Connect upper control arms to the axle. Remove the jack and lower the car to the ground.

Shock Absorbers

REMOVAL & INSTALLATION

1962–67 Chevy II

◆ **See Figure 16**

1. Raise the rear of the car and support the rear axle housing with a jack.
2. Remove the shock absorber lower mounting bolt from the shock absorber eye.
3. Withdraw the shock absorber upper mounting bracket bolts and remove the shock absorber.
4. Remove the nut, washer, bushing, and upper mounting bracket from the shock absorber.

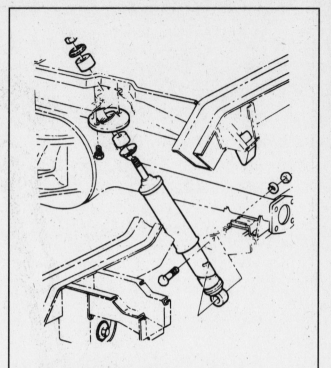

Fig. 16 Exploded view of the rear shock absorber mounting—1962–67 vehicles

To install:

5. Assemble the nut, washer, rubber brushings, and upper mounting bracket to the shock absorber and torque the nut 9–12 ft. lbs.
6. Position the shock absorber with its upper bracket to the floor pan and torque the bracket bolts to 9–12 ft. lbs. for 1962–64 models or 5–10 ft. lbs. for 1965–67 models.
7. Position the shock absorber eye in the lower bracket, fit the bolt with the nut toward the rear, and torque it to 45–55 ft. lbs.
8. Lower the car and check the shock absorber action.

1968 and Later Chevy II and Nova

◆ **See Figure 17**

1. Raise the rear of the car and support the rear axle housing with a jack.
2. Remove the shock absorber lower mounting bolt from the shock absorber eye.
3. Withdraw the shock absorber upper mounting bracket bolts and remove the shock absorber.

To install:

4. Position the shock absorber at its upper mounting bracket and loosely install the upper mounting bolts.
5. Position the shock absorber eye in the lower bracket, fit the bolt with the nut toward the rear, and torque to 45 ft. lbs. or 60 ft. lbs. on models equipped with optional special performance suspension.
6. Torque the upper mounting bolts to 15 ft. lbs.
7. Lower the car and check the shock absorber action.

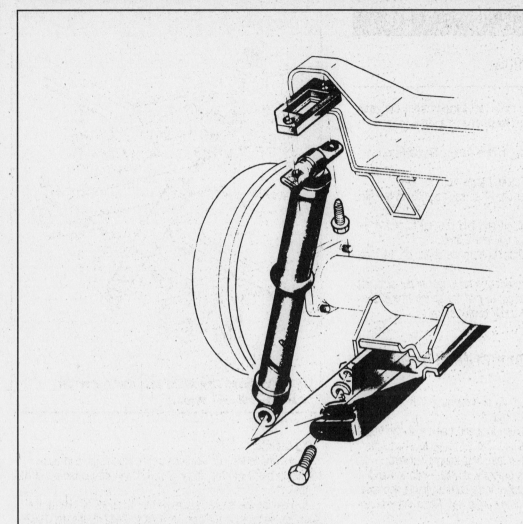

Fig. 17 Rear shock absorber mounting—1968–79 vehicles

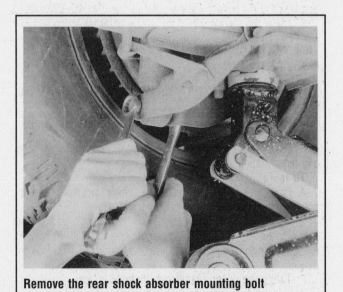

Remove the rear shock absorber mounting bolt

Remove the upper mounting bracket bolts, then remove the shock absorber

STEERING

All Chevy II and Nova models are fitted with a steering gear of the recirculating ball nut type. The ball nut, mounted on the worm gear, is driven by means of steel balls which circulate in helical grooves in both the worm and nut. Ball return guides attached to the nut serve to recirculate the two sets of balls in the grooves. As the steering wheel is turned to the right, the ball nut moves upward. When the wheel is turned to the left, the ball nut moves downward.

The sector teeth on the pinion shaft and the ball nut are designed so that they fit the tightest when the steering wheel is straight ahead. This mesh action is adjusted by an adjusting screw which moves the pinion shaft endwise until the teeth mesh properly. The worm bearing adjuster provides proper preloading of the upper and lower bearings.

Two types of power assist have been offered as optional equipment. A linkage-assist type, used on 1962–67 Chevy II models, has a pump which delivers an assist to a power cylinder attached to the steering linkage. Later models are equipped with an integral type of power steering gear. This type has a pump which delivers hydraulic pressure through two hoses to the steering gear itself.

Steering Wheel

REMOVAL & INSTALLATION

▶ See Figure 18

✳✳ CAUTION

Be very careful when removing the steering wheel from a car that is equipped with a collapsible steering column. A sharp blow or excessive pressure on the column could cause it to collapse, thereby destroying the steering column.

1. Disconnect the battery ground cable. Disconnect the chassis wiring harness from the steering column harness at the connector under the instrument panel.
2. Remove the horn button cap or the center ornament and retainer. Withdraw the three screws from the receiving cup.
3. Remove the receiving cup, belleville spring, bushing, and pivot ring.
4. Remove the retaining circlip with a suitable pair of pliers, if applicable.
5. Remove the steering wheel nut and washer.
6. Using a steering wheel puller, carefully remove the steering wheel.
7. Install the steering wheel using the reverse of the procedure above. Before installing the steering wheel, be sure that the directional signal control assembly is in the neutral position.

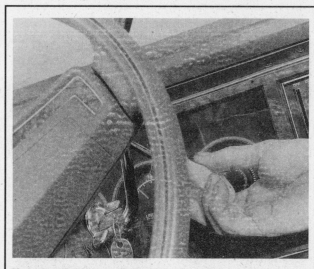

Unfasten the horn pad retaining screws . . .

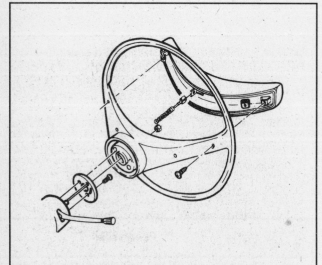

Fig. 18 Steering wheel and horn pad mounting

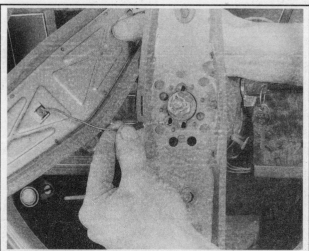

. . . then pull the horn pad away from the wheel and detach the electrical connector

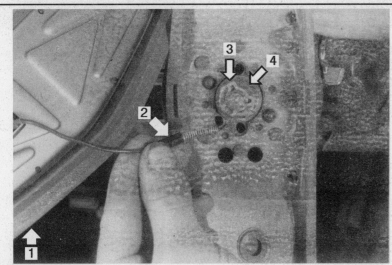

1. Horn pad
2. Horn pad electrical connector
3. Retaining circlip (snapring)
4. Steering wheel retaining nut

Steering wheel mounting components

If equipped, use snapring pliers to remove the retaining circlip

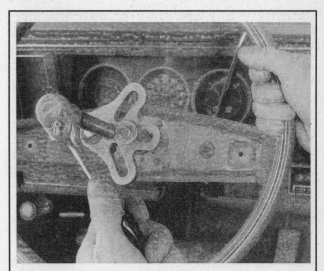

Use a suitable steering wheel puller to loosen . . .

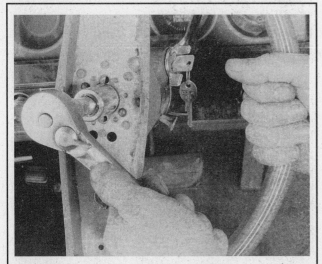

Remove the steering wheel attaching nut

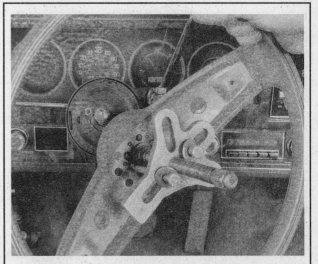

. . . then remove the steering wheel from the column

Turn Signal Switch

REMOVAL & INSTALLATION

1. Remove the steering wheel as described above.
2. Withdraw the turn signal lever arm mounting screws and remove the lever from the cancelling mechanism.
3. Withdraw the gearshift control lever retaining pin and remove the lever (on models so equipped).
4. Push in the hazard warning switch knob and unscrew the knob (if so equipped).
5. Remove the steering column mast jacket upper and lower covers.
6. Remove the automatic transmission dial indicator housing (on models so equipped).
7. Withdraw the three screws which secure the turn signal control assembly to the signal housing and remove the assembly.
8. Installation is the reverse of the removal procedure.

Ignition Switch (Column-Mounted)

REMOVAL & INSTALLATION

1969–79 Vehicles

All 1969 and later models have the ignition lock cylinder located on the upper right-side of the steering column. The ignition switch is inside the channel section of the brake pedal support. The switch is inaccessible unless the steering column is lowered.

1. Lower the steering column. The column must be carefully supported to prevent damage.
2. Remove the lock cylinder using the procedure for 1968 models which is in Section 6.

➡ **Pull the actuating rod for the switch up until a definite stop is felt, then push it down one detent to the Lock position.**

3. Remove the two switch screws and the switch assembly.
4. On installation, make sure that the switch and the lock are in the **LOCK** position. Do not use switch screws longer than the originals or the energy absorbing function of the column may be lost.

Power Steering Pump

REMOVAL & INSTALLATION

♦ **See Figure 19**

1. Remove the pump belt.
2. Remove the hoses at the pump and tape the openings shut to prevent contamination. Position the disconnected lines in a raised position to prevent leakage.

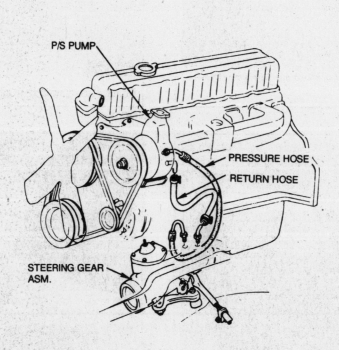

Fig. 19 View of the power steering pump and related system components—in-line 6-cylinder engine shown

Use a flare-end wrench to loosen . . .

. . . then disconnect the line from the power steering pump

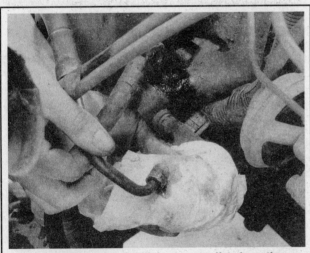

. . . then disconnect the high pressure line from the power steering pump

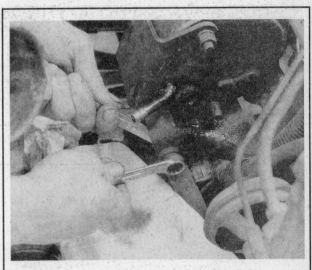

Remove the power steering pump mounting bolts . . .

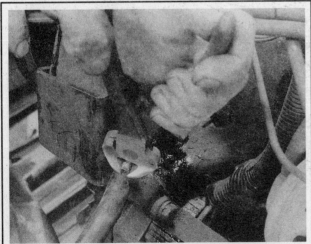

Use a pair of snips to cut the power steering pump fluid hose clamp . . .

. . . then remove the power steering pump from the engine

3. Loosen the retaining bolts and any braces, and remove the pump.

To install:

4. Install the pump on the engine with the retaining bolt hand-tight.

5. Connect and tighten the hose fittings.

6. Refill the pump with fluid and bleed by turning the pulley counterclockwise (viewed from the front). Stop the bleeding when air bubbles no longer appear.

7. Install the pump belt on the pulley and adjust the tension.

BLEEDING

1. Fill the fluid reservoir.

2. Let the fluid stand undisturbed for two minutes, then crank the engine for about two seconds. Refill reservoir if necessary.

3. Repeat Steps 1 and 2 above until the fluid level remains constant after cranking the engine.

4. Raise the front of the car until the wheels are off the ground, then start the engine. Increase the engine speed to about 1,500 rpm.

5. Turn the wheels to the left and right, checking the fluid level and refilling if necessary.

Tie-Rod Ends

REMOVAL & INSTALLATION

▶ **See Figure 20**

1. Matchmark the position of the tie-rod end for installation.

2. Remove the cotter pins and nuts from the tie-rod end studs.

3. Tap on the steering arm near the tierod end (use another hammer as backing) and pull down on the tie-rod, if necessary, to free it.

4. Remove the inner stud in the same manner as the outer.

5. Loosen the clamp bolts and unscrew the ends if they are being replaced.

To install:

6. Lubricate the tie-rod end threads with chassis grease if they were removed. Install each end assembly an equal distance from the sleeve.

7. Ensure that the tie-rod end stud threads and nut are clean. Install new seals and install the studs into the steering arms and relay rod.

8. Install the stud nuts. Tighten the outer end nut to 35 ft. lbs. and the inner nut to 60 ft. lbs.

9. Adjust the toe-in to specifications.

➡ **Before tightening the sleeve clamps, ensure that the clamps are positioned so that the adjusting sleeve slot is covered by the clamp.**

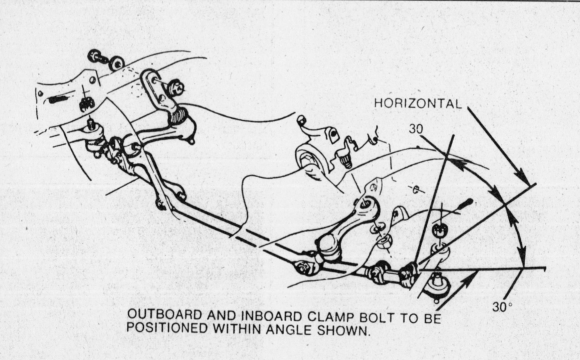

OUTBOARD AND INBOARD CLAMP BOLT TO BE POSITIONED WITHIN ANGLE SHOWN.

Fig. 20 View of the steering linkage mounting

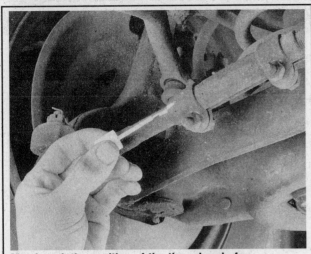

Matchmark the position of the tie-rod ends for installation purposes

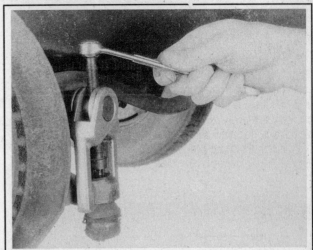

It may be necessary to use a steering linkage puller to loosen . . .

Use a pair of pliers to remove the cotter pin . . .

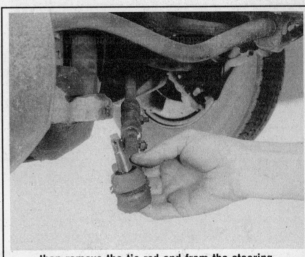

. . . then remove the tie-rod end from the steering knuckle

. . . then, remove the nut from the tie-rod end stud

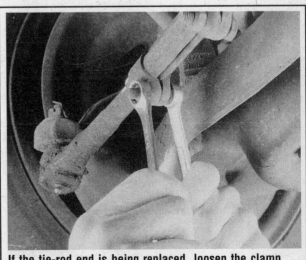

If the tie-rod end is being replaced, loosen the clamp bolts . . .

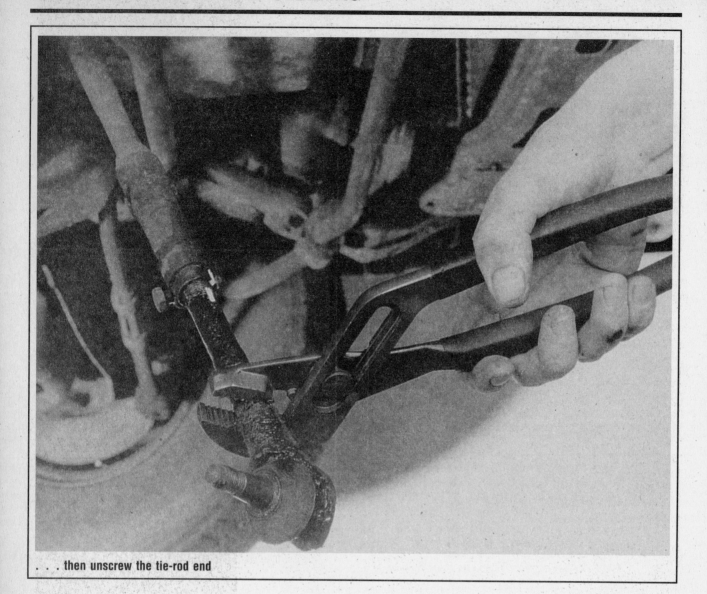

. . . then unscrew the tie-rod end

BRAKE SYSTEM 9-2
BASIC OPERATING PRINCIPLES 9-2
  DISC BRAKES 9-2
  DRUM BRAKES 9-3
  POWER BOOSTERS 9-3
SYSTEM DESCRIPTION 9-3
MASTER CYLINDER 9-3
  REMOVAL & INSTALLATION 9-3
  OVERHAUL 9-4
PRESSURE DIFFERENTIAL WARNING
 SWITCH AND COMBINATION
 VALVE 9-6
  REMOVAL & INSTALLATION 9-7
BLEEDING BRAKE SYSTEM 9-8
  PRESSURE BLEEDING 9-8
  MANUAL BLEEDING 9-8
FRONT DISC BRAKES 9-9
BRAKE PADS 9-9
  REMOVAL & INSTALLATION 9-9
BRAKE CALIPER 9-11
  REMOVAL & INSTALLATION 9-11
BRAKE DISC (ROTOR) 9-13
  REMOVAL & INSTALLATION 9-13
  INSPECTION 9-14
WHEEL BEARINGS 9-14
  ADJUSTMENT 9-14
  REMOVAL & INSTALLATION 9-14
  PACKING 9-15
DRUM BRAKES 9-15
BRAKE DRUMS 9-15
  REMOVAL & INSTALLATION 9-15
  INSPECTION 9-16
BRAKE SHOES 9-16
  ADJUSTMENT 9-16
  REMOVAL & INSTALLATION 9-16
WHEEL CYLINDERS 9-20
  OVERHAUL 9-20
WHEEL BEARINGS 9-21
PARKING BRAKE 9-21
CABLES 9-21
  ADJUSTMENT 9-21
  REMOVAL & INSTALLATION 9-21
COMPONENT LOCATIONS
 BRAKE MASTER CYLINDER AND
  RELATED COMPONENTS 9-7
 REAR DRUM BRAKES 9-19
SPECIFICATION CHARTS
 BRAKE SPECIFICATIONS 9-24

9

BRAKES

BRAKE SYSTEM 9-2
FRONT DISC BRAKES 9-9
DRUM BRAKES 9-15
PARKING BRAKE 9-21

BRAKE SYSTEM

Basic Operating Principles

Hydraulic systems are used to actuate the brakes of all modern automobiles. The system transports the power required to force the frictional surfaces of the braking system together from the pedal to the individual brake units at each wheel. A hydraulic system is used for two reasons.

First, fluid under pressure can be carried to all parts of an automobile by small pipes and flexible hoses without taking up a significant amount of room or posing routing problems.

Second, a great mechanical advantage can be given to the brake pedal end of the system, and the foot pressure required to actuate the brakes can be reduced by making the surface area of the master cylinder pistons smaller than that of any of the pistons in the wheel cylinders or calipers.

The master cylinder consists of a fluid reservoir along with a double cylinder and piston assembly. Double type master cylinders are designed to separate the front and rear braking systems hydraulically in case of a leak. The master cylinder coverts mechanical motion from the pedal into hydraulic pressure within the lines. This pressure is translated back into mechanical motion at the wheels by either the wheel cylinder (drum brakes) or the caliper (disc brakes).

Steel lines carry the brake fluid to a point on the vehicle's frame near each of the vehicle's wheels. The fluid is then carried to the calipers and wheel cylinders by flexible tubes in order to allow for suspension and steering movements.

In drum brake systems, each wheel cylinder contains two pistons, one at either end, which push outward in opposite directions and force the brake shoe into contact with the drum.

In disc brake systems, the cylinders are part of the calipers. At least one cylinder in each caliper is used to force the brake pads against the disc.

All pistons employ some type of seal, usually made of rubber, to minimize fluid leakage. A rubber dust boot seals the outer end of the cylinder against dust and dirt. The boot fits around the outer end of the piston on disc brake calipers, and around the brake actuating rod on wheel cylinders.

The hydraulic system operates as follows: When at rest, the entire system, from the piston(s) in the master cylinder to those in the wheel cylinders or calipers, is full of brake fluid. Upon application of the brake pedal, fluid trapped in front of the master cylinder piston(s) is forced through the lines to the wheel cylinders. Here, it forces the pistons outward, in the case of drum brakes, and inward toward the disc, in the case of disc brakes. The motion of the pistons is opposed by return springs mounted outside the cylinders in drum brakes, and by spring seals, in disc brakes.

Upon release of the brake pedal, a spring located inside the master cylinder immediately returns the master cylinder pistons to the normal position. The pistons contain check valves and the master cylinder has compensating ports drilled in it. These are uncovered as the pistons reach their normal position. The piston check valves allow fluid to flow toward the wheel cylinders or calipers as the pistons withdraw. Then, as the return springs force the brake pads or shoes into the released position, the excess fluid reservoir through the compensating ports. It is during the time the pedal is in the released position that any fluid that has

leaked out of the system will be replaced through the compensating ports.

Dual circuit master cylinders employ two pistons, located one behind the other, in the same cylinder. The primary piston is actuated directly by mechanical linkage from the brake pedal through the power booster. The secondary piston is actuated by fluid trapped between the two pistons. If a leak develops in front of the secondary piston, it moves forward until it bottoms against the front of the master cylinder, and the fluid trapped between the pistons will operate the rear brakes. If the rear brakes develop a leak, the primary piston will move forward until direct contact with the secondary piston takes place, and it will force the secondary piston to actuate the front brakes. In either case, the brake pedal moves farther when the brakes are applied, and less braking power is available.

All dual circuit systems use a switch to warn the driver when only half of the brake system is operational. This switch is usually located in a valve body which is mounted on the firewall or the frame below the master cylinder. A hydraulic piston receives pressure from both circuits, each circuit's pressure being applied to one end of the piston. When the pressures are in balance, the piston remains stationary. When one circuit has a leak, however, the greater pressure in that circuit during application of the brakes will push the piston to one side, closing the switch and activating the brake warning light.

In disc brake systems, this valve body also contains a metering valve and, in some cases, a proportioning valve. The metering valve keeps pressure from traveling to the disc brakes on the front wheels until the brake shoes on the rear wheels have contacted the drums, ensuring that the front brakes will never be used alone. The proportioning valve controls the pressure to the rear brakes to lessen the chance of rear wheel lock-up during very hard braking.

Warning lights may be tested by depressing the brake pedal and holding it while opening one of the wheel cylinder bleeder screws. If this does not cause the light to go on, substitute a new lamp, make continuity checks, and, finally, replace the switch as necessary.

The hydraulic system may be checked for leaks by applying pressure to the pedal gradually and steadily. If the pedal sinks very slowly to the floor, the system has a leak. This is not to be confused with a springy or spongy feel due to the compression of air within the lines. If the system leaks, there will be a gradual change in the position of the pedal with a constant pressure.

Check for leaks along all lines and at wheel cylinders. If no external leaks are apparent, the problem is inside the master cylinder.

DISC BRAKES

Instead of the traditional expanding brakes that press outward against a circular drum, disc brake systems utilize a disc (rotor) with brake pads positioned on either side of it. An easily-seen analogy is the hand brake arrangement on a bicycle. The pads squeeze onto the rim of the bike wheel, slowing its motion. Automobile disc brakes use the identical principle but apply the braking effort to a separate disc instead of the wheel.

The disc (rotor) is a casting, usually equipped with cooling fins between the two braking surfaces. This enables air to circulate between the braking surfaces making them less sensitive to heat buildup and more resistant to fade. Dirt and water do not drastically affect braking action since contaminants are thrown off by the centrifugal action of the rotor or scraped off the by the pads. Also, the equal clamping action of the two brake pads tends to ensure uniform, straight line stops. Disc brakes are inherently self-adjusting. There are three general types of disc brake:

1. A fixed caliper.
2. A floating caliper.
3. A sliding caliper.

The fixed caliper design uses two pistons mounted on either side of the rotor (in each side of the caliper). The caliper is mounted rigidly and does not move.

The sliding and floating designs are quite similar. In fact, these two types are often lumped together. In both designs, the pad on the inside of the rotor is moved into contact with the rotor by hydraulic force. The caliper, which is not held in a fixed position, moves slightly, bringing the outside pad into contact with the rotor. There are various methods of attaching floating calipers. Some pivot at the bottom or top, and some slide on mounting bolts. In any event, the end result is the same.

DRUM BRAKES

Drum brakes employ two brake shoes mounted on a stationary backing plate. These shoes are positioned inside a circular drum which rotates with the wheel assembly. The shoes are held in place by springs. This allows them to slide toward the drums (when they are applied) while keeping the linings and drums in alignment. The shoes are actuated by a wheel cylinder which is mounted at the top of the backing plate. When the brakes are applied, hydraulic pressure forces the wheel cylinder's actuating links outward. Since these links bear directly against the top of the brake shoes, the tops of the shoes are then forced against the inner side of the drum. This action forces the bottoms of the two shoes to contact the brake drum by rotating the entire assembly slightly (known as servo action). When pressure within the wheel cylinder is relaxed, return springs pull the shoes back away from the drum.

Most modern drum brakes are designed to self-adjust themselves during application when the vehicle is moving in reverse. This motion causes both shoes to rotate very slightly with the drum, rocking an adjusting lever, thereby causing rotation of the adjusting screw. Some drum brake systems are designed to self-adjust during application whenever the brakes are applied. This on-board adjustment system reduces the need for maintenance adjustments and keeps both the brake function and pedal feel satisfactory.

POWER BOOSTERS

Virtually all modern vehicles use a vacuum assisted power brake system to multiply the braking force and reduce pedal effort. Since vacuum is always available when the engine is operating, the system is simple and efficient. A vacuum diaphragm is located on the front of the master cylinder and assists the driver in applying the brakes, reducing both the effort and travel he must put into moving the brake pedal.

The vacuum diaphragm housing is normally connected to the intake manifold by a vacuum hose. A check valve is placed at the point where the hose enters the diaphragm housing, so that during periods of low manifold vacuum brakes assist will not be lost.

Depressing the brake pedal closes off the vacuum source and allows atmospheric pressure to enter on one side of the diaphragm. This causes the master cylinder pistons to move and apply the brakes. When the brake pedal is released, vacuum is applied to both sides of the diaphragm and springs return the diaphragm and master cylinder pistons to the released position.

If the vacuum supply fails, the brake pedal rod will contact the end of the master cylinder actuator rod and the system will apply the brakes without any power assistance. The driver will notice that much higher pedal effort is needed to stop the car and that the pedal feels harder than usual.

Vacuum Leak Test

1. Operate the engine at idle without touching the brake pedal for at least one minute.
2. Turn off the engine and wait one minute.
3. Test for the presence of assist vacuum by depressing the brake pedal and releasing it several times. If vacuum is present in the system, light application will produce less and less pedal travel. If there is no vacuum, air is leaking into the system.

System Operation Test

1. With the engine **OFF**, pump the brake pedal until the supply vacuum is entirely gone.
2. Put light, steady pressure on the brake pedal.
3. Start the engine and let it idle. If the system is operating correctly, the brake pedal should fall toward the floor if the constant pressure is maintained.

Power brake systems may be tested for hydraulic leaks just as ordinary systems are tested.

System Description

Standard brakes are the duo-servo, single-anchor drum type with bonded brake shoe linings. Beginning in 1965, segmented metallic linings were available as an extra cost option. Brake drums are made of cast iron. Front disc brakes became optional in 1967. From 1967 to 1968, the disc brakes used were the four-piston type. In 1969, a single-piston design was introduced. Single-piston front disc brakes are standard equipment on all 1975 and later models.

Master cylinders in use from 1962 through 1966 are of the single-cylinder and reservoir type. A dual reservoir master cylinder is used from 1967 through 1979. The front portion of the master cylinder wheels; the rear portion supplies the rear wheels. Power brakes have been available as an option since 1962.

Master Cylinder

REMOVAL & INSTALLATION

1. Disconnect the hydraulic line(s) at the master cylinder.
2. Remove the two retaining nuts and lockwashers that hold the cylinder to the firewall or vacuum booster.

Use a flare end wrench to loosen . . .

. . . then pull the master cylinder away from the firewall (or power booster, if so equipped)

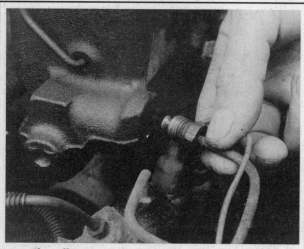

. . . then disconnect the brake line from the master cylinder

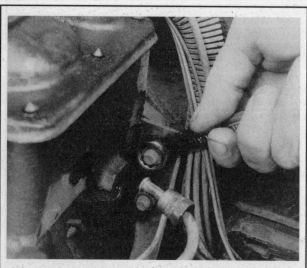

Unfasten the master cylinder retaining nuts . . .

➡On 1967 and later models, disconnect the pushrod at the brake pedal.

3. Remove the master cylinder, gasket, and rubber boot.
To install:
4. Position the master cylinder on the firewall, making sure the pushrod goes through the rubber boot into the piston.

➡On 1967 and later models, reconnect the pushrod clevis to the brake pedal.

5. Install the nuts and lockwashers.
6. Install the hydraulic line(s), then check brake pedal free-play.
7. Bleed the brakes as described later in this section.

➡Cars having disc brakes do not have a check valve in the front outlet port of the master cylinder. If one is installed, front disc will immediately wear out due to residual hydraulic pressure holding the pads against the rotor.

OVERHAUL

1962–66 Vehicles

1. Remove the master cylinder from the vehicle.
2. Secure the master cylinder in a vise and remove the pushrod assembly and protective boot. This exposes the lockring which, when removed, allows extraction of the piston stop, secondary cup, and piston.
3. Remove the cylinder end plug and push out the primary cup, spring, valve assembly, and seat.
4. Wash the component parts with denatured alcohol.
5. Carefully inspect the washed metal parts and the cylinder bore. A corroded cylinder must be replaced. Discoloration or stains can be removed with crocus cloth. When doing this, wrap the cloth around your finger and rotate the cylinder around the cloth.

✱✱ CAUTION

Do not polish the bore lengthwise as this can cause a fluid leak, which will lead to brake failure.

6. To reassemble, moisten the cylinder bore with brake fluid and replace the valve seat, valve assembly, and spring.

✳✳ CAUTION

Be sure the valve and seat are properly installed before proceeding. An incorrectly assembled check valve will distort and fail to provide a check valve seal, which will result in a reduction of brake pedal travel with a corresponding loss in braking.

7. Moisten the primary cup with brake fluid and install it, flat side out, and seated over the spring. The primary cup is distinguished by a brass support ring at its base.

8. Dip the secondary cup in brake fluid and slip it over the end of the piston.

9. Insert the completed assembly, with the bleeder brake end of the piston installed first. Secure the parts with the piston stop and the snapring, and install the end plug.

10. Attach the rubber boot and pushrod, and install the master cylinder.

11. Attach the brake pedal clevis and adjust the pushrod-to-piston clearance. Correct adjustment calls for a barely perceptible free pedal before piston/pushrod contact.

➡ **Overhaul of power brake master cylinders is the same as that for manual brake master cylinders.**

12. Bleed the brake system.

1967–79 Vehicles
◆ See Figure 1

1. Remove the master cylinder from the car.

2. Remove the mounting gasket and boot, and also the main cover, then purge the fluid from the unit.

3. Secure the cylinder in a vise and remove the pushrod retainer and the secondary piston stop bolt found inside the forward reservoir.

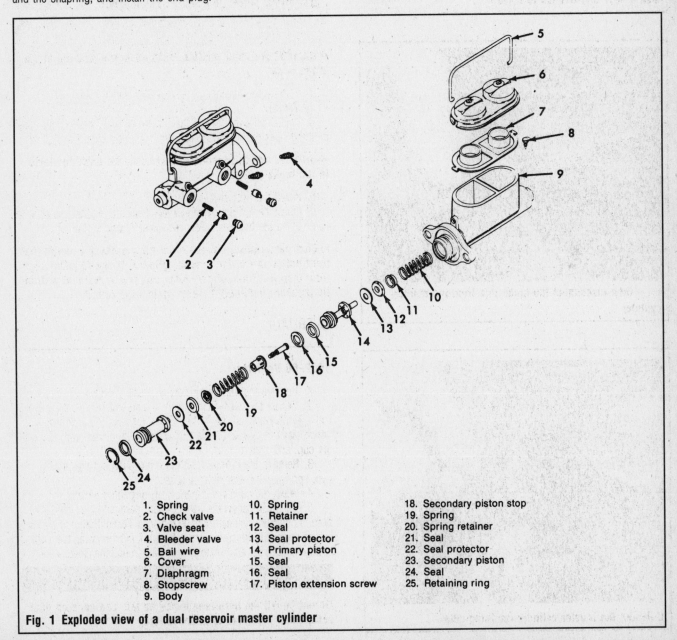

1. Spring	10. Spring	18. Secondary piston stop
2. Check valve	11. Retainer	19. Spring
3. Valve seat	12. Seal	20. Spring retainer
4. Bleeder valve	13. Seal protector	21. Seal
5. Bail wire	14. Primary piston	22. Seal protector
6. Cover	15. Seal	23. Secondary piston
7. Diaphragm	16. Seal	24. Seal
8. Stopscrew	17. Piston extension screw	25. Retaining ring
9. Body		

Fig. 1 Exploded view of a dual reservoir master cylinder

4. Compress the retaining ring and extract it along with the primary piston assembly.

5. Blow compressed air into the piston stop screw hole to force the secondary piston, spring, and retainer from the bore of the cylinder. An alternate method is to use hooked wire to snag and extract the secondary piston.

6. Check the brass tube fitting inserts and, if they are damaged, remove them. Leave undamaged inserts in place.

7. If replacement is necessary, thread a 6–32 x ⅝ in. self-tapping screw into the insert. Hook the end of the screw with a claw hammer and pry the insert free.

8. An alternate way of removing the inserts is to first drill the outlet holes to ¹³⁄₆₄ in. and thread them with a ¼ in.–20 tap. Position a thick washer over the hole to serve as a spacer, and then thread at ¼ in.–20 x ¾ in. hex head bolt into the insert and tighten the bolt until the insert is freed.

9. Use denatured alcohol and compressed air to clean the parts. Slight rust may be removed with crocus cloth.

10. Replace the brass tube inserts at this time by positioning them in their holes and threading a brake line tube nut into the outlet hole. Turn down the nut until the insert is seated.

11. Check the piston assemblies for correct identification and, when satisfied, position the replacement secondary seals in the twin grooves of the secondary piston.

12. The outside seal is correctly placed when its lips face the flat end of the piston.

13. Slip the primary seal and its protector over the end of the secondary piston opposite the secondary seals. The flat side of this seal should face the piston's compensating hole flange.

14. Replace the primary piston assembly with the assembled piece in the overhaul kit.

15. Moisten the cylinder bore and the secondary piston's inner and outer seals with brake fluid. Assemble the secondary piston

spring to its retainer and position them over the end of the primary seal.

16. Insert the combined spring and piston assembly into the cylinder and use a small wooden dowel or pencil to seat the spring against the end of the bore.

17. Moisten the primary piston seals with brake fluid and push it—pushrod receptacle end out—into the cylinder.

18. Keep the piston pushed in and snap the retaining ring into place.

19. Relax the pressure on the pistons and allow them to seek their static positions.

20. Replace the secondary piston stop screw and torque it to 25–40 inch lbs.

21. Replace the reservoir diaphragm and cover.

→**Overhaul of the main cylinder portion of power brake master cylinders is the same as that for manual brake master cylinders.**

22. Install the master cylinder, then bleed the brake system.

Pressure Differential Warning Switch and Combination Valve

◆ **See Figure 2**

This valve, mounted below the master cylinder, has both brake lines from the master cylinder connected to it and provides three functions on disc brake systems:

It meters or delays disc brake application until the shoes of the rear drum brakes contacts the drum.

It activates the brake failure warning light on the dash in the event of low pressure in one of the separate brake hydraulic systems.

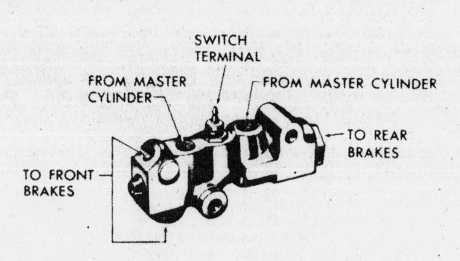

Fig. 2 View of a common combination valve

Finally, it acts as a proportioning valve which reduces rear brake hydraulic pressure during panic stop situations. This delays rear wheel skidding due to weight transfer to the front wheels.

Models with front drum brakes have a similar unit, however it provides only for activation of the brake failure warning light.

Both the pressure differential warning switch and the combination valve are nonadjustable and nonserviceable. They must be replaced if defective.

REMOVAL & INSTALLATION

1. Disconnect the battery negative cable.
2. Disconnect the electrical lead from the switch.
3. Place rags under the unit to absorb any spilled brake fluid.

4. Clean any dirt from the hydraulic lines and the switch/ valve assembly. Disconnect the hydraulic lines from the assembly. If necessary, loosen the line connections at the master cylinder. Tape the open line ends to prevent the entrance of dirt.

5. Remove the mounting screws and remove the switch/valve assembly.

To install:

6. Make sure that the new unit is clean and free of dust and lint. If in doubt, wash the new unit in clean brake fluid.

7. Place the new unit in position and install it to its mounting bracket with screws.

8. Remove the tape from the hydraulic lines and connect them to the unit. If necessary, tighten the line connections at the master cylinder.

9. Connect the electrical lead.
10. Connect the battery negative cable.
11. Bleed the brake systems.

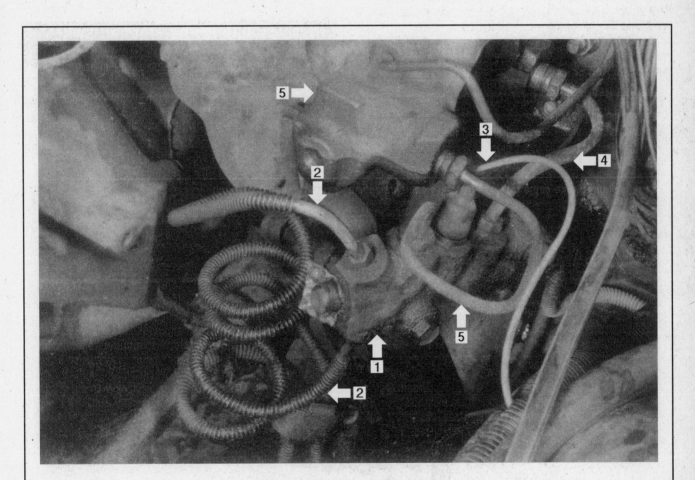

1. Combination/Proportioning valve
2. Brake lines (to front brakes)
3. Switch terminal/electrical connector
4. Brake lines (from master cylinder)
5. Master cylinder

Brake master cylinder and related components

Bleeding Brake System

The hydraulic brake system must be bled any time one of the lines is disconnected or air enters the system. This may be done manually or by the pressure method. The correct bleeding sequence is: left rear wheel cylinder, right rear, right front, and left front.

PRESSURE BLEEDING

1. Clean the top of the master cylinder, remove the cover, and attach the pressure bleeding adapter.

➡**On cars with front disc brakes, the spring-loaded plunger on the front of the proportioning valve must be depressed while bleeding. Wire or tape can be wrapped around the valve to hold the plunger in.**

2. Check the pressure bleeder reservoir for correct pressure and fluid level, then open the release valve.

3. Fasten a bleeder hose to the wheel cylinder bleeder nipple and submerge the free end of the hose in a transparent receptacle. The receptacle should contain enough brake fluid to cover the open end of the hose.

4. Open the wheel cylinder bleeder nipple and allow the fluid to flow until all bubbles disappear and an uncontaminated flow exists.

5. Close the nipple, remove the bleeder hose, and repeat the procedure on the other wheel cylinders in sequence.

MANUAL BLEEDING

An alternate to the pressure method of bleeding requires two people: one to depress the brake pedal and the other to open the bleeder nipples.

1. Clean the top of the master cylinder, remove the cover, and fill the reservoir.

➡**On cars with front disc brakes, the spring-loaded plunger on the front of the proportioning valve must be depressed while bleeding. Wire or tape can be wrapped around the valve to hold the plunger in.**

2. Attach a bleeder hose and a clear container as in the pressure bleeding procedure.

3. Have the assistant depress the brake pedal to the floor, then pause until the fluid flow stops and the bleeder nipple is closed.

4. Allow the pedal to return and repeat the procedure until a steady, bubble-free flow is seen.

5. Tighten the nipple and move on to the other wheels, in sequence.

6. Check the master cylinder level frequently during this procedure. If the reservoir runs dry, air will enter the system and the bleeding will have to be repeated.

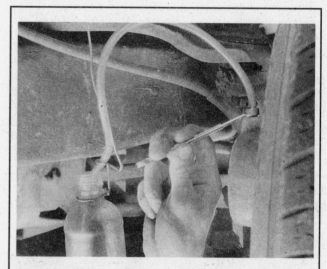

When bleeding the brakes, use fresh brake fluid from a sealed container—front disc brakes shown

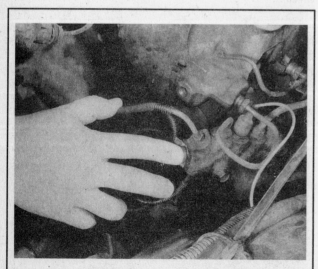

When bleeding front disc brakes, the plunger at the front of the proportioning valve must be depressed

Bleeding the rear drum brakes

FRONT DISC BRAKES

Brake Pads

REMOVAL & INSTALLATION

1967–68 Chevy II

1. Siphon off ⅔ of the brake fluid from the master cylinder.

➡**The insertion of the thicker replacement pads will push the caliper pistons back into their bores and will cause a full master cylinder to overflow.**

2. Jack the car up and support it with jackstands. Remove the wheel(s).
3. Extract and discard the pad retaining pin cotter key.
4. Remove the retaining pin and remove the brake pads.
5. Force the caliper pistons into their bores with a putty knife and install the replacement pads.
6. Install the retaining pin and insert a new cotter key.
7. Refill the master cylinder and bleed the system if necessary.

1969–79 Nova

▶ **See Figure 3**

1. Siphon off ⅔ of the brake fluid from the master cylinder.

➡**The insertion of the thicker replacement pads will push the caliper piston back into its bore and will cause a full master cylinder to overflow.**

2. Jack the car up and support it with jackstands. Remove the wheel(s).
3. Install a C-clamp on the caliper so that the solid side of the clamp rests against the back of the caliper and the screw end rests against the metal part of the outboard pad.
4. Tighten the clamp until the caliper moves enough to bottom the piston in its bore. Remove the clamp.

Use a C-clamp to bottom the caliper piston in its bore

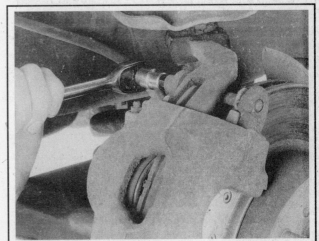

Unfasten the caliper mounting bolts using a hex-head socket

View of the front disc brake assembly—1977 Nova shown

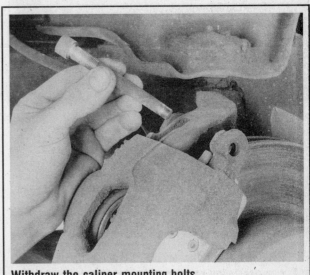

Withdraw the caliper mounting bolts . . .

. . . then lift the caliper off the rotor

Removing the inboard disc brake pad

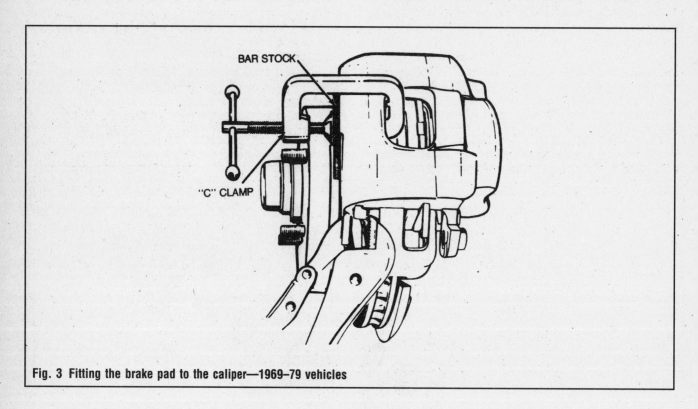

Fig. 3 Fitting the brake pad to the caliper—1969–79 vehicles

5. Remove the two allen head caliper mounting bolts enough to allow the caliper to be pulled off the disc.

6. Remove the inboard pad and dislodge the outboard pad. Place the caliper where it won't be supported by the brake hose.

7. Remove the pad support spring clip from the piston.

8. Remove the two bolt ear sleeves and the four rubber bushings from the ears.

9. Brake pads should be replaced when they are worn to within 1/32 in. of the rivet heads.

10. Check the inside of the caliper for leakage and the condition of the piston dust boot.

To install:

11. Lubricate the two new sleeves and four bushings with a silicone spray.

12. Install the bushings in each caliper ear. Install the two sleeves in the two inboard ears.

13. Install the pad support spring clip and the old pad into the center of the piston. You will then push this pad down to get the piston flat against the caliper. This part of the job is difficult and requires an assistant. While the assistant holds the caliper and loosens the bleeder valve to relieve pressure, you get a prybar and try to force the old pad in to make the piston flush with the

caliper surface. When it is flush, close the bleeder valve so that no air gets into the system.

➡**On models with wear sensors, make sure the wear sensor is toward the rear of the caliper.**

14. Position the outboard shoe with the ears of the shoes over the caliper ears and the tab at the bottom engaged in the caliper cutout.

15. With the two shoes in position, place the caliper over the brake disc and align the holes in the caliper with those of the mounting bracket.

✳✳ WARNING

Make certain that the brake hose is not twisted or kinked.

16. Install the mounting bracket bolts through the sleeves in the inboard caliper ears and through the mounting bracket, making sure that the ends of the bolts pass under the retaining ears on the inboard shoe.

17. Tighten the bolts into the bracket and tighten to 35 ft lbs. Bend over the outer pad ears.

18. Install the front wheel and lower the car.

19. Add fluid to the master cylinder reservoirs so the fluid level reaches ¼ in. from the top of the reservoir.

20. Test the brake pedal by pumping it to obtain a "hard" pedal. Check the fluid level again and add fluid as necessary. Do not remove the vehicle until a "hard" pedal is obtained. Bleed the brakes if necessary.

Brake Caliper

REMOVAL & INSTALLATION

1967–68 Chevy II

◆ **See Figure 4**

1. Raise the front of the car and place it on jackstands.

2. Remove the tire and wheel assembly on the side where the caliper is being removed.

3. Disconnect the brake hose at the support bracket. Tape the end of the line to prevent contamination.

4. Remove the cotter pin from the brake pad retaining pin and remove the pin.

5. Remove the brake pads and identify them as inboard and outboard if they are being reused.

6. Remove the U-shaped retainer from the hose fitting and pull the hose from the bracket.

7. Remove the two caliper retaining bolts and remove the caliper from its mounting bracket.

To install:

8. While holding the brake pistons in with a putty knife, mount the caliper over the disc. Be careful not to damage the piston boots on the edge of the disc.

9. Install the two mounting bolts and tighten to 130 ft lbs.

10. Install the brake pads. (See brake pad installation.)

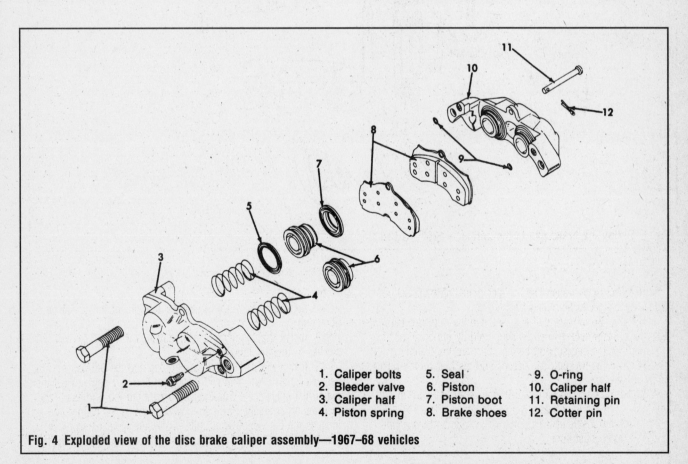

1. Caliper bolts	5. Seal	9. O-ring
2. Bleeder valve	6. Piston	10. Caliper half
3. Caliper half	7. Piston boot	11. Retaining pin
4. Piston spring	8. Brake shoes	12. Cotter pin

Fig. 4 Exploded view of the disc brake caliper assembly—1967–68 vehicles

11. Install the brake hose into the caliper, passing the female end through the support bracket.

12. Make sure that the tube line is clean and connect the brake line nut to the caliper.

13. Install the hose fitting into the support bracket and install the U-shaped retainer. Turn the steering wheel from side to side to make sure that the hose doesn't interfere with the tire. If it does, turn the hose end one or two points in the bracket until the interference is eliminated.

14. After performing the above check, install the steel tube connector and tighten it.

15. Partially lower the vehicle, then bleed the brakes as outlined in this section.

16. Install the wheel(s) and lower the car.

1969–79 Nova

▶ See Figure 5 and 6

1. Perform the removal steps for pad replacement.
2. Disconnect the brake hose and plug the line.
3. Remove the U-shaped retainer from the fitting.
4. Pull the hose from the frame bracket and remove the caliper with the hose attached.

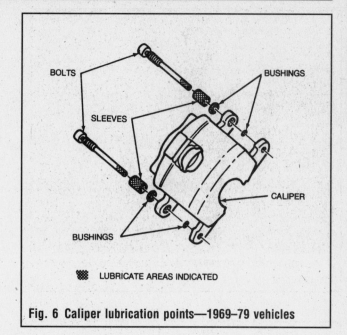

Fig. 6 Caliper lubrication points—1969–79 vehicles

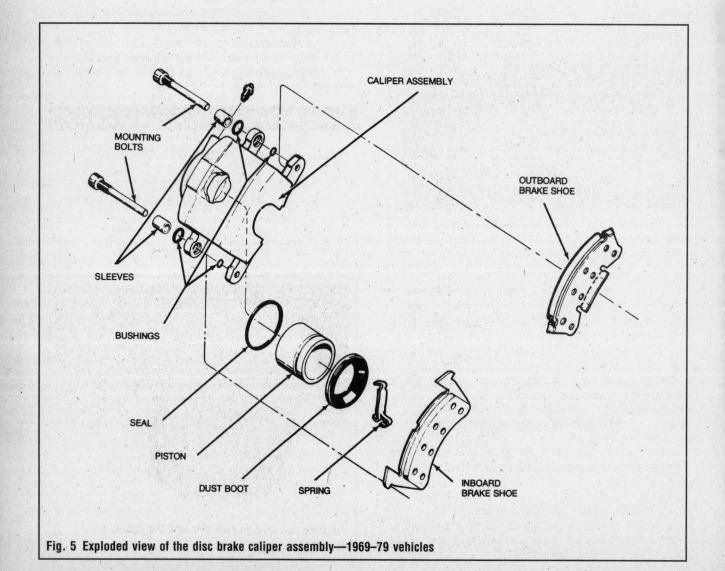

Fig. 5 Exploded view of the disc brake caliper assembly—1969–79 vehicles

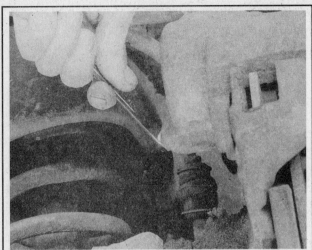

If the caliper is being replaced or overhauled, unfasten the retainer . . .

. . . then disconnect the brake fluid line from the rear of the caliper

5. Clean the outside of the caliper with denatured alcohol.

6. If the caliper is being removed for replacement or overhaul, remove the brake hose and discard the copper gasket.

7. Remove the brake fluid from the caliper.

8. Place clean rags inside the caliper opening to catch the piston when it is released.

9. Apply compressed air to the caliper fluid inlet hole and force the piston out of its bore. Do not blow the piston out, but use just enough pressure to ease it out.

10. Use a suitable prytool to pry the boot out of the caliper. Avoid scratching the bore.

11. Remove the piston seal from its groove in the caliper bore, using a plastic or wooden tool. *Do not use a metal tool of any type for this operation.*

12. Blow out all passages in the caliper and bleeder valve. Clean the piston and piston bore with fresh brake fluid.

13. Examine the piston for scoring, scratches, or corrosion. If any of these conditions exist, the piston must be replaced as it is plated and cannot be refinished.

14. Examine the bore for the same defects. Light rough spots may be removed by rotating crocus cloth, using finger-pressure, in the bore. Do not polish with an in-and-out motion or use any other abrasive.

15. Lubricate the piston bore and the new rubber parts with fresh brake fluid. Position the seal in the piston bore groove.

16. Lubricate the piston with brake fluid and assemble the boot into the piston groove so that the fold faces the open end of the piston.

17. Insert the piston into the bore, taking care not to unseat the seal.

18. Force the piston to the bottom of the bore. (This will require a force of 50–100 lbs.) Seat the boot lip around the caliper counterbore. Proper seating of the boot is very important for sealing out contaminants.

19. Install the brake hose into the caliper using a new copper gasket.

20. Lubricate the new sleeves and rubber bushings. Install the bushings in the caliper ears. Install the sleeves so that the end toward the disc pad is flush with the machined surface.

➡ **Lubrication of the sleeves and bushings is essential to ensure the proper operation of the sliding caliper design.**

21. Install the shoe support spring in the piston.

22. Install the disc pads in the caliper and remount the caliper on the hub. (See Disc Pad Replacement.)

23. Reconnect the brake hose to the steel brake line. Install the retainer clip. Bleed the brakes (see Bleeding Brake System).

24. Replace the wheels, check the brake fluid level, check the brake pedal travel, and road-test the vehicle.

Brake Disc (Rotor)

REMOVAL & INSTALLATION

1. Raise the car, support it with jackstands, and remove the wheel and tire assembly.

2. Remove the brake caliper as previously outlined.

3. Drill out the five rivets holding the disc to the hub.

The rotor can also be removed with the hub as an assembly

4. Remove the brake disc.

5. Remove the rivet stubs from the hub.

To install:

6. Install the disc on the hub, aligning the lug bolts with the holes in the disc.

7. Install the brake caliper and shoes as previously outlined.

8. Bleed the brakes, install the wheel, and lower the car.

INSPECTION

1. Tighten the spindle nut to remove all wheel bearing play.

2. Install a dial indicator on the caliper so that its feeler will contact the disc about 1 in. below its outer edge.

3. Turn the disc and observe the runout reading. If the reading exceeds 0.002 in., the disc should be replaced.

4. Minimum thickness dimensions are cast into the caliper for reference.

Wheel Bearings

Properly adjusted bearings have a slightly loose feeling. Wheel bearings must never be preloaded. Preloading will damage bearings and eventually spindles. If the bearings are too loose, they should be cleaned, inspected, and then adjusted.

Hold the tire at the top and bottom, and move the wheel in and out on the spindle. If the movement is greater than 0.008 in. for 1962–73 vehicles or 0.005 in. for 1974–79 vehicles, the bearings are too loose.

ADJUSTMENT

1. Raise and support the car by the lower control arm.

2. Remove the hub cap, then remove the dust cap from the hub.

3. Remove the cotter pin and spindle nut.

4. Spin the wheel forward by hand. Tighten the nut until snug to fully seat the bearings.

5. Back off the nut ¼–½ turn until it is just loose, then tighten it finger-tight.

6. Loosen the nut until either hole in the spindle lines up with a slot in the nut and then insert the cotter pin. This may appear to be too loose, but it is the correct adjustment. The spindle nut should not be even finger-tight.

7. Proper adjustment creates 0.001–0.008 in. of end-play for 1962–73 vehicles or 0.001–0.005 in. of end-play for 1974–79 vehicles.

REMOVAL & INSTALLATION

1. Remove the wheel and tire assembly, and the brake drum or brake caliper, as applicable.

2. Pry out the grease cap, cotter pin, spindle nut, and washer.

3. Remove the outer roller bearing assembly. Remove the hub assembly. The inner bearing assembly will remain in the hub and may be removed after prying out the inner seal. Discard the seal.

4. Clean all parts in solvent (air dry) and check for excessive wear or damage.

Remove the dust cap, using a suitable prytool

Use needlenose pliers to remove the cotter pin. Be sure to use a new cotter pin during installation

Remove the spindle nut and washer . . .

. . . then remove the outer wheel bearing

5. Using a hammer and drift, remove the bearing cups from the hub. When installing new cups, make sure that they are not cocked and that they are fully seated against the hub shoulder.
To install:
6. Using a high melting-point bearing lubricant, pack both inner and outer bearings.

DRUM BRAKES

Brake Drums

REMOVAL & INSTALLATION

1. Jack up the car so the wheels are off the ground.
2. Remove the wheel(s) from which the brake drum(s) are to be removed.

View of the rear drum brake assembly—1977 Nova shown

7. Place the inner bearing in the hub and install a new inner seal, making sure that the seal flange faces the bearing cup.
8. Carefully install the wheel hub over the spindle.
9. Using your hands, firmly press the outer bearing into the hub. Install the spindle washer and nut, and adjust as instructed above.
10. Install the caliper. Torque the two caliper mounting bolts to 35 ft. lbs.
11. Install the dust cap on the hub.
12. Install the wheel and lower the vehicle.

PACKING

Clean the wheel bearings thoroughly with solvent and check their condition before installation.

✳✳ WARNING

Do not blow the bearing dry with compressed air as this would allow the bearing to turn without lubrication.

Apply a sizable daub of lubricant to the palm of one hand. Using your other hand, work the bearing into the lubricant so that the grease is pushed through the rollers and out the other side. Keep rotating the bearing while continuing to push the lubricant through it.

Remove the brake drum by pulling it from the wheel studs

3. Pull off the brake drum. (It may be necessary to gently tap the rear edges of the drum to start it off the studs.)
4. If extreme resistance to removal is encountered, it will be necessary to retract the adjusting screw. Knock out the access hole in the brake drum and turn the adjuster to retract the linings.
To install:
5. Install the brake drums after adjusting the linings.
6. Install the drums in the same position on the hub or axle shaft as removed.

INSPECTION

Check the brake drums for any cracks, scores, grooves, or an out-of-round condition. Replace a cracked drum. Smooth slight scores with fine emery cloth. If scoring is extensive, have the drum turned. Never have a drum turned more than 0.060 in.

Brake Shoes

ADJUSTMENT

Rotate the star wheel adjuster until a slight drag is felt between the shoes and drum, then back off 1¼ turns on the adjuster. Backing the car and firmly braking will allow the self-adjusters to complete the adjustment.

REMOVAL & INSTALLATION

1. Raise the car and support it on jackstands.
2. Slacken the parking brake cable.
3. Remove the rear wheel and brake drum. The front wheel and brake drum may be removed as a unit by removing the spindle nut and cotter pin.
4. Free the brake shoe return springs, actuator pull-back spring, and link hold-down-pins and springs, and the actuator assembly.

➡**Special tools available from auto supply stores will ease spring and anchor pin removal, but the job may still be done with common hand tools.**

5. Remove the primary brake shoe and lining. On rear wheels, disconnect the adjusting mechanism and spring from the primary shoe.
6. On rear wheels, disconnect the parking brake lever from the secondary shoe and remove the shoe. (Front wheel shoes may be removed together.)

Using a specialized brake tool . . .

. . . unfasten the right-side brake shoe return spring

Use a commercially available spray to clean the drum brake components

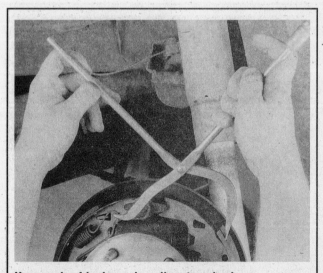
Use a pair of brake spring pliers to unhook . . .

. . . then remove the other brake shoe return spring

Use pliers or a specialized brake tool to unhook the hold-down spring . . .

Remove the actuator pull-back spring

. . . then remove the hold-down spring and actuator lever

Remove the actuating link

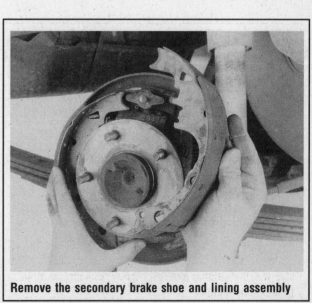

Remove the secondary brake shoe and lining assembly

Remove the brake adjusting mechanism

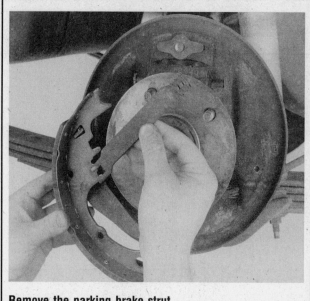

Remove the parking brake strut

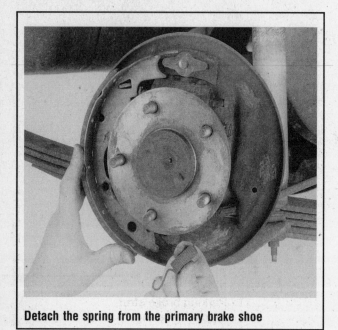

Detach the spring from the primary brake shoe

Remove the primary shoe and the parking brake lever

7. Clean and inspect all brake parts.
8. Check the wheel cylinder for seal condition and leaking.
9. Repack wheel bearings and replace the seals.
10. Inspect the replacement shoes for nicks or burrs, lubricate the backing plate contact points, brake cable and levers, and adjusting screws, and then assemble.
11. Make sure that the right- and left-hand adjusting screws are not mixed. You can prevent this by working on one side at a time. This will also provide you with a reference for reassembly.

The star wheel should be nearest the secondary shoe when correctly installed.
12. Reverse the removal procedure for assembly. When completed, make an initial adjustment as previously described.

➡**Maintenance procedures for the metallic lining option are the same as those for standard linings. Do not substitute these linings in standard drums, unless the drums have been honed to a 20-micro-inch finish and the shoes equipped with special heat-resistant springs.**

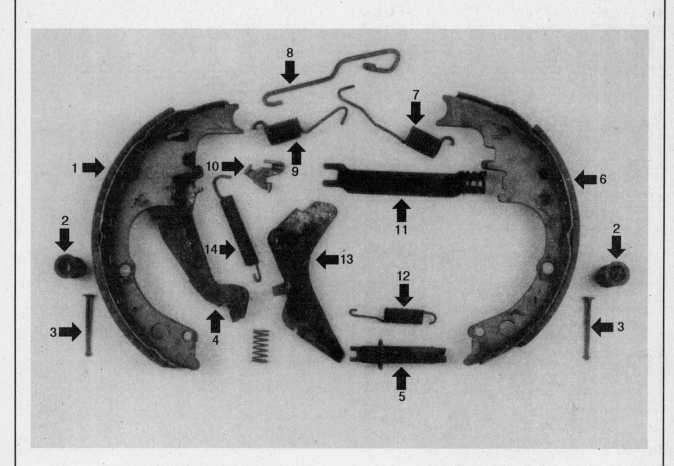

1. Primary brake shoe and lining
2. Hold-down spring
3. Hold-down pin
4. Parking brake lever
5. Adjusting screw
6. Secondary brake shoe and lining
7. Secondary return spring
8. Actuator link
9. Primary return spring
10. Pawl
11. Parking brake strut
12. Adjusting spring
13. Actuator lever
14. Actuator pull back spring

Exploded view of the rear drum brake components

Wheel Cylinders

▶ **See Figures 7, 8 and 9**

1. Raise and safely support the trunk with jackstands.
2. Remove the wheel and tire.
3. Back off the brake adjustment and remove the drum.
4. Disconnect and plug the brake line.
5. Remove the brake shoe pull-back springs.
6. Remove the screws securing the wheel cylinder to the backing plate. Later models have their wheel cylinders retained by a round retainer. To release the locking tabs, insert two awls into the access slots to bend the tabs back. Install the new retainer over the wheel cylinder abutment using a 1⅛ in. 12-point socket and socket extension.

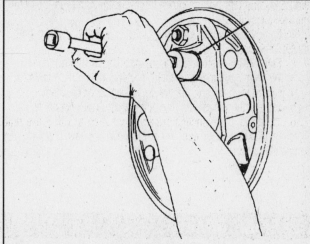

Fig. 9 Install the new retainer over the wheel cylinder using a 1 1/8 in. 12-point socket and extension

7. Disengage the wheel cylinder pushrods from the brake shoes and remove the wheel cylinder.
8. To install, place the wheel cylinder into position and tighten the retaining bolts to 180 inch lbs. Install the pushrods, then install the inlet tube and tighten to 120–280 inch lbs. Bleed the brake system.

OVERHAUL

▶ **See Figure 10**

Wheel cylinder overhaul procedures are similar to those for the master cylinder. Overhaul kits containing the necessary replacements are readily available. When rebuilding and installing the wheel cylinders, avoid introducing any contaminants into the sys-

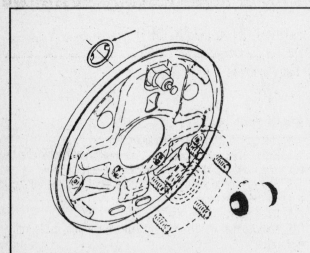

Fig. 7 Later model wheel cylinders are secured with a retaining ring

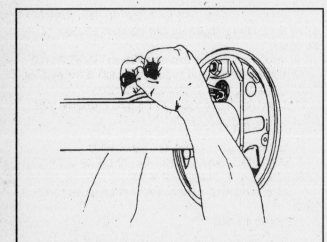

Fig. 8 Using two awls, simultaneously bend back the tabs on the retainer

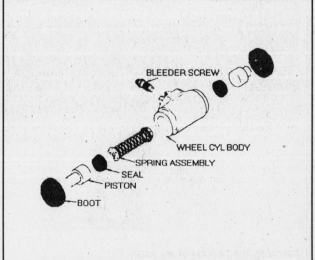

Fig. 10 Exploded view of a common wheel cylinder

tem. Cleaning and honing procedures are the same as those for the master cylinder.

1. Remove the boots from the cylinder ends with pliers and discard the boots.
2. Remove the pistons and cups and discard them.
3. Wash the cylinder and metal parts in denatured alcohol.
4. Blow the parts dry; do not use a rag to clean them.
5. Inspect the piston and replace it if it shows scratches.
6. Lubricate the cylinder bore and counterbore with brake fluid.
7. Install the rubber cups—flat side out—followed by the pistons—flat side in.

8. Insert new boots into the counterbores by hand. Do not lubricate the boots.
9. Front wheel cylinders are secured to the backing plate by a threaded anchor pin. Torque the pin to 65 ft lbs.

Wheel Bearings

Refer to the Front Disc Brakes—Wheel Bearings section for removal and installation, adjustment, and packing procedures.

PARKING BRAKE

Cables

ADJUSTMENT

1. Jack the rear of the car up and support it with jackstands.
2. Pull the parking brake on two notches from the fully released position.
3. Loosen the forward equalizer check nut and adjust the rear nut as necessary to obtain a light drag when the rear wheel is turned.
4. Tighten both check nuts.
5. Release the parking brake lever and check to see that there is no drag present when the wheel is turned.
6. Lower the car.

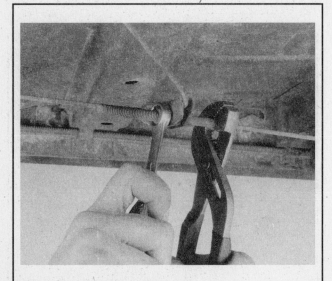

Adjusting the parking brake cable

REMOVAL & INSTALLATION

◆ **See Figure 11**

Front Cable

1962–76 VEHICLES

1. Disconnect the negative battery cable.
2. Remove the front cable from the swivel by removing the retaining clips and pulling the ball from the swivel.
3. Squeeze the locking fingers together and push the front cable out of the dash panel.
4. Raise the car on a hoist.
5. Remove the equalizer nut and remove the front cable from the equalizer.
6. Remove the cable clip at the frame and remove the front cable.

To install:

7. Route the stud end of the replacement cable through the frame and secure it with a clip.
8. Route the cable through the hole in the dash panel. Make sure that the locking fingers are fully expanded and secured in the cutout.
9. Install the cable ball into the swivel and install the clip.
10. Connect the stud end to the center cable at the equalizer. Adjust the parking brake as previously described.
11. Lower the car and reconnect the battery negative cable.

1977–79 VEHICLES

1. Remove the adjusting nut from the equalizer.
2. Remove the retainer clip from the rear portion of the front cable at the frame and from the lever arm.
3. Disconnect the front brake cable from the parking brake lever.
4. Remove the cable.

➡**On some models, it may be easier to install the new cable if a heavy cord is tied to either end of the cable to guide it through the openings.**

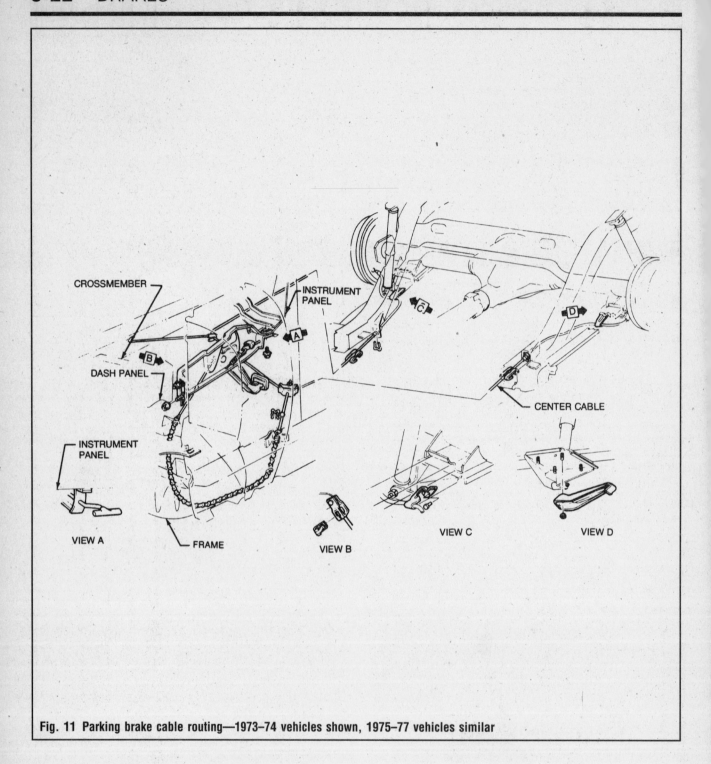

Fig. 11 Parking brake cable routing—1973–74 vehicles shown, 1975–77 vehicles similar

5. Reverse the removal procedure to install the new cable, and then adjust the parking brake.

Center and Rear Cables

1972–76 VEHICLES

1. Raise the car on a hoist.
2. Remove the equalizer nut and separate the front and center cables.

3. Remove the center cable from the cable connectors and remove the cable from the cable guides.
4. Remove the cable clip from the frame bracket and release the cable from the cable guides.
5. With brakes exposed, release the cable ball from the parking brake lever.
6. Squeeze the locking fingers together and pull the rear cable from the flange plate.

To install:

7. Route the rear cable through the flange plate and connect the ball to the lever. Ensure that the locking fingers are fully expanded on the flange plate.

8. Connect the cable to the cable guides, route the cable through the frame bracket, and install the clip.

9. Assemble the center and rear cables together with the connectors.

10. Connect the center cable guides, install the equalizer to the center cable, and install the front cable stud to the equalizer with the nut.

11. Apply and release the parking brake three times.

12. Adjust the parking brake as previously outlined.

13. Lower the car.

Center Cable

1977–79 VEHICLES

1. Raise the vehicle on a lift, and then remove the adjusting nut from the equalizer.

2. Unhook the connector at each end and then disengage hooks and guides.

To install:

3. Install the new cable in reverse order. Then, adjust parking brake as described above.

4. Finally, apply parking brake hard three times, and repeat parking brake adjustment.

Rear Cable

1977–79 VEHICLES

1. Remove the cable clip retainers.

2. Loosen the adjusting nut.

3. Disengage the rear cable at the connector.

4. Bend the retaining fingers and disengage the cable at the brake shoe operating lever.

5. Remove the assembly from the vehicle.

6. Install the new cable by reversing the removal procedure, and then adjust the parking brake.

Disengage the rear cable from the connector

Use a wrench to bend the rear cable retaining fingers . . .

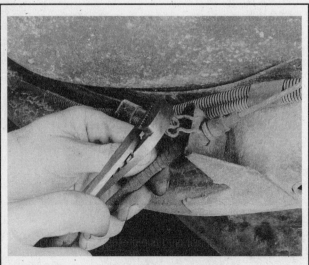

Remove the rear parking brake cable retainer

. . . then remove the rear parking brake cable from the backing plate

Brake Specifications
(All measurements are given in in.)

Year	Master Cylinder		Wheel Cylinder			Brake Disc or Drum Diameter		
			Front			Front		
	Disc	Drum	Disc	Drum	Rear	Disc	Drum	Rear
'62	—	1.0①	—	1.00	0.875	—	9.0	9.0
'63	—	1.0①	—	1.00	0.875	—	9.0	9.0
'64	—	1.0①	—	1.06	0.875	—	9.5	9.5
'65	—	1.0①	—	1.06	0.875	—	9.5	9.5
'66	—	1.0①	—	1.06	0.875	—	9.5	9.5
'67	1.00	1.0①	1.875	1.06	0.875	11.0	9.5	9.5
'68	1.125	1.0	2.063	1.125	0.875	11.0	9.5	9.5
'69	1.125	1.0	2.938	1.125	0.875	11.0	9.5	9.5
'70–'72	1.125②	1.0	2.938	1.125	0.875	11.0	9.5	9.5
'73–'74	1.125②	1.0	2.938	1.125	0.875	11.0	9.5	9.5
'75–'76④	0.9375③	—	2.938	—	0.875	11.0	—	9.5
'77	0.9375③	—	2.938	—	0.9375	11.0	—	9.5
'78	0.9375③	—	2.938	—	0.9375	11.0	—	9.5
'79	1.000③	—	2.9375	—	0.9375	11.0	—	9.5

① 0.875 with metallic linings
② 1.00 with power disc brakes
③ 1.125 with power disc brakes
④ Front disc brakes standard
— Not applicable

EXTERIOR 10-2
DOORS 10-2
   REMOVAL & INSTALLATION 10-2
   ADJUSTMENT 10-2
HOOD 10-3
   REMOVAL & INSTALLATION 10-3
   ALIGNMENT 10-3
TRUNK LID 10-4
   REMOVAL & INSTALLATION 10-4
   ALIGNMENT 10-5
BUMPERS 10-5
   REMOVAL & INSTALLATION 10-5
GRILLE 10-7
   REMOVAL & INSTALLATION 10-7
OUTSIDE MIRRORS 10-7
   REMOVAL & INSTALLATION 10-7
ANTENNA 10-8
   REMOVAL & INSTALLATION 10-8
INTERIOR 10-9
FRONT DOOR PANELS 10-9
   REMOVAL & INSTALLATION 10-9
REAR DOOR PANELS 10-13
   REMOVAL & INSTALLATION 10-13
DOOR LOCKS 10-13
   REMOVAL & INSTALLATION 10-13
FRONT DOOR GLASS 10-14
   REMOVAL & INSTALLATION 10-14
   ADJUSTMENT PROCEDURE 10-16
FRONT DOOR REGULATOR 10-17
   REMOVAL & INSTALLATION 10-17
FRONT DOOR ELECTRIC WINDOW
 MOTOR 10-17
   REMOVAL & INSTALLATION 10-17
REAR DOOR GLASS 10-17
   REMOVAL & INSTALLATION 10-17
REAR DOOR REGULATOR 10-17
   REMOVAL & INSTALLATION 10-17
REAR DOOR ELECTRIC WINDOW
 MOTOR 10-17
   REMOVAL & INSTALLATION 10-17
INSIDE REAR VIEW MIRROR 10-19
   REMOVAL & INSTALLATION 10-19
SEATS 10-19
   REMOVAL & INSTALLATION 10-19
POWER SEAT MOTOR 10-20
   REMOVAL & INSTALLATION 10-20

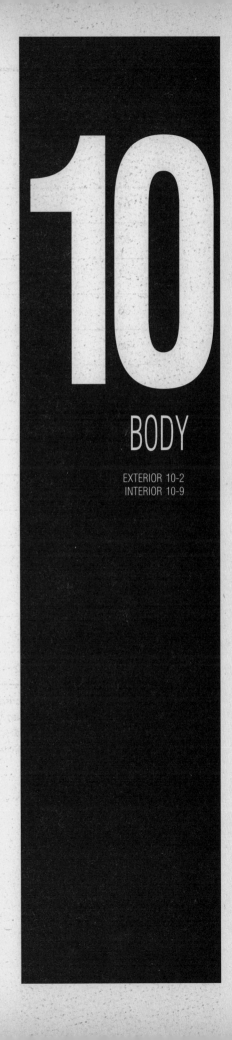

10

BODY

EXTERIOR 10-2
INTERIOR 10-9

EXTERIOR

Doors

REMOVAL & INSTALLATION

When removing the door, it is easier to remove the hinges with the door because the door side hinges are very accessible.

➡ **All factory installed door hardware attaching screws contain an epoxy thread-locking compound to ensure that the torque setting will be maintained. Service replacement screws may not contain a thread-locking compound. Such screws must be treated with No. 1052279 Loctite® 75 or equivalent. The adhesive is placed on the fastener prior to installation.**

1. Disconnect the negative battery cable. Mark the position of the door hinges-to-body to make the installation easier.

2. If equipped with power operated components, remove the trim panel and detach the inner panel water deflector enough to disconnect the wiring harness from the components. Separate and remove the rubber conduit and the wiring harness from the door.

3. Using an assistant (to support the door), remove the upper and lower hinge-to-body bolts. Remove the door from the vehicle.

4. To install, reverse the removal procedures. Torque the hinge-to-body bolt to 15–21 ft. lbs.

ADJUSTMENT

▶ **See Figures 1, 2 and 3**

The door adjustments are made possible through the use of floating anchor plates in the door and the body hinge pillars.

1. Remove the door lock striker from the body and allow the door to hang freely on its hinges.

2. Using a door hinge alignment tool, loosen the door hinge-to-body pillar bolts.

3. Using the tool attachments, adjust the door up/down and fore/aft.

➡ **If a rearward adjustment is made, it may be necessary to replace the jamb switch.**

4. At the door hinge pillar attachments, adjust the door in and out.

5. After adjusting the door, torque the door hinge-to-body pillar to 15–21 ft. lbs.

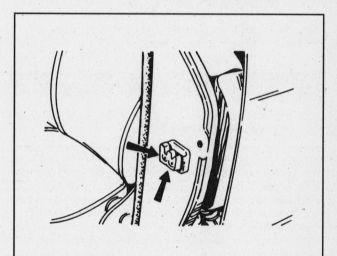

Fig. 2 The door striker can be adjusted in the directions shown

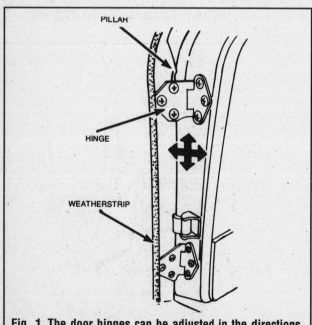

Fig. 1 The door hinges can be adjusted in the directions shown

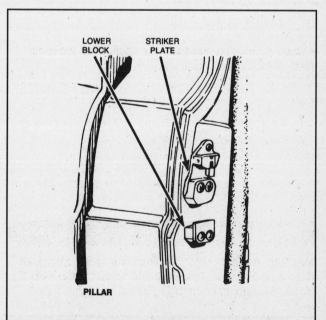

Fig. 3 View of the door striker plate and lower block

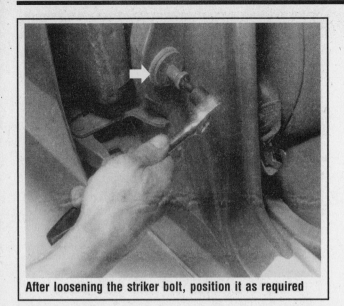

After loosening the striker bolt, position it as required

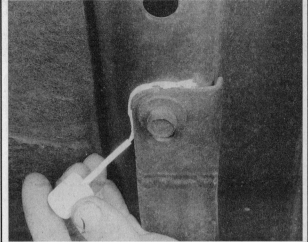

To remove the hood, first matchmark the position of the hinges on the hood

Hood

REMOVAL & INSTALLATION

1. Disconnect the negative battery cable. Using a scratch awl, scribe the hinge onto the hood. If equipped with a hood light, disconnect the electrical connector.

2. Using an assistant to support the hood, remove the hinge-to-hood bolts. Remove the hood.

3. To install, reverse the removal procedures. Check the hood alignment with the hood latch.

ALIGNMENT

▶ See Figures 4, 5, 6, 7 and 8

➡When aligning the hood and the latch, align the hood (first), then the latch (second).

Hood

The hood hinge-to-body mount is slotted to provide forward and rearward movement. Adjust the hood so that it is flush with the body sheet metal.

1. Using a scratch awl, scribe the hinge outline onto the hood.

2. Loosen the appropriate screws and shift the hood into proper alignment with the vehicles sheet metal.

✳✳ CAUTION

Make sure that the rear of the hood is properly positioned at the cowl seal; proper sealing will restrict fumes from the engine compartment from being pulled through the cowl vent.

3. After adjustment, tighten the appropriate screws.

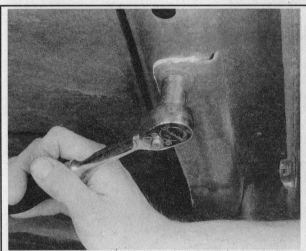

Unfasten the retaining bolts and remove the hood with the help of an assistant

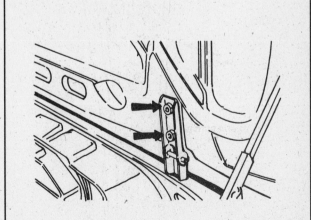

Fig. 4 Loosen the hinge bolts to permit fore, aft and horizontal adjustments

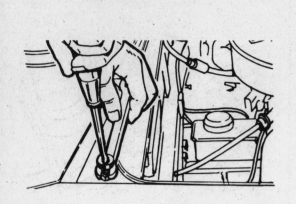

Fig. 5 The hood is adjusted vertically by the stop screws at the front and/or rear

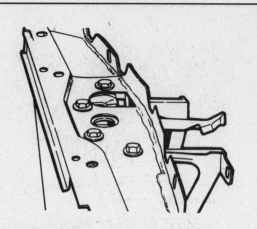

Fig. 8 The base of the hood lock can also be repositioned slightly to give more positive lock engagement

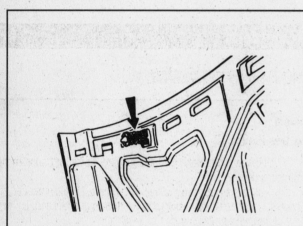

Fig. 6 The hood pin can be adjusted for proper lock engagement

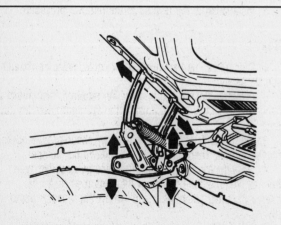

Fig. 7 The height of the hood at the rear is adjusted by loosening the bolts that attach the hinge to the body and moving the hood up or down

Latch

The hood latch assembly is mounted on a plate with elongated holes, which allow vertical adjustment.

Striker

The striker, on the hood, adjusts laterally to align with the hood latch assembly.

Trunk Lid

REMOVAL & INSTALLATION

◆ **See Figures 9 and 10**

1. Disconnect the negative battery cable. Open the trunk lid and place protective coverings over the rear fenders to protect the paint from damage.

2. Mark the location of the hinge-to-trunk lid bolts and disconnect the electrical connections and wiring from the lid, if equipped.

3. Using an assistant to support the lid, remove the hinge-to-lid bolts and the lid from the vehicle.

➡ **Some later vehicles use gas cushioned shock type assemblies to aid in supporting the trunk lid assembly. Remove the retaining clips and remove the shock assemblies from the trunk lid before removing the hinge retaining bolts.**

4. To install, reverse the removal procedures. Adjust the position of the trunk lid to the body. Rear compartment torque rods are adjustable to increase or decrease operating effort. To increase the amount of effort needed to raise the rear compartment lid or to decrease the amount of effort to close the lid, reposition the end of the rod to a lower torque rod adjusting notch. To decrease the amount of effort needed to raise the rear compartment lid or to increase the amount of effort to close the lid, reposition the end of the rod to a higher torque rod adjusting notch. Refer to the illustration. Prop the trunk lid in full-open position to keep lid

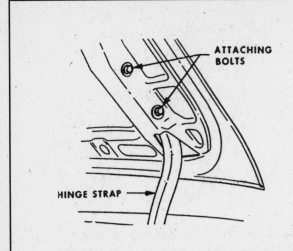

Fig. 9 Before removing the trunk lid bolts, matchmark the location of the hinges

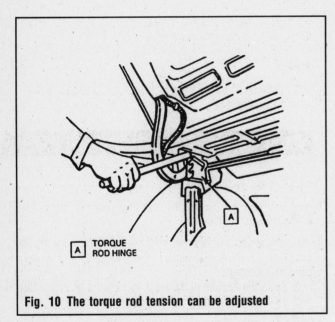

Fig. 10 The torque rod tension can be adjusted

from falling when torque rods are disengaged from the torque rod bracket.

ALIGNMENT

▶ **See Figure 11**

The trunk lid can be aligned slightly by loosening the hinge-to-lid bolts and shifting the lid into position.

➡**When adjusting the hinge/latch-to-body positions, be sure to use alignment marks as reference points.**

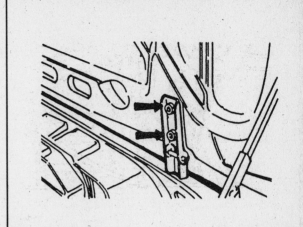

Fig. 11 Loosen the hinge bolts to permit fore, aft and horizontal adjustments

Bumpers

REMOVAL & INSTALLATION

Front
▶ **See Figure 12**

1. Disconnect the negative battery cable. Raise and support the vehicle safely.
2. Properly support the bumper. As required, disconnect all the necessary electrical connections at the turn signal assemblies and the cornering light housings.
3. On the vehicles without the energy absorber type bumper, remove the bolts from the frame and remove the bumper.
4. On vehicles equipped with the energy absorber type bumper, remove the bolts from the reinforcement to the energy absorber (each side) and remove the bumper assembly.
5. Installation is the reverse of the removal procedure.

Rear

1. Disconnect the negative battery cable. Raise and support the vehicle safely.
2. Properly support the bumper. As required, disconnect all the necessary electrical connections at the tail light assembly housings.
3. On the vehicles without the energy absorber type bumper, remove the bolts from the frame and remove the bumper.
4. On vehicles equipped with the energy absorber type bumper, remove the bolts from the reinforcement to the energy absorber (each side) and remove the bumper assembly.
5. Installation is the reverse of the removal procedure.

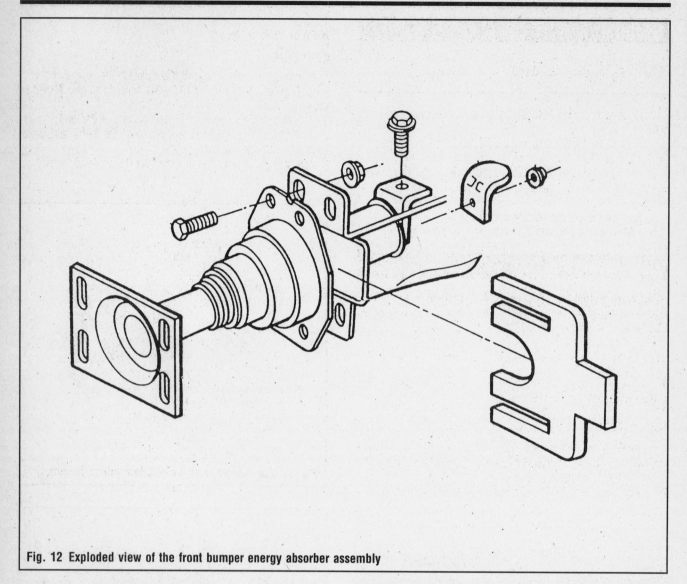

Fig. 12 Exploded view of the front bumper energy absorber assembly

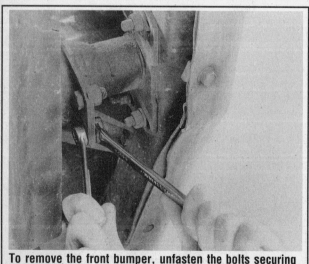

To remove the front bumper, unfasten the bolts securing it to the energy absorber

Remove the rear bumper in a similar manner to the front; remove the bolts securing it to the absorber

Grille

REMOVAL & INSTALLATION

1. Disconnect the negative battery cable. As required, open the hood.
2. Remove the sheet metal screws that retain the grille assembly to its mounting.
3. On some vehicles, the headlight trim rings may have to be removed before the grille assembly can be removed from the vehicle.
4. Remove the grille assembly from the vehicle.
5. Installation is the reverse of the removal procedure.

Outside Mirrors

➡ The mirror glass may be replaced by placing a piece of tape over the glass then breaking the mirror face. Adhesive back mirror faces are available.

REMOVAL & INSTALLATION

▶ See Figures 13, 14, 15 and 16

Standard Mirror

1. Remove the door trim panel.
2. Remove the mirror base to door outer panel stud nuts and remove the mirror from the door.
3. Install the base gasket and reverse the above to install.

Manual Remote Mirror

LEFT SIDE

1. Remove the door trim panel and detach the remote control lever. Peel back the insulator and water deflector to gain access to the mirror cable.
2. Detach the cable from any retaining tabs in the door.
3. Remove the attaching nuts and remove the mirror and cable assembly from the door.
4. Install the base gasket, then reverse the above to install.

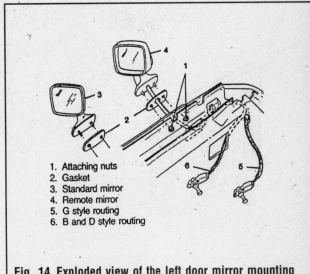

1. Attaching nuts
2. Gasket
3. Standard mirror
4. Remote mirror
5. G style routing
6. B and D style routing

Fig. 14 Exploded view of the left door mirror mounting

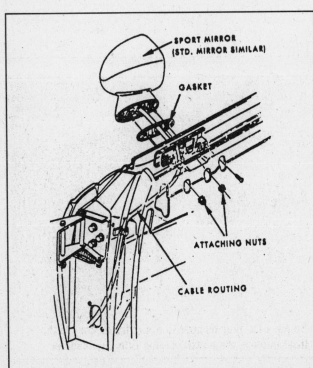

Fig. 13 Exploded view of the door mirror mounting (right side)

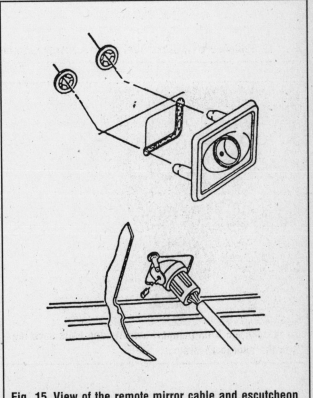

Fig. 15 View of the remote mirror cable and escutcheon

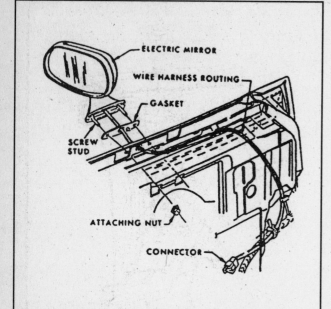

Fig. 16 Exploded view of the power mirror mounting—left side shown

RIGHT SIDE

1. Remove the door trim panel and detach the remote control lever. Peel back the insulator and water deflector to gain access to the mirror cable.

2. On models, with the instrument panel mounted control, remove the set screw from the control knob.

3. Remove the shroud side finishing panel as follows:

   a. Remove the sill plate screws and sill plate.

   b. Remove the litter container if so equipped.

   c. Remove the screw retaining the hinge pillar pinch-weld upper finishing lace.

   d. Grasp the shroud finishing panel at the forward edge toward the dash panel and pull inward to disengage the plastic retaining clip, and slide the panel rearward.

4. Feed the remote cable through the shroud and rubber conduit between the door and pillar and detach the cable from any retaining tabs in the door.

5. Remove the attaching nuts and remove the mirror and cable assembly from the door.

6. Reverse the above to install. Make sure the remote mirror operates properly before installing the trim.

Power Operated Mirror

1. Remove the door trim panel and disconnect the wire harness at the connector. Peel back the insulator pad and water deflector enough to gain access to the wire harness.

2. Detach the harness from any retaining tabs in the door.

3. Remove the attaching nuts and remove the mirror and harness assembly from the door.

4. Reverse the above to install. Make sure mirror operates correctly before installing the door panel.

Antenna

REMOVAL & INSTALLATION

Manual Type
♦ **See Figure 17**

1. Unscrew the mast from the top of the fender.

2. Unscrew the nut and the bezel from the top of the fender.

3. On later vehicles it may be necessary to remove a bolt/screw which retains the base of the antenna under the fender. This bolt/screw is accessible under the hood.

4. Disconnect the antenna lead from the antenna. On some later vehicles the antenna lead may even plug into another lead under the hood.

5. Reach under the fender and remove the antenna base.

6. When installing the antenna to the fender make sure the retaining nut is tight. A loose antenna or one that does not make good contact at the fender can cause radio interference.

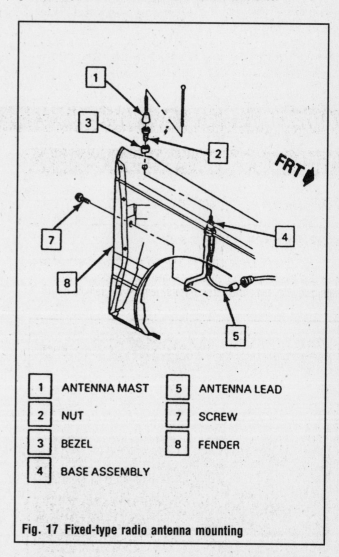

1	ANTENNA MAST	5	ANTENNA LEAD
2	NUT	7	SCREW
3	BEZEL	8	FENDER
4	BASE ASSEMBLY		

Fig. 17 Fixed-type radio antenna mounting

Power Type

◆ **See Figure 18**

➡The power antenna relay is located under the dash area in the convenience center.

1. Lower the antenna by turning off the radio or the ignition.

➡If the mast has failed in the UP position, and the mast or entire assembly is being replaced, the mast may be cut off to facilitate removal.

2. Disconnect the negative battery cable.

3. Remove the fender skirt attaching screws except those to the battery tray and radiator support.

➡On some vehicles there is an access plate which may reduce the amount of fender skirt bolts that have to be removed.

4. Pull down on the rear edge of the skirt and block with a 2″ × 4″ block of wood.

5. Remove the motor bracket attaching screws. Disconnect the motor electrical connections. Disconnect the antenna lead in wire. Remove the motor from the vehicle.

6. Reverse the above service procedures to install the assembly. Be sure the antenna mast is in the fully retracted position before installation.

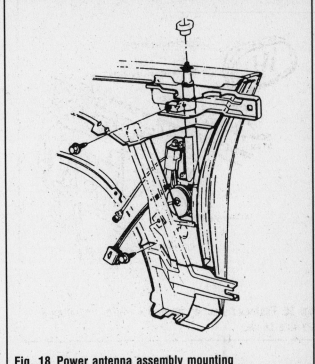

Fig. 18 Power antenna assembly mounting

INTERIOR

Front Door Panels

REMOVAL & INSTALLATION

◆ **See Figures 19, 20, 21 and 22**

1. Disconnect the negative battery cable. Remove the door handles and the locking knob from the inside of the doors. If equipped with remote control mirrors, remove the remote mirror escutcheon, then disengage the end of the mirror control cable from the escutcheon.

➡If equipped with door pull handles, remove the screws through the handle into the door inner panel.

2. If equipped with a switch cover plate in the door armrest, remove the cover plate screws, then disconnect the switches and the cigar lighter, if equipped from the electrical harness.

3. If equipped with an integral armrest, remove the screws in-

View of the vehicle interior—1977 Nova shown

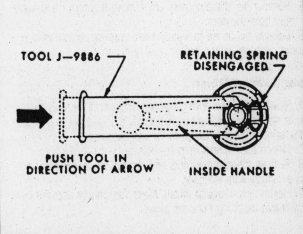

TOOL J—9886

RETAINING SPRING DISENGAGED

PUSH TOOL IN DIRECTION OF ARROW

INSIDE HANDLE

Fig. 19 A special tool is available to remove the clip from the inside door handle

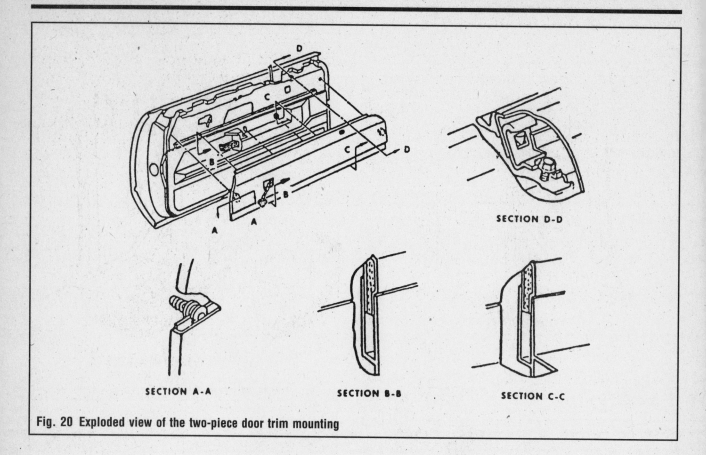

Fig. 20 Exploded view of the two-piece door trim mounting

serted through the pull cup into the armrest hanger support. If equipped with an armrest applied after the door trim installation, remove the armrest-to-inner panel screws.

4. If equipped with two-piece trim panels, disengage the retainer clips from the front and the rear of the upper trim panel, using tool No. BT-7323A, then lift the upper door trim and slide it slightly rearward to disengage it from the door inner panel at the beltline.

➡ **If equipped with electric switches in the door trim panel, disconnect the electrical connectors from the switch assembly.**

5. Along the upper edge of the lower trim panel, remove the mounting screws. At the lower edge of the panel, insert tool No. BT-7323A between the inner panel and the trim panel, then disengage the retaining clips from around the outer perimeter. To remove the lower panel, push the panel down and outward to disengage it from the door.

➡ **If equipped with courtesy lights, disconnect the wiring harness.**

6. If equipped with an insulator pad glued to the door inner panel, remove the pad with a putty knife by separating it from the inner panel.

7. To install, reverse the removal service removal procedures.

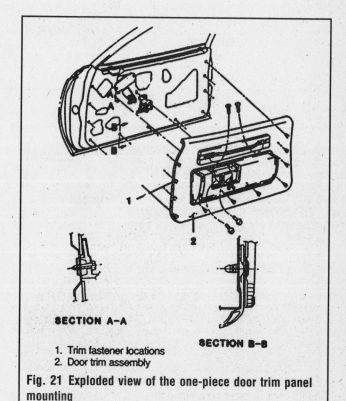

1. Trim fastener locations
2. Door trim assembly

Fig. 21 Exploded view of the one-piece door trim panel mounting

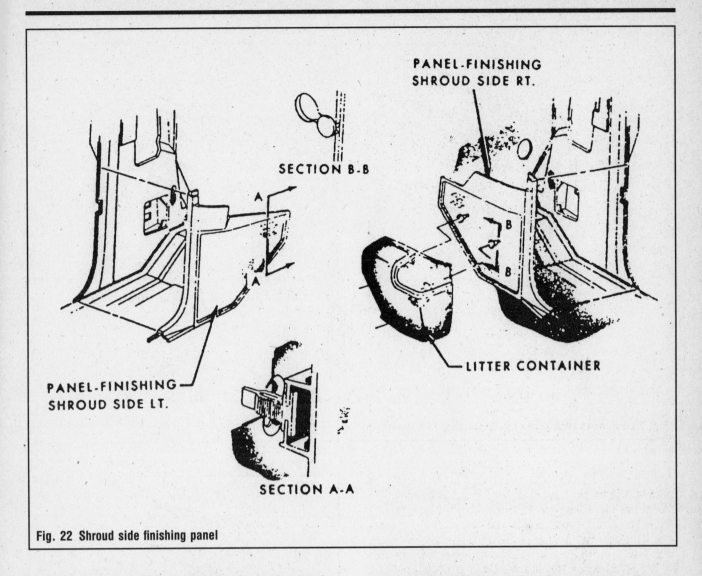

SECTION B-B

PANEL-FINISHING
SHROUD SIDE RT.

PANEL-FINISHING
SHROUD SIDE LT.

LITTER CONTAINER

SECTION A-A

Fig. 22 Shroud side finishing panel

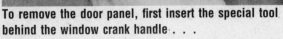

To remove the door panel, first insert the special tool behind the window crank handle . . .

. . . then remove the handle. Note the retaining clip (arrow)

Unfasten the door handle escutcheon retaining screw . . .

. . . then remove the armrest from the door trim panel

. . . then remove the inside door handle escutcheon

Unfasten the remaining door trim panel retainers . . .

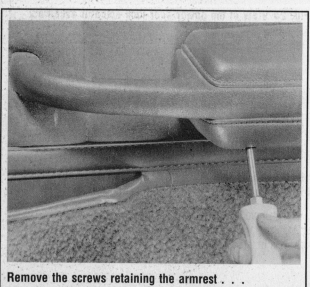

Remove the screws retaining the armrest . . .

. . . then remove the panel from the door

Rear Door Panels

REMOVAL & INSTALLATION

1. Disconnect the negative battery cable. Remove the door handles and the locking knob from the inside of the doors. If equipped with a switch cover plate in the door armrest, remove the cover plate screws, then disconnect the switch from the electrical harness.

➡**If equipped with door pull handles, remove the screws through the handle into the door inner panel.**

2. If equipped with an integral armrest, remove the screws inserted through the pull cup into the armrest hanger support. If equipped with an armrest applied after the door trim installation, remove the armrest-to-inner panel screws.

3. If equipped with two-piece trim panels, disengage the retainer clips from the front and the rear of the upper trim panel, using tool No. BT-7323A, then lift the upper door trim and slide it slightly rearward to disengage it from the door inner panel at the beltline.

4. Along the upper edge of the lower trim panel, remove the mounting screws. At the lower edge of the panel, insert tool No. BT-7323A between the inner panel and the trim panel, then disengage the retaining clips from around the outer perimeter. To remove the lower panel, push the panel down and outward to disengage it from the door.

➡**If equipped with courtesy lights, disconnect the wiring harness.**

5. If equipped with an insulator pad glued to the door inner panel, remove the pad (with a putty knife) by separating it from the inner panel.

6. To install, reverse the service removal procedures.

Door Locks

The door locks uses a fork bolt lock design which includes a safety interlock feature. The door is securely closed when the door lock fork bolt engages the striker bolt.

REMOVAL & INSTALLATION

◆ **See Figures 23 and 24**

➡**Never attempt to make repairs to the lock actuator assembly, replace the assembly.**

1. Disconnect the negative battery cable. Remove the door trim, then detach the insulator pad, if equipped and the inner panel water deflector enough to access the door lock.

2. Disconnect the electrical connector from the actuator assembly. If equipped with vacuum operated power locks, disconnect the vacuum line from the actuator assembly.

3. Remove the electric lock actuator by performing the following procedures;

Fig. 23 The door handle may be secured by rivets or screws

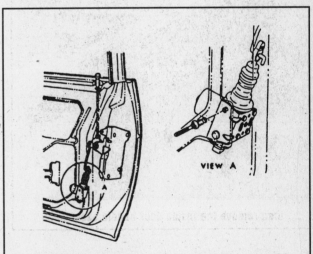

Fig. 24 View of the power door lock actuator assembly mounting

a. Using a center punch, drive the center pins out of pop rivets.

b. Using a ¼" drill bit, drill the heads off of the pop rivets.

c. Disconnect the lock actuator connecting rod and remove the lock actuator through the access hole.

➡**On some vehicles, it may be necessary to remove the inside handle, the lock and the connecting rod as a unit.**

4. Installation is the reverse of the removal procedure. When attaching the power door lock actuator to the door, use ¼" × ½" pop rivets or nuts and bolts.

Front Door Glass

REMOVAL & INSTALLATION

Closed Style Window Frame

1968–70 MODELS

♦ See Figure 25

1. Disconnect the negative battery cable. Remove the door panel.

2. If equipped, remove the front door ventilator. Loosen the window glass run channel lower retaining bolt. Remove the inner panel cam.

3. Slide the window lower sash channel cam off the window regulator lift arm and balance the arm rollers at the same time.

4. Remove the window outboard of the door upper frame and the window assembly.

5. Installation is the reverse of the service removal procedure.

1971–76 MODELS

1. Disconnect the negative battery cable. Remove the door panel.

2. Loosen the window stabilizer strips. Place the window in the ¾ down position.

3. Remove the window lower sash channel cam to glass retaining stud nuts. Tilt the front edge of the glass downward. Remove the inboard of the door upper frame and the window.

4. Installation is the reverse of the removal procedure. Adjust the window, as required.

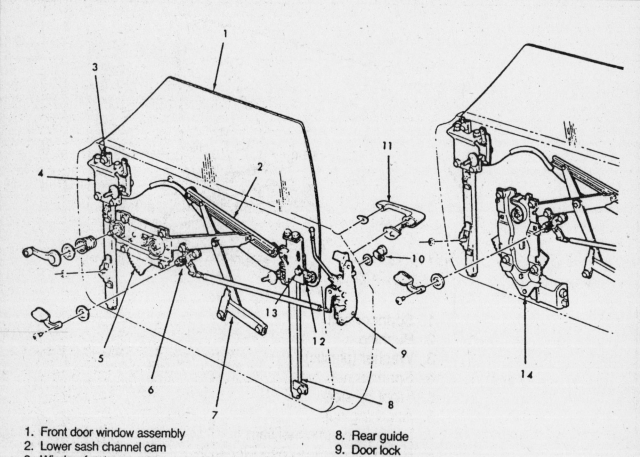

1. Front door window assembly
2. Lower sash channel cam
3. Window front upper stop
4. Front guide
5. Window regulator—manual
6. Door lock remote control
7. Inner panel cam
8. Rear guide
9. Door lock
10. Door lock cylinder
11. Door outside handle
12. Window rear upper stop (on window)
13. Window rear upper stop (on guide)
14. Window regulator—electric

Fig. 25 Front door glass and related components—1968–70 vehicles

1977–79 MODELS
▶ **See Figures 26 and 27**

1. Close the window and tape the glass to the door frame. Disconnect the negative battery cable. Remove the door panel.
2. Remove the bolts retaining the lower sash channel to the regulator sash. On coupe doors, remove the rubber down stop at the bottom of the door.
3. Attach the window regulator and lower the window regulator to the full down position. Remove the regulator sash.
4. While supporting the glass, remove the tape and lower the window to the full down position. Slide the glass forward and remove the guide clip from the window run channel.
5. Raise the glass while tilting it forward and remove it from the vehicle.
6. Installation is the reverse of the service removal procedure.

Open Style Window Frame
1968–70 MODELS

1. Disconnect the negative battery cable. Remove the door panel. Lower the window to the full down position. Remove the up-travel stop from the lower sash channel.
2. Roll the window ½ way up and remove the bolts that secure the lower window sash channel to the rear run channel guide plate. Disengage the guide plate from the sash channel.
3. Roll the window completely up. Remove the inner panel cam bolts. Tilt the upper corner of the glass inboard and rotate the glass counterclockwise until the lower sash channel cam is close to being parallel with the beltline.
4. Slide the glass rearward and disengage it from the regulator lift arm. Remove the glass from the vehicle.
5. Installation is the reverse of the removal procedure. Adjust the glass, as required.

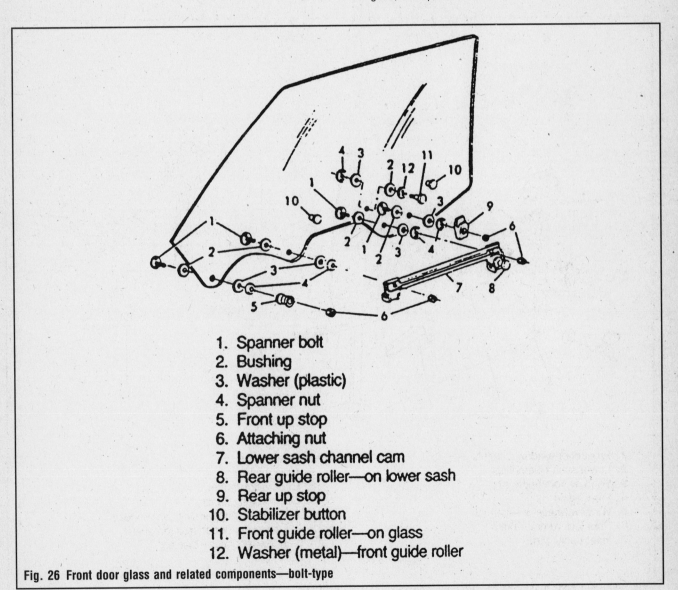

1. Spanner bolt
2. Bushing
3. Washer (plastic)
4. Spanner nut
5. Front up stop
6. Attaching nut
7. Lower sash channel cam
8. Rear guide roller—on lower sash
9. Rear up stop
10. Stabilizer button
11. Front guide roller—on glass
12. Washer (metal)—front guide roller

Fig. 26 Front door glass and related components—bolt-type

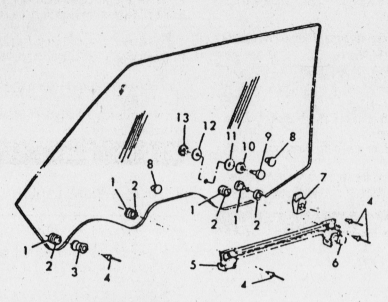

1. Rivet bushing
2. Rivet retainer
3. Front up stop
4. Rivet
5. Lower sash channel cam
6. Rear guide roller—on sash channel
7. Rear up stop
8. Stabilizer button
9. Front guide roller—on glass
10. Washer (metal)—front guide roller
11. Bushing
12. Washer (plastic)
13. Spanner nut

Fig. 27 Front door glass and related components—rivet-type

1971–76 MODELS

1. Disconnect the negative battery cable. Remove the door panel.

2. Remove the front and rear up-travel stops and stabilizer strips. Remove the glass bearing plate adjusting stud nut.

3. Turn the adjusting stud clockwise until the bearing plate is out of contact with the bearing button on the glass.

4. Remove the lower sash guide plate assembly to glass retaining bolts. Tilt the upper edge of the glass inboard to disengage it from the guide plate.

5. Remove the window glass from the vehicle by lifting straight up.

6. Installation is the reverse of the removal procedure. Adjust the glass, as required.

ADJUSTMENT PROCEDURE

1. Disconnect the negative battery cable. Remove the door panel.

2. To rotate the window, loosen the front and rear up-stops, adjust the inner panel cam and the up-stops, then tighten the screws.

3. To adjust the window's upper inboard and outboard edge, perform the following procedures:

    a. Position the window in the partially down position.

    b. Loosen the vertical guide upper support (lower) screws, which are accessible through the inner panel access holes.

    c. Loosen the pin assembly screws, the rear up-stop screw and the front belt stabilizer screw.

d. Adjust the vertical guide upper support and pin assembly (in or out as required, then tighten the screws, adjust and tighten the other components.

➡**When adjusting glass, make sure that it remains inboard of the blow-out clip, when cycled.**

4. If the window is too far forward or rearward, position the window partially down, loosen the vertical guide (upper and lower) screws, then adjust as required.

5. If the window is too high or low in it's Up position, adjust the front and rear up-travel stops.

6. If the window is too high or low in the Down position, adjust the down-travel stop.

7. If the window binds during the up and down operation, adjust the front and/or rear belt stabilizer pin assemblies.

Front Door Regulator

REMOVAL & INSTALLATION

1. Disconnect the negative battery cable. Remove the door panel. Remove the window glass.

2. If equipped with power windows, disconnect the electrical connector from the power window motor.

3. Remove the window regulator retaining bolts. Remove the window regulator from the vehicle.

4. Installation is the reverse of the service removal procedure.

Front Door Electric Window Motor

REMOVAL & INSTALLATION

1. Disconnect the negative battery cable. To properly remove the power window motor from the vehicle the window regulator must first be removed from the vehicle.

2. Refer to the Window Regulator Removal and Installation procedures for the proper information.

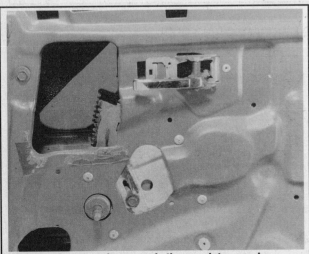

With the door panel removed, the regulator can be accessed

➡**The regulator arm is under tension, due to the mounting of the electric window motor, and if the following operation is not performed, serious damage could result.**

4. Drill a ¼″ hole through the regulator backing plate and sector gear. Install a ¹¹/₁₆″ bolt through the hole, but do not tighten the nut.

5. Remove the motor to regulator retaining bolts or rivets. Remove the motor from the regulator.

6. Installation is the reverse of the service removal procedure.

Rear Door Glass

REMOVAL & INSTALLATION

▸ **See Figures 28, 29 and 30**

1. Disconnect the negative battery cable. Remove the trim panel. Raise the window to the full up position and tape the glass to the door frame.

2. Remove the lower sash channel retaining bolts. Lower the window to the full down position. Remove the regulator sash.

3. Disengage the front edge of the glass from the glass channel retainer. Slide the glass forward and tilt it up slightly.

4. Using care, remove the glass from its mounting.

5. Installation is the reverse of the removal procedure. Before installing the trim panel, check for proper window operation.

Rear Door Regulator

REMOVAL & INSTALLATION

1. Disconnect the negative battery cable. Remove the trim panel. Remove the window.

2. Remove the regulator assembly retaining bolts or rivets. Remove the regulator from the vehicle.

3. Installation is the reverse of the service removal procedure.

Rear Door Electric Window Motor

REMOVAL & INSTALLATION

1. Disconnect the negative battery cable. Remove the trim panel. Remove the window.

2. Disconnect the electrical connection from the electrical motor assembly.

3. Remove the regulator retaining bolts or rivets and remove the regulator and window motor as an assembly.

➡**The regulator arm is under tension, due to the mounting of the electric window motor, and if the following operation is not performed, serious damage could result.**

4. Drill a ¼″ hole through the regulator backing plate and sector gear. Install a ¹¹/₁₆″ bolt through the hole, but do not tighten the nut.

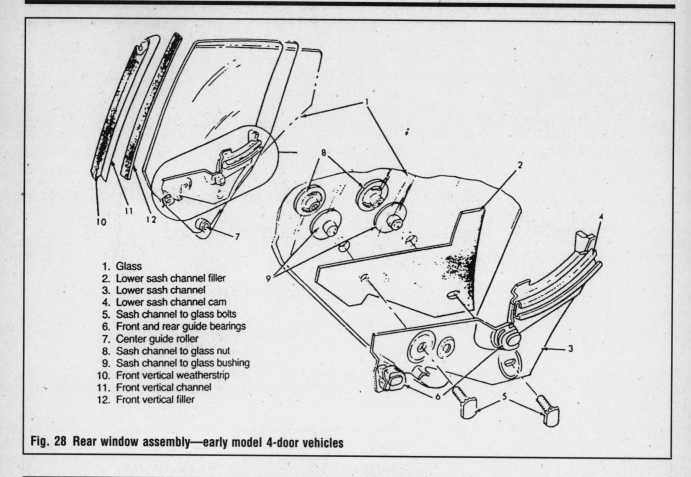

1. Glass
2. Lower sash channel filler
3. Lower sash channel
4. Lower sash channel cam
5. Sash channel to glass bolts
6. Front and rear guide bearings
7. Center guide roller
8. Sash channel to glass nut
9. Sash channel to glass bushing
10. Front vertical weatherstrip
11. Front vertical channel
12. Front vertical filler

Fig. 28 Rear window assembly—early model 4-door vehicles

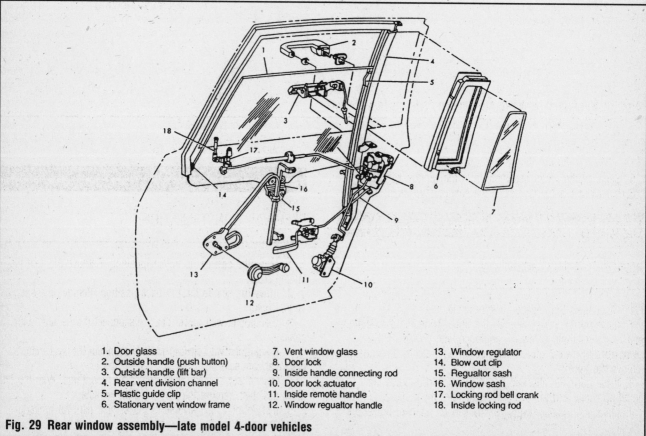

1. Door glass
2. Outside handle (push button)
3. Outside handle (lift bar)
4. Rear vent division channel
5. Plastic guide clip
6. Stationary vent window frame
7. Vent window glass
8. Door lock
9. Inside handle connecting rod
10. Door lock actuator
11. Inside remote handle
12. Window regualtor handle
13. Window regulator
14. Blow out clip
15. Regualtor sash
16. Window sash
17. Locking rod bell crank
18. Inside locking rod

Fig. 29 Rear window assembly—late model 4-door vehicles

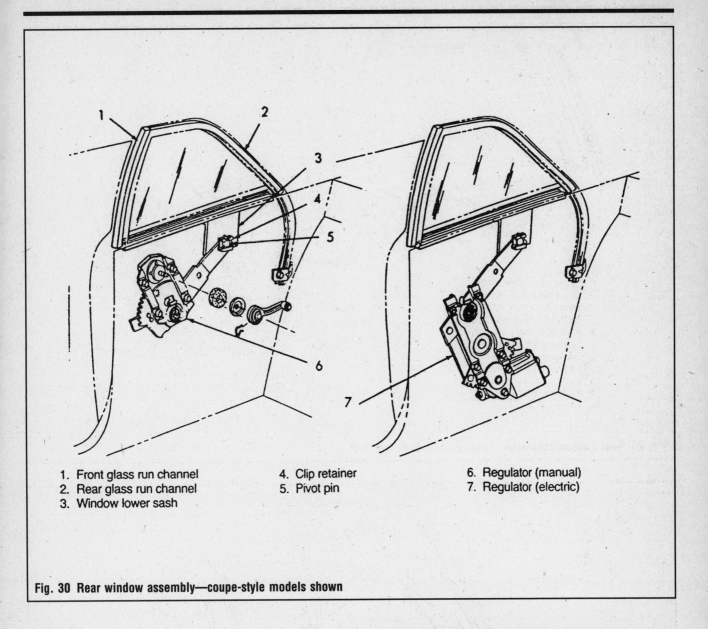

1. Front glass run channel
2. Rear glass run channel
3. Window lower sash
4. Clip retainer
5. Pivot pin
6. Regulator (manual)
7. Regulator (electric)

Fig. 30 Rear window assembly—coupe-style models shown

5. Separate the motor assembly from the window regulator.
6. Installation is the reverse of the service removal procedure.

Inside Rear View Mirror

REMOVAL & INSTALLATION

1. Disconnect the negative battery cable.
2. If the mirror is mounted on the upper windshield moulding, remove the retaining screws. If equipped with a map light, pull the mirror downward and disconnect the light electrical connector. Remove the mirror.
3. If the mirror is attached to the windshield, remove the mounting screw and remove the mirror from the vehicle.
4. Installation is the reverse of the service removal procedure.

Seats

REMOVAL & INSTALLATION

1. Move the seat to the full up position. Remove the seat retaining bolts.
2. Move the seat to the full back position. Remove the seat retaining bolts.
3. If equipped with power seats disconnect the negative battery cable.
4. If equipped with electric seats disconnect the seat motor electrical connector.
5. Disconnect the seat belts from their mountings. With the aid of an assistant, remove the seat from the vehicle.
6. Installation is the reverse of the service removal procedure.

Power Seat Motor

REMOVAL & INSTALLATION

▶ **See Figure 31**

1. Disconnect the negative battery cable. Disconnect the electrical harness connector.
2. Remove the seat retaining bolts. Remove the seat from the vehicle. Place it upside down on a protected workbench.
3. Disconnect the motor feed wires from the motor control relay.
4. Remove the motor mounting screws and the transmission-to-motor screws, then move the motor away to disengage it from the rubber coupling.
5. Installation is the reverse of the removal procedure.

➡ **When installing the motor, make sure that the rubber coupling is properly engaged at the motor and the transmission.**

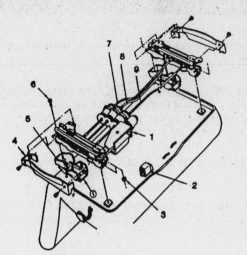

1. Transmission assembly
2. Seat relay
3. Nut
4. Adjuster track lower cover
5. Adjuster track upper cover
6. Adjuster-to-seat frame attaching bolts
7. Horizontal drive cable
8. Rear vertical drive cable
9. Front vertical drive cable

Fig. 31 View of the six-way power seat adjuster

GLOSSARY

AIR/FUEL RATIO: The ratio of air-to-gasoline by weight in the fuel mixture drawn into the engine.

AIR INJECTION: One method of reducing harmful exhaust emissions by injecting air into each of the exhaust ports of an engine. The fresh air entering the hot exhaust manifold causes any remaining fuel to be burned before it can exit the tailpipe.

ALTERNATOR: A device used for converting mechanical energy into electrical energy.

AMMETER: An instrument, calibrated in amperes, used to measure the flow of an electrical current in a circuit. Ammeters are always connected in series with the circuit being tested.

AMPERE: The rate of flow of electrical current present when one volt of electrical pressure is applied against one ohm of electrical resistance.

ANALOG COMPUTER: Any microprocessor that uses similar (analogous) electrical signals to make its calculations.

ARMATURE: A laminated, soft iron core wrapped by a wire that converts electrical energy to mechanical energy as in a motor or relay. When rotated in a magnetic field, it changes mechanical energy into electrical energy as in a generator.

ATMOSPHERIC PRESSURE: The pressure on the Earth's surface caused by the weight of the air in the atmosphere. At sea level, this pressure is 14.7 psi at 32°F (101 kPa at 0°C).

ATOMIZATION: The breaking down of a liquid into a fine mist that can be suspended in air.

AXIAL PLAY: Movement parallel to a shaft or bearing bore.

BACKFIRE: The sudden combustion of gases in the intake or exhaust system that results in a loud explosion.

BACKLASH: The clearance or play between two parts, such as meshed gears.

BACKPRESSURE: Restrictions in the exhaust system that slow the exit of exhaust gases from the combustion chamber.

BAKELITE: A heat resistant, plastic insulator material commonly used in printed circuit boards and transistorized components.

BALL BEARING: A bearing made up of hardened inner and outer races between which hardened steel balls roll.

BALLAST RESISTOR: A resistor in the primary ignition circuit that lowers voltage after the engine is started to reduce wear on ignition components.

BEARING: A friction reducing, supportive device usually located between a stationary part and a moving part.

BIMETAL TEMPERATURE SENSOR: Any sensor or switch made of two dissimilar types of metal that bend when heated or cooled due to the different expansion rates of the alloys. These types of sensors usually function as an on/off switch.

BLOWBY: Combustion gases, composed of water vapor and unburned fuel, that leak past the piston rings into the crankcase during normal engine operation. These gases are removed by the PCV system to prevent the buildup of harmful acids in the crankcase.

BRAKE PAD: A brake shoe and lining assembly used with disc brakes.

BRAKE SHOE: The backing for the brake lining. The term is, however, usually applied to the assembly of the brake backing and lining.

BUSHING: A liner, usually removable, for a bearing; an anti-friction liner used in place of a bearing.

CALIPER: A hydraulically activated device in a disc brake system, which is mounted straddling the brake rotor (disc). The caliper contains at least one piston and two brake pads. Hydraulic pressure on the piston(s) forces the pads against the rotor.

CAMSHAFT: A shaft in the engine on which are the lobes (cams) which operate the valves. The camshaft is driven by the crankshaft, via a belt, chain or gears, at one half the crankshaft speed.

CAPACITOR: A device which stores an electrical charge.

CARBON MONOXIDE (CO): A colorless, odorless gas given off as a normal byproduct of combustion. It is poisonous and extremely dangerous in confined areas, building up slowly to toxic levels without warning if adequate ventilation is not available.

CARBURETOR: A device, usually mounted on the intake manifold of an engine, which mixes the air and fuel in the proper proportion to allow even combustion.

CATALYTIC CONVERTER: A device installed in the exhaust system, like a muffler, that converts harmful byproducts of combustion into carbon dioxide and water vapor by means of a heat-producing chemical reaction.

CENTRIFUGAL ADVANCE: A mechanical method of advancing the spark timing by using flyweights in the distributor that react to centrifugal force generated by the distributor shaft rotation.

CHECK VALVE: Any one-way valve installed to permit the flow of air, fuel or vacuum in one direction only.

CHOKE: A device, usually a moveable valve, placed in the intake path of a carburetor to restrict the flow of air.

CIRCUIT: Any unbroken path through which an electrical current can flow. Also used to describe fuel flow in some instances.

CIRCUIT BREAKER: A switch which protects an electrical circuit from overload by opening the circuit when the current flow exceeds a predetermined level. Some circuit breakers must be reset manually, while most reset automatically.

COIL (IGNITION): A transformer in the ignition circuit which steps up the voltage provided to the spark plugs.

COMBINATION MANIFOLD: An assembly which includes both the intake and exhaust manifolds in one casting.

COMBINATION VALVE: A device used in some fuel systems that routes fuel vapors to a charcoal storage canister instead of venting them into the atmosphere. The valve relieves fuel tank pressure and allows fresh air into the tank as the fuel level drops to prevent a vapor lock situation.

COMPRESSION RATIO: The comparison of the total volume of the cylinder and combustion chamber with the piston at BDC and the piston at TDC.

CONDENSER: 1. An electrical device which acts to store an electrical charge, preventing voltage surges. 2. A radiator-like device in the air conditioning system in which refrigerant gas condenses into a liquid, giving off heat.

CONDUCTOR: Any material through which an electrical current can be transmitted easily.

CONTINUITY: Continuous or complete circuit. Can be checked with an ohmmeter.

COUNTERSHAFT: An intermediate shaft which is rotated by a mainshaft and transmits, in turn, that rotation to a working part.

CRANKCASE: The lower part of an engine in which the crankshaft and related parts operate.

CRANKSHAFT: The main driving shaft of an engine which receives reciprocating motion from the pistons and converts it to rotary motion.

CYLINDER: In an engine, the round hole in the engine block in which the piston(s) ride.

CYLINDER BLOCK: The main structural member of an engine in which is found the cylinders, crankshaft and other principal parts.

CYLINDER HEAD: The detachable portion of the engine, usually fastened to the top of the cylinder block and containing all or most of the combustion chambers. On overhead valve engines, it contains the valves and their operating parts. On overhead cam engines, it contains the camshaft as well.

DEAD CENTER: The extreme top or bottom of the piston stroke.

DETONATION: An unwanted explosion of the air/fuel mixture in the combustion chamber caused by excess heat and compression, advanced timing, or an overly lean mixture. Also referred to as "ping".

DIAPHRAGM: A thin, flexible wall separating two cavities, such as in a vacuum advance unit.

DIESELING: A condition in which hot spots in the combustion chamber cause the engine to run on after the key is turned off.

DIFFERENTIAL: A geared assembly which allows the transmission of motion between drive axles, giving one axle the ability to turn faster than the other.

DIODE: An electrical device that will allow current to flow in one direction only.

DISC BRAKE: A hydraulic braking assembly consisting of a brake disc, or rotor, mounted on an axle, and a caliper assembly containing, usually two brake pads which are activated by hydraulic pressure. The pads are forced against the sides of the disc, creating friction which slows the vehicle.

DISTRIBUTOR: A mechanically driven device on an engine which is responsible for electrically firing the spark plug at a predetermined point of the piston stroke.

DOWEL PIN: A pin, inserted in mating holes in two different parts allowing those parts to maintain a fixed relationship.

DRUM BRAKE: A braking system which consists of two brake shoes and one or two wheel cylinders, mounted on a fixed backing plate, and a brake drum, mounted on an axle, which revolves around the assembly.

DWELL: The rate, measured in degrees of shaft rotation, at which an electrical circuit cycles on and off.

ELECTRONIC CONTROL UNIT (ECU): Ignition module, module, amplifier or igniter. See Module for definition.

ELECTRONIC IGNITION: A system in which the timing and firing of the spark plugs is controlled by an electronic control unit, usually called a module. These systems have no points or condenser.

END-PLAY: The measured amount of axial movement in a shaft.

ENGINE: A device that converts heat into mechanical energy.

EXHAUST MANIFOLD: A set of cast passages or pipes which conduct exhaust gases from the engine.

FEELER GAUGE: A blade, usually metal, of precisely predetermined thickness, used to measure the clearance between two parts.

FIRING ORDER: The order in which combustion occurs in the cylinders of an engine. Also the order in which spark is distributed to the plugs by the distributor.

FLOODING: The presence of too much fuel in the intake manifold and combustion chamber which prevents the air/fuel mixture from firing, thereby causing a no-start situation.

FLYWHEEL: A disc shaped part bolted to the rear end of the crankshaft. Around the outer perimeter is affixed the ring gear. The starter drive engages the ring gear, turning the flywheel, which rotates the crankshaft, imparting the initial starting motion to the engine.

FOOT POUND (ft. lbs. or sometimes, ft.lb.): The amount of energy or work needed to raise an item weighing one pound, a distance of one foot.

FUSE: A protective device in a circuit which prevents circuit overload by breaking the circuit when a specific amperage is present. The device is constructed around a strip or wire of a lower amperage rating than the circuit it is designed to protect. When an amperage higher than that stamped on the fuse is present in the circuit, the strip or wire melts, opening the circuit.

GEAR RATIO: The ratio between the number of teeth on meshing gears.

GENERATOR: A device which converts mechanical energy into electrical energy.

HEAT RANGE: The measure of a spark plug's ability to dissipate heat from its firing end. The higher the heat range, the hotter the plug fires.

HUB: The center part of a wheel or gear.

HYDROCARBON (HC): Any chemical compound made up of hydrogen and carbon. A major pollutant formed by the engine as a byproduct of combustion.

HYDROMETER: An instrument used to measure the specific gravity of a solution.

INCH POUND (inch lbs.; sometimes in.lb. or in. lbs.): One twelfth of a foot pound.

INDUCTION: A means of transferring electrical energy in the form of a magnetic field. Principle used in the ignition coil to increase voltage.

INJECTOR: A device which receives metered fuel under relatively low pressure and is activated to inject the fuel into the engine under relatively high pressure at a predetermined time.

INPUT SHAFT: The shaft to which torque is applied, usually carrying the driving gear or gears.

INTAKE MANIFOLD: A casting of passages or pipes used to conduct air or a fuel/air mixture to the cylinders.

JOURNAL: The bearing surface within which a shaft operates.

KEY: A small block usually fitted in a notch between a shaft and a hub to prevent slippage of the two parts.

MANIFOLD: A casting of passages or set of pipes which connect the cylinders to an inlet or outlet source.

MANIFOLD VACUUM: Low pressure in an engine intake manifold formed just below the throttle plates. Manifold vacuum is highest at idle and drops under acceleration.

MASTER CYLINDER: The primary fluid pressurizing device in a hydraulic system. In automotive use, it is found in brake and hydraulic clutch systems and is pedal activated, either directly or, in a power brake system, through the power booster.

MODULE: Electronic control unit, amplifier or igniter of solid state or integrated design which controls the current flow in the ignition primary circuit based on input from the pick-up coil. When the module opens the primary circuit, high secondary voltage is induced in the coil.

NEEDLE BEARING: A bearing which consists of a number (usually a large number) of long, thin rollers.

OHM: (Ω) The unit used to measure the resistance of conductor-to-electrical flow. One ohm is the amount of resistance that limits current flow to one ampere in a circuit with one volt of pressure.

OHMMETER: An instrument used for measuring the resistance, in ohms, in an electrical circuit.

OUTPUT SHAFT: The shaft which transmits torque from a device, such as a transmission.

OVERDRIVE: A gear assembly which produces more shaft revolutions than that transmitted to it.

OVERHEAD CAMSHAFT (OHC): An engine configuration in which the camshaft is mounted on top of the cylinder head and operates the valve either directly or by means of rocker arms.

OVERHEAD VALVE (OHV): An engine configuration in which all of the valves are located in the cylinder head and the camshaft is located in the cylinder block. The camshaft operates the valves via lifters and pushrods.

OXIDES OF NITROGEN (NOx): Chemical compounds of nitrogen produced as a byproduct of combustion. They combine with hydrocarbons to produce smog.

OXYGEN SENSOR: Used with the feedback system to sense the presence of oxygen in the exhaust gas and signal the computer which can reference the voltage signal to an air/fuel ratio.

PINION: The smaller of two meshing gears.

PISTON RING: An open-ended ring which fits into a groove on the outer diameter of the piston. Its chief function is to form a seal between the piston and cylinder wall. Most automotive pistons have three rings: two for compression sealing; one for oil sealing.

PRELOAD: A predetermined load placed on a bearing during assembly or by adjustment.

PRIMARY CIRCUIT: The low voltage side of the ignition system which consists of the ignition switch, ballast resistor or resistance wire, bypass, coil, electronic control unit and pick-up coil as well as the connecting wires and harnesses.

PRESS FIT: The mating of two parts under pressure, due to the inner diameter of one being smaller than the outer diameter of the other, or vice versa; an interference fit.

RACE: The surface on the inner or outer ring of a bearing on which the balls, needles or rollers move.

REGULATOR: A device which maintains the amperage and/or voltage levels of a circuit at predetermined values.

RELAY: A switch which automatically opens and/or closes a circuit.

RESISTANCE: The opposition to the flow of current through a circuit or electrical device, and is measured in ohms. Resistance is equal to the voltage divided by the amperage.

RESISTOR: A device, usually made of wire, which offers a preset amount of resistance in an electrical circuit.

RING GEAR: The name given to a ring-shaped gear attached to a differential case, or affixed to a flywheel or as part of a planetary gear set.

ROLLER BEARING: A bearing made up of hardened inner and outer races between which hardened steel rollers move.

ROTOR: 1. The disc-shaped part of a disc brake assembly, upon which the brake pads bear; also called, brake disc. 2. The device mounted atop the distributor shaft, which passes current to the distributor cap tower contacts.

SECONDARY CIRCUIT: The high voltage side of the ignition system, usually above 20,000 volts. The secondary includes the ignition coil, coil wire, distributor cap and rotor, spark plug wires and spark plugs.

SENDING UNIT: A mechanical, electrical, hydraulic or electromagnetic device which transmits information to a gauge.

SENSOR: Any device designed to measure engine operating conditions or ambient pressures and temperatures. Usually electronic in nature and designed to send a voltage signal to an on-board computer, some sensors may operate as a simple on/off switch or they may provide a variable voltage signal (like a potentiometer) as conditions or measured parameters change.

SHIM: Spacers of precise, predetermined thickness used between parts to establish a proper working relationship.

SLAVE CYLINDER: In automotive use, a device in the hydraulic clutch system which is activated by hydraulic force, disengaging the clutch.

SOLENOID: A coil used to produce a magnetic field, the effect of which is to produce work.

SPARK PLUG: A device screwed into the combustion chamber of a spark ignition engine. The basic construction is a conductive core inside of a ceramic insulator, mounted in an outer conductive base. An electrical charge from the spark plug wire travels along the conductive core and jumps a preset air gap to a grounding point or points at the end of the conductive base. The resultant spark ignites the fuel/air mixture in the combustion chamber.

SPLINES: Ridges machined or cast onto the outer diameter of a shaft or inner diameter of a bore to enable parts to mate without rotation.

TACHOMETER: A device used to measure the rotary speed of an engine, shaft, gear, etc., usually in rotations per minute.

THERMOSTAT: A valve, located in the cooling system of an engine, which is closed when cold and opens gradually in response to engine heating, controlling the temperature of the coolant and rate of coolant flow.

TOP DEAD CENTER (TDC): The point at which the piston reaches the top of its travel on the compression stroke.

TORQUE: The twisting force applied to an object.

TORQUE CONVERTER: A turbine used to transmit power from a driving member to a driven member via hydraulic action, providing changes in drive ratio and torque. In automotive use, it links the driveplate at the rear of the engine to the automatic transmission.

TRANSDUCER: A device used to change a force into an electrical signal.

TRANSISTOR: A semi-conductor component which can be actuated by a small voltage to perform an electrical switching function.

TUNE-UP: A regular maintenance function, usually associated with the replacement and adjustment of parts and components in the electrical and fuel systems of a vehicle for the purpose of attaining optimum performance.

TURBOCHARGER: An exhaust driven pump which compresses intake air and forces it into the combustion chambers at higher than atmospheric pressures. The increased air pressure allows more fuel to be burned and results in increased horsepower being produced.

VACUUM ADVANCE: A device which advances the ignition timing in response to increased engine vacuum.

VACUUM GAUGE: An instrument used to measure the presence of vacuum in a chamber.

VALVE: A device which control the pressure, direction of flow or rate of flow of a liquid or gas.

VALVE CLEARANCE: The measured gap between the end of the valve stem and the rocker arm, cam lobe or follower that activates the valve.

VISCOSITY: The rating of a liquid's internal resistance to flow.

VOLTMETER: An instrument used for measuring electrical force in units called volts. Voltmeters are always connected parallel with the circuit being tested.

WHEEL CYLINDER: Found in the automotive drum brake assembly, it is a device, actuated by hydraulic pressure, which, through internal pistons, pushes the brake shoes outward against the drums.

ADD-ON ELECTRICAL EQUIPMENT 6-12
ADJUSTMENT (CLUTCH) 7-10
   LINKAGE & FREE-PLAY 7-10
ADJUSTMENTS (AUTOMATIC TRANSMISSION) 7-14
   DETENT CABLE 7-17
   DETENT SWITCH 7-17
   SHIFT LINKAGE 7-14
   THROTTLE VALVE LINKAGE 7-16
ADJUSTMENTS (MANUAL TRANSMISSION) 7-2
   LINKAGE 7-2
AIR CLEANER 1-18
   REMOVAL & INSTALLATION 1-18
AIR CONDITIONING 1-30
   DISCHARGING, EVACUATING & CHARGING 1-32
   GENERAL SERVICING PROCEDURES 1-31
   SAFETY PRECAUTIONS 1-30
   SYSTEM INSPECTION 1-32
AIR INJECTION REACTOR SYSTEM 4-10
   OPERATION 4-10
   REMOVAL & INSTALLATION 4-11
   SERVICE 4-11
AIR POLLUTION 4-2
ALTERNATOR 3-10
   ALTERNATOR PRECAUTIONS 3-10
   REMOVAL & INSTALLATION 3-11
ALTERNATOR AND REGULATOR SPECIFICATIONS 3-15
ANTENNA 10-8
   REMOVAL & INSTALLATION 10-8
AUTOMATIC TRANSMISSION 7-12
AUTOMATIC TRANSMISSION (FLUIDS AND LUBRICANTS) 1-45
   DRAIN & REFILL 1-46
   FLUID RECOMMENDATIONS 1-45
   LEVEL CHECK 1-45
AUTOMOTIVE EMISSIONS 4-3
AUTOMOTIVE POLLUTANTS 4-2
   HEAT TRANSFER 4-3
   TEMPERATURE INVERSION 4-2
AVOIDING THE MOST COMMON MISTAKES 1-2
AVOIDING TROUBLE 1-2
AXLE SHAFTS AND BEARINGS 7-25
   REMOVAL, OVERHAUL & INSTALLATION 7-25
BASIC OPERATING PRINCIPLES 9-2
   DISC BRAKES 9-2
   DRUM BRAKES 9-3
   POWER BOOSTERS 9-3
BATTERY (ENGINE ELECTRICAL) 3-13
   REMOVAL & INSTALLATION 3-13
BATTERY (ROUTINE MAINTENANCE) 1-23
   BATTERY FLUID 1-23
   CABLES 1-25
   CHARGING 1-26
   GENERAL MAINTENANCE 1-23
   REPLACEMENT 1-26
BATTERY AND STARTER SPECIFICATIONS 3-17
BATTERY, STARTING AND CHARGING SYSTEMS 3-4
   BASIC OPERATING PRINCIPLES 3-4
BELTS 1-26
   INSPECTION 1-26
   TENSION CHECKING & ADJUSTING 1-27
BLEEDING BRAKE SYSTEM 9-8
   MANUAL BLEEDING 9-8
   PRESSURE BLEEDING 9-8
BLOWER MOTOR 6-12
   REMOVAL & INSTALLATION 6-12
BODY LUBRICATION 1-54
   HOOD LATCH 1-54
BOLTS, NUTS AND OTHER THREADED RETAINERS 1-8
BRAKE CALIPER 9-11
   REMOVAL & INSTALLATION 9-11
BRAKE DISC (ROTOR) 9-13
   INSPECTION 9-14

MASTER
INDEX

REMOVAL & INSTALLATION 9-13
BRAKE DRUMS 9-15
  INSPECTION 9-16
  REMOVAL & INSTALLATION 9-15
BRAKE MASTER CYLINDER AND RELATED COMPONENTS 9-7
BRAKE PADS 9-9
  REMOVAL & INSTALLATION 9-9
BRAKE SHOES 9-16
  ADJUSTMENT 9-16
  REMOVAL & INSTALLATION 9-16
BRAKE SPECIFICATIONS 9-24
BRAKE SYSTEM 9-2
BREAK-IN PROCEDURE 3-54
BREAKER POINT IGNITION SYSTEM 2-9
BREAKER POINTS AND CONDENSER 2-9
  REMOVAL & INSTALLATION 2-9
BUMPERS 10-5
  REMOVAL & INSTALLATION 10-5
CABLES 9-21
  ADJUSTMENT 9-21
  REMOVAL & INSTALLATION 9-21
CAMSHAFT 3-40
  REMOVAL & INSTALLATION 3-40
CAPACITIES 1-65
CARBURETOR 5-32
  OVERHAUL 5-32
  REMOVAL & INSTALLATION 5-32
CARBURETOR SPECIFICATIONS—CARTER CARBURETORS 5-34
CARTER AFB-4 BARREL CARBURETOR 5-18
  ADJUSTMENTS 5-18
CARTER AVS-4 BARREL CARBURETOR 5-19
  ADJUSTMENTS 5-19
CARTER YF-1 BARREL CARBURETOR 5-7
  ADJUSTMENTS 5-7
CATALYTIC CONVERTER 4-15
  OPERATION 4-15
CHASSIS GREASING 1-54
CIRCUIT BREAKERS 6-25
CIRCUIT PROTECTION 6-25
CLUTCH 7-5
COIL SPRINGS (FRONT SUSPENSION) 8-5
  REMOVAL & INSTALLATION 8-5
COIL SPRINGS (REAR SUSPENSION) 8-16
  REMOVAL & INSTALLATION 8-16
COMPLETING THE REBUILDING PROCESS 3-54
COMPONENT LOCATIONS
  BRAKE MASTER CYLINDER AND RELATED COMPONENTS 9-7
  FRONT SUSPENSION COMPONENTS—LATE MODEL NOVA 8-4
  HEI DISTRIBUTOR COMPONENTS 3-9
  MAINTENANCE COMPONENT LOCATIONS—EARLY MODEL V8
   ENGINE 1-16
  MAINTENANCE COMPONENT LOCATIONS—LATE MODEL NOVA
   INLINE ENGINE 1-17
  REAR DRUM BRAKES 9-19
  REAR SUSPENSION 8-14
CONTROLLED COMBUSTION SYSTEM (CCS) 4-6
  OPERATION 4-6
  SERVICE 4-6
CONVENTIONAL IGNITION SYSTEM 3-10
  REMOVAL & INSTALLATION 3-10
COOLING 1-55
  ENGINE 1-55
  TRANSMISSION 1-55
COOLING SYSTEM 1-48
  COOLING SYSTEM INSPECTION 1-50
  DRAIN & REFILL 1-51
  FLUID RECOMMENDATIONS 1-49
  FLUSHING & CLEANING THE SYSTEM 1-52

LEVEL CHECK 1-50
CRANKCASE EMISSIONS 4-5
CRANKCASE VENTILATION FILTER 1-22
  REMOVAL & INSTALLATION 1-22
CRANKSHAFT AND CONNECTING ROD SPECIFICATIONS 3-25
CYLINDER BLOCK 3-65
  RECONDITIONING 3-65
CYLINDER BORE, PISTON, AND RING SPECIFICATIONS 1962–77 3-28
CYLINDER HEAD (ENGINE MECHANICAL) 3-32
  REMOVAL AND INSTALLATION 3-32
CYLINDER HEAD (ENGINE REBUILDING) 3-54
  RECONDITIONING 3-54
DC GENERATOR 3-10
  REMOVAL & INSTALLATION 3-10
DESIGN (ENGINE MECHANICAL) 3-18
DETERMINING AXLE RATIO (REAR AXLE) 7-28
  1962 VEHICLES 7-28
  1963 VEHICLES 7-28
  1964 VEHICLES 7-28
  1965 VEHICLES 7-28
  1966 VEHICLES 7-29
  1967 VEHICLES 7-29
  1968 VEHICLES 7-29
  1969 VEHICLES 7-29
  1970 VEHICLES 7-29
  1971 VEHICLES 7-30
  1972 VEHICLES 7-30
  1973–74 VEHICLES 7-30
  1975–77 VEHICLES 7-30
DO'S 1-7
DON'TS 1-8
DOOR LOCKS 10-13
  REMOVAL & INSTALLATION 10-13
DOORS 10-2
  ADJUSTMENT 10-2
  REMOVAL & INSTALLATION 10-2
DRIVELINE 7-21
DRIVEN DISC AND PRESSURE PLATE 7-6
  REMOVAL & INSTALLATION 7-6
DRIVESHAFT AND U-JOINTS 7-22
  DRIVESHAFT REMOVAL & INSTALLATION 7-22
  U-JOINT OVERHAUL 7-24
DRUM BRAKES 9-15
DWELL ANGLE 2-10
  ADJUSTMENT 2-10
  DWELL VARIATION TEST 2-11
EARLY FUEL EVAPORATION SYSTEM 4-14
  OPERATION 4-14
EMISSION CONTROLS 4-6
ENGINE (ENGINE MECHANICAL) 3-31
  REMOVAL & INSTALLATION 3-31
  SEPARATING THE TRANSMISSION FROM THE ENGINE 3-32
ENGINE (FLUIDS AND LUBRICANTS) 1-42
  OIL CHANGE 1-43
  OIL FILTER CHANGES 1-44
  OIL LEVEL CHECK 1-42
ENGINE (SERIAL NUMBER IDENTIFICATION) 1-14
ENGINE ELECTRICAL 3-2
ENGINE MECHANICAL 3-18
ENGINE OVERHAUL TIPS 3-52
  INSPECTION TECHNIQUES 3-52
  OVERHAUL TIPS 3-52
  REPAIRING DAMAGED THREADS 3-52
  TOOLS 3-52
ENGINE REBUILDING 3-52
ENGLISH TO METRIC CONVERSION CHARTS 1-68
EVAPORATIVE CANISTER 1-22
  SERVICING 1-22

EVAPORATIVE EMISSION CONTROL SYSTEM 4-7
   OPERATION 4-7
   SERVICE 4-7
EVAPORATIVE EMISSIONS 4-5
EXHAUST GAS RECIRCULATION SYSTEM 4-13
   OPERATION 4-13
   REMOVAL & INSTALLATION 4-14
EXHAUST GASES 4-3
   CARBON MONOXIDE 4-4
   HYDROCARBONS 4-3
   NITROGEN 4-4
   OXIDES OF SULFUR 4-4
   PARTICULATE MATTER 4-4
EXHAUST MANIFOLD 3-37
   REMOVAL & INSTALLATION 3-37
EXHAUST SYSTEM 3-50
EXTERIOR 10-2
FASTENERS, MEASUREMENTS AND CONVERSIONS 1-8
FIRING ORDERS 2-8
FLAME ARRESTER 1-22
FLASHERS 6-25
   REPLACEMENT 6-25
FLUID DISPOSAL 1-41
FLUID PAN 7-19
   REMOVAL & INSTALLATION 7-19
FLUIDS AND LUBRICANTS 1-41
FRONT DISC BRAKES 9-9
FRONT DOOR ELECTRIC WINDOW MOTOR 10-17
   REMOVAL & INSTALLATION 10-17
FRONT DOOR GLASS 10-14
   ADJUSTMENT PROCEDURE 10-16
   REMOVAL & INSTALLATION 10-14
FRONT DOOR PANELS 10-9
   REMOVAL & INSTALLATION 10-9
FRONT DOOR REGULATOR 10-17
   REMOVAL & INSTALLATION 10-17
FRONT END ALIGNMENT 8-11
   CAMBER 8-12
   CASTER 8-12
   TOE-IN 8-12
FRONT SUSPENSION 8-4
FRONT SUSPENSION COMPONENTS—LATE MODEL NOVA 8-4
FUEL AND ENGINE OIL RECOMMENDATIONS 1-41
   ENGINE OIL 1-41
   FUEL 1-41
FUEL FILTER 1-19
   REMOVAL & INSTALLATION 1-19
FUEL PUMP 5-2
   REMOVAL & INSTALLATION 5-2
FUEL SYSTEM 5-2
FUSES 6-25
FUSES AND CIRCUIT BREAKERS 6-26
FUSIBLE LINKS 6-25
   REPLACEMENT 6-25
FUSIBLE LINKS—1962–77 6-28
FUSIBLE LINKS—1978–79 6-28
GENERAL ENGINE SPECIFICATIONS 3-19
GENERAL INFORMATION (EXHAUST SYSTEM) 3-50
   COMPONENT REPLACEMENT 3-51
   SPECIAL TOOLS 3-51
GENERAL INFORMATION (HIGH ENERGY IGNITION) 2-13
GENERAL RECOMMENDATIONS 1-55
GENERATOR AND REGULATOR SPECIFICATIONS 3-14
GRILLE 10-7
   REMOVAL & INSTALLATION 10-7
HANDLING A TRAILER 1-56
HEADLIGHTS 6-19
   AIMING 6-21

   REMOVAL & INSTALLATION 6-19
HEATER 6-12
HEATER CORE 6-12
   REMOVAL & INSTALLATION 6-12
HEI DISTRIBUTOR COMPONENTS 3-9
HEI ELECTRONIC IGNITION SYSTEM 3-5
   REMOVAL & INSTALLATION 3-6
   TROUBLESHOOTING 3-5
HIGH ENERGY IGNITION 2-13
HITCH (TONGUE) WEIGHT 1-55
HOLLEY CARBURETORS 5-34
HOLLEY 4150, 4160-4 BARREL CARBURETORS 5-29
   ADJUSTMENTS 5-29
HOOD 10-3
   ALIGNMENT 10-3
   REMOVAL & INSTALLATION 10-3
HOSES 1-29
   INSPECTION 1-29
   REMOVAL & INSTALLATION 1-29
HOW TO BUY A USED VEHICLE 1-60
HOW TO USE THIS BOOK 1-2
HYDRAULIC TAPPETS 2-13
   ADJUSTMENT 2-13
IDLE SPEED ADJUSTMENT—1971 5-4
IDLE SPEED ADJUSTMENT—1972 5-4
IDLE SPEED ADJUSTMENT—1973 5-5
IDLE SPEED ADJUSTMENT—1974–75 5-5
IDLE SPEED AND MIXTURE ADJUSTMENTS 2-15
IGNITION SWITCH (COLUMN-MOUNTED) 8-20
   REMOVAL & INSTALLATION 8-20
IGNITION SWITCH (DASH-MOUNTED) 6-17
   REMOVAL & INSTALLATION 6-17
IGNITION TIMING 2-13
INDUSTRIAL POLLUTANTS 4-2
INSIDE REAR VIEW MIRROR 10-19
   REMOVAL & INSTALLATION 10-19
INSTRUMENT PANEL 6-17
INTAKE MANIFOLD 3-37
   REMOVAL & INSTALLATION 3-37
INTERIOR 10-9
JACKING 1-57
JACKING PRECAUTIONS 1-59
JUMP STARTING A DEAD BATTERY 1-56
JUMP STARTING PRECAUTIONS 1-56
JUMP STARTING PROCEDURE 1-57
LEAF SPRINGS 8-14
   REMOVAL & INSTALLATION 8-14
LIGHT BULB SPECIFICATIONS 1962–77 6-29
LIGHT BULB SPECIFICATIONS 1978–79 6-28
LIGHTING 6-19
LOWER BALL JOINT 8-9
   INSPECTION 8-9
   REMOVAL & INSTALLATION 8-9
LOWER CONTROL ARM 8-11
   REMOVAL & INSTALLATION 8-11
LUBRICATION AND MAINTENANCE SCHEDULE 1-63
MAGNETIC PULSE DISTRIBUTOR 2-11
MAINTENANCE COMPONENT LOCATIONS—EARLY MODEL V8
   ENGINE 1-16
MAINTENANCE COMPONENT LOCATIONS—LATE MODEL NOVA INLINE
   ENGINE 1-17
MAINTENANCE OR REPAIR? 1-2
MANUAL STEERING GEAR 1-53
   FLUID RECOMMENDATION 1-53
MANUAL TRANSMISSION 7-2
MANUAL TRANSMISSION (FLUIDS AND LUBRICANTS) 1-45
   DRAIN & REFILL 1-45
   FLUID RECOMMENDATIONS 1-45

LEVEL CHECK 1-45
MASTER CYLINDER (BRAKE SYSTEM) 9-3
  OVERHAUL 9-4
  REMOVAL & INSTALLATION 9-3
MASTER CYLINDER (FLUIDS AND LUBRICANTS) 1-52
  FLUID RECOMMENDATONS 1-52
  LEVEL CHECK 1-52
MECHANICAL TAPPETS 2-14
  ADJUSTMENT 2-14
NATURAL POLLUTANTS 4-2
NEUTRAL SAFETY SWITCH 7-18
  ADJUSTMENTS 7-18
  REMOVAL & INSTALLATION 7-18
1962–67 VEHICLES WITHOUT AIR (IDLE SPEED AND MIXTURE
  ADJUSTMENTS) 2-15
1962–68 ENGINE OIL VISCOSITY RECOMMENDATIONS (FLUIDS AND
  LUBRICANTS) 1-42
1967 VEHICLES WITH AIR (IDLE SPEED AND MIXTURE
  ADJUSTMENTS) 2-15
1968–69 VEHICLES (IDLE SPEED AND MIXTURE
  ADJUSTMENTS) 2-15
1969–71 RECOMMENDED SAE VISCOSITY NUMBER 1-42
1970 VEHICLES (IDLE SPEED AND MIXTURE ADJUSTMENTS) 2-15
  4-153 ENGINES 2-16
  6-230/250 ENGINES 2-16
  8-307 ENGINES 2-16
  8-350 (300 HP) ENGINES 2-16
1971–72 VEHICLES (IDLE SPEED AND MIXTURE
  ADJUSTMENTS) 2-16
  6-250 ENGINES 2-16
  8-307 (200 HP) AND 350 (245 HP) ENGINES 2-16
  8-350 (270 HP) ENGINES 2-16
1972–77 RECOMMENDED SAE VISCOSITY NUMBER 1-42
1973 VEHICLES (IDLE SPEED AND MIXTURE ADJUSTMENTS) 2-16
  6-250 ENGINES 2-17
  8-307, 350 (2 BBL) ENGINES 2-17
  8-350 (4 BBL) ENGINES 2-17
1974 VEHICLES (IDLE SPEED AND MIXTURE ADJUSTMENTS) 2-17
  6-250 ENGINES 2-17
  8-350 (2 BBL) ENGINES 2-17
  8-350 (4 BBL) ENGINES 2-17
1975 VEHICLES (IDLE SPEED AND MIXTURE ADJUSTMENTS) 2-17
1976–77 VEHICLES (IDLE SPEED AND MIXTURE
  ADJUSTMENTS) 2-17
  1 BBL CARBURETORS 2-17
  2 BBL & 4 BBL CARBURETORS 2-17
1978–79 RECOMMENDED SAE VISCOSITY NUMBER 1-42
1978–79 VEHICLES (IDLE SPEED AND MIXTURE
  ADJUSTMENTS) 2-18
OIL PAN 3-44
  REMOVAL & INSTALLATION 3-44
OIL PUMP 3-45
  REMOVAL & INSTALLATION 3-45
OUTSIDE MIRRORS 10-7
  REMOVAL & INSTALLATION 10-7
PARKING BRAKE 9-21
PCV VALVE 1-20
  REMOVAL & INSTALLATION 1-20
PISTON CLEARANCE SPECIFICATIONS 3-29
PISTONS AND CONNECTING RODS 3-43
  INSPECTION 3-43
  INSTALLATION 3-43
  REMOVAL 3-43
POSITIVE CRANKCASE VENTILATION SYSTEM 4-6
  OPERATION 4-6
  SERVICE 4-6
POWER SEAT MOTOR 10-20
  REMOVAL & INSTALLATION 10-20

POWER STEERING PUMP (FLUIDS AND LUBRICANTS) 1-53
  FLUID RECOMMENDATION & LEVEL CHECK 1-53
POWER STEERING PUMP (STEERING) 8-20
  BLEEDING 8-22
  REMOVAL & INSTALLATION 8-20
PRELIMINARY ADJUSTMENTS 5-3
  IDLE SOLENOID 5-6
  IDLE SPEED AND MIXTURE 5-3
PRESSURE DIFFERENTIAL WARNING SWITCH AND COMBINATION
  VALVE 9-6
  REMOVAL & INSTALLATION 9-7
RADIATOR 3-46
  REMOVAL & INSTALLATION 3-46
RADIO 6-13
RADIO RECEIVER 6-13
  REMOVAL & INSTALLATION 6-13
REAR AXLE 7-25
REAR AXLE (FLUIDS AND LUBRICANTS) 1-47
  DRAIN & REFILL 1-47
  FLUID RECOMMENDATIONS 1-47
  LEVEL CHECK 1-47
REAR DOOR ELECTRIC WINDOW MOTOR 10-17
  REMOVAL & INSTALLATION 10-17
REAR DOOR GLASS 10-17
  REMOVAL & INSTALLATION 10-17
REAR DOOR PANELS 10-13
  REMOVAL & INSTALLATION 10-13
REAR DOOR REGULATOR 10-17
  REMOVAL & INSTALLATION 10-17
REAR DRUM BRAKES 9-19
REAR MAIN OIL SEAL 3-45
  REMOVAL & INSTALLATION 3-45
REAR SUSPENSION (COMPONENT LOCATIONS) 8-14
REAR SUSPENSION 8-14
RING GAP SPECIFICATIONS 3-30
RING SIDE CLEARANCE 3-29
ROCHESTER B-1 BARREL CARBURETOR 5-6
  ADJUSTMENTS 5-6
ROCHESTER BC-1 BARREL CARBURETOR 5-8
  ADJUSTMENTS 5-8
ROCHESTER BV-1 BARREL CARBURETOR 5-9
  ADJUSTMENTS 5-9
ROCHESTER CARBURETORS—1962–76 5-35
ROCHESTER CARBURETORS—1967–76 5-38
ROCHESTER 4GC-4 BARREL CARBURETOR 5-15
  ADJUSTMENTS 5-15
ROCHESTER 4MV, 4MC, M4MC SPECIFICATIONS—1977–79 5-44
ROCHESTER 4MV QUADRAJET-4 BARREL CARBURETOR 5-21
  ADJUSTMENTS 5-21
ROCHESTER ME SPECIFICATIONS—1977–79 5-43
ROCHESTER M4MC, M4MCA QUADRAJET-4 BARREL
  CARBURETORS 5-24
  ADJUSTMENTS 5-24
ROCHESTER MV-1 BARREL CARBURETOR 5-10
  ADJUSTMENTS 5-10
ROCHESTER 1ME-1 BARREL CARBURETORS 5-11
  ADJUSTMENTS 5-11
ROCHESTER 2GC SPECIFICATIONS—1977–79 5-43
ROCHESTER 2GC-2 BARREL CARBURETOR 5-13
  ADJUSTMENT 5-13
ROCHESTER 2GV-2 BARREL CARBURETOR 5-12
  ADJUSTMENTS 5-12
ROCKER ARMS 3-36
  REMOVAL & INSTALLATION 3-36
ROUTINE MAINTENANCE 1-16
SAFETY PRECAUTIONS 6-2
SEAT BELT/STARTER INTERLOCK SYSTEM 6-18
  DISABLING THE SEATBELT INTERLOCK SYSTEM 6-18

GENERAL INFORMATION 6-18
SEATBELT SYSTEM 6-17
SEATS 10-19
   REMOVAL & INSTALLATION 10-19
SERIAL NUMBER IDENTIFICATION 1-14
SERVICING YOUR VEHICLE SAFELY 1-7
SHOCK ABSORBERS (REAR SUSPENSION) 8-16
   REMOVAL & INSTALLATION 8-16
SHOCK ABSORBERS (WHEELS) 8-6
   REMOVAL & INSTALLATION 8-6
SIGNAL AND MARKER LIGHTS 6-21
   REMOVAL & INSTALLATION 6-21
SPARK PLUG WIRES 2-7
   REMOVAL & INSTALLATION 2-8
   TESTING 2-7
SPARK PLUGS 2-2
   INSPECTION & GAPPING 2-4
   REMOVAL & INSTALLATION 2-3
   SPARK PLUG HEAT RANGE 2-2
SPARK PLUGS AND WIRING 2-2
SPECIAL TOOLS 1-6
SPECIFICATION CHARTS
   ALTERNATOR AND REGULATOR SPECIFICATIONS 3-15
   BATTERY AND STARTER SPECIFICATIONS 3-17
   BRAKE SPECIFICATIONS 9-24
   CAPACITIES 1-65
   CARBURETOR SPECIFICATIONS—CARTER CARBURETORS 5-34
   CRANKSHAFT AND CONNECTING ROD SPECIFICATIONS 3-25
   CYLINDER BORE, PISTON, AND RING SPECIFICATIONS
    1962–77 3-28
   ENGLISH TO METRIC CONVERSION CHARTS 1-68
   FUSES AND CIRCUIT BREAKERS 6-26
   FUSIBLE LINKS—1962–77 6-27
   FUSIBLE LINKS—1978–79 6-27
   GENERAL ENGINE SPECIFICATIONS 3-19
   GENERATOR AND REGULATOR SPECIFICATIONS 3-14
   HOLLEY CARBURETORS 5-34
   IDLE SPEED ADJUSTMENT—1971 5-4
   IDLE SPEED ADJUSTMENT—1972 5-4
   IDLE SPEED ADJUSTMENT—1973 5-5
   IDLE SPEED ADJUSTMENT—1974–75 5-5
   LIGHT BULB SPECIFICATIONS 1962–77 6-28
   LIGHT BULB SPECIFICATIONS 1978–79 6-27
   LUBRICATION AND MAINTENANCE SCHEDULE 1-63
   1962–68 ENGINE OIL VISCOSITY RECOMMENDATIONS 1-42
   1969–71 RECOMMENDED SAE VISCOSITY NUMBER 1-42
   1972–77 RECOMMENDED SAE VISCOSITY NUMBER 1-42
   1978–79 RECOMMENDED SAE VISCOSITY NUMBER 1-42
   PISTON CLEARANCE SPECIFICATIONS 3-29
   RING GAP SPECIFICATIONS 3-30
   RING SIDE CLEARANCE 3-29
   ROCHESTER CARBURETORS—1962–76 5-35
   ROCHESTER CARBURETORS—1967–76 5-38
   ROCHESTER 4MV, 4MC, M4MC SPECIFICATIONS—1977–79 5-44
   ROCHESTER ME SPECIFICATIONS—1977–79 5-43
   ROCHESTER 2GC SPECIFICATIONS—1977–79 5-43
   STANDARD AND METRIC CONVERSION FACTORS 1-13
   STANDARD TORQUE SPECIFICATIONS AND FASTENER
    MARKINGS 1-10
   TORQUE SPECIFICATIONS 3-31
   TUNE-UP SPECIFICATIONS 2-19
   VALVE SPECIFICATIONS 3-23
   WHEEL ALIGNMENT SPECIFICATIONS 8-13
STANDARD AND METRIC CONVERSION FACTORS 1-13
STANDARD TORQUE SPECIFICATIONS AND FASTENER
   MARKINGS 1-10
STANDARD AND METRIC MEASUREMENTS 1-12
STARTER 3-12

REMOVAL & INSTALLATION 3-12
STEERING 8-18
STEERING WHEEL 8-18
   REMOVAL & INSTALLATION 8-18
SYSTEM DESCRIPTION 9-3
THERMOSTAT 3-49
   REMOVAL & INSTALLATION 3-49
TIE-ROD ENDS 8-22
   REMOVAL & INSTALLATION 8-22
TIMING 2-13
   INSPECTION & ADJUSTMENT 2-13
TIMING CHAIN 3-39
   REMOVAL & INSTALLATION 3-39
TIMING GEAR/CHAIN COVER 3-38
   OIL SEAL REPLACEMENT 3-39
   REMOVAL & INSTALLATION 3-38
TIPS 1-60
   ROAD TEST CHECKLIST 1-62
   USED VEHICLE CHECKLIST 1-61
TIRES AND WHEELS 1-37
   CARE OF SPECIAL WHEELS 1-40
   INFLATION & INSPECTION 1-38
   TIRE DESIGN 1-38
   TIRE ROTATION 1-37
   TIRE STORAGE 1-38
TOOLS AND EQUIPMENT 1-3
TORQUE 1-9
   TORQUE ANGLE METERS 1-12
   TORQUE WRENCHES 1-11
TORQUE SPECIFICATIONS 3-31
TOWING THE VEHICLE 1-56
TRAILER TOWING 1-55
TRAILER WEIGHT 1-55
TRAILER WIRING 6-24
TRANSMISSION (AUTOMATIC TRANSMISSION) 7-20
   REMOVAL & INSTALLATION 7-20
TRANSMISSION (MANUAL TRANSMISSION) 7-5
   REMOVAL & INSTALLATION 7-5
TRANSMISSION (SERIAL NUMBER IDENTIFICATION) 1-15
TRANSMISSION CONTROLLED SPARK SYSTEM 4-8
   OPERATION 4-8
TROUBLESHOOTING 6-3
   BASIC TROUBLESHOOTING THEORY 6-4
   TEST EQUIPMENT 6-4
   TESTING 6-6
TRUNK LID 10-4
   ALIGNMENT 10-5
   REMOVAL & INSTALLATION 10-4
TUNE-UP SPECIFICATIONS 2-19
TURN SIGNAL SWITCH 8-20
   REMOVAL & INSTALLATION 8-20
**UNDERSTANDING AND TROUBLESHOOTING ELECTRICAL
  SYSTEMS 6-2**
UNDERSTANDING AUTOMATIC TRANSMISSIONS 7-12
   HYDRAULIC CONTROL SYSTEM 7-13
   PLANETARY GEARBOX 7-12
   SERVOS & ACCUMULATORS 7-13
   TORQUE CONVERTER 7-12
UNDERSTANDING BASIC ELECTRICITY 6-2
   AUTOMOTIVE CIRCUITS 6-3
   CIRCUITS 6-2
   SHORT CIRCUITS 6-3
   THE WATER ANALOGY 6-2
UNDERSTANDING ELECTRICITY 3-2
   BASIC CIRCUITS 3-2
   TROUBLESHOOTING 3-3
UNDERSTANDING REAR AXLES 7-25
UNDERSTANDING THE CLUTCH 7-5

UNDERSTANDING THE ENGINE 3-18
UNDERSTANDING THE MANUAL TRANSMISSION 7-2
UPPER BALL JOINT 8-7
  INSPECTION 8-7
  REMOVAL & INSTALLATION 8-8
UPPER CONTROL ARM 8-10
  REMOVAL & INSTALLATION 8-10
VACUUM DIAGRAMS 4-16
VALVE GUIDES 3-36
VALVE LASH 2-13
VALVE LASH ADJUSTMENT 3-41
  HYDRAULIC LIFTERS 3-41
  MECHANICAL LIFTERS 3-41
VALVE LIFTERS 3-41
  REMOVAL & INSTALLATION 3-41
VALVE SPECIFICATIONS 3-23
VEHICLE 1-14
VOLTAGE REGULATOR 3-11
  REMOVAL & INSTALLATION 3-11
WARNING BUZZER AND LIGHT 6-17
  GENERAL INFORMATION 6-17
WATER PUMP 3-48
  REMOVAL & INSTALLATION 3-48
WHEEL ALIGNMENT SPECIFICATIONS 8-13
WHEEL ASSEMBLY 8-2

  INSPECTION 8-2
  REMOVAL & INSTALLATION 8-2
WHEEL BEARINGS (DRUM BRAKES) 9-21
WHEEL BEARINGS (FLUIDS AND LUBRICANTS) 1-54
WHEEL BEARINGS (FRONT DISC BRAKES) 9-14
  ADJUSTMENT 9-14
  PACKING 9-15
  REMOVAL & INSTALLATION 9-14
WHEEL CYLINDERS 9-20
  OVERHAUL 9-20
WHEEL LUG STUDS 8-2
  REPLACEMENT 8-2
WHEELS 8-2
WHERE TO BEGIN 1-2
WINDSHIELD WIPER MOTOR 6-15
  REMOVAL & INSTALLATION 6-15
WINDSHIELD WIPERS 6-15
WINDSHIELD WIPERS (ROUTINE MAINTENANCE) 1-32
  ELEMENT (REFILL) CARE & REPLACEMENT 1-32
WIPER TRANSMISSION 6-16
  REMOVAL & INSTALLATION 6-16
WIRING DIAGRAMS 6-30
WIRING HARNESSES 6-8
  WIRING REPAIR 6-8